Susanne Stelling

THE MARXIST READER

THE MARXIST READER

The Most Significant and Enduring
Works of Marxism

with
Commentary and Notes by
Emile Burns

Illustrated

AVENEL BOOKS
New York

This 1982 edition is published by Avenel Books,
distributed by Crown Publishers, Inc.

Substantial portions of this book appeared previously in
The Handbook of Marxism.

Manufactured in the United States of America

Library of Congress Cataloging in Publication Data
Main entry under title:

The Marxist reader.

Abridged ed. of: A handbook of Marxism/[edited by] Emile Burns. 1935.
1. Socialism—Addresses, essays, lectures.
2. Communism—Addresses, essays, lectures.
I. Burns, Emile, 1889–   . II. A Handbook of Marxism.
HX39.M362   1982   335.4   82-11799
ISBN 0-517-38766-2

h g f e d c b a

CONTENTS

6

FOREWORD

WHAT WAS IT in Marxism that propelled John Reed, Emma Goldman, and legions, continents, armies, and nations of others? Were these merely words? Decidedly not. For the poet in Reed, there was the brilliance, the passion beyond the prose. Karl Marx lived, after all, perhaps without realizing it, in the high romantic age.

It was to take the passage of tumultuous decades, two merciless major wars, hysterical, life-killing blacklists and countless transformed lives wearing every color of the planetary palette, before this rhetoric would stand willingly naked before us. Now, out of the immediate context, we see that these words will, clearly, never die.

The Communist Manifesto is the keynote speech of worlds, generations, and cultures. Frequently compared to the Bible and the Koran, it is no opiate. It is said to have heralded a secular religion, yet nobody, this time, walked on water. And nobody parted the sea to allow armies to amble through, except with words. The miracle, this time, lay in the transformation of universal rage into action, and action into power. And power into a history that seared the pages as it wrote itself.

"A specter is haunting Europe...."

Could Eliot or Yeats, or Shakespeare have said it better? Marx, the prophet and visionary, was writing the manifesto of a party that didn't yet exist. Written in haste in six weeks, totalling only 12,000 words (shorter than the various introductions often accompanying it), *The Communist Manifesto* is the most renowned pamphlet in all of human history.

Karl Marx, from a long line of rabbis, was baptized, with

his family, into the Lutheran Church by a father attempting to save his career. Young Karl took a wife four years his elder, Jenny von Westphalen, the daughter of a Prussian aristocrat and descendent of barons and earls, from a family of Lutheran officials. This was, perhaps, his first revolutionary act. After a thoroughly bohemian college career at a school known for its partying, Marx spent only one or two years making his own living.

Later, his head faithfully bent to his mission in the research rooms at the British Museum, Marx was supported by cash donations from Friedrich Engels, the son of a capitalist in the textile business. Engels, having represented his father's Manchester office, retired at fifty and joined the hunt on the English countryside alongside the gentry. Engels's *The Origin of The Family* may have been founded on the principles of the Great Peace of the Iroquois, but *The Communist Manifesto* came directly from his observation of the treatment of the workers in his father's mills.

Karl Marx knew life as a five-letter word: exile. While Engels was more isolated from society by a common-law marriage than by his politics, Marx spent most of his life on the Prussian police "wanted" list. Treves, the German city where he was born, was held by Prussia, and boasted the most tyranically reactionary police state in Europe. Marx was greatly in sympathy with exiled German socialists, and was eventually exiled from Paris, Brussels, and Cologne.

When Marx and Engels wrote *The Communist Manifesto* they were unknowns in their late twenties who despised soldiers and despotic states. While they worked, they knew of no communist states, no revolutionary governments, or trade unions of any size. (The trade union leaders Marx was likely to meet wore gold watch chains across their portly stomachs.) Every country in the world except those on the American continents and Switzerland was a monarchy ruled absolutely by a king, emperor, czar or sultan. There were millions of slaves in America, and in Great Britain, most men were too poor to qualify to vote. Every country was "backward," and over 90 percent of the world lived in undeniable poverty. All worlds were in ferment.

Inspired by Marx, Nicolai Lenin took up the cry. Like Marx, he had his taste of the aristocracy—being the son of a nobleman—and of exile. A determining event in his life was the hanging of his brother for an attempted assassination of the czar. Lenin himself was arrested, imprisoned for a year, and spent three years as an exile in Siberia.

Joseph Stalin, too, made the trip to Siberia, and escaped no less than three times. Earlier, in a spell of ecclesiastical prescience, church officials had him expelled from a religious seminary for "unreliability." There are those who would not employ that word, but the man to whom Lenin gave the name Stalin, meaning "steel," was in line for religious pursuits of a different order.

Those were the days when one man's presence could fan the flames of revolution. Lenin took a train to Russia, in 1917, with the cooperation of Germany, with the idea that his presence alone would weaken the entire Russian nation. The men behind these writings swept across national and ethnic boundaries. They touched religious emotions. Dictatorship was not a dirty word...as long as it was ascribed to the proletariat, a term lifted from the Ancient Romans by the far-seeing Marx.

Emile Burns's introduction gives these classic works a you-are-there feeling. He comments, for instance, that Engels's *Introduction to the Class Struggles in France* had been sabotaged by a German editor, who deleted Engels's blueprints for insurrection, thereby leaving the impression on the reader that Engels was merely a restless burgher. "Now, insurrection is an art quite as much as war or any other..." says Engels in his work on German revolution and counterrevolution. With as much chilling understatement, Marx begins *The Civil War in France:* "On September 4, 1870, when the working men of Paris proclaimed the Republic...."

The scissors-bearing editors never stopped trying. According to Burns, "Social Democratic philistine" was printed as "German philistine," again destroying the message in Engels's *Introduction to the Civil War in France*. And Marx, ever sure that he was destined to be the intellectual master of the world (he was half right), described his *Theses on Feuerbach* as "notes hurriedly scribbled down for later elaboration, absolutely not intended for publication, but they are invaluable as the first document in which is deposited the brilliant germ of the new world outlook." In these notes is found the profound, and powerfully accurate call to action: "The philosophers have only *interpreted* the world in various ways; the point however is to *change* it."

PATRICIA HORAN

New York City
1982

ACKNOWLEDGMENT

The publisher would like to express appreciation for the advice and consultation given by Jake Goldberg on this Avenel Books edition.

INTRODUCTION

FOR SOME YEARS there has been an increasing interest in the theories and general outlook of what is known as Marxism.

The purpose of this book is to set out these theories in the most authoritative form possible—in the words of the founders of Marxism and of the greatest of their followers. It is therefore a collection of extracts from their writings, selected so as to give the reader the most comprehensive account of Marxism possible within the limits of a single volume.

The founders of Marxism were Karl Marx and Friedrich Engels. Marx was born in Prussia in 1818; his father was a lawyer, and he himself studied jurisprudence at Berlin University. But by 1842 he had entered the political arena as editor of an opposition paper which within six months was suppressed by the government of Prussia. From then on he was virtually a political exile, living in Paris and Brussels, and finally settling in London after a brief return to Cologne during the German revolution of 1848–9.

Engels was also born in Prussia, in 1820; his father was a manufacturer. From 1842 Engels worked in a commercial house in Manchester—at the same time studying English conditions. In 1844, he met Marx in Paris, and from then on the two were close friends, jointly developing the theories which were afterwards to be known as Marxism. Of his part in their work, Engels writes: "I cannot deny that both before and during my forty years' collaboration with Marx I had a certain independent share in laying the formulations, and more particularly in elaborating the theory. But the greater part of its leading basic principles, particularly in the realm of economics and history, and, above all, its final clear formulation, belong to Marx... Marx was a genius; we others were at best talented. Without him the theory would not be what it is to-day. It therefore rightly bears his name."

After Marx's death in 1883, Engels was able to complete, from Marx's notes, the unfinished second and third volumes of *Capital*, before his own death in 1895.

The wide range of their works is indicated by the extracts given in this book. But it is impossible to list the innumerable articles which Marx and Engels contributed to the Press (for many years these were Marx's only regular sources of income), their correspondence, and the many documents which they drafted for political and trade union organisations. All through their lives they were closely associated with the practical work of organising the labour movement; they were particularly identified with the International Workingmen's Association (the "First International," founded in 1864), and even after its collapse continued to guide the policy of the rising labour organisations in many countries.

The book opens with *The Communist Manifesto* (1848), the joint work in which Marx and Engels set out their general view of history and class struggle, showing the development of human society through the changing forms of production and the conflict of classes, and indicating the inevitable overthrow of capitalism by the working class; this was the first scientific programme of the Socialist movement.

This is followed by a series of extracts from subsequent writings, in which this historical viewpoint is reinforced and developed in relation to contemporary events—especially the revolutionary events of 1848–51 in France and Germany and the Paris Commune of 1871. This group of historical writings is of particular importance for the development of the theory of revolution; they formed the basis of the further extension of the theory by Lenin.

The next two extracts are taken from the more general philosophical writings of Marx and Engels, in which the standpoint of dialectical materialism is explained and applied: *German Ideology*, and *Feuerbach*. Social science is further developed in the chapters taken from Engels's *The Origin of the Family, Private Property and the State*, showing the present-day family as the outcome of a long process of development, changing as the mode of production changed, and presenting the State as the product of the division of society into classes, and the instrument of class domination. Chapters from Engels's *The Housing Question* and Marx's *The Poverty of Philosophy* complete this group.

Marx's introduction to *The Critique of Political Economy* then prepares the way for the most vital chapters from the best known—at least by name—of Marx's works: *Capital*, the analysis of the capitalist system of production which is the basis of Marxist economics. The historical chapters are given first (following Marx's recommendation for the general reader). Of the chapters on economic theory it has only been possible to include those dealing with the most fundamental points, especially the labour theory of value, surplus value, accumulation and reproduction of capital, and the falling tendency of the rate of profit.

When Engels died, in 1895, the theories of Marxism had already begun to undergo the process of mirepresentation and corruption which was to transform important sections of the socialist movement into a movement of social reform within capitalism. At this time, however, there appeared in the Russian socialist movement the man who was destined to defend and develop Marxism and to vindicate it in the greatest class struggle in history—Vladimir Ilyich Ulianov, later known by his pen-name, N. Lenin.

Lenin was born in 1870: his father was an inspector of schools in the Tsarist civil service. The family belonged to the Liberal intelligentsia; Lenin's elder brother, Alexander, was hanged in 1887 for complicity in a plot to assassinate the Tsar. Lenin studied law, and was admitted to the Bar; but after 1893 he devoted himself entirely to the socialist movement.

He was in prison in 1896, and in exile in Siberia from 1897 to 1900, after which he went abroad, living mainly in Paris, London, Switzerland and Galicia. At the end of 1905 the revolutionary development enabled him to return to Russia; but he had to leave again at the end of 1907. After the March revolution of 1917 he reached Russia once more; was forced to take refuge in Finland in August; and finally returned to Russia immediately before the revolution of November, 1917. In 1918 he was severely wounded in an attempt on his life, and although he was able to work for another four years, he never completely recovered, and died in January, 1924.

As with Marx and Engels, Lenin's works were written in the midst of continuous political activity: to him the theory and practice of Marxism were inseparable. His essay on Marxism, *The Teachings of Karl Marx,* is an extraordinarily clear statement; it serves here as a summing up of the writings of Marx and Engels and as an introduction to those of Lenin himself. Lenin's essential problem was to form in Russia, out of the mixed anarchist-revolutionary-democratic-liberal groups of the 'nineties, an organised party of the working class with a clear understanding of Marxism. His earlier writings are all directed to this aim—the selections given, from *Our Programme* (1898) and *What is to be Done?* (1900), show his theoretical approach, which was finally victorious in the London Conference of 1903, when the Russian Social Democratic Labour Party split into the Bolsheviks (= majority following Lenin) and the Mensheviks (= minority, opposed to Lenin).

Then follows *The Revolution of 1905,* in which Lenin analyses what he afterwards called the "dress rehearsal" of the November revolution of 1917. After the final defeat of this "dress rehearsal" in 1907, Lenin returned to the theoretical fight for Marxism.

Lenin's defence of Marxism continued through the years preceding the war; it reached a new stage in *Imperialism*— written during the war, and showing the basis of reformist tendencies in the labour movement. Some essential passages are reprinted here, and are followed by chapters from *The State and Revolution*—a work of extreme theoretical importance, bringing together and extending the conclusions reached by Marx and Engels on this subject.

Joseph Djugashvili (Stalin) was born in 1879, in the Caucasus. He was of peasant stock, though his father worked in a boot factory. In 1898 Stalin joined the Russian Social Democratic Labour Party, and went through imprisonment and exile to Siberia by 1904. He escaped from exile, and thereafter was definitely associated with the Bolshevik section of the Party, meeting Lenin in 1905. He was repeatedly arrested, and from 1913 to 1916 was in exile in Siberia, but came to Petrograd after the March revolution of 1917. He supported Lenin in the Party discussions, and was elected to the committees for political and organisational leadership of the November insurrection. In 1922 he became one of the secretaries and the political leader of the Communist Party of the Soviet Union.

Next to Lenin, Stalin was the most consistent Marxist in the leadership of the revolution, especially in his understanding of the part played by the revolutionary party, and of revolutionary strategy in connection with the national movements and the peasantry. Two of his articles on these subjects, *The October Revolution and the National Question* and *The October Revolution and the Question of the Middle Strata,* are therefore included at this point.

After these works, Stalin's statement on "The Party" is given—setting out the methods of work of a revolutionary Marxist party.

Readers who are familiar with the works of Marx, Engels, Lenin and Stalin will inevitably be disappointed that some work or passage which they think of vital significance is not included in this book. The selection has aimed at giving the reader who is *not* familiar with Marxism as clear and comprehensive a view of Marxist theories as can be given in one volume. This has necessarily meant the exclusion of works and passages of great value. In any case, while the book will be of immense value to everyone who wants to know what Marxism is, and will be of use as a reference book even to advanced students of Marxism, I hope that it will serve merely as an introduction to the study of some of the complete works of Marx, Engels, Lenin and Stalin.

I must express my thanks to Messrs. George Allen and Unwin Ltd. (the successors to Swan Sonnenschein & Co., Ltd.), Charles H. Kerr and Company, Martin Lawrence Ltd., and Modern Books Ltd., as well as to the Editorial Boards of the *Communist International* and of the *Labour Monthly*, who have allowed me to use English translations of which they had the copyright.

At the head of each work or passage the author's name and the English title of the work are given. Then follows a brief bibliographical note (printed in italics), giving the date when the work was first published or written, and the date and publishers of the (in my view) best current English translation. A further note, explaining the circumstances in which the work was written and its special significance in the development of Marxism, is enclosed in heavy square brackets.

Then follows the text of the work itself. In the case of shorter works, detailed references to the passages selected are unnecessary, and have not been given; in the case of longer works, the chapter heads and sub-heads will enable the enquiring reader to identify the passage in any edition of the complete work.

The glossaries at the end of the book will help the reader who finds unfamiliar names and terms in the text.

EMILE BURNS

Working men of all countries, unite! (*The Communist Manifesto*)
All lithographs in this book, with the exception of the first
illustration in *Capital*, are by Lynd Ward.

Karl Marx and Friedrich Engels

THE COMMUNIST MANIFESTO

Published 1848. Authorised English translation of 1888, edited by Engels and with prefaces by Engels and Marx, republished by Martin Lawrence Ltd., 1934.

[Engels wrote in the 1888 preface: "The Manifesto was published as the platform of the Communist League, a workingmen's association, first exclusively German, later on international. . . . At a Congress of the League, held in London in November 1847, Marx and Engels were commissioned to prepare for publication a complete theoretical and practical party programme. Drawn up in German in January 1848, the manuscript was sent to the printer in London a few weeks before the French revolution of February 24th."

The Communist League was dissolved in 1852, but the Manifesto became " undoubtedly the most widespread, the most international production of all Socialist literature, the common platform acknowledged by millions of workingmen from Siberia to California."

In their earlier writings Marx and Engels had developed the materialist conception of history ; in *The Communist Manifesto* this was first embodied in a programme for the political party of the working class. The Manifesto was called *Communist* and not *Socialist* because, as Engels explains, the word Socialist was associated with the Utopians on the one hand, and on the other with " the most multifarious social quacks, who by all manner of tinkering professed to redress, without any danger to capital and profit, all sorts of social grievances." But " whatever portion of the working class had become convinced of the insufficiency of mere political revolutions, and had proclaimed the necessity of a total social change, called itself Communist."

The Manifesto has inspired all revolutionary socialism ;

it is the most concise statement and the most important single document of Marxism.]

THE COMMUNIST MANIFESTO

A SPECTRE is haunting Europe—the spectre of Communism. All the powers of old Europe have entered into a holy alliance to exorcise this spectre : Pope and Tsar, Metternich and Guizot, French Radicals and German police-spies.

Where is the party in opposition that has not been decried as communistic by its opponents in power ? Where is the Opposition that has not hurled back the branding reproach of Communism, against the more advanced opposition parties, as well as against its reactionary adversaries ?

Two things result from this fact :

I. Communism is already acknowledged by all European powers to be itself a power.

II. It is high time that Communists should openly, in the face of the whole world, publish their views, their aims, their tendencies, and meet this nursery tale of the spectre of Communism with a manifesto of the party itself.

To this end, Communists of various nationalities have assembled in London, and sketched the following manifesto, to be published in the English, French, German, Italian, Flemish and Danish languages :

I : BOURGEOIS AND PROLETARIANS[1]

The history of all hitherto existing society[2] is the history of class struggles.

[1] By bourgeoisie is meant the class of modern capitalists, owners of the means of social production and employers of wage-labour. By proletariat, the class of modern wage-labourers who, having no means of production of their own, are reduced to selling their labour power in order to live.

[2] That is, all *written* history. In 1847, the pre-history of society, the social organisation existing previous to recorded history, was all but

Freeman and slave, patrician and plebeian, lord and serf, guild-master[1] and journeyman, in a word, oppressor and oppressed, stood in constant opposition to one another, carried on an uninterrupted, now hidden, now open fight, a fight that each time ended, either in a revolutionary reconstitution of society at large, or in the common ruin of the contending classes.

In the earlier epochs of history, we find almost everywhere a complicated arrangement of society into various orders, a manifold gradation of social rank. In ancient Rome we have patricians, knights, plebeians, slaves ; in the Middle Ages, feudal lords, vassals, guild-masters, journeymen, apprentices, serfs ; in almost all of these classes, again, subordinate gradations.

The modern bourgeois society that has sprouted from the ruins of feudal society has not done away with class antagonisms. It has but established new classes, new conditions of oppression, new forms of struggle in place of the old ones.

Our epoch, the epoch of the bourgeoisie, possesses, however, this distinctive feature : it has simplified the class antagonisms. Society as a whole is more and more splitting up into two great hostile camps, into two great classes directly facing each other—bourgeoisie and proletariat.

From the serfs of the Middle Ages sprang the chartered

---

unknown. Since then Haxthausen [August von, 1792–1866] discovered common ownership of land in Russia, Maurer [Georg Ludwig von] proved it to be the social foundation from which all Teutonic races started in history, and, by and by, village communities were found to be, or to have been, the primitive form of society everywhere from India to Ireland. The inner organisation of this primitive communistic society was laid bare, in its typical form, by Morgan's [Henry, 1818–1881] crowning discovery of the true nature of the *gens* and its relation to the *tribe*. With the dissolution of these primæval communities, society begins to be differentiated into separate and finally antagonistic classes. I have attempted to retrace this process of dissolution in *Der Ursprung der Familie, des Privateigenthums und des Staats*, 2nd edition, Stuttgart, 1886. (*The Origin of the Family, Private Property and the State.*)

[1] Guild-master, that is a full member of a guild, a master within, not a head of a guild.

burghers of the earliest towns. From these burgesses the first elements of the bourgeoisie were developed.

The discovery of America, the rounding of the Cape, opened up fresh ground for the rising bourgeoisie. The East-Indian and Chinese markets, the colonisation of America, trade with the colonies, the increase in the means of exchange and in commodities generally, gave to commerce, to navigation, to industry, an impulse never before known, and thereby, to the revolutionary element in the tottering feudal society, a rapid development.

The feudal system of industry, in which industrial production was monopolised by closed guilds, now no longer sufficed for the growing wants of the new markets. The manufacturing system took its place. The guild-masters were pushed aside by the manufacturing middle class ; division of labour between the different corporate guilds vanished in the face of division of labour in each single workshop.

Meantime the markets kept ever growing, the demand ever rising. Even manufacture no longer sufficed. Thereupon, steam and machinery revolutionised industrial production. The place of manufacture was taken by the giant, modern industry, the place of the industrial middle class, by industrial millionaires, the leaders of whole industrial armies, the modern bourgeois.

Modern industry has established the world market, for which the discovery of America paved the way. This market has given an immense development to commerce, to navigation, to communication by land. This development has, in its turn, reacted on the extension of industry ; and in proportion as industry, commerce, navigation, railways extended, in the same proportion the bourgeoisie developed, increased its capital, and pushed into the background every class handed down from the Middle Ages.

We see, therefore, how the modern bourgeoisie is itself the product of a long course of development, of a series of revolutions in the modes of production and of exchange.

Each step in the development of the bourgeoisie was accompanied by a corresponding political advance of that class. An oppressed class under the sway of the feudal nobility, an armed and self-governing association in the mediæval commune[1]; here independent urban republic (as in Italy and Germany), there taxable " third estate " of the monarchy (as in France) ; afterwards, in the period of manufacture proper, serving either the semi-feudal or the absolute monarchy as a counterpoise against the nobility, and, in fact, corner-stone of the great monarchies in general, the bourgeoisie has at last, since the establishment of Modern Industry and of the world market, conquered for itself, in the modern representative State, exclusive political sway. The executive of the modern State is but a committee for managing the common affairs of the whole bourgeoisie.

The bourgeoisie, historically, has played a most revolutionary part.

The bourgeoisie, wherever it has got the upper hand, has put an end to all feudal, patriarchal, idyllic relations. It has pitilessly torn asunder the motley feudal ties that bound man to his " natural superiors," and has left no other nexus between man and man than naked self-interest, than callous " cash payment." It has drowned the most heavenly ecstasies of religious fervour, of chivalrous enthusiasm, of philistine sentimentalism, in the icy water of egotistical calculation. It has resolved personal worth into exchange value, and in place of the numberless indefeasible chartered freedoms, has set up that single, unconscionable freedom— Free Trade. In one word, for exploitation, veiled by religious and political illusions, it has substituted naked, shameless, direct, brutal exploitation.

[1] " Commune " was the name taken, in France, by the nascent towns even before they had conquered from their feudal lords and masters, local self-government and political rights as " the Third Estate." Generally speaking, for the economical development of the bourgeoisie, England is here taken as the typical country, for its political development, France.

The bourgeoisie has stripped of its halo every occupation hitherto honoured and looked up to with reverent awe. It has converted the physician, the lawyer, the priest, the poet, the man of science, into its paid wage-labourers.

The bourgeoisie has torn away from the family its sentimental veil, and has reduced the family relation to a mere money relation.

The bourgeoisie has disclosed how it came to pass that the brutal display of vigour in the Middle Ages, which reactionaries so much admire, found its fitting complement in the most slothful indolence. It has been the first to show what man's activity can bring about. It has accomplished wonders far surpassing Egyptian pyramids, Roman aqueducts, and Gothic cathedrals ; it has conducted expeditions that put in the shade all former Exoduses of nations and crusades.

The bourgeoisie cannot exist without constantly revolutionising the instruments of production, and thereby the relations of production, and with them the whole relations of society. Conservation of the old modes of production in unaltered form, was, on the contrary, the first condition of existence for all earlier industrial classes. Constant revolutionising of production, uninterrupted disturbance of all social conditions, everlasting uncertainty and agitation distinguish the bourgeois epoch from all earlier ones. All fixed, fast-frozen relations, with their train of ancient and venerable prejudices and opinions, are swept away, all new-formed ones become antiquated before they can ossify. All that is solid melts into air, all that is holy is profaned, and man is at last compelled to face with sober senses his real conditions of life and his relations with his kind.

The need of a constantly expanding market for its products chases the bourgeoisie over the whole surface of the globe. It must nestle everywhere, settle everywhere, establish connections everywhere.

The bourgeoisie has through its exploitation of the world market given a cosmopolitan character to production and consumption in every country. To the great chagrin of re-actionaries, it has drawn from under the feet of industry the national ground on which it stood. All old-established national industries have been destroyed or are daily being destroyed. They are dislodged by new industries, whose introduction becomes a life and death question for all civilised nations, by industries that no longer work up in-digenous raw material, but raw material drawn from the remotest zones ; industries whose products are consumed, not only at home, but in every quarter of the globe. In place of the old wants, satisfied by the production of the country, we find new wants, requiring for their satisfaction the pro-ducts of distant lands and climes. In place of the old local and national seclusion and self-sufficiency, we have inter-course in every direction, universal inter-dependence of nations. And as in material, so also in intellectual produc-tion. The intellectual creations of individual nations be-come common property. National one-sidedness and narrow-mindedness become more and more impossible, and from the numerous national and local literatures there arises a world literature.

The bourgeoisie, by the rapid improvement of all instru-ments of production, by the immensely facilitated means of communication, draws all, even the most barbarian, nations into civilisation. The cheap prices of its commodities are the heavy artillery with which it batters down all Chinese walls, with which it forces the barbarians' intensely obstin-ate hatred of foreigners to capitulate. It compels all nations, on pain of extinction, to adopt the bourgeois mode of pro-duction ; it compels them to introduce what it calls civilisa-tion into their midst, i.e., to become bourgeois themselves. In one word, it creates a world after its own image.

The bourgeoisie has subjected the country to the rule of the towns. It has created enormous cities, has greatly in-creased the urban population as compared with the rural, and has thus rescued a considerable part of the population from the idiocy of rural life. Just as it has made the country dependent on the towns, so it has made barbarian and semi-barbarian countries dependent on the civilised ones, nations of peasants on nations of bourgeois, the East on the West.

The bourgeoisie keeps more and more doing away with the scattered state of the population, of the means of production, and of property. It has agglomerated population, centralised means of production, and has concentrated property in a few hands. The necessary consequence of this was political centralisation. Independent, or but loosely connected provinces, with separate interests, laws, governments and systems of taxation, became lumped together into one nation, with one government, one code of laws, one national class interest, one frontier and one customs tariff.

The bourgeoisie, during its rule of scarce one hundred years, has created more massive and more colossal productive forces than have all preceding generations together. Subjection of nature's forces to man, machinery, application of chemistry to industry and agriculture, steam-navigation, railways, electric telegraphs, clearing of whole continents for cultivation, canalisation of rivers, whole populations conjured out of the ground—what earlier century had even a presentiment that such productive forces slumbered in the lap of social labour?

We see then ; the means of production and of exchange, on whose foundation the bourgeoisie built itself up, were generated in feudal society. At a certain stage in the development of these means of production and of exchange, the conditions under which feudal society produced and exchanged, the feudal organisation of agriculture and manufacturing industry, in one word, the feudal relations of property became no longer compatible with the already developed productive forces ; they became so many fetters. They had to be burst asunder ; they were burst asunder.

Into their place stepped free competition, accompanied by a social and political constitution adapted to it, and by the economical and political sway of the bourgeois class.

A similar movement is going on before our own eyes. Modern bourgeois society with its relations of production, of exchange and of property, a society that has conjured up such gigantic means of production and of exchange, is like the sorcerer who is no longer able to control the powers of the nether world whom he has called up by his spells. For many a decade past the history of industry and commerce is but the history of the revolt of modern productive forces against modern conditions of production, against the property relations that are the conditions for the existence of the bourgeoisie and of its rule. It is enough to mention the commercial crises that by their periodical return put the existence of the entire bourgeois society on its trial, each time more threateningly. In these crises a great part not only of the existing products, but also of the previously created productive forces, are periodically destroyed. In these crises there breaks out an epidemic that, in all earlier epochs, would have seemed an absurdity—the epidemic of over-production. Society suddenly finds itself put back into a state of momentary barbarism ; it appears as if a famine, a universal war of devastation had cut off the supply of every means of subsistence ; industry and commerce seem to be destroyed. And why ? Because there is too much civilisation, too much means of subsistence, too much industry, too much commerce. The productive forces at the disposal of society no longer tend to further the development of the conditions of bourgeois property ; on the contrary, they have become too powerful for these conditions, by which they are fettered, and so soon as they overcome these fetters, they bring disorder into the whole of bourgeois society, endanger the existence of bourgeois property. The conditions of bourgeois society are too narrow to comprise the wealth created by them. And how does the bourgeoisie get over these crises ? On the one hand by enforced destruction of a mass of productive forces ; on the other, by the conquest of new markets, and by the more thorough

exploitation of the old ones. That is to say, by paving the
way for more extensive and more destructive crises, and
by diminishing the means whereby crises are prevented.

The weapons with which the bourgeoisie felled feudalism
to the ground are now turned against the bourgeoisie itself.

But not only has the bourgeoisie forged the weapons that
bring death to itself; it has also called into existence the
men who are to wield those weapons—the modern working
class—the proletarians.

In proportion as the bourgeoisie, i.e., capital, is developed,
in the same proportion is the proletariat, the modern working class, developed—a class of labourers, who live only so
long as they find work, and who find work only so long as
their labour increases capital. These labourers, who must
sell themselves piecemeal, are a commodity, like every other
article of commerce, and are consequently exposed to all
the vicissitudes of competition, to all the fluctuations of the
market.

Owing to the extensive use of machinery and to division
of labour, the work of the proletarians has lost all individual character, and, consequently, all charm for the workman. He becomes an appendage of the machine, and it is
only the most simple, most monotonous, and most easily
acquired knack, that is required of him. Hence, the cost of
production of a workman is restricted, almost entirely, to
the means of subsistence that he requires for his maintenance, and for the propagation of his race. But the price of
a commodity, and therefore, also of labour, is equal to its
cost of production. In proportion, therefore, as the repul-
siveness of the work increases, the wage decreases. Nay,
more, in proportion as the use of machinery and division of
labour increases, in the same proportion the burden of toil
also increases, whether by prolongation of the working
hours, by increase of the work exacted in a given time, or
by increased speed of the machinery, etc.

Modern industry has converted the little workshop of the
patriarchal master into the great factory of the industrial

capitalist. Masses of labourers, crowded into the factory, are organised like soldiers. As privates of the industrial army they are placed under the command of a perfect hierarchy of officers and sergeants. Not only are they slaves of the bourgeois class, and of the bourgeois state ; they are daily and hourly enslaved by the machine, by the over-looker, and, above all, by the individual bourgeois manu-facturer himself. The more openly this despotism proclaims gain to be its end and aim, the more petty, the more hateful and the more embittering it is.

The less the skill and exertion of strength implied in manual labour, in other words, the more modern industry becomes developed, the more is the labour of men super-seded by that of women. Differences of age and sex have no longer any distinctive social validity for the working class. All are instruments of labour, more or less expensive to use, according to their age and sex.

No sooner is the exploitation of the labourer by the manu-facturer so far at an end that he receives his wages in cash than he is set upon by the other portions of the bourgeoisie, the landlord, the shopkeeper, the pawnbroker, etc.

The lower strata of the middle class—the small trades-people, shopkeepers, and retired tradesmen generally, the handicraftsmen and peasants—all these sink gradually into the proletariat, partly because their diminutive capital does not suffice for the scale on which modern industry is carried on, and is swamped in the competition with the large capitalists, partly because their specialised skill is rendered worthless by new methods of production. Thus the prole-tariat is recruited from all classes of the population.

The proletariat goes through various stages of develop-ment. With its birth begins its struggle with the bourgeoisie. At first the contest is carried on by individual labourers, then by the work people of a factory, then by the operatives of one trade, in one locality, against the individual bour-geois who directly exploits them. They direct their attacks not against the bourgeois conditions of production, but against the instruments of production themselves ; they destroy imported wares that compete with their labour, they smash to pieces machinery, they set factories ablaze, they seek to restore by force the vanished status of the workman of the Middle Ages.

At this stage the labourers still form an incoherent mass scattered over the whole country, and broken up by their mutual competition. If anywhere they unite to form more compact bodies, this is not yet the consequence of their own active union, but of the union of the bourgeoisie, which class, in order to attain its own political ends, is compelled to set the whole proletariat in motion, and is moreover yet, for a time, able to do so. At this stage, therefore, the proletarians do not fight their enemies, but the enemies of their enemies, the remnants of absolute monarchy, the land-owners, the non-industrial bourgeois, the petty bourgeoisie. Thus the whole historical movement is concentrated in the hands of the bourgeoisie ; every victory so obtained is a victory for the bourgeoisie.

But with the development of industry the proletariat not only increases in number ; it becomes concentrated in greater masses, its strength grows, and it feels that strength more. The various interests and conditions of life within the ranks of the proletariat are more and more equalised, in proportion as machinery obliterates all distinctions of labour, and nearly everywhere reduces wages to the same low level. The growing competition among the bourgeois, and the resulting commercial crises, make the wages of the workers ever more fluctuating. The unceasing improvement of machinery, ever more rapidly developing, makes their livelihood more and more precarious ; the collisions between individual workmen and individual bourgeois take more and more the character of collisions between two classes. Thereupon the workers begin to form combinations (trades' unions) against the bourgeois ; they club together in order to keep up the rate of wages ; they found permanent associations in order to make provision beforehand for these occasional revolts. Here and there the contest breaks out into riots.

Now and then the workers are victorious, but only for a time. The real fruit of their battles lies, not in the immediate result, but in the ever expanding union of the workers. This union is helped on by the improved means of communication that are created by modern industry, and that place the workers of different localities in contact with one another. It was just this contact that was needed to centralise the numerous local struggles, all of the same character, into one national struggle between classes. But every class struggle is a political struggle. And that union, to attain which the burghers of the Middle Ages, with their miserable highways, required centuries, the modern proletarians, thanks to railways, achieve in a few years.

This organisation of the proletarians into a class, and consequently into a political party, is continually being upset again by the competition between the workers themselves. But it ever rises up again, stronger, firmer, mightier. It compels legislative recognition of particular interests of the workers, by taking advantage of the divisions among the bourgeoisie itself. Thus the ten-hours' bill in England was carried.

Altogether, collisions between the classes of the old society further in many ways the course of development of the proletariat. The bourgeoisie finds itself involved in a constant battle. At first with the aristocracy ; later on, with those portions of the bourgeoisie itself, whose interests have become antagonistic to the progress of industry ; at all times with the bourgeoisie of foreign countries. In all these battles it sees itself compelled to appeal to the proletariat, to ask for its help, and thus to drag it into the political arena. The bourgeoisie itself, therefore, supplies the proletariat with its own elements of political and general education, in other words, it furnishes the proletariat with weapons for fighting the bourgeoisie.

Further, as we have already seen, entire sections of the

ruling classes are, by the advance of industry, precipitated into the proletariat, or are at least threatened in their conditions of existence. These also supply the proletariat with fresh elements of enlightenment and progress.

Finally, in times when the class struggle nears the decisive hour, the process of dissolution going on within the ruling class, in fact within the whole range of old society, assumes such a violent, glaring character that a small section of the ruling class cuts itself adrift and joins the revolutionary class, the class that holds the future in its hands. Just as, therefore, at an earlier period, a section of the nobility went over to the bourgeoisie, so now a portion of the bourgeoisie goes over to the proletariat, and, in particular, a portion of the bourgeois ideologists, who have raised themselves to the level of comprehending theoretically the historical movement as a whole.

Of all the classes that stand face to face with the bourgeoisie to-day, the proletariat alone is a really revolutionary class. The other classes decay and finally disappear in the face of modern industry ; the proletariat is its special and essential product.

The lower middle class, the small manufacturer, the shopkeeper, the artisan, the peasant, all these fight against the bourgeoisie, to save from extinction their existence as fractions of the middle class. They are therefore not revolutionary, but conservative. Nay, more, they are reactionary, for they try to roll back the wheel of history. If by chance they are revolutionary, they are so only in view of their impending transfer into the proletariat ; they thus defend not their present, but their future interests ; they desert their own standpoint to place themselves at that of the proletariat.

The " dangerous class," the social scum, that passively rotting mass thrown off by the lowest layers of old society, may, here and there, be swept into the movement by a proletarian revolution ; its conditions of life, however, prepare it far more for the part of a bribed tool of reactionary intrigue.

In the conditions of the proletariat, those of old society at large are already virtually swamped. The proletarian is without property ; his relation to his wife and children has no longer anything in common with the bourgeois family relations ; modern industrial labour, modern subjection to capital, the same in England as in France, in America as in Germany, has stripped him of every trace of national character. Law, morality, religion, are to him so many bourgeois prejudices, behind which lurk in ambush just as many bourgeois interests.

All the preceding classes that got the upper hand, sought to fortify their already acquired status by subjecting society at large to their conditions of appropriation. The proletarians cannot become masters of the productive forces of society, except by abolishing their own previous mode of appropriation, and thereby also every other previous mode of appropriation. They have nothing of their own to secure and to fortify ; their mission is to destroy all previous securities for, and insurances of, individual property.

All previous historical movements were movements of minorities, or in the interest of minorities. The proletarian movement is the self-conscious, independent movement of the immense majority, in the interest of the immense majority. The proletariat, the lowest stratum of our present society, cannot stir, cannot raise itself up, without the whole superincumbent strata of official society being sprung into the air.

Though not in substance, yet in form, the struggle of the proletariat with the bourgeoisie is at first a national struggle. The proletariat of each country must, of course, first of all settle matters with its own bourgeoisie.

In depicting the most general phases of the development of the proletariat, we traced the more or less veiled civil war, raging within existing society, up to the point where that war breaks out into open revolution, and where the violent overthrow of the bourgeoisie lays the foundation for the sway of the proletariat.

Hitherto, every form of society has been based, as we have already seen, on the antagonism of oppressing and oppressed classes. But in order to oppress a class, certain conditions must be assured to it under which it can, at least, continue its slavish existence. The serf, in the period of serfdom, raised himself to membership in the commune, just as the petty bourgeois, under the yoke of feudal absolutism, managed to develop into a bourgeois. The modern labourer, on the contrary, instead of rising with the progress of industry, sinks deeper and deeper below the conditions of existence of his own class. He becomes a pauper, and pauperism develops more rapidly than population and wealth. And here it becomes evident that the bourgeoisie is unfit any longer to be the ruling class in society and to impose its conditions of existence upon society as an over-riding law. It is unfit to rule because it is incompetent to assure an existence to its slave within his slavery, because it cannot help letting him sink into such a state, that it has to feed him, instead of being fed by him. Society can no longer live under this bourgeoisie; in other words, its existence is no longer compatible with society.

The essential condition for the existence and for the sway of the bourgeois class is the formation and augmentation of capital; the condition for capital is wage-labour. Wage-labour rests exclusively on competition between the labourers. The advance of industry, whose involuntary promoter is the bourgeoisie, replaces the isolation of the labourers, due to competition, by their revolutionary combination, due to association. The development of modern industry, therefore, cuts from under its feet the very foundation on which the bourgeoisie produces and appropriates products. What the bourgeoisie therefore produces, above all, are its own grave-diggers. Its fall and the victory of the proletariat are equally inevitable.

II : PROLETARIANS AND COMMUNISTS

In what relation do the Communists stand to the proletarians as a whole?

The Communists do not form a separate party opposed to other working class parties.

They have no interests separate and apart from those of the proletariat as a whole.

They do not set up any sectarian principles of their own, by which to shape and mould the proletarian movement.

The Communists are distinguished from the other working class parties by this only : 1. In the national struggles of the proletarians of the different countries, they point out and bring to the front the common interests of the entire proletariat, independently of all nationality. 2. In the various stages of development which the struggle of the working class against the bourgeoisie has to pass through, they always and everywhere represent the interests of the movement as a whole.

The Communists, therefore, are on the one hand, practically, the most advanced and resolute section of the working class parties of every country, that section which pushes forward all others ; on the other hand, theoretically, they have over the great mass of the proletariat the advantage of clearly understanding the line of march, the conditions, and the ultimate general results of the proletarian movement.

The immediate aim of the Communists is the same as that of all the other proletarian parties : formation of the proletariat into a class, overthrow of the bourgeois supremacy, conquest of political power by the proletariat.

The theoretical conclusions of the Communists are in no way based on ideas or principles that have been invented, or discovered, by this or that would-be universal reformer.

They merely express, in general terms, actual relations springing from an existing class struggle, from a historical movement going on under our very eyes. The abolition of existing property relations is not at all a distinctive feature of Communism.

All property relations in the past have continually been subject to historical change consequent upon the change in historical conditions.

The French revolution, for example, abolished feudal property in favour of bourgeois property.

The distinguishing feature of Communism is not the abolition of property generally but the abolition of bourgeois property. But modern bourgeois private property is the final and most complete expression of the system of producing and appropriating products that is based on class antagonisms, on the exploitation of the many by the few.

In this sense, the theory of the Communists may be summed up in the single sentence : Abolition of private property.

We Communists have been reproached with the desire of abolishing the right of personally acquiring property as the fruit of a man's own labour, which property is alleged to be the groundwork of all personal freedom, activity and independence.

Hard-won, self-acquired, self-earned property ! Do you mean the property of the petty artisan and of the small peasant, a form of property that preceded the bourgeois form ? There is no need to abolish that ; the development of industry has to a great extent already destroyed it, and is still destroying it daily.

Or do you mean modern bourgeois private property ?

But does wage-labour create any property for the labourer ? Not a bit. It creates capital, i.e., that kind of property which exploits wage-labour and which cannot increase except upon condition of begetting a new supply of wage-labour for fresh exploitation. Property, in its present form, is based on the antagonism of capital and wage-labour. Let us examine both sides of this antagonism.

To be a capitalist is to have not only a purely personal,

but a social, *status* in production. Capital is a collective product, and only by the united action of many members, nay, in the last resort, only by the united action of all members of society, can it be set in motion.

Capital is therefore not a personal, it is a social power.

When, therefore, capital is converted into common property, into the property of all members of society, personal property is not thereby transformed into social property. It is only the social character of the property that is changed. It loses its class character.

Let us now take wage-labour.

The average price of wage-labour is the minimum wage, i.e., that quantum of the means of subsistence which is absolutely requisite to keep the labourer in bare existence as a labourer. What, therefore, the wage-labourer appropriates by means of his labour merely suffices to prolong and reproduce a bare existence. We by no means intend to abolish this personal appropriation of the products of labour, an appropriation that is made for the maintenance and reproduction of human life, and that leaves no surplus wherewith to command the labour of others. All that we want to do away with is the miserable character of this appropriation, under which the labourer lives merely to increase capital, and is allowed to live only in so far as the interest of the ruling class requires it.

In bourgeois society, living labour is but a means to increase accumulated labour. In Communist society, accumulated labour is but a means to widen, to enrich, to promote the existence of the labourer.

In bourgeois society, therefore, the past dominates the present ; in Communist society, the present dominates the past. In bourgeois society capital is independent and has individuality, while the living person is dependent and has no individuality.

And the abolition of this state of things is called by the bourgeois abolition of individuality and freedom ! And rightly so. The abolition of bourgeois individuality, bourgeois independence, and bourgeois freedom is undoubtedly aimed at.

By freedom is meant, under the present bourgeois conditions of production, free trade, free selling and buying.

But if selling and buying disappears, free selling and buying disappears also. This talk about free selling and buying, and all the other " brave words " of our bourgeoisie about freedom in general, have a meaning, if any, only in contrast with restricted selling and buying, with the fettered traders of the Middle Ages, but have no meaning when opposed to the Communist abolition of buying and selling, of the bourgeois conditions of production, and of the bourgeoisie itself.

You are horrified at our intending to do away with private property. But in your existing society, private property is already done away with for nine-tenths of the population ; its existence for the few is solely due to its non-existence in the hands of those nine-tenths. You reproach us, therefore, with intending to do away with a form of property, the necessary condition for whose existence is the non-existence of any property for the immense majority of society.

In one word, you reproach us with intending to do away with your property. Precisely so ; that is just what we intend.

From the moment when labour can no longer be converted into capital, money, or rent, into a social power capable of being monopolised, i.e., from the moment when individual property can no longer be transformed into bourgeois property, into capital, from that moment, you say, individuality vanishes.

You must, therefore, confess that by " individual " you mean no other person than the bourgeois, than the middle class owner of property. This person must, indeed, be swept out of the way, and made impossible.

Communism deprives no man of the power to appropriate the products of society ; all that it does is to deprive him of the power to subjugate the labour of others by means of such appropriation.

It has been objected that upon the abolition of private property all work will cease, and universal laziness will overtake us.

According to this, bourgeois society ought long ago to have gone to the dogs through sheer idleness ; for those of its members who work acquire nothing, and those who acquire anything do not work. The whole of this objection is but another expression of the tautology : There can no longer be any wage-labour when there is no longer any capital.

All objections urged against the Communistic mode of producing and appropriating material products have, in the same way, been urged against the Communistic modes of producing and appropriating intellectual products. Just as to the bourgeois the disappearance of class property is the disappearance of production itself so the disappearance of class culture is to him identical with the disappearance of all culture.

That culture, the loss of which he laments, is, for the enormous majority, a mere training to act as a machine.

But don't wrangle with us so long as you apply, to our intended abolition of bourgeois property, the standard of your bourgeois notions of freedom, culture, law, etc. Your very ideas are but the outgrowth of the conditions of your bourgeois production and bourgeois property, just as your jurisprudence is but the will of your class made into a law for all, a will whose essential character and direction are determined by the economical conditions of existence of your class.

The selfish misconception that induces you to transform into eternal laws of nature and of reason, the social forms springing from your present mode of production and form of property—historical relations that rise and disappear in the progress of production—this misconception you share with every ruling class that has preceded you. What you see clearly in the case of ancient property, what you admit in the case of feudal property, you are of course forbidden to admit in the case of your own bourgeois form of property.

Abolition of the family ! Even the most radical flare up at this infamous proposal of the Communists.

On what foundation is the present family, the bourgeois family, based ? On capital, on private gain. In its completely developed form this family exists only among the bourgeoisie. But this state of things finds its complement in the practical absence of the family among the proletarians, and in public prostitution.

The bourgeois family will vanish as a matter of course when its complement vanishes, and both will vanish with the vanishing of capital.

Do you charge us with wanting to stop the exploitation of children by their parents ? To this crime we plead guilty.

But, you will say, we destroy the most hallowed of relations, when we replace home education by social.

And your education ! Is not that also social, and determined by the social conditions under which you educate, by the intervention, direct or indirect, of society, by means of schools, etc. ? The Communists have not invented the intervention of society in education ; they do but seek to alter the character of that intervention, and to rescue education from the influence of the ruling class.

The bourgeois claptrap about the family and education, about the hallowed correlation of parent and child, becomes all the more disgusting the more, by the action of modern industry, all family ties among the proletarians are torn asunder, and their children transformed into simple articles of commerce and instruments of labour.

But you Communists would introduce community of women, screams the whole bourgeoisie in chorus.

The bourgeois sees in his wife a mere instrument of production. He hears that the instruments of production are to be exploited in common, and, naturally, can come to no other conclusion than that the lot of being common to all will likewise fall to the women.

He has not even a suspicion that the real point aimed at is to do away with the status of women as mere instruments of production.

For the rest, nothing is more ridiculous than the virtuous indignation of our bourgeois at the community of women which, they pretend, is to be openly and officially established by the Communists. The Communists have no need to introduce community of women ; it has existed almost from time immemorial.

Our bourgeois, not content with having the wives and daughters of their proletarians at their disposal, not to speak of common prostitutes, take the greatest pleasure in seducing each other's wives.

Bourgeois marriage is in reality a system of wives in common and thus, at the most, what the Communists might possibly be reproached with is that they desire to introduce, in substitution for a hypocritically concealed, an openly legalised community of women. For the rest, it is self-evident that the abolition of the present system of production must bring with it the abolition of the community of women springing from that system, i.e., of prostitution both public and private.

The Communists are further reproached with desiring to abolish countries and nationality.

The working men have no country. We cannot take from them what they have not got. Since the proletariat must first of all acquire political supremacy, must rise to be the leading class of the nation, must constitute itself *the* nation, it is, so far, itself national, though not in the bourgeois sense of the word.

National differences and antagonisms between peoples are daily more and more vanishing, owing to the development of the bourgeoisie, to freedom of commerce, to the world market, to uniformity in the mode of production and in the conditions of life corresponding thereto.

The supremacy of the proletariat will cause them to vanish still faster. United action of the leading civilised countries at least is one of the first conditions for the emancipation of the proletariat.

In proportion as the exploitation of one individual by another is put an end to, the exploitation of one nation by another will also be put an end to. In proportion as the antagonism between classes within the nation vanishes, the hostility of one nation to another will come to an end.

The charges against Communism made from a religious, a philosophical and, generally, from an ideological stand-point are not deserving of serious examination.

Does it require deep intuition to comprehend that man's ideas, views, and conceptions, in one word, man's conscious-ness, changes with every change in the conditions of his material existence, in his social relations and in his social life ?

What else does the history of ideas prove than that in-tellectual production changes its character in proportion as material production is changed ? The ruling ideas of each age have ever been the ideas of its ruling class.

When people speak of ideas that revolutionise society, they do but express the fact that within the old society the elements of a new one have been created, and that the dissolution of the old ideas keeps even pace with the dis-solution of the old conditions of existence.

When the ancient world was in its last throes, the ancient religions were overcome by Christianity. When Christian ideas succumbed in the eighteenth century to rationalist ideas, feudal society fought its death-battle with the then revolutionary bourgeoisie. The ideas of religious liberty and freedom of conscience merely gave expression to the sway of free competition within the domain of knowledge.

" Undoubtedly," it will be said, " religious, moral, philo-sophical and juridical ideas have been modified in the course of historical development. But religion, morality, philosophy, political science, and law constantly survived this change."

" There are, besides, eternal truths, such as Freedom, Justice, etc., that are common to all states of society. But Communism abolishes eternal truths, it abolishes all religion, and all morality, instead of constituting them on a new basis ; it therefore acts in contradiction to all past historical experience."

What does this accusation reduce itself to ? The history of all past society has consisted in the development of class antagonisms, antagonisms that assumed different forms at different epochs.

But whatever form they may have taken, one fact is common to all past ages, viz., the exploitation of one part of society by the other. No wonder, then, that the social consciousness of past ages, despite all the multiplicity and variety it displays, moves within certain common forms, or general ideas, which cannot completely vanish except with the total disappearance of class antagonisms.

The Communist revolution is the most radical rupture with traditional property relations ; no wonder that its development involves the most radical rupture with traditional ideas.

But let us have done with the bourgeois objections to Communism.

We have seen above that the first step in the revolution by the working class is to raise the proletariat to the position of ruling class, to win the battle of democracy.

The proletariat will use its political supremacy to wrest, by degrees, all capital from the bourgeoisie, to centralise all instruments of production in the hands of the State, i.e., of the proletariat organised as the ruling class ; and to increase the total of productive forces as rapidly as possible.

Of course, in the beginning, this cannot be effected except by means of despotic inroads on the rights of property, and on the conditions of bourgeois production ; by means of measures, therefore, which appear economically insufficient and untenable, but which, in the course of the movement, outstrip themselves, necessitate further inroads upon the old social order, and are unavoidable as a means of entirely revolutionising the mode of production.

These measures will, of course, be different in different countries.

Nevertheless in the most advanced countries, the following will be pretty generally applicable :

1. Abolition of property in land and application of all rents of land to public purposes.

2. A heavy progressive or graduated income tax.

3. Abolition of all right of inheritance.

4. Confiscation of the property of all emigrants and rebels.

5. Centralisation of credit in the hands of the State, by means of a national bank with State capital and an exclusive monopoly.

6. Centralisation of the means of communication and transport in the hands of the State.

7. Extension of factories and instruments of production owned by the State ; the bringing into cultivation of waste lands, and the improvement of the soil generally in accordance with a common plan.

8. Equal obligation of all to work. Establishment of industrial armies, especially for agriculture.

9. Combination of agriculture with manufacturing industries ; gradual abolition of the distinction between town and country, by a more equable distribution of the population over the country.

10. Free education for all children in public schools. Abolition of children's factory labour in its present form. Combination of education with industrial production, etc.

When, in the course of development, class distinctions have disappeared, and all production has been concentrated in the hands of a vast association of the whole nation, the public power will lose its political character. Political power, properly so called, is merely the organised power of one class for oppressing another. If the proletariat during its contest with the bourgeoisie is compelled, by the force of circumstances, to organise itself as a class ; if, by means of a revolution, it makes itself the ruling class, and, as such, sweeps away by force the old conditions of production, then it will, along with these conditions, have swept away the conditions for the existence of class antagonisms and of classes generally, and will thereby have abolished its own supremacy as a class.

In place of the old bourgeois society, with its classes and class antagonisms, we shall have an association in which the free development of each is the condition for the free development of all.

III : SOCIALIST AND COMMUNIST LITERATURE

1. Reactionary Socialism

a. Feudal Socialism

Owing to their historical position, it became the vocation of the aristocracies of France and England to write pamphlets against modern bourgeois society. In the French revolution of July 1830, and in the English reform agitation, these aristocracies again succumbed to the hateful upstart. Thenceforth, a serious political struggle was altogether out of the question. A literary battle alone remained possible. But even in the domain of literature the old cries of the restoration period[1] had become impossible.

In order to arouse sympathy, the aristocracy was obliged to lose sight, apparently, of its own interests, and to formulate its indictment against the bourgeoisie in the interest of the exploited working class alone. Thus the aristocracy took their revenge by singing lampoons on their new master, and whispering in his ears sinister prophecies of coming catastrophe.

In this way arose feudal socialism : half lamentation, half lampoon ; half echo of the past, half menace of the future ; at times, by its bitter, witty and incisive criticism, striking

[1] Not the English Restoration, 1660 to 1689, but the French Restoration, 1814 to 1830.

the bourgeoisie to the very heart's core, but always ludicrous in its effect, through total incapacity to comprehend the march of modern history.

The aristocracy, in order to rally the people to them, waved the proletarian alms-bag in front for a banner. But the people so often as it joined them saw on their hind-quarters the old feudal coats of arms and deserted with loud and irreverent laughter.

One section of the French Legitimists and "Young England," exhibited this spectacle.

In pointing out that their mode of exploitation was different to that of the bourgeoisie, the feudalists forget that they exploited under circumstances and conditions that were quite different, and that are now antiquated. In showing that, under their rule, the modern proletariat never existed, they forget that the modern bourgeoisie is the necessary offspring of their own form of society.

For the rest, so little do they conceal the reactionary character of their criticism that their chief accusation against the bourgeoisie amounts to this, that under the bourgeois régime a class is being developed which is destined to cut up root and branch the old order of society.

What they upbraid the bourgeoisie with is not so much that it creates a proletariat as that it creates a *revolutionary* proletariat.

In political practice, therefore, they join in all coercive measures against the working class ; and in ordinary life, despite their high-faluting phrases, they stoop to pick up the golden apples dropped from the tree of industry, and to barter truth, love, and honour for traffic in wool, beetroot-sugar, and potato spirits.[1]

---

[1] This applies chiefly to Germany where the landed aristocracy and squirearchy have large portions of their estates cultivated for their own account by stewards, and are, moreover, extensive beetroot-sugar manufacturers and distillers of potato spirits. The wealthier British aristocracy are, as yet, rather above that ; but they, too, know how to make up for declining rents by lending their names to floaters of more or less shady joint-stock companies.

As the parson has ever gone hand in hand with the landlord, so has Clerical Socialism with Feudal Socialism.

Nothing is easier than to give Christian asceticism a Socialist tinge. Has not Christianity declaimed against private property, against marriage, against the State? Has it not preached in the place of these, charity and poverty, celibacy and mortification of the flesh, monastic life and Mother Church? Christian Socialism is but the holy water with which the priest consecrates the heart-burnings of the aristocrat.

b. Petty Bourgeois Socialism

The feudal aristocracy was not the only class that was ruined by the bourgeoisie, not the only class whose conditions of existence pined and perished in the atmosphere of modern bourgeois society. The mediæval burgesses and the small peasant proprietors were the precursors of the modern bourgeoisie. In those countries which are but little developed, industrially and commercially, these two classes still vegetate side by side with the rising bourgeoisie.

In countries where modern civilisation has become fully developed, a new class of petty bourgeois has been formed, fluctuating between proletariat and bourgeoisie, and ever renewing itself as a supplementary part of bourgeois society. The individual members of this class, however, are being constantly hurled down into the proletariat by the action of competition, and, as modern industry develops, they even see the moment approaching when they will completely disappear as an independent section of modern society, to be replaced, in manufactures, agriculture and commerce, by overlookers, bailiffs and shopmen.

In countries like France, where the peasants constitute far more than half of the population, it was natural that writers who sided with the proletariat against the bourgeoisie should use, in their criticism of the bourgeois régime, the standard of the peasant and petty bourgeois, and from the standpoint of these intermediate classes should take up the cudgels for the working class. Thus arose petty bourgeois Socialism. Sismondi was the head of this school, not only in France but also in England.

This school of Socialism dissected with great acuteness the contradictions in the conditions of modern production. It laid bare the hypocritical apologies of economists. It proved, incontrovertibly, the disastrous effects of machinery and division of labour ; the concentration of capital and land in a few hands ; overproduction and crises ; it pointed out the inevitable ruin of the petty bourgeois and peasant, the misery of the proletariat, the anarchy in production, the crying inequalities in the distribution of wealth, the industrial war of extermination between nations, the dissolution of old moral bonds, of the old family relations, of the old nationalities.

In its positive aims, however, this form of Socialism aspires either to restoring the old means of production and of exchange, and with them the old property relations, and the old society, or to cramping the modern means of production and of exchange within the framework of the old property relations that have been, and were bound to be exploded by those means. In either case, it is both reactionary and Utopian.

Its last words are : Corporate guilds for manufacture ; patriarchal relations in agriculture.

Ultimately, when stubborn historical facts had dispersed all intoxicating effects of self-deception, this form of Socialism ended in a miserable fit of the blues.

c. German or " True " Socialism

The Socialist and Communist literature of France, a literature that originated under the pressure of a bourgeoisie in power, and that was the expression of the struggle against this power, was introduced into Germany at a time when the bourgeoisie in that country had just begun its contest with feudal absolutism.

German philosophers, would-be philosophers, and men of letters eagerly seized on this literature, only forgetting that when these writings immigrated from France into Germany, French social conditions had not immigrated along with them. In contact with German social conditions, this French literature lost all its immediate practical significance, and assumed a purely literary aspect. Thus, to the German philosophers of the eighteenth century, the demands of the " Practical Reason " in general—and the utterance of the will of the first French Revolution were nothing more than the demands of revolutionary French bourgeoisie—signified in their eyes the laws of pure will, of will as it was bound to be, of true human will generally.

The work of the German *literati* consisted solely in bringing the new French ideas into harmony with their ancient philosophical conscience, or, rather, in annexing the French ideas without deserting their own philosophic point of view.

This annexation took place in the same way in which a foreign language is appropriated, namely, by translation.

It is well known how the monks wrote silly lives of Catholic saints *over* the manuscripts on which the classical works of ancient heathendom had been written. The German *literati* reversed this process with the profane French literature. They wrote their philosophical nonsense beneath the French original. For instance, beneath the French criticism of the economic functions of money, they wrote " alienation of humanity," and beneath the French criticism of the bourgeois State they wrote, " dethronement of the category of the general," and so forth.

The introduction of these philosophical phrases at the back of the French historical criticisms they dubbed " Philosophy of Action," " True Socialism," " German Science of Socialism," " Philosophical Foundation of Socialism," and so on.

The French Socialist and Communist literature was thus completely emasculated. And, since it ceased in the hands of the German to express the struggle of one class with the other, he felt conscious of having overcome " French one-sidedness " and of representing, not true requirements, but the requirements of truth ; not the interests of the proletariat, but the interests of human nature, of man in general, who belongs to no class, has no reality, who exists only in the misty realm of philosophical phantasy.

This German Socialism, which took its schoolboy task so seriously and solemnly, and extolled its poor stock-in-trade in such mountebank fashion, meanwhile gradually lost its pedantic innocence.

The fight of the German and especially of the Prussian bourgeoisie against feudal aristocracy and absolute monarchy, in other words, the liberal movement, became more earnest.

By this, the long-wished-for opportunity was offered to " True " Socialism of confronting the political movement with the Socialist demands, of hurling the traditional anathemas against liberalism, against representative government, against bourgeois competition, bourgeois freedom of the press, bourgeois legislation, bourgeois liberty and equality, and of preaching to the masses that they had nothing to gain, and everything to lose, by this bourgeois movement. German Socialism forgot, in the nick of time, that the French criticism, whose silly echo it was, presupposed the existence of modern bourgeois society, with its corresponding economic conditions of existence, and the political constitution adapted thereto, the very things whose attainment was the object of the pending struggle in Germany.

To the absolute governments, with their following of parsons, professors, country squires and officials, it served as a welcome scarecrow against the threatening bourgeoisie.

It was a sweet finish after the bitter pills of floggings and bullets with which these same governments, just at that time, dosed the German working class risings.

While this " True " Socialism thus served the governments as a weapon for fighting the German bourgeoisie, it, at the same time, directly represented a reactionary interest, the interest of the German Philistines. In Germany the petty bourgeois class, a relic of the sixteenth century, and since then constantly cropping up again under various forms, is the real social basis of the existing state of things.

To preserve this class is to preserve the existing state of things in Germany. The industrial and political supremacy of the bourgeoisie threatens it with certain destruction— on the one hand, from the concentration of capital ; on the other, from the rise of a revolutionary proletariat. " True " Socialism appeared to kill these two birds with one stone. It spread like an epidemic

The robe of speculative cobwebs, embroidered with flowers of rhetoric, steeped in the dew of sickly sentiment, this transcendental robe in which the German Socialists wrapped their sorry " eternal truths," all skin and bone, served to wonderfully increase the sale of their goods amongst such a public.

And on its part, German Socialism recognised, more and more, its own calling as the bombastic representative of the petty bourgeois Philistine.

It proclaimed the German nation to be the model nation, and the German petty Philistine to be the typical man. To every villainous meanness of this model man it gave a hidden, higher, socialistic interpretation, the exact contrary of its real character. It went to the extreme length of directly opposing the " brutally destructive " tendency of Communism, and of proclaiming its supreme and impartial contempt of all class struggles. With very few exceptions, all the so-called Socialist and Communist publications that now (1847) circulate in Germany belong to the domain of this foul and enervating literature.

2. *Conservative or Bourgeois Socialism*

A part of the bourgeoisie is desirous of redressing social grievances, in order to secure the continued existence of bourgeois society.

To this section belong economists, philanthropists, humanitarians, improvers of the condition of the working class, organisers of charity, members of societies for the prevention of cruelty to animals, temperance fanatics, hole-and-corner reformers of every imaginable kind. This form of Socialism has, moreover, been worked out into complete systems.

We may cite Proudhon's *Philosophie de la Misère* (Philosophy of Poverty) as an example of this form.

The socialistic bourgeois want all the advantages of modern social conditions without the struggles and dangers necessarily resulting therefrom. They desire the existing state of society minus its revolutionary and disintegrating elements. They wish for a bourgeoisie without a proletariat. The bourgeoisie naturally conceives the world in which it is supreme to be the best ; and bourgeois Socialism develops this comfortable conception into various more or less complete systems. In requiring the proletariat to carry out such a system, and thereby to march straightway into the social New Jerusalem, it but requires in reality that the proletariat should remain within the bounds of existing society, but should cast away all its hateful ideas concerning the bourgeoisie.

A second and more practical, but less systematic, form of this Socialism sought to depreciate every revolutionary movement in the eyes of the working class, by showing that no mere political reform, but only a change in the material conditions of existence, in economical relations, could be of any advantage to them. By changes in the material conditions of existence, this form of Socialism, however, by no means understands abolition of the bourgeois relations of production, an abolition that can be effected only by a revolution, but administrative reforms, based on the continued existence of these relations ; reforms, therefore, that in no respect affect the relations between capital and labour, but, at the best, lessen the cost, and simplify the administrative work of bourgeois government.

Bourgeois Socialism attains adequate expression, when, and only when, it becomes a mere figure of speech.

Free trade : for the benefit of the working class. Protective duties : for the benefit of the working class. Prison reform : for the benefit of the working class. This is the last word and the only seriously meant word of bourgeois Socialism.

It is summed up in the phrase : the bourgeois is a bourgeois—for the benefit of the working class.

3. Critical-Utopian Socialism and Communism

We do not here refer to that literature which, in every great modern revolution, has always given voice to the demands of the proletariat, such as the writings of Babeuf and others.

The first direct attempts of the proletariat to attain its own ends, made in times of universal excitement, when feudal society was being overthrown—these attempts necessarily failed, owing to the then undeveloped state of the proletariat, as well as to the absence of the economic conditions for its emancipation, conditions that had yet to be produced, and could be produced by the impending bourgeois epoch alone. The revolutionary literature that accompanied these first movements of the proletariat had necessarily a reactionary character. It inculcated universal asceticism and social levelling in its crudest form.

The Socialist and Communist systems properly so called, those of St. Simon, Fourier, Owen and others, spring into existence in the early undeveloped period, described above, of the struggle between proletariat and bourgeoisie (see Section I. Bourgeois and Proletarians).

The founders of these systems see, indeed, the class antagonisms, as well as the action of the decomposing elements in the prevailing form of society. But the proletariat, as yet in its infancy, offers to them the spectacle of a class without any historical initiative or any independent political movement.

Since the development of class antagonism keeps even pace with the development of industry, the economic situation, as they find it, does not as yet offer to them the material conditions for the emancipation of the proletariat. They therefore search after a new social science, after new social laws, that are to create these conditions.

Historical action is to yield to their personal inventive action ; historically created conditions of emancipation to phantastic ones ; and the gradual, spontaneous class organisation of the proletariat to an organisation of society specially contrived by these inventors. Future history resolves itself, in their eyes, into the propaganda and the practical carrying out of their social plans.

In the formation of their plans they are conscious of caring chiefly for the interests of the working class, as being the most suffering class. Only from the point of view of being the most suffering class does the proletariat exist for them.

The undeveloped state of the class struggle, as well as their own surroundings, causes Socialists of this kind to consider themselves far superior to all class antagonisms. They want to improve the condition of every member of society, even that of the most favoured. Hence, they habitually appeal to society at large, without distinction of class ; nay, by preference, to the ruling class. For how can people, when once they understand their system, fail to see in it the best possible plan of the best possible state of society ?

Hence, they reject all political, and especially all revolutionary action ; they wish to attain their ends by peaceful means, and endeavour, by small experiments, necessarily doomed to failure, and by the force of example, to pave the way for the new social gospel.

Such phantastic pictures of future society, painted at a time when the proletariat is still in a very undeveloped state and has but a phantastic conception of its own position, correspond with the first instinctive yearnings of that class for a general reconstruction of society.

But these Socialist and Communist publications contain

also a critical element. They attack every principle of existing society. Hence they are full of the most valuable materials for the enlightenment of the working class. The practical measures proposed in them—such as the abolition of the distinction between town and country, of the family, of the carrying on of industries for the account of private individuals, and of the wage-system, the proclamation of social harmony, the conversion of the functions of the State into a mere superintendence of production—all these proposals point solely to the disappearance of class antagonisms which were, at that time, only just cropping up, and which, in these publications, are recognised in their earliest, indistinct and undefined forms only. These proposals, therefore, are of a purely Utopian character.

The significance of Critical-Utopian Socialism and Communism bears an inverse relation to historical development. In proportion as the modern class struggle develops and takes definite shape, this phantastic standing apart from the contest, these phantastic attacks on it, lose all practical value and all theoretical justification. Therefore, although the originators of these systems were, in many respects, revolutionary, their disciples have, in every case, formed mere reactionary sects. They hold fast by the original views of their masters, in opposition to the progressive historical development of the proletariat. They, therefore, endeavour, and that consistently, to deaden the class struggle and to reconcile the class antagonisms. They still dream of experimental realisation of their social Utopias, of founding isolated *phalansteres*, of establishing " Home Colonies," or setting up a " Little Icaria "[1]—pocket editions of the New Jerusalem—and to realise all these castles in the air, they are compelled to appeal to the feelings and purses of the bourgeois. By degrees they sink into the category of the reactionary conservative Socialists depicted above, differing

[1] *Phalansteres* were socialist colonies on the plan of Charles Fourier ; Icaria was the name given by Cabet to his Utopia and, later on, to his American Communist colony.

from these only by more systematic pedantry, and by their fanatical and superstitious belief in the miraculous effects of their social science.

They, therefore, violently oppose all political action on the part of the working class ; such action, according to them, can only result from blind unbelief in the new gospel.

The Owenites in England, and the Fourierists in France, respectively, oppose the Chartists and the *Reformistes*.

IV : POSITION OF THE COMMUNISTS IN RELATION TO THE VARIOUS EXISTING OPPOSITION PARTIES

Section II has made clear the relations of the Communists to the existing working class parties, such as the Chartists in England and the Agrarian Reformers in America.

The Communists fight for the attainment of the immediate aims, for the enforcement of the momentary interests of the working class ; but in the movement of the present, they also represent and take care of the future of that movement. In France the Communists ally themselves with the Social-Democrats,[1] against the conservative and radical bourgeoisie, reserving, however, the right to take up a critical position in regard to phrases and illusions tradition-ally handed down from the great Revolution.

In Switzerland they support the Radicals, without losing sight of the fact that this party consists of antagonistic ele-ments, partly of Democratic Socialists, in the French sense, partly of radical bourgeois.

In Poland they support the party that insists on an agrarian revolution as the prime condition for national emancipation, that party which fomented the insurrection of Cracow in 1846.

In Germany they fight with the bourgeoisie whenever it

[1] The party then represented in Parliament by Ledru-Rollin, in litera-ture by Louis Blanc [1811–1882], in the daily press by the *Reform*. The name of Social-Democracy signifies, with these its inventors, a section of the Democratic or Republican Party more or less tinged with Socialism.

acts in a revolutionary way, against the absolute monarchy, the feudal squirearchy, and the petty bourgeoisie.

But they never cease, for a single instant, to instil into the working class the clearest possible recognition of the hostile antagonism between bourgeoisie and proletariat, in order that the German workers may straightway use, as so many weapons against the bourgeoisie, the social and political conditions that the bourgeoisie must necessarily introduce along with its supremacy, and in order that, after the fall of the reactionary classes in Germany, the fight against the bourgeoisie itself may immediately begin.

The Communists turn their attention chiefly to Germany, because that country is on the eve of a bourgeois revolution that is bound to be carried out under more advanced conditions of European civilisation and with a much more developed proletariat than that of England was in the seventeenth, and of France in the eighteenth century, and because the bourgeois revolution in Germany will be but the prelude to an immediately following proletarian revolution.

In short, the Communists everywhere support every revolutionary movement against the existing social and political order of things.

In all these movements they bring to the front, as the leading question in each, the property question, no matter what its degree of development at the time.

Finally, they labour everywhere for the union and agreement of the democratic parties of all countries.

The Communists disdain to conceal their views and aims. They openly declare that their ends can be attained only by the forcible overthrow of all existing social conditions. Let the ruling classes tremble at a Communist revolution. The proletarians have nothing to lose but their chains. They have a world to win.

Working men of all countries, unite !

(NOTE : The footnotes were written by Engels for the English edition of 1888.)

Karl Marx

ADDRESS TO THE COMMUNIST LEAGUE (1850)

Drafted by Marx, and adopted by the Central Executive of the Communist League, March 1850. Translation by Max Beer published in the Labour Monthly, September 1922.

[The *Communist Manifesto* of 1848 was the general programme of the Communist League ; the 1850 Address was the practical working out of the revolutionary principles of the *Manifesto* for the next round of the revolutionary struggle. It is of particular importance for its insistence on the need for a separate working-class party which, when the bourgeois democratic governments took power, should set up its own alternative authority " either in the form of local executives and communal councils, or workers' clubs or workers' committees " thus foreshadowing the Soviets of March – November 1917.]

ADDRESS TO THE COMMUNIST LEAGUE (1850)

ADDRESS OF THE CENTRAL AUTHORITY TO THE LEAGUE

BRETHREN,—During the last two years of revolution (1848–9) the League doubly justified its existence. First, by the vigorous activity of our members ; in all places and movements where they happened to be at that time they were foremost in the Press, on the barricades, and on the battlefields of the proletariat, the only revolutionary class in society. Secondly, through the League's conception of the whole upheaval, as enunciated in the circular letter of the Congresses and the Central Executive in 1847, and

The proletarians have nothing to lose but their chains.
(*The Communist Manifesto*)

particularly in *The Communist Manifesto*. This conception has been verified by the actual happenings of the last two years. Moreover, the views of the present-day social conditions, which we in former years used to propagate in secret meetings and writings, are now public property and are preached in the market-places and at the street corners.

On the other hand, the former rigid organisation of the League has considerably loosened, a great number of members who directly participated in the revolution have come to the conclusion that the time for secret organisation was past, and that public propaganda alone would be sufficient. Various districts and communities lost contact with the Central Authority and have not resumed it. While the Democratic Party, the party of the petty bourgeoisie, enlarged and strengthened their organisation, the working-class party lost its cohesion, or formed local organisations for local purposes, and therefore was dragged into the democratic movement and so came under the sway of the petty bourgeoisie. This state of things must be put an end to; the independence of the working class must be restored. The Central Authority, as far back as the winter of 1848–9, saw the necessity for reorganisation and sent the missionary, Joseph Moll, but this mission had no lasting result. After the defeat of the revolutionary movement in Germany and France in June, 1849, nearly all the members of the Central Authority reunited in London, supplemented by new revolutionary forces, and took the work of the reorganisation seriously in hand.

This reorganisation can only be accomplished by a special missionary, and the Central Authority thinks it most important that the missionary should start on his journey at this moment when a new upheaval is imminent ; when therefore the working-class Party should be thoroughly organised and act unanimously and independently, if it does not wish again to be exploited and taken in tow by the bourgeoisie, as in 1848.

.   .   .   .

We have told you, brethren, as far back as in 1848, that
German Liberalism would soon come to power and would
at once use it against the working class. You have seen how
this has been fulfilled. It was the bourgeoisie who after the
victorious movement of March, 1848, took the reins of
government, and the first use they made of their power was
to force back the working men, their allies in the fight
against absolutism, to their former oppressed condition.
They could not achieve their purpose without the assistance
of the defeated aristocracy, to whom they even transferred
governmental power, securing, however, for themselves the
ultimate control of the Government through the budget. . . .

The part which the Liberals played in 1848, this treach-
erous rôle will at the next revolution be played by the
democratic petty bourgeoisie, who, among the parties
opposing the Government, are now occupying the same
position which the Liberals occupied prior to the March
revolution. This democratic party, which is more dangerous
to the working men than the Liberal Party was, consists of
the following three elements :

(i) The more progressive members of the upper bourgeoisie, whose object it is to sweep away all remnants
of feudalism and absolutism ;

(ii) The democratic-constitutional petty bourgeoisie,
whose main object it is to establish a democratic
federation of the Germanic States ;

(iii) The republican petty bourgeoisie, whose ideal it is
to turn Germany into a sort of Swiss republic. These
republicans are calling themselves " reds " and
" social democrats " because they have the pious wish
to remove the pressure of large capital upon the smaller
one, and of the big bourgeoisie upon the petty
bourgeoisie.

All these parties, after the defeat they have suffered, are
calling themselves republicans or reds, just as in France

the republican petty bourgeoisie are calling themselves socialists. Where, however, they have the opportunity of pursuing their aims by constitutional methods they are using their old phraseology and are showing by deed that they have not changed at all. It is a matter of course that the changed name of that party does not alter their attitude towards the working class ; it merely proves that in their struggle against the united forces of absolutism and large capitalists they require the support of the proletariat.

The petty bourgeois democratic party in Germany is very powerful. It embraces not only the great majority of the town population, the small traders and craftsmen, but also the peasantry and the agricultural labourers, in so far as the latter have not yet come into contact with the proletariat of the towns. The revolutionary working class acts in agreement with that party as long as it is a question of fighting and overthrowing the Aristocratic-Liberal coalition ; in all other things the revolutionary working class must act independently. The democratic petty bourgeoisie, far from desiring to revolutionise the whole society, are aiming only at such changes of the social conditions as would make their life in existing society more comfortable and profitable. They desire above all a reduction of national expenditure through a decrease of bureaucracy, and the imposition of the main burden of taxation on the landowners and capitalists. They demand, likewise, the establishment of State banks and laws against usury, so as to ease the pressure of the big capitalist upon the small traders and to get from the State cheap credit. They demand also the full mobilisation of the land, so as to do away with all remnants of manorial rights. For these purposes they need a democratic constitution which would give them the majority in Parliament, municipality, and parish.

With a view to checking the power and the growth of big capital the democratic party demand a reform of the laws of inheritance and legacies, likewise the transfer of the public services and as many industrial undertakings as possible to the State and municipal authorities. As to the working men—well, they should remain wage workers : for whom, however, the democratic party would procure higher wages, better labour conditions, and a secure existence. The democrats hope to achieve that partly through State and municipal management and through welfare institutions. In short, they hope to bribe the working class into quiescence, and thus to weaken their revolutionary spirit by momentary concessions and comforts.

The democratic demands can never satisfy the party of the proletariat. While the democratic petty bourgeoisie would like to bring the revolution to a close as soon as their demands are more or less complied with, it is our interest and our task to make the revolution permanent, to keep it going until all the ruling and possessing classes are deprived of power, the governmental machinery occupied by the proletariat, and the organisation of the working classes of all lands is so far advanced that all rivalry and competition among themselves has ceased ; until the more important forces of production are concentrated in the hands of the proletarians. With us it is not a matter of reforming private property, but of abolishing it ; not of hushing up the class antagonism, but of abolishing the classes ; not of ameliorating the existing society, but of establishing a new one. There is doubt that, with the further development of the revolution, the petty bourgeois democracy may for a time become the most influential party in Germany. The question is, therefore, what should be the attitude of the proletariat, and particularly of the League, towards it :

(i) During the continuation of the present conditions in which the petty bourgeois democracy is also oppressed ?

(ii) In the ensuing revolutionary struggles which would give them momentary ascendancy ?

(iii) After those struggles, during the time of their ascendancy over the defeated classes and the proletariat ?

(i) At the present moment when the democratic petty bourgeoisie are everywhere oppressed, they lecture the proletariat, exhorting it to effect a unification and conciliation ; they would like to join hands and form one great opposition party, embracing within its folds all shades of democracy. That is, they would like to entangle the proletariat in a party organisation in which the general social democratic phrases predominate, behind which their particular interests are concealed, and in which the particular proletarian demands should not, for the sake of peace and concord, be brought forward. Such a unification would be to the exclusive benefit of the petty bourgeois democracy and to the injury of the proletariat. The organised working class would lose its hard-won independence and would become again a mere appendage of the official bourgeois democracy. Such a unification must be resolutely opposed.

Instead of allowing themselves to form the chorus of the bourgeois democracy, the working men, and particularly the League, must strive to establish next to the official democracy an independent, a secret as well as a legal organisation of the working-class party, and to make each community the centre and nucleus of working-class societies in which the attitude and the interests of the proletariat should be discussed independently of bourgeois influences. How little the bourgeois democrats care for an alliance in which the proletarians should be regarded as co-partners with equal rights and equal standing is shown by the attitude of the Breslau democrats, who in their organ the *Oder-Zeitung* are attacking those working men who are independently organised, and whom they nick-name socialists, subjecting them to severe persecutions. The gist of the matter is this : In case of an attack on a common adversary no special union is necessary ; in the fight with such an enemy the interests of both parties, the middle-class democrats and the working-class party, coincide for the moment, and both parties will carry it on by a temporary understanding. This was so in the past, and will be so in the

future. It is a matter of course that in the future sanguinary
conflicts, as in all previous ones, the working men by their
courage, resolution, and self-sacrifice will form the main
force in the attainment of victory. As hitherto, so in the
coming struggle, the petty bourgeoisie as a whole will
maintain an attitude of delay, irresolution, and inactivity
as long as possible, in order that, as soon as victory is
assured, they may arrogate it to themselves and call upon
the workers to remain quiet, return to work, avoid so-called
excesses, and thus to shut off the workers from the fruits of
victory. It is not in the power of the workers to prevent
the petty bourgeois democrats from doing that ; but it is
within their power to render their ascendancy over the
armed proletariat difficult, and to dictate to them such
terms as shall make the rule of the bourgeois democracy
carry within itself from the beginning the germ of dissolution, and its ultimate substitution by the rule of the proletariat considerably facilitated.

The workers, above all during the conflict and immediately afterwards, must try as much as ever possible to
counteract all bourgeois attempts at appeasement, and
compel the democrats to carry out their present terrorist
phrases. They must act in such a manner that the revolutionary excitement does not subside immediately after the
victory. On the contrary, they must endeavour to maintain
it as long as possible. Far from opposing so-called excesses
and making examples of hated individuals or public
buildings to which hateful memories are attached by
sacrificing them to popular revenge, such deeds must not
only be tolerated, but their direction must be taken in hand.
During the fight and afterwards the workers must seize
every opportunity to present their own demands beside
those of the bourgeois democrats. They must demand
guarantees for the workers as soon as the democrats propose
to take over the reins of government. If necessary, they
must exact these guarantees, and generally see to it that
the new rulers should bind themselves to every possible

concession and promise, which is the surest way to compromise them. The workers must not be swept off their feet
by the general elation and enthusiasm for the new order of
things which usually follow upon street battles ; they must
quench all ardour by a cool and dispassionate conception of
the new conditions, and must manifest open distrust of the
new Government. Beside the official Government they
must set up a revolutionary workers' Government, either in
the form of local executives and communal councils, or
workers' clubs or workers' committees, so that the bourgeois
democratic Governments not only immediately lose all
backing among the workers, but from the commencement find themselves under the supervision and threats of
authorities, behind whom stands the entire mass of the
working class. In short, from the first moment of victory
we must no longer direct our distrust against the beaten
reactionary enemy, but against our former allies, against
the party who are now about to exploit the common victory
for their own ends only.

(ii) In order that this party, whose betrayal of the
workers will begin with the first hour of victory, should be
frustrated in its nefarious work, it is necessary to organise
and arm the proletariat. The arming of the whole proletariat with rifles, guns, and ammunition must be carried
out at once ; we must prevent the revival of the old bourgeois militia, which has always been directed against the
workers. Where the latter measure cannot be carried out,
the workers must try to organise themselves into an independent guard, with their own chiefs and general staff, to
put themselves under the order, not of the Government, but
of the revolutionary authorities set up by the workers.
Where workers are employed in State service they must
arm and organise in special corps, with chiefs chosen by
themselves, or form part of the proletarian guard. Under no
pretext must they give up their arms and equipment, and
any attempt at disarmament must be forcibly resisted.
Destruction of the influence of bourgeois democracy over

the workers, immediate independent and armed organisation of the workers, and the exaction of the most irksome
and compromising terms from the bourgeois democracy,
whose triumph is for the moment unavoidable—these are
the main points which the proletariat, and therefore also
the League, has to keep in eye during and after the coming
upheaval.

(iii) As soon as the new Government is established they
will commence to fight the workers. In order to be able
effectively to oppose the petty bourgeois democracy, it is in
the first place necessary that the workers should be independently organised in clubs, which should soon be centralised.
The central authority, after the overthrow of the existing
Governments, will at the earliest opportunity transfer its
headquarters to Germany, immediately call together a
congress, and make the necessary proposals for the centralisation of the workers' clubs under an Executive Committee,
who will have their headquarters in the centre of the
movement. The rapid organisation, or at least the establishment of a provincial union of the workers' clubs, is one of
the most important points in our considerations for invigor-
ating and developing the Workers' Party. The next result
of the overthrow of the existing Government will be the
election of a national representation. The proletariat must
see to it first that no worker shall be deprived of his suffrage
by the trickery of the local authorities or Government
commissioners ; secondly, that beside the bourgeois
democratic candidates there shall be put up everywhere
working-class candidates, who, as far as possible, shall be
members of the League, and for whose success all must
work with every possible means. Even in constituencies
where there is no prospect of our candidate being elected,
the workers must nevertheless put up candidates in order
to maintain their independence, to steel their forces, and to
bring their revolutionary attitude and party views before the
public. They must not allow themselves to be diverted
from this work by the stock argument that to split the vote

of the democrats means assisting the reactionary parties. All such talk is but calculated to cheat the proletariat. The advance which the Proletarian Party will make through its independent political attitude is infinitely more important than the disadvantage of having a few more reactionaries in the national representation. The victorious democrats could, if they liked, even prevent the reactionary party having any success at all, if they only used their newly won power with sufficient energy.

The first point which will bring the democrats into conflict with the proletariat is the abolition of all feudal rights. The petty bourgeois democrats, following the example of the first French Revolution, will hand over the lands as private property to the peasants ; that is, they will leave the agricultural labourers as they are, and will but create a petty bourgeois peasantry, who will pass through the same cycle of material and spiritual misery in which the French peasant now finds himself.

The workers, in the interest of the agricultural proletariat as well as in their own, must oppose all such plans. They must demand that the confiscated feudal lands shall be nationalised and converted into settlements for the associated groups of the landed proletariat ; all the advantages of large-scale agriculture shall be put at their disposal ; these agricultural colonies, worked on the co-operative principle, shall be put in the midst of the crumbling bourgeois property institutions. Just as the democrats have combined with the small peasantry, so we must fight shoulder to shoulder with the agricultural proletariat. Further, the democrat will either work directly for a federal republic, or at least, if they cannot avoid the republic one and indivisible, will seek to paralyse the centralisation of government by granting the greatest possible independence to the municipalities and provinces. The workers must set their face against this plan, not only to secure the one and indivisible German republic, but to concentrate as much power as possible in the hands of the Central Government.

They need not be misled by democratic platitudes about
freedom of the communes, self-determination, &c. In a
country like Germany, where there are so many mediæval
remnants to be swept away and so much local and provincial obstinacy to be overcome, under no circumstances
must parishes, towns, and provinces be allowed to be made
into obstacles in the way of the revolutionary activity which
must emanate from the centre. That the Germans should
have to fight and bleed, as they have done hitherto, for
every advance over and over again in every town and in
every province separately cannot be tolerated. As in France
in 1793, so it is to-day the task of the revolutionary party
in Germany to centralise the nation.

We have seen that the democrats will come to power in
the next phase of the movement, and that they will be
obliged to propose measures of a more or less socialistic
nature. It will be asked what contrary measures should be
proposed by the workers. Of course they cannot in the
beginning propose actual communist measures, but they
can (i) compel the democrats to attack the old social order
from as many sides as possible, disturb their regular procedure and compromise themselves, and concentrate in
the hands of the State as much as possible of the productive forces, means of transport, factories, railways, &c.
(ii) The measures of the democrats, which in any case are
not revolutionary but merely reformist, must be pressed
to the point of turning them into direct attacks on private
property ; thus, for instance, if the petty bourgeoisie propose to purchase the railways and factories, the workers
must demand that such railways and factories, being the
property of the reactionaries, shall simply be confiscated
by the State without compensation. If the democrats propose proportional taxation, the workers must demand
progressive taxation ; if the democrats themselves declare
for a moderate progressive tax, the workers must insist on
a tax so steeply graduated as to cause the collapse of large
capital ; if the democrats propose the regulation of the

National Debt, the workers must demand State bankruptcy. The demands of the workers will depend on the proposals and measures of the democrats.

If the German workers will only come to power and to the enforcement of their class interests after a prolonged revolutionary development, they will at least gain the certainty that the first act of this revolutionary drama will coincide with the victory of their class in France, and this will surely accelerate the movement of their own emancipation. But they themselves must accomplish the greater part of the work ; they must be conscious of their class interests and take up the position of an independent party. They must not be diverted from their course of proletarian independence by the hypocrisy of the democratic petty bourgeoisie. Their battle-cry must be : " The revolution in permanence."

Friedrich Engels

INTRODUCTION TO THE CLASS STRUGGLES IN FRANCE
(1848 – 50)

Written in March 1895, and published, with essential passages omitted, in the German Social Democratic paper " Vorwärts." The complete original text is in the English edition of " The Class Struggles in France," published in 1934 by Martin Lawrence Ltd.

[In writing this introduction in 1895, Engels was able to draw on the experience of forty-five years of class struggles in Europe since Marx wrote *The Class Struggles in France*. It therefore serves as a general introduction also to the extracts given from Marx's works covering later periods ; its particular significance is its examination of the failure of earlier working class revolts, its conclusions on insurrectionary tactics, and its emphasis on the growth of the German Social Democratic Party. It is of special interest to note that the editor of *Vorwärts*, Wilhelm Liebknecht, cut out a number of passages in which Engels drew lessons for future insurrections, thus leaving the impression on the reader that Engels had abandoned his revolutionary ideas, and had become a peaceful worshipper of legality. The text given below is complete ; the passages omitted by *Vorwärts* in 1895 are printed in italics and enclosed in square brackets.]

INTRODUCTION TO THE CLASS STRUGGLES IN FRANCE

THIS newly republished work was Marx's first attempt, with the aid of his materialist conception, to explain a section of contemporary history from the given economic situation. In *The Communist Manifesto*, the theory was applied in broad outline to the whole of modern history, while in the articles by Marx and myself in the *Neue Rheinische Zeitung*, it was constantly used to interpret political events of the day. Here, on the other hand, the question was to demonstrate the inner causal connection in the course of a development which extended over some years, a development as critical, for the whole of Europe, as it was typical ; that is, in accordance with the conception of the author, to trace political events back to the effects of what are, in the last resort, economic causes.

In judging the events and series of events of day-to-day history, it will never be possible for anyone to go right back to the final economic causes. Even to-day, when the specialised technical press provides such rich materials, in

England itself it still remains impossible to follow day by day the movement of industry and trade in the world market and the changes which take place in the methods of production, in such a way as to be able to draw the general conclusion, at any point of time, from these very complicated and ever changing factors : of these factors, the most important, into the bargain, generally operate a long time in secret before they suddenly and violently make themselves felt on the surface. A clear survey of the economic history of a given period is never contemporaneous ; it can only be gained subsequently, after collecting and sifting of the material has taken place. Statistics are a necessary help here, and they always lag behind. For this reason, it is only too often necessary, in the current history of the time, to treat the most decisive factor as constant, to treat the economic situation existing at the beginning of the period concerned as given and unalterable for the whole period, or else to take notice only of such changes in this situation as themselves arise out of events clearly before us, and as, therefore, can likewise be clearly seen. Hence, the materialist method has here often to limit itself to tracing political conflicts back to the struggles between the interests of the social classes and fractions of classes encountered as the result of economic development, and to show the particular political parties as the more or less adequate political expression of these same classes and fractions of classes.

It is self-evident that this unavoidable neglect of contemporaneous changes in the economic situation, of the very basis of all the proceedings subject to examination, must be a source of error. But all the conditions of a comprehensive presentation of the history of the day unavoidably imply sources of error—which, however, keeps nobody from writing contemporary history.

When Marx undertook this work, the sources of error mentioned were, to a still greater degree, impossible to avoid. It was quite impossible during the period of the

Revolution of 1848–9 to follow the economic transformations which were being consummated at the same time, or even to keep a general view of them. It was just the same during the first months of exile in London, in the autumn and winter of 1849–50. But that was just the time when Marx began this work. And, in spite of these unfavourable circumstances, his exact knowledge both of the economic situation in France and of the political history of that country since the February Revolution made it possible for him to give a picture of events which laid bare their inner connections in a way never attained since, and which later brilliantly withstood the double test instituted by Marx himself.

The first test resulted from the fact that after the spring of 1850 Marx once again found leisure for economic studies, and first of all took up the economic history of the last ten years. In this study, what he had earlier deduced, half *a priori*, from defective material, was made absolutely clear to him by the facts themselves, namely, that the world trade crisis of 1847 had been the true mother of the February and March Revolutions and that the industrial prosperity which had been returning gradually since the middle of 1848, and which attained full bloom in 1849 and 1850, was the revivifying force of the newly strengthened European reaction. That was decisive. Whereas in the three first articles (which appeared in the January, February and March numbers of the *Neue Rheinische Zeitung, politischökonomische Revue*, Hamburg, 1850) there was still the expectation of an imminent new upsurge of revolutionary energy, the historical review written by Marx and myself for the last number, which was published in the autumn of 1850 (a double number, May to October), breaks once and for all with these illusions : " A new revolution is only possible as a result of a new crisis. It is just as certain, however, as this." But that was the only essential change which had to be made. There was absolutely nothing to alter in the interpretation of events given in the earlier chapters, or in the causal connections established therein, as the continuation of the narrative from March 10, up to the autumn of 1850 in the review in question, proves. I have therefore included this continuation as the fourth article in the present new edition.

The second test was even more severe. Immediately after Louis Bonaparte's *coup d'état* of December 2, 1851. Marx worked out anew the history of France from February 1848, up to this event, which concluded the revolutionary period for the time being. (*The Eighteenth Brumaire of Louis Bonaparte*. Third edition, Meissner, Hamburg, 1885.) In this brochure the period which we had depicted in our present publication is again dealt with, although more briefly. Compare this second production, written in the light of decisive events which happened over a year later, with our present publication, and it will be found that the author had very little to change.

The thing which still gives this work of ours a quite special significance is that, for the first time, it expresses the formula in which, by common agreement, the workers' parties of all countries in the world briefly summarise their demand for economic reconstruction : the appropriation by society of the means of production. In the second chapter, in connection with the " right to work," which is characterised as " the first clumsy formula wherein the revolutionary aspirations of the proletariat are summarised," it is said : " But behind the right to work stands the power over capital ; behind the power over capital, the appropriation of the means of production, their subjection to the associated working class and, therefore, the abolition of wage labour as well as of capital and of their mutual relationships." Thus, here, for the first time, the proposition is formulated by which modern working class socialism is equally sharply differentiated both from all the different shades of feudal, bourgeois, petty-bourgeois, etc., socialism and also from the confused community of goods of Utopian and spontaneous worker-communism. If, later, Marx extended the formula to appropriation of the means of exchange also, this extension, which, in any case, was self-evident after *The Communist Manifesto*, only expressed a corollary to the main proposition. A few wiseacres in England have of late added that the " means of distribution " should also be handed over to society. It would be difficult for these gentlemen to say what these economic means of distribution are, as distinct from the means of production and exchange ; unless political means of distribution are meant, taxes, poor relief, including the *Sachsenwald* and other endowments. But, first, these are means of distribution now already in collective possession, either of the state or of the commune, and, secondly, it is precisely these we wish to abolish.

When the February Revolution broke out, we all of us, as far as our conception of the conditions and the course of revolutionary movements was concerned, were under the spell of previous historical experience, namely that of France. It was, indeed, the latter which had dominated the whole of European history since 1789, and from which now once again the signal had gone forth for general revolutionary change. It was therefore natural and unavoidable that our conceptions of the nature and the path of the " social " revolution proclaimed in Paris in February 1848, of the revolution of the proletariat, were strongly coloured by memories of the models of 1789-1830. Moreover, when the Paris upheaval found its echo in the victorious insurrections in Vienna, Milan and Berlin ; when the whole of Europe right up to the Russian frontier was swept into the movement ; when in Paris the first great battle for power between the proletariat and the bourgeoisie was joined ; when the very victory of their class so shook the bourgeoisie of all countries that they fled back into the arms of the monarchist-feudal reaction which had just been overthrown—for us, under the circumstances of the time, there could be no doubt that the great decisive struggle had broken out, that it would have to be fought out in a single, long and changeful period of revolution, but that it could only end with the final victory of the proletariat.

After the defeats of 1849 we in no way shared the illusions of the vulgar democracy grouped around the would-be provisional governments *in partibus*. This vulgar democracy reckoned on a speedy and finally decisive victory of the " people " over the " usurpers " ; we looked to a long struggle, after the removal of the " usurpers," between the antagonistic elements concealed within this " people " itself. Vulgar democracy expected a renewed outbreak from day to day ; we declared as early as autumn 1850 that at least the first chapter of the revolutionary period was closed and that nothing further was to be expected until the outbreak of a new world crisis. For this reason we were excommunicated, as traitors to the revolution, by the very people who later, almost without exception, have made their peace with Bismarck—so far as Bismarck found them worth the trouble.

But we, too, have been shown to have been wrong by history, which has revealed our point of view of that time to have been an illusion. It has done even more : it has not merely destroyed our error of that time ; it has also completely transformed the conditions under which the proletariat has to fight. The mode of struggle of 1848 is to-day obsolete from every point of view, and this is a point which deserves closer examination on the present occasion.

All revolutions up to the present day have resulted in the displacement of one definite class rule by another ; all ruling classes up till now have been only minorities as against the ruled mass of the people. A ruling minority was thus overthrown ; another minority seized the helm of state and remodelled the state apparatus in accordance with its own interests. Thus was on every occasion the minority group able and called to rule by the degree of economic development, and just for that reason, and only for that

reason, it happened that the ruled majority either participated in the revolution on the side of the former or else
passively acquiesced in it. But if we disregard the concrete
content of each occasion, the common form of all these
revolutions was that they were minority revolutions. Even
where the majority took part, it did so—whether wittingly
or not—only in the service of a minority ; but because of
this, or simply because of the passive, unresisting attitude
of the majority, this minority acquired the appearance of
being the representative of the whole people.

As a rule, after the first great success, the victorious
minority became divided ; one half was pleased with what
had been gained, the other wanted to go still further, and
put forward new demands, which, to a certain extent at
least, were also in the real or apparent interests of the great
mass of the people. In individual cases these more radical
demands were realised, but often only for the moment ;
the more moderate party again gained the upper hand,
and what had eventually been won was wholly or partly
lost again ; the vanquished shrieked of treachery, or ascribed
their defeat to accident. But in truth the position was
mainly this : the achievements of the first victory were only
safeguarded by the second victory of the more radical
party ; this having been attained, and, with it, what was
necessary for the moment, the radicals and their achievements vanished once more from the stage.

All revolutions of modern times, beginning with the
great English revolution of the seventeenth century, showed
these features, which appeared inseparable from every
revolutionary struggle. They appeared applicable, also, to
the struggles of the proletariat for its emancipation ; all the
more applicable, since in 1848 there were few people who
had any idea at all of the direction in which this emancipation was to be sought. The proletarian masses themselves,
even in Paris, after the victory, were still absolutely in the
dark as to the path to be taken. And yet the movement was
there, instinctive, spontaneous, irrepressible. Was not this

just the situation in which a revolution had to succeed, led certainly by a minority, but this time not in the interests of the minority, but in the real interests of the majority ? If, in all the longer revolutionary periods, it was so easy to win the great masses of the people by the merely plausible and delusive views of the minorities thrusting themselves forward, how could they be less susceptible to ideas which were the truest reflex of their economic position, which were nothing but the clear, comprehensible expression of their needs, of needs not yet understood by themselves, but only vaguely felt ? To be sure, this revolutionary mood of the masses had almost always, and usually very speedily, given way to lassitude or even to a revulsion to its opposite, so soon as illusion evaporated and disappointment set in. But here it was not a question of delusive views, but of giving effect to the very special interests of the great majority itself, interests which at that time were certainly by no means clear to this great majority, but which must soon enough become clear in the course of giving practical effect to them, by their convincing obviousness. And if now, as Marx showed in the third article, in the spring of 1850, the development of the bourgeois republic that had arisen out of the " social " revolution of 1848 had concentrated the real power in the hands of the big bourgeoisie—monarchistically inclined as it was—and, on the other hand, had grouped all the other social classes, peasants as well as petty bourgeoisie, round the proletariat, so that, during and after the common victory, not they, but the proletariat grown wise by experience, must become the decisive factor—was there not every prospect here of turning the revolution of the minority into the revolution of the majority ?

History has proved us, and all who thought like us, wrong. It has made it clear that the state of economic development on the Continent at that time was not, by a long way, ripe for the removal of capitalist production ; it has proved this by the economic revolution which, since

1848, has seized the whole of the Continent, has really caused big industry for the first time to take root in France, Austria, Hungary, Poland and, recently, in Russia, while it has made Germany positively an industrial country of the first rank—all on a capitalist basis, which in the year 1848, therefore, still had great capacity for expansion. But it is just this industrial revolution which has everywhere for the first time produced clarity in the class relationships, which has removed a number of transition forms handed down from the manufacturing period and in Eastern Europe even from guild handicraft, and has created a genuine bourgeoisie and a genuine large-scale industrial proletariat and pushed them into the foreground of social development. But, owing to this, the struggle of these two great classes, which, apart from England, existed in 1848 only in Paris and, at the most, a few big industrial centres, has been spread over the whole of Europe and has reached an intensity such as was unthinkable in 1848. At that time the many obscure evangels of the sects, with their panaceas; to-day the one generally recognised, transparently clear theory of Marx, sharply formulating the final aims of the struggle. At that time the masses, sundered and differing according to locality and nationality, linked only by the feeling of common suffering, undeveloped, tossed to and fro in their perplexity from enthusiasm to despair ; to-day a great international army of Socialists, marching irresistibly on and growing daily in number, organisation, discipline, insight and assurance of victory. If even this mighty army of the proletariat has still not reached its goal, if, a long way from winning victory with one mighty stroke, it has slowly to press forward from position to position in a hard, tenacious struggle, this only proves, once and for all, how impossible it was in 1848 to win social reconstruction by a simple surprise attack.

A bourgeoisie split into two monarchist sections adhering to two dynasties, a bourgeoisie, however, which demanded, above all, peace and security for its financial operations, faced with a proletariat vanquished, indeed, but still a constant menace, a proletariat round which petty bourgeois and peasants grouped themselves more and more—the continual threat of a violent outbreak, which, nevertheless, offered no prospect of a final solution—such was the situation, as if created for the *coup d'état* of the third, the pseudo-democratic pretender, Louis Bonaparte. On December 2, 1851, by means of the army, he put an end to the tense situation and secured for Europe the assurance of domestic tranquillity, in order to give it the blessing of a new era of wars. The period of revolutions from below was concluded for the time being ; there followed a period of revolutions from above.

The imperial reaction of 1851 gave a new proof of the unripeness of the proletarian aspirations of that time. But it was itself to create the conditions under which they were bound to ripen. Internal tranquillity ensured the full development of the new industrial boom ; the necessity of keeping the army occupied and of diverting the revolutionary currents outwards produced wars, in which Bonaparte, under the pretext of asserting " the principle of nationality," sought to sneak annexations for France. His imitator, Bismarck, adopted the same policy for Prussia ; he made his *coup d'état*, his revolution from above, in 1868, against the German Confederation and Austria, and no less against the Prussian *Konfliktskammer*. But Europe was too small for two Bonapartes and historical irony so willed it that Bismarck overthrew Bonaparte, and King William of Prussia not only established the little German Empire, but also the French Republic. The general result, however, was that in Europe the autonomy and internal unity of the great nations, with the exception of Poland, had become a fact. Within relatively modest limits, it is true, but, for all that, on a scale large enough to allow the development of the working class to proceed without finding national complications any longer a serious obstacle. The grave-diggers of the Revolution of 1848 had become the executors of its will. And alongside of them rose threateningly the heir of 1848, the proletariat, in the International.

After the war of 1870–1, Bonaparte vanishes from the stage and Bismarck's mission is fulfilled, so that he can now sink back again into the ordinary *Junker*. The period, however, is brought to a close by the Paris Commune. An underhand attempt by Thiers to steal the cannon of the Paris National Guard, called forth a victorious rising. It was shown once more that, in Paris, none but a proletarian revolution is any longer possible. After the victory power fell, wholly of its own accord, and quite undisputed, into the hands of the working class. And once again, twenty years after the time described in this work of ours, it was proved how impossible, even then, was this rule of the working class. On the one hand, France left Paris in the lurch, looked on while it bled from the bullets of Mac-Mahon ; on the other hand, the Commune was consumed in unfruitful strife between the two parties which divided it, the Blanquists (the majority) and the Proudhonists (the minority), neither of which knew what was to be done. The victory which came as a gift in 1871 remained just as unfruitful as the surprise attack of 1848.

It was believed that the militant proletariat had been finally buried with the Paris Commune. But, completely to the contrary, it dates its most powerful advance from the Commune and the Franco-German war. The recruitment of the whole of the population able to bear arms into armies that could be counted in millions, and the introduction of firearms, projectiles and explosives of hitherto undreamt of efficacy created a complete revolution in all warfare. This, on the one hand, put a sudden end to the Bonapartist war period and insured peaceful industrial development, since any war other than a world war of unheard of cruelty and absolutely incalculable outcome had become an impossibility. On the other hand, it caused military expenditure to rise in geometrical progression, and thereby forced up taxes to exorbitant levels and so drove the poorer classes

of people into the arms of Socialism. The annexation of
Alsace-Lorraine, the most immediate cause of the mad
competition in armaments, might set the French and German bourgeoisie chauvinistically at each other's throats ;
for the workers of the two countries it became a new bond of
unity. And the anniversary of the Paris Commune became the
first universal commemoration day of the whole proletariat.

The war of 1870–1 and the defeat of the Commune had
transferred the centre of gravity of the European workers'
movement for the time being from France to Germany, as
Marx foretold. In France it naturally took years to recover
from the bloodletting of May 1871. In Germany, on the
other hand, where industry was, in addition, furthered (in
positively hot-house fashion) by the blessing of the French
milliards and developed more and more quickly, Social-
Democracy experienced a much more rapid and enduring
growth. Thanks to the understanding with which the
German workers made use of the universal suffrage introduced in 1866, the astonishing growth of the Party is made
plain to all the world by incontestable figures. 1871,
102,000 ; 1874, 352,000 ; 1877, 493,000 Social-Democratic
votes. Then came recognition of this advance by high
authority in the shape of the Anti-Socialist Law : the Party
was temporarily disrupted ; the number of votes sank to
312,000 in 1881. But that was quickly overcome, and then,
though oppressed by the Exceptional Law, without press,
without external organisation and without the right of
combination or meeting, the rapid expansion really began :
1884, 550,000 ; 1887, 763,000 ; 1890, 1,427,000 votes.
Then the hand of the state was paralysed. The Anti-
Socialist Law disappeared ; socialist votes rose to 1,787,000,
over a quarter of all the votes cast. The government and
the ruling classes had exhausted all their expedients—
uselessly, to no purpose, and without success. The tangible
proofs of their impotence, which the authorities, from night
watchman to the imperial chancellor, had had to accept—
and that from the despised workers—these proofs were

counted in millions. The state was at the end of its Latin, the workers only at the beginning of theirs.

But the German workers did a second great service to their cause in addition to the first, which they rendered by their mere existence as the strongest, best disciplined and most rapidly growing Socialist Party. They supplied their comrades of all countries with a new weapon, and one of the sharpest, when they showed them how to use universal suffrage.

There had long been universal suffrage in France, but it had fallen into disrepute through the misuse to which the Bonapartist government had put it. After the Commune there was no workers' party to make use of it. Also in Spain it had existed since the republic, but in Spain boycott of the elections was ever the rule of all serious opposition parties. The Swiss experiences of universal suffrage, also, were anything but encouraging for a workers' party. The revolutionary workers of the Latin countries had been wont to regard the suffrage as a snare, as an instrument of government trickery. It was otherwise in Germany. *The Communist Manifesto* had already proclaimed the winning of universal suffrage, of democracy, as one of the first and most important tasks of the militant proletariat, and Lassalle had again taken up this point. When Bismarck found himself compelled to introduce the franchise as the only means of interesting the mass of the people in his plans, our workers immediately took it in earnest and sent August Bebel to the first constituent Reichstag. And from that day on they have used the franchise in a way which has paid them a thousandfold and has served as a model to the workers of all countries. The franchise has been, in the words of the French Marxist programme, " *transformé, de moyen de duperie qu'il a été jusqu'ici, en instrument d'émancipation* "—they have transformed it from a means of deception, which it was heretofore, into an instrument of emancipation. And if universal suffrage had offered no other advantage than that it allowed us to count our numbers every three years ; that by the regularly established, unexpectedly rapid rise in the number of votes it increased in equal measure the workers' certainty of victory and the dismay of their opponents, and so became our best means of propaganda ; that it accurately informed us concerning our own strength and that of all hostile parties, and thereby provided us with a measure of proportion for our actions second to none, safeguarding us from untimely timidity as much as from untimely foolhardiness—if this had been the only advantage we gained from the suffrage, then it would still have been more than enough. But it has done much more than this. In election agitation it provided us with a means, second to none, of getting in touch with the mass of the people, where they still stand aloof from us ; of forcing all parties to defend their views and actions against our attacks before all the people ; and, further, it opened to our representatives in the Reichstag a platform from which they could speak to their opponents in Parliament and to the masses without, with quite other authority and freedom than in the Press or at meetings. Of what avail to the government and the bourgeoisie was their Anti-Socialist Law when election agitation and socialist speeches in the Reichstag continually broke through it ?

With this successful utilisation of universal suffrage, an entirely new mode of proletarian struggle came into force, and this quickly developed further. It was found that the state institutions, in which the rule of the bourgeoisie is organised, offer still further opportunities for the working class to fight these very state institutions. They took part in elections to individual diets, to municipal councils and to industrial courts ; they contested every post against the bourgeoisie in the occupation of which a sufficient part of the proletariat had its say. And so it happened that the bourgeoisie and the government came to be much more afraid of the legal than of the illegal action of the workers' party, of the results of elections than of those of rebellion.

For here, too, the conditions of the struggle had essentially changed. Rebellion in the old style, the street fight with barricades, which up to 1848 gave everywhere the final decision, was to a considerable extent obsolete.

Let us have no illusions about it : a real victory of an insurrection over the military in street fighting, a victory as between two armies, is one of the rarest exceptions. But the insurgents, also, counted on it just as rarely. For them it was solely a question of making the troops yield to moral influences, which, in a fight between the armies of two warring countries do not come into play at all, or do so to a much less degree. If they succeed in this, then the troops fail to act, or the commanding officers lose their heads, and the insurrection wins. If they do not succeed in this, then, even where the military are in the minority, the superiority of better equipment and training, of unified leadership, of the planned employment of the military forces and of discipline makes itself felt. The most that the insurrection can achieve in actual tactical practice is the correct construction and defence of a single barricade. Mutual support ; the disposition and employment of reserves ; in short, the co-operation and harmonious working of the individual detachments, indispensable even for the defence of one quarter of the town, not to speak of the whole of a large town, are at best defective, and mostly not attainable at all ; concentration of the military forces at a decisive point is, of course, impossible. Hence the passive defence is the prevailing form of fight : the attack will rise here and there, but only by way of exception, to occasional advances and flank assaults ; as a rule, however, it will be limited to occupation of the positions abandoned by the retreating troops. In addition, the military have, on their side, the disposal of artillery and fully equipped corps of skilled engineers, resources of war which, in nearly every case, the insurgents entirely lack. No wonder, then, that even the barricade struggles conducted with the greatest heroism—Paris, June 1848 ; Vienna, October 1848 ; Dresden, May 1849—ended with the defeat of the insurrection, so soon as the leaders of the attack, unhampered by political considerations, acted from the purely military standpoint, and their soldiers remained reliable.

The numerous successes of the insurgents up to 1848 were due to a great variety of causes. In Paris in July 1830 and February 1848, as in most of the Spanish street fights, there stood between the insurgents and the military a civic militia, which either directly took the side of the insurrection, or else by its lukewarm, indecisive attitude caused the troops likewise to vacillate, and supplied the insurrection with arms into the bargain. Where this citizens' guard opposed the insurrection from the outset, as in June 1848 in Paris, the insurrection was vanquished. In Berlin in 1848, the people were victorious partly through a considerable accession of new fighting forces during the night and the morning of the 19th, partly as a result of the exhaustion and bad victualling of the troops, and, finally, partly as a result of the paralysed command. But in all cases the fight was won because the troops failed to obey, because the officers lost their power of decision or because their hands were tied.

Even in the classic time of street fighting, therefore, the barricade produced more of a moral than a material effect. It was a means of shaking the steadfastness of the military. If it held out until this was attained, then victory was won ; if not, there was defeat. [*This is the main point, which must be kept in view, likewise when the chances of contingent future street fights are examined.*]

The chances, however, were in 1849 already pretty poor. Everywhere the bourgeoisie had thrown in its lot with the governments, " culture and property " had hailed and feasted the military moving against the insurrections. The spell of the barricade was broken ; the soldier no longer saw behind it " the people," but rebels, agitators, plunderers, levellers, the scum of society ; the officer had in the course of time become versed in the tactical forms of street fighting, he no longer marched straight ahead and without cover

against the improvised breastwork, but went round it
through gardens, yards and houses. And this was now
successful, with a little skill, in nine cases out of ten.

But since then there have been very many more changes,
and all in favour of the military. If the big towns have
become considerably bigger, the armies have become
bigger still. Paris and Berlin have, since 1848, grown less
than fourfold, but their garrisons have grown more than
that. By means of the railways, the garrisons can, in twenty-
four hours, be more than doubled, and in forty-eight hours
they can be increased to huge armies. The arming of this
enormously increased number of troops has become incomparably more effective. In 1848 the smooth-bore percussion
muzzle-loader, to-day the small-calibre magazine breech-
loading rifle, which shoots four times as far, ten times as
accurately and ten times as fast as the former. At that time
the relatively ineffective round-shot and grape-shot of the
artillery ; to-day the percussion shells, of which one is
sufficient to demolish the best barricade. At that time the
pick-axe of the sapper for breaking through walls ; to-day
the dynamite cartridge.

On the other hand, all the conditions on the insurgents'
side have grown worse. An insurrection with which all
sections of the people sympathise will hardly recur ; in the
class struggle all the middle sections will never group themselves round the proletariat so exclusively that the reactionary parties gathered round the bourgeoisie well-nigh
disappear. The " people," therefore, will always appear
divided, and with this a powerful lever, so extraordinarily
effective in 1848, is lacking. Even if more soldiers who have
seen service were to come over to the insurrectionists, the
arming of them becomes so much the more difficult. The
hunting and luxury guns of the gunshops—even if not
previously made unusable by removal of part of the lock
by the police—are far from being a match for the magazine
rifle of the soldier, even in close fighting. Up to 1848 it was
possible to make the necessary ammunition oneself out of

powder and lead ; to-day the cartridges differ for each rifle, and are everywhere alike only in one point, that they are a special product of big industry, and therefore not to be prepared *ex tempore*, with the result that most rifles are useless as long as one does not possess the ammunition specially suited to them. And, finally, since 1848 the newly built quarters of the big towns have been laid out in long, straight, broad streets, as though made to give full effect to the new cannons and rifles. The revolutionary would have to be mad, who himself chose the working class districts in the North and East of Berlin for a barricade fight. [*Does that mean that in the future the street fight will play no further role ? Certainly not. It only means that the conditions since 1848 have become far more unfavourable for civil fights, far more favourable for the military. A future street fight can therefore only be victorious when this unfavourable situation is compensated by other factors. Accordingly, it will occur more seldom in the beginning of a great revolution than in its further progress, and will have to be undertaken with greater forces. These, however, may then well prefer, as in the whole Great French Revolution on September 4 and October 31, 1870, in Paris, the open attack to the passive barricade tactics.*]

Does the reader now understand why the ruling classes decidedly want to bring us to where the guns shoot and the sabres slash ? Why they accuse us to-day of cowardice, because we do not betake ourselves without more ado into the street, where we are certain of defeat in advance ? Why they so earnestly implore us to play for once the part of cannon fodder ?

The gentlemen pour out their prayers and their challenges for nothing, for nothing at all. We are not so stupid. They might just as well demand from their enemy in the next war that he should take up his position in the line formation of old Fritz, or in the columns of whole divisions *à la* Wagram and Waterloo, and with the flintlock in his hands at that. If the conditions have changed in the case of war between nations, this is no less true in the case of the class struggle.

The time of surprise attacks, of revolutions carried through
by small conscious minorities at the head of unconscious
masses, is past. Where it is a question of a complete transformation of the social organisation, the masses themselves
must also be in it, must themselves already have grasped
what is at stake, what they are going in for [*with body and
soul*]. The history of the last fifty years has taught us that.
But in order that the masses may understand what is to
be done, long, persistent work is required, and it is just
this work which we are now pursuing, and with a success
which drives the enemy to despair.

In the Latin countries, also, it is being more and more
recognised that the old tactics must be revised. Everywhere
[*the unprepared onslaught has gone into the background, everywhere*]
the German example of utilising the suffrage, of winning
all posts accessible to us, has been imitated. In France,
where for more than a hundred years the ground has been
undermined by revolution after revolution, where there is
no single party which has not done its share in conspiracies,
insurrections and all other revolutionary actions ; in
France, where, as a result, the government is by no means
sure of the army and where, in general, the conditions for
an insurrectionary *coup de main* are far more favourable
than in Germany—even in France the Socialists are realising more and more that no lasting victory is possible for
them, unless they first win the great mass of the people, i.e.,
in this case, the peasants. Slow propaganda work and parliamentary activity are being recognised here, too, as the
most immediate tasks of the Party. Successes were not lacking. Not only have a whole series of municipal councils
been won ; fifty Socialists have seats in the Chambers, and
they have already overthrown three ministries and a
President of the Republic. In Belgium last year the workers
enforced the franchise, and have been victorious in a
quarter of the constituencies. In Switzerland, in Italy, in
Denmark, yes, even in Bulgaria and Rumania the Socialists
are represented in the Parliaments. In Austria all parties

agree that our admission to the Reichsrat can no longer
be withheld. We will get in, that is certain; the only question still in dispute is : by which door ? And even in Russia,
when the famous *Zemsky Sobor* meets, that National Assembly to which young Nicholas offers such vain resistance,
even there we can reckon with certainty on also being
represented in it.

Of course, our foreign comrades do not renounce their
right to revolution. The right to revolution is, after all, the
only real " historical right," the only right on which all
modern states without exception rest, Mecklenburg included,
whose aristocratic revolution was ended in 1755 by the
" hereditary settlement," the glorious charter of feudalism
still valid to-day. The right to revolution is so incontestably
recognised in the general conciousness that even General
von Boguslawski derives the right to a *coup d'état*, which he
vindicates for his Kaiser, solely from this popular right.

But whatever may happen in other countries, German
Social-Democracy has a special situation and therewith,
at least in the first instance, a special task. The two million
voters, whom it sends to the ballot box, together with the
young men and women, who stand behind them as non-
voters, form the most numerous, most compact mass, the
decisive " *shock force* " of the international proletarian army.
This mass already supplies over a fourth of the recorded
votes ; and as the by-elections to the Reichstag, the diet
elections in individual states, the municipal council and
industrial court elections demonstrate, it increases uninterruptedly. Its growth proceeds as spontaneously, as
steadily, as irresistibly, and at the same time as tranquilly
as a natural process. All government interventions have
proved powerless against it. We can count even to-day on
two and a half million voters. If it continues in this fashion,
by the end of the century we shall conquer the greater part
of the middle section of society, petty bourgeois and small
peasants, and grow into the decisive power in the land,
before which all other powers will have to bow, whether

they like it or not. To keep this growth going without interruption until of itself it gets beyond the control of the ruling
governmental system [*not to fritter away this daily increasing
shock force in advance guard fighting, but to keep it intact until the
day of the decision,*] that is our main task. And there is only
one means by which the steady rise of the socialist fighting
forces in Germany could be momentarily halted, and even
thrown back for some time : a clash on a big scale with the
military, a bloodbath like that of 1871 in Paris. In the long
run that would also be overcome. To shoot out of the world
a party which numbers millions—all the magazine rifles
of Europe and America are not enough for this. But the
normal development would be impeded, [*the shock force
would, perhaps, not be available at the critical moment,*] *the decisive
struggle* would be delayed, protracted and attended by
heavy sacrifices.

The irony of world history turns everything upside down.
We, the " revolutionaries," the " rebels "—we are thriving
far better on legal methods than on illegal methods and
revolt. The parties of order, as they call themselves, are
perishing under the legal conditions created by themselves.
They cry despairingly with Odilon Barrot : *la légalité nous tue*,
legality is the death of us ; whereas we, under this legality,
get firm muscles and rosy cheeks and look like eternal life.
And if we are not so crazy as to let ourselves be driven into
street fighting in order to please them, then nothing else
is finally left for them but themselves to break through this
legality so fatal to them.

Meanwhile they make new laws against revolution. Again
everything is turned upside down. These anti-revolt fanatics
of to-day, are they not themselves the rebels of yesterday ?
Have we, perchance, evoked the civil war of 1866 ? Have
we driven the King of Hanover, the Elector of Hesse, the
Duke of Nassau from their hereditary, lawful domains, and
annexed these hereditary domains ? And do these rebels
against the German Confederation and three crowns by
the grace of God complain of overthrow ? *Quis tulerit*

Gracchos de seditione querentes? Who could allow the Bismarck worshippers to rail at revolt?

Let them, nevertheless, put through their anti-revolt bills, make them still worse, transform the whole penal law into india-rubber, they will achieve nothing but a new proof of their impotence. In order seriously to hit Social-Democracy, they will have to resort to quite other measures. They can only hold in check the Social-Democratic revolt which is just now doing so well by keeping within the law, by revolt on the part of the parties of order, which cannot live without breaking the laws. Herr Rössler, the Prussian bureaucrat, and Herr von Boguslawski, the Prussian general, have shown them the only way in which the workers, who refuse to let themselves be lured into street fighting, can still, perhaps, be held in check. Breach of the constitution, dictatorship, return to absolutism, *regis voluntas suprema lex!* Therefore, only courage, gentlemen; here is no backing out of it; here you are in for it!

But do not forget that the German Empire, just as all small states and generally all modern states, is a product of contract; of the contract, firstly, of the princes with one another and, secondly, of the princes with the people. If one side breaks the contract, the whole contract falls to the ground; the other side is then also no longer bound [*as Bismarck showed us so beautifully in 1866. If, therefore, you break the constitution of the Reich, then the Social-Democracy is free, can do and refrain from doing what it will as against you. But what it will do then it will hardly give away to you to-day!*]

It is now, almost to the year, sixteen hundred years since a dangerous party of revolt made a great commotion in the Roman Empire. It undermined religion and all the foundations of the state; it flatly denied that Cæsar's will was the supreme law; it was without a fatherland, international; it spread over all countries of the Empire from Gaul to Asia, and beyond the frontiers of the Empire. It had long carried on an underground agitation in secret; for a considerable time, however, it had felt itself strong

enough to come out into the open. This party of revolt, who
were known by the name of christians, was also strongly
represented in the army ; whole legions were christian.
When they were ordered to attend the sacrificial ceremonies
of the pagan established church, in order to do the honours
there, the soldier rebels had the audacity to stick peculiar
emblems—crosses—on their helmets in protest. Even the
wonted barrack cruelties of their superior officers were
fruitless. The Emperor Diocletian could no longer quietly
look on while order, obedience and discipline in his army
were being undermined. He intervened energetically, while
there was still time. He passed an anti-Socialist, I should say,
anti-christian, law. The meetings of the rebels were forbidden,
their meeting halls were closed or even pulled down, the
christian badges, crosses, etc., were, like the red handker-
chiefs in Saxony, prohibited. Christians were declared incapable of holding offices in the state, they were not to be
allowed even to become corporals. Since there were not
available at that time judges so well trained in " respect of
persons " as Herr von Köller's anti-revolt bill assumes, the
christians were forbidden out of hand to seek justice before
a court. This exceptional law was also without effect. The
christians tore it down from the walls with scorn ; they are
even supposed to have burnt the Emperor's palace in
Nicomedia over his head. Then the latter revenged himself by the great persecution of christians in the year 303,
according to our chronology. It was the last of its kind.
And it was so effective that seventeen years later the army
consisted overwhelmingly of christians, and the succeeding
autocrat of the whole Roman Empire, Constantine, called
the Great by the priests, proclaimed christianity as the
state religion.

Karl Marx

THE CLASS STRUGGLES IN FRANCE (1848 – 50)

Articles published in the " Neue Rheinische Zeitung," 1850. English edition published in 1934 by Martin Lawrence Ltd.

[The four articles which form this work covered every stage of the long struggles in France between 1848 and 1850, which led on to the imperial restoration of 1851. The passages selected show the earlier stages, up to the defeat of the proletarian uprising in June 1848 ; the later stages are covered in the extracts subsequently given from Marx's later work, *The Eighteenth Brumaire of Louis Bonaparte.* Marx's analysis shows the characteristic form of the bourgeois revolution—its use of the workers against the more reactionary forces, and then its disarming and suppression of the workers' forces when the new bourgeois government is established.]

———

THE CLASS STRUGGLES IN FRANCE

FROM FEBRUARY TO JUNE 1848

(From Ch. I)

WITH the exception of a few short chapters, every important part of the annals of the revolution from 1848 to 1849 carries the heading : Defeat of the revolution !

But what succumbed in these defeats was not the revolution. It was the pre-revolutionary traditional appendages, results of social relationships, which had not yet come to the point of sharp class antagonisms—persons, illusions, conceptions, projects, from which the revolutionary party before the February Revolution was not free, from which it could be freed, not by the victory of February, but only by a series of defeats.

In a word : revolutionary advance made headway not by its immediate tragi-comic achievements, but on the contrary by the creation of a powerful, united counter-revolution, by the creation of an opponent, by fighting whom the party of revolt first ripened into a real revolutionary party.

To prove this is the task of the following pages.

I. THE DEFEAT OF JUNE 1848

After the July Revolution, when the Liberal banker, Laffitte, led his godfather, the Duke of Orleans, in triumph to the Hôtel de Ville, he let fall the words : " From now on the bankers will rule." Laffitte had betrayed the secret of the revolution.

It was not the French bourgeoisie that ruled under Louis Philippe, but a fraction of it, bankers, Stock Exchange kings, railway kings, owners of coal and iron works and forests, a section of landed proprietors that rallied round them—the so-called finance aristocracy. It sat on the throne, it dictated laws in the Chambers, it conferred political posts from cabinet portfolios to the tobacco bureau.

The real industrial bourgeoisie formed part of the official opposition, i.e., it was represented only as a minority in the Chambers. Its opposition was expressed all the more decisively, the more unalloyed the autocracy of the finance aristocracy became, and the more it itself imagined that its domination over the working-class was ensured after the mutinies of 1832, 1834 and 1839, which had been drowned in blood. *Grandin*, the Rouen manufacturer, the most fanatical instrument of bourgeois reaction, in the Constituent Assembly, as well as in the legislative National Assembly, was the most violent opponent of Guizot in the Chamber of Deputies. *Leon Faucher*, later renowned for his impotent endeavours to push himself forward as the Guizot of the French counter-revolution, in the last days of Louis Philippe, waged a war of the pen for industry against speculation and its train bearer, the government. *Bastiat* agitated against the ruling system in the name of Bordeaux and the whole of wine-producing France.

The petty bourgeoisie of all degrees, and the peasantry also, were completely excluded from political power. Finally, in the official opposition or entirely outside the *pays légal*, there were the ideological representatives and spokesmen of the above classes, their savants, lawyers, doctors, etc., in a word : their so-called talents.

The July monarchy, owing to its financial need, was dependent from the beginning on the big bourgeoisie, and its dependence on the big bourgeoisie was the inexhaustible source of a growing financial need. It was impossible to subordinate state administration to the interests of national production, without balancing the budget, establishing a balance between state expenses and income. And how was this balance to be established, without limiting state expenditure, i.e., without encroaching on interests which were so many supports of the ruling system, and without redistributing taxes, i.e., without putting a considerable share of the burden of taxes on the shoulders of the big bourgeoisie itself?

Rather the fraction of the bourgeoisie that ruled and legislated through the Chambers had a direct interest in state indebtedness. The state deficit was even the main object of its speculation and played the chief rôle in its enrichment. At the end of each year a new deficit. After expiry of four or five years a new loan. And every new loan offered new opportunities to the finance aristocracy for defrauding the state which was kept artificially on the verge of bankruptcy—it had to contract with the bankers under the most unfavourable conditions. Each new loan gave a further opportunity for plundering the public that had invested its capital in state bonds, by stock exchange manipulations into the secrets of which the government and the majority in the Chambers were admitted. In general, the fluctuation of state credits and the possession of state secrets gave the bankers and their associates in the Chambers and on the throne the possibility of evoking sudden, extraordinary fluctuations in the quotations of state bonds, the result of which was always bound to be the ruin of a mass of smaller capitalists and the fabulously rapid enrichment of the big gamblers. If the state deficit was in the direct interest of the ruling fraction of the bourgeoisie, then it is clear why extraordinary state expenditure in the last years of Louis Philippe's government was far more than double the extraordinary state expenditure under Napoleon; indeed, reached a yearly sum of nearly 400,000,000 francs, whereas the whole annual export of France seldom attained a volume amounting to 750,000,000 francs. The enormous sums which, in this way, flowed through the hands of the state, facilitated, moreover, swindling contracts for deliveries, bribery, defalcations and all kinds of roguery. The defrauding of the state, just as it occurred on a large scale in connection with loans, was repeated in detail, in the state works. The relationship between Chamber and government multiplied itself as the relationship between individual departments and individual *entrepreneurs*.

In the same way as the ruling class exploited state expenditure in general and state loans, they exploited the building of railways. The Chambers piled the main burdens on the state, and secured the golden fruits to the speculating finance aristocracy. One recalls the scandals in the Chamber of Deputies when by chance it came out that all the members of the majority, including a number of ministers, had taken part as shareholders in the very railway construction which as legislators they caused to be carried out afterwards at the cost of the state.

On the other hand, the smallest financial reform was wrecked by the influence of the bankers. For example, the postal reform. Rothschild protested. Was it permissible for the state to curtail sources of income out of which interest was to be paid on its ever increasing debt?

The July monarchy was nothing other than a joint stock

company for the exploitation of French national wealth, the dividends of which were divided amongst ministers, Chambers, 240,000 voters and their adherents. Louis Philippe was the director of this company—Robert Macaire on the throne. Trade, industry, agriculture, shipping, the interests of the industrial bourgeoisie, were bound to be continually prejudiced and endangered under this system. The bourgeoisie in the July days had inscribed on its banner : *gouvernement à bon marché,* cheap government.

While the finance aristocracy made the laws, was at the head of the administration of the State, had command of all the organised public powers, dominated public opinion through facts and through the Press, the same prostitution, the same shameless cheating, the same mania to get rich, was repeated in every sphere, from the Court to the Café Borgne, to get rich not by production, but by pocketing the already available wealth of others. In particular there broke out, at the top of bourgeois society, an unbridled display of unhealthy and dissolute appetites, which clashed every moment with the bourgeois laws themselves, wherein the wealth having its source in gambling naturally seeks its satisfaction, where pleasure becomes *crapuleux,* where gold, dirt and blood flow together. The finance aristocracy, in its mode of acquisition as well as in its pleasures, is nothing but the resurrection of the *lumpenproletariat* at the top of bourgeois society.

And the non-ruling sections of the French bourgeoisie cried : corruption ! The people cried : *à bas les grands voleurs! à bas les assassins!* when in 1847, on the most prominent stages of bourgeois society, the same scenes were publicly enacted which regularly lead the *lumpenproletariat* to brothels, to workhouses and lunatic asylums, before the Bench, to bagnos and to the scaffold. The industrial bourgeoisie saw its interests endangered, the petty bourgeoisie was filled with moral indignation, the imagination of the people was offended, Paris was flooded with pamphlets—" *la dynastie Rothschild,*" " *les juifs rois de l'époque,*" etc.

—in which the rule of the finance aristocracy was denounced and stigmatised with greater or less wit.

Rien pour la gloire ! Glory brings no profit ! *La paix partout et toujours !* War depresses the quotations of the Three and Four per Cents ! the France of the Bourse Jews had inscribed on her banner. Her foreign policy was therefore lost in a series of mortifications to French national feeling, which reacted all the more vigorously when the robbery of Poland was brought to an end with the annexation of Cracow by Austria, and when Guizot came out actively on the side of the Holy Alliance in the Swiss separatist war. The victory of the Swiss liberals in this mimic war raised the self-respect of the bourgeois opposition in France ; the bloody uprising of the people in Palermo worked like an electric shock on the paralysed masses of the people and awoke their great revolutionary memories and passions.

The eruption of the general discontent was finally accelerated and the sentiment for revolt ripened by two economic world-events.

The potato blight and the bad harvests of 1845 and 1846 increased the general ferment among the people. The high cost of living of 1847 called forth bloody conflicts in France as well as on the rest of the Continent. As against the shameless orgies of the finance aristocracy, the struggle of the people for the first necessities of life ! At Buzançais the hunger rioters executed ; in Paris the over-satiated *escrocs* snatched from the courts by the Royal family.

The second great economic event which hastened the outbreak of the revolution was a general commercial and industrial crisis in England. Already heralded in the autumn of 1845 by the wholesale reverses of the speculators in railway shares, delayed during 1846 by a number of incidents such as the impending abolition of the corn duties, in the autumn of 1847 the crisis finally burst forth with the bankruptcy of the London grocers, on the heels of which followed the insolvencies of the land banks and the closing of the factories in the English industrial districts.

The after-effect of this crisis on the Continent had not yet
spent itself when the February Revolution broke out.

The devastation of trade and industry caused by the
economic epidemic made the autocracy of the finance aristocracy still more unbearable. Throughout the whole of
France the bourgeois opposition evoked the banquet agitation for an electoral reform which should win for them the
majority in the Chambers and overthrow the Ministry of
the Bourse. In Paris the industrial crisis had, in particular,
the result of throwing a number of manufacturers and big
traders, who under the existing circumstances could no
longer do any business in the foreign market, on to the home
market. They set up large establishments, the competition
of which ruined the *épiciers* and *boutiquiers en masse.* Hence
the innumerable bankruptcies among this section of the
Paris bourgeoisie, and hence their revolutionary action in
February. It is known how Guizot and the Chambers
answered the reform proposals with a plain challenge, how
Louis Philippe too late resolved on a Ministry led by
Barrot, how hand-to-hand fighting took place between the
people and the army, how the army was disarmed by the
passive conduct of the National Guard, how the July
monarchy had to give way to a Provisional Government.

The Provisional Government which emerged from the
February barricades necessarily mirrored in its composition
the different parties which shared in the victory. It could
not be anything but a compromise between the different
classes which together had overturned the July throne, but
whose interests were mutually antagonistic. A large
majority of its members consisted of representatives of the
bourgeoisie. The republican petty bourgeoisie were represented by Ledru-Rollin and Flocon, the republican bourgeoisie by the people from the *National,* the dynastic
opposition by Cremieux, Dupont de l'Eure, etc. The
working class had only two representatives, Louis Blanc and
Albert. Finally, Lamartine as a member of the Provisional
Government ; that was actually no real interest, no definite

class ; that was the February Revolution itself, the common uprising with its illusions, its poetry, its imagined content and its phrases. For the rest, the spokesman of the February Revolution, by his position and his views, belonged to the bourgeoisie.

If Paris, as a result of political centralisation, rules France, the workers, in moments of revolutionary earth-quakes, rule Paris. The first act in the life of the Provisional Government was an attempt to escape from this over-powering influence, by an appeal from intoxicated Paris to sober France. Lamartine disputed the right of the barri-cade fighters to proclaim the republic, on the ground that only the majority of Frenchmen had that right ; they must await their votes, the Parisian proletariat must not besmirch its victory by a usurpation. The bourgeoisie allowed the proletariat only one usurpation—that of fighting.

Up to noon on February 25, the republic had not yet been proclaimed ; on the other hand, the whole of the Ministries had already been divided among the bourgeois elements of the Provisional Government and among the generals, bankers and lawyers of the *National*. But the workers were this time determined not to put up with any swindling like that of July 1830. They were ready to take up the fight anew and to enforce the republic by force of arms. With this message, Raspail betook himself to the Hôtel de Ville. In the name of the Parisian proletariat he commanded the Provisional Government to proclaim the republic ; if this order of the people were not fulfilled within two hours, he would return at the head of 200,000 men. The bodies of the fallen were scarcely cold, the barri-cades were not yet cleared away, the workers not yet dis-armed, and the only force which could be opposed to them was the National Guard. Under these circumstances the prudent state doubts and juristic scruples of conscience of the Provisional Government suddenly vanished. The inter-val of two hours had not expired before all the walls of Paris were resplendent with the tremendous historical words:

République française ! Liberté, Egalité, Fraternité !

Even the memory of the limited aims and motives which drove the bourgeoisie into the February Revolution was extinguished by the proclamation of the republic on the basis of universal suffrage. Instead of a few small fractions of the bourgeoisie, whole classes of French society were suddenly hurled into the circle of political power, forced to leave the boxes, the stalls and the gallery and to act in person upon the revolutionary stage ! With the constitutional monarchy the semblance of a state power independently confronting bourgeois society also vanished, as well as the whole series of subordinate struggles which this semblance of power called forth !

The proletariat, by dictating the republic to the Provisional Government and through the Provisional Government to the whole of France, stepped into the foreground forthwith as an independent party, but at the same time challenged the whole of bourgeois France to enter the lists against it. What it won was the terrain for the fight for its revolutionary emancipation, but in no way this emancipation itself !

The first thing that the February republic had to do was rather to complete the rule of the bourgeoisie by allowing, besides the finance aristocracy, all the propertied classes to enter the circle of political power. The majority of the great landowners, the Legitimists, were emancipated from the political nullity to which they had been condemned by the July Monarchy. Not for nothing had the *Gazette de France* agitated in common with the opposition papers, not for nothing had Laroche-Jaquelin taken the side of the revolution in the session of the Chamber of Deputies on February 24. The nominal proprietors, who form the great majority of the French people, the peasants, were put by universal suffrage in the position of arbiters of the fate of France. The February republic finally brought the rule of the bourgeoisie clearly into prominence, since it struck off the crown behind which Capital kept itself concealed.

Just as the workers in the July days had fought and won the bourgeois monarchy, so in the February days they fought and won the bourgeois republic. Just as the July monarchy had to proclaim itself as a monarchy surrounded by republican institutions, so the February republic was forced to proclaim itself a republic surrounded by social institutions. The Parisian proletariat compelled this concession, too.

Marche, a worker, dictated the decree by which the newly formed Provisional Government pledged itself to secure the existence of the workers by work, to provide work for all citizens, etc. And when, a few days later, it forgot its promises and seemed to have lost sight of the proletariat, a mass of 20,000 workers marched on the Hôtel de Ville with the cry : Organisation of labour ! Formation of a special Ministry of Labour ! The Provisional Government, with reluctance and after long debates, nominated a permanent, special commission, charged with finding means of improving the lot of the working classes ! This commission consisted of delegates from the corporations of Parisian artisans and was presided over by Louis Blanc and Albert. The Luxembourg was assigned to it as a meeting place. In this way the representatives of the working class were exiled from the seat of the Provisional Government, the bourgeois section of which held the real state power and the reins of administration exclusively in its hands, and side by side with the Ministries of Finance, Trade and Public Works, side by side with the banks and the bourse, there arose a socialist synagogue whose high priests, Louis Blanc and Albert, had the task of discovering the promised land, of preaching the new gospel and of occupying the attention of the Parisian proletariat. Unlike any profane state power, they had no budget, no executive authority at their disposal. With their heads they had to break the pillars of bourgeois society. While the Luxembourg sought the philosopher's stone, in the Hôtel de Ville they minted the current coinage.

And yet the claims of the Parisian proletariat, so far as they went beyond the bourgeois republic, could win no other existence than the nebulous one of the Luxembourg.

In common with the bourgeoisie the workers had made the February Revolution, and alongside the bourgeoisie they sought to put through their interests, just as they had installed a worker in the Provisional Government itself alongside the bourgeois majority. Organisation of labour ! But wage labour is the existing bourgeois organisation of labour. Without it there is no capital, no bourgeoisie, no bourgeois society. Their own Ministry of Labour ! But the Ministries of Finance, of Trade, of Public Works—are not these the bourgeois Ministries of Labour ? And alongside these a proletarian Ministry of Labour must be a Ministry of impotence, a Ministry of pious wishes, a commission of the Luxembourg. Just as the workers thought to emancipate themselves side by side with the bourgeoisie, so they opined they would be able to consummate a proletarian revolution within the national walls of France, side by side with the remaining bourgeois nations. But French production relations are conditioned by the foreign trade of France, by her position on the world market and the laws thereof ; how should France break them without a European revolutionary war, which would strike back at the despot of the world market, England ?

A class in which the revolutionary interests of society are concentrated, so soon as it has risen up, finds directly in its own situation the content and the material of its revolutionary activity : foes to be laid low, measures, dictated by the needs of the struggle, to be taken ; the consequences of its own deeds drive it on. It makes no theoretical inquiries into its own task. The French working class had not attained this standpoint ; it was still incapable of accomplishing its own revolution.

The development of the industrial proletariat is, in general, conditioned by the development of the industrial bourgeoisie. Only under its rule the proletariat wins the

extensive national existence which can raise its revolution
to a national one and itself creates the modern means of
production, which become just so many means of its
revolutionary emancipation. Only bourgeois rule tears up
the roots of feudal society and levels the ground on which a
proletarian revolution is alone possible. In France industry
is more developed and the bourgeoisie more revolutionary
than elsewhere on the Continent. But was not the February
Revolution directed immediately against the finance aristocracy? This fact proved that the industrial bourgeoisie
did not rule France. The industrial bourgeoisie can only
rule where modern industry shapes all property relations
in conformity with itself, and industry can only win this
power when it has conquered the world market, for national
bounds are not wide enough for its development. But
French industry, to a great extent, maintains its command
even of the national market only through a more or less
modified system of prohibitive duties. If, therefore, the
French proletariat, at the moment of a revolution, possesses
in Paris actual power and influence which spur it on to a
drive beyond its means, in the rest of France it is crowded
into single, scattered industrial centres, being almost lost
in the superior numbers of peasants and petty bourgeois.
The struggle against capital in its developed, modern form,
in its culminating phase the struggle of the industrial wage
worker against the industrial bourgeois, is in France partially a fact, which after the February days could supply
the national content of the revolution so much the less,
since the struggle against capital's secondary modes of
exploitation, that of the peasants against the usury in
mortgages, of the petty bourgeois against the wholesale
dealer, banker and manufacturer, in a word, against
bankruptcy, was still hidden in the general uprising against
the general finance aristocracy. Nothing is more under-
standable, then, than that the Paris proletariat sought to
put through its own interests along with those of the bourgeoisie, instead of enforcing them as the revolutionary

interests of society itself, and that it let the red flag be lowered to the tricolour. The French workers could not take a step forward, could not touch a hair of the bourgeois order before the course of the revolution had forced the mass of the nation, peasants and petty bourgeois, standing between the proletariat and the bourgeoisie and in revolt not against this order, against the rule of capital, to attach itself to the proletariat as its vanguard. The workers could only buy this victory through the huge defeat of June.

To the Luxembourg commission, this creation of the Paris workers, remains the merit of having disclosed from the European tribune the secret of the revolution of the nineteenth century : the emancipation of the proletariat. The *Moniteur* raged when it had to propagate officially the " wild ravings " which up to that time lay buried in the apocryphal writings of the Socialists and only reached the ears of the bourgeoisie from time to time as remote, half terrifying, half ludicrous legends. Europe awoke astonished from its bourgeois doze. In the ideas of the proletarians, therefore, who confused the finance aristocracy with the bourgeoisie in general ; in the imagination of good old republicans who denied the very existence of classes or, at most, admitted them as a result of the constitutional monarchy ; in the hypocritical phrases of the sections of the bourgeoisie up till now excluded from power, the rule of the bourgeoisie was abolished with the introduction of the republic. All the royalists were transformed into republicans and all the millionaires of Paris into workers. The phrase which corresponded to this imagined liquidation of class relations was *fraternité*, universal fraternisation and brotherhood. This pleasant abstraction from class antagonisms, this sentimental equalisation of contradictory class interests, this fantastic elevation above the class struggle, *fraternité*, this was the special catch-cry of the February Revolution. The classes were divided by a mere misunderstanding and Lamartine baptised the Provisional

Government on February 24 as " *un gouvernement qui suspende ce malentendu terrible qui existe entre les différentes classes.*" The Parisian proletariat revelled in this generous intoxication of fraternity. . . .

The Provisional Government, having honoured the bill drawn on the state by the old bourgeois society, succumbed to the latter. It had become the hard pressed debtor of bourgeois society instead of confronting it as the pressing creditor that had to collect the revolutionary debts of many years. It had to consolidate the shaky bourgeois relationship, in order to fulfil obligations which are only to be fulfilled within these relationships. Credit becomes a condition of life for it and the concessions to the proletariat, the promises made to it, become so many fetters which had to be struck off. The emancipation of the workers— even as a phrase—became an unbearable danger to the new republic, for it was a standing protest against the restoration of credit, which rests on undisturbed and untroubled recognition of the existing economic class relations. Therefore, it was necessary to have done with the workers.

The February Revolution had cast the army out of Paris. The National Guard, i.e., the bourgeoisie in its different grades, formed the sole power. Alone, however, it did not feel itself a match for the proletariat. Moreover, it was forced slowly and bit by bit to open its ranks and allow armed proletarians to enter the National Guard, albeit after the most tenacious resistance and after setting up a hundred different obstacles. There consequently remained but one way out : to set one part of the proletariat against the other.

For this purpose the Provisional Government formed 24 battalions of Mobile Guards, each of a thousand men, out of young men from 15 to 20 years. They belonged for the most part to the *lumpenproletariat*, which, in all big towns, form a mass strictly differentiated from the industrial proletariat, a recruiting ground for thieves and criminals of all kinds, living on the crumbs of society, people without a definite trade, vagabonds, *gens sans feu et sans aveu*, with differences according to the degree of civilisation of the nation to which they belong, but never renouncing their *lazzaroni* character ; at the youthful age at which the Provisional Government recruited them, thoroughly malleable, capable of the most heroic deeds and the most exalted sacrifices, as of the basest banditry and the dirtiest corruption. The Provisional Government paid them 1 franc 50 centimes a day, i.e., it bought them. It gave them their own uniform, i.e., it made them outwardly distinct from the blouse of the workers. They had assigned to them as leaders, partly officers from the standing army ; partly they themselves elected young sons of the bourgeoisie whose rhodomontades about death for the fatherland and devotion to the republic captivated them.

And so the Paris proletariat was confronted with an army, drawn from its own midst, of 24,000 young, strong and foolhardy men. It gave cheers for the Mobile Guard on its marches through Paris. It recognised in it its champions of the barricades. It regarded it as the proletarian guard in opposition to the bourgeois National Guard. Its error was pardonable.

Besides the Mobile Guard, the Government decided to gather round itself an industrial army of workers. A hundred thousand workers thrown on the streets through the crisis and the revolution were enrolled by the Minister Marie in so-called National *Ateliers*. Under this grand name was hidden nothing but the employment of the workers on tedious, monotonous, unproductive earthworks at a wage of 23 sous. English *workhouses* in the open—that is what these National *Ateliers* were. The Provisional Government believed that it had formed in them a second proletarian army against the workers themselves. This time the bourgeoisie was mistaken in the National *Ateliers*, just as the workers were mistaken in the Mobile Guard. It had created an army for mutiny.

But one purpose was achieved.

National *Ateliers*—that was the name of the people's workshops, which Louis Blanc preached in the Luxembourg. The *Ateliers* of Marie, devised in direct antagonism to the Luxembourg, thanks to the common name, offered occasion for a plot of errors worthy of the Spanish comedy of servants. The Provisional Government itself secretly spread the report that these National *Ateliers* were the discovery of Louis Blanc, and this seemed the more plausible because Louis Blanc, the prophet of the National *Ateliers*, was a member of the Provisional Government. And in the half naïve, half intentional confusion of the Paris bourgeoisie, in the artificially maintained opinion of France and of Europe, these workhouses were the first realisation of socialism, which was put in the pillory with them.

In their title, though not in their content, the National *Ateliers* were the embodied protest of the proletariat against bourgeois industry, bourgeois credit and the bourgeois republic. The whole hate of the bourgeoisie was therefore turned upon them. At the same time, it had found in them the point against which it could direct the attack, as soon as it was strong enough to break openly with the February illusions. All the discontent, all the ill humour of the petty bourgeois was simultaneously directed against these National *Ateliers*, the common target. With real fury they reckoned up the sums that the proletarian loafers swallowed, while their own situation became daily more unbearable. A state pension for sham labour, that is socialism ! they growled to themselves. They sought the basis of their misery in the National *Ateliers*, the declarations of the Luxembourg, the marches of the workers through Paris. And no one was more fantastic about the alleged machinations of the Communists than the petty bourgeoisie who hovered hopelessly on the brink of bankruptcy.

Thus in the approaching *mêlée* between bourgeoisie and

proletariat, all the advantages, all the decisive posts, all the middle sections of society were in the hands of the bourgeoisie, at the same time as the waves of the February Revolution rose high over the whole Continent, and each new post brought a new bulletin of revolution, now from Italy, now from Germany, now from the remotest parts of South-Eastern Europe, and maintained the general exuberance of the people, giving it constant testimony of a victory that it had already lost. . . .

In the Constituent National Assembly, which met on May 4, the bourgeois republicans, the republicans of the *National* had the upper hand. Legitimists and even Orleanists at first only dared to show themselves under the mask of bourgeois republicanism. Only in the name of the republic could the fight against the proletariat be undertaken.

The republic dates from May 4, not from February 25, i.e., the republic recognised by the French people; it is not the republic which the Paris proletariat thrust upon the Provisional Government, not the republic with social institutions, not the dream picture which hovered before the fighters on the barricades. The republic proclaimed by the National Assembly, the sole legitimate republic, is the republic which is no revolutionary weapon against the bourgeois order, but rather its political reconstitution, the political re-consolidation of bourgeois society, in a word, the bourgeois republic. From the tribune of the National Assembly this contention resounded and in the entire republican and anti-republican bourgeois Press it found its echo.

And we have seen how the February republic in reality was not and could not be other than a bourgeois republic ; how the Provisional Government, nevertheless, was forced by the immediate pressure of the proletariat to announce it as a republic with social institutions, how the Paris proletariat was still incapable of going beyond the bourgeois republic otherwise than in ideas, in imagination ; how it everywhere acted in its service when it really came to action ; how the promises made to it became an unbearable danger for the new republic ; how the whole life process of the Provisional Government was comprised in a continuous fight against the demands of the proletariat.

In the National Assembly all France sat in judgment on the Paris proletariat. It broke immediately with the social illusions of the February Revolution ; it roundly proclaimed the bourgeois republic, nothing but the bourgeois republic. It at once excluded the representatives of the proletariat, Louis Blanc and Albert, from the Executive Commission appointed by it ; it threw out the proposal of a special Labour Ministry, and received with stormy applause the statement of the Minister Trélat : " The question is merely one of bringing labour back to its old conditions."

But all this was not enough. The February republic was won by the workers with the passive support of the bourgeoisie. The proletarians regarded themselves, and rightly, as the victors of February, and they made the proud claims of victors. They had to be vanquished on the streets, they had to be shown that they were worsted as soon as they fought, not with the bourgeoisie, but against the bourgeoisie. Just as the February republic, with its socialist concessions, required a battle of the proletariat, united with the bourgeoisie, against monarchy, so a second battle was necessary in order to sever the republic from the socialist concessions, in order to officially work out the bourgeois republic as dominant. The bourgeoisie had to refute the demands of the proletariat with arms in its hands. And the real birthplace of the bourgeois republic is not the February victory ; it is the June defeat.

The proletariat hastened the decision when, on the 15th of May, it pushed into the National Assembly, sought in vain to recapture its revolutionary influence and only delivered its energetic leaders to the jailers of the bourgeoisie. *Il faut en finir !* This situation must end ! With this cry the National Assembly gave vent to its determination to force the proletariat into a decisive struggle. The Executive Commission issued a series of provocative decrees, such as that prohibiting congregation of the people, etc. From the tribune of the Constituent National Assembly, the workers were directly provoked, insulted and derided. But the real point of the attack was, as we have seen, the National *Ateliers*. The Constituent National Assembly imperiously pointed these out to the Executive Commission, which only waited to hear its own plan put forward as the command of the National Assembly.

The Executive Commission began by making entry into the National *Ateliers* more difficult, by turning the day wage into a piece wage, by banishing workers not born in Paris to Sologne, ostensibly for the construction of earthworks. These earthworks were only a rhetorical formula with which to gloss over their expulsion, as the workers, returning disillusioned, announced to their comrades. Finally, on June 21, a decree appeared in the *Moniteur*, which ordered the forcible expulsion of all unmarried workers from the National *Ateliers*, or their enrolment in the army.

The workers were left no choice : they had to starve or start to fight. They answered on June 22 with the tremendous insurrection in which the first great battle was joined between the two classes that split modern society. It was a fight for the preservation or annihilation of the bourgeois order. The veil that shrouded the republic was torn to pieces.

It is well known how the workers, with unexampled bravery and talent, without chiefs, without a common plan, without means and, for the most part, lacking weapons, held in check for five days the army, the Mobile Guard, the Parisian National Guard, and the National Guard that streamed in from the provinces. It is well known how the bourgeoisie compensated itself for the mortal anguish it underwent by unheard of brutality, and massacred over 3,000 prisoners. . . .

The Paris proletariat was forced into the June insurrection by the bourgeoisie. In this lay its doom. Neither its immediate admitted needs drove it to want to win the forcible overthrow of the bourgeoisie, nor was it equal to this task. The *Moniteur* had to inform it officially that the time was past when the republic saw any occasion to do honour to its illusions, and its defeat first convinced it of the truth that the slightest improvement in its position remains an Utopia within the bourgeois republic, an Utopia that becomes a crime as soon as it wants to realise it. In place of its demands, exuberant in form, but petty and even still bourgeois in content, the concession of which it wanted to wring from the February republic, there appeared the bold slogan of revolutionary struggle : Overthrow of the bourgeoisie ! Dictatorship of the working class !

By making its burial place the birth place of the bourgeois republic, the proletariat compelled the latter to come out forthwith in its pure form as the state whose admitted object is to perpetuate the rule of capital, the slavery of labour. With constant regard to the scarred, irreconcilable, unconquerable enemy—unconquerable because its existence is the condition of its own life—bourgeois rule, freed from all fetters, was bound to turn immediately into bourgeois terrorism. With the proletariat removed for the time being from the stage and bourgeois dictatorship recognised officially, the middle sections, in the mass, had more and more to side with the proletariat as their position became more unbearable and their antagonism to the bourgeoisie became more acute. Just as earlier in its upsurge, so now they had to find in its defeat the cause of their misery.

If the June insurrection raised the self-reliance of the bourgeoisie all over the Continent, and caused it to league itself openly with the feudal monarchy against the people, what was the first sacrifice to this alliance ? The Continental bourgeoisie itself. The June defeat prevented it from consolidating its rule and from bringing the people, half satisfied and half out of humour, to a standstill at the lowest stage of the bourgeois revolution.

Finally, the defeat of June divulged to the despotic powers of Europe the secret that France under all conditions must maintain peace abroad in order to be able to wage civil war at home. Thus the peoples who had begun the fight for their national independence were abandoned to the superior power of Russia, Austria and Prussia, but, at the same time, the fate of these national revolutions was subordinated to the fate of the proletarian revolution, robbed of its apparent independence, its independence of the great social revolution. The Hungarian shall not be free, nor the Pole, nor the Italian, as long as the worker remains a slave !

Finally, with the victory of the Holy Alliance, Europe took on a form that makes every fresh proletarian upheaval in France directly coincide with a world war. The new French revolution is forced to leave its national soil forthwith and conquer the European terrain, on which alone the revolution of the nineteenth century can be carried through.

Only through the defeat of June, therefore, were all the conditions created under which France can seize the initiative of the European revolution. Only after baptism in the blood of the June insurgents did the tricolour become the flag of the European revolution—the red flag.

And we cry : *The revolution is dead !—Long live the revolution !*

Karl Marx

THE EIGHTEENTH BRUMAIRE
OF LOUIS BONAPARTE

*First published 1852, in " Die Revolution," a monthly journal
issued in New York. English edition, Martin Lawrence Ltd., 1935.*

[With the restoration of the French monarchy in December 1851, the class struggles which began in France in 1848 were temporarily ended, and Marx was enabled to sum up the experiences of the whole revolutionary period. In *The Class Struggles in France* he traced the detailed history of 1848–50 ; in *The Eighteenth Brumaire* he drew conclusions which form the classical theoretical analysis of the bourgeois revolution, and the part played in it by the lower middle class and the proletariat.]

THE EIGHTEENTH BRUMAIRE OF
LOUIS BONAPARTE

HEGEL REMARKS somewhere that all great, historical facts and personages occur, as it were, twice. He forgot to add : the first time as tragedy, the second as farce. Caussidière for Danton, Louis Blanc for Robespierre, the Mountain of 1848 to 1851 for the Mountain of 1793 to 1795, the Nephew for the Uncle. And the same caricature occurs in the circumstances in which the second edition of the Eighteenth Brumaire is taking place.

Men make their own history, but they do not make it just as they please ; they do not make it under circumstances chosen by themselves, but under circumstances directly found, given and transmitted from the past. The tradition of all the dead generations weighs like an incubus on the brain of the living. And just when they seem engaged in

revolutionising themselves and things, in creating something
entirely new, precisely in such epochs of revolutionary crisis
they anxiously conjure up the spirits of the past to their
service and borrow from them names, battle slogans and
costumes in order to present the new scene of world history
in this time-honoured disguise and this borrowed language.
Thus Luther donned the mask of the Apostle Paul, the
Revolution of 1789–1814 draped itself alternately as the
Roman Republic and the Roman Empire, and the Revolution of 1848 knew of nothing better to do than to parody
in turn 1789, and the revolutionary tradition of 1793 to
1795. In like manner the beginner, who has learnt a new
language, always translates it back into his mother tongue,
but he has assimilated the spirit of the new language and
can produce freely in it only when he moves in it without
calling to mind his ancestral tongue.

But closer consideration of this historical conjuring with
the dead reveals at once a salient difference. Camille
Desmoulins, Danton, Robespierre, Saint-Just, Napoleon,
the heroes, as well as the parties and the masses of the old
French Revolution, performed the task of their time in
Roman costume and with Roman phrases, the task of
releasing and establishing modern *bourgeois* society. The first
mentioned knocked the feudal basis to pieces and cut off
the feudal heads which had grown from it. The other created
inside France the conditions under which free competition
could first be developed, the parcelled landed property
exploited, the unfettered productive power of the nation
employed, and outside the French borders he everywhere
swept the feudal form away, so far as it was necessary
to furnish bourgeois society in France with a suitable
up-to-date environment on the European Continent.
The new social formation once established, the antediluvian Colossuses disappeared and with them the resur-
rected Romans—the Brutuses, Gracchi, Publicolas, the
Tribunes, the Senators and Cæsar himself. Bourgeois
society in its sober reality had begotten its true interpreters

and mouthpieces in the Says, Cousins, Roler-Collards, Benjamin Constants and Guizots ; its real military leaders sat behind the office desks, and the hog-headed Louis XVIII was its political chief. Wholly absorbed in the production of wealth and in the peaceful struggle of competition, it no longer comprehended that ghosts from the days of Rome had watched over its cradle. But unheroic as bourgeois society is, yet in its birth it had need of heroism and sacrifice in the classically austere traditions of the Roman Republic ; its gladiators found the ideals and the art forms, the self-deceptions that they needed, in order to conceal from themselves the bourgeois limitations of the content of their struggles and to keep their passion at the height of the great historical tragedy. Similarly, at another stage of development, a century earlier, Cromwell and the English people had borrowed speech, passions and illusions from the Old Testament for their bourgeois revolution. When the real aim had been achieved, when the bourgeois transformation of English society had been accomplished, Locke supplanted Habakkuk.

The awakening of the dead in those revolutions therefore served the purpose of glorifying the new struggles, not of parodying the old ; of magnifying the given tasks in imagination, not of fleeing back from their solution in reality ; of finding once more the spirit of revolution, not of making its ghost walk again.

From 1848 to 1851 only the ghost of the old Revolution walked, from Marrast, the *Républicain en gants jaunes*, who disguised himself as the old Bailly, to the adventurer who hides his trivially repulsive features under the iron death mask of Napoleon. An entire people, which had imagined that by a revolution it had increased its power of action, suddenly finds itself set back into a dead epoch and, so that no doubt as to the relapse may be possible, the old calendar again appears, the old chronology, the old names, the old edicts, which have long become a subject of antiquarian erudition, and the old henchmen, who had long seemed dead and rotting. The nation appears to itself like that mad English-man in Bedlam, who fancies that he lives in the times of the ancient Pharaohs and daily bemoans the hard labour that he must perform in the Ethiopian mines as a gold digger, immured in this subterranean prison, a dimly burning lamp fastened to his head, the slaves' overseer behind him with a long whip, and at the exits a confused mass of bar-barian mercenaries, who understand neither the forced labourers in the mines nor one another, since they have no common speech. " And all this is expected of me," groans the mad Englishman, " of me, a free-born Briton, in order to make gold for the old Pharaohs." " In order to pay the debts of the Bonaparte family," sighs the French nation. The Englishman, so long as he was in his right mind, could not get rid of the fixed idea of making gold. The French, so long as they were engaged in revolution, could not get rid of the memory of Napoleon, as the election of December 10, 1848, proved. From the perils of revolution their longings went back to the flesh-pots of Egypt, and December 2, 1851, was the answer. They have not only the caricature of the old Napoleon, they have caricatured the old Napoleon himself as he would inevitably appear in the middle of the nineteenth century.

The social revolution of the nineteenth century cannot draw its poetry from the past, but only from the future. It cannot make a beginning until it has stripped off all superstition of the past. Earlier revolutions required world-historical recollections in order to drug themselves concerning their own content. In order to arrive at its own content, the revolution of the nineteenth century must let the dead bury their dead. There the phrase went beyond the content ; here the content goes beyond the phrase.

The February Revolution was a sudden attack, a taking of the old society by *surprise*, and the people proclaimed this unexpected *stroke* as a world-historical deed, opening the new epoch. On December 2 the February Revolution is conjured away by a cardsharper's trick, and what seems overthrown is no longer the monarchy ; it is the liberal concessions that were wrung from it by century-long struggles. Instead of *society* having conquered a new content for itself, the *state* only appears to have returned to its oldest form, to the shamelessly open domination of the sword and the club. This is the answer to the *coup de main* of February 1848, given by the *coup de tête* of December, 1851. Easy come, easy go. Meanwhile the interval has not passed by unused. During the years 1848–1851 French society has made up, and that by an abbreviated, because revolutionary, method for the studies and experiences which, in a regular, so to speak, text-book development would have had to precede the February Revolution if it was to be more than a disturbance of the surface. Society now seems to have fallen back behind its point of departure ; it has in truth first to create for itself the revolutionary point of departure, the situation, the relationships, the conditions, under which modern revolution alone becomes serious.

Bourgeois revolutions, like those of the eighteenth century, storm more swiftly from success to success ; their dramatic effects outdo each other ; men and things seem set in sparkling brilliants ; ecstasy is the everyday spirit ; but they are short lived ; soon they have attained their zenith, and a long depression lays hold of society before it learns to assimilate soberly the results of its storm and stress period. Proletarian revolutions, on the other hand, like those of the nineteenth century, criticise themselves constantly, interrupt themselves continually in their own course, come back to the apparently accomplished in order to recommence it afresh, deride with unmerciful thoroughness the inadequacies, weaknesses and paltrinesses of their first attempts, seem to throw down their adversary only in order that he may draw new strength from the earth and rise again more gigantic before them, recoil ever and anon from the infinite immensity of their own aims, until the situation has been created which makes all turning back impossible, and the conditions themselves cry out :

Hic Rhodus, hic salta !

The first period from February 24, or the overthrow of Louis Philippe, to May 4, 1848, the meeting of the Constituent Assembly, the February period proper, may be described as the *prologue* of the Revolution. Its character was officially expressed in the fact that the government improvised by it declared itself to be *provisional* and, like the government, everything that was instigated, attempted or enunciated during this period, proclaimed itself to be *provisional*. Nothing and nobody ventured to claim for themselves the right of existence and of real action. All the elements that had prepared or determined the Revolution, the dynastic opposition, the republican bourgeoisie, the democratic-republican petty bourgeoisie and the social-democratic workers, provisionally found their place in the February *government*.

It could not be otherwise. The February days originally intended an electoral reform, by which the circle of the politically privileged among the possessing class itself was to be widened and the exclusive domination of the aristocracy of finance overthrown. When it came to the actual conflict, however, when the people mounted the barricades, the National Guard maintained a passive attitude, the army offered no serious resistance and the monarchy ran away, the republic appeared to be a matter of course. Every party construed it in its own sense. Having been won by the proletariat by force of arms, the proletariat impressed its stamp on it and proclaimed it to be a *social republic*. There was thus indicated the general content of modern revolution, which stood in most singular contradiction to everything that, with the material at hand, with the degree of education attained by the masses, under the given circumstances and relationships, could be immediately realised in practice. On the other hand, the claims of all the remaining elements that had participated in the February Revolution were recognised by the lion's share that they obtained in the government. In no period do we therefore find a more confused mixture of high-flown phrases and actual uncertainty and clumsiness, of more enthusiastic striving for innovation and more deeply rooted domination of the old routine, of more apparent harmony of the whole society and more profound estrangement of its elements. While the Paris proletariat still revelled in the vision of the wide prospects that had opened before it and indulged in seriously meant discussions on social problems, the old powers of society had grouped themselves, assembled, deliberated and found an unexpected support in the mass of the nation, the peasants and petty bourgeois, who all at once stormed on to the political stage, after the barriers of the July monarchy had fallen.

The *second period*, from May 4, 1848, to the end of May 1849, is the period of the *Constitution*, the *foundation of the bourgeois republic*. Directly after the February days the dynastic opposition had not only been surprised by the republicans, the republicans by the socialists, but all France had been surprised by Paris. The National Assembly, which had met on May 4, 1848, having emerged from the national elections, represented the nation. It was a living protest against the presumptuous aspirations of the February days and was to reduce the results of the Revolution to the bourgeois scale. In vain the Paris proletariat, which immediately grasped the character of this National Assembly, attempted on May 15, a few days after it met, forcibly to deny its existence, to dissolve it, to disintegrate once more into its constituent parts the organic form in which the proletariat was threatened by the reactionary spirit of the nation. As is known, May 15 had no other result save that of removing Blanqui and his comrades, that is, the real leaders of the proletarian party, the revolutionary communists, from the public stage for the entire duration of the cycle we are considering.

The *bourgeois monarchy* of Louis Philippe can only be followed by the bourgeois republic, that is, if a limited section of the bourgeoisie formerly ruled in the name of the king, the whole of the bourgeoisie will now rule in the name of the people. The demands of the Paris proletariat are Utopian nonsense of which an end must be made. To this declaration of the Constituent National Assembly the Paris proletariat replied with the *June Insurrection*, the most colossal event in the history of European civil wars. The bourgeois republic triumphed. On its side stood the aristocracy of finance, the industrial bourgeoisie, the middle class, the petty bourgeois, the army, the *lumpenproletariat* organised as the Mobile Guard, the intellectual lights, the clergy, and the rural population. On the side of the Paris proletariat stood none but itself. More than three thousand insurgents were butchered after the victory, and fifteen thousand were transported without trial. With this defeat the proletariat passes into the background of the revolutionary stage. It attempts to press forward again on every occasion, as soon as the movement appears to make a fresh start, but with ever decreased expenditure of strength and always more insignificant results. As soon as one of the social strata situated above it gets into revolutionary ferment, it enters into an alliance with it and so shares all the defeats that the different parties suffer one after another. But these subsequent blows become steadily weaker the more they are distributed over the entire surface of society. Its more important leaders in the Assembly and the Press successively fall victims to the courts, and ever more equivocal figures come to the fore. In part it throws itself into *doctrinaire experiments, exchange banks and workers' associations, hence into a movement in which it renounces the revolutionising of the old world by means of its own great, combined resources, and seeks, rather, to achieve its salvation behind society's back,*

*in private fashion, within its limited conditions of existence, and
hence inevitably suffers shipwreck.* It seems to be unable either to
rediscover revolutionary greatness in itself or to win new
energy from the alliances newly entered into, until *all
classes* with which it contended in June themselves lie
prostrate beside it. But at least it succumbs with the honours
of the great, world-historical struggle ; not only France, but
all Europe trembles at the June earthquake, while the
ensuing defeats of the upper classes are so cheaply bought
that they require bare-faced exaggeration by the victorious
party to be able to pass for events at all and become the
more ignominious the further the defeated party is removed
from the proletariat.

The defeat of the June insurgents, to be sure, had now
prepared and levelled the ground on which the bourgeois
republic could be founded and built up, but it had shown
at the same time that in Europe there are other questions
involved than that of " republic or monarchy." It had
revealed that here *bourgeois republic* signifies the unlimited
despotism of one class over other classes. It had proved that
in lands with an old civilisation, with a developed formation
of classes, with modern conditions of production and with
an intellectual consciousness into which all traditional ideas
had been dissolved by centuries of effort, *the republic* signifies
in general only the political form of the revolution of bourgeois society
and not its *conservative form of life*, as, for example, in the
United States of North America, where, though classes,
indeed, already exist, they have not yet become fixed, but
continually change and interchange their elements in a
constant state of flux, where the modern means of production, instead of coinciding with a stagnant surplus population, rather supply the relative deficiency of heads and
hands and where, finally, the feverishly youthful movement
of material production, that has a new world to make its
own, has allowed neither time nor opportunity to abolish
the old spirit world.

During the June days all classes and parties had united

in the *party of order* against the proletarian class, as the *party of anarchy*, of socialism, of communism. They had " saved " society from " the enemies of society." They had given out the watchwords of the old society, " *property, family, religion, order*," to their army as passwords and proclaimed to the counter-revolutionary crusaders : " In this sign you will conquer ! " From that moment as soon as one of the numerous parties which had gathered under this sign against the June insurgents seeks to hold the revolutionary battle-field in its own class interests, it goes down before the cry : " Property, family, religion, order." Society is saved just as often as the circle of its rulers contracts, as a more ex-clusive interest is maintained against a wider one. Every demand of the simplest bourgeois financial reform, of the most ordinary liberalism, of the most formal republicanism, of the most insipid democracy, is simultaneously castigated as an " attempt on society " and stigmatised as " socialism." And, finally, the high priests of " religion and order " themselves are driven with kicks from their Pythian tripods, hauled out of their beds in the darkness of night, stuck in prison-vans, thrown into dungeons or sent into exile ; their temple is razed to the ground, their mouths are sealed, their pens broken, their law torn to pieces in the name of religion, of property, of family, of order. Bourgeois fanatics for order are shot down on their balconies by mobs of drunken soldiers, their domestic sanctuaries profaned, their houses bombarded for amusement—in the name of property, of family, of religion and of order. Finally the scum of bourgeois society forms *the holy phalanx of order* and the hero Crapulinsky installs himself in the Tuileries as the " *saviour of society*." . . .

Legitimists and Orleanists, as we have said, formed the two great sections of the Party of Order. Was that which held these sections fast to their pretenders and kept them apart from one another, nothing but lily and tricolour, house of Bourbon and house of Orleans, different shades of royalty, was it the confession of faith in royalty at all ?

Under the Bourbons, large landed property had governed
with its priests and lackeys; under the Orleans, high finance,
large-scale industry, wholesale trade, that is, *capital*,
governed with its retinue of advocates, professors and
orators. The Legitimate Monarchy was merely the political
expression of the hereditary rule of the lords of the soil, as
the July Monarchy was only the political expression of the
usurping rule of the bourgeois *parvenus*. What kept the two
sections apart, therefore, was not any so-called principles,
it was their material conditions of existence, two different
kinds of property, it was the old antagonism of town and
country, the rivalry between capital and landed property.
That at the same time old memories, personal enmities,
fears and hopes, prejudices and illusions, sympathies and
antipathies, convictions, articles of faith and principles
bound them to one or the other royal house, who is there
that denies this? Upon the different forms of property,
upon the social conditions of existence rises an entire superstructure of distinct and characteristically formed senti-
ments, illusions, modes of thought and views of life. The
entire class creates and forms them out of its material
foundations and out of the corresponding social relations.
The single individual who derives them through tradition
and education may imagine that they form the real motives
and the starting-point of his action. If Orleanists and
Legitimists, if each section sought to make itself and the
other believe that loyalty to their two royal houses separated
them, it later proved to be the case that it was rather their
divided interests which forbade the uniting of the two royal
houses. And as in private life one distinguishes between
what a man thinks and says of himself and what he really
is and does, still more in historical struggles must one
distinguish the phrases and fancies of the parties from their
real organism and their real interests, their conception of
themselves from their reality. Orleanists and Legitimists
found themselves side by side in the republic with equal
claims. If each side wished to effect the *restoration* of its *own*

royal house against the other, that merely signifies that
the *two great interests* into which the *bourgeoisie* is split—
landed property and capital—sought each to restore its
own supremacy and the subordination of the other. We
speak of two interests of the bourgeoisie, for large landed
property, despite its feudal coquetry and pride of race, has
been rendered thoroughly bourgeois by the development
of modern society. Thus the Tories in England long
imagined that they were enthusiastic about the monarchy,
the church and the beauties of the old English Constitution, until the day of danger wrung from them the
confession that they are only enthusiastic about *ground
rent.* . . .

Against this coalition of the bourgeoisie, a coalition between petty bourgeois and workers had been formed, the
so-called *Social-Democratic* Party. The petty bourgeoisie
saw that they were badly rewarded after the June days of
1848, their material interests imperilled and the democratic
guarantees which were to secure the assertion of these
interests endangered by the counter-revolution. Accordingly, they came closer to the workers. On the other hand,
their parliamentary representation, the Mountain, thrust
aside during the dictatorship of the bourgeois republicans,
had, in the last half of the life of the Constituent Assembly,
reconquered its lost popularity through the struggle with
Bonaparte and the royalist ministers. It had concluded
an alliance with the socialist leaders. In February 1849,
banquets celebrated the reconciliation. A joint programme
was drafted, joint election committees were set up and joint
candidates put forward. From the social demands of the
proletariat the revolutionary point was broken off and a
democratic turn given to them ; from the democratic
claims of the petty bourgeoisie the purely political form was
stripped off and their socialist point thrust forward. Thus
arose *Social-Democracy*. The new *Mountain*, the result of this
combination, apart from some supernumeraries from the
working class and some socialist sectarians, contained the

same elements as the old Mountain, only numerically stronger. But in the course of development it had changed with the class that it represented. The peculiar character of Social-Democracy is epitomised in the fact that democratic-republican institutions are demanded not as a means of doing away with both the extremes, capital and wage-labour, but of weakening their antagonism and transforming it into harmony. However different the means proposed for the attainment of this end may be, however much it may be trimmed with more or less revolutionary notions, the content remains the same. This content is the transformation of society in a democratic way, but a transformation within the bounds of the petty bourgeoisie. Only, one must not form the narrow-minded notion that the petty bourgeoisie, on principle, wishes to enforce an egoistic class interest. Rather, it believes that the *special* conditions of its emancipation are the *general* conditions under which modern society can alone be saved and the class struggle avoided. Just as little must one imagine that the democratic representatives are all shopkeepers or enthusiastic champions of shopkeepers. According to their education and their individual position they may be separated from them as widely as heaven from earth. What makes them representatives of the petty bourgeoisie is the fact that in their minds they do not go beyond the limits which the latter do not go beyond in life, that they are consequently driven theoretically to the same tasks and solutions to which material interest and social position practically drive the latter. This is, in general, the relationship of the *political and literary representatives* of a class to the class that they represent. . . .

But the revolutionary threats of the petty bourgeois and their democratic representatives are mere attempts to intimidate the antagonist. And when they have run into a blind alley, when they have sufficiently compromised themselves to make it necessary to give effect to their threats, then this happens in an ambiguous fashion that avoids

nothing so much as the means to the end and tries to find
an excuse for defeat. The blaring overture that announced
the struggle dies away in a dejected snarl ; as soon as it is
to begin, the actors cease to take themselves *au sérieux*,
and the action collapses completely, like a pricked
balloon.

No party exaggerates its powers more than the democrats,
none deludes itself more irresponsibly over the situation.
When a section of the army had voted for it, the Mountain
was now convinced that the army would revolt for it. And
on what grounds ? On grounds which, from the standpoint
of the troops, had no other meaning than that the revolutionaries took the side of the Roman soldiers against the
French soldiers. On the other hand, the recollections of
June, 1848, were still too fresh to allow of anything but a
profound aversion on the part of the proletariat against the
National Guard and a thorough-going mistrust of the
democratic chiefs on the part of the leaders of the secret
societies. To adjust these differences, it was necessary for
great common interests to be at stake. The violation of an
abstract paragraph of the Constitution could not provide
these interests. Had not the Constitution been repeatedly
violated, according to the assurance of the democrats
themselves ? Had not the most popular journals branded it
as counter-revolutionary botch-work ? But the democrat,
because he represents the petty bourgeoisie, therefore a
transition class, in which interests of two classes simultaneously lose their point, imagines himself elevated above
class antagonism generally. The democrats concede that a
privileged class confronts them, but they, along with all the
rest of the surrounding nation, form the *people*. What they
represent are the *people's rights* ; what interests them are the
people's interests. Accordingly, when a struggle is impending,
they do not need to examine the interests and positions of
the different classes. They do not need to consider their own
resources too critically. They have merely to give the signal
and the people, with all its inexhaustible resources, will fall

upon the *oppressors*. If in the performance their interests now prove to be uninteresting and their power to be impotence, then the fault lies either with pernicious sophists, who split the *indivisible people* into different hostile camps, or the army was too brutalised and blinded to apprehend the pure aims of democracy as best for itself, or the whole thing has been wrecked by a detail in its execution, or else an unforeseen accident has for this time spoilt the game. In any case, the democrat comes out of the most disgraceful defeat just as immaculate as he went into it innocent, with the new-won conviction that he is bound to conquer, not that he himself and his party have to give up the old standpoint, but, on the contrary, that conditions have to ripen in his direction. . . .

But the revolution is thoroughgoing. It is still in process of passing through purgatory. It does its work methodically. By December 2, 1851, it had completed one half of its preparatory work ; it is now completing the other half. First it perfected the parliamentary power, in order to be able to overthrow it. Now that it has attained this, it perfects the *executive power*, reduces it to its purest expression, isolates it, sets it up against itself as the sole object, in order to concentrate all its forces of destruction against it. And when it has done its second half of its preliminary work, Europe will leap from her seat and exultantly exclaim : " Well grubbed, old mole ! "

This executive power with its monstrous bureaucratic and military organisation, with its artificial state machinery embracing wide strata, with a host of officials numbering half a million, besides an army of another half million, this appalling parasitic growth, which enmeshes the body of French society like a net and chokes all its pores, sprang up in the days of the absolute monarchy, with the decay of the feudal system, which it helped to hasten. The seignorial privileges of the landowners and towns became transformed into so many attributes of the state power, the feudal dignitaries into paid officials and the motley pattern of conflicting mediæval plenary powers into the regulated plan of a state authority, whose work is divided and centralised as in a factory. The first French Revolution, with its task of breaking all local, territorial, urban and provincial independent powers in order to create the bourgeois unity of the nation, was bound to develop what the absolute monarchy had begun—centralisation, but at the same time the extent, the attributes and the agents of governmental authority. Napoleon perfected this state machinery. The Legitimist monarchy and the July monarchy added nothing but a greater division of labour, growing in the same measure that the division of labour within bourgeois society created new groups of interests, and, therefore, new material for state administration. Every *common* interest was straightway severed from society, counterposed to it as a higher, *general* interest, snatched from the self-activity of society's members and made an object of governmental activity from the bridge, the school-house and the communal property of a village community to the railways, the national wealth and the national university of France. The parliamentary republic, finally, in its struggle against the revolution, found itself compelled to strengthen, along with the repressive measures, the resources and centralisation of governmental power. All the revolutions perfected this machine instead of smashing it up. The parties that contended in turn for domination regarded the possession of this huge state edifice as the principal spoils of the victor.

But under the absolute monarchy, during the first Revolution, and under Napoleon, bureaucracy was only the means of preparing the class rule of the bourgeoisie. Under the Restoration, under Louis Philippe and under the parliamentary republic, it was the instrument of the ruling class, however much it strove for power of its own. . . .

Friedrich Engels

GERMANY: REVOLUTION AND COUNTER-REVOLUTION

First published in 1851 and 1852, as a series of articles in the New York " Daily Tribune." Published in book form, with other writings of Engels referring to the same period, by Martin Lawrence Ltd., 1933.

[These articles, describing and analysing the 1848–9 revolutions in Central Europe, were written by Engels and edited by Marx, in whose name they were printed. The combined analysis of the military and political events of the period is characteristic of Engels ; the distinction between the classes and sections of classes involved in the revolution is clearly brought out and related to the actual course of events. Only one brief passage, from the article dated London, August 1852, is given below : it is the classical statement of the principles of insurrection, and was used by Lenin in his letters from Finland to the Bolsheviks in Petersburg just before the November revolution of 1917.]

GERMANY: REVOLUTION AND COUNTER-REVOLUTION

. . . Now, insurrection is an art quite as much as war or any other, and subject to certain rules of proceeding, which, when neglected, will produce the ruin of the party neglecting them. Those rules, logical deductions from the nature of the parties and the circumstances one has to deal with in such a case, are so plain and simple that the short experience of 1848 had made the Germans pretty well acquainted with them. Firstly, never play with insurrection unless you are fully prepared to face the consequences of your play.

Insurrection is a calculus with very indefinite magnitudes the value of which may change every day ; the forces opposed to you have all the advantage of organisation, discipline, and habitual authority ; unless you bring strong odds against them you are defeated and ruined. Secondly, the insurrectionary career once entered upon, act with the greatest determination, and on the offensive. The defensive is the death of every armed rising ; it is lost before it measures itself with its enemies. Surprise your antagonists while their forces are scattering, prepare new successes, however small, but daily ; keep up the moral ascendancy which the first successful rising has given to you ; rally those vacillating elements to your side which always follow the strongest impulse, and which always look out for the safer side ; force your enemies to a retreat before they can collect their strength against you ; in the words of Danton, the greatest master of revolutionary policy yet known, *de l'audace, de l'audace, encore de l'audace !* . . .

Karl Marx

THE CIVIL WAR IN FRANCE

Three Addresses of the General Council of the International Working Men's Association, drafted by Marx, and dated July 23, 1870, September 9, 1870, and May 30, 1871. English edition, Martin Lawrence Ltd., 1933.

[Marx was one of the Corresponding Secretaries of the International Working Men's Association—the " First International," founded in 1864. In the course of the Franco-Prussian war of 1870–1 he drafted statements on the war and the Paris Commune, which were adopted by the General Council of the Association and issued to its members in Europe and the United States. The Address dated May 30, 1871—two days after the last forces of the Paris Commune had been overpowered—is not only a record of events but an analysis of the Paris Commune itself—showing its place in history, the features which distinguished it from all previous revolutions, the reasons for its ultimate defeat. The most essential passages are given below.]

THE CIVIL WAR IN FRANCE

ADDRESS OF THE GENERAL COUNCIL OF THE INTERNATIONAL WORKING MEN'S ASSOCIATION

To All The Members of the Association in Europe and in the United States

ON SEPTEMBER 4, 1870, when the working men of Paris proclaimed the Republic, which was almost instantaneously acclaimed throughout France, without a single voice of dissent, a cabal of place-hunting barristers, with Thiers for their statesman and Trochu for their general, took hold of the Hôtel de Ville. At that time they were imbued with so fanatical a faith in the mission of Paris to represent France in all epochs of historical crisis, that, to legitimatise their usurped titles as Governors of France, they thought it quite sufficient to produce their lapsed mandates as representatives of Paris. In our second address on the late war, five days after the rise of these men, we told you who they were. Yet, in the turmoil of surprise, with the real leaders of the working class still shut up in Bonapartist prisons and the Prussians already marching upon Paris, Paris bore with their assumption of power, on the express condition that it was to be wielded for the single purpose of national defence. Paris, however, was not to be defended without arming its working class, organising them into an effective force, and training their ranks by the war

itself. But Paris armed was the Revolution armed. A victory
of Paris over the Prussian aggressor would have been a
victory of the French workman over the French capitalist
and his State parasites. In this conflict between national
duty and class interest, the Government of National Defence did not hesitate one moment to turn into a Government of National Defection.

The first step they took was to send Thiers on a roving
tour to all the Courts of Europe there to beg mediation by
offering the barter of the Republic for a king. Four months
after the commencement of the siege, when they thought
the opportune moment come for breaking the first word of
capitulation, Trochu, in the presence of Jules Favre and
others of his colleagues, addressed the assembled mayors
of Paris in these terms :

" The first question put to me by my colleagues on the
very evening of September 4 was this : Paris, can it, with
any chance of success stand a siege by the Prussian army ?
I did not hesitate to answer in the negative. Some of my
colleagues here present will warrant the truth of my words
and the persistence of my opinion. I told them, in these very
terms, that, under the existing state of things, the attempt
of Paris to hold out a siege by the Prussian army would be
a folly. Without doubt, I added, it would be an heroic
folly ; but that would be all. . . . The events (managed by
himself) have not given the lie to my prevision." This nice
little speech of Trochu was afterwards published by M.
Corbon, one of the mayors present.

Thus, on the very evening of the proclamation of the
Republic, Trochu's "plan" was known to his colleagues to
be the capitulation of Paris. If national defence had been
more than a pretext for the personal government of Thiers,
Favre and Co., the upstarts of September 4 would have
abdicated on the 5th—would have initiated the Paris
people into Trochu's " plan," and called upon them to
surrender at once, or to take their own fate into their own
hands. Instead of this, the infamous impostors resolved

upon curing the heroic folly of Paris by a regimen of famine and broken heads, and to dupe her in the meanwhile by ranting manifestoes, holding forth that Trochu, " the Governor of Paris, will never capitulate," and Jules Favre, the Foreign Minister, will " not cede an inch of our territory, nor a stone of our fortresses." In a letter to Gambetta, that very same Jules Favre avows that what they were " defending " against were not the Prussian soldiers, but the working men of Paris. During the whole continuance of the siege the Bonapartist cut-throats, whom Trochu had wisely intrusted with the command of the Paris army, exchanged, in their intimate correspondence, ribald jokes at the well-understood mockery of defence (see, for instance, the correspondence of Alphonse Simon Guiod, supreme commander of the artillery of the Army of Defence of Paris and Grand Cross of the Legion of Honour, to Suzanne, general of division of artillery, a correspondence published by the *Journal officiel* of the Commune). The mask of imposture was at last dropped on January 28, 1871. With the true heroism of utter self-debasement, the Government of National Defence, in their capitulation, came out as the Government of France by Bismarck's permission—a part so base that Louis Bonaparte himself had, at Sedan, shrunk from accepting it. After the events of March 18, on their wild flight to Versailles, the *capitulards* left in the hands of Paris the documentary evidence of their treason, to destroy which, as the Commune says in its manifesto to the provinces, " those men would not recoil from a sea of blood." . . .

The capitulation of Paris, by surrendering to Prussia, not only Paris, but all France, closed the long-continued intrigues or treason with the enemy, which the usurpers of September 4 began, as Trochu himself said, on that very same day. On the other hand, it initiated the civil war they were now to wage with the assistance of Prussia, against the Republic and Paris. The trap was laid in the very terms of the capitulation. At that time above one-third

of the territory was in the hands of the enemy, the capital
was cut off from the provinces, all communications were
disorganised. To elect under such circumstances a real
representation of France was impossible unless ample time
were given for preparation. In view of this the capitulation
stipulated that a National Assembly must be elected within
eight days ; so that in many parts of France the news of
the impending election arrived on its eve only. This assembly, moreover, was, by an express clause of the capitulation, to be elected for the sole purpose of deciding on
peace or war, and, eventually, to conclude a treaty of peace.
The population could not but feel that the terms of the
armistice rendered the continuation of the war impossible,
and that for sanctioning the peace imposed by Bismarck,
the worst men in France were the best. But not content with
these precautions, Thiers, even before the secret of the
armistice had been broached to Paris, set out for an elec-
tioneering tour through the provinces, there to galvanise
back into life the Legitimist party, which now, along with
the Orleanists, had to take the place of the then impossible
Bonapartists. He was not afraid of them. Impossible as a
government of modern France, and therefore contemptible
as rivals, what party were more eligible as tools of counter-
revolution than the party whose action, in the words of
Thiers himself (Chamber of Deputies, January 5, 1833),
" had always been confined to the three resources of foreign
invasion, civil war, and anarchy " ? They verily believed
in the advent of their long-expected retrospective millen-
nium. There were the heels of foreign invasion trampling
upon France ; there was the downfall of an Empire, and
the captivity of a Bonaparte ; and there they were themselves. The wheel of history has evidently rolled back to
stop at the "Chambre introuvable" of 1816. In the assemblies of the Republic, 1848–51, they had been represented
by their educated and trained Parliamentary champions ;
it was the rank-and-file of the party which now rushed in—
all the Pourceaugnacs of France.

As soon as this assembly of " Rurals " had met at Bordeaux, Thiers made it clear to them that the peace preliminaries must be assented to at once, without even the honours of a Parliamentary debate, as the only condition on which Prussia would permit them to open the war against the Republic and Paris, its stronghold. The counter-revolution had, in fact, no time to lose. The Second Empire had more than doubled the national debt, and plunged all the large towns into heavy municipal debts. The war had fearfully swelled the liabilities, and mercilessly ravaged the resources of the nation. To complete the ruin, the Prussian Shylock was there with his bond for the keep of half a million of his soldiers on French soil, his indemnity of five milliards and interest at 5 per cent on the unpaid instalments thereof. Who was to pay the bill ? It was only by the violent overthrow of the Republic that the appropriators of wealth could hope to shift on to the shoulders of its producers the cost of a war which they, the appropriators, had themselves originated. Thus, the immense ruin of France spurred on these patriotic representatives of land and capital, under the very eyes and patronage of the invader, to graft upon the foreign war a civil war—a slave-holders' rebellion. . . .

Armed Paris was the only serious obstacle in the way of counter-revolutionary conspiracy. Paris was, therefore, to be disarmed. On this point the Bordeaux Assembly was sincerity itself. If the roaring rant of its Rurals had not been audible enough, the surrender of Paris by Thiers to the tender mercies of the triumvirate of Vinoy the *Décembriseur*, Valentin the Bonapartist *gendarme*, and Aurelles de Paladine the Jesuit general, would have cut off even the last subterfuge of doubt. But while insultingly exhibiting the true purpose of the disarmament of Paris, the conspirators asked her to lay down her arms on a pretext which was the most glaring, the most barefaced of lies. The artillery of the Paris National Guard, said Thiers, belonged to the State, and to the State it must be returned. The fact is this : From the very day of the capitulation, by which Bismarck's prisoners had signed the surrender of France, but reserved to themselves a numerous bodyguard for the express purpose of cowing Paris, Paris stood on the watch. The National Guard reorganised themselves and intrusted their supreme control to a Central Committee elected by their whole body, save some fragments of the old Bonapartist formation. On the eve of the entrance of the Prussians into Paris, the Central Committee took measures for the removal to Montmartre, Belleville, and La Villette of the cannon and mitrailleuses treacherously abandoned by the *capitulards* in and about the very quarters the Prussians were to occupy. That artillery had been furnished by the subscriptions of the National Guard. As their private property, it was officially recognised in the capitulation of January 28, and on that very title exempted from the general surrender, into the hands of the conqueror, of arms belonging to the Government. And Thiers was so utterly destitute of even the flimsiest pretext for initiating the war against Paris, that he had to resort to the flagrant lie of the artillery of the National Guard being State property !

The seizure of her artillery was evidently but to serve as the preliminary to the general disarmament of Paris, and, therefore, of the Revolution of the 4th September. But that Revolution had become the legal status of France. The Republic, its work, was recognised by the conqueror in the terms of the capitulation. After the capitulation, it was acknowledged by all the foreign Powers, and in its name the National Assembly had been summoned. The Paris working-men's revolution of September 4 was the only legal title of the National Assembly seated at Bordeaux, and of its executive. Without it, the National Assembly would at once have to give way to the Corps Legislatif, elected in 1869 by universal suffrage under French, not under Prussian, rule, and forcibly dispersed by the arm of the Revolution. Thiers and his ticket-of-leave men would have had to capitulate for safe conducts signed by Louis Bonaparte,

to save them from a voyage to Cayenne. The National
Assembly, with its power of attorney to settle the terms of
peace with Prussia, was but an incident of that Revolution,
the true embodiment of which was still armed Paris, which
had initiated it, undergone for it a five-months' siege, with
its horrors of famine, and made her prolonged resistance,
despite Trochu's plan, the basis of an obstinate war of
defence in the provinces. And Paris was now either to lay
down her arms at the insulting behest of the rebellious
slaveholders of Bordeaux, and acknowledge that her Revolution of September 4 meant nothing but a simple transfer
of power from Louis Bonaparte to his Royal rivals ; or
she had to stand forward as the self-sacrificing champion
of France, whose salvation from ruin, and whose regeneration were impossible, without the revolutionary overthrow
of the political and social conditions that had engendered
the second Empire, and, under its fostering care, matured
into ·utter rottenness. Paris, emaciated by a five-months'
famine, did not hesitate one moment. She heroically resolved to run all the hazards of a resistance against the
French conspirators, even with Prussian cannon frowning
upon her from her own forts. Still, in its abhorrence of the
civil war into which Paris was to be goaded, the Central
Committee continued to persist in a merely defensive attitude, despite the provocations of the Assembly, the usurpa-
tions of the Executive, and the menacing concentration of
troops in and around Paris.

Thiers opened the civil war by sending Vinoy, at the
head of a multitude of *sergents-de-ville* and some regiments
of the line, upon a nocturnal expedition against Montmartre, there to seize, by surprise, the artillery of the
National Guard. It is well known how this attempt broke
down before the resistance of the National Guard and
the fraternisation of the line with the people. Aurelles de
Paladine had printed beforehand his bulletin of victory, and
Thiers held ready the placards announcing his measures of
coup d'état. Now these had to be replaced by Thiers's appeals,

imparting his magnanimous resolve to leave the National
Guard in the possession of their arms, with which, he said,
he felt sure they would rally round the Government against
the rebels. Out of 300,000 National Guards only 300 re-
sponded to this summons to rally round little Thiers against
themselves. The glorious working-men's Revolution of
March 18 took undisputed sway of Paris. The Central
Committee was its provisional Government. Europe
seemed, for a moment, to doubt whether its recent sensa-
tional performances of state and war had any reality in
them or whether they were the dreams of a long bygone
past. . . .

On the dawn of the 18th of March, Paris arose to the
thunderburst of " Vive la Commune ! " What is the Commune, that sphinx so tantalising to the bourgeois mind ?

" The proletarians of Paris," said the Central Committee
in its manifesto of the 18th March, " amidst the failures
and treasons of the ruling classes, have understood that the
hour has struck for them to save the situation by taking
into their own hands the direction of public affairs. . . .
They have understood that it is their imperious duty and
their absolute right to render themselves masters of their
own destinies, by seizing upon the governmental power."
But the working class cannot simply lay hold of the ready-
made State machinery, and wield it for its own purposes.

The centralised State power, with its ubiquitous organs of
standing army, police, bureaucracy, clergy, and judicature
—organs wrought after the plan of a systematic and hierarchic division of labour—originates from the days of absolute monarchy, serving nascent middle-class society as a
mighty weapon in its struggles against feudalism. Still, its
development remained clogged by all manner of mediæval
rubbish, seignorial rights, local privileges, municipal and
guild monopolies and provincial constitutions. The gigantic
broom of the French Revolution of the eighteenth century
swept away all these relics of bygone times, thus clearing
simultaneously the social soil of its last hindrances to the

superstructure of the modern State edifice raised under the
First Empire, itself the offspring of the coalition wars of old
semi-feudal Europe against modern France. During the
subsequent *régimes* the Government, placed under parliamentary control—that is, under the direct control of the
propertied classes—became not only a hotbed of huge
national debts and crushing taxes ; with its irresistible
allurements of place, pelf, and patronage, it became not
only the bone of contention between the rival factions and
adventurers of the ruling classes ; but its political character
changed simultaneously with the economic changes of
society. At the same pace at which the progress of modern
industry developed, widened, intensified the class antagonism between capital and labour, the State power assumed more and more the character of the national power
of capital over labour, of a public force organised for social
enslavement, of an engine of class despotism. After every
revolution marking a progressive phase in the class struggle,
the purely repressive character of the State power stands
out in bolder and bolder relief. The revolution of 1830,
resulting in the transfer of Government from the landlords
to the capitalists transferred it from the more remote to
the more direct antagonists of the working men. The
bourgeois Republicans, who, in the name of the Revolution of February, took the State power, used it for the June
massacres, in order to convince the working class that
" social " republic meant the republic ensuring their social
subjection, and in order to convince the royalist bulk of the
bourgeois and landlord class that they might safely leave
the cares and emoluments of government to the bourgeois " Republicans." However, after their one heroic
exploit of June, the bourgeois Republicans had, from the
front, to fall back to the rear of the " Party-of-Order "—a
combination formed by all the rival fractions and factions
of the appropriating class in their now openly declared
antagonism to the producing classes. The proper form of
their joint stock Government was the *Parliamentary Republic*,

with Louis Bonaparte for its President. Theirs was a *régime* of avowed class terrorism and deliberate insult towards the " vile multitude." If the Parliamentary Republic, as M. Thiers said, " divided them (the different fractions of the ruling class) least," it opened an abyss between that class and the whole body of society outside their spare ranks. The restraints by which their own divisions had under former *régimes* still checked the State power were removed by their union ; and in view of the threatening upheaval of the proletariat, they now used that State power mercilessly and ostentatiously as the national war engine of capital against labour. In their uninterrupted crusade against the producing masses they were, however, bound not only to invest the executive with continually increased powers of repression, but at the same time to divest their own parliamentary stronghold—the National Assembly—one by one, of all its own means of defence against the Executive. The Executive, in the person of Louis Bonaparte, turned them out. The natural offspring of the " Party-of-Order " Republic was the Second Empire.

The Empire, with the *coup d'état* for its certificate of birth, universal suffrage for its sanction, and the sword for its sceptre, professed to rest upon the peasantry, the large mass of producers not directly involved in the struggle of capital and labour. It professed to save the working class by breaking down Parliamentarism, and, with it, the undisguised subserviency of Government to the propertied classes. It professed to save the propertied classes by upholding their economic supremacy over the working class ; and, finally, it professed to unite all classes by reviving for all the chimera of national glory. In reality, it was the only form of government possible at a time when the bourgeoisie had already lost, and the working class had not yet required the faculty of ruling the nation. It was acclaimed throughout the world as the saviour of society. Under its sway, bourgeois society, freed from political cares, attained a development unexpected even by itself. Its industry and commerce expanded to colossal dimensions ; financial swindling celebrated cosmopolitan orgies ; the misery of the masses was set off by a shameless display of gorgeous, meretricious, and debased luxury. The State power, apparently soaring high above society, was at the same time itself the greatest scandal of that society and the very hotbed of all its corruptions. Its own rottenness and the rottenness of the society it had saved, were laid bare by the bayonet of Prussia, herself eagerly bent upon transferring the supreme seat of that *régime* from Paris to Berlin. Imperialism is, at the same time, the most prostitute and the ultimate form of the State power which nascent middle-class society had commenced to elaborate as a means of its own emancipation from feudalism, and which full-grown bourgeois society had finally transformed into a means for the enslavement of labour by capital.

The direct antithesis to the Empire was the Commune. The cry of " Social Republic," with which the revolution of February was ushered in by the Paris proletariat, did but express a vague aspiration after a Republic that was not only to supersede the monarchical form of class-rule, but class-rule itself. The Commune was the positive form of that Republic.

Paris, the central seat of the old governmental power, and, at the same time, the social stronghold of the French working class, had risen in arms against the attempt of Thiers and the Rurals to restore and perpetuate that old governmental power bequeathed to them by the Empire. Paris could resist only because, in consequence of the siege, it had got rid of the army, and replaced it by a National Guard, the bulk of which consisted of working men. This fact was now to be transformed into an institution. The first decree of the Commune, therefore, was the suppression of the standing army, and the substitution for it of the armed people.

The Commune was formed of the municipal councillors, chosen by universal suffrage in various wards of the town,

responsible and revocable at short terms. The majority of
its members were naturally working men, or acknowledged
representatives of the working class. The Commune was to
be a working, not a parliamentary body, executive and
legislative at the same time. Instead of continuing to be the
agent of the Central Government, the police was at once
stripped of its political attributes, and turned into the
responsible and at all times revocable agent of the Commune. So were the officials of all other branches of the
Administration. From the members of the Commune
downwards, the public service had to be done at *workmen's
wages*. The vested interests and the representation allow-
ances of the high dignitaries of State disappeared along
with the high dignitaries themselves. Public functions
ceased to be the private property of the tools of the Central
Government. Not only municipal administration, but the
whole initiative hitherto exercised by the State was laid
into the hands of the Commune.

Having once got rid of the standing army and the police,
the physical force elements of the old Government, the
Commune was anxious to break the spiritual force of repression, the " parson-power," by the disestablishment and
disendowment of all churches as proprietary bodies. The
priests were sent back to the recess of private life, there to
feed upon the alms of the faithful in imitation of their
predecessors, the Apostles. The whole of the educational
institutions were opened to the people gratuitously, and at
the same time cleared of all interference of Church and
State. Thus, not only was education made accessible to all,
but science itself freed from the fetters which class prejudice
and governmental force had imposed upon it.

The judicial functionaries were to be divested of that
sham independence which had but served to mask their
abject subserviency to all succeeding governments, to which
in turn they had taken, and broken, the oaths of allegiance.
Like the rest of public servants, magistrates and judges
were to be elective, responsible and revocable.

The Paris Commune was, of course, to serve as a model to all the great industrial centres of France. The communal *régime* once established in Paris and the secondary centres, the old centralised Government would in the provinces, too, have to give way to the self-government of the producers. In a rough sketch of national organisation which the Commune had no time to develop, it states clearly that the Commune was to be the political form of even the smallest country hamlet, and that in the rural districts the standing army was to be replaced by a national militia, with an extremely short term of service. The rural communes of every district were to administer their common affairs by an assembly of delegates in the central town, and these district assemblies were again to send deputies to the National Delegation in Paris, each delegate to be at any time revocable and bound by the *mandat impératif* (formal instructions) of his constituents. The few but important functions which still would remain for a central government were not to be suppressed, as has been intentionally misstated, but were to be discharged by Communal and, therefore, strictly responsible agents. The unity of the nation was not to be broken ; but, on the contrary, to be organised by the Communal constitution, and to become a reality by the destruction of the State power which claimed to be the embodiment of that unity independent of, and superior to, the nation itself, from which it was but a parasitic excrescence. While the merely repressive organs of the old governmental power were to be amputated, its legitimate functions were to be wrested from an authority usurping pre-eminence over society itself, and restored to the responsible agents of society. Instead of deciding once in three or six years which member of the ruling class was to represent the people in Parliament, universal suffrage was to serve the people, constituted in Communes, as individual suffrage serves every other employer in the search for the workmen and managers in his business. And it is well known that companies, like individuals, in matters of real business generally know how to put the right man in the right place, and, if they for once make a mistake, to redress it promptly. On the other hand, nothing could be more foreign to the spirit of the Commune than to supersede universal suffrage by hierarchic investiture.

It is generally the fate of completely new historical creations to be mistaken for the counterpart of older and even defunct forms of social life, to which they may bear a certain likeness. Thus, this new Commune, which breaks the modern State power, has been mistaken for a reproduction of the mediæval Communes, which first preceded, and afterwards became the substratum of, that very State power. The communal constitution has been mistaken for an attempt to break up into a federation of small States, as dreamt of by Montesquieu and the Girondins, that unity of great nations which, if originally brought about by political force, has now become a powerful coefficient of social production. The antagonism of the Commune against the State power has been mistaken for an exaggerated form of the ancient struggle against over-centralisation. Peculiar historical circumstances may have prevented the classical development, as in France, of the bourgeois form of government, and may have allowed, as in England, completion of the great central State organs by corrupt vestries, jobbing councillors, ferocious poor-law guardians in the towns, and virtually hereditary magistrates in the counties. The Communal Constitution would have restored to the social body all the forces hitherto absorbed by the State parasite feeding upon, and clogging the free movement of, society. By this one act it would have initiated the regeneration of France. The provincial French middle-class saw in the Commune an attempt to restore the sway their order had held over the country under Louis Philippe, and which, under Louis Napoleon, was supplanted by the pretended rule of the country over the towns. In reality, the Communal Constitution brought the rural producers under the intellectual lead of the central towns of their districts, and

there secured to them, in the working man, the natural
trustees of their interests. The very existence of the Commune involved, as a matter of course, local municipal
liberty, but no longer as a check upon the now superseded
State power. It could only enter into the head of a Bismarck,
who, when not engaged on his intrigues of blood and iron,
always likes to resume his old trade, so befitting his mental
calibre, of contributor to *Kladderadatsch* (the Berlin *Punch*),
it could only enter in such a head, to ascribe to the Paris
Commune aspirations after the caricature of the old French
municipal organisation of 1791, the Prussian municipal
constitution which degrades the town governments to mere
secondary wheels in the police machinery of the Prussian
State. The Commune made that catchword of bourgeois
revolutions, cheap government, a reality by destroying the
two greatest sources of expenditure—the standing army
and State functionarism. Its very existence presupposed the
non-existence of monarchy, which, in Europe at least, is
the normal incumbrance and indispensable cloak of class-
rule. It supplied the Republic with the basis of really
democratic institutions. But neither cheap government nor
the " true Republic " was its ultimate aim ; they were its
mere concomitants.

The multiplicity of interpretations to which the Commune has been subjected, and the multiplicity of interests
which construed it in their favour, show that it was a
thoroughly expansive political form, while all previous
forms of government had been emphatically repressive.
Its true secret was this. It was essentially a working-class
government, the produce of the struggle of the producing
against the appropriating class, the political form at last
discovered under which to work out the economical
emancipation of Labour.

Except on this last condition, the Communal Constitution would have been an impossibility and a delusion. The
political rule of the producer cannot co-exist with the
perpetuation of his social slavery. The Commune was,

therefore, to serve as a lever for uprooting the economical foundations upon which rests the existence of classes, and therefore of class-rule. With labour emancipated, every man becomes a working man, and productive labour ceases to be a class attribute.

It is a strange fact. In spite of all the tall talk and all the immense literature, for the last sixty years, about Emancipation of Labour, no sooner do the working men anywhere take the subject into their own hands with a will, than uprises at once all the apologetic phraseology of the mouth-pieces of present society with its two poles of Capital and Wage-slavery (the landlord now is but the sleeping partner of the capitalist), as if capitalist society was still in its purest state of virgin innocence, with its antagonisms still undeveloped, with its delusions still unexploded, with its prostitute realities not yet laid bare. The Commune, they exclaim, intends to abolish property, the basis of all civilisation ! Yes, gentlemen, the Commune intended to abolish that class-property which makes the labour of the many the wealth of the few. It aimed at the expropriation of the ex-propriators. It wanted to make individual property a truth by transforming the means of production, land and capital, now chiefly the means of enslaving and exploiting labour, into mere instruments of free and associated labour. But this is Communism, " impossible " Communism ! Why, those members of the ruling classes who are intelligent enough to perceive the impossibility of continuing the present system—and they are many—have become the obtrusive and full-mouthed apostles of co-operative production. If co-operative production is not to remain a sham and a snare ; if it is to supersede the Capitalist system ; if united co-operative societies are to regulate national production upon a common plan, thus taking it under their own control, and putting an end to the constant anarchy and periodical convulsions which are the fatality of capitalist production—what else, gentlemen, would it be but Communism, " possible " Communism ?

The working class did not expect miracles from the Commune. They have no ready-made Utopias to introduce *par décret du peuple*. They know that in order to work out their own emancipation, and along with it that higher form to which present society is irresistibly tending, by its own economical agencies they will have to pass through long struggles, through a series of historic processes, transforming circumstances and men. They have no ideals to realise, but to set free the elements of the new society with which old collapsing bourgeois society itself is pregnant. In the full consciousness of their historic mission, and with the heroic resolve to act up to it, the working class can afford to smile at the coarse invective of the gentlemen's gentlemen with the pen and inkhorn, and at the didactic patronage of well-wishing bourgeois-doctrinaires, pouring forth their ignorant platitudes and sectarian crotchets in the oracular tone of scientific infallibility.

When the Paris Commune took the management of the revolution in its own hands ; when plain working men for the first time dared to infringe upon the Governmental privilege of their " natural superiors," and, under circumstances of unexampled difficulty, performed their work modestly, conscientiously, and efficiently—performed it at salaries the highest of which barely amounted to one-fifth of what, according to high scientific authority, is the minimum required for a secretary to a certain metropolitan school board—the old world writhed in convulsions of rage at the sight of the Red Flag, the symbol of the Republic of Labour, floating over the Hôtel de Ville.

And yet, this was the first revolution in which the working class was openly acknowledged as the only class capable of social initiative, even by the great bulk of the Paris middle-class—shop-keepers, tradesmen, merchants—the wealthy capitalist alone excepted. The Commune had saved them by a sagacious settlement of that ever recurring cause of dispute among the middle-class themselves—the debtor and creditor accounts. The same portion of the middle-class,

THE CIVIL WAR IN FRANCE

after they had assisted in putting down the working-men's insurrection of June 1848, had been at once unceremoniously sacrificed to their creditors by the then Constituent Assembly. But this was not their only motive for now rallying round the working-class. They felt there was but one alternative—the Commune, or the Empire—under whatever name it might reappear. The Empire had ruined them economically by the havoc it made of public wealth, by the wholesale financial swindling it fostered, by the props it lent to the artificially accelerated centralisation of capital, and the concomitant expropriation of their own ranks. It had suppressed them politically, it had shocked them morally by its orgies, it had insulted their Voltairianism by handing over the education of their children to the *frères Ignorantins*, it had revolted their national feeling as Frenchmen by precipitating them headlong into a war which left only one equivalent for the ruins it made—the disappearance of the Empire. In fact, after the exodus from Paris of the high Bonapartist and capitalist *Bohème*, the true middle-class Party-of-Order came out in the shape of the " Union Republicaine," enrolling themselves under the colours of the Commune and defending it against the wilful misconstruction of Thiers. Whether the gratitude of this great body of the middle-class will stand the present severe trial, time must show.

The Commune was perfectly right in telling the peasants that " its victory was their only hope." Of all the lies hatched at Versailles and re-echoed by the glorious European penny-a-liner, one of the most tremendous was that the Rurals represented the French peasantry. Think only of the love of the French peasant for the men to whom, after 1815, he had to pay the milliard of indemnity ! In the eyes of the French peasant, the very existence of a great landed proprietary is in itself an encroachment on his conquests of 1789. The bourgeoisie, in 1848, had burdened his plot of land with the additional tax of forty-five cents in the franc ; but then it did so in the name of the revolution ;

while now it had fomented a civil war against the revolution, to shift on the peasant's shoulders the chief load of the five milliards of indemnity to be paid to the Prussians. The Commune, on the other hand, in one of its first proclamations, declared that the true originators of the war would be made to pay its cost. The Commune would have delivered the peasant of the blood tax, would have given him a cheap government, transformed his present bloodsuckers, the notary, advocate, executor, and other judicial vampires, into salaried communal agents, elected by, and responsible to himself. It would have freed him of the tyranny of the *garde champêtre*, the gendarme, and the prefect ; would have put enlightenment by the schoolmaster in the place of stultification by the priest. And the French peasant is, above all, a man of reckoning. He would find it extremely reasonable that the pay of the priest, instead of being extorted by the tax-gatherer, should only depend upon the spontaneous action of the parishioners' religious instincts. Such were the great immediate boons which the rule of the Commune—and that rule alone—held out to the French peasantry. It is, therefore, quite superfluous here to expatiate upon the more complicated but vital problems which the Commune alone was able, and at the same time compelled, to solve in favour of the peasant, viz., the hypothecary debt, lying like an incubus upon his parcel of soil, the *proletariat foncier* (the rural proletariat), daily growing upon it, and his expropriation from it enforced, at a more rapid rate, by the very development of modern agriculture and the competition of capitalist farming.

The French peasant had elected Louis Bonaparte president of the Republic ; but the Party-of-Order created the Empire. What the French peasant really wants he commenced to show in 1849 and 1850, by opposing his maire to the Government's prefect, his schoolmaster to the Government's priest, and himself to the Government's gendarme. All the laws made by the Party-of-Order in January and February 1850, were avowed measures of repression against the peasant. The peasant was a Bonapartist, because the great Revolution, with all its benefits to him, was, in his eyes, personified in Napoleon. This delusion, rapidly breaking down under the Second Empire (and in its very nature hostile to the Rurals), this prejudice of the past, how could it have withstood the appeal of the Commune to the living interests and urgent wants of the peasantry?

The Rurals—this was, in fact, their chief apprehension—knew that three months' free communication of Communal Paris with the provinces would bring about a general rising of the peasants, and hence their anxiety to establish a police blockade around Paris, so as to stop the spread of the rinderpest.

If the Commune was thus the true representative of all the healthy elements of French society, and therefore the truly national Government, it was, at the same time, a working men's Government, as the bold champion of the emancipation of labour, emphatically international. Within sight of the Prussian army, that had annexed to Germany two French provinces, the Commune annexed to France the working people all over the world.

The second Empire had been the jubilee of cosmopolitan blacklegism, the rakes of all countries rushing in at its call for a share in its orgies and in the plunder of the French people. Even at this moment the right hand of Thiers is Ganesco, the foul Wallachian, and his left hand is Markowski, the Russian spy. The Commune admitted all foreigners to the honour of dying for the immortal cause. Between the foreign war lost by their treason, and the civil war fomented by their conspiracy with the foreign invader, the bourgeoisie had found the time to display their patriotism by organising police-hunts upon the Germans in France. The Commune made a German working man its Minister of Labour. Thiers, the bourgeoisie, the Second Empire, had continually deluded Poland by loud professions of sympathy, while in reality betraying her to, and doing the dirty work of Russia. The Commune honoured the heroic sons of Poland by placing them at the head of the defenders of Paris. And, to broadly mark the new era of history, it was conscious of initiating, under the eyes of the conquering Prussians on the one side and of the Bonapartist army, led by Bonapartist generals, on the other, the Commune pulled down that colossal symbol of martial glory, the Vendôme column.

The great social measure of the Commune was its own working existence. Its special measures could but betoken the tendency of a government of the people by the people. Such were the abolition of the nightwork of journeyman bakers ; the prohibition, under penalty, of the employers' practice to reduce wages by levying upon their workpeople fines under manifold pretexts—a process in which the employer combines in his own person the parts of legislator, judge, and executioner, and filches the money to boot. Another measure of this class was the surrender, to associations of workmen, under reserve of compensation, of all closed workshops and factories, no matter whether the respective capitalists had absconded or preferred to strike work.

The financial measures of the Commune, remarkable for their sagacity and moderation, could only be such as were compatible with the state of a besieged town. . . . . . .

At last, when treachery had opened the gates of Paris to General Douai, on May 21, Thiers, on the 22nd, revealed to the Rurals the " goal " of his conciliation comedy, which they had so obstinately persisted in not understanding. " I told you a few days ago that we were approaching *our goal* : to-day I came to tell you *the goal* is reached. The victory of order, justice, and civilisation is at last won ! "

So it was. The civilisation and justice of bourgeois order comes out in its lurid light whenever the slaves and drudges of that order rise against their masters. Then this civilisation and justice stand forth as undisguised savagery and lawless revenge. Each new crisis in the class struggle between the appropriator and the producer brings out this fact more glaringly. Even the atrocities of the bourgeois in June 1848, vanish before the ineffable infamy of 1871. The self-sacrificing heroism with which the population of Paris—men, women, and children—fought for eight days after the entrance of the Versaillese, reflects as much the grandeur of their cause as the infernal deeds of the soldiery reflect the innate spirit of that civilisation of which they are the mercenary vindicators. A glorious civilisation, indeed, the great problem of which is how to get rid of the heaps of corpses it made after the battle was over !

To find a parallel for the conduct of Thiers and his bloodhounds we must go back to the times of Sulla and the two Triumvirates of Rome. The same wholesale slaughter in cold blood ; the same disregard, in massacre, of age and sex, the same system of torturing prisoners ; the same proscriptions, but this time of a whole class ; the same savage hunt after concealed leaders, lest one might escape ; the same denunciations of political and private enemies ; the same indifference for the butchery of entire strangers to the feud. There is but this difference, that the Romans had no *mitrailleuses* for the despatch, in the lump, of the proscribed, and that they had not " the law in their hands," nor on their lips the cry of " civilisation."

And after those horrors, look upon the other, still more hideous, face of that bourgeois civilisation as described by its own Press !

" With stray shots," writes the Paris correspondent of a London Tory paper, " still ringing in the distance, and untended wounded wretches dying amid the tombstones of Père la Chaise—with 6,000 terror-stricken insurgents wandering in an agony of despair in the labyrinth of the catacombs, and wretches hurried through the streets to be shot down in scores by the mitrailleuse—it is revolting to see the *cafés* filled with the votaries of absinthe, billiards, and dominoes ; female profligacy perambulating the boulevards, and the sound of revelry disturbing the night from the *cabinets particuliers* of fashionable restaurants." M.

Edouard Hervé writes in the *Journal de Paris*, a Versaillist journal suppressed by the Commune : " The way in which the population of Paris (!) manifested its satisfaction yesterday was rather more than frivolous, and we fear it will grow worse as time progresses. Paris has now a *fête* day appearance, which is sadly out of place ; and, unless we are to be called the *Parisiens de la décadence*, this sort of thing must come to an end." And then he quotes the passage from Tacitus : " Yet, on the morrow of that horrible struggle—began once more to wallow in the voluptuous slough which was destroying its body and polluting its soul —*ali prælia et vulnera, alibi balnea popinæque*—(here fights and wounds, there baths and restaurants)." M. Hervé only forgets to say that the " population of Paris " he speaks of is but the population of the Paris of M. Thiers—the *francs-fileurs* returning in throngs from Versailles, Saint Denis, Rueil, and Saint Germain—*the* Paris of the " Decline." . . .

That after the most tremendous war of modern times, the conquering and the conquered hosts should fraternise for the common massacre of the proletariat — this unparalleled event does indicate, not, as Bismarck thinks, the final repression of a new society upheaving, but the crumbling into dust of bourgeois society. The highest heroic effort of which old society is still capable is national war ; and this is now proved to be a mere governmental humbug, intended to defer the struggle of the classes, and to be thrown aside as soon as that class struggle bursts out in civil war. Class-rule is no longer able to disguise itself in a national uniform ; the national Governments are *one* as against the proletariat.

After Whit-Sunday, 1871, there can be neither peace nor truce possible between the working men of France and the appropriators of their produce. The iron hand of a mercenary soldiery may keep for a time both classes tied down in common oppression. But the battle must break out again and again in ever-growing dimensions, and there can be no

doubt as to who will be the victor in the end—the appropriating few, or the immense working majority. And the
French working class is only the advanced guard of the
modern proletariat.

While the European Governments thus testify, before
Paris, to the international character of class rule, they cry
down the International Working Men's Association—the
international counter-organisation of labour against the
cosmopolitan of capital—as the head fountain of all these
disasters. Thiers denounced it as the despot of labour, pretending to be its liberator. Picard ordered that all communications between the French Internationals and those abroad
should be cut off ; Count Jaubet, Thiers's mummified ac-
complice of 1835, declares it the great problem of all
civilised governments to weed it out. The Rurals roar
against it, and the whole European Press joins the chorus.
An honourable French writer, completely foreign to our
Association, speaks as follows : " The members of the Central Committee of the National Guard, as well as the
greater part of the members of the Commune, are the most
active, intelligent, and energetic minds of the International
Working Men's Association . . . men who are thoroughly
honest, sincere, intelligent, devoted, pure, and fanatical
in the *good* sense of the word." The police-tinged bourgeois
mind naturally figures to itself the International Working
Men's Association as acting in the manner of a secret conspiracy, its central body ordering, from time to time, explosions in different countries. Our Association is, in fact,
nothing but the international bond between the most
advanced working men in the various countries of the
civilised world. Wherever, in whatever shape, and under
whatever conditions the class struggle obtains any consistency, it is but natural that members of our association
should stand in the foreground. The soil out of which it
grows is modern society itself. It cannot be stamped out
by any amount of carnage. To stamp it out, the Government would have to stamp out the despotism of capital

over labour—the condition of their own parasitical existence.

Working-men's Paris, with its Commune, will be for ever
celebrated as the glorious harbinger of a new society. Its
martyrs are enshrined in the great heart of the working
class. Its exterminators history has already nailed to that
eternal pillory from which all the prayers of their priests
will not avail to redeem them.

Friedrich Engels

INTRODUCTION TO THE CIVIL WAR IN FRANCE

*Written in 1891 ; contained in English edition of " The Civil War
in France " published by Martin Lawrence Ltd., 1933.*

[Engels wrote this introduction on March 18, 1891, the
twentieth anniversary of the Paris Commune. It is of special
importance for its analysis of the State. In the last paragraph, Engels wrote "Social Democratic philistine" ; the
German Social Democratic Party printed these words as
". German philistine," thus obscuring Engels's criticism of
the Social Democrats who were against the dictatorship
of the proletariat.]

INTRODUCTION TO THE CIVIL WAR IN FRANCE

. . . Thanks to the economic and political development of
France since 1789, for fifty years the position in Paris has

been such that no Revolution could break out there without
assuming a proletarian character, that is to say, without the
proletariat, which had bought victory with its blood,
advancing its own demands after victory had been won.
These demands were more or less unclear and even confused, corresponding to the state of evolution reached by the
workers of Paris at the particular period, but the ultimate
purpose of them all was the abolition of the class antagonism between capitalists and workers. It is true that no
one could say how this was to be brought about. But the
demand itself, however indefinite it still was in its formulation, contained a threat to the existing order of society ; the
workers who put it forward were still armed, and therefore
the disarming of the workers was the first commandment
for whatever bourgeois group was at the helm of the State.
Hence, after every revolution won by the workers, a new
struggle, ending with the defeat of the workers.

This happened for the first time in 1848. The liberal
bourgeoisie of the Parliamentary opposition held banquets
in support of the reform of the franchise, which was designed
to secure supremacy for their Party. Forced more and more,
in their struggle with the government, to appeal to the
people, they had to allow the radical and republican sections of the bourgeoisie and petty bourgeoisie gradually to
take the lead. But behind these stood the revolutionary
workers, and since 1830 these had acquired far more political independence than the bourgeoisie, and even the
republicans, imagined. At the moment of the crisis between
the Government and the opposition, the workers opened
battle on the streets ; Louis Philippe vanished, and with him
the franchise reforms ; and in their place arose the Republic,
hailed by the victorious workers themselves as a " social "
Republic. No one, however, was clear as to what this social
republic was to imply ; not even the workers themselves.
But they now had arms in their hands, and were a power
in the State. Therefore, as soon as the bourgeois republicans
in control felt the ground under their feet a little firmer,

their first aim was to disarm the workers. This was carried into effect by driving them into the revolt of June 1848 : by direct breach of faith, by open defiance and the attempt to banish the unemployed to a distant province. And then followed a blood-bath of defenceless prisoners the like of which has not been seen since the days of the civil wars which led to the overthrow of the Roman Republic. It was the first time that the bourgeoisie showed to what insane cruelties of revenge they will resort, the moment that the proletariat ventures to take its stand against them as a class apart, with its own interests and demands. And yet 1848 was only child's play compared with their frenzy in 1871.

Punishment followed hard at heel. If the proletariat was not yet able to rule France, the bourgeoisie could no longer do so. At least not at that period, when it had not yet a majority in favour of the monarchy, and was divided into three dynastic parties and a fourth republican party. Their internal dissensions allowed the adventurer Louis Bonaparte to take possession of all the strategic points—army, police, and the administrative machinery and, on December 2, 1851, to torpedo that last stronghold of the bourgeoisie, the National Assembly. The Second Empire opened—the exploitation of France by a band of political and financial adventurers, but at the same time also an industrial development such as had never been possible under the narrowminded and timorous system of Louis Philippe, with its exclusive domination by only a small section of the big bourgeoisie.

Louis Bonaparte took the political power from the capitalists under the pretext of protecting them, the bourgeoisie, from the workers, and on the other hand the workers from them ; but in compensation for this his rule encouraged speculation and industrial activity—in a word the rise and enrichment of the whole bourgeoisie to an extent which was hitherto unknown. To an even greater extent, it is true, corruption and mass robbery developed, clustering round the imperial Court, and drawing their heavy percentages from this enrichment.

But the Second Empire was the appeal to French Chauvinism, the demand for the restoration of the frontiers of the First Empire, which had been lost in 1814, or at least those of the First Republic. A French Empire within the frontiers of the old monarchy and, in fact, within the even more amputated frontiers of 1815—such a thing was impossible for any long duration of time. Hence the necessity for brief wars and the extension of frontiers. But no extension of frontiers was so dazzling to the imagination of the French Chauvinists as the extension which would take in the German left bank of the Rhine. One square mile on the Rhine was more to them than ten in the Alps or anywhere else. Given the Second Empire, the demand for the restoration to France of the left bank of the Rhine, either all at once or by degrees, was merely a question of time. The time came with the Prusso-Austrian war of 1866 ; swindled by Bismarck and by his own over-cunning, vacillating policy in regard to the expected "territorial compensation," there was now nothing left for Napoleon but war, which broke out in 1870 and drove him first to Sedan, and thence to Wilhelmshohe.

The inevitable result was the Paris Revolution of September 4, 1870. The Empire collapsed like a house of cards, and the Republic was again proclaimed. But the enemy was standing at the gates ; the armies of the Empire were either hopelessly beleaguered in Metz or held captive in Germany. In this dire situation the people allowed the Paris deputies to the former legislative body to constitute themselves into a " Government of National Defence." They were the more ready to allow this because, for the purposes of defence, all Parisians capable of bearing arms had enrolled in the National Guard and were armed, so that now the workers constituted a great majority. But almost at once the antagonism between the almost completely bourgeois government and the armed proletariat

broke into open conflict. On October 31 workers' battalions stormed the town hall, and captured some members
of the government. Treachery, the government's breach of
its undertakings, and the intervention of some petty bourgeois battalions set them free again, and in order not to
occasion the outbreak of civil war inside a city which was
already beleaguered by foreign armies, they left the former
government in office.

At last, on January 8, 1871, Paris, almost starving, capitu-
lated ; but with honours unprecedented in the history of
war. The forts were surrendered, the outer wall disarmed,
the weapons of the regiments of the line and of the mobile
guard were handed over, and the troops considered prisoners of war. But the National Guard kept their weapons
and guns, and only entered into an armistice with the
victors, who themselves did not dare enter Paris in triumph.
They only dared to occupy a tiny corner of Paris, which,
into the bargain, consisted partly of public parks, and even
this they only occupied for a few days ! And during this
time they, who had maintained their encirclement of Paris
for 131 days, were themselves encircled by the armed
workers of Paris, who kept a sharp watch that no " Prussian " should overstep the narrow bounds of the corner
yielded up to the foreign conquerors. Such was the respect
which the Paris workers inspired in the army before which
all the armies of the Empire had laid down their arms ; and
the Prussian Junkers, who had come to take revenge at
the very centre of the revolution, were compelled to stand
by respectfully, and salute just precisely this armed
revolution !

During the war the Paris workers had confined themselves to demanding the vigorous prosecution of the fight.
But now, when peace had come with the capitulation of
Paris, at this moment Thiers, the new head of the government, was compelled to realise that the supremacy of the
propertied classes—large landowners and capitalists—was
in constant danger so long as the workers of Paris had arms

in their hands. His first action was to attempt to disarm them. On March 18 he sent troops of the line with orders to deprive the National Guard of the artillery belonging to them, which had been constructed during the siege of Paris and had been paid for by subscription. The attempt did not come off ; Paris rallied as one man in defence of the guns, and war between Paris and the French government sitting at Versailles was declared. The Central Committee of the National Guard, which up to then had carried on the government, handed in its resignation to the National Guard, after it had first decreed the abolition of the scandalous Paris " Morality Police." On the 30th the Commune abolished conscription and the standing army, and declared that the National Guard, in which all citizens capable of bearing arms were to be enrolled, was to be the sole armed force. They released the citizens from all payments of rent for dwelling houses from October 1870 to April, taking also into account amounts already paid in advance, and stopped all sales of articles pledged in the hands of the municipal pawnshops. On the same day the foreigners elected to the Commune were confirmed in office, because " the flag of the Commune is the flag of the World Republic."

On April 1 it was decided that the highest salary received by any employee of the Commune, and therefore also by its members themselves, might not exceed 6,000 francs. On the following day the Commune decreed the separation of the Church from the State, and the abolition of all State payments for religious purposes as well as the transformation of all Church property into national property ; on April 8 this was followed up by a decree excluding from the schools all religious symbols, pictures, dogmas, prayers—in a word, " all that belongs to the sphere of the individual's conscience "—and this decree was gradually applied. On the 5th, in reply to the shooting, day after day, of soldiers of the Commune captured by the Versailles troops, a decree was issued ordering the imprisonment of hostages, but it was never carried into effect. On the 6th the guillotine was brought out by the 137th battalion of the National Guard, and publicly burnt, amid great popular rejoicing. On the 12th the Commune decided that the Column of Victory on the Place Vendôme, which had been cast from captured guns by Napoleon after the war of 1809, should be demolished, as the symbol of chauvinism and incitement to national hatreds. This decree was carried out on May 16. On April 16 the Commune ordered a statistical registration of factories which had been closed down by the manufacturers, and the working out of plans for the carrying on of these factories by workers formerly employed in them, who were to be organised in co-operative societies ; and also plans for the organisation of these co-operatives in one great Union. On the 20th the Commune abolished night work for bakers, and also the workers' registration cards, which since the Second Empire had been run as a monopoly by nominees of the police —exploiters of the first rank; the issuing of these registration cards was transferred to the mayors of the twenty districts of Paris. On April 30 the Commune ordered the closing of the pawnshops, on the ground that they were a form of individual exploitation of the worker, and stood in contradiction with the right of the workers to their instruments of labour and to credit. On May 5 it ordered the demolition of the Chapel of Atonement, which had been built in expiation of the execution of Louis XVI.

Thus, from March 18 onwards the class character of the Paris movement, which had previously been pushed into the background by the fight against the foreign invaders, emerged sharply and clearly. As almost without exception workers, or recognised representatives of the workers, sat in the Commune, its decisions bore a decidedly proletarian character. Either they decreed reforms which the republican bourgeoisie had failed to pass only out of cowardice, but which provided a necessary basis for the free activity of the working class—such as the adoption of the principle that *in relation to the State*, religion is a purely private affair—or they promulgated decrees which were in the direct interests of the working class and to some extent cut at the foundations of the old order of society. In a beleaguered city, however, it was possible to do no more than make a start in the realisation of all these measures. And from the beginning of May on all their energies were required for the fight against the ever-growing armies assembled by the Versailles government.

On April 7 the Versailles troops had captured the Seine crossing at Neuilly, on the west front of Paris ; on the other hand they were driven back with heavy losses by General Eudes in an attack on the south front. Paris was continuously bombarded and, moreover, by the very people who had stigmatised as a sacrilege the bombardment of the same city by the Prussians. These same people now besought the Prussian government to hasten the return of the French soldiers who had been taken prisoner at Sedan and Metz, in order that they might recapture Paris for them. From the beginning of May the gradual arrival of these troops gave the Versailles forces a decided ascendancy. This already became evident when, on April 23, Thiers broke off the negotiations for the exchange, proposed by the Commune, of the Archbishop of Paris and a whole number of other priests held as hostages in Paris, for only one man, Blanqui, who had twice been elected to the Commune but was a prisoner in Clairvaux. And even more in the changed attitude of Thiers ; previously procrastinating and double-faced, he now suddenly became insolent, threatening, brutal. The Versailles forces took the redoubt of Moulin Saquet on the south front, on May 3 ; on the 9th Fort Issy, which had been completely reduced to ruins by gunfire ; and on the 14th Fort Vanves. On the west front they advanced gradually, their weight of numbers capturing the villages and buildings which extended up to the city wall, and at last reached the wall itself ; on the 11th, thanks to treachery and the carelessness of the National Guards stationed there, they succeeded in forcing their way into the city. The Prussians who held the northern and eastern forts allowed the Versailles troops to advance across the land north of the city, which was forbidden ground to them under the armistice, and thus to march forward and attack on a long front, which the Parisians naturally thought covered by the armistice, and therefore held only with weak forces. As a result of this, only a weak resistance was put up in the western half of Paris, the luxury quarter proper; it grew stronger and more tenacious the nearer the attacking troops approached the eastern half, the real working-class quarter. It was only after eight days' fighting that the last defenders of the Commune were overwhelmed on the heights of Belleville and Menilmontant; and then the massacre of defenceless men, women and children, which had been raging all through the week on an increasing scale, reached its zenith. The breech-loaders could no longer kill fast enough; the vanquished workers were shot down in hundreds by mitrailleuse fire. The " Wall of the Federals " at the Père Lachaise cemetery, where the final mass murder was consummated, is still standing to-day, a mute but eloquent testimonial to the savagery of which the ruling class is capable, as soon as the working class dares to demand its rights. Then came mass arrests; when the slaughter of them all proved to be impossible, the shooting of victims arbitrarily selected from the prisoners' ranks, and the removal of the rest to great camps, where they had to await trial by courts-martial. The Prussian troops surrounding the northern half of Paris had orders not to allow any fugitives to pass; but the officers often shut their eyes when the soldiers paid more obedience to the dictates of humanity than to their general's orders; particular honour is due to the Saxon army corps for its humane conduct in letting through many workers who had obviously been fighting for the Commune.

To-day, when after twenty years we look back at the work and historical significance of the Paris Commune of 1871, we find that it is necessary to supplement the account given in *The Civil War in France* with a few additional points.

The members of the Commune were divided into a majority, the Blanquists, who had also been predominant in the Central Committee of the National Guard ; and a minority : members of the International Working Men's Association, chiefly consisting of adherents of the Proudhon school of Socialism. The great majority of the Blanquists at that time were Socialists only by revolutionary and proletarian instinct ; only a few had attained greater clarity. on the essential principles, through Vaillant, who was familiar with German scientific Socialism. It is therefore comprehensible that in the economic sphere much was neglected which, as we see to-day, the Commune should have done. The hardest thing to understand is the holy awe with which they remained standing outside the gates of the Bank of France. This was also a serious political mistake. The bank in the hands of the Commune—this would have been worth more than ten thousand hostages. It would have meant that the whole of the French bourgeoisie would have brought pressure to bear on the Versailles government in favour of peace with the Commune. But what is more astonishing is the correctness of so much that was actually done by the Commune, composed as it was of Blanquists and Proudhonists. Naturally the Proudhonists were chiefly responsible for the economic decrees of the Commune, for their praiseworthy and their less praiseworthy aspects ; as the Blanquists were for its political achievements and failings. And in both cases the irony of history willed—as often happens when doctrinaires come into power—that both did the opposite of what the doctrines of their school prescribed.

Proudhon, the Socialist of small farmers and mastercraftsmen, regarded the principle of association with positive hatred. He said of it that there was more bad than good in it ; that it was by nature sterile, even harmful, because it was a fetter on the freedom of the workers ; that it was a pure dogma, unproductive and burdensome, in conflict as

much with the freedom of the workers as with economy of
labour ; that its disadvantages multiplied more swiftly than
its advantages; that, as compared with it, competition, division of labour and private property were sources of economic strength. Only for the exceptional cases—as Proudhon
called them—of large-scale industry and large industrial
units, such as railways, was there any place for the association of workers. (Cf. *Idéé Générale de la Révolution*, 3 *étude*.)

And by 1871, even in Paris, the great centre of handicrafts, large-scale industry had already to such a degree
ceased to be an exceptional case, that by far the most
important decree of the Commune instituted an organisation of large-scale industry and even of manufacture which
was not based only on the association of workers in each
factory, but also aimed at combining all these associations
in one great Union ; in short an organisation which as
Marx quite rightly says in *The Civil War* must necessarily
have led in the end to Communism, that is to say, the
direct antithesis of the Proudhon doctrine. And, therefore,
the Commune was also the grave of the Proudhon school
of Socialism. To-day this school is no longer to be found in
French working-class circles ; among the Possibilists no less
than among the "Marxists," the Marxian theory now rules
there unchallenged. Only among the " radical " bourgeoisie can Proudhonists still be found.

The Blanquists fared no better. Brought up in the school
of conspiracy, and held together by the severe discipline
which went with it, they worked on the theory that a pro-
portionately small number of resolute, well-organised men
would be able, at a given favourable moment, not only to
seize the helm of the State, but also by energetic and relentless action, to keep power until they succeeded in drawing
the mass of the people into the revolution and ranging them
round the small band of leaders. This conception involved,
above all, the strictest dictatorship and centralisation of all
power in the hands of the new revolutionary government.
And what did the Commune, with its majority of these same

Blanquists, actually do? In all its proclamations to the French in the provinces the Commune proposed to them a free federation of all French Communes with Paris, a national organisation, which for the first time was really to be created by the nation itself. It was precisely the oppressing power of the former centralised government— the army, political police and bureaucracy which Napoleon had created in 1789 and since then had been taken over by every new government and used against its opponents— it was precisely this power which should have fallen everywhere, just as it had already fallen in Paris.

The Commune was compelled to recognise from the outset that the working class, once come to power, could not carry on business with the old State machine ; that in order not to lose again its but newly won supremacy, this working class must, on the one hand, do away with all the old repressive machinery previously used against it, and on the other, safeguard itself against its own deputies and officials, by declaring them all, without exception, subject to recall at any moment. What had been the special characteristics of the former State? Society had created its own organs to look after its common interests, first through the simple division of labour. But these organs, at whose head was the State power, had in the course of time, in pursuance of their own special interests, transformed themselves from the servants of society into the masters of society ; as can be seen for example, not only in the hereditary monarchy, but equally also in the democratic republic. There is no country in which "politicians" form a more powerful and distinct section of the nation than in North America. There each of the two great parties which alternately succeed each other in power is itself in turn controlled by people who make a business of politics, who speculate on seats in the legislative assemblies of the Union as well as of the separate States, or who make a living by carrying on agitation for their party and on its victory are rewarded with positions. It is common knowledge that the Americans have been striving for thirty years to shake off this yoke, which has become intolerable, and that in spite of all they can do they continue to sink ever deeper in this quicksand of corruption. It is precisely in America that we have the best example of the growing independence of the State power in opposition to society, whose mere instrument it was originally intended to be. Here there was no dynasty, no nobility, no standing army, beyond the few men keeping watch on the Indians ; no bureaucracy with permanent posts or the right to pensions. And nevertheless we find here two great groups of political speculators, who alternately take possession of the State machine, and exploit it by the most corrupt means and for the most corrupt ends —and the nation is powerless against these two great cartels of politicians, who are ostensibly its servants but in reality exploit and plunder it.

Against this transformation of the State and the organs of the State from the servants of society into masters of society—a process which had been inevitable in all previous States—the Commune made use of two infallible expedients. In the first place, it filled all posts—administrative, judicial and educational—by election on the basis of universal suffrage of all concerned, with the right of these electors to recall their delegate at any time. And in the second place, all officials, high or low, were paid only the wages received by other workers. The highest salary paid by the Commune to anyone was 6,000 francs. In this way an effective barrier to place-hunting and careerism was set up, even apart from the imperative mandates to delegates to representative bodies which were also added in profusion.

This shattering of the former State power and its replacement by a new and really democratic State is described in detail in the third section of *The Civil War*. But it was necessary to dwell briefly here once more on some of its features because in Germany particularly the superstitious faith in the State has been carried over from philosophy into the general consciousness of the bourgeoisie and even of many workers. According to the philosophical conception the State is the " realisation of the idea " or, translated into philosophical language, the Kingdom of God on earth ; the sphere in which eternal truth and justice is or should be realised. And from this follows a superstitious reverence for the State and everything connected with it, which takes root the more readily as people from their childhood are accustomed to imagine that the affairs and interests common to the whole of society could be managed and safeguarded in any other way than as in the past, that is through the State and its well-paid officials. And people think they are taking quite an extraordinarily bold step forward when they rid themselves of faith in a hereditary monarchy and become partisans of a democratic republic. In reality, however, the State is nothing more than a machine for the oppression of one class by another, and indeed in the democratic republic no less than in the monarchy ; and at best an evil inherited by the proletariat after its victorious struggle for class supremacy whose worst sides the proletariat, just like the Commune, will have at the earliest possible moment to lop off, until such time as a new generation, reared under new and free social conditions, will be able to throw on the scrap-heap all the useless lumber of the State.

Of late the Social Democratic philistine has once more been filled with wholesome terror at the words : Dictatorship of the Proletariat. Well and good, gentlemen, do you want to know what this dictatorship looks like ? Look at the Paris Commune. That was the Dictatorship of the Proletariat.

London, on the twentieth anniversary of the Paris Commune, *March 18, 1891.*

F. ENGELS.

Opposite: The manuscript, *German Ideology,* was sent to the printers, but practical difficulties prevented its publication.

Karl Marx and Friedrich Engels

GERMAN IDEOLOGY

Written in 1845–6 : only one section was published as an article in 1847 : other parts were published in periodicals after Marx's death. Complete text first published by the Marx-Engels Institute in 1932. No English edition exists.

[In the preface to *The Critique of Political Economy* Marx explains that when Engels and he settled in Brussels in

1845, " we decided to work out together the contrast
between our view and the idealism of the German philosophy, in fact to settle our accounts with our former
philosophic conscience. The plan was carried out in the
form of a criticism of the post-Hegelian philosophy." The
manuscript, *German Ideology,* was sent to the printers, but
practical difficulties prevented its publication. *German
Ideology* is largely polemical, but is still of extreme importance for its clear statement of the difference between the
standpoints of idealism, materialism and dialectical
materialism. A part of the first section, which deals with
the contrast between the materialist and the idealist conception, is given below.]

GERMAN IDEOLOGY

THE CONTRAST BETWEEN THE MATERIALIST AND THE IDEALIST CONCEPTION

Ideology in General, German Philosophy in Particular

THE PREMISES from which we start are not arbitrary,
they are not dogmas ; they are real premises, from which
abstraction can be made only in imagination. They are
real individuals, their action and their material conditions
of life, both those which they find in existence and those
produced through their own action. These premises can
therefore be verified in a purely empirical way.

The first premise of all human history is of course the
existence of living human individuals. The first fact to be
established is therefore the physical organisation of these
individuals and their consequent relation to the rest of
nature. We cannot here, of course, go into either the
physical characteristics of men themselves, or the natural
conditions found by men—the geological, oro-hydro-
graphical, climatic and other conditions. All historical

work must start on the basis of these natural conditions and
their modification in the course of history through the
action of men.

Men may be distinguished from animals by consciousness,
religion, or anything else. They begin to differentiate
themselves from animals as soon as they begin to *produce*
their means of subsistence, a step which is conditioned by
their physical organisation. By producing their means of
existence men indirectly produce their material life itself.

The mode in which men produce their means of existence
depends in the first place on the nature of the means of
existence themselves—those which they find at their disposal and have to reproduce.

This mode of production must not be considered merely
from the aspect that it is the reproduction of the physical
existence of individuals. It is rather, in fact, a definite form
of activity of these individuals, a definite form of expressing
their life, their definite *mode of life*. As individuals express
their life, so they are. What they are therefore coincides
with their production—*what* they produce as well as *how*
they produce. What individuals are therefore depends on
the material conditions of their production.

This production first makes its appearance with the
increase of population. It in turn itself presupposes *intercourse*
of the individuals among themselves. The form of this
intercourse is again determined by production. . . .

The fact is therefore that definite individuals, who are
productively active in a definite way, enter into these
definite social and political relations. In every single
instance empirical observation must show the connection
of the social and political structure with production—
empirically and without any mystification and speculation.
The social structure and the State always arise from the
life-process of definite individuals, but of these individuals,
not as they may appear in their own or other people's
ideas, but as they *really* are, that is, as they act, produce in
a material way, therefore as they produce under definite

limitations, presuppositions and conditions which are material and independent of their will.

The production of ideas, concepts, of consciousness, is at first directly interwoven with the material activity and the material intercourse of men, the language of actual life. Conception, thought, the mental intercourse of men, then still appear as the direct efflux of their material relations. The same is true of mental production, as expressed in the language of the politics, laws, morality, religion and metaphysics of a people. Men are the producers of their concepts, ideas, etc.—but real, producing men, as they are conditioned by a definite development of their productive forces and the intercourse, up to its most far-reaching forms, which corresponds with these. Consciousness can never be anything else than conscious existence, and the existence of men is their actual life-process. If in all ideology men and their relations appear upside down, as in a camera obscura, this phenomenon arises just as much from their historical life-process as the reversal of objects on the retina does from their directly physical life-process.

In direct contrast to German philosophy, which descends from heaven to earth, here the ascent is made from earth to heaven. That is to say, we do not start from what men say, imagine, conceive, nor from men as described, thought of, imagined and conceived, in order thence and thereby to reach corporeal men ; we start from real, active men, and from their life-process also show the development of the ideological reflexes and echoes of this life-process. Even the phantasmagoria in men's brains are necessary supplements of their material life-process, empirically demonstrable and bound up with material premises. Morals, religion, metaphysics and all other ideology and the corresponding forms of consciousness thus no longer maintain the appearance of independence. They have no history, they have no development ; but men, developing their material production and their material intercourse, change, along with this their real existence, also their thinking and the products of their thought. It is not consciousness that determines life, but life that determines consciousness. In the first mode of observation, the starting point is consciousness taken as the living individual ; in the second, in conformity with actual life, it is the real living individual himself, and consciousness is considered only as *his* consciousness.

This mode of observation is not without a basis. It sets out from real premises, and never for a moment leaves them. Its premises are men not in any imaginary isolation and state of fixation, but in their actual empirically observable process of development in definite conditions. From the moment this active life-process is shown, history ceases to be a collection of dead facts, as it is with the empiricists, themselves still abstract, or an imaginary activity of imaginary persons, as it is with the idealists.

There, where speculation ends, with real life, real positive science therefore begins, the representation of practical activity, of the practical process of the development of men. The empty phrases of consciousness break off ; real knowledge must take their place. With the representation of reality, independent philosophy loses the medium for its existence. Its place can at best be taken by a collection of the most general results which can be extracted from observation of men's historical development. The abstractions in themselves, separated from actual history, have absolutely no value. They can only serve to facilitate the arrangement of the historical material, to indicate the sequence of its separate strata. But they do not, like philosophy, in any way provide a recipe or formula by which the historical epochs can be neatly trimmed. On the contrary, the difficulty begins precisely when a start is made with the examination and arrangement, the actual presentation, of the material, whether of a past epoch or of the present. The overcoming of these difficulties is conditioned by premises which cannot be given at this stage, but can only result from the study of the real life-process and the action of individuals of every epoch.

Friedrich Engels

LUDWIG FEUERBACH

*First published as a series of articles in " Die Neue Zeit," 1886 ;
English edition, Martin Lawrence Ltd., 1934.*

[Engels wrote these articles by way of a review of a book
on Feuerbach by Starcke. In the preface to the first reprint
in book form (1888), Engels explains that at the time when
he was asked to write the review, classical German philosophy was experiencing " a kind of rebirth abroad " at the
same time as the world outlook represented by Marx and
himself was spreading, and therefore : " a short, connected
account of our relation to the Hegelian philosophy, of our
point of departure as well as of our separation from it,
appeared to me to be required more and more. Equally,
a full acknowledgment of the influence which Feuerbach,
more than any other post-Hegelian philosopher, had upon
us during our period of storm and stress, appeared to me
to be an undischarged debt of honour." *Ludwig Feuerbach*
is therefore an extremely valuable statement of the distinction between materialism and idealism, and between mechanical and dialectical materialism ; the passages given
below not only state these differences, but in themselves
illustrate the dialectical approach to philosophical
questions.]

LUDWIG FEUERBACH

IDEALISM AND MATERIALISM

THE GREAT BASIC QUESTION of all philosophy, especially of modern philosophy, is that concerning the relation
of thinking and being. From the very early times when men,
still completely ignorant of the structure of their own bodies,

under the stimulus of dream apparitions[1] came to believe
that their thinking and sensation were not activities of their
bodies, but of a distinct soul which inhabits the body and
leaves it at death—from this time, men have been driven to
reflect about the relation between this soul and the outside
world. If in death it took leave of the body and lived on,
there was no occasion to invent yet another distinct death
for it. Thus arose the idea of its immortality which at that
stage of development appeared not at all as a consolation
but as a fate against which it was no use fighting, and often
enough, as among the Greeks, as a positive misfortune. Not
religious desire for consolation, but the quandary arising
from the common universal ignorance of what to do with
this soul (once its existence had been accepted) after the
death of the body—led in a general way to the tedious notion of personal immortality. In an exactly similar manner
the first gods arose through the personification of natural
forces. And these gods in the further development of religions assumed more and more an extra-mundane form, until finally by a process of abstraction, I might almost say of
distillation, occurring naturally in the course of man's intellectual development, out of the many more or less limited and
mutually limiting gods there arose in the minds of men the
idea of the one exclusive god of the monotheistic religions.

Thus the question of the relation of thinking to being, the
relation of spirit to nature—the paramount question of the
whole of philosophy—has, no less than all religion, its roots
in the narrow-minded and ignorant notions of savagery.
But this question could for the first time be put forward in
its whole acuteness, could achieve its full significance, only
after European society had awakened from the long hiber-
nation of the Christian Middle Ages. The question of the

---

[1] Among savages and lower barbarians the idea is still universal that
the human forms which appear in dreams are souls which have temporarily left their bodies ; the real man is therefore held responsible for
acts committed by his dream apparition against the dreamer. Thus B.
Imthurn found this belief current, for example, among the Indians of
Guiana in 1884.

position of thinking in relation to being, a question which,
by the way, had played a great part also in the scholasticism
of the Middle Ages, the question : which is primary, spirit
or nature—that question, in relation to the Church, was
sharpened into this : " Did god create the world or has
the world been in existence eternally ? "

The answers which the philosophers gave to this question
split them into two great camps. Those who asserted the
primacy of spirit to nature and, therefore, in the last instance, assumed world creation in some form or other—
(and among the philosophers, Hegel, for example, this creation often becomes still more intricate and impossible than
in Christianity)—comprised the camp of idealism. The
others, who regarded nature as primary, belong to the
various schools of materialism.

These two expressions, idealism and materialism, primarily signify nothing more than this ; and here also they
are not used in any other sense. What confusion arises when
some other meaning is put into them will be seen below.

But the question of the relation of thinking and being has
yet another side : in what relation do our thoughts about
the world surrounding us stand to this world itself ? Is our
thinking capable of the cognition of the real world ? Are
we able in our ideas and notions of the real world to produce a correct reflection of reality ? In philosophical
language this question is called the question of the " identity
of thinking and being," and the overwhelming majority of
philosophers give an affirmative answer to this question.
With Hegel, for example, its affirmation is self-evident ; for
what we perceive in the real world is precisely its thought-
content—that which makes the world a gradual realisation
of the absolute idea, which absolute idea has existed somewhere from eternity, independent of the world and before
the world. But it is manifest without more ado that thought
can know a content which is from the outset a thought-
content. It is equally manifest that what is here to be proved
is already tacitly contained in the presupposition. But that

in no way prevents Hegel from drawing the further conclusion from his proof of the identity of thinking and being that his philosophy, because it is correct for his own thinking, is therefore the only correct one, and that the identity of thinking and being must prove its validity by mankind immediately translating his philosophy from theory into practice and transforming the whole world according to Hegelian principles. This is an illusion which he shares with well-nigh all philosophers.

In addition there is yet another set of different philosophers—those who question the possibility of any cognition (or at least of an exhaustive cognition) of the world. To them, among the moderns, belong Hume and Kant, and they have played a very important rôle in philosophical development. What is decisive in the refutation of this view has already been said by Hegel—in so far as this was possible from an idealist standpoint. The materialistic additions made by Feuerbach are more ingenious than profound. The most telling refutation of this as of all other philosophical fancies is practice, viz., experiment and industry. If we are able to prove the correctness of our conception of a natural process by making it ourselves, bringing it into being out of its conditions and using it for our own purposes into the bargain, then there is an end of the Kantian incomprehensible " thing-in-itself." The chemical substances produced in the bodies of plants and animals remained just such " things-in-themselves " until organic chemistry began to produce them one after another, whereupon the " thing-in-itself " became a thing for us, as, for instance, alizarin, the colouring matter of the madder, which we no longer trouble to grow in the madder roots in the field, but produce much more cheaply and simply from coal tar. For three hundred years the Copernican solar system was an hypothesis with a hundred, a thousand or ten thousand chances to one in its favour, but still always an hypothesis. But when Leverrier, by means of the data provided by this system, not only deduced the necessity of

the existence of an unknown planet, but also calculated
the position in the heavens which this planet must necessarily occupy, and when Galle really found this planet, the
Copernican system was proved. If, nevertheless, the Neo-
Kantians are attempting to resurrect the Kantian conception in Germany and the agnostics that of Hume in England (where in fact it had never ceased to survive), this is
—in view of their theoretical and practical refutation
accomplished long ago—scientifically a regression and
practically merely a shamefaced way of surreptitiously
accepting materialism, while denying it before the world.

But during this long period from Descartes to Hegel and
from Hobbes to Feuerbach, the philosophers were by no
means impelled, as they thought they were, solely by the
force of pure reason. On the contrary. What really pushed
them forward was the powerful and ever more rapidly on-
rushing progress of natural science and industry. Among
the materialists this was plain on the surface, but the idealist
systems also filled themselves more and more with a materialist content and attempted pantheistically to reconcile the
antithesis between mind and matter. Thus, ultimately, the
Hegelian system represents merely a materialism idealistic-
ally turned upside down in method and content.

It is, therefore, comprehensible that Starcke in his charac-
terisation of Feuerbach first of all investigates the latter's
position in regard to this fundamental question of the relation of thinking and being. After a short introduction, in
which the views of the preceding philosophers, particularly
since Kant, are described in unnecessarily ponderous philosophical language, and in which Hegel, by an all too for-
malistic adherence to certain passages of his work, gets far
less than his due, there follows a detailed description of
the course of development of Feuerbach's " metaphysics "
itself, as this course was reconstructed out of the sequence
of those writings of this philosopher which have a bearing
here. This description is industriously and carefully elaborated, only, like the whole book, it is loaded with a ballast

of philosophical phraseology by no means everywhere unavoidable, which is the more disturbing in its effect, the
less the author keeps to the manner of expression of one
and the same school, or even of Feuerbach himself, and
the more he interjects expressions of very different schools
—especially of the tendencies now rampant and calling
themselves philosophical.

The course of evolution of Feuerbach is that of an
Hegelian—a never quite orthodox Hegelian, it is true—
into a materialist ; an evolution which at a definite stage
necessitates a complete rupture with the idealist system of
his predecessor. With irresistible force Feuerbach is finally
forced to the realisation that the Hegelian pre-mundane
existence of the " absolute idea," the " pre-existence of the
logical categories " before the world existed, is nothing
more than the fantastic survival of the belief in the existence
of an extra-mundane creator ; that the material, sensuously
perceptible world to which we ourselves belong is the only
reality ; and that our consciousness and thinking, however
supra-sensuous they may seem, are the product of a material, bodily organ, the brain. Matter is not a product of
mind, but mind itself is merely the highest product of matter. This is, of course, pure materialism. But, having got so
far, Feuerbach stops short. He cannot overcome the customary philosophical prejudice, prejudice not against the
thing but against the name materialism. He says : " To
me materialism is the foundation of the edifice of human
essence and knowledge, but to me it is not what it is to the
physiologist, to the natural scientist in the narrower sense,
for example, Moleschott, and necessarily so indeed from
their standpoint and profession, the building itself. Backwards I fully agree with the materialists ; but not forwards."

Here Feuerbach lumps together the materialism that is a
general world outlook resting upon a definite conception of
the relation between matter and mind, and the special form
in which this world outlook was expressed at a definite stage
of historical development, viz., in the eighteenth century.

More than that, he confuses it with the shallow and vulgarised form in which the materialism of the eighteenth
century continues to exist to-day in the minds of naturalists
and physicians, the form which was preached on their tours
in the 'fifties by Büchner, Vogt and Moleschott. But just
as idealism underwent a series of stages of development, so
also did materialism. With each epoch-making discovery
even in the sphere of natural science it has to change its
form ; and after history also was subjected to materialistic
treatment, here also a new avenue of development has
opened.

The materialism of the last century was predominantly
mechanical, because at that time, of all natural sciences,
mechanics and indeed only the mechanics of solid bodies—
celestial and terrestrial—in short, the mechanics of gravity,
had come to any definite close. Chemistry at that time
existed only in its infantile, phlogistic form. Biology still
lay in swaddling clothes ; vegetable and animal organisms
had been only roughly examined and were explained as the
result of purely mechanical causes. As the animal was to
Descartes, so was man a machine to the materialists of the
eighteenth century. This exclusive application of the standards of mechanics to processes of a chemical and organic
nature—in which processes, it is true, the laws of mechanics
are also valid, but are pushed into the background by other
and higher laws—constitutes a specific but at that time
inevitable limitation of classical French materialism.

The second specific limitation of this materialism lay in
its inability to comprehend the universe as a process—as
matter developing in an historical process. This was in
accordance with the level of the natural science of that time,
and with the metaphysical, i.e., anti-dialectical manner of
philosophising connected with it. Nature, it was known,
was in constant motion. But according to the ideas of that
time, this motion turned eternally in a circle and therefore
never moved from the spot ; it produced the same results
over and over again. This conception was at that time

inevitable. The Kantian theory of the origin of the solar
system had been put forward but recently and was regarded
merely as a curiosity. The history of the development of the
earth, geology, was still totally unknown, and the conception that the animate natural beings of to-day are the result
of a long sequence of development from the simple to the
complex could not at that time scientifically be put forward at all. The unhistorical view of nature was therefore
inevitable. We have the less reason to reproach the philosophers of the eighteenth century on this account, since the
same thing is found in Hegel. According to him, nature,
as a mere " alienation " of the idea, is incapable of development in time—capable only of extending its manifoldness
in space, so that it displays simultaneously and alongside of
one another all the stages of development comprised in it,
and is condemned to an eternal repetition of the same process. This absurdity of a development in space, but outside
of time—the fundamental condition of all development—
Hegel imposes upon nature just at the very time when
geology, embryology, the physiology of plants and animals,
and organic chemistry were being built up, and when everywhere on the basis of these new sciences brilliant fore-
shadowings of the later theory of evolution were appearing
(e.g., Goethe and Lamarck). But the system demanded it ;
hence the method, for the sake of the system, had to become untrue to itself.

This same unhistorical conception prevailed also in the
domain of history. Here the struggle against the remnants
of the Middle Ages blurred the view. The Middle Ages
were regarded as a mere interruption of history by a thousand years of universal barbarism. The great progress made
in the Middle Ages—the extension of the area of European
culture, the bringing into existence there of great nations,
capable of survival, and finally the enormous technical progress of the fourteenth and fifteenth centuries—all this was
not seen. Consequently a rational insight into the great
historical inter-connections was made impossible, and

history served at best as a collection of examples and illustrations for the use of philosophers.

The vulgarising pedlars who in Germany in the 'fifties busied themselves with materialism by no means overcame the limitations of their teachers. All the advances of natural science which had been made in the meantime served them only as new proofs against the existence of a creator of the world ; and, in truth, it was quite outside their scope to develop the theory any further. Though idealism was at the end of its tether and was dealt a death blow by the Revolution of 1848, it had the satisfaction of seeing that materialism had for the moment fallen lower still. Feuerbach was unquestionably right when he refused to take responsibility for this materialism ; only he should not have confounded the doctrines of these hedge-preachers with materialism in general. . . .

DIALECTICAL MATERIALISM

Strauss, Bauer, Stirner, Feuerbach—these were the offshoots of Hegelian philosophy, in so far as they did not abandon the field of philosophy. Strauss, after his *Life of Jesus* and *Dogmatics*, produced only literary studies in philosophy and ecclesiastical history after the fashion of Renan. Bauer only achieved something in the field of the history of the origin of Christianity, though what he did here was important. Stirner remained a curiosity, even after Bakunin blended him with Proudhon and labelled the blend " anarchism." Feuerbach alone was of significance as a philosopher. But not only did philosophy—claimed to soar above all sciences and to be the all comprehensive science of sciences—remain for him an impassable barrier, an unassailable holy thing, but as a philosopher, too, he stopped half way ; the lower half of him was materialist, the upper half idealist. He was incapable of disposing of Hegel through criticism ; he simply threw him aside as useless, while he himself, compared with the encyclopædic wealth of the

Hegelian system, achieved nothing positive beyond a grandiloquent religion of love and a meagre, impotent system of morals.

Out of the dissolution of the Hegelian school, however, there developed still another tendency, the only one which has borne real fruit. And this tendency is essentially connected with the name of Marx.[1]

The separation from the Hegelian school was here also the result of a return to the materialist standpoint. That means it was resolved to comprehend the real world—nature and history—just as it presents itself to everyone who approaches it free from pre-conceived idealist fancies. It was decided relentlessly to sacrifice every idealist fancy which could not be brought into harmony with the facts conceived in their own and not in a fantastic connection. And materialism means nothing more than this. But here the materialistic world outlook was taken really seriously for the first time and was carried through consistently—at least in its basic features—in all domains of knowledge concerned.

Hegel was not simply put aside. On the contrary, one started out from his revolutionary side described above, from the dialectical method. But in its Hegelian form this method was unusable. According to Hegel, dialectics is the self-development of the concept. The absolute concept does not only exist—where unknown—from eternity, it is also

---

[1] Here I may be permitted to make a personal explanation. Lately repeated reference has been made to my share in this theory, and so I can hardly avoid saying a few words here to settle this particular point. I cannot deny that both before and during my forty years' collaboration with Marx I had a certain independent share in laying the formulations, and more particularly in elaborating the theory. But the greater part of its leading basic principles, particularly in the realm of economics and history, and, above all, its final, clear formulation, belong to Marx. What I contributed—at any rate with the exception of a few special studies—Marx could very well have done without me. What Marx accomplished I would not have achieved. Marx stood higher, saw farther, and took a wider and quicker view than all the rest of us. Marx was a genius ; we others were at best talented. Without him the theory would not be what it is to-day. It therefore rightly bears his name.

the actual living soul of the whole existing world. It develops into itself through all the preliminary stages which are treated at length in the *Logic* and which are all included in it. Then it " alienates " itself by changing into nature, where, without consciousness of itself, disguised as the necessity of nature, it goes through a new development and finally comes again to self-consciousness in man. This self-consciousness then elaborates itself again in history from the crude form until finally the absolute concept again comes to itself completely in the Hegelian philosophy. According to Hegel, therefore, the dialectical development apparent in nature and history, i.e., the causal inter-connection of the progressive movement from the lower to the higher, which asserts itself through all zigzag movements and temporary setbacks, is only a miserable copy of the self-movement of the concept going on from eternity, no one knows where, but at all events independently of any thinking human brain. This ideological reversal had to be done away with. We comprehended the concepts in our heads once more materialistically—as images of real things instead of regarding the real things as images of this or that stage of development of the absolute concept. Thus dialectics reduced itself to the science of the general laws of motion—both of the external world and of human thought —two sets of laws which are identical in substance, but differ in their expression in so far as the human mind can apply them consciously, while in nature and also up to now for the most part in human history, these laws assert themselves unconsciously in the form of external necessity in the midst of an endless series of seeming accidents. Thereby the dialectic of the concept itself became merely the conscious reflex of the dialectical motion of the real world and the dialectic of Hegel was placed upon its head ; or rather, turned off its head, on which it was standing before, and placed upon its feet again. And this materialist dialectic which for years has been our best working tool and our sharpest weapon was, remarkably enough, discovered not only by us, but also independently of us and even of Hegel by a German worker, Joseph Dietzgen.

In this way, however, the revolutionary side of Hegelian philosophy was again taken up and at the same time freed from the idealist trammels which in Hegel's hands had prevented its consistent execution. The great basic thought that the world is not to be comprehended as a complex of ready-made *things*, but as a complex of *processes*, in which the things apparently stable no less than their mind-images in our heads, the concepts, go through an uninterrupted change of coming into being and passing away, in which, in spite of all seeming accidents and of all temporary retrogression, a progressive development asserts itself in the end—this great fundamental thought has, especially since the time of Hegel, so thoroughly permeated ordinary consciousness that in this generality it is scarcely ever contradicted. But to acknowledge this fundamental thought in words and to apply it in reality in detail to each domain of investigation are two different things. If, however, investigation always proceeds from this standpoint, the demand for final solutions and eternal truths ceases once for all ; one is always conscious of the necessary limitation of all acquired knowledge, of the fact that it is conditioned by the circumstances in which it was acquired. On the other hand, one no longer permits oneself to be imposed upon by the antitheses, insuperable for the still common old metaphysics, between true and false, good and bad, identical and different, necessary and accidental. One knows that these antitheses have only a relative validity ; that that which is recognised now as true has also its latent false side which will later manifest itself, just as that which is now regarded as false has also its true side by virtue of which it could previously have been regarded as true. One knows that what is maintained to be necessary is composed of sheer accidents and that the so-called accidental is the form behind which necessity hides itself—and so on.

The old method of investigation and thought which

Hegel calls " metaphysical," which preferred to investigate
things as given, as fixed and stable, a method the relics of
which still strongly haunt people's minds, had a good deal
of historical justification in its day. It was necessary first to
examine things before it was possible to examine processes.
One had first to know what a particular thing was before
one could observe the changes going on in connection with
it. And such was the case with natural science. The old
metaphysics which accepted things as finished objects arose
from a natural science which investigated dead and living
things as finished objects. But when this investigation had
progressed so far that it became possible to take the decisive
step forward of transition to the systematic investigation of
the changes which these things undergo in nature itself,
then the last hour of the old metaphysics sounded in the
realm of philosophy also. And in fact, while natural science
up to the end of the last century was predominantly a
collecting science, a science of finished things, in our century
it is essentially a *classifying* science, a science of the processes,
of the origin and development of these things and of the
inter-connection which binds all these natural processes
into one great whole. Physiology, which investigates the
processes occurring in plant and animal organisms ; embryology, which deals with the development of individual
organisms from germ to maturity ; geology, which investigates the gradual formation of the earth's surface—all these
are the offspring of our century.

But, above all, there are three great discoveries which
had enabled our knowledge of the inter-connection of
natural processes to advance by leaps and bounds : first,
the discovery of the cell as the unit from whose multiplica-
tion and differentiation the whole plant and animal body
develops—so that not only is the development and growth
of all higher organisms recognised to proceed according to
a single general law, but also, in the capacity of the cell to
change, the way is pointed out by which organisms can
change their species and thus go through a more than

individual development. Second, the transformation of
energy, which has demonstrated that all the so-called forces
operative in the first instance in inorganic nature—mechanical force and its complement, so-called potential
energy, heat, radiation (light or radiant heat), electricity,
magnetism and chemical energy—are different forms of
manifestation of universal motion, which pass into one another in definite proportions so that in place of a certain
quantity of the one which disappears, a certain quantity of
another makes its appearance and thus the whole motion of
nature is reduced to this incessant process of transformation
from one form into another. Finally, the proof which Darwin first developed in connected form that the stock of
organic products of nature surrounding us to-day, including
mankind, is the result of a long process of evolution from
a few original unicellular germs, and that these again have
arisen from protoplasm or albumen which came into
existence by chemical means.

Thanks to these three great discoveries and the other
immense advances in natural science, we have now arrived
at the point where we can demonstrate as a whole the inter-
connection between the processes in nature not only in
particular spheres but also in the inter-connection of these
particular spheres themselves, and so can present in an
approximately systematic form a comprehensive view of the
inter-connection in nature by means of the facts provided
by empirical natural science itself. To furnish this comprehensive view was formerly the task of so-called natural
philosophy. It could do this only by putting in place of
the real but as yet unknown inter-connections ideal and
imaginary ones, filling out the missing facts by figments of
the mind and bridging the actual gaps merely in imagination. In the course of this procedure it conceived many
brilliant ideas and foreshadowed many later discoveries,
but it also produced a considerable amount of nonsense,
which indeed could not have been otherwise. To-day, when
one needs to comprehend the results of natural scientific

investigation only dialectically, that is, in the sense of their own inter-connections, in order to arrive at a " system of nature " sufficient for our time ; when the dialectical character of this inter-connection is forcing itself against their will even into the metaphysically-trained minds of the natural scientists, to-day this natural philosophy is finally disposed of. Every attempt at resurrecting it would be not only superfluous but a *step backwards*. . . .

Karl Marx

THESES ON FEUERBACH

Written in 1845 : first published as an appendix in the 1888 edition of Engels's " Ludwig Feuerbach " : English edition of this book, containing Marx's Theses, Martin Lawrence Ltd., 1934.

[In the preface to the 1888 edition of *Ludwig Feuerbach*, Engels says that he found the eleven theses on Feuerbach in an old notebook of Marx's. " These are notes hurriedly scribbled down for later elaboration, absolutely not intended for publication, but they are invaluable as the first document in which is deposited the brilliant germ of the new world outlook."]

THESES ON FEUERBACH

(Jotted down in Brussels in the spring of 1845)

I

THE CHIEF DEFECT of all hitherto existing materialism —that of Feuerbach included—is that the object, reality, sensuousness, is conceived only in the form of the *object* or *contemplation* but not as *human sensuous activity, practice,* not subjectively. Thus it happened that the *active* side, in opposition to materialism, was developed by idealism—but only abstractly, since, of course, idealism does not know real sensuous activity as such. Feuerbach wants sensuous objects, really differentiated from the thought-objects, but he does not conceive human activity itself as activity *through objects.* Consequently, in the *Essence of Christianity,* he regards the theoretical attitude as the only genuinely human attitude, while practice is conceived and fixed only in its dirty-Jewish form of appearance. Hence he does not grasp the significance of " revolutionary," of practical-critical, activity.

II

The question whether objective truth can be attributed to human thinking is not a question of theory but is a practical question. In practice man must prove the truth, i.e., the reality and power, the " this-sidedness " of his thinking. The dispute over the reality or non-reality of thinking which is isolated from practice is a purely scholastic question.

III

The materialist doctrine that men are products of circumstances and upbringing and that, therefore, changed men are products of other circumstances and changed upbringing, forgets that circumstances are changed precisely by men and that the educator must himself be educated. Hence this doctrine necessarily arrives at dividing society into two parts, of which one towers above society (in Robert Owen, for example).

The coincidence of the changing of circumstances and of human activity can only be conceived and rationally understood as revolutionising practice.

IV

Feuerbach starts out from the fact of religious self-alienation, the duplication of the world into a religious, imaginary world and a real one. His work consists in the dissolution of the religious world into its secular basis. He overlooks the fact that after completing this work, the chief thing still remains to be done. For the fact that the secular foundation lifts itself above itself and establishes itself in the clouds as an independent realm is only to be explained by the self-cleavage and self-contradictoriness of this secular basis. The latter must itself, therefore, first be understood in its contradiction and then, by the removal of the contradiction, revolutionised in practice. Thus, for instance, once the earthly family is discovered to be the secret of the holy family, the former must then itself be theoretically criticised and radically changed in practice.

V

Feuerbach, not satisfied with *abstract thinking*, appeals to *sensuous contemplation*, but he does not conceive sensuousness as a practical, human-sensuous activity.

VI

Feuerbach resolves the religious essence into the human. But the human essence is no abstraction inherent in each single individual. In its reality it is the *ensemble* of the social relations.

Feuerbach, who does not attempt the criticism of this real essence, is consequently compelled :

1. To abstract from the historical process and to fix the religious sentiment as something for itself and to presuppose an abstract—*isolated*—human individual.

2. The human essence, therefore, can with him be comprehended only as " genus," as a dumb internal generality which merely *naturally* unites the many individuals.

VII

Feuerbach, consequently, does not see that the " religious sentiment " is itself a *social product*, and that the abstract individual whom he analyses belongs in reality to a particular form of society.

VIII

Social life is essentially *practical*. All mysteries which mislead theory to mysticism find their rational solution in human practice and in the comprehension of this practice.

IX

The highest point attained by contemplative materialism, i.e., materialism which does not understand sensuousness as practical activity, is the outlook of single individuals in " civil society."

X

The standpoint of the old materialism is " civil society " ; the standpoint of the new is *human* society or socialised humanity.

XI

The philosophers have only *interpreted* the world in various ways ; the point however is to *change* it.

Opposite: Prostitution, for a woman, is a crime; for a man, a slight moral blemish, easily tolerated. (*The Origin of the Family*)

Friedrich Engels

THE ORIGIN OF THE FAMILY, PRIVATE PROPERTY AND THE STATE

First published in 1884. The only English edition now available was published by Kerr, Chicago. As the translation is not satisfactory the chapters given below have been specially re-translated.

[In 1877 Lewis H. Morgan's *Ancient Society* was published by Macmillan. Its sub-title was: "Researches in the Lines

of Human Progress from Savagery through Barbarism to Civilisation." This book was greatly appreciated by Marx and Engels, and Engels says in the preface to his own work that Marx had himself intended to write on this subject, to examine the material collected by Morgan and show that it confirms, in relation to ancient society, the materialist conception of history. After Marx's death in 1883, Engels, making use of Marx's notes, wrote *The Origin of the Family*. This book traces the development of the family as a social institution, its relation to the prevailing mode of production ; the changes in the family arising from changing forms of production which also brought private property as an institution ; the division of society into classes ; and the emergence of the State. In the course of the book Engels sums up Morgan's material, on the successive stages of the consanguine family (group intermarriage of brothers and sisters, own and collateral) ; the punaluan family (group intermarriage of several sisters with each other's husbands, not necessarily related ; or of several brothers with each other's wives, not necessarily related) ; the pairing family (marriage between single pairs, without exclusive cohabitation, and terminable) ; the patriarchal (marriage of one man with several wives) ; and finally monogamy. The basis of early social organisation was the gens, or group of related persons, all descent at first being traced through the mother, and later through the father. A wider grouping was the tribe, uniting several gentes (which might be organised in an intermediate group, the phratry) ; and several tribes formed a confederation ultimately merging into a people or a nation. Engels shows the connection of these groupings and changes with production ; the passages reprinted below are his summing up on the Family and on the State.]

THE ORIGIN OF THE FAMILY, PRIVATE PROPERTY AND THE STATE

THE FAMILY

(Ch. II)

. . . Accordingly we have three principal forms of marriage, which in the main correspond to the three principal stages of human development. For the period of savagery, the group marriage ; for barbarism, the pairing marriage ; for civilisation, monogamy supplemented by adultery and prostitution. Between the pairing marriage and monogamy there intervened, at the highest stage of barbarism, the right of men to female slaves, and polygamy.

As our whole exposition has shown, the progress which manifests itself in this succession is linked with the peculiarity that the sexual freedom of the group marriage is more and more taken away from women, but not from men. And in fact the group marriage continues to exist for men actually up to the present time. What for a woman is a crime drawing in its train grave legal and social consequences, for a man is regarded as honourable or at worst as a slight moral blemish, easily tolerated. But the more the hetærism of antiquity is altered, in our age, by capitalist commodity production and is adapted to this, the more it is transformed into unconcealed prostitution, the more demoralising are its effects. And in fact it demoralises men far more than women. Prostitution degrades, among women, only the unfortunate ones to whose lot it falls, and even these not at all to the extent that is commonly believed. On the other hand, it degrades the character of the whole world of men. A long engagement particularly is in nine cases out of ten actually a preparatory school for marital infidelity.

We are now approaching a social revolution in which the former economic foundations of monogamy will just as surely disappear as those of its complement, prostitution.

Monogamy arose from the concentration of great riches
in a single hand—that of the man—and from the need
to bequeath these riches to the children of that man and
not of any other. And for this purpose the monogamy
of the woman was necessary, not that of the man, so that
this monogamy of the woman did not at all stand in the
way of open or concealed polygamy on the part of the man.
The coming social revolution, however, through the
transformation at least of the infinitely greater portion
of permanent, heritable wealth—the means of production—
into social property, will reduce this whole solicitude for
inheritance to a minimum. If then monogamy came into
being from economic causes, will it disappear when these
causes disappear ? It would be possible to answer, not
without justice : far from disappearing, it will then on the
contrary be fully realised for the first time. For with the
transformation of the means of production into social
property there will disappear also wage-labour, the proletariat, and therefore also the necessity for a certain—
statistically calculable—number of women to surrender
themselves for money. Prostitution disappears, monogamy,
instead of collapsing, at last becomes a reality—even for
men.

The position of men is therefore in any case very much
altered. But also the position of women, of *all* women,
undergoes a significant change. With the transfer of the
means of production into common ownership the individual
family ceases to be the economic unit of society. Private
house-keeping is transformed into a social industry. The
care and education of children becomes a public affair ;
society looks after all children equally, whether they are
legitimate or not. And this puts an end to the anxiety
about the " consequences," which is now the most essential
social—moral as well as economic—factor that deters a
girl from giving herself without reluctance to the man she
loves. Will that not be cause enough to bring about
the gradual establishment of an unconstrained sexual

intercourse, and with this also a more lenient public opinion in regard to maidenly honour and womanly shame? And finally, have we not seen that in the modern world monogamy and prostitution are, it is true, contradictions, but inseparable contradictions, poles of the same social conditions? Can prostitution disappear without dragging monogamy down with it into the abyss?

Here a new factor comes into play, a factor which, at the time when monogamy developed, existed at most in germ : individual sex-love.

Before the middle ages there can be no question of individual sex-love. That personal beauty, intimate intercourse, sympathetic tastes, and so forth, awakened the desire for sexual intercourse among people of opposite sexes; that both to men and to women it was not a matter of absolute indifference with whom they entered into this most intimate relationship—this goes without saying. But there is an infinite distance between that and our sex-love. Throughout the whole ancient world marriages were arranged by the parents for the partners, and the latter were easily reconciled. The little portion of marital love known to antiquity is not any subjective inclination, but an objective duty, not a ground but a correlative of marriage. Love relationships in the modern sense only make their appearance in antiquity outside of official society. The shepherds of whose joys and sorrows in love Theocritus and Moschus sing, the Daphnis and Chloë of Longos, were simple slaves who had no share in the State, the free citizens' sphere of life. Apart from slaves we find love affairs only as products of the disintegration of the old world in its decline, and with women who also stood outside official society, with hetæræ, that is, with " barbarians " or freed slaves : in Athens from the eve of its ruin onwards, in Rome at the time of the Cæsars. If love affairs really developed between free men and women citizens, it was only through adultery. And to the classical love poet of antiquity, old Anakreon, sex-love in our sense was of so

little concern that even the sex of the loved one was a
matter of absolute indifference to him.

Our sex-love is essentially different from the simple
sexual desire, the Eros, of the ancients. In the first place
it presupposes that the love is reciprocated by the loved
one ; to this extent the woman stands on the same footing
as the man, while in the Eros of antiquity she was by no
means always asked. Secondly, our sex-love has a degree
of intensity and duration which makes both lovers feel
that non-possession and separation are a very great, if
not the greatest, misfortune. In order to ensure mutual
possession they risk high stakes, even staking their lives—
a thing which in antiquity happened only in adultery.
And finally a new moral standard arises by which sexual
intercourse is judged ; we not only ask whether it was within
or without the marriage tie, but also whether it sprang
from love and reciprocated love or not. Of course this new
standard has fared no better in feudal or bourgeois practice
than any other moral standard—it is simply ignored. But
also it fares no worse. It is recognised to the same extent
as previous standards—in theory, on paper. And at present
it can ask no more than this.

At the point where antiquity ended its progress towards
sex-love, the middle ages took it up—in adultery. We have
already spoken of the knightly love which gave rise to the
songs. From this love, urging violation of the marriage tie,
to the love which is to be the foundation of marriage, is
still a long road, and this road was never fully traversed
by the knights. Even when we pass from the frivolous
Latin race to the virtuous Germans, we find in the *Nibe-
lungenlied* that although in her heart Kriemhild is not less
in love with Siegfried than he is with her, when Gunther
tells her that he has promised her to a knight whom he does
not name, she simply answers : " You have no need to ask
me ; as you bid me, so will I ever be ; the man whom you,
lord, give me to wed, that man will I gladly take in troth."
It does not even enter her head that her love can in any way

come into consideration in this matter. Gunther asks for Brünhild, Etzel for Kriemhild, although they have never seen each other ; the same is true of the suit of Gutrun Sigebant of Ireland for the Norwegian Ute, of Hetel of Hegelingen's suit for Hilde of Ireland ; and finally of Siegfried of Morland, Hartmut of Ormanien and Herwig of Zeeland, in their suit for Gutrun—and in this case for the first time it happens that Gutrun voluntarily decides in favour of the last-named of the three. As a rule the young prince's bride is selected by his parents, if they are still living, and if not, by the prince himself on the advice of the great feudal lords, whose views in all cases carry considerable weight. And it cannot be otherwise. For the knight or baron, as the head of the land himself, marriage is a political act, an occasion for the extension of power through new alliances ; the interest of the *house* must be decisive, not the wishes of the individual. In such circumstances how can love reach the position in which it has the decisive say in marriage ?

The same held good for the guild member in the towns of the middle ages. The privileges protecting him, the clauses of the guild charters, the artificial lines of demarcation which legally cut him off, both from the other guilds, and from other members of his own guild and from his own journeymen and apprentices, already sufficiently narrowed down the circle within which he might select a suitable spouse. And in that complicated system it was certainly not his individual fancy, but the interests of the family, which decided who was the most suitable spouse within that circle.

In the infinitely greater majority of cases, therefore, marriage remained, up to the close of the middle ages, what it had been from the very beginning—a matter which the partners did not decide. In the earliest stages men and women were already married when they came into the world—married to an entire group of the opposite sex. In the later forms of group marriage probably similar relations existed, but within continually contracting groups. In the pairing marriage it was customary for the mothers to arrange the marriages of their children ; here too the decisive considerations are the new ties of kinship which can win for the young couple a stronger position in the gens and tribe. And when, with the pre-dominance of private over communal property and the growing concern for inheritance, patriarchy and mono-gamy came to dominate, marriage then became completely dependent on economic considerations. The *form* of marri-age by purchase disappeared, but the practice itself came to be more and more consistently applied, so that not only the woman but also the man acquired a price—based not on his personal characteristics but on his property. From the very beginning the conception that the mutual inclin-ation of the contracting parties should be the ground, out-weighing all others, for the marriage was completely unheard of in the practice of the ruling classes. Anything of this sort occurred at best in romance, or—among the oppressed classes, who did not count.

Such was the state of things which capitalist production found in existence when, following the epoch of geographi-cal discoveries, it set out to conquer the world through trade and manufacture. It might have assumed that this mode of marriage suited it exceptionally well ; and such was the case. And yet—the irony of history knows no limit—it was capitalist production which was destined to make the decisive breach in this mode of marriage. By trans-forming everything into commodities, it destroyed all inherited, traditional relationships, it set up, in place of time-honoured custom and historical right, purchase and sale and " free " contract. The English jurist H. S. Maine thought he had made an immense discovery when he stated that our whole progress as compared with former epochs, consisted in the fact that we had passed from status to contract, from inherited and traditional conditions to those brought into being by voluntary contract—a statement which, in so far as it is correct, was already, as a matter of fact, contained in *The Communist Manifesto.*

The making of contracts, however, requires people who can freely dispose of their persons, actions and possessions, and meet each other on the basis of equal rights. It was precisely the creation of these "free" and "equal" people that was one of the principal functions of capitalist society. And although at first it happened only in a half-conscious way, and moreover disguised in religious wrappings, by the time of the Lutheran and Calvinist Reformation it was an established principle that man is only fully responsible for his actions when he acts with complete freedom of will, and that it is a moral obligation to resist all coercion to an immoral act. But how did this fit in with former practice in the arrangement of marriages? According to the bourgeois conception, marriage was a contract, a juridical matter, and indeed the most important of all contracts, because it disposed of the body and mind of the two human beings for the period of their life. It is true that at that time, from a formal standpoint, it was entered into voluntarily; it could not be completed without the assent of the persons concerned. But everyone knew only too well how this assent was obtained, and who were the real contracting parties to the marriage. But if real freedom of decision was required for all other contracts, why not also in this one? Had not the two young people who were to be united in marriage also the right to dispose freely of themselves, of their body and its organs? Had not sex-love come into fashion through the knights, and, in contrast to the adulterous love of the age of chivalry, was not the love of one's own spouse its proper bourgeois form? And if it was the duty of married people to love each other, was it not equally the duty of lovers to marry each other and no one else? Was not the right of lovers superior to the right of parents, relatives and other traditional marriage brokers and agents? If the right of free personal investigation made its way unchecked into the

church and religion, how could it stand still in face of the
older generation's intolerable claim to dispose over the
body, soul, property, weal and woe of young persons ?

These questions had to be raised at a period which
loosened all the old ties of society and shattered all inherited
conceptions. The world had suddenly become almost
ten times bigger ; instead of a quadrant of a hemisphere,
the whole globe now lay before the eyes of the West Europeans, who hastened to take possession of the other seven
quadrants. And along with the old narrow barriers of
their native land, the thousand-year old barriers of mediæval conventional thought were also broken down. An
infinitely wider horizon opened out before both the out-
ward and the inward gaze of man. What mattered the
prospects offered by respectability, or the honourable
guild privileges inherited through generations, to the
young man tempted by the wealth of India, the gold and
silver mines of Mexico and Potosis ? It was the knight-
errant period of the bourgeoisie ; it had too its romance
and its amorous enthusiasms, but on a bourgeois footing,
and in the last analysis, with bourgeois aims.

So it came about that the rising bourgeoisie, especially
in the protestant countries where existing institutions
were most severely shaken, more and more came to recognise freedom of contract also in marriage, and developed
it in the way described above. Marriage remained class
marriage, but a certain degree of free choice within the
class was allowed to the partners. And on paper, in ethical
theory and poetic description, nothing was more firmly
established than that every marriage is immoral which does
not rest on mutual sex-love and really free contract between
husband and wife. In a word, the love-marriage was
proclaimed as a human right, and indeed not only as
droit de l'homme, but even by way of exception as *droit de la
femme*.

This human right, however, differed in one respect
from all other so-called human rights. While the latter,

in practice, remained restricted to the ruling class, the bourgeoisie, and were directly or indirectly curtailed for the oppressed class, the proletariat, in the case of the former the irony of history once more lived up to its reputation. The ruling class remained dominated by the familiar economic influences, and therefore only in exceptional cases provided instances of really freely contracted marriages, while these, as we have seen, were the rule among the oppressed class.

Full freedom of marriage can therefore only become generally established when the abolition of capitalist production and of the property relations created by it has done away with all the economic considerations which still exert such powerful influence on the choice of a spouse. For then no motive other than mutual affection will be left.

And as sex-love is by its nature exclusive—although this exclusiveness is now fully effective only in the woman—the marriage based on sex-love is by its nature individual marriage. We have seen how right Bachofen was when he considered the advance from group marriage to individual marriage as primarily due to the woman. Only the further step forward from the pairing marriage to monogamy can be credited to the men ; and the essence of this, historically, was to change for the worse the position of women and to make easier the infidelity of the men. If now the economic considerations because of which women acquiesce in this customary infidelity of their husbands—concern for their own means of existence and still more for their children's future—also disappear, to judge from all previous experience the equality of the woman resulting from this will have an infinitely stronger tendency to make men really monogamous than to make women polyandrous.

But what will quite positively disappear from monogamy are all the features impressed on it through its origin in property relations ; these are in the first place the predominance of the man, and secondly, indissolubility. The predominance of the man in marriage is the simple consequence of his economic predominance, and will disappear of itself along with the latter. The indissolubility of marriage is partly a consequence of the economic situation in which monogamy arose, and partly a tradition from the period when the connection between this economic situation and monogamy was as yet not fully understood and was pushed to extremes by religion. To-day it is already broken through at a thousand points. If only the marriage based on love is moral, then also only the marriage in which love continues to exist. The duration of an attack of sex-love for an individual is however very different for different individuals, especially among men, and if affection definitely comes to an end, or is supplanted by a new passionate love, this makes divorce a benefit for both partners as well as for society. The only thing people will be spared will be having to wade through the useless mire of a divorce case.

What we can now anticipate as to the way in which sex relations will be ordered after capitalist production has been swept away is mainly negative, limited for the most part to the features that will disappear. But what new features will come into being? The answer will be given when a new generation has grown up ; a generation of men who never in their life chanced to buy a woman's surrender for money or any other social instrument of power ; and a generation of women who have never happened to give themselves to a man for any consideration other than real love, nor to refuse themselves to the man they love from fear of the economic consequences. When such people have come into existence, they will not care a brass farthing what people think to-day about how they should act ; they will make their own practice for themselves, and their own public opinion, measured by this practice, as to the practice of each individual—and that will be the end of it.

Let us, however, turn back to Morgan, from whom we have moved a considerable distance. The historical investigation of the social institutions developed during the period of civilisation goes beyond the limits of his book. He therefore deals only very briefly with the fate of monogamy during this epoch. He too sees in the development of the monogamous family a step forward, an approximation to the complete equality of the sexes, though he does not regard this goal as having been attained. But, he says :

"When the fact is accepted that the family has passed through four successive forms, and is now in a fifth, the question at once arises whether this form can be permanent in the future. The only answer that can be given is, that it must advance as society advances, and change as society changes, even as it has done in the past. It is the creature of the social system, and will reflect its culture. As the monogamian family has improved greatly since the commencement of civilisation, and very sensibly in modern times, it is at least supposable that it is capable of still further improvement until the equality of the sexes is attained. Should the monogamian family in the distant future fail to answer the requirements of society, assuming the continuous progress of civilisation, it is impossible to predict the nature of its successor."

BARBARISM AND CIVILISATION

(Ch. IX)

We have now traced the dissolution of gens society in its three main distinct types among the Greeks, Romans and Germans. In conclusion we examine the general economic conditions which had already undermined the gens organisation of society by the later stage of barbarism, and completely abolished it with the advent of civilisation. Here Marx's *Capital* will be as necessary to us as Morgan's book.

Making its appearance at the middle stage, and further developing at the later stage of savagery, the gens, so far as we can judge from our material, reached its most flourishing period at the lower stage of barbarism. We therefore start from this stage of development.

At this stage—here the American Redskins must serve as our example—gens society is fully developed. A tribe has divided itself into several, but as a rule two, separate gentes ; as the population increases these original gentes split into several daughter gentes, in relation to which the mother gens now appears as a phratry. The tribe itself splits into several tribes, in each of which we find, as a rule, the old gentes ; at least in some cases the related tribes are held together by a confederacy. This simple organisation is fully adequate for the social conditions from which it sprang. It is nothing more than the natural grouping peculiar to these social conditions ; it is able to adjust all the conflicts which can arise within a society so organised. External adjustments are made by war ; war may end with the annihilation of the tribe, but never with its subjection. It is the magnificent but at the same time the limiting feature of gens society that it had no place for domination and subjection. Within gens society there was as yet no distinction between rights and obligations; the question whether participation in public affairs, revenge for the murder of kinsmen or other expiatory act, is a right or a duty, does not exist for the Indian ; it would seem to him as absurd as the question whether eating, sleeping, hunting is a right or a duty. Just as little can a division of the tribe and the gens into different classes take place. And this leads us to investigate the economic basis of this state of things.

The population is extremely sparse : it is dense only at the place where the tribe lives, round which extend in a wide circle first the hunting ground, and then the neutral protective forest which separates it from other tribes. The division of labour is purely natural ; it exists only between the two sexes. The man wages war, goes hunting and fishing, procures the raw material of food and the tools required for these. The woman looks after the house and the preparation of food and clothing, cooks, weaves and sews. Each is master in the appropriate sphere : the man in the forest, the woman in the house. Each owns the tools made and used by each : the man owns the weapons and the instruments for hunting and fishing, the woman the household equipment. The housekeeping is communal for several families, often a great many.[1] Whatever is used and made in common is common property : the house, the garden, the long-boat. Here, therefore, and as yet only here, exists that " self-made property " falsely ascribed by jurists and economists to civilised society—the last fictitious legal subterfuge on which modern capitalist property still rests.

But men did not everywhere remain stationary at this stage. In Asia they came across animals which could be tamed and bred when tamed. The wild buffalo cow had to be hunted ; the tame one provided a calf each year and milk besides. A number of the most advanced tribes—Aryans, Semites, perhaps also Turanians—made their chief occupation at first the taming, and only later also the breeding and tending of cattle. Pastoral tribes separated themselves off from the general mass of barbarians : *the first great social division of labour.* The pastoral tribes produced not only more but also different means of existence as compared with other barbarians. They had not only milk, milk products and meat in greater quantity than other barbarians, but also skins, wool, goat-hair and spun and woven materials which increased in quantity with the mass of raw material. And this for the first time made regular exchange possible. At earlier stages only

---

[1] Especially on the North West Coast of America—see Bancroft. Among the Haidahs on Queen Charlotte's Island there are households with up to 700 persons under one roof. Among the Nootkas whole tribes used to live under one roof.

occasional exchanges could take place ; special ability in the making of weapons and tools might lead to a transitory division of labour. Thus indisputable traces of workplaces for stone tools of the Neolithic period have been found at many places ; the experts who there perfected their skill probably worked for the account of the commune, as the permanent handicraftsmen of the Indian gens communes still do. In no case, at this stage, could any other exchange arise than that within the tribe, and this remained an exceptional incident. But, in contrast to this, after the separation of the pastoral tribes we find all the conditions ripe for exchange between the members of different tribes, for its development and establishment as a regular institution.

Originally tribe exchanged with tribe, through their respective heads of the gens ; but when the herds began to pass into individual ownership, individual exchange began to predominate more and more, and eventually became the only form. The chief article, however, which the pastoral tribes gave to their neighbours in exchange was cattle ; cattle became the commodity by which all other commodities were valued and which was everywhere willingly accepted in exchange for these—in a word, cattle assumed the function of money and performed the services of money already at this stage. Such was the necessity and speed with which the need for a money commodity developed right at the very beginning of commodity exchange.

Horticulture, which was probably unknown to the Asiatics in the lower stage of barbarism, made its appearance among them at the latest in the middle stage of barbarism, as the forerunner of agriculture. The climate of the Turanian plateau makes pastoral life impossible without supplies of fodder for the long and severe winter ; here the cultivation of grass and corn was therefore a necessary condition. This is also true of the steppes north of the Black Sea. But when once corn had been won for

the cattle, it soon became food for men also. The cultivated
land still remained the property of the tribe ; at first it was
handed over to the gens, by this later to the household
and ultimately to individuals for their use : they might
have certain rights of possession in this land, but nothing
more than that.

Of the industrial achievements of this stage two are
especially important. The first is the weaving loom, the
second the smelting of metal ores and the working of metal.
Copper and tin, and bronze, an alloy of these, were far the
most important ; bronze provided usable tools and weapons,
but could not displace stone tools ; only iron could do
this, and as yet men did not understand how to win iron.
Gold and silver began to be used for ornament and decor-
ation, and must already have been set at a high value as
compared with copper and bronze.

The increase of production in all branches—cattle
raising, agriculture, home handicrafts—gave human labour
power the capacity to produce a larger product than was
necessary for its maintenance. Simultaneously it increased
the daily amount of labour which fell to the lot of each
member of the gens, the house commune or the individual
family. The bringing in of new labour forces became
desirable. These were provided by war : prisoners of war
were transformed into slaves.

In the general historical conditions then prevailing the
first great social division of labour, with its increase of the
productivity of labour and therefore of wealth, and its
widening of the field of production, necessarily brought
slavery in its train. From the first great social division
of labour sprang the first great cleavage of society into
two classes : masters and slaves, exploiters and exploited.

Up to the present we do not know how and when the
herds passed from the common possession of the tribe
or the gens into the property of the individual heads of
families. It must, however, have taken place mainly at
this stage. With the herds and the other new forms of

wealth, however, a revolution came over the family. It had always been the man's business to procure the means of existence, and the instruments required for this had been produced by him and were his property. The herds were the new means of existence ; their initial taming and subsequent tending were the work of the man. The cattle therefore belonged to him, to him also belonged the commodities and slaves taken in exchange for cattle. All the surplus which the acquisition of the means of.living now yielded fell to the man ; the woman shared in the enjoyment of this surplus, but she had no share in its ownership. The " savage " warrior and hunter had been content with the second place in the house, below the woman ; the " milder " herdsman, boasting of his property, pushed himself forward to the first place, and the woman back to the second. And she could not complain. The division of labour in the family had regulated the division of property between man and woman ; it had remained the same, and yet now it turned the former household relations upside-down, merely because the division of labour outside the family had become different. The same cause which had secured for the woman her former dominion in the house— her restriction to household work—this same cause now ensured the dominion of the man in the house : the woman's household work had now dwindled in comparison with the man's labour in procuring the means of existence ; the latter was all-important, the former an insignificant adjunct. It is already clear at this point that the emancipation of woman, her equalisation with man, is and remains impossible so long as the woman is excluded from the productive work of society and remains restricted to private household work. The emancipation of woman first becomes possible when she is able, on an extensive, social scale, to participate in production, and household work claims her attention only to an insignificant extent. And this for the first time has been made possible by modern large-scale industry, which not only admits women's labour over a wide range, but absolutely demands it, and also strives to transform private household work more and more into a public industry.

With the *de facto* dominion of the man in the house the last barrier to his exclusive dominion had fallen. This exclusive dominion was confirmed and perpetuated by the overthrow of the matriarchy and the introduction of the patriarchy, the gradual transition from the pairing family to monogamy. But this brought a rupture in the old gens organisation of society : the individual family became a power and rose up menacingly confronting the gens.

The next step brings us to the highest stage of barbarism, the period in which all civilised peoples passed through their heroic age : the period of the iron sword, but also of the iron ploughshare and axe. Iron had become usable by man—the last and most important of all raw materials which played a revolutionary part in history, the last— until the potato. Iron extended agriculture to wider areas, clearing more extensive stretches of forest ; it provided handicraft with a tool of a hardness and cutting power that no stone or any other known metal could withstand. But all this was a gradual process ; the first iron was often even softer than bronze. Stone weapons therefore only slowly disappeared ; not only in the Song of Hildebrand, but even at Hastings in the year 1066 stone axes were still brought to battle. But the advance now proceeded irresistibly, with fewer checks and at a more rapid pace. The town, with its stone walls, towers and battlements encircling stone or brick houses, became the central seat of the tribe or tribal federation—a mighty step forward in architecture, but also an indication of greater danger and need of protection. Wealth grew rapidly, but as the wealth of individuals ; weaving, metal-working and the other handicrafts, more and more separating themselves apart, developed increasing variety and technical skill in production ; in addition to corn, leguminous plants and fruit, agriculture now yielded oil and wine, which man had learnt to make. Such manifold activities could no longer be carried on by the same individual. *The second great division of labour* took place : handicraft was separated off from agriculture. The continuous rise of production, and with it, of the productivity of labour, raised the value of human labour power. Slavery, in the preceding period still coming into existence and sporadic, now became an essential part of the social system ; slaves ceased to be mere auxiliaries, and were driven in dozens to work in the fields and workplaces. With the cleavage of production into the two great branches, agriculture and handicraft, arose production directly for exchange, the production of commodities ; and with this, trade, not only within the tribe and at the fringes of the tribal territory, but also already overseas. But all of this as yet in very undeveloped form ; the precious metals began to be the predominant and general money commodities, but as yet in unminted form, exchanging simply on the basis of their as yet uncloaked weight.

The distinction between rich and poor made its appearance, alongside that between freemen and slaves—with the new division of labour, a new cleavage of society into classes. The differences of property as between the heads of individual families burst asunder the old communal households wherever they had continued to exist, and with these, the joint cultivation of land for account of this house-commune. Agricultural land was transferred to individual families for their use, first for a period, and later in permanence ; the transition to full private ownership was completed gradually and parallel with the transition from the pairing marriage to monogamy. The individual family begins to become the economic unit in society.

The increasing density of the population necessitated closer consolidation within the tribe as well as externally. Everywhere the related tribes found it necessary to form

confederations, and soon even to merge, and consequently
to merge the separate tribal territories into an aggregate
territory of the nation. The chief of the nation's army—
rex, basileus, thiudans—became an indispensable, permanent official. The national assembly sprang up, where it
did not already exist. The chief of the army, council
and national assembly constituted the organs of a gens
society developed into a military democracy. Military,
because war and the organisation for war had now become
regular functions of national life. The wealth of neighbours
excited the greed of nations to whom the acquisition
of wealth already appeared as one of the first aims of life.
They were barbarians : to them pillage seemed easier
and even more honourable than acquisition by labour.
War, previously only waged in revenge for attacks or to
extend territory which had become insufficient, was then
carried on for the sake of pure pillage, and became a
permanent branch of industry. It is not for nothing that
menacing walls rose high, encircling the newly fortified
towns : in the ditches under them gaped the grave of gens
society, and their turrets were already towering into
civilisation. And the same process was going on within
them. Wars of robbery increased the power of the supreme
military chief, as well as that of the subordinate chieftains ;
the customary choice of successors within the same family
was gradually transformed, especially since the introduction
of patriarchy, into what was at first a tolerated, then a
claimed, and finally a usurped heredity ; the foundations
of the hereditary monarchy and hereditary nobility were
laid. In this way the organs of gens society were gradually
torn from their roots in the people, in the gens, phratry
and tribe ; and the entire gens organisation of society was
transformed into its opposite : from an organisation of
tribes for the free ordering of their affairs it became an
organisation for the pillage and oppression of neighbouring
peoples, and its organs accordingly changed from instruments of the peoples' will into independent organs of

domination and repression in relation to their own people. But this would never have been possible had not the greed for wealth cleft the members of the gens into rich and poor ; had not " the property differences within the same gens transformed the identity of interests into antagonisms of the members of the gens " (Marx) ; and had not the extension of slavery already begun to lead to the acquisition of the means of subsistence by labour being regarded as an activity only fit for slaves, more dishonourable than pillage.

.   .   .   .

And with this we reach the threshold of civilisation. The period opens with a new step forward in the division of labour. At the lower stage men produced only for their own immediate needs ; the acts of exchange which may have taken place were isolated, and covered only accidental surpluses which arose. At the middle stage of barbarism we find already among the pastoral peoples property in the form of cattle, which when the herds reach a certain size regularly yields a surplus over their own requirements ; and at the same time, a division of labour between pastoral peoples and backward tribes without herds. That is to say, two different stages of production in existence alongside each other, and hence the conditions for regular exchange. The later stage of barbarism shows us the further division of labour between agriculture and handicraft, and with this the production of a constantly growing portion of the products of labour directly for exchange ; and the raising of exchange between individual producers into a necessity of life for society. Civilisation strengthened and increased all these divisions of labour which it found in existence, particularly through the sharpening of the antagonism between town and country. (In this process the town may, from an economic standpoint, rule the country, or the country the town, as in the middle ages.) And to these existing divisions it adds a third division of labour, peculiar to it, and of decisive importance : it creates a class which is no longer engaged in production, but only in the exchange of the products—the *merchants*. All previous tendencies to the formation of classes were as yet exclusively connected with production ; they separated the people engaged in production into those directing the work and those carrying it out, or into producers on a larger and producers on a smaller scale. Now for the first time a class arose which, without in any way participating in production, won for itself the directing rôle over production as a whole and threw the producers into economic subjection ; a class which made itself the indispensable mediator between every two producers and exploited them both. Under the pretext of relieving the producers of the trouble and risk of exchange, and extending the sale of their products to the most distant markets, and thereby becoming the most useful class of the population, a class of parasites was formed, real social bloodsuckers, who as compensation for very slight actual services skimmed the cream off both home and foreign production, rapidly acquired enormous wealth and corresponding social influence, and precisely because of this throughout the period of civilisation attained ever fresh honours and ever greater control of production, until it ultimately brought to light a product of its own : the periodical commercial crises.

At the stage of development we are now considering, however, the young merchant class had as yet not the faintest inkling of the great things that lay before it. But it built itself up and made itself indispensable, and that sufficed. With it, however, metallic money, minted coin, developed, and with metallic money a new means to the dominion of the non-producer over the producer and his production. The commodity of commodities, which contained hidden within itself all other commodities, was discovered ; the charm which can transform itself at will into any desirable and desired thing. Whoever had it controlled the world of production—and who above all others had it ? The merchant. In his hand the cult of money was secure. He made sure that it became evident how low in the dust all commodities, and with them all producers of commodities, must prostrate themselves in face of money. He demonstrated in a practical way that all other forms of wealth were merely empty illusion in comparison with this embodiment of wealth as such. Never again did the power of money show itself with such primordial crudity and violence as in this its period of youth. After the sale of commodities for money came the loaning of money, and with this, interest and usury. And no legislation of later epochs hurled the debtor so helplessly and irretrievably at the usurious creditor's feet as the legislation of ancient Athens and Rome—and both arose spontaneously, as customary rights, without any pressure other than economic.

Alongside the wealth in commodities and slaves, alongside of money wealth, there now also appeared wealth in land. The possessive rights held by individuals in the parcels of land originally allocated to them by the gens or tribe had now been consolidated to such an extent that these parcels now belonged to them by inheritance. In the most recent period the chief aim for which they strove was liberation from the claim of the corporate gens to these parcels, since this claim had become a fetter to them. They rid themselves of this fetter—but soon after, also of their new landed property. The full, unrestricted ownership of the lands means not only the possibility of possessing the land intact and without limit ; it means also the possibility of disposing of it. So long as the land was the property of the gens, this possibility did not exist. But when the new landowner finally struck off the fetter of the paramount right of the gens and the tribe to the land, he also tore away the bond that up to then had bound him indissolubly to the land. What this meant was made clear to him by money, which was invented simultaneously with private property in land. The land could now become a commodity that was sold or mortgaged. Property in land was no sooner introduced than mortgages also were discovered (see Athens). Just as hetærism and prostitution clung to the heels of monogamy, so now the mortgage clung to the heels of property in land. You wanted full, unrestricted, alienable property in land ; very well, then, you have it—*tu l'as voulu, Georges Dandin !*

Thus, with the extension of trade, money and money usury, property in land and mortgages, the concentration and centralisation of wealth in the hands of a numerically small class went rapidly ahead, and alongside it the increasing impoverishment of the masses and the increasing mass of poor people. The new aristocracy of wealth, in so far as it was not already identical from the outset with the old tribal nobility, pushed the latter eventually into the background (in Athens, in Rome, and among the Germans). And alongside this division of freemen into classes based on wealth there took place, especially in Greece, an immense increase in the number of slaves[1] whose forced labour formed the foundation on which the superstructure of the entire society was built up.

Let us now turn to consider what had become of the gens organisation in the course of this social revolution. As against the new elements which had grown up without its aid, the gens organisation was powerless. Its presupposition was that the members of a gens, or even of a tribe, lived united in the same territory, occupied it exclusively. That had long ceased to be the case. Everywhere gentes and tribes were intermingled ; everywhere slaves, " clients," " barbarians " lived right among the citizens. The settled domicile which had been won only towards the end of the middle stage of barbarism was ever and again broken through by the mobility and change of domicile resulting

---

[1] In Corinth at the zenith of its power the number of slaves was 460,000 ; in Ægina 470,000—in both cases ten times the population of free citizens.

from trade, alteration of occupation and changes in the
ownership of land. The members of the gens could no
longer meet together to take cognisance of their own
common affairs ; only unimportant things, such as religious
festivals, were still here and there maintained. Alongside
the needs and interest for the safeguarding of which the
gens councils were appropriate and competent, out of
the revolution in productive relations and the consequent
change in the social structure new needs and interests
had arisen, which were not only unknown to the old gens
organisation but even cut across it in every way. The
interests of the handicraft groups which had arisen through
the division of labour, the special interests of the town
as opposed to the country, required new organs : each of
these groups, however, was composed of people of the
most diverse gentes, phratries and tribes, and even included
" barbarians " ; these organs had therefore to be formed
outside the gens organisation, alongside of it, and hence in
opposition to it.—And again each gens began to experience
this conflict of interests, which reached its highest point
in the union of rich and poor, usurers and debtors within
the same gens and the same tribe. In addition there was
the mass of the new population, outside of the gens groupings, who, as in Rome, might become a power in the land,
and yet was too numerous to be gradually absorbed in the
families and tribes based on blood relationship. Over
against this mass stood the gens groups as closed, privileged
associations ; the primitive natural democracy had been
transformed into a hated aristocracy. And finally, the
gens organisation had grown up in a society which knew
no internal contradictions, and was only suited to such a
society. It had no means of coercion other than public
opinion. But now a society had arisen which, by virtue
of its entire economic conditions of life, had been compelled
to split into freemen and slaves, into exploiting rich and
exploited poor ; a society which not only could not again
reconcile these contradictions, but necessarily drove them

to an ever sharpened point. Such a society could only continue to exist either in constant open conflict of these classes with one another, or under the rule of a third power, which, seemingly standing above the conflicting classes, suppressed their open conflict, and allowed the class struggle to be fought out at most on the economic field, in so-called legal form. The gens organisation of society had ceased to live. It had been burst asunder by the division of society into classes. It was replaced by the *State*.

·   ·   ·   ·   ·   ·   ·   ·

In the foregoing pages we have considered in detail the three chief forms in which the State arose on the ruins of the gens organisation. Athens provided the purest, the classical form : here the State sprang directly and predominantly from the class contradictions which developed within gens society itself. In Rome gens society grew into a closed aristocracy surrounded by a numerically large plebs which was outside the gens organisation and had no rights but was subject to obligations ; the victory of the plebs burst asunder the old organisation based on kinship, and set up on its ruins the State, in which both the gens aristocracy and the plebs were soon completely fused. Among the German conquerors of the Roman Empire, finally, the State arose directly from the conquest of large foreign territories, for the control of which the gens organisation was not adapted. But because this conquest involved neither any serious struggle with the former population, nor a more advanced division of labour ; because the victors' level of economic development was almost the same as that of the vanquished, and the economic basis of society therefore remained the same—for these reasons the gens organisation of society was able to continue in existence for many centuries in the altered, territorial form of the Mark, and even for a time to rejuvenate itself in modified form in the later noble and patrician families ; in fact even in peasant families, as in Ditmarsh.[1]

The State is therefore by no means a power imposed on society from the outside ; just as little is it " the reality of the moral idea," " the image and reality of reason," as Hegel asserted. Rather, it is a product of society at a certain stage of development ; it is the admission that this society has become entangled in an insoluble contradiction with itself, that it is cleft into irreconcilable antagonisms which it is powerless to dispel. But in order that these antagonisms, classes with conflicting economic interests, may not consume themselves and society in sterile struggle, a power apparently standing above society becomes necessary, whose purpose is to moderate the conflict and keep it within the bounds of " order " ; and this power arising out of society, but placing itself above it, and increasingly separating itself from it, is the State.

In contrast with the ancient organisation of the gens, the first distinguishing characteristic of the State is the grouping of the subjects of the State on a territorial basis. The old gens organisations, built up and held together by ties of blood, had become inadequate, largely because they presupposed that the members of the gens were bound to a definite territory, and this had long ceased to be the case. The territory had stood still, but men had become mobile. The territorial division was therefore taken as the starting point, and the citizens were allowed to exercise their rights and obligations at the place where they settled, without regard to gens and tribe. This organisation of the subjects of a State on the basis of their attachment to a particular place is common to all States. To us, therefore, it seems natural ; but we have seen what bitter and pro-tracted struggles had to be passed through before it was

---

[1] The first historian who had at least an approximate idea of the nature of the gens was Niebuhr ; and this—but also undoubtedly the erroneous conceptions he embodied in it—he owed to his acquaintance with the families in Ditmarsh.

able, in Athens and Rome, to replace the old organisation based on kinship.

The second is the establishment of a *public force*, which is no longer absolutely identical with the population organising itself as an armed power. This special public force is necessary, because a self-acting armed organisation of the population has become impossible since the cleavage of society into classes. The slaves also formed part of the population; the 90,000 Athenian citizens constituted only a privileged class as against the 365,000 slaves. The national army of the Athenian democracy was an aristocratic public force as against the slaves, and held them in check; but in order to hold the citizens in check, as noted above, a gendarmerie also was necessary. This public force exists in every State; it consists not merely of armed men, but of material appendages, prisons and repressive institutions of all kinds, of which gens society knew nothing. It may be very insignificant, almost infinitesimal, in societies where class contradictions are still undeveloped and in outlying areas, as at certain periods and in certain parts of the United States of America. It grows stronger, however, in proportion as the class antagonisms within the State grow sharper, and with the growth in size and population of the adjacent States. We have only to look at our present-day Europe, where class struggle and rivalry in conquest have screwed up the public power to such a pitch that it threatens to devour the whole of society and even the State itself.

For the maintenance of this public force, contributions from the citizens are necessary—*taxes*. To gens society these were completely unknown. We, however, nowadays know more than enough about them. With the advance of civilisation even these become inadequate; the State draws bills on the future, it contracts loans, *State debts*. Of these, too, ancient Europe can tell a tale.

Having at their disposal the public force and the right to exact taxes, the officials now stand as organs of society *above* society. The free, voluntary respect which was accorded to the organs of the gens form of government does not satisfy them, even if they could have it ; as representatives of a force alien to society, respect for them had to be established through exceptional laws, thanks to which they enjoyed a special sanctity and inviolability. The shabbiest police servant of the civilised State has more " authority " than all the organs of gens society put together ; but the most powerful prince and the greatest statesman or military chief of a civilised State may well envy the least among the chiefs of the gens the unconstrained and uncontested respect which was paid to him. The latter stood right in the middle of society ; the former is compelled to pose as something outside of and above society.

As the State arose out of the need to hold class antagonisms in check, but as it, at the same time, arose in the midst of the conflict of these classes, it is, as a rule, the State of the most powerful, economically dominant class, which by virtue thereof becomes also the dominant class politically, and thus acquires new means of holding down and exploiting the oppressed class. Thus the ancient State was above all the slaveowners' State for holding down the slaves, as the feudal State was the organ of the nobles for holding down the peasantry, bondmen and serfs, and the modern representative State is the instrument of the exploitation of wage-labour by capital. By way of exception, however, there are periods when the warring classes so nearly attain equilibrium that the State power, ostensibly appearing as a mediator, assumes for the moment a certain independence in relation to both. Such were the absolute monarchies of the seventeenth and eighteenth centuries, which balanced the nobles and burghers against each other ; the Bonapartism of the First and particularly the Second Empire in France, which played off the proletariat against the bourgeoisie and the bourgeoisie against the proletariat. The latest achievement of this kind, in which both ruler and subjects appear equally ridiculous, is the New German Imperial Bismarckian Nation : here the capitalists and the workers are balanced against each other and both equally fleeced by the degenerate and boorish country-squires of Prussia.

Moreover in most States that have existed in history the rights conceded to citizens have been graded on the basis of property, and thereby the fact has been directly expressed that the State is an organisation of the possessing class for protection against the non-possessing class. This was already the case in the Athenian and Roman classes based on property. This was the case in the feudal State of the middle ages, in which political power was graded in accordance with the ownership of land. And it is the case in the electoral register of the modern representative States. This political recognition of property differences is, however, by no means essential. On the contrary, it indicates a low stage of development of the State. The highest form of State, the democratic republic, which in our modern social relations is becoming more and more an unavoidable necessity, and is the form of State in which alone the last decisive battle between proletariat and bourgeoisie can be fought out—the democratic republic no longer has any official cognisance of property differences. In it, wealth wields its power indirectly, but all the more effectively. On the one hand in the form of direct corruption of the officials—America is the classical example of this ; on the other hand in the form of the alliance between the government and the stock exchange, which comes about all the more easily the more the public debt increases and the more share companies concentrate in their hands not only transport but even production, and in turn find their own centre of gravity in the stock exchange. Apart from America, the most recent republic of France is a striking example of this, and even honest Switzerland has played her part on this field. On the other hand, that a democratic republic is not essential for this fraternal alliance between government and stock exchange is proved, in addition to England, by the new German Empire, where it is impossible to say which of the two universal suffrage has the more exalted, Bismarck or Bleichröder. And in the last analysis the possessing class rules directly by means of universal suffrage. So long as the oppressed class, that is, in our case, the proletariat, is not yet ripe for self-liberation, so long will it, that is, the majority, regard the existing social order as the only possible one, and be politically the tail of the capitalist class, its extreme left wing. In the degree, however, that it matures towards its self-emancipation, to that degree it constitutes itself as its own party, elects its own representatives and not those of the capitalists. Universal suffrage is therefore the measure of the maturity of the working class ; in the State of to-day it cannot and never will be anything more. But this in any case is enough. On the day when the thermometer of universal suffrage indicates boiling-point among the workers, they as well as the capitalists will know where they are.

The State, therefore, has not existed from all eternity. There have been societies which managed without it, which had no conception of the State and State power. At a certain stage of economic development, which was necessarily bound up with the cleavage of society into classes, the State became a necessity owing to this cleavage. We are now rapidly approaching a stage in the development of production at which the existence of these classes has not only ceased to be a necessity, but is becoming a positive hindrance to production. They will disappear as inevitably as they arose at an earlier age. Along with them the State will inevitably disappear. The society that organises production anew on the basis of a free and equal association of the producers will put the whole State machine where it will then belong : in the museum of antiquities, side by side with the spinning wheel and the bronze axe.

·　·　·　·　·　·　·　·　·

Civilisation is therefore, in accordance with the above analysis, the stage of development of society in which the division of labour, the exchange between individuals arising therefrom, and the production of commodities embracing both of these, reach full development and revolutionise the whole of earlier society.

Production at all earlier stages of society was essentially collective, just as consumption also was on the basis of direct distribution of the products within larger or smaller communal groupings. This collective production took place within extremely narrow limits; but it brought with it the domination of the producers over their process of production and their product. They knew what became of their product : they consumed it, it did not leave their hands ; and so long as production was carried on on this basis, it could not grow beyond the control of the producers, nor beget any spectral, extraneous forces in opposition to them, as in civilisation is always and inevitably the case.

But slowly the division of labour penetrated this process of production and appropriation, it raised appropriation by individuals into the prevailing rule, and thereby begot exchange between individuals—we have investigated above how it did this. By degrees the production of commodities became the dominant form.

With the production of commodities, production no longer for the use of the producer but for exchange, the products necessarily change hands. The producer gives away his product in exchange ; he no longer knows what becomes of it. When money, and with money the merchant, steps in as intermediary between the producers, the process of exchange becomes still more complicated, the ultimate fate of the products still more uncertain. There are many merchants, and none of them knows what the other is doing. Commodities now already not merely pass from hand to hand, they move also from market to market ; the producers have lost control over the total production of the group in which they live, and the traders have not taken over this control. Products and production become subject to chance.

But chance is only one pole of an interrelation whose other pole is necessity. In nature, where also chance seems to rule, we have long since established in each separate field the inner necessity and subjection to law which runs through this chance. But what is true of Nature is true also of society. The more a social activity, a series of social processes, becomes too powerful for men's conscious control, gets beyond them, and the more it seems left to the purest chance, all the more surely, as though with elemental necessity, the immanent laws peculiar to this chance work themselves out within it. Such laws govern also the accidents of commodity production and exchange ; they face individual producers and traders as hostile, in the beginning even unrecognised, forces, whose nature must first be laboriously investigated and established. These economic laws of commodity production are modified with the various stages of development of this form of production ; but in one form or another the whole period of civilisation is dominated by them. And even to this day the product dominates the producer ; even to this day the aggregate production of society is regulated not by a jointly-devised plan, but by blind laws which make themselves felt with elemental force, ending with the storms of the periodical commercial crises.

We saw above that at a rather early stage of development of production human labour power became able to produce a considerably greater product than was necessary for the maintenance of the producers, and that this stage of production was in the main the same as that in which the division of labour and exchange between individuals made their appearance. After that it was not long before the great " truth " was discovered that man also can be a commodity ; that human strength is exchangeable and usable, by the transformation of a man into a slave.

Hardly had men begun to exchange when they themselves began to be exchanged. The active became the passive, whether men liked it or not.

With slavery, which in civilisation reached its most complete development, came the first great cleavage of society into an exploiting and an exploited class. This cleavage lasted throughout the whole period of civilisation. Slavery is the first form of exploitation, the form proper to the world of antiquity ; it was followed by serfdom in the middle ages, and wage labour in the more recent period. These are the three great forms of subjection, characteristic of the three great epochs of civilisation ; open, and more recently disguised, slavery continues throughout, side by side with the later forms.

The stage of commodity production at which civilisation begins is marked, from the economic standpoint, by the introduction of (1) metallic money, and with it money capital, interest and usury ; (2) merchants, as a class of intermediaries between the producers ; (3) the private ownership of land, and mortgages ; and (4) slave labour as the prevailing form of production. The form of the family which corresponds to civilisation and reaches definite ascendancy with it is monogamy, the domination of the man over the woman, and the individual family as the economic unit of society. The combining link of civilised society is the State, which in all typical periods without exception is the State of the ruling class, and in all cases continues to be in essence a machine for holding down the oppressed and exploited class. A further characteristic of civilisation is : on the one hand the establishment of the opposition between town and country as the basis of the entire social division of labour ; and on the other hand the introduction of the testament through which the property owner can dispose of his property even after his death. This institution, which struck a blow straight in the face of the former gens organisation, was unknown in Athens until the time of Solon ; in Rome it was introduced at an early date, though we do not know exactly when[1] ; among the Germans it was the priests who introduced it, in order that the devout German might without hindrance bequeath his heritage to the church.

With this fundamental constitution civilisation has accomplished things of which the old gens society was quite incapable. But it has accomplished them by setting in motion the basest impulses and passions of man and developing these at the cost of all his other talents. Sheer greed has been the driving spirit of civilisation from its first day up to now : wealth, and more wealth, and still more wealth—the wealth not of society but of the wretched individual, its sole decisive goal. If in pursuit of this goal the progressive development of science, and at recurrent periods the highest achievements of art, fell into its lap, it was only because without these the full conquest of wealth of our time would not have been possible.

As the basis of civilisation is the exploitation of one class by another class, its whole development moved within a permanent contradiction. Each advance of production is at the same time a step backwards in the position of the oppressed class, that is, of the immense majority. Each benefit for some is necessarily a disadvantage for the others ; each new liberation of one class is a new oppression for another class. The most striking proof of this is given

---

[1] Part II of Lassalle's *System of Inherited Rights* depends mainly on the proposition that the Roman testament is as old as Rome itself, that in Roman history there was never " a period without the testament " ; that, on the contrary, the testament had come into existence in pre-Roman days, through the cult of the dead. Lassalle, as a faithful Hegelian, derives Roman legal dispositions not from the social conditions of the Romans, but from the " speculative conceptions " of the will, and because of this arrives at this totally unhistorical assertion. It is not to be wondered at in a book which, on the basis of these same " speculative conceptions," comes to the conclusion that the transfer of property was a purely subsidiary matter in Roman inheritance. Lassalle not only believes in the illusions of the Roman jurists, especially those of the earlier period ; he even surpasses them.

by the introduction of machinery, the effects of which are now known throughout the world. And if among barbarians, as we saw, the distinction between rights and obligations can hardly as yet be made, civilisation makes the distinction and contrast between these clear even to the most stupid, inasmuch as it bestows on one class to all intents and purposes all the rights, and on the other class, on the contrary, to all intents and purposes all the obligations.

But this has not to be so. What is good for the ruling class has also to be good for the whole of society, with which the ruling class identifies itself. The further civilisation advances, therefore, the more it is compelled to cover up the evil conditions necessarily created by it with the cloak of charity, to palliate them or deny their existence ; in short, to introduce a conventional hypocrisy which was unknown either to earlier forms of society or even to the first stages of civilisation, and finally culminates in the assertion that the exploitation of the oppressed class is carried on by the exploiting class simply and solely in the interests of the exploited class itself ; and if the latter does not understand this, and even grows rebellious, this is the most base ingratitude to the benefactors and exploiters.[1]

And now to conclude with Morgan's judgment on civilisation :

> Since the advent of civilisation the outgrowth of property has been so immense, its forms so diversified, its uses so expanding and its management so intelligent in the interests of its

[1] I originally intended, when dealing with Morgan's and my own views, also to take account of the brilliant critique of civilisation which is to be found scattered through Charles Fourier's works. Unfortunately I have not the time for this. I only note that already in Fourier's writings monogamy and property in land are treated as the chief characteristics of civilisation, and that he calls it a war of the rich against the poor. Similarly, his insight was deep enough to understand even then that in all imperfect societies which are split into antagonisms the economic units are the individual families (*les familles incohérentes*).

owners, that it has become, on the part of the people, an unmanageable power. The human mind stands bewildered in the presence of its own creation. The time will come, nevertheless, when human intelligence will rise to the mastery over property and define the relations of the State to the property it protects, as well as the obligations and the limits of the rights of its owners. The interests of society are paramount to individual interests, and the two must be brought into just and harmonious relations. A mere property career is not the final destiny of mankind, if progress is to be the law of the future as it has been of the past. The time which has passed away since civilisation began is but a fragment of the past duration of man's existence ; and but a fragment of the ages yet to come. The dissolution of society bids fair to become the termination of a career of which property is the end and aim ; because such a career contains the elements of self-destruction. Democracy in government, brotherhood in society, equality in rights and privileges, and universal education, foreshadow the next higher plane of society to which experience, intelligence and knowledge are steadily tending. It will be a revival, in a higher form, of the liberty, equality and fraternity of the ancient gentes.

Friedrich Engels

THE HOUSING QUESTION

First published in 1872, in the form of articles in the Leipzig Social Democratic paper " Volksstaat " ; English edition, Martin Lawrence Ltd., 1935.

[In the late 'sixties and early 'seventies of last century the housing shortage became acute in Germany, owing to the rapid industrial development of that period. The German Press was full of articles on the housing question, and a

number of " solutions " were put forward, including some
which professed to be socialist, but in fact represented
" mere social patchwork." Engels protested against such
articles being printed in the socialist Press ; the Editors of
Volksstaat invited him to write a critical examination of
them. Engels therefore wrote these articles, showing that
the housing shortage is only one feature of the capitalist
mode of production and the class relations of capitalism,
and can never be " solved " so long as these class relations
exist. The articles are mainly polemic, but also state positive
Marxist principles, indicating the revolutionary solution of
the housing question.]

THE HOUSING QUESTION

HOW PROUDHON SOLVES THE HOUSING QUESTION

. . . The so-called housing shortage, which plays such a
great rôle in the Press nowadays, does not consist in the
fact that the working class generally lives in bad, overcrowded and unhealthy dwellings. *This* shortage is not
something peculiar to the present ; it is not even one of the
sufferings peculiar to the modern proletariat in contradistinction to all earlier oppressed classes. On the contrary,
all oppressed classes in all periods suffered more or less
uniformly from it. In order to make an end of *this* housing
shortage there is only *one* means : to abolish altogether the
exploitation and oppression of the working class by the
ruling class. What is meant to-day by housing shortage is
the peculiar intensification of the bad housing conditions
of the workers as the result of the sudden rush of population
to the big towns ; a colossal increase in rents, a still further
aggravation of overcrowding in the individual houses, and,
for some, the impossibility of finding a place to live in at
all. And *this* housing shortage gets talked of so much only

because it does not limit itself to the working class but has affected the petty bourgeoisie also.

The housing shortage from which the workers and part of the petty bourgeoisie suffer in our modern big cities is one of the numerous *smaller*, secondary evils which result from the present-day capitalist mode of production. It is not at all a direct result of the exploitation of the worker *as a* worker by the capitalists. This exploitation is the basic evil which the social revolution strives to abolish by abolishing the capitalist mode of production. The corner-stone of the capitalist mode of production is, however, the fact that our present social order enables the capitalists to buy the labour power of the worker at its value, but to extract from it much more than its value by making the worker work longer than is necessary in order to reproduce the price paid for the labour power. The surplus value produced in this fashion is divided among the whole class of capitalists and landowners together with their paid servants, from the Pope and the Kaiser, down to the night watchman and below. We are not concerned here as to how this distribution comes about, but this much is certain : that all those who do not work can live only from fragments of this surplus value which reach them in one way or another. (See Marx's *Capital* where this was worked out for the first time.)

The distribution of this surplus value, produced by the working class and taken from it without payment, among the non-working classes proceeds amid extremely edifying squabblings and mutual swindling. In so far as this distribution takes place by means of buying and selling, one of its chief methods is the cheating of the buyer by the seller, and in retail trade, particularly in the big towns, this has become an absolute condition of existence for the sellers. When, however, the worker is cheated by his grocer or his baker, either in regard to the price or the quality of the commodity, this does not happen to him in his specific capacity as a worker. On the contrary, as soon as a certain average level of cheating has become the social rule in any place, it must in the long run be levelled out by a corresponding increase in wages. The worker appears before the small shopkeeper as a buyer, that is, as the owner of money or credit, and hence not at all in his capacity as a worker, that is, as a seller of labour power. The cheating may hit him, and the poorer class as a whole, harder than it hits the richer social classes, but it is not an evil which hits him exclusively or is peculiar to his class.

And it is just the same with the housing shortage. The growth of the big modern cities gives the land in certain areas, particularly in those which are centrally situated, an artificial and often colossally increasing value ; the buildings erected on these areas depress this value, instead of increasing it, because they no longer correspond to the changed circumstances. They are pulled down and replaced by others. This takes place above all with workers' houses which are situated centrally and whose rents, even with the greatest overcrowding, can never, or only very slowly, increase above a certain maximum. They are pulled down and in their stead shops, warehouses and public buildings are erected. Through its Haussmann in Paris, Bonapartism exploited this tendency tremendously for swindling and private enrichment. But the spirit of Haussmann has also been abroad in London, Manchester and Liverpool, and seems to feel itself just as much at home in Berlin and Vienna. The result is that the workers are forced out of the centre of the towns towards the outskirts ; that workers' dwellings, and small dwellings in general, become rare and expensive and often altogether unobtainable, for under these circumstances the building industry, which is offered a much better field for speculation by more expensive houses, builds workers' dwellings only by way of exception.

This housing shortage therefore certainly hits the worker harder than it hits any more prosperous class, but it is just as

little an evil which burdens the working class exclusively
as the cheating of the shopkeeper, and it must, as far as the
working class is concerned, when it reaches a certain level
and attains a certain permanency similarly find a certain
economic adjustment.

It is with just such sufferings as these, which the
working class endures in common with other classes,
and particularly the petty bourgeoisie, that petty-
bourgeois socialism, to which Proudhon belongs, prefers
to occupy itself. And thus it is not at all accidental that our
German Proudhonist occupies himself chiefly with the
housing question, which, as we have seen, is by no means
exclusively a working-class question ; and that, on the contrary, he declares it to be a true, exclusively working-class
question.

" As the *wage worker* is in relation to the *capitalist*, so is
the *tenant* in relation to the *house owner*."

This is totally untrue.

In the housing question we have two parties confronting
each other : the tenant and the landlord or house owner.
The former wishes to purchase from the latter the temporary
use of a dwelling ; he has money or credit, even if he has to
buy this credit from the house owner himself at a usurious
price as an addition to the rent. It is simple commodity
sale ; it is not an operation between proletarian and
bourgeois, between worker and capitalist. The tenant—
even if he is a worker—appears as *a man with money* ; he must
already have sold his own particular commodity, his labour
power, in order to appear with the proceeds as the buyer
of the use of a dwelling, or he must be in a position to give a
guarantee of the impending sale of this labour power. The
peculiar results which attend the sale of labour power to
the capitalist are completely absent here. The capitalist
causes the purchased labour power firstly to produce its
own value and secondly to produce a surplus value which
remains in his hands for the time being, subject to its
distribution among the capitalist class. In this case therefore

an extra value is produced, the total sum of the existing value is increased. In the rent transaction the situation is quite different. No matter how much the landlord may over-reach the tenant it is still only a transfer of already *existing*, previously *produced* value, and the total sum of values possessed by the landlord and the tenant *together* remains the same after as it was before. The worker is always cheated of a part of the product of his labour, whether that labour is paid for by the capitalist below, above, or at its value. The tenant, on the other hand, is cheated only when he is compelled to pay for the dwelling above its value. It is, therefore, a complete misrepresentation of the relation between landlord and tenant to attempt to make it equivalent to the relation between worker and capitalist. On the contrary, we are dealing here with a quite ordinary commodity transaction between two citizens, and this transaction proceeds according to the economic laws which govern the sale of commodities in general and in particular the sale of the commodity, land property. The building and maintenance costs of the house, or of the part of the house in question, enters first of all into the calculation ; the land value, determined by the more or less favourable situation of the house, comes next ; the state of the relation between supply and demand existing at the moment is finally decisive. . . .

. . . How is the housing question to be solved then ? In present-day society just as any other social question is solved : by the gradual economic adjustment of supply and demand, a solution which ever reproduces the question itself anew and therefore is no solution. How a social revolution would solve this question depends not only on the circumstances which would exist in each case, but is also connected with still more far-reaching questions, among which one of the most fundamental is the abolition of the antithesis between town and country. As it is not our task to create Utopian systems for the arrangement of the future society, it would be more than idle to go into the question here

But one thing is certain : there are already in existence sufficient buildings for dwellings in the big towns to remedy immediately any real " housing *shortage*," given rational utilisation of them. This can naturally only take place by the expropriation of the present owners and by quartering in their houses the homeless or those workers excessively overcrowded in their former houses. Immediately the proletariat has conquered political power such a measure dictated in the public interests will be just as easy to carry out as other expropriations and billetings are by the existing state. . . .

HOW THE BOURGEOISIE SOLVES THE HOUSING QUESTION

. . . It is the essence of bourgeois socialism to want to maintain the basis of all the evils of present-day society and at the same time to want to abolish the evils themselves. As already pointed out in *The Communist Manifesto*, the bourgeois socialist " is desirous of redressing social grievances in order to secure the continued existence of bourgeois society," he wants " *a bourgeoisie without a proletariat*." We have already seen that Dr. Sax formulates the question in exactly the same fashion. The solution he finds in the solution of the housing question. He is of the opinion that :

> by improving the housing of the working classes it would be possible successfully to remedy the material and spiritual misery which has been described and thereby—by a radical improvement of the housing conditions *alone*—to raise the greater part of these classes out of the morass of their often hardly human conditions of existence to the pure heights of material and spiritual well-being.

Incidentally, it is in the interests of the bourgeoisie to disguise the fact of the existence of a proletariat created by the bourgeois production relations and determining the continued existence of these production relations. And, therefore, Dr. Sax tells us (p. 21) that the expression working classes is to be understood as including all

" impecunious social classes," " and in general, people in a small way, such as handicraftsmen, widows, pensioners (!), subordinate officials, etc.," as well as actual workers. Bourgeois socialism extends its hand to the petty-bourgeois variety.

Whence then comes the housing shortage? How did it arise? As a good bourgeois, Dr. Sax is not supposed to know that it is a necessary product of the bourgeois social order ; that it cannot fail to be present in a society in which the great masses of the workers are exclusively dependent upon wages, that is to say, on the sum of foodstuffs necessary for their existence and for the propagation of their kind ; in which improvements of the existing machinery continually throw masses of workers out of employment ; in which violent and regularly recurring industrial vacillations determine on the one hand the existence of a large reserve army of unemployed workers, and on the other hand drive large masses of the workers temporarily unemployed on to the streets ; in which the workers are crowded together in masses in the big towns, at a quicker rate than dwellings come into existence for them under existing conditions ; in which, therefore, there must always be tenants even for the most infamous pigsties ; and in which finally the house owner in his capacity as capitalist has not only the right, but, in view of the competition, to a certain extent also the duty, of ruthlessly making as much out of his property in house rent as he possibly can. In such a society the housing shortage is no accident ; it is a necessary institution and it can be abolished together with all its effects on health, etc., only if the whole social order from which it springs is fundamentally refashioned. That, however, bourgeois socialism dare not know. It dare not explain the housing shortage from the existing conditions. And therefore nothing remains for it but to explain the housing shortage by means of moral phrases as the result of the baseness of human beings, as the result of original sin, so to speak. . . .

. . . In any case, Dr. Sax has solved the question raised in the beginning : the worker " *becomes a capitalist* " by acquiring his own little house.

Capital is the command over the unpaid labour of others. The house of the worker can only become capital therefore if he rents it to a third person and appropriates a part of the labour product of this third person in the form of rent. By the fact that the worker lives in it himself the house is prevented from becoming capital, just as a coat ceases to be capital the moment I buy it from the tailor and put it on. The worker who owns a little house to the value of a thousand thalers is certainly no longer a proletarian, but one must be Dr. Sax to call him a capitalist.

However, the capitalist character of our worker has still another side. Let us assume that in a given industrial area it has become the rule that each worker owns his own little house. In this case *the working class of that area lives rent free* ; expenses for rent no longer enter into the value of its labour power. Every reduction in the cost of production of labour power, that is to say, every permanent price reduction in the worker's necessities of life, is equivalent "on the basis of the iron laws of political economy " to a reduction in the value of labour power and will therefore finally result in a corresponding fall in wages. Wages would fall on an average corresponding to the average sum saved on rent, that is, the worker would pay rent for his own house, but not, as formerly, in money to the house owner, but in unpaid labour to the factory owner for whom he works. In this way the savings of the worker invested in his little house would certainly become capital to some extent, but not capital for him, but for the capitalist employing him.

Dr. Sax is thus unable to succeed even on paper in turning his worker into a capitalist.

Incidentally, what has been said above applies to all

so-called social reforms which aim at saving or cheapening the means of subsistence of the worker. Either they become general and then they are followed by a corresponding reduction of wages, or they remain quite isolated experiments, and then their very existence as isolated exceptions proves that their realisation on a general scale is incompatible with the existing capitalist mode of production. Let us assume that in a certain area a general introduction of consumers' co-operatives succeeds in reducing the cost of foodstuffs for the workers by 20 per cent ; in the long run wages would fall in that area by approximately 20 per cent, that is to say, in the same proportion as the foodstuffs in question enter into the means of subsistence of the workers. If the worker, for example, spends three-quarters of his weekly wage on these foodstuffs, then wages would finally fall by three-quarters of $20 = 15$ per cent. In short, as soon as any such savings reform has become general, the worker receives in the same proportion less wages, as his savings permit him to live cheaper. Give every worker a saved independent income of 52 thalers a year and his weekly wage must finally fall by one thaler. Therefore : the more he saves the less he will receive in wages. He saves therefore not in his own interests, but in the interests of the capitalist. Is anything else necessary in order " to stimulate in the most powerful fashion the primary economic virtue, thrift " ? . . .

. . . It is perfectly clear that the existing state is neither able nor willing to do anything to remedy the housing difficulty. The state is nothing but the organised collective power of the possessing classes, the landowners and the capitalists as against the exploited classes, the peasants and the workers. What the individual capitalists (and it is here only a question of these because in this matter the landowner who is also concerned acts primarily as a capitalist) do not want, their state also does not want. If therefore the *individual* capitalists deplore the housing shortage, but can hardly be persuaded even superficially to palliate its most terrifying consequences, then the *collective* capitalist, the state, will not do much more. At the most it will see to it that the measure of superficial palliation which has become standard is carried out everywhere uniformly. And we have already seen that this is the case. . . .

Karl Marx

THE POVERTY OF PHILOSOPHY

Published 1847 ; English edition : Martin Lawrence Ltd., 1935.

[This was written as a reply to Proudhon's *The Philosophy of Poverty*, a work referred to in *The Communist Manifesto* as an example of " conservative or bourgeois socialism "— the form of socialism put forward by a section of the capitalist class which is " desirous of redressing social grievances, in order to secure the continued existence of bourgeois society." In *The Poverty of Philosophy* Marx not only criticised Proudhon's 'variety of " socialism " and philosophical confusion, but developed in a positive form the fundamental ideas which he and Engels had by then clearly formulated for themselves. The first section of the book represents an early statement of Marxist economic theory, leading on to *The Critique of Political Economy* and *Capital*. The second section, from which the following passages are taken, criticises Proudhon's philosophical conceptions and indicates the Marxist viewpoint.]

THE POVERTY OF PHILOSOPHY
THE METAPHYSICS OF POLITICAL ECONOMY

HERE we are, right in Germany! We shall now have to talk metaphysics while talking political economy. And in this again we shall but follow M. Proudhon's " contradictions." Just now he forced us to speak English, to become ourselves to some extent English. Now the scene is changing. M. Proudhon is transporting us to our dear fatherland and is forcing us to resume, whether we like it or not, our capacity as German.

If the Englishman transforms men into hats, the German transforms hats into ideas. The Englishman is Ricardo, rich banker and distinguished economist ; the German is Hegel, simple professor of philosophy at the University of Berlin.

Louis XV, the last absolute monarch and representative of the decadence of French royalty, had attached to his person a doctor who was himself France's first economist. This doctor, this economist, represented the imminent and certain triumph of the French bourgeoisie. Doctor Quesnay made a science out of political economy ; he summarised it in his famous *Tableau Économique* [*Economic Table*]. Besides the thousand and one commentaries which have appeared on this table, we possess one by the doctor himself. It is the " analysis of the economic table," followed by " seven *important observations*."

M. Proudhon is another Dr. Quesnay. He is the Quesnay of the metaphysics of political economy.

Now metaphysics—indeed all philosophy—can be summed up, according to Hegel, in method. We must, therefore, try to elucidate the method of M. Proudhon, which is at least as foggy as the *Economic Table*. It is for this reason that we are making seven more or less important observations. If Dr. Proudhon is not pleased with our observations, well, then, he will have to become an Abbé Baudeau and give the " explanation of the economico-metaphysical method " himself.

First Observation

" We are not giving a *history according to the order in time*, but *according to the sequence of ideas*. Economic *phases* or *categories* are in their *manifestation* sometimes contemporary, sometimes inverted. . . . Economic theories have none the less their *logical sequence* and their *serial relation in the understanding* : it is this order that we flatter ourselves to have discovered." (Proudhon, Vol. I, p. 146.)

M. Proudhon most certainly wanted to frighten the French by flinging quasi-Hegelian phrases at them. So we have to deal with two men ; firstly with M. Proudhon, and then with Hegel. How does M. Proudhon distinguish himself from other economists ? And what part does Hegel play in M. Proudhon's political economy ?

Economists express the relations of bourgeois production, the division of labour, credit, money, etc., as fixed, immutable, eternal categories. M. Proudhon, who has these ready-made categories before him, wants to explain to us the act of formation, the genesis of these categories, principles, laws, ideas, thoughts.

Economists explain how production takes place in the above-mentioned relations, but what they do not explain is how these relations themselves are produced, that is, the historical movement which gave them birth. M. Proudhon, taking these relations for principles, categories, abstract thoughts, has merely to put into *order* these thoughts, which are to be found alphabetically arranged at the end of every treatise on political economy. The economists' material is the active, energetic life of man ; M. Proudhon's material is the dogmas of the economists. But the moment we cease to pursue the historical movement of production-relations, of which the categories are but the theoretical expression, the moment we try to see in these categories no more than ideas, spontaneous thoughts, independent of real relations, we are forced to attribute the origin of these thoughts to the movement of pure reason. How does pure,

eternal, impersonal reason give rise to these thoughts?
How does it proceed in order to produce them?

If we had M. Proudhon's intrepidity in the matter of
Hegelianism we should say : it is distinguished in itself from
itself. What does this mean? Impersonal reason, having
outside itself neither a base on which it can pose itself, nor
an object to which it can oppose itself, nor a subject with
which it can compose itself, is forced to turn head over
heels, in posing itself, opposing itself and composing itself—
position, opposition, composition. Or, to speak Greek—we
have thesis, antithesis and synthesis. For those who do
not know the Hegelian language, we shall give the conse-
crating formula : affirmation, negation and negation of the
negation. That is what language means. It is certainly not
Hebrew (with due apologies to M. Proudhon) ; but it is
the language of this pure reason, separate from the individual. Instead of the ordinary individual with his ordinary
manner of speaking and thinking we have nothing but this
ordinary manner in itself—without the individual.

Is it surprising that everything in the final abstraction—
for we have here an abstraction, and not an analysis—
presents itself as a logical category? Is it surprising that,
if you let drop little by little all that constitutes the individuality of a house, making an abstraction first of the
materials of which it is composed, then of the form that
distinguishes it, you end up with nothing but a body ; that,
if you make an abstraction of the limits of this body, you
soon have nothing but a space—that if, finally, you make
an abstraction of the dimensions of this space, there is
absolutely nothing left but pure quantity, the logical
category? If we abstract thus from every subject all the
alleged accidents, animate or inanimate, men or things,
we are right in saying that in the final abstraction, the only
substance left is the logical categories. Thus the metaphysicians who, in making these abstractions, think they are
making analyses, and who, the more they detach themselves from things, imagine themselves to be getting all the

nearer to the point of penetrating to their core—these metaphysicians in turn are right in saying that things here below are embroideries of which the logical categories constitute the canvas. This is what distinguishes the philosopher from the Christian. The Christian, in spite of logic, has only one incarnation of the *Logos* ; the philosopher has never finished with incarnations. If all that exists, all that lives on land and under water can be reduced by abstraction to a logical category—if the whole real world can be drowned thus in a world of abstractions, in the world of logical categories—who need be astonished at it ?

All that exists, all that lives on earth and under water, exists and lives only by some kind of movement. Thus the movement of history produces social relations ; industrial movement gives us industrial products, etc.

Just as by dint of abstraction we have transformed everything into a logical category, so one has only to make an abstraction of every characteristic distinctive of different movements to attain movement in its abstract condition— purely formal movement, the purely logical formula of movement. If one finds in logical categories the substance of all things, one imagines one has found in the logical formula of movement the *absolute method*, which not only explains all things, but also implies the movement of things.

It is of this absolute method that Hegel speaks in these terms : " Method is the absolute, unique, supreme, infinite force, which no object can resist ; it is the tendency of reason to find itself again, to recognise itself in all things." (*Logik*, Vol. III.) All things being reduced to a logical category, and every movement, every act of production, to method, it follows naturally that every aggregate of products and production, of objects and of movement, can be reduced to a form of applied metaphysics. What Hegel has done for religion, law, etc., M. Proudhon seeks to do for political economy.

So what is this absolute method ? The abstraction of movement. What is the abstraction of movement ? Movement in abstract condition. What is movement in abstract condition ? The purely logical formula of movement or the movement of pure reason. Wherein does the movement of pure reason consist ? In posing itself, opposing itself, composing itself, in formulating itself as thesis, antithesis, synthesis ; or, yet again, in affirming itself, negating itself and negating its negation.

How does reason manage to affirm itself, to pose itself in a definite category ? That is the business of reason itself and of its apologists.

But once it has managed to pose itself as a thesis, this thesis, this thought, opposed to itself, splits up into two contradictory thoughts—the positive and the negative, the yes and the no. The struggle between these two antagonistic elements comprised in the antithesis constitutes the dialectical movement. The yes becoming no, the no becoming yes, the yes becoming both yes and no, the no becoming both no and yes, the contraries balance, neutralise, paralyse each other. The fusion of these two contradictory thoughts constitutes a new thought, which is the synthesis of them. This thought splits up once again into two contradictory thoughts, which in turn establish a new synthesis. Of this travail is born a group of thoughts. This group of thoughts follows the same dialectic movement as the simple category, and has a contradictory group as antithesis. Of these two groups of thoughts is born a new group of thoughts, which is the synthesis of them.

Just as from the dialectic movement of the simple categories is born the group, so from the dialectic movement of the groups is born the series, and from the dialectic movement of the series is born the entire system.

Apply this method to the categories of political economy, and you have the logic and metaphysics of political economy, or, in other words, you have the economic categories that everybody knows, translated into a little-known language which makes them look as if they had newly blossomed forth in an intellect of pure reason ; so much do these categories seem to engender one another, to be linked up with, intertwined with one another, by the very working of the dialectic movement. The reader must not get alarmed at these metaphysics with all their scaffolding of categories, groups, series and systems. M. Proudhon, in spite of all the trouble he has taken to scale the heights of the *system of contradictions*, has never been able to raise himself above the first two rungs of simple thesis and antithesis ; and even these he has mounted only twice, and on one of these two occasions he fell over backwards.

Up to now we have expounded only the dialectics of Hegel. We shall see later how M. Proudhon has succeeded in reducing it to the meanest proportions. Thus, for Hegel, all that has happened and is still happening is only just what is happening in his own mind. Thus the philosophy of history is nothing but the history of philosophy, of his own philosophy. There is no longer a " history according to the order in time," there is only " the sequence of ideas in the understanding." He thinks he is constructing the world by the movement of thought, whereas he is merely reconstructing systematically and classifying by the absolute method the thoughts which are in the minds of all.

Second Observation

Economic categories are only the theoretical expressions, the abstractions of the social relations of production. M. Proudhon, holding things upside-down like a true philosopher, sees in actual relations nothing but the incarnation of these principles, of these categories, which were slumbering—so M. Proudhon the philosopher tells us—in the bosom of the " impersonal reason of humanity."

M. Proudhon the economist understands well enough that men make cloth, linen or silk materials in definite relations of production. But what he has not understood is that these definite social relations are just as much produced by men as linen, flax, etc. Social relations are closely bound up with productive forces. In acquiring new productive forces men change their mode of production ; and in changing their mode of production they change their way of earning their living—they change all their social relations. The hand-mill gives you society with the feudal lord ; the steam-mill, society with the industrial capitalist.

The same men who establish their social relations in conformity with their material productivity, produce also principles, ideas and categories, in conformity with their social relations.

Thus these ideas, these categories, are as little eternal as the relations they express. They are *historical and transitory products*.

There is a continual movement of growth in productive forces, of destruction in social relations, of formation in ideas ; the only immutable thing is the abstraction of movement—*mors immortalis*.

Third Observation

The production relations of every society form a whole. M. Proudhon considers economic relations as so many social phases, engendering one another, resulting one from the other like the antithesis from the thesis, and realising in their logical sequence the impersonal reason of humanity.

The only drawback to this method is that when he comes to examine a single one of these phases, M. Proudhon cannot explain it without having recourse to all the other relations of society ; which relations, however, he has not yet contrived to engender by means of his dialectic movement. When, after that, M. Proudhon, by means of pure reason, proceeds to give birth to these other phases, he treats them as if they were new-born babes. He forgets that they are of the same age as the first.

Thus, to arrive at the constitution of value, which for him is the basis of all economic evolutions, he could not do without division of labour, competition, etc. Yet in the *series*, in the *understanding* of M. Proudhon, in the *logical sequence*, these relations were still non-existent.

In constructing the edifice of an ideological system by means of the categories of political economy, the limbs of the social system are dislocated. The different limbs of society are converted into so many separate societies, following one upon the other. How, indeed, could the single logical formula of movement, of sequence, of time, explain the structure of society, in which all relations co-exist simultaneously and support one another ?

Fourth Observation

Let us see now to what modifications M. Proudhon subjects Hegel's dialectics, when he applies it to political economy.

For him, M. Proudhon, every economic category has two sides—one good, the other bad. He looks upon these categories as the petty bourgeois looks upon the great men of history : *Napoleon* was a great man ; he did a lot of good ; he also did a lot of harm.

The *good side* and the *bad side*, the *advantages* and the *drawbacks*, taken together form for M. Proudhon the *contradiction* in every economic category.

The problem to be solved : to keep the good side, while eliminating the bad.

Slavery is an economic category like any other. Thus it also must have its two sides. Let us leave alone the bad side and talk about the good side of slavery. Needless to say we are dealing only with direct slavery, with Negro slavery in Surinam, in Brazil, in the Southern States of North America.

Direct slavery is just as much the pivot of bourgeois industry as machinery, credits, etc. Without slavery you have no cotton ; without cotton you have no modern industry. It is slavery that has given the colonies their value ; it is the colonies that have created world trade, and it is world trade that is the pre-condition of large-scale industry. Thus slavery is an economic category of the greatest importance.

Without slavery, North America, the most progressive of countries, would be transformed into a patriarchal country. Wipe out North America from the map of the world, and you will have anarchy—the complete decay of modern commerce and civilisation. Abolish slavery and you will have wiped America off the map of nations.[1]

Thus slavery, because it is an economic category, has always existed among the institutions of the peoples. Modern nations have been able to disguise slavery in their own countries, but they have imposed it without disguise upon the New World.

What would M. Proudhon do to save slavery ? He would formulate the *problem* thus : preserve the good side of this economic category, eliminate the bad.

Hegel has no problems to formulate. He has only dialectics. M. Proudhon has nothing of Hegel's dialectics but the language. For him the dialectic movement is his own dogmatic distinction between good and bad.

Let us for a moment consider M. Proudhon himself as a category. Let us examine his good and his bad side, his advantages and his drawbacks.

If he has the advantage over Hegel of formulating problems which he reserves the right of solving for the greater good of humanity, he has the drawback of being stricken with sterility when it is a question of engendering a new

[1] " This was perfectly correct for the year 1847. At that time the world trade of the United States was limited to the import of immigrants and industrial products, and the export of cotton and tobacco, that is, of the products of slave labour. The northern states produced principally corn and meat for the slave states. It was only when the North produced corn and meat for export and also became an industrial country, and when the American cotton monopoly had to face powerful competition in India, Egypt, Brazil, etc., that the abolition of slavery became possible. And even then this led to the ruin of the South, which did not succeed in replacing the open Negro slavery by the disguised slavery of Indian and Chinese coolies." [*Note by F. Engels to the German edition, 1885.*]

category by dialectical birth-throes. What constitutes dialectical movement is the co-existence of two contradictory sides, their conflict and their fusion into a new category. The very formulation of the problem as one of eliminating the bad side cuts short the dialectic movement. It is not the category which is posed and opposed to itself, by its contradictory nature, it is M. Proudhon who gets excited, perplexed and frets himself between the two sides of the category.

Caught thus in a blind alley, from which it is difficult to escape by legal means, M. Proudhon takes a real flying leap which transports him at one bound into a new category. Then it is that to his astonished gaze is revealed the *sequence in the understanding*.

He takes hold of the first category that comes handy and attributes to it arbitrarily the quality of supplying a remedy for the drawbacks of the category to be purified. Thus, if we are to believe M. Proudhon, taxes remedy the drawbacks of monopoly ; the balance of trade, the drawbacks of taxes ; landed property, the drawbacks of credit.

By taking the economic categories thus successively, one by one, and making one the *antidote* to the other, M. Proudhon manages to make with this mixture of contradictions and antidotes to contradictions, two volumes of contradictions which he rightly entitles : *The System of Economic Contradictions.*

Fifth Observation

" In the absolute reason all these ideas . . . are equally simple and general. . . . In fact, we attain knowledge only by a *sort of scaffolding* of our ideas. But truth in itself is independent of these dialectical symbols and freed from the combinations of our minds." (Proudhon, Vol. II, p. 97.)

Here all of a sudden, by a kind of switch-over of which we now know the secret, the metaphysics of political economy has become an illusion ! Never has M. Proudhon spoken more truly. Indeed, from the moment the process of the dialectic movement is reduced to the simple process of opposing good to bad, of posing problems tending to eliminate the bad, and of administering one category as an antidote to another, the categories are deprived of all spontaneity ; the idea " ceases to *function* " ; there is no life left in it. It is no longer posed or decomposed into categories. The sequence of categories has become a *sort of scaffolding*. Dialectics has ceased to be the movement of absolute reason. There is no longer any dialectics but only, at the most, an absolutely pure morality.

When M. Proudhon spoke of the *series in the understanding*, of the *logical sequence of categories*, he declared positively that he did not want to give *history according to the order in time*, that is, in M. Proudhon's view, the historical sequence in which the categories have *manifested* themselves. Thus for him everything happened in the *pure ether of reason*. Everything was to be derived from this ether by means of dialectics. Now that he has to put this dialectics into practice his reason defaults. M. Proudhon's dialectics runs counter to Hegel's dialectics, and now we have M. Proudhon reduced to saying that the order in which he gives his economic categories is not the order in which they engender one another. Economic evolutions are no longer the evolutions of reason itself.

What, then, does M. Proudhon give us ? Real history, which is, according to M. Proudhon's understanding, the sequence in which the categories have *manifested* themselves in order of time ? No ! History as it takes place in the idea itself ? Still less ! That is, neither the profane history of the categories, nor their sacred history ! What history does he give us, then ? The history of his own contradictions. Let us see how they go, and how they drag M. Proudhon in their train.

Before entering upon this examination, which gives rise to the sixth important observation, we have yet another important observation to make.

Let us grant with M. Proudhon that true history, history

according to the order in time, is the historical sequence in which ideas, categories and principles have manifested themselves.

Each principle has had its own century in which to manifest itself. The principle of authority, for example, had the eleventh century, just as the principle of individualism had the eighteenth century. In due sequence, it was the century that belonged to the principle, and not the principle that belonged to the century. In other words it was the principle that made the history, and not the history that made the principle. When, consequently, in order to save principles as much as to save history, we ask ourselves why such a principle was manifested in the eleventh or in the eighteenth century rather than in any other, we are necessarily forced to examine minutely what men were like in the eleventh century, what they were like in the eighteenth, what were their respective needs, their productive forces, their mode of production, the raw materials of their production—in short, what were the relations between man and man which resulted in all these conditions of existence. To get to the bottom of all these questions—what is this but to study the real, profane history of men in every century and to present these men as both the authors and the actors of their own drama ? But the moment you present men as the actors and authors of their own history, you arrive—by a detour—at the real starting point, because you have abandoned those eternal principles of which you spoke at the outset.

M. Proudhon has not even gone far enough along the cross-road which an ideologist takes to reach the main road of history.

Sixth Observation

Let us take this cross-road with M. Proudhon.

We shall concede that economic relations, viewed as *immutable laws, eternal principles, ideal categories*, existed before active and energetic men did ; we shall concede further that these laws, principles and categories had, since the beginning of time, slumbered " in the impersonal reason of humanity." We have already seen that, in all these changeless and motionless eternities, there is no history left ; there is at most history in the idea, that is, history reflected in the dialectic movement of pure reason. M. Proudhon, by saying that, in the dialectic movement, ideas are no longer *differentiated*, has done away with both the *shadow of movement* and the *movement of shadows*, by means of which one could still have created at least a semblance of history. Instead of that, he imputes to history his own impotence. He lays the blame on everything, even the French language. " It is not correct then," says M. Proudhon, the philosopher, " to say that something *happens*, that something is produced : in civilisation as in the universe, everything has existed, has acted, from eternity. *This applies to the whole of social economy.*" (Vol. II, p. 102.)

So great is the productive force of the contradictions which *function* and which make M. Proudhon function, that, in trying to explain history, he is forced to deny it ; in trying to explain the successive appearance of social relations, he denies that *anything* can appear : in trying to explain production, with all its phases, he questions whether *anything can be produced* !

Thus, for M. Proudhon, there is no longer any history : no longer any sequence of ideas. And yet his book still exists ; and it is just this book which is, to use his own expression, " *history according to the sequence of ideas.*" How shall we find a formula, for M. Proudhon is a man of formulas, to help him to clear, *in a single leap*, all these contradictions ?

To this end he has invented a new reason, which is neither the pure and virgin absolute reason, nor the common reason of men living and acting in different periods, but a reason quite apart—the reason of the person, Society —of the subject, *Humanity*—which under the pen of M. Proudhon figures at times also as *social genius, general reason,*

or finally as *human reason*. This reason, decked out under so
many names, betrays itself nevertheless, at every moment,
as the individual reason of M. Proudhon, with his good and
his bad side, his antidotes and his problems.

" Human reason does not create truth," hidden in the
depths of absolute, eternal reason. It can only unveil it.
But such truth as it has unveiled up to now is incomplete,
insufficient and consequently contradictory. Thus, economic categories, being themselves truths discovered, revealed
by human reason, by the social genius, are equally incomplete and contain within themselves the germ of contradiction. Before M. Proudhon, the social genius saw only
the *antagonistic elements*, and not the *synthetic formula*, both
hidden simultaneously in *absolute reason*. Economic relations, which merely realise on earth just these insufficient
truths, these incomplete categories, these contradictory
ideas, are consequently contradictory in themselves, and
present the two sides, one good, the other bad.

To find complete truth, the Idea, in all its fullness, the
synthetic formula that is to annihilate the contradiction,
this is the problem of the social genius. This again is why,
in M. Proudhon's illusion, this same social genius has been
harried from one category to another without ever, despite
all its battery of categories, having been able to snatch
from God, or from absolute reason, a synthetic formula.

" At first, society (the social genius) states a primary fact,
puts forward a *hypothesis* . . . a veritable antinomy whose antagonistic results develop in the social economy in the same way
as its consequences could have been deduced in the mind ; so
that industrial movement, following in all things the deduction
of ideas, splits up into two currents, one of useful effects, the
other of subversive results. To bring harmony into the constitution of this two-sided principle, and to solve this antinomy,
society gives rise to a *second*, which will soon be followed by a
third ; and *progress of the social genius* will take place in this
manner, until, having exhausted all its contradictions—I suppose, but it is not proved that there is a limit to human contradictions—it returns at one leap to all its former positions and
with a single formula solves all its problems." (Vol. I, p. 135.)

Just as the *antithesis* was before turned into an *antidote*, so now the *thesis* becomes a *hypothesis*. This change of terms, coming from M. Proudhon, has no longer anything surprising for us ! Human reason, which is anything but pure, having only incomplete vision, encounters at every step new problems to be solved. Every new thesis which it discovers in absolute reason and which is the negation of the first thesis, becomes for it a synthesis, which it accepts rather naïvely as the solution of the problem in question. It is thus that this reason tortures itself in ever renewing contradictions until, coming to the end of its contradictions, it perceives that all its theses and syntheses are merely contradictory hypotheses. In its perplexity, " human reason, the social genius, returns at one leap to all its former positions and, in a single formula, solves all its problems." This unique formula, by the way, constitutes M. Proudhon's true discovery. It is *constituted value*.

Hypotheses are made only in view of a certain aim. The aim that the social genius, speaking through the mouth of M. Proudhon, set itself in the first place, was to eliminate the bad in every economic category, in order to have nothing left but the good. For him, the good, the supreme well-being, the real practical aim, is *equality*. And why did the social genius aim at equality rather than inequality, fraternity, catholicism or any other principle ? Because " humanity has successively realised so many separate hypotheses only in view of a superior hypothesis," which precisely is equality. In other words : because equality is M. Proudhon's ideal, he imagines that the division of labour, credit, the workshop, that all economic relations were invented merely for the benefit of equality, and yet they always end up by turning against it. Since history and the fiction of M. Proudhon contradict each other at every step, the latter concludes that there is a contradiction. If there is a contradiction, it exists only between his fixed idea and real movement.

Henceforth the good side of an economic relation is that

which affirms equality ; the bad side, that which negates
it and affirms inequality. Every new category is a hypothesis of the social genius to eliminate the inequality engendered by the preceding hypothesis. In short, equality
is the *primordial intention*, the *mystical tendency*, the *providential
aim* that the social genius has constantly before its eyes as
it twists round in the circle of economic contradictions.
Thus *Providence* is the locomotive which makes the whole
of M. Proudhon's economic baggage move better than his
pure, volatilised reason. He has devoted to Providence a
whole chapter, which follows the one on taxes.

Providence, providential aim, this is the great word
used to-day to explain the movement of history. In fact,
this word explains nothing. It is at most a rhetorical form,
one of the various ways of paraphrasing facts.

It is a fact that in Scotland landed property acquired a
new value by the development of English industry. This
industry opened up new outlets for wool. In order to
produce wool on a large scale, arable land had to be transformed into pasturage. To effect this transformation, the
estates had to be concentrated. To concentrate the estates,
small holdings had first to be abolished, thousands of
tenants had to be driven from their native soil and a few
shepherds in charge of millions of sheep to be installed in
their place. Thus, by successive transformations, landed
property in Scotland has resulted in the driving out of men
by sheep. Now say that the providential aim of the institution of landed property in Scotland was to have men
driven out by sheep, and you will have made providential
history.

Of course, the tendency towards equality belongs to our
century. To say now that all former centuries, with entirely
different needs, means of production, etc., worked pro-
videntially for the realisation of equality, is, firstly, to substitute the means and the men of our century for the men
and the means of earlier centuries and to misunderstand
the historical movement by which the successive generations

transformed the results acquired by the generations that preceded them. Economists know well enough that the very thing that was for the one a finished product was for the other but the raw material for new production.

Suppose, as M. Proudhon does, that the social genius produced, or rather improvised, the feudal lords with the providential aim of transforming the *settlers* into *responsible* and *equally-placed* workers : and you will have effected a substitution of aims and of persons worthy of the Providence that instituted landed property in Scotland, in order to give itself the malicious pleasure of driving out men by sheep.

But since M. Proudhon takes such a tender interest in Providence, we refer him to the *History of Political Economy* of M. de Villeneuve-Bargemont, who likewise goes in pursuit of a providential aim. This aim, however, is not equality, but catholicism.

Seventh and Last Observation

Economists have a singular method of procedure. There are only two kinds of institutions for them, artificial and natural. The institutions of feudalism are artificial institutions, those of the bourgeoisie are natural institutions. In this they resemble the theologians, who likewise establish two kinds of religion. Every religion which is not theirs is an invention of men, while their own religion is an emanation from God. When they say that present-day relations— the relations of bourgeois production—are natural, the economists imply that these are the relations in which wealth is created and productive forces developed in conformity with the laws of nature. Thus these relations are themselves natural laws independent of the influence of time. They are eternal laws which must always govern society. Thus there has been history, but there is no longer any. There has been history, since there were the institutions of feudalism, and in these institutions of feudalism we find quite different production relations from those of bourgeois society, which the economists try to pass off as natural and consequently eternal.

Feudalism also had its proletariat—serfdom, which contained all the germs of the bourgeoisie. Feudal production also had two antagonistic elements which are likewise designated by the name of *good side* and *bad side*, without considering that it is always the bad side that in the end triumphs over the good side. It is the bad side that produces the movement which makes history, by providing a struggle. If, during the epoch of the domination of feudalism, the economists, enthusiastic over the knightly virtues, the harmony between rights and duties, the patriarchal life of the towns, the prosperous condition of domestic industry in the countryside, the development of industry organised into corporations, guilds and fraternities, in short, everything that constitutes the good side of feudalism, had set themselves the problem of eliminating everything that cast a shadow on this picture—serfdom, privileges, anarchy—what would have happened ? All the elements which called forth the struggle would have been destroyed, and the development of the bourgeoisie nipped in the bud. One would have set oneself the absurd problem of eliminating history.

After the triumph of the bourgeoisie there was no longer any question of the good or the bad side of feudalism. The bourgeoisie took possession of the productive forces it had developed under feudalism. All the old economic forms, the corresponding civil relations, the political state which was the official expression of the old civil society, were smashed.

Thus feudal production, to be judged properly, must be considered as a mode of production founded on antagonism. It must be shown how wealth was produced within this antagonism, how the productive forces were developed at the same time as class antagonisms, how one of the classes, the bad side, the drawback of society, went on growing until the material conditions for its emancipation had attained full maturity. Is not this as good as saying that the mode of production, the relations in which productive forces are developed, are anything but eternal laws, but that they correspond to a definite development of men and of their productive forces, and that a change in men's productive forces necessarily brings about a change in their production-relations ? As it is a matter of prime concern not to be deprived of the fruits of civilisation, of the acquired productive forces, the traditional forms in which they were produced must be smashed. From this moment the revolutionary class becomes conservative.

The bourgeoisie begins with a proletariat which is itself a relic of the proletariat of feudal times. In the course of its historical development, the bourgeoisie necessarily develops its antagonistic character, which at first is more or less disguised, existing only in a latent state. As the bourgeoisie develops, there develops in its bosom a new proletariat, a modern proletariat ; there develops a struggle between the proletarian class and the bourgeois class, a struggle which, before being felt, perceived, appreciated, understood, avowed and proclaimed aloud by the two sides, expresses itself, to start with, merely in partial and momentary conflicts, in subversive acts. On the other hand, if all the members of the modern bourgeoisie have the same interests in so far as they form a class as against another class they have opposite, antagonistic interests inasmuch as they stand face to face with one another. This opposition of interests results from the economic conditions of their bourgeois life. From day to day it thus becomes clearer that the production-relations in which the bourgeoisie moves have not a simple uniform character, but a dual character ; that in the self-same relations in which wealth is produced, misery is produced also ; that in the self-same relations in which there is a development of the productive forces, there is also a driving force of repression ; that these relations produce *bourgeois wealth*, i.e., the wealth of the bourgeois class, only by continually annihilating the wealth of the individual members of this class and by producing an ever-growing proletariat.

The more the antagonistic character comes to light, the more the economists, the scientific representatives of bourgeois production, find themselves in conflict with their own theory ; and different schools arise.

We have the *fatalist* economists, who in their theory are as indifferent to what they call the drawbacks of bourgeois production as the bourgeois themselves are in practice to the sufferings of the proletarians who help them to acquire wealth. In this fatalist school there are the Classics and the Romantics. The Classics, like Adam Smith and Ricardo, represent a bourgeoisie which, while still struggling with the relics of feudal society, works only to purge economic relations of feudal taints, to increase the productive forces and to give a new upsurge to industry and commerce. The proletariat that takes part in this struggle and is absorbed in this feverish labour experiences only passing, accidental sufferings, and itself regards them as such. The economists like Adam Smith and Ricardo, who are the historians of this epoch, have no other mission than that of showing how wealth is acquired in bourgeois production-relations, of formulating these relations into categories, laws, and of showing how superior these laws, categories, are for the production of wealth to the laws and categories of feudal society. Misery is in their eyes merely the pang which accompanies every childbirth, in nature as in industry.

The Romantics belong to our own age, in which the bourgeoisie is in direct opposition to the proletariat ; in which misery is engendered in as great abundance as wealth. The economists now pose as blasé fatalists, who, from their elevated position, cast a proudly disdainful glance at the human locomotives who manufacture wealth. They copy all the developments, given by their predecessors, and the indifference which to the latter was merely naïveté becomes to them coquetry.

Next comes the *humanitarian school*, which takes to heart

the bad side of present-day production-relations. It seeks, by way of easing its conscience, to palliate to a certain extent the real contrasts ; it sincerely deplores the distress of the proletariat, the unbridled competition of the bourgeois among themselves ; it counsels the workers to be sober, to work hard and to have few children ; it advises the bourgeois to put a reasoned ardour into production. The whole theory of this school rests on interminable distinctions between theory and practice, between principles and results, between idea and application, between form and content, between essence and reality, between right and fact, between the good side and the bad side.

The *philanthropic* school is the humanitarian school carried to perfection. It denies the necessity of antagonism ; it wants to turn all men into bourgeois ; it wants to realise theory in so far as it is distinguished from practice and contains no antagonism. It goes without saying that, in theory, it is easy to make an abstraction of the contradictions that are met with at every moment in actual reality. This theory would therefore become idealised reality. The philanthropists, then, want to retain the categories which express bourgeois relations, without the antagonism which constitutes them and is inseparable from them. They think they are seriously fighting bourgeois practice, and they are more bourgeois than the others.

Just as the *economists* are the scientific representatives of the bourgeois class, so the *Socialists* and the *Communists* are the theoreticians of the proletarian class. So long as the proletariat is not yet sufficiently developed to constitute a class, and consequently so long as the struggle itself of the proletariat with the bourgeoisie has not assumed a political character, and the productive forces are not yet sufficiently developed in the bosom of the bourgeoisie itself to enable us to catch a glimpse of the material conditions necessary for the emancipation of the proletariat and for the formation of a new society, these theoreticians are merely Utopians who, to meet the wants of the oppressed classes,

improvise systems and go in search of a regenerating science.
But in the measure that history moves forward and with it
the struggle of the proletariat assumes clearer outlines,
they no longer need to seek science in their minds ; they
have only to take note of what is happening before their
eyes and to become the mouthpiece of this. So long as they
look for science and merely make systems, so long as they
are at the beginning of the struggle, they see in misery
nothing but misery, without seeing in it the revolutionary,
subversive side, which will overthrow the old society.
From this moment, science, produced by the historical
movement and associating itself with it in full recognition
of its cause, has ceased to be doctrinaire and has become
revolutionary. . . .

Karl Marx

A CONTRIBUTION TO
THE CRITIQUE OF POLITICAL
ECONOMY

*First published in 1859. English edition, Chas. H. Kerr & Co.,
Chicago, 1904.*

[This work, which is an analysis of Commodities and
Money, was originally intended by Marx as the first part
of a much longer work which was to cover : " Capital,
landed property, wage labour, State, foreign trade, world
market." This idea, however, later took shape in *Capital,*
which is not a continuation of *The Critique of Political Economy,* but a complete work, the early chapters of which
summarise the analysis made in *The Critique* of Commodities

and Money. In particular, however, the treatment of Money in *The Critique* is much more detailed than the corresponding treatment in Vol. I of *Capital*. The unique feature of *The Critique* is the author's preface, in which Marx explains how he and Engels developed their theories, and summarises the conclusions which inspired their work. The main part of this preface is given below. It has been retranslated, as the Kerr translation is not altogether satisfactory.]

A CONTRIBUTION TO THE CRITIQUE OF POLITICAL ECONOMY

AUTHOR'S PREFACE

. . . My investigations led to the conclusion that legal relations as well as forms of State could not be understood from themselves, nor from the so-called general development of the human mind, but, on the contrary, are rooted in the material conditions of life, the aggregate of which Hegel, following the precedent of the English and French of the eighteenth century, grouped under the name of " civil society "; but that the anatomy of civil society is to be found in political economy. My study of the latter, begun in Paris, was continued in Brussels, whither I migrated in consequence of an expulsion order issued by M. Guizot. The general conclusion I arrived at—and once reached, it served as the guiding thread in my studies—can be briefly formulated as follows : In the social production of their means of existence men enter into definite, necessary relations which are independent of their will, productive relationships which correspond to a definite stage of development of their material productive forces. The aggregate of these productive relationships constitutes the economic structure of society, the real basis on which a juridical and political superstructure arises, and to which definite forms of social consciousness correspond. The mode of production of the material means of existence conditions the whole process of social, political and intellectual life. It is not the consciousness of men that determines their existence, but, on the contrary, it is their social existence that determines their consciousness. At a certain stage of their development the material productive forces of society come into contradiction with the existing productive relationships, or, what is but a legal expression for these, with the property relationships within which they had moved before. From forms of development of the productive forces these relationships are transformed into their fetters. Then an epoch of social revolution opens. With the change in the economic foundation the whole vast superstructure is more or less rapidly transformed. In considering such revolutions it is necessary always to distinguish between the material revolution in the economic conditions of production, which can be determined with scientific accuracy, and the juridical, political, religious, æsthetic or philosophic—in a word, ideological forms wherein men become conscious of this conflict and fight it out. Just as we cannot judge an individual on the basis of his own opinion of himself, so such a revolutionary epoch cannot be judged from its own consciousness ; but on the contrary this consciousness must be explained from the contradictions of material life, from the existing conflict between social productive forces and productive relationships. A social system never perishes before all the productive forces have developed for which it is wide enough ; and new, higher productive relationships never come into being before the material conditions for their existence have been brought to maturity within the womb of the old society itself. Therefore, mankind always sets itself only such problems as it can solve ; for when we look closer we will always find that the problem itself only arises when the material conditions for its solution are already present or at

THE CRITIQUE OF POLITICAL ECONOMY 269

least in process of coming into being. In broad outline, the Asiatic, the ancient, the feudal and the modern bourgeois modes of production can be indicated as progressive epochs in the economic system of society. Bourgeois productive relationships are the last antagonistic form of the social process of production—antagonistic in the sense not of individual antagonism, but of an antagonism arising out of the conditions of the social life of individuals ; but the productive forces developing within the womb of bourgeois society at the same time create the material conditions for the solution of this antagonism. With this social system, therefore, the pre-history of human society comes to a close. . . .

Karl Marx

CAPITAL

This work is in three volumes : I. " Capitalist Production " ; II. " Capitalist Circulation " ; III. " Capitalist Production as a Whole." The separate volumes were first published (in German) in 1867, 1885 and 1894—the second and third being completed by Engels after Marx's death in 1883. An English translation of Vol. I was first published in 1886 by Swan Sonnenschein & Co. ; the only complete English translation of the three volumes is published by Charles H. Kerr & Co., Chicago.

[*Capital* was the completion of the detailed analysis of capitalism which Marx had already begun in his earlier works, especially *The Critique of Political Economy* (1859). At that time, as to-day, most writers on political economy regarded the existing system of production—capitalism— as the absolutely final and unalterable form of social production. Marx, starting from the standpoint of dialectical materialism, saw the historical succession of systems of production—primitive communism, the slave system, feudalism, capitalism—and capitalism itself as a passing historical phase, to be succeeded by socialism. His economic work was therefore directed towards discovering and stating the economic laws which brought capitalism into existence, controlled its development, and eventually produced contradictions insoluble within capitalism ; as he wrote in the preface to Vol. I : " It is the ultimate aim of this work to lay bare the economic law of motion of modern society."

It is an enormous work : the three volumes in the Kerr edition make almost 2,500 pages. (Additional material, originally intended by Marx to complete *Capital*, was edited by Karl Kautsky after Engels's death, and published in German in a further three volumes under the title of *Theories of Surplus Value*. These have not yet been translated into English.)

As a whole, *Capital* is not light reading ; no fundamental study of economics could be. But the legend that it is dull and pompously long-winded is carefully cultivated by those whose antagonism to the style is a result of their antagonism to Marx's conclusions. It is characteristic of this outlook that most economics students in British universities have no first-hand knowledge of Marx ; they meet him only in refutations which inevitably distort Marx's theories.

The historical sections of *Capital* are in fact extremely interesting and vivid ; Marx himself suggested that these should be read first by the general reader. Other sections are of compelling interest because of their clear analysis and almost prophetical conclusions, which history is to-day confirming in more and more obvious ways. And if the abstract theory and arithmetical illustrations require great concentration, this is equally true of any scientific work.

The selection of passages from *Capital* is extraordinarily difficult, owing to the careful development of the main theme and the logical dependence of successive chapters, apart from the wide range of the work as a whole. It has been necessary to concentrate on a few of the key points for the understanding of Marx's economic theory : the general historical analysis, which comes at the end of Vol. I, is given first, and this is followed by the economic analysis, from the study of value and surplus value to the accumulation of surplus value as capital and the falling tendency of the rate of profit, with the resultant difficulties for capitalism.

It has not been possible to include even portions of many other sections which are perhaps of equal importance—in particular, the whole theory of Capitalist Circulation, dealt with in Vol. II, and the study of ground rent. But the passages given below cover the most fundamental points—those which are most hotly contested by the opponents of Marxism.

The chapter references given show the chapter in the Kerr edition from which the passages are taken ; they do not mean that the whole chapter is given, as in many cases illustrations and elaborations of particular points have had to be omitted.]

CAPITAL

THE SECRET OF PRIMITIVE ACCUMULATION
(Vol. I, Ch. XXVI)

WE HAVE SEEN how money is changed into capital ; how through capital surplus-value is made, and from surplus-value more capital. But the accumulation of capital presupposes surplus-value ; surplus-value presupposes capitalistic production ; capitalistic production presupposes the pre-existence of considerable masses of capital and of labour-power in the hands of producers of commodities. The whole movement, therefore, seems to turn in a vicious circle, out of which we can only get by supposing a primitive accumulation (previous accumulation of Adam Smith) preceding capitalistic accumulation ; an accumulation not the result of the capitalist mode of production, but its starting point.

This primitive accumulation plays in Political Economy about the same part as original sin in theology. Adam bit the apple, and thereupon sin fell on the human race. Its origin is supposed to be explained when it is told as an anecdote of the past. In times long gone by there were two sorts of people ; one, the diligent, intelligent, and, above all, frugal élite ; the other, lazy rascals, spending their substance, and more, in riotous living. The legend of theological original sin tells us certainly how man came to be condemned to eat his bread in the sweat of his brow ; but the history of economic original sin reveals to us that there are people to whom this is by no means essential. Never mind ! Thus it came to pass that the former sort accumulated wealth, and the latter sort had at last nothing to sell except their own skins. And from this original sin dates the poverty' of the great majority that, despite all its labour, has up to now nothing to sell but itself, and the wealth of the few that increases constantly although they have long ceased to work. Such insipid childishness is every day preached to us in the defence of property. M. Thiers, e.g., had the assurance to repeat it with all the solemnity of a statesman, to the French people, once so *spirituel*. But as soon as the question of property crops up, it becomes a sacred duty to proclaim the intellectual food of the infant as the one thing fit for all ages and for all stages of development. In actual history it is notorious that conquest, enslavement, robbery, murder, briefly force, play the great part. In the tender annals of Political Economy, the idyllic reigns from time immemorial. Right and " labour " were from all time the sole means of enrichment, the present year of course always excepted. As a matter of fact, the methods of primitive accumulation are anything but idyllic.

In themselves, money and commodities are no more capital than are the means of production and of subsistence. They want transforming into capital. But this transformation itself can only take place under certain circumstances that centre in this, viz., that two very different kinds of

commodity-possessors must come face to face and into contact ; on the one hand, the owners of money, means of
production, means of subsistence, who are eager to increase
the sum of values they possess, by buying other people's
labour-power ; on the other hand, free labourers, the sellers
of their own labour-power, and therefore the sellers of
labour. Free labourers, in the double sense that neither they
themselves form part and parcel of the means of production,
as in the case of slaves, bondsmen, &c., nor do the means
of production belong to them, as in the case of peasant-
proprietors ; they are, therefore, free from, unencumbered
by any means of production of their own. With this polarisa-
tion of the market for commodities, the fundamental conditions of capitalist production are given. The capitalist system presupposes the complete separation of the labourers
from all property in the means by which they can realise
their labour. As soon as capitalist production is once on its
own legs, it not only maintains this separation, but reproduces it on a continually extending scale. The process,
therefore, that clears the way for the capitalist system, can
be none other than the process which takes away from the
labourer the possession of his means of production ; a process that transforms, on the one hand, the social means of
subsistence and of production into capital, on the other, the
immediate producers into wage-labourers. The so-called
primitive accumulation, therefore, is nothing else than the
historical process of divorcing the producer from the means
of production. It appears as primitive, because it forms the
pre-historic stage of capital and of the mode of production
corresponding with it.

The economic structure of capitalistic society has grown
out of the economic structure of feudal society. The dissolution of the latter set free the elements of the former.

The immediate producer, the labourer, could only dispose of his own person after he had ceased to be attached
to the soil and ceased to be the slave, serf, or bondsman of
another. To become a free seller of labour-power, who

carries his commodity wherever he finds a market, he must
further have escaped from the régime of the guilds, their
rules for apprentices and journeymen, and the impediments
of their labour regulations. Hence, the historical movement
which changes the producers into wage-workers, appears,
on the one hand, as their emancipation from serfdom and
from the fetters of the guilds, and this side alone exists for
our bourgeois historians. But, on the other hand, these new
freedmen became sellers of themselves only after they had
been robbed of all their own means of production, and of
all the guarantees of existence afforded by the old feudal
arrangements. And the history of this, their expropriation,
is written in the annals of mankind in letters of blood and
fire.

The industrial capitalists, these new potentates, had on
their part not only to displace the guild masters of handicrafts, but also the feudal lords, the possessors of the sources
of wealth. In this respect their conquest of social power
appears as the fruit of a victorious struggle both against
feudal lordship and its revolting prerogatives, and against
the guilds and the fetters they laid on the free development
of production and the free exploitation of man by man.
The chevaliers d'industrie, however, only succeed in sup-
planting the chevaliers of the sword by making use of events
of which they themselves were wholly innocent. They have
risen by means as vile as those by which the Roman freed-
man once on a time made himself the master of his *patronus*.

The starting-point of the development that gave rise to
the wage-labourer as well as to the capitalist, was the servitude of the labourer. The advance consisted in a change of
form of this servitude, in the transformation of feudal exploitation into capitalist exploitation. To understand its
march, we need not go back very far. Although we come
across the first beginnings of capitalist production as early
as the fourteenth or fifteenth century, sporadically, in
certain towns of the Mediterranean, the capitalistic era
dates from the sixteenth century. Wherever it appears, the

The servitude of the worker. (*Capital*, "Primitive Accumulation")
Lithograph by Hugo Gellert.

abolition of serfdom has been long effected, and the highest development of the middle ages, the existence of sovereign towns, has been long on the wane.

In the history of primitive accumulation, all revolutions are epoch-making that act as levers for the capitalist class in course of formation ; but, above all, those moments when great masses of men are suddenly and forcibly torn from their means of subsistence, and hurled as free and " unattached " proletarians on the labour market. The expropriation of the agricultural producer, of the peasant, from the soil, is the basis of the whole process. The history of this expropriation, in different countries, assumes different aspects, and runs through its various phases in different orders of succession, and at different periods. In England alone, which we take as our example, has it the classic form.

EXPROPRIATION OF THE AGRICULTURAL POPULATION FROM THE LAND
(Vol. I, Ch. XXVII)

In England, serfdom had practically disappeared in the last part of the fourteenth century. The immense majority of the population consisted then, and to a still larger extent in the fifteenth century, of free peasant proprietors, whatever was the feudal title under which their right of property was hidden. In the larger seignorial domains, the old bailiff, himself a serf, was displaced by the free farmer. The wage-labourers of agriculture consisted partly of peasants, who utilised their leisure time by working on the large estates, partly of an independent special class of wage-labourers, relatively and absolutely few in numbers. The latter also were practically at the same time peasant farmers, since, besides their wages, they had allotted to them arable land to the extent of four or more acres, together with their cottages. Besides they, with the rest of the peasants, enjoyed the usufruct of the common land, which gave pasture to their cattle, furnished them with timber, fire-wood, turf, etc. In all countries of Europe, feudal production is characterised by division of the soil amongst the greatest possible number of sub-feudatories. The might of the feudal lord, like that of the sovereign, depended not on the length of his rent roll, but on the number of his subjects, and the latter depended on the number of peasant proprietors. Although, therefore, the English land, after the Norman conquest, was distributed in gigantic baronies, one of which often included some 900 of the old Anglo-Saxon lordships, it was bestrewn with small peasant properties, only here and there interspersed with great seignorial domains. Such conditions, together with the prosperity of the towns so characteristic of the fifteenth century, allowed of that wealth of the people which Chancellor Fortescue so eloquently paints in his " Laudes legum Angliæ " ; but it excluded the possibility of capitalistic wealth.

The prelude of the revolution that laid the foundation of the capitalist mode of production was played in the last third of the fifteenth, and the first decade of the sixteenth century. A mass of free proletarians was hurled on the labour-market by the breaking-up of the bands of feudal retainers, who, as Sir James Steuart well says, " everywhere uselessly filled house and castle." Although the royal power, itself a product of bourgeois development, in its strife after absolute sovereignty forcibly hastened on the dissolution of these bands of retainers, it was by no means the sole cause of it. In insolent conflict with king and parliament, the great feudal lords created an incomparably larger proletariat by the forcible driving of the peasantry from the land, to which the latter had the same feudal right as the lord himself, and by the usurpation of the common lands. The rapid rise of the Flemish wool manufactures, and the corresponding rise in the price of wool in England, gave the direct impulse to these evictions. The old nobility had been devoured by the great feudal wars. The new nobility was the child of its time, for which money was the power of all powers. Transformation of arable land into sheep-walks was, therefore, its cry. . . .

The process of forcible expropriation of the people received in the sixteenth century a new and frightful impulse from the Reformation, and from the consequent colossal spoliation of the church property. The Catholic church was, at the time of the Reformation, feudal proprietor of a great part of the English land. The suppression of the monasteries, etc., hurled their inmates into the proletariat. The estates of the church were to a large extent given away to rapacious royal favourites, or sold at a nominal price to speculating farmers and citizens, who drove out, *en masse*, the hereditary sub-tenants and threw their holdings into one. The legally guaranteed property of the poorer folk in a part of the church's tithes was tacitly confiscated. " Pauper ubique jacet," cried Queen Elizabeth, after a journey through England. In the 43rd year of her reign the nation was obliged to recognise pauperism officially by the introduction of a poor-rate. " The authors of this law seem to have been ashamed to state the grounds of it, for [contrary to traditional usage] it has no preamble whatever." By the 16th of Charles I., ch. 4, it was declared perpetual, and in fact only in 1834 did it take a new and harsher form. These immediate results of the Reformation were not its most lasting ones. The property of the church formed the religious bulwark of the traditional conditions of landed property. With its fall these were no longer tenable.

Even in the last decade of the seventeenth century, the yeomanry, the class of independent peasants, were more numerous than the class of farmers. They had formed the backbone of Cromwell's strength, and, even according to the confession of Macaulay, stood in favourable contrast to the drunken squires and to their servants, the country clergy, who had to marry their master's cast-off mistresses. About 1750, the yeomanry had disappeared, and so had, in the last decade of the eighteenth century, the last trace of the common land of the agricultural labourer. We leave on one side here the purely economic causes of the agricultural revolution. We deal only with the forcible means employed.

After the restoration of the Stuarts, the landed proprietors carried, by legal means, an act of usurpation, effected everywhere on the Continent without any legal formality. They abolished the feudal tenure of land, i.e., they got rid of all its obligations to the State, " indemnified " the State by taxes on the peasantry and the rest of the mass of the people, vindicated for themselves the rights of modern private property in estates to which they had only a feudal title, and, finally, passed those laws of settlement, which, *mutatis mutandis*, had the same effect on the English agricultural labourer, as the edict of the Tartar Boris Godunof on the Russian peasantry.

The " glorious Revolution " brought into power, along with William of Orange, the landlord and capitalist appropriators of surplus-value. They inaugurated the new era by practising on a colossal scale thefts of State lands, thefts that had been hitherto managed more modestly. These estates were given away, sold at a ridiculous figure, or even annexed to private estates by direct seizure. All this happened without the slightest observation of legal etiquette. The crown lands thus fraudulently appropriated, together with the robbery of the Church estates, as far as these had not been lost again during the republican revolution, form the basis of the to-day princely domains of the English oligarchy. The bourgeois capitalists favoured the operation with the view, among others, to promoting free trade in land, to extending the domain of modern agriculture on the large farm-system, and to increasing their supply of the free agricultural proletarians ready to hand. Besides, the new landed aristocracy was the natural ally of the new bankocracy, of the newly-hatched *haute finance*, and of the large manufacturers, then depending on protective duties. The English bourgeoisie acted for its own interest quite as wisely as did the Swedish bourgeoisie who, reversing the process, hand in hand with their economic allies, the

peasantry, helped the kings in the forcible resumption of
the Crown lands from the oligarchy. This happened since
1604 under Charles X. and Charles XI.

Communal property—always distinct from the State property just dealt with—was an old Teutonic institution which
lived on under cover of feudalism. We have seen how the
forcible usurpation of this, generally accompanied by the
turning of arable into pasture land, begins at the end of the
fifteenth and extends into the sixteenth century. But, at
that time, the process was carried on by means of individual acts of violence against which legislation, for a hundred and fifty years, fought in vain. The advance made by
the eighteenth century shows itself in this, that the law itself becomes now the instrument of the theft of the people's
land, although the large farmers make use of their little independent methods as well. The parliamentary form of the
robbery is that of Acts for enclosures of Commons, in other
words, decrees by which the landlords grant themselves the
people's land as private property, decrees of expropriation
of the people. Sir F. M. Eden refutes his own crafty special
pleading, in which he tries to represent communal property
as the private property of the great landlords who have taken
the place of the feudal lords, when he, himself, demands
a " general Act of Parliament for the enclosure of Commons " (admitting thereby that a parliamentary *coup d'état*
is necessary for its transformation into private property),
and moreover calls on the legislature for the indemnifica-
tion for the expropriated poor.

Whilst the place of the independent yeoman was taken
by tenants at will, small farmers on yearly leases, a servile
rabble dependent on the pleasure of the landlords, the
systematic robbery of the Communal lands helped especially, next to the theft of the State domains, to swell those
large farms, that were called in the eighteenth century
capital farms or merchant farms, and to "set free" the agricultural populations as proletarians for manufacturing
industry.

The eighteenth century, however, did not yet recognise as fully as the nineteenth the identity between national wealth and the poverty of the people. Hence the most vigorous polemic, in the economic literature of that time, on the " enclosure of commons." . . .

In the nineteenth century, the very memory of the connexion between the agricultural labourer and the communal property had, of course, vanished. To say nothing of more recent times, have the agricultural population received a farthing of compensation for the 3,511,770 acres of common land which between 1801 and 1831 were stolen from them and by parliamentary devices presented to the landlords by the landlords ?

The last process of wholesale expropriation of the agricultural population from the soil is, finally, the so-called clearing of estates, i.e., the sweeping men off them. All the English methods hitherto considered culminated in " clearing." As we saw in the picture of modern conditions given in a former chapter, where there are no more independent peasants to get rid of, the " clearing " of cottages begins ; so that the agricultural labourers do not find on the soil cultivated by them even the spot necessary for their own housing. But what " clearing of estates " really and properly signifies, we learn only in the promised land of modern romance, the Highlands of Scotland. There the process is distinguished by its systematic character, by the magnitude of the scale on which it is carried out at one blow (in Ireland landlords have gone to the length of sweeping away several villages at once ; in Scotland areas as large as German principalities are dealt with), finally by the peculiar form of property, under which the embezzled lands were held. . . .

The spoliation of the church's property, the fraudulent alienation of the State domains, the robbery of the common lands, the usurpation of feudal and clan property, and its transformation into modern private property under circumstances of reckless terrorism, were just so many idyllic methods of primitive accumulation. They conquered the field for capitalistic agriculture, made the soil part and parcel of capital, and created for the town industries the necessary supply of a " free " and outlawed proletariat.

GENESIS OF THE CAPITALIST FARMER
(Vol. I, Ch. XXIX)

Now that we have considered the forcible creation of a class of outlawed proletarians, the bloody discipline that turned them into wage-labourers, the disgraceful action of the State which employed the police to accelerate the accumulation of capital by increasing the degree of exploitation of labour, the question remains : whence came the capitalists originally ? For the expropriation of the agricultural population creates, directly, none by great landed proprietors. As far, however, as concerns the genesis of the farmer, we can, so to say, put our hand on it, because it is a slow process evolving through many centuries. The serfs, as well as the free small proprietors, held land under very different tenures, and were therefore emancipated under very different economic conditions. In England the first form of the farmer is the bailiff, himself a serf. His position is similar to that of the old Roman *villicus*, only in a more limited sphere of action. During the second half of the fourteenth century he is replaced by a farmer, whom the landlord provides with seed, cattle and implements. His condition is not very different from that of the peasant. Only he exploits more wage-labour. Soon he becomes a métayer, a half-farmer. He advances one part of the agricultural stock, the landlord the other. The two divide the total product in proportions determined by contract. This form quickly disappears in England, to give place to the farmer proper, who makes his own capital breed by employing wage-labourers, and pays a part of the surplus product, in money or in kind, to the landlord as rent. So long, during the fifteenth century, as the independent peasant and the farm-labourer working for himself as well as for wages, enriched themselves by their own labour, the circumstances of the farmer, and his field of production, were equally mediocre. The agricultural revolution which commenced in the last third of the fifteenth century, and continued during almost the whole of the sixteenth (excepting, however, its last decade), enriched him just as speedily as it impoverished the mass of the agricultural people.

The usurpation of the common lands allowed him to augment greatly his stock of cattle, almost without cost, whilst they yielded him a richer supply of manure for the tillage of the soil. To this was added in the sixteenth century a very important element. At that time the contracts for farms ran for a long time, often for 99 years. The progressive fall in the value of the precious metals, and therefore of money, brought the farmers golden fruit. Apart from all the other circumstances discussed above, it lowered wages. A portion of the latter was now added to the profits of the farm. The continuous rise in the price of corn, wool, meat, in a word of all agricultural produce, swelled the money capital of the farmer without any action on his part, whilst the rent he paid (being calculated on the old value of money), diminished in reality. Thus they grew rich at the expense both of their labourers and their landlords. No wonder, therefore, that England, at the end of the sixteenth century, had a class of capitalist farmers, rich, considering the circumstances of the time.

REACTION OF THE AGRICULTURAL REVOLUTION ON INDUSTRY : CREATION OF THE HOME MARKET FOR INDUSTRIAL CAPITAL

(Vol. I, Ch. XXX)

The expropriation and expulsion of the agricultural population, intermittent but renewed again and again, supplied, as we saw, the town industries with a mass of proletarians, entirely unconnected with the corporate guilds and unfettered by them ; a fortunate circumstance that makes old A. Anderson (not to be confounded with James Anderson) in his *History of Commerce*, believe in the direct intervention of Providence. We must still pause a moment on this element of primitive accumulation. The thinning-out of the independent, self-supporting peasants not only brought about the crowding together of the industrial proletariat, in the way that Geoffroy Saint Hilaire explained the condensation of cosmical matter at one place, by its rarefaction at another. In spite of the smaller numbers of its cultivators, the soil brought forth as much or more produce, after as before, because the revolution in the conditions of landed property was accompanied by improved methods of culture, greater co-operation, concentration of the means of production, etc., and because not only were the agricultural wage-labourers put on the strain more intensely, but the field of production on which they worked for themselves became more and more contracted. With the setting free of a part of the agricultural population, therefore, their former means of nourishment were also set free. They were now transformed into material elements of variable capital. The peasant, expropriated and cast adrift, must buy their value in the form of wages, from his new master, the industrial capitalist. That which holds good of the means of subsistence holds with the raw materials of industry dependent upon home agriculture. They were transformed into an element of constant capital. Suppose, e.g., a part of the Westphalian peasants, who, at the time of Frederic II, all spun flax, forcibly expropriated and hunted from the soil ; and the other part that remained, turned into day-labourers of large farmers. At the same time arise large establishments for flax-spinning and weaving, in which the men " set free " now work for wages. The flax looks exactly as before. Not a fibre of it is changed, but a new social soul has popped into its body. It forms now a part of the constant capital of the master manufacturer. Formerly divided among a number of small producers, who cultivated it themselves and with their families spun it in retail fashion,

it is now concentrated in the hand of one capitalist, who
sets others to spin and weave it for him. The extra labour
expended in flax-spinning realised itself formerly in extra
income to numerous peasant families, or maybe, in Frederic
II's time, in taxes *pour le roi de Prusse*. It realises itself
now in profit for a few capitalists. The spindles and looms,
formerly scattered over the face of the country, are now
crowded together in a few great labour-barracks, together
with the labourers and the raw material. And spindles,
looms, raw material, are now transformed, from means of
independent existence for the spinners and weavers, into
means for commanding them and sucking out of them unpaid labour. One does not perceive, when looking at the
large manufactories and the large farms, that they have
originated from the throwing into one of many small centres
of production, and have been built up by the expropriation
of many small independent producers. Nevertheless, the
popular intuition was not at fault. In the time of Mirabeau,
the lion of the Revolution, the great manufactories were
still called manufactures réunies, workshops thrown into
one, as we speak of fields thrown into one. . . .

The expropriation and eviction of a part of the agricultural population not only set free for industrial capital
the labourers, their means of subsistence, and material for
labour ; it also created the home market.

In fact, the events that transformed the small peasants
into wage-labourers, and their means of subsistence and of
labour into material elements of capital, created, at the
same time, a home-market for the latter. Formerly, the
peasant family produced the means of subsistence and the
raw materials, which they themselves, for the most part,
consumed. These raw materials and means of subsistence
have now become commodities ; the large farmer sells
them, he finds his market in manufactures. Yarn, linen,
coarse woollen stuffs—things whose raw materials had been
within the reach of every peasant family, had been spun
and woven by it for its own use—were now transformed

into articles of manufacture, to which the country districts
at once served for markets. The many scattered customers,
whom stray artisans until now had found in the numerous
small producers working on their own account, concentrate
themselves now into one great market provided for by industrial capital. Thus, hand in hand with the expropriation
of the self-supporting peasants, with their separation from
their means of production, goes the destruction of rural
domestic industry, the process of separation between manufacture and agriculture. And only the destruction of rural
domestic industry can give the internal market of a country
that extension and consistence which the capitalist mode of
production requires. Still the manufacturing period, properly so-called, does not succeed in carrying out this transformation radically and completely. It will be remembered
that manufacture, properly so-called, conquers but partially
the domain of national production, and always rests on the
handicrafts of the town and the domestic industry of the
rural districts as its ultimate basis. If it destroys these in
one form, in particular branches, at certain points, it calls
them up again elsewhere, because it needs them for the
preparation of raw material up to a certain point. It produces, therefore, a new class of small villagers who, while
following the cultivation of the soil as an accessory calling,
find their chief occupation in industrial labour, the products of which they sell to the manufacturers directly, or
through the medium of merchants. This is one, though not
the chief, cause of a phenomenon which, at first, puzzles
the student of English history. From the last third of the
fifteenth century he finds continually complaints, only
interrupted at certain intervals, about the encroachment
of capitalist farming in the country districts, and the progressive destruction of the peasantry. On the other hand,
he always finds this peasantry turning up again, although
in diminished number, and always under worse conditions.
The chief reason is : England is at one time chiefly a culti-
vator of corn, at another chiefly a breeder of cattle, in

alternate periods, and with these the extent of peasant cultivation fluctuates. Modern Industry alone, and finally, supplies, in machinery, the lasting basis of capitalistic agriculture, expropriates radically the enormous majority of the agricultural population, and completes the separation between agriculture and rural domestic industry, whose roots —spinning and weaving—it tears up. It therefore also, for the first time, conquers for industrial capital the entire home market.

GENESIS OF THE INDUSTRIAL CAPITALIST
(Vol. I, Ch. XXXI)

The genesis of the industrial capitalist did not proceed in such a gradual way as that of the farmer. Doubtless many small guild-masters, and yet more independent small artisans, or even wage-labourers, transformed themselves into small capitalists, and (by gradually extending exploitation of wage-labour and corresponding accumulation) into full-blown capitalists. In the infancy of capitalist production, things often happened as in the infancy of mediæval towns, where the question, which of the escaped serfs should be master and which servant, was in great part decided by the earlier or later date of their flight. The snail's-pace of this method corresponded in no wise with the commercial requirements of the new world-market that the great discoveries of the end of the fifteenth century created. But the middle age had handed down two distinct forms of capital, which mature in the most different economic social formations, and which, before the era of the capitalist mode of production, are considered as capital *quand même*— usurer's capital and merchant's capital. . . .

The money capital formed by means of usury and commerce was prevented from turning into industrial capital, in the country by the feudal constitution, in the towns by the guild organisation. These fetters vanished with the dissolution of feudal society, with the expropriation and partial eviction of the country population. The new manufacturers

were established at sea-ports, or in inland points beyond
the control of the old municipalities and their guilds. Hence
in England an embittered struggle of the corporate towns
against these new industrial nurseries.

The discovery of gold and silver in America, the extirpa-
tion, enslavement and entombment in mines of the aboriginal
population, the beginning of the conquest and looting of the
East Indies, the turning of Africa into a warren for the commercial hunting of black-skins, signalised the rosy dawn of
the era of capitalist production. These idyllic proceedings
are the chief momenta of primitive accumulation. On their
heels treads the commercial war of the European nations,
with the globe for a theatre. It begins with the revolt of
the Netherlands from Spain, assumes giant dimensions in
England's anti-jacobin war, and is still going on in the
opium wars against China, etc.

The different momenta of primitive accumulation dis-
tribute themselves now, more or less in chronological order,
particularly over Spain, Portugal, Holland, France, and
England. In England at the end of the seventeenth century,
they arrive at a systematical combination, embracing the
colonies, the national debt, the modern mode of taxation,
and the protectionist system. These methods depend in part
on brute force, e.g., the colonial system. But they all employ the power of the State, the concentrated and organised
force of society, to hasten, hothouse fashion, the process of
transformation of the feudal mode of production into the
capitalist mode, and to shorten the transition. Force is the
midwife of every old society pregnant with a new one. It
is itself an economic power.

Of the Christian colonial system, W. Howitt, a man who
makes a specialty of Christianity, says : " The barbarities
and desperate outrages of the so-called Christian race,
throughout every region of the world, and upon every
people they have been able to subdue, are not to be paral-
leled by those of any other race, however fierce, however
untaught, and however reckless of mercy and of shame, in

any age of the earth." The history of the colonial administration of Holland—and Holland was the head capitalistic nation of the seventeenth century—" is one of the most extraordinary relations of treachery, bribery, massacre, and meanness." Nothing is more characteristic than their system of stealing men, to get slaves for Java. The men stealers were trained for this purpose. The thief, the interpreter, and the seller, were the chief agents in this trade, native princes the chief sellers. The young people stolen were thrown into the secret dungeons of Celebes, until they were ready for sending to the slave-ships. An official report says : " This one town of Macassar, e.g., is full of secret prisons, one more horrible than the other, crammed with unfortunates, victims of greed and tyranny fettered in chains, forcibly torn from their families." To secure Malacca, the Dutch corrupted the Portuguese governor. He let them into the town in 1641. They hurried at once to his house and assassinated him, to " abstain " from the payment of £21,875, the price of his treason. Wherever they set foot, devastation and depopulation followed. Banjuwangi, a province of Java in 1750 numbered over 80,000 inhabitants, in 1811 only 18,000. Sweet commerce !

The English East India Company, as is well known, obtained, besides the political rule in India, the exclusive monopoly of the tea-trade, as well as of the Chinese trade in general and of the transport of goods to and from Europe. But the coasting trade of India and between the islands, as well as the internal trade of India, were the monopoly of the higher employés of the company. The monopolies of salt, opium, betel and other commodities, were inexhaustible mines of wealth. The employés themselves fixed the price and plundered at will the unhappy Hindus. The Governor-General took part in this private traffic. His favourites received contracts under conditions whereby they, cleverer than the alchemists, made gold out of nothing. Great fortunes sprang up like mushrooms in a day ; primitive accumulation went on without the advance of a shilling. The trial of Warren Hastings swarms with such cases. Here is an instance. A contract for opium was given to a certain Sullivan at the moment of his departure on an official mission to a part of India far removed from the opium district. Sullivan sold his contract to one Binn for £40,000 ; Binn sold it the same day for £60,000, and the ultimate purchaser who carried out the contract declared that after all he realised an enormous gain. According to one of the lists laid before Parliament, the Company and its employés from 1757–66 got £6,000,000 from the Indians as gifts. Between 1769 and 1770, the English manufactured a famine by buying up all the rice and refusing to sell it again, except at fabulous prices.[1]

The treatment of the aborigines was, naturally, most frightful in plantation-colonies destined for export trade only, such as the West Indies, and in rich and well-populated countries, such as Mexico and India, that were given over to plunder. But even in the colonies properly so-called, the Christian character of primitive accumulation did not belie itself. Those sober virtuosi of Protestantism, the Puritans of New England, in 1703, by decrees of their assembly, set a premium of £40 on every Indian scalp and every captured red-skin : in 1720 a premium of £100 on every scalp ; in 1744, after Massachusetts Bay had proclaimed a certain tribe as rebels, the following prices : for a male scalp of 12 years and upwards £100 (new currency), for a male prisoner £105, for women and children prisoners £50, for scalps of women and children £50. Some decades later, the colonial system took its revenge on the descendants of the pious pilgrim fathers, who had grown seditious in the meantime. At English instigation and for English pay they were tomahawked by red-skins. The British Parliament, proclaimed blood-hounds and scalping as " means that God and Nature had given into its hand."

[1] In the year 1866 more than a million Hindus died of hunger in the province of Orissa alone. Nevertheless, the attempt was made to enrich the Indian treasury by the price at which the necessaries of life were sold to the starving people.

The colonial system ripened, like a hot-house, trade and
navigation. The "societies Monopolia" of Luther were
powerful levers for concentration of capital. The colonies
secured a market for the budding manufactures, and,
through the monopoly of the market, an increased accumulation. The treasures captured outside Europe by undisguised looting, enslavement, and murder, floated back
to the mother-country and were there turned into capital.
Holland, which first fully developed the colonial system,
in 1648 stood already in the acme of its commercial greatness. It was "in almost exclusive possession of the East
Indian trade and the commerce between the south-east and
north-west of Europe. Its fisheries, marine, manufactures,
surpassed those of any other country. The total capital of
the Republic was probably more important than that of
all the rest of Europe put together." Gülich forgets to add
that by 1648, the people of Holland were more overworked,
poorer and more brutally oppressed than those of all the
rest of Europe put together.

To-day industrial supremacy implies commercial supremacy. In the period of manufacture properly so-called,
it is, on the other hand, the commercial supremacy that
gives industrial predominance. Hence the preponderant
rôle that the colonial system plays at that time. It was " the
strange God " who perched himself on the altar cheek by
jowl with the old Gods of Europe, and one fine day with
a shove and a kick chucked them all of a heap. It proclaimed
surplus-value making as the sole end and aim of humanity.

The system of public credit, i.e., of national debts, whose
origin we discover in Genoa and Venice as early as the
middle ages, took possession of Europe generally during the
manufacturing period. The colonial system with its mari-
time trade and commercial wars served as a forcing-house
for it. Thus it first took root in Holland. National debts,
i.e., the alienation of the State—whether despotic, constitutional or republican—marked with its stamp the capitalistic
era. The only part of the so-called national wealth that

actually enters into the collective possessions of modern peoples is—their national debt.[1] Hence, as a necessary consequence, the modern doctrine that a nation becomes the richer the more deeply it is in debt. Public credit becomes the *credo* of capital. And with the rise of national debt-making, want of faith in the national debt takes the place of the blasphemy against the Holy Ghost, which may not be forgiven.

The public debt becomes one of the most powerful levers of primitive accumulation. As with the stroke of an enchanter's wand, it endows barren money with the power of breeding and thus turns it into capital, without the necessity of its exposing itself to the troubles and risks inseparable from its employment in industry or even in usury. The State-creditors actually give nothing away, for the sum lent is transformed into public bonds, easily negotiable, which go on functioning in their hands just as so much hard cash would. But further, apart from the class of lazy annuitants thus created, and from the improvised wealth of the financiers, middlemen between the government and the nation—as also apart from the tax-farmers, merchants, private manufacturers, to whom a good part of every national loan renders the service of a capital fallen from heaven—the national debt has given rise to joint-stock companies, to dealings in negotiable effects of all kinds, and to agiotage, in a word to stock-exchange gambling and the modern bankocracy.

At their birth the great banks, decorated with national titles, were only associations of private speculators, who placed themselves by the side of governments, and, thanks to the privileges they received, were in a position to advance money to the State. Hence the accumulation of the national debt has no more infallible measure than the successive rise in the stock of these banks, whose full development dates

---

[1] William Cobbett remarks that in England all public institutions are designated " royal " ; as compensation for this, however, there is the " national " debt.

from the founding of the Bank of England in 1694. The
Bank of England began with lending its money to the
Government at 8 per cent ; at the same time it was em-
powered by Parliament to coin money out of the same
capital, by lending it again to the public in the form of
bank-notes. It was allowed to use these notes for discounting
bills, making advances on commodities, and for buying the
precious metals. It was not long ere this credit-money,
made by the bank itself, became the coin in which the
Bank of England made its loans to the State, and paid, on
account of the State, the interest on the public debt. It was
not enough that the bank gave with one hand and took
back more with the other ; it remained, even whilst receiving, the eternal creditor of the nation down to the last
shilling advanced. Gradually it became inevitably the
receptacle of the metallic hoard of the country, and the
centre of gravity of all commercial credit. What effect was
produced on their contemporaries by the sudden uprising
of this brood of bankocrats, financiers, rentiers, brokers,
stock-jobbers, etc., is proved by the writings of that time,
e.g., by Bolingbroke's.

With the national debt arose an international credit system, which often conceals one of the sources of primitive
accumulation in this or that people. Thus the villainies of
the Venetian thieving system formed one of the secret bases
of the capital-wealth of Holland to whom Venice in her
decadence lent large sums of money. So also was it with
Holland and England. By the beginning of the eighteenth
century the Dutch manufactures were far outstripped. Holland had ceased to be the nation preponderant in commerce
and industry. One of its main lines of business, therefore,
from 1701–76, is the lending out of enormous amounts
of capital, especially to its great rival England. The same
thing is going on to-day between England and the United
States. A great deal of capital, which appears to-day in the
United States without any certificate of birth, was yesterday, in England, the capitalised blood of children.

As the national debt finds its support in the public revenue, which must cover the yearly payments for interest, etc., the modern system of taxation was the necessary complement of the system of national loans. The loans enable the government to meet extraordinary expenses, without the tax-payers feeling it immediately, but they necessitate, as a consequence, increased taxes. On the other hand, the raising of taxation caused by the accumulation of debts contracted one after another, compels the government always to have recourse to new loans for new extraordinary expenses. Modern fiscality, whose pivot is formed by taxes on the most necessary means of subsistence (thereby increasing their price), thus contains within itself the germ of automatic progression. Over-taxation is not an incident, but rather a principle. In Holland, therefore, where this system was first inaugurated, the great patriot, De Witt, has in his *Maxims* extolled it as the best system for making the wage-labourer submissive, frugal, industrious, and overburdened with labour. The destructive influence that it exercises on the condition of the wage-labourer concerns us less, however, here than the forcible expropriation, resulting from it, of peasants, artisans, and, in a word, all elements of the lower middle-class. On this there are not two opinions, even among the bourgeois economists. Its expropriating efficacy is still further heightened by the system of protection, which forms one of its integral parts.

The great part that the public debt, and the fiscal system corresponding with it, has played in the capitalisation of wealth and the expropriation of the masses, has led many writers, like Cobbett, Doubleday and others, to seek in this, incorrectly, the fundamental cause of the misery of the modern peoples.

The system of protection was an artificial means of manufacturing manufacturers, of expropriating independent labourers, of capitalising the national means of production and subsistence, of forcibly abbreviating the transition from the mediæval to the modern mode of production. The European States tore one another to pieces about the patent of this invention, and, once entered into the service of the surplus-value makers, did not merely lay under contribution in the pursuit of this purpose their own people, indirectly through protective duties, directly through export premiums. They also forcibly rooted out, in their dependent countries, all industry, as, e.g., England did with the Irish woollen manufacture. On the continent of Europe, after Colbert's example, the process was much simplified. The primitive industrial capital, here, came in part directly out of the State treasury. " Why," cries Mirabeau, " why go so far to seek the cause of the manufacturing glory of Saxony before the war ? 180,000,000 of debts contracted by the sovereigns ! "

Colonial system, public debts, heavy taxes, protection, commercial wars, etc., these children of the true manufacturing period, increase gigantically during the infancy of Modern Industry. The birth of the latter is heralded by a great slaughter of the innocents. Like the royal navy, the factories were recruited by means of the press-gang. Blasé as Sir F. M. Eden is as to the horrors of the expropriation of the agricultural population from the soil, from the last third of the fifteenth century to his own time ; with all the self-satisfaction with which he rejoices in this process, " essential " for establishing capitalistic agriculture and " the due proportion between arable and pasture land "— he does not show, however, the same economic insight in respect to the necessity of child-stealing and child-slavery for the transformation of manufacturing exploitation into factory exploitation, and the establishment of the " true relation " between capital and labour-power. He says : " It may, perhaps, be worthy the attention of the public to consider, whether any manufacture, which, in order to be carried on successfully, requires that cottages and workhouses should be ransacked for poor children ; that they should be employed by turns during the greater part of

the night and robbed of that rest which, though indispensable to all, is most required by the young ; and that numbers
of both sexes, of different ages and dispositions, should be
collected together in such a manner that the contagion of
example cannot but lead to profligacy and debauchery ;
will add to the sum of individual or national felicity ? "

" In the counties of Derbyshire, Nottinghamshire, and
more particularly in Lancashire," says Fielden, " the
newly-invented machinery was used in large factories built
on the sides of streams capable of turning the water-wheel.
Thousands of hands were suddenly required in these places,
remote from towns ; and Lancashire, in particular, being,
till then, comparatively thinly populated and barren, a
population was all that she now wanted. The small and
nimble fingers of little children being by very far the most
in request, the custom instantly sprang up of procuring
apprentices from the different parish workhouses of London,
Birmingham, and elsewhere. Many, many thousands of
these little, hapless creatures were sent down into the north,
being from the age of 7 to the age of 13 or 14 years.
The custom was for the master to clothe his apprentices
and to feed and lodge them in an " apprentice house "
near the factory ; overseers were appointed to see to the
works, whose interest it was to work the children to the
utmost, because their pay was in proportion to the quantity
of work that they could exact. Cruelty was, of course, the
consequence. . . . In many of the manufacturing districts,
but particularly, I am afraid, in the guilty county to which
I belong [Lancashire], cruelties the most heart-rending
were practised upon the unoffending and friendless creatures who were thus consigned to the charge of master
manufacturers ; they were harassed to the brink of death
by excess of labour . . . were flogged, fettered and tortured
in the most exquisite refinement of cruelty ; . . . they were
in many cases starved to the bone while flogged to their
work and . . . even in some instances . . . were driven to
commit suicide . . . The beautiful and romantic valleys of

Derbyshire, Nottinghamshire and Lancashire, secluded from the public eye, became the dismal solitudes of torture, and of many a murder. The profits of manufactures were enormous ; but this only whetted the appetite that it should have satisfied, and therefore the manufacturers had recourse to an expedient that seemed to secure to them those profits without any possibility of limit ; they began the practice of what is termed ' night-working,' that is, having tired one set of hands, by working them throughout the day, they had another set ready to go on working throughout the night ; the day-set getting into the beds that the night-set had just quitted, and in their turn again, the night-set getting into the beds that the day-set quitted in the morning. It is a common tradition in Lancashire, that the beds *never get cold*."

With the development of capitalist production during the manufacturing period, the public opinion of Europe had lost the last remnant of shame and conscience. The nations bragged cynically of every infamy that served them as a means to capitalistic accumulation. Read, e.g., the naïve Annals of Commerce of the worthy A. Anderson. Here it is trumpeted forth as a triumph of English statecraft that at the Peace of Utrecht, England extorted from the Spaniards by the Asiento Treaty the privilege of being allowed to ply the negro-trade, until then only carried on between Africa and the English West Indies, between Africa and Spanish America as well. England thereby acquired the right of supplying Spanish America until 1743 with 4,800 negroes yearly. This threw, at the same time, an official cloak over British smuggling. Liverpool waxed fat on the slave-trade. This was its method of primitive accumulation. And, even to the present day, Liverpool "respectability " is the Pindar of the slave-trade which—compare the work of Aikin [1795] already quoted—" has coincided with that spirit of bold adventure which has characterised the trade of Liverpool and rapidly carried it to its present state of prosperity ; has occasioned vast employment for shipping and sailors, and greatly augmented the demand for the manufactures of the country " (p. 339). Liverpool employed in the slave-trade, in 1730, 15 ships ; in 1751, 53 ; in 1760, 74 ; in 1770, 96 ; and in 1792, 132.

Whilst the cotton industry introduced child-slavery in England, it gave in the United States a stimulus to the transformation of the earlier, more or less patriarchal slavery, into a system of commercial exploitation. In fact, the veiled slavery of the wage-earners in Europe needed, for its pedestal, slavery pure and simple in the new world·

Tantæ molis erat, to establish the " eternal laws of Nature " of the capitalist mode of production, to complete the process of separation between labourers and conditions of labour, to transform, at one pole, the social means of production and subsistence into capital, at the opposite pole, the mass of the population into wage-labourers, into " free labouring poor," that artificial product of modern society. If money, according to Augier, " comes into the world with a congenital blood-stain on one cheek," capital comes dripping from head to foot, from every pore, with blood and dirt.

HISTORICAL TENDENCY OF CAPITALIST ACCUMULATION

(Vol. I, Ch. XXXII)

What does the primitive accumulation of capital, i.e., its historical genesis, resolve itself into ? In so far as it is not immediate transformation of slaves and serfs into wage-labourers, and therefore a mere change of form, it only means the expropriation of the immediate producers, i.e., the dissolution of private property based on the labour of its owner. Private property, as the antithesis to social, collective property, exists only where the means of labour and the external conditions of labour belong to private individuals. But according as these private individuals are labourers or not labourers, private property has a different character. The numberless shades, that it at first sight presents, correspond to the intermediate stages lying between these two extremes. The private property of the labourer in his means of production is the foundation of petty industry, whether agricultural, manufacturing or both ; petty industry, again, is an essential condition for the development of social production and of the free individuality of the labourer himself. Of course, this petty mode of production exists also under slavery, serfdom, and other states of dependence. But it flourishes, it lets loose its whole energy, it attains its adequate classical form only where the labourer is the private owner of his own means of labour set in action by himself : the peasant of the land which he cultivates, the artisan of the tool which he handles as a virtuoso. This mode of production pre-supposes parcelling of the soil, and scattering of the other means of production. As it excludes the concentration of these means of production, so also it excludes co-operation, division of labour within each separate process of production, the control over, and the productive application of the forces of Nature by society, and the free development of the social productive powers. It is compatible only with a system of production, and a society, moving within narrow and more or less primitive bounds. To perpetuate it would be, as Pecqueur rightly says, " to decree universal mediocrity." At a certain stage of development it brings forth the material agencies for its own dissolution. From that moment new forces and new passions spring up in the bosom of society ; but the old social organisation fetters them and keeps them down. It must be annihilated ; it is annihilated. Its annihilation, the transformation of the individualised and scattered means of production into socially concentrated ones, of the pigmy property of the many into the huge property of the few, the expropriation of the great mass of the people from the soil, from the means of subsistence, and from the means of labour, this fearful and painful expropriation of the mass of the people forms the prelude to the history of capital. It comprises a series of forcible methods, of which we have passed in review only those that have been epoch-making as methods of the primitive accumulation of capital. The expropriation of the immediate producers was accomplished with merciless vandalism, and under the stimulus of passions the most infamous, the most sordid, the pettiest, the most meanly odious. Self-earned private property, that is based, so to say, on the fusing together of the isolated, independent labouring-individual with the conditions of his labour, is supplanted by capitalistic private property, which rests on exploitation of the nominally free labour of others, i.e., on wages-labour.

As soon as this process of transformation has sufficiently decomposed the old society from top to bottom, as soon as the labourers are turned into proletarians, their means of labour into capital, as soon as the capitalist mode of production stands on its own feet, then the further socialisation of labour and further transformation of the land and other means of production into socially exploited and, therefore, common means of production, as well as the further expropriation of private proprietors, takes a new form. That which is now to be expropriated is no longer the labourer working for himself, but the capitalist exploiting many labourers. This expropriation is accomplished by the action of the immanent laws of capitalistic production itself, by the centralisation of capital. One capitalist always kills many. Hand in hand with this centralisation, or this expropriation of many capitalists by few, develop, on an ever extending scale, the co-operative form of the labour-process, the conscious technical application of science, the methodical cultivation of the soil, the transformation of the instruments of labour into instruments of labour only usable in common, the economising of all means of production by their use as the means of production of combined, socialised labour, the entanglement of all peoples in the net of the world-market, and this, the international character of the capitalistic régime. Along with the constantly

diminishing number of the magnates of capital, who usurp
and monopolise all advantages of this process of transformation, grows the mass of misery, oppression, slavery, degrada-
tion, exploitation ; but with this too grows the revolt of
the working-class, a class always increasing in numbers,
and disciplined, united, organised by the very mechanism
of the process of capitalist production itself. The monopoly
of capital becomes a fetter upon the mode of production,
which has sprung up and flourished along with, and under
it. Centralisation of the means of production and socialisation of labour at last reach a point where they become
incompatible with their capitalist integument. This integument is burst asunder. The knell of capitalist private property sounds. The expropriators are expropriated.

The capitalist mode of appropriation, the result of the
capitalist mode of production, produces capitalist private
property. This is the first negation of individual private
property, as founded on the labour of the proprietor. But
capitalist production begets, with the inexorability of a law
of Nature, its own negation. It is the negation of negation.
This does not re-establish private property for the producer,
but gives him individual property based on the acquisi-
tions of the capitalist era : i.e., on co-operation and the
possession in common of the land and of the means of
production.

The transformation of scattered private property, arising
from individual labour, into capitalist private property is,
naturally, a process, incomparably more protracted, violent, and difficult, than the transformation of capitalistic
private property, already practically resting on socialised
production, into socialised property. In the former case, we
had the expropriation of the mass of the people by a few
usurpers ; in the latter, we have the expropriation of a few
usurpers by the mass of the people.

COMMODITIES

(Vol. I, Ch. I)

The Two Factors of a Commodity : Use-Value and Value (the Substance of Value and the Magnitude of Value)

The wealth of those societies in which the capitalist mode of production prevails, presents itself as " an immense accumulation of commodities," its unit being a single commodity. Our investigation must therefore begin with the analysis of a commodity.

A commodity is, in the first place, an object outside us, a thing that by its properties satisfies human wants of some sort or another. The nature of such wants, whether, for instance, they spring from the stomach or from fancy, makes no difference. Neither are we here concerned to know how the object satisfies these wants, whether directly as means of subsistence, or indirectly as means of production.

Every useful thing, as iron, paper, etc., may be looked at from the two points of view of quality and quantity. It is an assemblage of many properties, and may therefore be of use in various ways. To discover the various use of things is the work of history. So also is the establishment of socially-recognised standards of measure for the quantities of these useful objects. The diversity of these measures has its origin partly in the diverse nature of the objects to be measured, partly in convention.

The utility of a thing makes it a use-value. But this utility is not a thing of air. Being limited by the physical properties of the commodity, it has no existence apart from that commodity. A commodity, such as iron, corn, or a diamond, is therefore, so far as it is a material thing, a use-value, something useful. This property of a commodity is independent of the amount of labour required to appropriate its useful qualities. When treating of use-value, we always assume to be dealing with definite quantities, such as dozens of watches, yards of linen, or tons of iron. The use-values of commodities furnish the material for a special study, that of the commercial knowledge of commodities. Use-values become a reality only by use or consumption : they also constitute the substance of all wealth, whatever may be the social form of that wealth. In the form of society we are about to consider, they are, in addition, the material depositories of exchange value.

Exchange value, at first sight, presents itself as a quantitative relation, as the proportion in which values in use of one sort are exchanged for those of another sort, a relation constantly changing with time and place. Hence exchange value appears to be something accidental and purely relative, and consequently an intrinsic value, i.e., an exchange value that is inseparably connected with, inherent in commodities, seems a contradiction in terms. Let us consider the matter a little more closely.

A given commodity, e.g., a quarter of wheat is exchanged for x blacking, y silk, or z gold, etc.—in short, for other commodities in the most different proportions. Instead of one exchange value, the wheat has, therefore, a great many. But since x blacking, y silk, or z gold, etc., each represent the exchange value of one quarter of wheat, x blacking, y silk, z gold, etc., must as exchange values be replaceable by each other, or equal to each other. Therefore, first : the valid exchange values of a given commodity express something equal ; secondly, exchange value, generally, is only the mode of expression, the phenomenal form, of something contained in it, yet distinguishable from it.

Let us take two commodities, e.g., corn and iron. The proportions in which they are exchangeable, whatever those proportions may be, can always be represented by an equation in which a given quantity of corn is equated to some quantity of iron : e.g., 1 quarter corn $=x$ cwt. iron. What does this equation tell us ? It tells us that in two different things—in 1 quarter of corn and x cwt. of iron, there exists in equal quantities something common to both. The two things must therefore be equal to a third, which in itself is neither the one nor the other. Each of them, so far as it is exchange value, must therefore be reducible to this third.

A simple geometrical illustration will make this clear. In order to calculate and compare the areas of rectilinear figures, we decompose them into triangles. But the area of the triangle itself is expressed by something totally different from its visible figure, namely, by half the product of the base into the altitude. In the same way the exchange values of commodities must be capable of being expressed in terms of something common to them all, of which thing they represent a greater or less quantity.

This common " something " cannot be either a geometrical, a chemical, or any other natural property of commodities. Such properties claim our attention only in so far as they affect the utility of those commodities, make them use-values. But the exchange of commodities is evidently an act characterised by a total abstraction from use-value. Then one use-value is just as good as another, provided only it be present in sufficient quantity. Or, as old Barbon says, " one sort of wares are as good as another, if the values be equal. There is no difference or distinction in things of equal value. . . . An hundred pounds' worth of lead or iron, is of as great value as one hundred pounds' worth of silver or gold." As use-values, commodities are, above all, of different qualities, but as exchange values they are merely different quantities, and consequently do not contain an atom of use-value.

If then we leave out of consideration the use-value of commodities, they have only one common property left, that of being products of labour. But even the product of labour itself has undergone a change in our hands. If we make abstraction from its use-value, we make abstraction at the same time from the material elements and shapes that make the product a use-value, we see in it no longer a table, a house, yarn, or any other useful thing. Its existence as a material thing is put out of sight. Neither can it any longer be regarded as the product of the labour of the joiner, the mason, the spinner, or of any other definite kind of productive labour. Along with the useful qualities of the products themselves, we put out of sight both the useful character of the various kinds of labour embodied in them, and the concrete forms of that labour ; there is nothing left but what is common to them all ; all are reduced to one and the same sort of labour, human labour in the adstract.

Let us now consider the residue of each of these products ; it consists of the same unsubstantial reality in each, a mere congelation of homogeneous human labour, of labour-power expended without regard to the mode of its expenditure. All that these things now tell us is, that human labour-power has been expended in their production, that human labour is embodied in them. When looked at as crystals of this social substance, common to them all, they are—Values.

We have seen that when commodities are exchanged, their exchange value manifests itself as something totally independent of their use-value. But if we abstract from their use-value, there remains their Value as defined above. Therefore, the common substance that manifests itself in the exchange value of commodities, whenever they are exchanged, is their value. The progress of our investigation will show that exchange value is the only form in which the value of commodities can manifest itself or be expressed. For the present, however, we have to consider the nature of value independently of this, its form.

A use-value, or useful article, therefore, has value only because human labour in the abstract has been embodied or materialised in it. How, then, is the magnitude of this value to be measured ? Plainly, by the quantity of the value-creating substance, the labour, contained in the article. The quantity of labour, however, is measured by its duration, and labour-time in its turn finds its standard in weeks, days, and hours.

Some people might think that if the value of a commodity is determined by the quantity of labour spent on

it, the more idle and unskilful the labourer, the more valuable would his commodity be, because more time would
be required in its production. The labour, however, that
forms the substance of value is homogeneous human
labour, expenditure of one uniform labour-power. The
total labour-power of society, which is embodied in the
sum total of the values of all commodities produced by that
society, counts here as one homogeneous mass of human
labour-power, composed though it be of innumerable individual units. Each of these units is the same as any other,
so far as it has the character of the average labour-power of
society, and takes effect as such ; that is, so far as it requires
for producing a commodity, no more time than is needed
on an average, no more than is socially necessary. The
labour-time socially necessary is that required to produce
an article under the normal conditions of production, and
with the average degree of skill and intensity prevalent at
the time. The introduction of power looms into England
probably reduced by one half the labour required to weave
a given quantity of yarn into cloth. The hand-loom weavers,
as a matter of fact, continued to require the same time as
before ; but for all that, the product of one hour of their
labour represented after the change only half an hour's
social labour, and consequently fell to one half its former
value.

We see then that that which determines the magnitude of
the value of any article is the amount of labour socially
necessary, or the labour-time socially necessary for its production. Each individual commodity, in this connection,
is to be considered as an average sample of its class. Commodities, therefore, in which equal quantities of labour are
embodied, or which can be produced in the same time,
have the same value. The value of one commodity is to
the value of any other, as the labour-time necessary for
the production of the one is to that necessary for the production of the other. " As values, all commodities are only
definite masses of congealed labour-time."

The value of a commodity would therefore remain constant, if the labour-time required for its production also remained constant. But the latter changes with every variation in the productiveness of labour. This productiveness is determined by various circumstances, amongst others, by the average amount of skill of the workmen, the state of science, and the degree of its practical application, the social organisation of production, the extent and capabilities of the means of production, and by physical conditions. For example, the same amount of labour in favourable seasons is embodied in eight bushels of corn, and in unfavourable, only in four. The same labour extracts from rich mines more metal than from poor mines. Diamonds are of very rare occurrence on the earth's surface, and hence their discovery costs, on an average, a great deal of labour-time. Consequently much labour is represented in a small compass. Jacob doubts whether gold has ever been paid for at its full value. This applies still more to diamonds. According to Eschwege, the total produce of the Brazilian diamond mines for the eighty years ending in 1823 had not realised the price of one and a half years' average produce of the sugar and coffee plantations of the same country, although the diamonds cost much more labour, and therefore represented more value. With richer mines, the same quantity of labour would embody itself in more diamonds and their value would fall. If we could succeed at a small expenditure of labour, in converting carbon into diamonds, their value might fall below that of bricks. In general, the greater the productiveness of labour, the less is the labour-time required for the production of an article, the less is the amount of labour crystallised in that article, and the less is its value ; and vice versa, the less the productiveness of labour, the greater is the labour-time required for the production of an article, and the greater is its value. The value of a commodity, therefore, varies directly as the quantity, and inversely as the productiveness, of the labour incorporated in it.

A thing can be a use-value, without having value. This is the case whenever its utility to man is not due to labour. Such are air, virgin soil, natural meadows, etc. A thing can be useful, and the product of human labour, without being a commodity. Whoever directly satisfies his wants with the produce of his own labour, creates, indeed, use-values, but not commodities. In order to produce the latter, he must not only produce use-values, but use-values for others, social use-values. Lastly, nothing can have value, without being an object of utility. If the thing is useless, so is the labour contained in it ; the labour does not count as labour, and therefore creates no value. . . .

The Fetishism of Commodities and the Secret thereof

A commodity appears, at first sight, a very trivial thing, and easily understood. Its analysis shows that it is, in reality, a very queer thing, abounding in metaphysical subtleties and theological niceties. So far as it is a value in use, there is nothing mysterious about it, whether we consider it from the point of view that by its properties it is capable of satisfying human wants, or from the point that those properties are the product of human labour. It is as clear as noon-day, that man, by his industry, changes the forms of the materials furnished by nature, in such a way as to make them useful to him. The form of wood, for instance, is altered, by making a table out of it. Yet, for all that the table continues to be that common, every-day thing, wood. But, so soon as it steps forth as a commodity, it is changed into something transcendent. It not only stands with its feet on the ground, but, in relation to all other commodities, it stands on its head, and evolves out of its wooden brain grotesque ideas, far more wonderful than " table-turning " ever was.

The mystical character of commodities does not originate, therefore, in their use-value. Just as little does it proceed from the nature of the determining factors of value.

For, in the first place, however varied the useful kinds of
labour, or productive activities, may be, it is a physiological
fact that they are functions of the human organism, and
that each such function, whatever may be its nature or
form, is essentially the expenditure of human brain, nerves,
muscles, etc. Secondly, with regard to that which forms
the ground-work for the quantitative determination of
value, namely, the duration of that expenditure, or the
quantity of labour, it is quite clear that there is a palpable
difference between its quantity and quality. In all states of
society, the labour-time that it costs to produce the means
of subsistence must necessarily be an object of interest to
mankind, though not of equal interest in different stages of
development. And lastly, from the moment that men in any
way work for one another, their labour assumes a social form.

Whence, then, arises the enigmatical character of the
product of labour, so soon as it assumes the form of commodities ? Clearly from this form itself. The equality of all
sorts of human labour is expressed objectively by their products all being equally values ; the measure of the expenditure of labour-power by the duration of that expenditure,
takes the form of the quantity of value of the products of
labour ; and finally, the mutual relations of the producers,
within which the social character of their labour affirms
itself, take the form of a social relation between the products.

A commodity is therefore a mysterious thing, simply because in it the social character of men's labour appears to
them as an objective character stamped upon the product
of that labour ; because the relation of the producers to
the sum total of their own labour is presented to them as
a social relation, existing not between themselves, but between the products of their labour. This is the reason why
the products of labour become commodities, social things
whose qualities are at the same time perceptible and im-
perceptible by the senses. In the same way the light from
an object is perceived by us not as the subjective excitation
of our optic nerve, but as the objective form of something

outside the eye itself. But, in the act of seeing, there is at all events an actual passage of light from one thing to another, from the external object to the eye. There is a physical relation between physical things. But it is different with commodities. There, the existence of the things *quâ* commodities, and the value relation between the products of labour which stamps them as commodities, have absolutely no connection with their physical properties and with the material relations arising therefrom. There it is a definite social relation between men, that assumes, in their eyes, the fantastic form of a relation between things. In order, therefore, to find an analogy, we must have recourse to the mist-enveloped regions of the religious world. In that world the productions of the human brain appear as independent beings endowed with life, and entering into relation both with one another and the human race. So it is in the world of commodities with the products of men's hands. This I call the Fetishism which attaches itself to the products of labour, so soon as they are produced as commodities, and which is therefore inseparable from the production of commodities.

This Fetishism of commodities has its origin, as the foregoing analysis has already shown, in the peculiar social character of the labour that produces them.

As a general rule, articles of utility become commodities, only because they are products of the labour of private individuals or groups of individuals who carry on their work independently of each other. The sum total of the labour of all these private individuals forms the aggregate labour of society. Since the producers do not come into social contact with each other until they exchange their products, the specific social character of each producer's labour does not show itself except in the act of exchange. In other words, the labour of the individual asserts itself as a part of the labour of society, only by means of the relations which the act of exchange establishes directly between the products, and indirectly, through them, between the producers. To the latter, therefore, the relations connecting the labour of

one individual with that of the rest appear, not as direct
social relations between individuals at work, but as what
they really are, material relations between persons and
social relations between things. It is only by being exchanged that the products of labour acquire, as values, one
uniform social status, distinct from their varied forms of
existence as objects of utility. This division of a product
into a useful thing and a value becomes practically important, only when exchange has acquired such an extension
that useful articles are produced for the purpose of being
exchanged, and their character as values has therefore to
be taken into account, beforehand, during production.
From this moment the labour of the individual producer
acquires socially a two-fold character. On the one hand, it
must, as a definite useful kind of labour, satisfy a definite
social want, and thus hold its place as part and parcel of
the collective labour of all, as a branch of a social division
of labour that has sprung up spontaneously. On the other
hand, it can satisfy the manifold wants of the individual
producer himself, only in so far as the mutual exchange-
ability of all kinds of useful private labour is an established
social fact, and therefore the private useful labour of each
producer ranks on an equality with that of all others. The
equalisation of the most different kinds of labour can be the
result only of an abstraction from their inequalities, or of
reducing them to their common denominator, viz., expenditure of human labour power or human labour in the
abstract. The two-fold social character of the labour of the
individual appears to him, when reflected in his brain, only
under those forms which are impressed upon that labour in
everyday practice by the exchange of products. In this way,
the character that his own labour possesses of being socially
useful takes the form of the condition that the product must
be not only useful, but useful for others, and the social
character that his particular labour has of being the equal
of all other particular kinds of labour takes the form that
all the physically different articles that are the products of

labour have one common quality, viz., that of having value.

Hence, when we bring the products of our labour into relation with each other as values, it is not because we see in these articles the material receptacles of homogeneous human labour. Quite the contrary ; whenever, by an exchange, we equate as values our different products, by that very act we also equate, as human labour, the different kinds of labour expended upon them. We are not aware of this, nevertheless we do it. Value, therefore, does not stalk about with a label describing what it is. It is value, rather, that converts every product into a social hieroglyphic. Later on, we try to decipher the hieroglyphic, to get behind the secret of our own social products ; for to stamp an object of utility as a value is just as much a social product as language. The recent scientific discovery that the products of labour, so far as they are values, are but material expressions of the human labour spent in their production marks, indeed, an epoch in the history of the development of the human race, but by no means dissipates the mist through which the social character of labour appears to us to be an objective character of the products themselves. The fact that in the particular form of production with which we are dealing, viz., the production of commodities, the specific social character of private labour carried on independently consists in the equality of every kind of that labour, by virtue of its being human labour, which character, therefore, assumes in the product the form of value— this fact appears to the producers, notwithstanding the discovery above referred to, to be just as real and final as the fact that, after the discovery by science of the component gases of air, the atmosphere itself remained unaltered.

What, first of all, practically concerns producers when they make an exchange is the question, how much of some other product they get for their own ? in what proportions the products are exchangeable ? When these proportions have, by custom, attained a certain stability, they appear to result from the nature of the products, so that, for

instance, one ton of iron and two ounces of gold appear as
naturally to be of equal value, as a pound of gold and a
pound of iron in spite of their different physical and chemical qualities appear to be of equal weight. The character of
having value, when once impressed upon products, obtains
fixity only by reason of their acting and re-acting upon each
other as quantities of value. These quantities vary continually, independently of the will, foresight and action of the
producers. To them, their own social action takes the form
of the action of objects, which rule the producers instead of
being ruled by them. It requires a fully developed production of commodities before, from accumulated experience
alone, the scientific conviction springs up that all the different kinds of private labour, which are carried on independently of each other, and yet as spontaneously developed
branches of the social division of labour, are continually
being reduced to the quantitive proportions in which society
requires them. And why ? Because, in the midst of all the
accidental and ever fluctuating exchange-relations between
the products, the labour-time socially necessary for · their
production forcibly asserts itself like an over-riding law of
nature. The law of gravity thus asserts itself when a house
falls about our ears. The determination of the magnitude
of value by labour-time is therefore a secret, hidden under
the apparent fluctuations in the relative values of commodities. Its discovery, while removing all appearance of mere
accidentality from the determination of the magnitude of
the values of products, yet in no way alters the mode in
which that determination takes place.

Man's reflections on the forms of social life, and consequently, also, his scientific analysis of those forms, take a
course directly opposite to that of their actual historical
development. He begins, post festum, with the results of the
process of development ready to hand before him. The
characters that stamp products as commodities, and whose
establishment is a necessary preliminary to the circulation
of commodities, have already acquired the stability of

natural, self-understood forms of social life, before man seeks
to decipher, not their historical character, for in his eyes
they are immutable, but their meaning. Consequently it
was the analysis of the prices of commodities that alone
led to the determination of the magnitude of value, and it
was the common expression of all commodities in money
that alone led to the establishment of their characters as
values. It is, however, just this ultimate money form of the
world of commodities that actually conceals, instead of disclosing, the social character of private labour, and the social
relations between the individual producers. When I state
that coats or boots stand in a relation to linen, because it is
the universal incarnation of abstract human labour, the
absurdity of the statement is self-evident. Nevertheless,
when the producers of coats and boots compare those
articles with linen, or, what is the same thing, with gold or
silver, as the universal equivalent, they express the relation
between their own private labour and the collective labour
of society in the same absurd form.

The categories of bourgeois economy consist of such like
forms. They are forms of thought expressing with social
validity the conditions and relations of a definite, historically determined mode of production, viz., the production of
commodities. The whole mystery of commodities, all the
magic and necromancy that surrounds the products of
labour as long as they take the form of commodities,
vanishes therefore, so soon as we come to other forms of
production.

Since Robinson Crusoe's experiences are a favourite
theme with political economists, let us take a look at him
on his island. Moderate though he be, yet some few wants
he has to satisfy, and must therefore do a little useful work
of various sorts, such as making tools and furniture, taming
goats, fishing and hunting. Of his prayers and the like we
take no account, since they are a source of pleasure to him,
and he looks upon them as so much recreation. In spite of
the variety of his work, he knows that his labour, whatever

its form, is but the activity of one and the same Robinson, and consequently, that it consists of nothing but different modes of human labour. Necessity itself compels him to apportion his time accurately between his different kinds of work. Whether one kind occupies a greater space in his general activity than another, depends on the difficulties, greater or less as the case may be, to be overcome in attaining the useful effect aimed at. This our friend Robinson soon learns by experience, and having rescued a watch, ledger, and pen and ink from the wreck, commences, like a true-born Briton, to keep a set of books. His stock-book contains a list of the objects of utility that belong to him, of the operations necessary for their production ; and lastly, of the labour time that definite quantities of those objects have, on an average, cost him. All the relations between Robinson and the objects that form this wealth of his own creation, are here so simple and clear as to be intelligible without exertion, even to Mr. Sedley Taylor. And yet those relations contain all that is essential to the determination of value.

Let us now transport ourselves from Robinson's island bathed in light to the European middle ages shrouded in darkness. Here, instead of the independent man, we find everyone dependent, serfs and lords, vassals and suzerains, laymen and clergy. Personal dependence here characterises the social relations of production just as much as it does the other spheres of life organised on the basis of that production. But for the very reason that personal dependence forms the ground-work of society, there is no necessity for labour and its products to assume a fantastic form different from their reality. They take the shape, in the transactions of society, of services in kind and payments in kind. Here the particular and natural form of labour, and not, as in a society based on production of commodities, its general abstract form is the immediate social form of labour. Compulsory labour is just as properly measured by time, as commodity-producing labour ; but every serf knows that

Robinson Crusoe did a little useful work, such as making tools. (*Capital*, "The Fetishism of Commodities")

what he expends in the service of his lord is a definite quantity of his own personal labour-power. The tithe to be rendered to the priest is more matter of fact than his blessing. No matter, then, what we may think of the parts played by the different classes of people themselves in this society, the social relations between individuals in the performance of their labour, appear at all events as their own mutual personal relations, and are not disguised under the shape of social relations between the products of labour.

For an example of labour in common or directly associated labour, we have no occasion to go back to that spontaneously developed form which we find on the threshold of the history of all civilised races. We have one close at hand in the patriarchal industries of a peasant family, that produces corn, cattle, yarn, linen, and clothing for home use. These different articles are, as regards the family, so many products of its labour, but as between themselves, they are not commodities. The different kinds of labour, such as tillage, cattle tending, spinning, weaving and making clothes, which result in the various products, are in themselves, and such as they are, direct social functions, because functions of the family, which just as much as a society based on the production of commodities, possesses a spontaneously developed system of division of labour. The distribution of the work within the family, and the regulation of the labour-time of the several members, depend as well upon differences of age and sex as upon natural conditions varying with the seasons. The labour-power of each individual, by its very nature, operates in this case merely as a definite portion of the whole labour-power of the family, and therefore, the measure of the expenditure of individual labour-power by its duration, appears here by its very nature as a social character of their labour.

Let us now picture to ourselves, by way of change, a community of free individuals, carrying on their work with the means of production in common, in which the labour-power of all the different individuals is consciously applied as the combined labour-power of the community. All the characteristics of Robinson's labour are here repeated, but with this difference, that they are social, instead of individual. Everything produced by him was exclusively the result of his own personal labour, and therefore simply an object of use for himself. The total product of our community is a social product. One portion serves as fresh means of production and remains social. But another portion is consumed by the members as means of subsistence. A distribution of this portion amongst them is consequently necessary. The mode of this distribution will vary with the productive organisation of the community, and the degree of historical development attained by the producers. We will assume, but merely for the sake of a parallel with the production of commodities, that the share of each individual producer in the means of subsistence is determined by his labour-time. Labour-time would, in that case, play a double part. Its apportionment in accordance with a definite social plan maintains the proper proportion between the different kinds of work to be done and the various wants of the community. On the other hand, it also serves as a measure of the portion of the common labour borne by each individual and of his share in the part of the total product destined for individual consumption. The social relations of the individual producers, with regard both to their labour and to its products, are in this case perfectly simple and intelligible, and that with regard not only to production but also to distribution.

The religious world is but the reflex of the real world. And for a society based upon the production of commodities, in which the producers in general enter into social relations with one another by treating their products as commodities and values, whereby they reduce their individual private labour to the standard of homogeneous human labour—for such a society, Christianity with its *cultus* of abstract man, more especially in its bourgeois developments, Protestantism, Deism, etc., is the most fitting form of religion. In the ancient Asiatic and other ancient modes of production, we find that the conversion of products into commodities, and therefore the conversion of men into producers of commodities, holds a subordinate place, which, however, increases in importance as the primitive communities approach nearer and nearer to their dissolution. Trading nations, properly so called, exist in the ancient world only in its interstices, like the gods of Epicurus in the Intermundia, or like Jews in the pores of Polish society. Those ancient social organisms of production are, as compared with bourgeois society, extremely simple and transparent. But they are founded either on the immature development of man individually, who has not yet severed the umbilical cord that unites him with his fellow men in a primitive tribal community, or upon direct relations of subjection. They can arise and exist only when the development of the productive power of labour has not risen beyond a low stage, and when, therefore, the social relations within the sphere of material life, between man and man, and between man and Nature, are correspondingly narrow. This narrowness is reflected in the ancient worship of Nature, and in the other elements of the popular religions. The religious reflex of the real world can, in any case, only then finally vanish when the practical relations of everyday life offer to man none but perfectly intelligible and reasonable relations with regard to his fellow men and to nature.

The life-process of society, which is based on the process of material production, does not strip off its mystical veil until it is treated as production by freely associated men, and is consciously regulated by them in accordance with a settled plan. This, however, demands for society a certain material ground-work or set of conditions of existence which in their turn are the spontaneous product of a long and painful process of development.

Political economy has indeed analysed, however incompletely, value and its magnitude, and has discovered what lies beneath these forms. But it has never once asked the question why labour is represented by the value of its product and labour-time by the magnitude of that value. These formulæ, which bear stamped upon them in unmistakable letters, that they belong to a state of society; in which the process of production has the mastery over man, instead of being controlled by him, such formulæ appear to the bourgeois intellect to be as much a self-evident necessity imposed by nature as productive labour itself. Hence forms of social production that preceded the bourgeois form, are treated by the bourgeoisie in much the same way as the Fathers of the Church treated pre-Christian religions. . . .

MONEY, OR THE CIRCULATION OF COMMODITIES
(Vol. I, Ch. III)
The Measure of Values

Throughout this work, I assume, for the sake of simplicity, gold as the money-commodity.

The first chief function of money is to supply commodities with the material for the expression of their values, or to represent their values as magnitudes of the same denomination, qualitatively equal, and quantitatively comparable. It thus serves as a *universal measure of value*. And only by virtue of this function does gold, the equivalent commodity *par excellence*, become money.

It is not money that renders commodities commensurable. Just the contrary. It is because all commodities, as values, are realised human labour, and therefore commensurable, that their values can be measured by one and the same special commodity, and the latter be converted into the common measure of their values, i.e., into money. Money as a measure of value, is the phenomenal form that must of necessity be assumed by that measure of value which is immanent in commodities, labour-time.

The expression of the value of a commodity in gold—x commodity $A = y$ money-commodity—is its money-form or price. A single equation, such as 1 ton of iron $= 2$ ounces of gold, now suffices to express the value of the iron in a socially valid manner. There is no longer any need for this equation to figure as a link in the chain of equations that express the values of all other commodities, because the equivalent commodity, gold, now has the character of money. The general form of relative value has resumed its original shape of simple or isolated relative value. On the other hand, the expanded expression of relative value, the endless series of equations, has now become the form peculiar to the relative value of the money-commodity. The series itself, too, is now given, and has social recognition in the prices of actual commodities. We have only to read the quotations of a price-list backwards, to find the magnitude of the value of money expressed in all sorts of commodities. But money itself has no price. In order to put it on an equal footing with all other commodities in this respect, we should be obliged to equate it to itself as its own equivalent.

The price or money-form of commodities is, like their form of value generally, a form quite distinct from their palpable bodily form ; it is, therefore, a purely ideal or mental form. Although invisible, the value of iron, linen and corn has actual existence in these very articles : it is ideally made perceptible by their equality with gold, a relation that, so·to say, exists only in their own heads. Their owner must, therefore, lend them his tongue, or hang a ticket on them, before their prices can be communicated to the outside world. Since the expression of the value of commodities in gold is a merely ideal act, we may use for this purpose imaginary or ideal money. Every trader knows, that he is far from having turned his goods into money, when he has expressed their value in a price or in imaginary money, and that it does not require the least bit of real gold, to estimate in that metal millions of pounds' worth of goods. When, therefore, money serves as a measure of value, it is employed only as imaginary or ideal money. This circumstance has given rise to the wildest theories. But, although the money that performs the functions of a measure of value is only ideal money, price depends entirely upon the actual substance that is money. The value, or in other words, the quantity of human labour contained in a ton of iron, is expressed in imagination by such a quantity of the money-commodity as contains the same amount of labour as the iron. According, therefore, as the measure of value is gold, silver, or copper, the value of the ton of iron will be expressed by very different prices, or will be represented by very different quantities of those metals respectively.

If, therefore, two different commodities, such as gold and silver, are simultaneously measures of value, all commodities have two prices—one a gold-price, the other a silver-price. These exist quietly side by side, so long as the ratio of the value of silver to that of gold remains unchanged, say, at 15 : 1. Every change in their ratio disturbs the ratio which exists between the gold-prices and the silver-prices of commodities, and thus proves, by facts, that a double standard of value is inconsistent with the functions of a standard.

Commodities with definite prices present themselves under the form : a commodity $A=x$ gold ; b commodity B $=z$ gold ; c commodity $C=y$ gold, etc., where a, b, c, represent definite quantities of the commodities A, B, C and x, z, y, definite quantities of gold. The values of these commodities are, therefore, changed in imagination into so many different quantities of gold. Hence, in spite of the confusing variety of the commodities themselves, their values become magnitudes of the same denomination, gold-magnitudes. They are now capable of being compared with each other and measured, and the want becomes technically felt of comparing them with some fixed quantity of gold as a unit measure. This unit, by subsequent division into aliquot parts, becomes itself the standard or scale. Before they become money, gold, silver, and copper already possess such standard measures in their standards of weight, so that, for example, a pound weight, while serving as the unit, is, on the one hand, divisible into ounces, and, on the other, may be combined to make up hundredweights. It is owing to this that, in all metallic currencies, the names given to the standards of money or of price were originally taken from the pre-existing names of the standards of weight.

As *measure of value* and as *standard of price*, money has two entirely distinct functions to perform. It is the measure of value inasmuch as it is the socially recognised incarnation of human labour ; it is the standard of price inasmuch as it is a fixed weight of metal. As the measure of value it serves to convert the values of all the manifold commodities into prices, into imaginary quantities of gold ; as the standard of price it measures those quantities of gold. The measure of values measures commodities considered as values ; the standard of price measures, on the contrary, quantities of gold by a unit quantity of gold, not the value of one quantity of gold by the weight of another. In order to make gold a standard of price, a certain weight must be fixed upon as the unit. In this case, as in all cases of measuring quantities of the same denomination, the establishment of an unvarying unit of measure is all-important. Hence, the less the unit is subject to variation, so much the better does the standard of price fulfil its office. But only in so far as it is itself a product of labour, and, therefore, potentially variable in value, can gold serve as a measure of value.

It is, in the first place, quite clear that a change in the value of gold does not, in any way, affect its function as a standard of price. No matter how this value varies, the proportions between the values of different quantities of the metal remain constant. However great the fall in its value, 12 ounces of gold still have 12 times the value of 1 ounce ; and in prices, the only thing considered is the relation between different quantities of gold. Since, on the other hand, no rise or fall in the value of an ounce of gold can alter its weight, no alteration can take place in the weight of its aliquot parts. Thus gold always renders the same service as an invariable standard of price, however much its value may vary.

In the second place, a change in the value of gold does not interfere with its functions as a measure of value. The change affects all commodities simultaneously, and, therefore, *cœteris paribus*, leaves their relative values *inter se*, unaltered, although those values are now expressed in higher or lower gold-prices.

Just as when we estimate the value of any commodity by a definite quantity of the use-value of some other commodity, so in estimating the value of the former in gold, we assume nothing more than that the production of a given quantity of gold costs, at the given period, a given amount of labour. As regards the fluctuations of prices generally, they are subject to the laws of elementary relative value investigated in a former chapter.

A general rise in the prices of commodities can result only, either from a rise in their values—the value of money remaining constant—or from a fall in the value of money, the values of commodities remaining constant. On the other hand, a general fall in prices can result only, either from a fall in the values of commodities—the value of money remaining constant—or from a rise in the value of money, the values of commodities remaining constant. It therefore by no means follows, that a rise in the value of money necessarily implies a proportional fall in the prices of commodities ; or that a fall in the value of money implies a proportional rise in prices. Such change of price holds good only in the case of commodities whose value remains constant. With those, for example, whose value rises, simultaneously with, and proportionally to, that of money, there is no alteration in price. And if their value rise either slower or faster than that of money, the fall or rise in their prices will be determined by the difference between the change in their value and that of money ; and so on.

Let us now go back to the consideration of the price-form.

By degrees there arises a discrepancy between the current money names of the various weights of the precious metal figuring as money, and the actual weights which those

names originally represented. This discrepancy is the result
of historical causes, among which the chief are : (1) The
importation of foreign money into an imperfectly developed
community. This happened in Rome in its early days, where
gold and silver coins circulated at first as foreign commodities. The names of these foreign coins never coincide with
those of the indigenous weights. (2) As wealth increases,
the less precious metal is thrust out þy the more precious
from its place as a measure of value, copper by silver, silver
by gold, however much this order of sequence may be in
contradiction with poetical chronology. The word pound,
for instance, was the money-name given to an actual pound
weight of silver. When gold replaced silver as a measure of
value, the same name was applied according to the ratio
between the values of silver and gold, to perhaps one-
fifteenth of a pound of gold. The word pound, as a money-
name, thus becomes differentiated from the same word as
a weight-name. (3) The debasing of money carried on for
centuries by kings and princes to such an extent that, of
the original weights of the coins, nothing in fact remained
but the names.

These historical causes convert the separation of the
money-name from the weight-name into an established
habit with the community. Since the standard of money is
on the one hand purely conventional, and must on the other
hand find general acceptance, it is in the end regulated by
law. A given weight of one of the precious metals, an ounce
of gold, for instance, becomes officially divided into aliquot
parts, with legally bestowed names, such as pound, dollar,
etc. These aliquot parts, which henceforth serve as units of
money, are then sub-divided into other aliquot parts with
legal names, such as shilling, penny, etc. But, both before
and after these divisions are made, a definite weight of metal
is the standard of metallic money. The sole alteration consists in the sub-division and denomination.

The prices, or quantities of gold, into which the values
of commodities are ideally changed, are therefore now

expressed in the names of coins, or in the legally valid names of the sub-divisions of the gold standard. Hence, instead of saying : A quarter of wheat is worth an ounce of gold ; we say, it is worth £3 17s. 10½d. In this way commodities express by their prices how much they are worth, and money serves as *money of account* whenever it is a question of fixing the value of an article in its money-form.

The name of a thing is something distinct from the qualities of that thing. I know nothing of a man, by knowing that his name is Jacob. In the same way with regard to money, every trace of a value-relation disappears in the names pound, dollar, franc, ducat, etc. The confusion caused by attributing a hidden meaning to these cabalistic signs is all the greater, because these money-names express both the values of commodities, and, at the same time, aliquot parts of the weight of the metal that is the standard of money. On the other hand, it is absolutely necessary that value, in order that it may be distinguished from the varied bodily forms of commodities, should assume this material and unmeaning, but, at the same time, purely social form.

Price is the money-name of the labour realised in a commodity. Hence the expression of the equivalence of a commodity with the sum of money constituting its price is a tautology, just as in general the expression of the relative value of a commodity is a statement of the equivalence of two commodities. But although price, being the exponent of the magnitude of a commodity's value, is the exponent of its exchange-ratio with money, it does not follow that the exponent of this exchange-ratio is necessarily the exponent of the magnitude of the commodity's value. Suppose two equal quantities of socially necessary labour to be respectively represented by 1 quarter of wheat and £2 (nearly ½ oz. of gold), £2 is the expression in money of the magnitude of the value of the quarter of wheat, or is its price. If now circumstances allow of this price being raised to £3, or compel it to be reduced to £1, then although £1 and £3 may be too small or too great properly to express the magnitude of the wheat's value, nevertheless they are its prices, for they are, in the first place, the form under which its value appears, i.e., money ; and in the second place, the exponents of its exchange-ratio with money. If the conditions of production, in other words, if the productive power of labour remain constant, the same amount of social labour-time must, both before and after the change in price, be expended in the reproduction of a quarter of wheat. This circumstance depends, neither on the will of the wheat producer, nor on that of the owners of other commodities.

Magnitude of value expresses a relation of social production, it expresses the connection that necessarily exists between a certain article and the portion of the total labour-time of society required to produce it. As soon as magnitude of value is converted into price, the above necessary relation takes the shape of a more or less accidental exchange-ratio between a single commodity and another, the money-commodity. But this exchange-ratio may express either the real magnitude of that commodity's value, or the quantity of gold deviating from that value, for which, according to circumstances, it may be parted with. The possibility, therefore, of quantitative incongruity between price and magnitude of value, or the deviation of the former from the latter, is inherent in the price-form itself. This is no defect, but, on the contrary, admirably adapts the price-form to a mode of production whose inherent laws impose themselves only as the mean of apparently lawless irregularities that compensate one another.

The price-form, however, is not only compatible with the possibility of a quantitative incongruity between magnitude of value and price, i.e. between the former and its expression in money, but it may also conceal a qualitative inconsistency, so much so, that, although money is nothing but the value-form of commodities, price ceases altogether to express value. Objects that in themselves are no commodities, such as conscience, honour, etc., are capable of being offered

for sale by their holders, and of thus acquiring, through
their price, the form of commodities. Hence an object may
have a price without having value. The price in that case
is imaginary, like certain quantities in mathematics. On
the other hand, the imaginary price-form may sometimes
conceal either a direct or indirect real value-relation ; for
instance, the price of uncultivated land, which is without
value, because no human labour has been incorporated
in it.

Price, like relative value in general, expresses the value of
a commodity (e.g., a ton of iron), by stating that a given
quantity of the equivalent (e.g., an ounce of gold), is directly
exchangeable for iron. But it by no means states the con-
verse, that iron is directly exchangeable for gold. In order,
therefore, that a commodity may in practice act effectively
as exchange value, it must quit its bodily shape, must transform itself from mere imaginary into real gold, although to
the commodity such transubstantiation may be more difficult than to the Hegelian " concept," the transition from
" necessity " to " freedom," or to a lobster the casting of
his shell, or to Saint Jerome the putting off of the old Adam.
Though a commodity may, side by side with its actual form
(iron, for instance), take in our imagination the form of
gold, yet it cannot at one and the same time actually be
both iron and gold. To fix its price, it suffices to equate it
to gold in imagination. But to enable it to render to its
owner the service of a universal equivalent, it must be actually replaced by gold. If the owner of the iron were to go
to the owner of some other commodity offered for exchange,
and were to refer him to the price of the iron as proof that
it was already money, he would get the same answer as
St. Peter gave in heaven to Dante, when the latter recited
the creed—

> *Assai bene è trascorsa*
> *D'esta moneta già la lega e'l peso,*
> *Ma dimmi se tu l'hai nella tua borsa.*

A price therefore implies both that a commodity is exchangeable for money, and also that it must be so exchanged. On the other hand, gold serves as an ideal measure of value, only because it has already, in the process of exchange, established itself as the money-commodity. Under the ideal measure of values there lurks the hard cash. . . .

THE GENERAL FORMULA FOR CAPITAL
(Vol. I, Ch. IV)

The circulation of commodities is the starting point of capital. The production of commodities, their circulation, and that more developed form of their circulation called commerce, these form the historical ground-work from which it rises. The modern history of capital dates from the creation in the sixteenth century of a world-embracing commerce and a world-embracing market.

If we abstract from the material substance of the circulation of commodities, that is, from the exchange of the various use-values, and consider only the economic forms produced by this process of circulation, we find its final result to be money : this final product of the circulation of commodities is the first form in which capital appears.

As a matter of history, capital, as opposed to landed property, invariably takes the form at first of money ; it appears as moneyed wealth, as the capital of the merchant and of the usurer. But we have no need to refer to the origin of capital in order to discover that the first form of appearance of capital is money. We can see it daily under our very eyes. All new capital, to commence with, comes on the stage, that is, on the market, whether of commodities, labour, or money, even in our days, in the shape of money that by a definite process has to be transformed into capital.

The first distinction we notice between money that is money only, and money that is capital, is nothing more than a difference in their form of circulation.

The simplest form of the circulation of commodities is C—M—C, the transformation of commodities into money, and the change of the money back again into commodities ; or selling in order to buy. But alongside of this form we find another specifically different form : M—C—M, the transformation of money into commodities, and the change of commodities back again into money ; or buying in order to sell. Money that circulates in the latter manner is thereby transformed into, becomes capital, and is already potentially capital.

Now let us examine the circuit M—C—M a little closer. It consists, like the other, of two antithetical phases. In the first phase, M—C, or the purchase, the money is changed into a commodity. In the second phase, C—M, or the sale, the commodity is changed back again into money. The combination of these two phases constitutes the single movement whereby money is exchanged for a commodity and the same commodity is again exchanged for money ; whereby a commodity is bought in order to be sold, or, neglecting the distinction in form between buying and selling, whereby a commodity is bought with money, and then money is bought with a commodity. The result, in which the phases of the process vanish, is the exchange of money for money, M—M. If I purchase 2,000 lbs. of cotton for £100, and resell the 2,000 lbs. of cotton for £110, I have, in fact, exchanged £100 for £110, money for money.

Now it is evident that the circuit M—C—M would be absurd and without meaning if the intention were to exchange by this means two equal sums of money, £100 for £100. The miser's plan would be far simpler and surer ; he sticks to his £100 instead of exposing it to the dangers of circulation. And yet, whether the merchant who has paid £100 for his cotton sells it for £110, or lets it go for £100, or even £50, his money has, at all events, gone through a characteristic and original movement, quite different in kind from that which it goes through in the hands of the peasant who sells corn, and with the money thus set free buys clothes. We have therefore to examine first the distinguishing characteristics of the forms of the circuits M—C—M and C—M—C, and in doing this the real difference that underlies the mere difference of form will reveal itself.

Let us see, in the first place, what the two forms have in common.

Both circuits are resolvable into the same two antithetical phases, C—M, a sale, and M—C, a purchase. In each of these phases the same material elements—a commodity, and money, and the same economical dramatis personæ, a buyer and a seller—confront one another. Each circuit is the unity of the same two antithetical phases, and in each case this unity is brought about by the intervention of three contracting parties, of whom one only sells, another only buys, while the third both buys and sells.

What, however, first and foremost distinguishes the circuit C—M—C from the circuit M—C—M, is the inverted order of succession of the two phases. The simple circulation of commodities begins with a sale and ends with a purchase, while the circulation of money as capital begins with a purchase and ends with a sale. In the one case both the starting-point and the goal are commodities, in the other they are money. In the first form the movement is brought about by the intervention of money, in the second by that of a commodity.

In the circulation C—M—C, the money is in the end converted into a commodity, that serves as a use-value ; it is spent once for all. In the inverted form, M—C—M, on the contrary, the buyer lays out money in order that, as a seller, he may recover money. By the purchase of his commodity he throws money into circulation, in order to withdraw it again by the sale of the same commodity. He lets the money go, but only with the sly intention of getting it back again. The money, therefore, is not spent, it is merely advanced.

In the circuit C—M—C, the same piece of money changes its place twice. The seller gets it from the buyer and pays it

away to another seller. The complete circulation, which begins with the receipt, concludes with the payment, of money
for commodities. It is the very contrary in the circuit M—
C—M. Here it is not the piece of money that changes its
place twice, but the commodity. The buyer takes it from the
hands of the seller and passes it into the hands of another
buyer. Just as in the simple circulation of commodities the
double change of place of the same piece of money effects
its passage from one hand into another, so here the double
change of place of the same commodity brings about the
reflux of the money to its point of departure.

Such reflux is not dependent on the commodity being
sold for more than was paid for it. This circumstance influences only the amount of the money that comes back.
The reflux itself takes place, so soon as the purchased commodity is resold, in other words, so soon as the circuit M—
C—M is completed. We have here, therefore, a palpable
difference between the circulation of money as capital, and
its circulation as mere money.

The circuit C—M—C comes completely to an end, so
soon as the money brought in by the sale of one commodity
is abstracted again by the purchase of another.

If, nevertheless, there follows a reflux of money to its
starting point, this can only happen through a renewal or
repetition of the operation. If I sell a quarter of corn for
£3, and with this £3 buy clothes, the money, so far as I am
concerned, is spent and done with. It belongs to the clothes
merchant. If I now sell a second quarter of corn, money
indeed flows back to me, not however as a sequel to the first
transaction, but in consequence of its repetition. The money
again leaves me, so soon as I complete this second transaction by a fresh purchase. Therefore, in the circuit C—
M—C, the expenditure of money has nothing to do
with its reflux. On the other hand, in M—C—M, the reflux of the money is conditioned by the very mode of its
expenditure. Without this reflux, the operation fails, or
the process is interrupted and incomplete, owing to the

absence of its complementary and final phase, the sale.

The circuit C—M—C starts with one commodity, and finishes with another, which falls out of circulation and into consumption. Consumption, the satisfaction of wants, in one word, use-value, is its end and aim. The circuit M—C—M, on the contrary, commences with money and ends with money. Its leading motive, and the goal that attracts it, is therefore mere exchange value.

In the simple circulation of commodities, the two extremes of the circuit have the same economic form. They are both commodities, and commodities of equal value. But they are also use-values differing in their qualities, as, for example, corn and clothes. The exchange of products, of the different materials in which the labour of society is embodied, forms here the basis of the movement. It is otherwise in the circulation M—C—M, which at first sight appears purposeless, because tautological. Both extremes have the same economic form. They are both money, and therefore are not qualitatively different use-values ; for money is but the converted form of commodities, in which their particular use-values vanish. To exchange £100 for cotton, and then this same cotton again for £100, is merely a roundabout way of exchanging money for money, the same for the same, and appears to be an operation just as purposeless as it is absurd. One sum of money is distinguishable from another only by its amount. The character and tendency of the process M—C—M, is therefore not due to any qualitative difference between its extremes, both being money, but solely to their quantitative difference. More money is withdrawn from circulation at the finish than was thrown into it at the start. The cotton that was bought for £100 is perhaps resold for £100 + £10 or £110. The exact form of this process is therefore M—C—M', where M' = $M + \triangle M$ = the original sum advanced, plus an increment. This increment or excess over the original value I call " surplus-value." The value originally advanced, therefore, not only remains intact while in circulation, but adds

to itself a surplus-value or expands itself. It is this movement that converts it into capital.

Of course it is also possible, that in C—M—C, the two
extremes C—C, say corn and clothes, may represent different quantities of value. The farmer may sell his corn above
its value, or may buy the clothes at less than their value.
He may, on the other hand, " be done " by the clothes
merchant. Yet, in the form of circulation now under consideration, such differences in value are purely accidental.
The fact that the corn and the clothes are equivalents, does
not deprive the process of all meaning, as it does in M—
C—M. The equivalence of their values is rather a necessary
condition to its normal course.

The repetition or renewal of the act of selling in order to
buy, is kept within bounds by the very object it aims at,
namely, consumption or the satisfaction of definite wants, an
aim that lies altogether outside the sphere of circulation. But
when we buy in order to sell, we, on the contrary, begin and
end with the same thing, money, exchange-value ; and
thereby the movement becomes interminable. No doubt,
M becomes $M + \triangle M$, £100 become £110. But when viewed
in their qualitative aspect alone, £110 are the same as £100,
namely money ; and considered quantitatively, £110 is,
like £100, a sum of definite and limited value. If now, the
£110 be spent as money, they cease to play their part. They
are no longer capital. Withdrawn from circulation, they
become petrified into a hoard, and though they remained
in that state till doomsday, not a single farthing would
accrue to them. If, then, the expansion of value is once
aimed at, there is just the same inducement to augment
the value of the £110 as that of the £100 ; for both are but
limited expressions for exchange-value, and therefore both
have the same vocation to approach, by quantitative increase,
as near as possible to absolute wealth. Momentarily, indeed,
the value originally advanced, the £100 is distinguishable
from the surplus value of £10 that is annexed to it during
circulation ; but the distinction vanishes immediately.

At the end of the process we do not receive with one hand the original £100, and with the other, the surplus value of £10. We simply get a value of £110, which is in exactly the same condition and fitness for commencing the expanding process, as the original £100 was. Money ends the movement only to begin it again. Therefore, the final result of every separate circuit, in which a purchase and consequent sale are completed, forms of itself the starting-point of a new circuit. The simple circulation of commodities—selling in order to buy—is a means of carrying out a purpose unconnected with circulation, namely, the appropriation of use-values, the satisfaction of wants. The circulation of money as capital is, on the contrary, an end in itself, for the expansion of value takes place only within this constantly renewed movement. The circulation of capital has therefore no limits. Thus the conscious representative of this movement, the possessor of money becomes a capitalist. His person, or rather his pocket, is the point from which the money starts and to which it returns. The expansion of value, which is the objective basis or main-spring of the circulation M—C—M, becomes his subjective aim, and it is only in so far as the appropriation of ever more and more wealth in the abstract becomes the sole motive of his operations, that he functions as a capitalist, that is, as capital personified and endowed with consciousness and a will. Use-values must therefore never be looked upon as the real aim of the capitalist ; neither must the profit on any single transaction. The restless never-ending process of profit-making alone is what he aims at. This boundless greed after riches, this passionate chase after exchange value, is common to the capitalist and the miser ; but while the miser is merely a capitalist gone mad, the capitalist is a rational miser. The never-ending augmentation of exchange value, which the miser strives after, by seeking to save his money from circulation, is attained by the more acute capitalist, by constantly throwing it afresh into circulation.

The independent form, i.e., the money-form, which the

value of commodities assumes in the case of simple circulation, serves only one purpose, namely, their exchange, and
vanishes in the final result of the movement. On the other
hand, in the circulation M—C—M, both the money and
the commodity represent only different modes of existence
of value itself, the money its general mode, and the commodity its particular, or, so to say, disguised mode. It is
constantly changing from one form to the other without
thereby becoming lost, and thus assumes an automatically
active character. If now we take in turn each of the two
different forms which self-expanding value successively
assumes in the course of its life, we then arrive at these two
propositions : Capital is money : Capital is commodities.
In truth, however, value is here the active factor in a process, in which, while constantly assuming the form in turn
of money and commodities, it at the same time changes in
magnitude, differentiates itself by throwing off surplus value
from itself ; the original value, in other words, expands
spontaneously. For the movement, in the course of which
it adds surplus value, is its own movement, its expansion,
therefore, is automatic expansion. Because it is value, it has
acquired the occult quality of being able to add value to
itself. It brings forth living offspring, or, at the least, lays
golden eggs.

Value, therefore, being the active factor in such a process,
and assuming at one time the form of money, at another
that of commodities, but through all these changes preserving itself and expanding, it requires some independent
form, by means of which its identity may at any time be
established. And this form it possesses only in the shape of
money. It is under the form of money that value begins and
ends, and begins again, every act of its own spontaneous
generation. It began by being £100, it is now £110, and so
on. But the money itself is only one of the two forms of
value. Unless it takes the form of some commodity, it does
not become capital. There is here no antagonism, as in the
case of hoarding, between the money and commodities.

The capitalist knows that all commodities, however scurvy they may look, or however badly they may smell, are in faith and in truth money, inwardly circumcised Jews, and what is more, a wonderful means whereby out of money to make more money.

In simple circulation, C—M—C, the value of commodities attained at the most a form independent of their use-values, i.e., the form of money ; but that same value now in the circulation M—C—M, or the circulation of capital, suddenly presents itself as an independent substance, endowed with a motion of its own, passing through a life-process of its own, in which money and commodities are mere forms which it assumes and casts off in turn. Nay, more : instead of simply representing the relations of commodities, it enters now, so to say, into private relations with itself. It differentiates itself as original value from itself as surplus-value ; as the father differentiates himself from himself *quâ* the son, yet both are one and of one age : for only by the surplus value of £10 does the £100 originally advanced become capital, and so soon as this takes place, so soon as the son, and by the son, the father, is begotten, so soon does their difference vanish, and they again become one, £110.

Value therefore now becomes value in process, money in process, and, as such, capital. It comes out of circulation, enters into it again, preserves and multiplies itself within its circuit, comes back out of it with expanded bulk, and begins the same round ever afresh. M—M′, money which begets money, such is the description of Capital from the mouths of its first interpreters, the Mercantilists.

Buying in order to sell, or, more accurately, buying in order to sell dearer, M—C—M′ appears certainly to be a form peculiar to one kind of capital alone, namely, merchants' capital. But industrial capital too is money, that is changed into commodities, and by the sale of these commodities, is reconverted into more money. The events that take place outside the sphere of circulation, in the interval between the buying and selling, do not affect the form of this movement. Lastly, in the case of interest-bearing capital, the circulation M—C—M′ appears abridged. We have its result without the intermediate stage, in the form M—M′, *en style lapidaire* so to say, money that is worth more money, value that is greater than itself.

M—C—M′ is therefore in reality the general formula of capital as it appears prima facie within the sphere of circulation. . . .

CONTRADICTIONS IN THE GENERAL FORMULA OF CAPITAL
(Vol. I, Ch. V)

The form which circulation takes when money becomes capital, is opposed to all the laws we have hitherto investigated bearing on the nature of commodities, value and money, and even of circulation itself. What distinguishes this form from that of the simple circulation of commodities is the inverted order of succession of the two antithetical processes, sale and purchase. How can this purely formal distinction between these processes change their character as it were by magic?

But that is not all. This inversion has no existence for two out of the three persons who transact business together. As capitalist, I buy commodities from A and sell them again to B, but as a simple owner of commodities, I sell them to B and then purchase fresh ones from A. A and B see no difference between the two sets of transactions. They are merely buyers or sellers. And I on each occasion meet them as a mere owner of either money or commodities, as a buyer or a seller, and, what is more, in both sets of transactions, I am opposed to A only as a buyer and to B only as a seller, to the one only as money, to the other only as commodities, and to either of them as capital or a capitalist, or as representative of anything that is more than money or commodities, or that can produce any effect beyond what money and commodities can. For me the purchase from A and the sale to B are part of a series. But the connection between the two acts exists for me alone. A does not trouble himself about my transaction with B, nor does B about my business with A. And if I offered to explain to them the meritorious nature of my action in inverting the order of succession, they would probably point out to me that I was mistaken as to that order of succession, and that the whole transaction, instead of beginning with a purchase and ending with a sale, began, on the contrary, with a sale and was concluded with a purchase. In truth, my first act, the purchase, was from the standpoint of A, a sale, and my second act, the sale, was from the standpoint of B, a purchase. Not content with that, A and B would declare that the whole series was superfluous and nothing but hokus pokus ; that for the future A would buy direct from B, and B sell direct to A. Thus the whole transaction would be reduced to a single act forming an isolated, non-complemented phase in the ordinary circulation of commodities, a mere sale from A's point of view, and from B's, a mere purchase. The inversion, therefore, of the order of succession, does not take us outside the sphere of the simple circulation of commodities, and we must rather look, whether there is in this simple circulation anything permitting an expansion of the value that enters into circulation, and, consequently, a creation of surplus value.

Let us take the process of circulation in a form under which it presents itself as a simple and direct exchange of commodities. This is always the case when two owners of commodities buy from each other, and on the settling day the amounts mutually owing are equal and cancel each other. The money in this case is money of account and serves to express the value of the commodities by their prices, but is not, itself, in the shape of hard cash, confronted with them. So far as regards use-values, it is clear that both parties may gain some advantage. Both part with goods that, as use-values, are of no service to them, and receive others that they can make use of. And there may also be a further gain. A, who sells wine and buys corn, possibly produces more wine, with given labour-time, than farmer B could, and B, on the other hand, more corn than wine-grower A could. A, therefore, may get, for the same exchange value, more corn, and B more wine, than each would respectively get without any exchange by producing his own corn and wine. With reference, therefore, to use-value, there is good ground for saying that " exchange is a transaction by which both sides gain." It is otherwise with exchange value. " A man who has plenty of wine and no corn treats with a man who has plenty of corn and no wine ; an exchange takes place between them of corn to the value of 50, for wine of the same value. This act produces no increase of exchange value either for the one or the other ; for each of them already possessed, before the exchange, a value equal to that which he acquired by means of that operation." The result is not altered by introducing money, as a medium of circulation, between the commodities, and making the sale and the purchase two distinct acts. The value of a commodity is expressed in its price before it goes into circulation, and is therefore a precedent condition of circulation, not its result.

Abstractedly considered, that is, apart from circumstances not immediately flowing from the laws of the simple circula-tion of commodities, there is in an exchange nothing (if we except the replacing of one use-value by another) but a metamorphosis, a mere change in the form of the com-modity. The same exchange value, i.e., the same quantity of incorporated social labour, remains throughout in the hands of the owner of the commodity first in the shape of his own commodity, then in the form of the money for which he exchanged it, and lastly, in the shape of the commodity he buys with that money. This change of form does not imply a change in the magnitude of the value. But the change, which the value of the commodity undergoes in this process, is limited to a change in its money form. This form exists first as the price of the commodity offered for sale, then as an actual sum of money, which, however, was already expressed in the price, and lastly, as the price of an equivalent commodity. This change of form no more implies, taken alone, a change in the quantity of value, than does the change of a £5 note into sovereigns, half sovereigns and shillings. So far therefore as the circulation of commodities effects a change in the form alone of their values, and is free from disturbing influences, it must be the exchange of equivalents. Little as Vulgar-Economy knows about the nature of value, yet whenever it wishes to consider the phenomena of circulation in their purity, it assumes that supply and demand are equal, which amounts to this, that their effect is nil. If therefore, as regards the use-values exchanged, both buyer and seller may possibly gain something, this is not the case as regards the exchange values. Here we must rather say, " Where equality exists there can be no gain." It is true, commodities may be sold at prices deviating from their values, but these deviations are to be considered as infractions of the laws of the exchange of commodities, which in its normal state is an exchange of equivalents, consequently, no method for increasing value.

Hence, we see that behind all attempts to represent the circulation of commodities as a source of surplus value, there lurks a *quid pro quo*, a mixing up of use-value and exchange value. For instance, Condillac says : " It is not true that on an exchange of commodities we give value for value. On the contrary, each of the two contracting parties in every case, gives a less for a greater value. . . . If we really exchanged equal values, neither party could make a profit. And yet, they both gain, or ought to gain. Why ? The value of a thing consists solely in its relation to our wants. What is more to the one is less to the other, and vice versa. . . . It is not to be assumed that we offer for sale articles required for our own consumption. . . . We wish to part with a useless thing, in order to get one that we need ; we want to give less for more. . . . It was natural to think that, in an exchange, value was given for value, whenever each of the articles exchanged was of equal value with the same quantity of gold. . . . But there is another point to be considered in our calculation. The question is, whether we both exchange something superfluous for something necessary." We see in this passage, how Condillac not only confuses use-value with exchange value, but in a really childish manner assumes, that in a society, in which the production of commodities is well developed, each producer produces his own means of subsistence, and throws into circulation only the excess over his own requirements. Still, Condillac's argument is frequently used by modern economists, more especially when the point is to show that the exchange of commodities in its developed form, commerce, is productive of surplus value. For instance, " Commerce . . . adds value to products, for the same products in the hands of consumers, are worth more than in the hands of producers, and it may strictly be considered an act of production." But commodities are not paid for twice over, once on account of their use-value, and again on account of their value. And though the use-value of a commodity is more serviceable to the buyer than to the seller, its money form is more serviceable to the seller. Would he otherwise sell it ? We might therefore just as well say that the buyer performs " strictly an act of production," by converting stockings, for example, into money.

If commodities, or commodities and money, of equal exchange value, and consequently equivalents, are exchanged, it is plain that no one abstracts more value from, than he throws into, circulation. There is no creation of surplus value. And, in its normal form, the circulation of commodities demands the exchange of equivalents. But in actual practice, the process does not retain its normal form. Let us, therefore, assume an exchange of non-equivalents.

In any case the market for commodities is only frequented by owners of commodities, and the power which these persons exercise over each other, is no other than the power of their commodities. The material variety of these commodities is the material incentive to the act of exchange, and makes buyers and sellers mutually dependent, because none of them possesses the object of his own wants, and each holds in his hand the object of another's wants. Besides these material differences of their use-values, there is only one other difference between commodities, namely, that between their bodily form and the form into which they are converted by sale, the difference between commodities and money. And consequently the owners of commodities are distinguishable only as sellers, those who own commodities, and buyers, those who own money.

Suppose then, that by some inexplicable privilege, the seller is enabled to sell his commodities above their value, what is worth 100 for 110, in which case the price is nominally raised 10 per cent. The seller therefore pockets a surplus value of 10. But after he has sold he becomes a buyer. A third owner of commodities comes to him now as seller, who in this capacity also enjoys the privilege of selling his commodities 10 per cent too dear. Our friend gained 10 as a seller only to lose it again as a buyer. The nett result is, that all owners of commodities sell their goods to one another at 10 per cent above their value, which comes precisely to the same as if they sold them at their true value. Such a general and nominal rise of prices has the same effect as if the values had been expressed in weight of silver instead of in weight of gold. The nominal prices of commodities would rise, but the real relation between their values would remain unchanged.

Let us make the opposite assumption, that the buyer has the privilege of purchasing commodities under their value. In this case it is no longer necessary to bear in mind that he in his turn will become a seller. He was so before he became buyer ; he had already lost 10 per cent in selling before he gained 10 per cent as buyer. Everything is just as it was.

The creation of surplus value, and therefore the conversion of money into capital, can consequently be explained neither on the assumption that commodities are sold above their value, nor that they are bought below their value.

The problem is in no way simplified by introducing irrelevant matters after the manner of Col. Torrens : " Effectual demand consists in the power and inclination (!), on the part of consumers, to give for commodities, either by immediate or circuitous barter, some greater portion of . . . capital than their production costs." In relation to circulation, producers and consumers meet only as buyers and sellers. To assert that the surplus value acquired by the producer has its origin in the fact that consumers pay for commodities more than their value, is only to say in other words : The owner of commodities possesses, as a seller, the privilege of selling too dear. The seller has himself produced the commodities or represents their producer, but the buyer has to no less extent produced the commodities represented by his money, or represents their producer. The distinction between them is, that one buys and the other sells. The fact that the owner of the commodities, under the designation of producer, sells them over their value, and under the designation of consumer, pays too much for them, does not carry us a single step further.

To be consistent therefore, the upholders of the delusion that surplus value has its origin in a nominal rise of prices or in the privilege which the seller has of selling too dear, must assume the existence of a class that only buys and does not sell, i.e., only consumes and does not produce. The existence of such a class is inexplicable from the standpoint we have so far reached, viz., that of simple circulation. But let us anticipate. The money with which such a class is constantly making purchases, must constantly flow into their pockets, without any exchange, gratis, by might or right, from the pockets of the commodity-owners themselves. To sell commodities above their value to such a class, is only to crib back again a part of the money previously given to it. The towns of Asia Minor thus paid a yearly money tribute to ancient Rome. With this money Rome purchased from them commodities, and purchased them too dear. The provincials cheated the Romans, and thus got back from their conquerors, in the course of trade, a portion of the tribute. Yet, for all that, the conquered were the really cheated. Their goods were still paid for with their own money. That is not the way to get rich or to create surplus value.

Let us therefore keep within the bounds of exchange where sellers are also buyers, and buyers, sellers. Our difficulty may perhaps have arisen from treating the actors as personifications instead of as individuals.

A may be clever enough to get the advantage of B or C without their being able to retaliate. A sells wine worth £40 to B, and obtains from him in exchange corn to the value of £50. A has converted his £40 into £50, has made more money out of less, and has converted his commodities into capital. Let us examine this a little more closely. Before the exchange we had £40 worth of wine in the hands of A, and £50 worth of corn in those of B, a total value of £90. After the exchange we have still the same total value of £90. The value in circulation has not increased by one iota, it is only distributed differently between A and B. What is a loss of value to B is surplus value to A ; what is " minus " to one is " plus " to the other. The same change would have taken place if A, without the formality of an exchange, had directly stolen the £10 from B. The sum of the values in circulation can clearly not be augmented by any change in their distribution, any more than the quantity of the precious metals in a country by a Jew selling a Queen Ann's farthing for a guinea. The capitalist class, as a whole, in any country, cannot overreach themselves.

Turn and twist then as we may, the fact remains unaltered. If equivalents are exchanged, no surplus value results, and if non-equivalents are exchanged, still no surplus value. Circulation, or the exchange of commodities, begets no value.

The reason is now therefore plain why, in analysing the

standard form of capital, the form under which it determines the economical organisation of modern society, we
entirely left out of consideration its most popular, and, so to
say, antediluvian forms, merchants' capital and moneylenders' capital.

The circuit M—C—M', buying in order to sell dearer, is
seen most clearly in genuine merchants' capital. But the
movement takes place entirely within the sphere of circulation. Since, however, it is impossible, by circulation alone,
to account for the conversion of money into capital, for the
formation of surplus value, it would appear, that merchants'
capital is an impossibility, so long as equivalents are exchanged ; that, therefore, it can only have its origin in the
twofold advantage gained, over both the selling and the
buying producers, by the merchant who parasitically shoves
himself in between them. It is in this sense that Franklin
says, " war is robbery, commerce is generally cheating." If
the transformation of merchants' money into capital is to be
explained otherwise than by the producers being simply
cheated, a long series of intermediate steps would be necessary, which, at present, when the simple circulation of commodities forms our only assumption, are entirely wanting.

What we have said with reference to merchants' capital,
applies still more to moneylenders' capital. In merchants'
capital, the two extremes, the money that is thrown upon
the market, and the augmented money that is withdrawn
from the market, are at least connected by a purchase and
a sale, in other words by the movement of the circulation.
In moneylenders' capital the form M—C—M' is reduced
to the two extremes without a mean, M—M', money exchanged for more money, a form that is incompatible with
the nature of money, and therefore remains inexplicable
from the standpoint of the circulation of commodities.
Hence Aristotle : " since chrematistic is a double science,
one part belonging to commerce, the other to economic,
the latter being necessary and praiseworthy, the former
based on circulation and with justice disapproved (for it is

not based on Nature, but on mutual cheating), therefore
the usurer is most rightly hated, because money itself is
the source of his gain, and is not used for the purposes for
which it was invented. For it originated for the exchange of
commodities, but interest makes out of money, more money.
Hence its name (τόκος interest and offspring). For the begotten are like those who beget them. But interest is money
of money, so that of all modes of making a living, this is the
most contrary to nature."

In the course of our investigation, we shall find that both
merchants' capital and interest-bearing capital are deriva-
tive forms, and at the same time it will become clear, why
these two forms appear in the course of history before the
modern standard form of capital.

We have shown that surplus value cannot be created by
circulation, and, therefore, that in its formation, something
must take place in the background, which is not apparent in
the circulation itself. But can surplus value possibly originate anywhere else than in circulation, which is the sum total
of all the mutual relations of commodity-owners, as far as
they are determined by their commodities? Apart from
circulation, the commodity-owner is in relation only with
his own commodity. So far as regards value, that relation is
limited to this, that the commodity contains a quantity of
his labour, that quantity being measured by a definite social
standard. This quantity is expressed by the value of the
commodity, and since the value is reckoned in money of account, this quantity is also expressed by the price, which we
will suppose to be £10. But his labour is not represented
both by the value of the commodity, and by a surplus over
that value, not by a price of 10 that is also a price of 11, not
by a value that is greater than itself. The commodity-owner
can, by his labour, create value, but not self-expanding
value. He can increase the value of his commodity, by adding fresh labour, and therefore more value to the value in
hand, by making, for instance, leather into boots. The same
material has now more value, because it contains a greater

quantity of labour. The boots have therefore more value than the leather, but the value of the leather remains what it was ; it has not expanded itself, has not, during the making of the boots, annexed surplus value. It is therefore impossible that outside the sphere of circulation, a producer of commodities can, without coming into contact with other commodity-owners, expand value, and consequently convert money or commodities into capital.

It is therefore impossible for capital to be produced by circulation, and it is equally impossible for it to originate apart from circulation. It must have its origin both in circulation and yet not in circulation.

We have, therefore, got a double result.

The conversion of money into capital has to be explained on the basis of the laws that regulate the exchange of commodities, in such a way that the starting-point is the exchange of equivalents. Our friend, Moneybags, who as yet is only an embryo capitalist, must buy his commodities at their value, must sell them at their value, and yet at the end of the process must withdraw more value from circulation than he threw into it at starting. His development into a full-grown capitalist must take place, both within the sphere of circulation and without it. These are the conditions of the problem. Hic Rhodus, hic salta !

THE BUYING AND SELLING OF LABOUR-POWER
(Vol. I, Ch. VI)

The change of value that occurs in the case of money intended to be converted into capital, cannot take place in the money itself, since in its function of means of purchase and of payment, it does no more than realise the price of the commodity it buys or pays for ; and, as hard cash, it is value petrified, never varying. Just as little can it originate in the second act of circulation, the re-sale of the commodity, which does no more than transform the article from its bodily form back again into its money form. The

change must, therefore, take place in the commodity bought
by the first act, M—C, but not in its value, for equivalents
are exchanged, and the commodity is paid for at its full
value. We are, therefore, forced to the conclusion that the
change originates in the use-value, as such, of the commodity, i.e., in its consumption. In order to be able to extract value from the consumption of a commodity, our
friend, Moneybags, must be so lucky as to find, within the
sphere of circulation, in the market, a commodity, whose
use-value possesses the peculiar property of being a source
of value, whose actual consumption, therefore, is itself an
embodiment of labour, and, consequently, a creation of
value. The possessor of money does find on the market such
a special commodity in capacity for labour or labour-power.

By labour-power or capacity for labour is to be understood the aggregate of these mental and physical capabilities existing in a human being, which he exercises whenever
he produces a use-value of any description.

But in order that our owner of money may be able to find
labour-power offered for sale as a commodity, various conditions must first be fulfilled. The exchange of commodities of itself implies no other relations of dependence than
those which result from its own nature. On this assumption, labour-power can appear upon the market as a commodity only if, and so far as, its possessor, the individual
whose labour-power it is, offers it for sale, or sells it, as a
commodity. In order that he may be able to do this, he
must have it at his disposal, must be the untrammelled
owner of his capacity for labour, i.e., of his person. He and
the owner of money meet in the market, and deal with
each other as on the basis of equal rights, with this difference alone, that one is buyer, the other seller ; both, therefore, equal in the eyes of the law. The continuance of this
relation demands that the owner of the labour-power should
sell it only for a definite period, for if he were to sell it rump
and stump, once for all, he would be selling himself, converting himself from a free man into a slave, from an owner

of a commodity into a commodity. He must constantly look upon his labour-power as his own property, his own commodity, and this he can only do by placing it at the disposal of the buyer temporarily, for a definite period of time. By this means alone can he avoid renouncing his rights of ownership over it.

The second essential condition to the owner of money finding labour-power in the market as a commodity is this —that the labourer instead of being in the position to sell commodities in which his labour is incorporated, must be obliged to offer for sale as a commodity that very labour-power, which exists only in his living self.

In order that a man may be able to sell commodities other than labour-power, he must of course have the means of production, as raw material, implements, etc. No boots can be made without leather. He requires also the means of subsistence. Nobody—not even " a musician of the future " can live upon future products, or upon use-values in an unfinished state ; and ever since the first moment of his appearance on the world's stage, man always has been, and must still be a consumer, both before and while he is producing. In a society where all products assume the form of commodities, these commodities must be sold after they have been produced ; it is only after their sale that they can serve in satisfying the requirements of their producer. The time necessary for their sale is superadded to that necessary for their production.

For the conversion of his money into capital, therefore, the owner of money must meet in the market with the free labourer, free in the double sense, that as a free man he can dispose of his labour-power as his own commodity, and that on the other hand he has no other commodity for sale, is short of everything necessary for the realisation of his labour-power.

The question why this free labourer confronts him in the market has no interest for the owner of money, who regards the labour market as a branch of the general market for commodities. And for the present it interests us just as little. We cling to the fact theoretically, as he does practically. One thing, however, is clear—nature does not produce on the one side owners of money or commodities, and on the other men possessing nothing but their own labour-power. This relation has no natural basis, neither is its social basis one that is common to all historical periods. It is clearly the result of a past historical development, the product of many economical revolutions, of the extinction of a whole series of older forms of social production.

So, too, the economical categories, already discussed by us, bear the stamp of history. Definite historical conditions are necessary that a product may become a commodity. It must not be produced as the immediate means of subsistence of the producer himself. Had we gone further, and inquired under what circumstances all, or even the majority of products take the form of commodities, we should have found that this can only happen with production of a very specific kind, capitalist production. Such an inquiry, however, would have been foreign to the analysis of commodities. Production and circulation of commodities can take place, although the great mass of the objects produced are intended for the immediate requirements of their producers, are not turned into commodities, and consequently social production is not yet by a long way dominated in its length and breadth by exchange value, the appearance of products as commodities presupposed such a development of the social division of labour, that the separation of use-value from exchange value, a separation which first begins with barter, must already have been completed. But such a degree of development is common to many forms of society, which in other respects present the most varying historical features. On the other hand, if we consider money, its existence implies a definite stage in the exchange of commodities. The particular functions of money which it performs, either as the mere equivalent of commodities, or as means of circulation, or means of payment, as hoard or as universal money, point, according to the extent and relative preponderance of the one function or the other, to very different stages in the process of social production. Yet we know by experience that a circulation of commodities relatively primitive, suffices for the production of all these forms. Otherwise with capital. The historical conditions of its existence are by no means given with the mere circulation of money and commodities. It can spring into life, only when the owner of the means of production and subsistence meets in the market with the free labourer selling his labour-power. And this one historical condition comprises a world's history. Capital, therefore, announces from its first appearance a new epoch in the process of social production.

We must now examine more closely this peculiar commodity, labour-power. Like all others it has a value. How is that value determined ?

The value of labour-power is determined, as in the case of every other commodity, by the labour-time necessary for the production, and consequently also the reproduction, of this special article. So far as it has value, it represents no more than a definite quantity of the average labour of society incorporated in it. Labour-power exists only as a capacity, or power of the living individual. Its production consequently presupposes his existence. Given the individual, the production of labour-power consists in his reproduction of himself or his maintenance. For his maintenance he requires a given quantity of the means of subsistence. Therefore the labour-time requisite for the production of labour-power reduces itself to that necessary for the production of those means of subsistence ; in other words, the value of labour-power is the value of the means of subsistence necessary for the maintenance of the labourer. Labour-power, however, becomes a reality only by its exercise ; it sets itself in action only by working. But thereby a definite quantity of human muscle, nerve, brain, etc., is wasted, and these require to be restored. This increased expenditure demands a larger income. If the owner of labour-power works to-day, to-morrow he must again be able to repeat the same process in the same conditions as regards health and strength. His means of subsistence must therefore be sufficient to maintain him in his normal state as a labouring individual. His natural wants, such as food, clothing, fuel, and housing, vary according to the climatic and other physical conditions of his country. On the other hand, the number and extent of his so-called necessary wants, as also the modes of satisfying them, are themselves the product of historical development, and depend therefore to a great extent on the degree of civilisation of a country, more particularly on the conditions under which, and consequently on the habits and degree of comfort in which, the class of free labourers has been formed. In contradistinction therefore to the case of other commodities, there enters into the determination of the value of labour-power a historical and moral element. Nevertheless, in a given country, at a given period, the average quantity of the means of subsistence necessary for the labourer is practically known.

The owner of labour-power is mortal. If then his appearance in the market is to be continuous, and the continuous conversion of money into capital assumes this, the seller of labour-power must perpetuate himself, " in the way that every living individual perpetuates himself, by procreation." The labour-power withdrawn from the market by wear and tear and death, must be continually replaced by, at the very least, an equal amount of fresh labour-power. Hence the sum of the means of subsistence necessary for the production of labour-power must include the means necessary for the labourer's substitutes, i.e., his children, in order that this race of peculiar commodity-owners may perpetuate its appearance in the market.

In order to modify the human organism, so that it may acquire skill and handiness in a given branch of industry, and become labour-power of a special kind, a special education or training is requisite, and this, on its part, costs an equivalent in commodities of a greater or less amount. This amount varies according to the more or less complicated character of the labour-power. The expenses of this education (excessively small in the case of ordinary labour-power), enter *pro tanto* into the total value spent in its production.

The value of labour-power resolves itself into the value of a definite quantity of the means of subsistence. It therefore varies with the value of these means or with the quantity of labour requisite for their production.

Some of the means of subsistence, such as food and fuel, are consumed daily, and a fresh supply must be provided daily. Others such as clothes and furniture last for longer periods and require to be replaced only at longer intervals. One article must be bought or paid for daily, another weekly, another quarterly, and so on. But in whatever way the sum total of these outlays may be spread over the year, they must be covered by the average income, taking one day with another. If the total of the commodities required daily for the production of labour-power$=A$, and those required weekly$=B$, and those required quarterly$=C$, and so on, the daily average of these commodities$=\dfrac{365A + 52B + 4C + \text{etc.}}{365}$ Suppose that in this mass of commodities requisite for the average day there are embodied six hours of social labour, then there is incorporated daily in labour-power half a day's average social labour, in other words, half a day's labour is requisite for the daily production of labour-power. This quantity of labour forms the value of a day's labour-power or the value of the labour-power daily reproduced. If half a day's average social labour is incorporated in three shillings, then three shillings is the price corresponding to the value of a day's labour-power. If its owner therefore offers it for sale at three shillings a day, its selling price is equal to its value, and according to our supposition, our friend Moneybags, who is intent upon converting his three shillings into capital, pays this value.

The minimum limit of the value of labour-power is determined by the value of the commodities, without the daily supply of which the labourer cannot renew his vital energy, consequently by the value of those means of subsistence that are physically indispensable. If the price of labour-power fall to this minimum, it falls below its value, since under such circumstances it can be maintained and developed only in a crippled state. But the value of every commodity is determined by the labour-time requisite to turn it out so as to be of normal quality. . . .

We now know how the value paid by the purchaser to the possessor of this peculiar commodity, labour-power, is determined. The use-value which the former gets in exchange, manifests itself only in the actual usufruct, in the consumption of the labour-power. The money owner buys everything necessary for this purpose, such as raw material, in the market, and pays for it at its full value. The consumption of labour-power is at one and the same time the production of commodities and of surplus value. The consumption of labour-power is completed, as in the case of every other commodity, outside the limits of the market or of the sphere of circulation. Accompanied by Mr. Moneybags and by the possessor of labour-power, we therefore take leave for a time of this noisy sphere, where everything takes place on the surface and in view of all men, and follow them both into the hidden abode of production, on whose threshold there stares us in the face " No admittance except on business." Here we shall see, not only how capital produces, but how capital is produced. We shall at last force the secret of profit making.

This sphere that we are deserting, within whose boundaries the sale and purchase of labour-power goes, is in fact a very Eden of the innate rights of man. There alone rule Freedom, Equality, Property and Bentham. Freedom, because both buyer and seller of a commodity, say of labour-power, are constrained only by their own free will. They contract as free agents, and the agreement they come to is but the form in which they give legal expression to their common will. Equality, because each enters into relation with the other, as with a simple owner of commodities, and they exchange equivalent for equivalent. Property, because each disposes only of what is his own. And Bentham, because each looks only to himself. The only force that brings them together and puts them in relation with each other, is the selfishness, the gain and the private interests of each. Each looks to himself only, and no one troubles himself about the rest, and just because they do so, do they all, in accordance with the pre-established harmony of things, or under the auspices of an all-shrewd providence, work together to their mutual advantage, for the common weal and in the interest of all.

On leaving this sphere of simple circulation or of exchange of commodities, which furnishes the " Free-trader Vulgaris " with his views and ideas, and with the standard by which he judges a society based on capital and wages, we think we can perceive a change in the physiognomy of our dramatis personæ. He who before was the money owner now strides in front as capitalist ; the possessor of labour-power follows as his labourer. The one with an air of importance, smirking, intent on business ; the other, timid and holding back, like one who is bringing his own hide to market and has nothing to expect but—a hiding.

THE LABOUR PROCESS AND THE PROCESS OF PRODUCING SURPLUS VALUE
(Vol. I, Ch. VII)

The Labour Process or the Production of Use-Values

. . . Let us now return to our would-be capitalist. We left him just after he had purchased, in the open market, all the necessary factors of the labour-process ; its objective factors, the means of production, as well as its subjective factor, labour-power. With the keen eye of an expert, he had selected the means of production and the kind of labour-power best adapted to his particular trade, be it spinning, bootmaking, or any other kind. He then proceeds to consume the commodity, the labour-power that he has just bought, by causing the labourer, the impersonation of that labour-power, to consume the means of production by his labour. The general character of the labour-process is evidently not changed by the fact that the labourer works for the capitalist instead of for himself; moreover, the particular methods and operations employed in bootmaking or spinning are not immediately changed by the intervention of the capitalist. He must begin by taking the labour-power as he finds it in the market, and consequently be satisfied with labour of such a kind as would be found in the period immediately preceding the rise of the capitalists. Changes in the methods of production by the subordination of labour to capital, can take place only at a later period, and therefore will have to be treated of in a later chapter.

The labour-process, turned into the process by which the capitalist consumes labour-power, exhibits two characteristic phenomena. First, the labourer works under the control of the capitalist to whom his labour belongs; the capitalist taking good care that the work is done in a proper manner, and that the means of production are used with intelligence, so that there is no unnecessary waste of raw material, and no wear and tear of the implements beyond what is necessarily caused by the work.

Secondly, the product is the property of the capitalist and not that of the labourer, its immediate producer. Suppose that a capitalist pays for a day's labour-power at its value; then the right to use that power for a day belongs to him, just as much as the right to use any other commodity, such as a horse that he has hired for the day. To the purchaser of a commodity belongs its use, and the seller of labour-power, by giving his labour, does no more, in reality, than part with the use-value that he has sold. From the instant he steps into the workshop, the use-value of his labour-power, and therefore also its use, which is labour, belongs to the capitalist. By the purchase of labour-power, the capitalist incorporates labour, as a living ferment, with the lifeless constituents of the product. From his point of view, the labour-process is nothing more than the consumption of the commodity purchased, i.e., of labour-power ; but this consumption cannot be effected except by supplying the labour-power with the means of production. The labour-process is a process between things that the capitalist has purchased, things that have become his property. The product of this process also belongs, therefore, to him, just as much as does the wine which is the product of a process of fermentation completed in his cellar.

The Production of Surplus Value

The product appropriated by the capitalist is a use-value, as yarn, for example, or boots. But, although boots are, in one sense, the basis of all social progress, and our capitalist is a decided " progressist," yet he does not manufacture boots for their own sake. Use-value is, by no means, the thing " qu'on aime pour lui-même " in the production of commodities. Use-values are only produced by capitalists, because, and in so far as, they are the material substratum, the depositaries of exchange value. Our capitalist has two objects in view : in the first place, he wants to produce a use-value that has a value in exchange, that is to say, an article destined to be sold, a commodity ; and secondly, he desires to produce a commodity whose value shall be greater than the sum of the values of the commodities used in its production, that is, of the means of production and the labour-power, that he purchased with his good money in the open market. His aim is to produce not only a use-value, but a commodity also ; not only use-value, but value ; not only value, but at the same time surplus value.

It must be borne in mind, that we are now dealing with the production of commodities, and that, up to this point, we have only considered one aspect of the process. Just as commodities are, at the same time, use-values and values, so the process of producing them must be a labour-process, and at the same time, a process of creating value.

Let us now examine production as a creation of value.

We know that the value of each commodity is determined by the quantity of labour expended on and materialised in it, by the working-time necessary, under given social conditions, for its production. This rule also holds good in the case of the product that accrued to our capitalist, as the result of the labour-process carried on for him. Assuming this product to be 10 lbs. of yarn, our first step is to calculate the quantity of labour realised in it.

For spinning the yarn, raw material is required ; suppose in this case 10 lbs. of cotton. We have no need at present to investigate the value of this cotton, for our capitalist has, we will assume, bought it at its full value, say of ten shillings. In this price the labour required for the production of the cotton is already expressed in terms of the average labour of society. We will further assume that the wear and tear of the spindle, which, for our present purpose, may represent all other instruments of labour employed, amounts to the value of two shillings. If, then, twenty-four hours' labour, or two working days, are required to produce the quantity of gold represented by twelve shillings, we have here, to begin with, two days' labour already incorporated in the yarn.

We must not let ourselves be misled by the circumstance that the cotton has taken a new shape while the substance of the spindle has to a certain extent been used up. By the general law of value, if the value of 40 lbs. of yarn=the value of 40 lbs. of cotton + the value of a whole spindle, i.e., if the same working time is required to produce the commodities on either side of this equation, then 10 lbs. of yarn are an equivalent for 10 lbs. of cotton, together with one-fourth of a spindle. In the case we are considering the same working time is materialised in the 10 lbs. of yarn on the one hand, and in the 10 lbs. of cotton and the fraction of a spindle on the other. Therefore, whether value appears in cotton, in a spindle, or in yarn, makes no difference in the amount of that value. The spindle and cotton, instead of resting quietly side by side, join together in the process, their forms are altered, and they are turned into yarn ; but their value is no more affected by this fact than it would be if they had been simply exchanged for their equivalent in yarn.

The labour required for the production of the cotton, the raw material of the yarn, is part of the labour necessary to produce the yarn, and is therefore contained in the yarn. The same applies to the labour embodied in the spindle, without whose wear and tear the cotton could not be spun.

Hence, in determining the value of the yarn, or the labour-time required for its production, all the special processes carried on at various times and in different places, which were necessary, first to produce the cotton and the wasted portion of the spindle, and then with the cotton and spindle to spin the yarn, may together be looked on as different and successive phases of one and the same process. The whole of the labour in the yarn is past labour ; and it is a matter of no importance that the operations necessary for the production of its constituent elements were carried on at times which, referred to the present, are more remote than the final operation of spinning. If a definite quantity of labour, say thirty days, is requisite to build a house, the total amount of labour incorporated in it is not altered by the fact that the work of the last day is done twenty-nine days later than that of the first. Therefore the labour contained in the raw material and the instruments of labour can be treated just as if it were labour expended in an earlier stage of the spinning process, before the labour of actual spinning commenced.

The values of the means of production, i.e., the cotton and the spindle, which values are expressed in the price of twelve shillings, are therefore constituent parts of the value of the yarn, or, in other words, of the value of the product.

Two conditions must nevertheless be fulfilled. First, the cotton and spindle must concur in the production of a use-value ; they must in the present case become yarn. Value is independent of the particular use-value by which it is borne, but it must be embodied in a use-value of some kind. Secondly, the time occupied in the labour of production must not exceed the time really necessary under the given social conditions of the case. Therefore, if no more than 1 lb. of cotton be requisite to spin 1 lb. of yarn, care must be taken that no more than this weight of cotton is consumed in the production of 1 lb. of yarn ; and similarly with regard to the spindle. Though the capitalists have a hobby, and use a gold instead of a steel spindle, yet the only labour that counts for anything in the value of the yarn is that which would be required to produce a steel spindle, because no more is necessary under the given social conditions.

We now know what portion of the value of the yarn is owing to the cotton and the spindle. It amounts to twelve shillings or the value of two days' work. The next point for our consideration is, what portion of the value of the yarn is added to the cotton by the labour of the spinner.

We have now to consider this labour under a very different aspect from that which it had during the labour-process ; there, we viewed it solely as that particular kind of human activity which changes cotton into yarn ; there, the more the labour was suited to the work, the better the yarn, other circumstances remaining the same. The labour of the spinner was then viewed as specifically different from other kinds of productive labour, different on the one hand in its special aim, viz., spinning, different, on the other hand, in the special character of its operations, in the special nature of its means of production and in the special use-value of its product. For the operation of spinning, cotton and spindles are a necessity, but for making rifled cannon they would be of no use whatever. Here, on the contrary, where we consider the labour of the spinner only so far as it is value-creating, i.e., a source of value, his labour differs in no respect from the labour of the man who bores cannon, or (what here more nearly concerns us), from the labour of the cotton-planter and spindle-maker incorporated in the means of production. It is solely by reason of this identity, that cotton planting, spindle making and spinning, are capable of forming the component parts, differing only quantitatively from each other, of one whole, namely, the value of the yarn. Here, we have nothing more to do with the quality, the nature and the specific character of the labour, but merely with its quantity. And this simply requires to be calculated. We proceed upon the assumption that spinning is simple, unskilled labour, the average labour of a given state of society. Hereafter we shall see that the contrary assumption would make no difference.

While the labourer is at work his labour constantly undergoes a transformation : from being motion, it becomes an object without motion ; from being the labourer working, it becomes the thing produced. At the end of one hour's spinning, that act is represented by a definite quantity of yarn ; in other words, a definite quantity of labour, namely that of one hour, has become embodied in the cotton. We say labour, i.e., the expenditure of his vital force by the spinner, and not spinning labour, because the special work of spinning counts here, only so far as it is the expenditure of labour-power in general, and not in so far as it is the specific work of the spinner.

In the process we are now considering it is of extreme importance that no more time be consumed in the work of transforming the cotton into yarn than is necessary under the given social conditions. If under normal, i.e., average social conditions of production, a pounds of cotton ought to be made into b pounds of yarn by one hour's labour, then a day's labour does not count as 12 hours' labour unless 12 a pounds of cotton have been made into 12 b pounds of yarn ; for in the creation of value, the time that is socially necessary alone counts.

Not only the labour, but also the raw material and the product now appear in quite a new light, very different from that in which we viewed them in the labour-process pure and simple. The raw material serves now merely as an absorbent of a definite quantity of labour. By this absorption it is in fact changed into yarn, because it is spun, because labour-power in the form of spinning is added to it ; but the product, the yarn, is now nothing more than a measure of the labour absorbed by the cotton. If in one hour $1\frac{2}{3}$ lbs. of cotton can be spun into $1\frac{2}{3}$ lbs. of yarn, then 10 lbs. of yarn indicate the absorption of six hours' labour. Definite quantities of product, these quantities being determined by experience, now represent nothing but definite quantities of labour, definite masses of crystallised labour-time. They are nothing more than the materialisation of so many hours or so many days of social labour.

We are here no more concerned about the facts, that the labour is the specific work of spinning, that its subject is cotton and its product yarn, than we are about the fact that the subject itself is already a product and therefore raw material. If the spinner, instead of spinning, were working in a coal-mine, the subject of his labour, the coal, would be supplied by Nature ; nevertheless, a definite quantity of extracted coal, a hundredweight, for example, would represent a definite quantity of absorbed labour.

We assumed, on the occasion of its sale, that the value of a day's labour-power is three shillings, and that six hours' labour are incorporated in that sum ; and consequently that this amount of labour is requisite to produce the necessaries of life daily required on an average by the labourer. If now our spinner by working for one hour, can convert $1\frac{2}{3}$ lbs. of cotton into $1\frac{2}{3}$ lbs. of yarn, it follows that in six hours he will convert 10 lbs. of cotton into 10 lbs. of yarn. Hence, during the spinning process, the cotton absorbs six hours' labour. The same quantity of labour is also embodied in a piece of gold of the value of three shillings. Consequently by the mere labour of spinning, a value of three shillings is added to the cotton.

Let us now consider the total value of the product, the 10 lbs. of yarn. Two and a half days' labour have been embodied in it, of which two days were contained in the cotton and in the substance of the spindle worn away, and half a day was absorbed during the process of spinning. This two and a half days' labour is also represented by a piece of gold of the value of fifteen shillings. Hence, fifteen shillings is an adequate price for the 10 lbs. of yarn, or the price of one pound is eighteenpence.

Our capitalist stares in astonishment. The value of the product is exactly equal to the value of the capital advanced. The value so advanced has not expanded, no surplus value has been created, and consequently money has not been converted into capital. The price of the yarn is fifteen shillings, and fifteen shillings were spent in the open market upon the constituent elements of the product, or, what amounts to the same thing, upon the factors of the labour-process ; ten shillings were paid for the cotton, two shillings for the substance of the spindle worn away, and three shillings for the labour-power. The swollen value of the yarn is of no avail, for it is merely the sum of the values formerly existing in the cotton, the spindle, and the labour-power ; out of such a simple addition of existing values, no surplus value can possibly arise. These separate values are now all concentrated in one thing ; but so they were also in the sum of fifteen shillings, before it was split up into three parts, by the purchase of the commodities.

There is in reality nothing very strange in this result. The value of one pound of yarn being eighteenpence, if our capitalist buys 10 lbs. of yarn in the market, he must pay fifteen shillings for them. It is clear that, whether a man buys his house ready built, or gets it built for him, in neither case will the mode of acquisition increase the amount of money laid out on the house.

Our capitalist, who is at home in his vulgar economy, exclaims : " Oh ! but I advanced my money for the express purpose of making more money." The way to Hell is paved with good intentions, and he might just as easily have intended to make money, without producing at all. He threatens all sorts of things. He won't be caught napping again. In future he will buy the commodities in the market, instead of manufacturing them himself. But if all his brother capitalists were to do the same, where would he find his commodities in the market ? And his money he cannot eat. He tries persuasion. " Consider my abstinence ; I might have played ducks and drakes with the fifteen shillings ; but instead of that I consumed it productively, and made yarn with it." Very well, and by way of reward he is now in possession of good yarn instead of a bad conscience ; and as for playing the part of a miser, it would never do for him to relapse into such bad ways as that ; we have seen before to what results such asceticism leads. Besides, where nothing is, the king has lost his rights : whatever may be the merit of his abstinence, there is nothing wherewith specially to remunerate it, because the value of the product is merely the sum of the values of the commodities that were thrown into the process of production. Let him therefore console himself with the reflection that virtue is its own reward. But no, he becomes importunate. He says : " The yarn is of no use to me : I produced it for sale." In that case let him sell it, or, still better, let him for the future produce only things for satisfying his personal wants, a remedy that his physician M'Culloch has already prescribed as infallible against an epidemic of over-production. He now gets obstin- ate. " Can the labourer," he asks, " merely with his arms and legs, produce commodities out of nothing ? Did I not supply him with the materials, by means of which, and in which alone, his labour could be embodied ? And as the greater part of society consists of such ne'er-do-weels, have I not rendered society incalculable service by my instru- ments of production, my cotton and my spindle, and not only society, but the labourer also, whom in addition I have provided with the necessaries of life ? And am I to be allowed nothing in return for all this service ? " Well, but has not the labourer rendered him the equivalent service of changing his cotton and spindle into yarn ? Moreover, there is here no question of service. A service is nothing more than the useful effect of a use-value, be it of a commodity, or be it of labour. But here we are dealing with exchange value. The capitalist paid to the labourer a value of three shillings, and the labourer gave him back an exact equivalent in the value of three shillings, added by him to the cotton : he gave him value for value. Our friend, up to this time so purse-proud, suddenly assumes the modest demeanour of his own workman, and exclaims : " Have I myself not worked ? Have I not performed the labour of superintendence and of overlooking the spinner ? And does not this labour, too, create value?" His overlooker and his manager try to hide their smiles. Meanwhile, after a hearty laugh, he re-assumes his usual mien. Though he chanted to us the whole creed of the economists, in reality, he says, he would not give a brass farthing for it. He leaves this and all suchlike subterfuges and juggling tricks to the professors of political economy, who are paid for it. He himself is a practical man ; and though he does not always consider what he says outside his business, yet in his business he knows what he is about.

Let us examine the matter more closely. The value of a day's labour-power amounts to three shillings, because on our assumption half a day's labour is embodied in that quantity of labour-power, i.e., because the means of subsistence that are daily required for the production of labour-power, cost half a day's labour. But the past labour that is embodied in the labour-power, and the living labour that it can call into action ; the daily cost of maintaining it, and its daily expenditure in work, are two totally different things. The former determines the exchange value of the labour-power, the latter is its use-value. The fact that half a day's labour is necessary to keep the labourer alive during twenty-four hours, does not in any way prevent him from working a whole day. Therefore, the value of labour-power, and the value which that labour-power creates in the labour-process, are two entirely different magnitudes ; and this difference of the two values was what the capitalist had in view, when he was purchasing the labour-power. The useful qualities that labour-power possesses, and by virtue of which it makes yarn or boots, were to him nothing more than a *conditio sine qua non* ; for in order to create value, labour must be expended in a useful manner. What really influenced him was the specific use-value which this commodity possesses of being *a source not only of value, but of more value than it has itself*. This is the special service that the capitalist expects from labour-power, and in this transaction he acts in accordance with the " eternal laws " of the exchange of commodities. The seller of labour-power, like the seller of any other commodity, realises its exchange value, and parts with its use-value. He cannot take the one without giving the other. The use-value of labour-power, or in other words, labour, belongs just as little to its seller, as the use-value of oil after it has been sold belongs to the dealer who has sold it. The owner of the money has paid the value of a day's labour-power ; his, therefore, is the use of it for a day ; a day's labour belongs to him. The circumstance, that on the one hand the daily sustenance of labour-power costs only half a day's labour, while on the other hand the very same labour-power can work during a whole day, that consequently the value which its use during one day creates, is double what he pays for that use, this circumstance is, without doubt, a piece of good luck for the buyer, but by no means an injury to the seller.

Our capitalist foresaw this state of things, and that was the cause of his laughter. The labourer therefore finds, in the workshop, the means of production necessary for working, not only during six, but during twelve hours. Just as during the six hours' process our 10 lbs. of cotton absorbed six hours' labour, and became 10 lbs. of yarn, so now, 20 lbs. of cotton will absorb twelve hours' labour and be changed into 20 lbs. of yarn. Let us now examine the product of this prolonged process. There is now materialised in this 20 lbs. of yarn the labour of five days, of which four days are due to the cotton and the lost steel of the spindle, the remaining day having been absorbed by the cotton during the spinning process. Expressed in gold, the labour of five days is thirty shillings. This is therefore the price of the 20 lbs. of yarn, giving, as before, eighteenpence as the price of a pound. But the sum of the values of the commodities that entered into the process amounts to twenty-seven shillings. The value of the yarn is thirty shillings. Therefore the value of the product is one-ninth greater than the value advanced for its production ; twenty-seven shillings have been transformed into thirty shillings ; a surplus value of three shillings has been created. The trick has at last succeeded ; money has been converted into capital.

Every condition of the problem is satisfied, while the laws that regulate the exchange of commodities have been in no way violated. Equivalent has been exchanged for equivalent. For the capitalist as buyer paid for each commodity, for the cotton, the spindle and the labour-power, its full value. He then did what is done by every purchaser of commodities ; he consumed their use-value. The consumption of the labour-power, which was also the process of producing commodities, resulted in 20 lbs. of yarn, having a value of thirty shillings. The capitalist, formerly a buyer, now returns to market as a seller, of commodities. He sells his yarn at eighteenpence a pound, which is its exact value. Yet for all that he withdraws three shillings more from circulation than he originally threw into it. This metamorphosis, this conversion of money into capital, takes place both within the sphere of circulation and also outside it ; within the circulation, because conditioned by the purchase of the labour-power in the market ; outside the circulation because what is done within it is only a stepping-stone to the production of surplus value, a process which is entirely confined to the sphere of production. Thus " tout est pour le mieux dans le meilleur des mondes possibles."

By turning his money into commodities that serve as the material elements of a new product, and as factors in the labour-process, by incorporating living labour with their dead substance, the capitalist at the same time converts value, i.e., past, materialised, and dead labour into capital, into value big with value, a live monster that is fruitful and multiplies.

CONSTANT CAPITAL AND VARIABLE CAPITAL
(Vol. I, Ch. VIII)

. . . While productive labour is changing the means of production into constituent elements of a new product, their value undergoes a metempsychosis. It deserts the consumed body, to occupy the newly created one. But this transmigration takes place, as it were, behind the back of the labourer. He is unable to add new labour, to create new value, without at the same time preserving old values, and this, because the labour he adds must be of a specific useful kind ; and he cannot do work of a useful kind, without employing products as the means of production of a new product, and thereby transferring their value to the new product. The property therefore which labour-power in action, living labour, possesses of preserving value, at the same time that it adds it, is a gift of Nature which costs the labourer nothing, but which is very advantageous to the capitalist inasmuch as it preserves the existing value of his capital. So long as trade is good, the capitalist is too much absorbed in money-grubbing to take notice of this gratuitous gift of labour. A violent interruption of the labour-process by a crisis makes him sensitively aware of it.

As regards the means of production, what is really consumed is their use-value, and the consumption of this use-value by labour results in the product. There is no consumption of their value, and it would therefore be inaccurate to say that it is reproduced. It is rather preserved ; not by reason of any operation it undergoes itself in the process ; but because the article in which it originally exists, vanishes, it is true, but vanishes into some other article. Hence, in the value of the product, there is a re-appearance of the value of the means of production, but there is, strictly speaking, no reproduction of that value. That which is produced is a new use-value in which the old exchange value re-appears.

It is otherwise with the subjective factor of the labour-process, with labour-power in action. While the labourer, by virtue of his labour being of a specialised kind that has a special object, preserves and transfers to the product the value of the means of production, he at the same time, by the mere act of working, creates each instant an additional or new value. Suppose the process of production to be stopped just when the workman has produced an equivalent for the value of his own labour-power, when, for example, by six hours' labour, he has added a value of three shillings. This value is the surplus, of the total value of the product, over the portion of its value that is due to the means of production. It is the only original bit of value formed during this process, the only portion of the value of the product created by this process. Of course, we do not forget that this new value only replaces the money advanced by the capitalist in the purchase of the labour-power, and spent by the labourer on the necessaries of life. With regard to the money spent, the new value is merely a reproduction ; but, nevertheless, it is an actual, and not, as in the case of the value of the means of production, only an apparent, reproduction. The substitution of one value for another is here effected by the creation of new value.

We know, however, from what has gone before, that the labour-process may continue beyond the time necessary to reproduce and incorporate in the product a mere equivalent for the value of the labour-power. Instead of the six hours that are sufficient for the latter purpose, the process may continue for twelve hours. The action of labour-power, therefore, not only reproduces its own value, but produces value over and above it. This surplus value is the difference between the value of the product and the value of the elements consumed in the formation of that product, in other words, of the means of production and the labour-power.

By our explanation of the different parts played by the various factors of the labour-process in the formation of the product's value, we have, in fact, disclosed the characters of the different functions allotted to the different elements of capital in the process of expanding its own value. The surplus of the total value of the product, over the sum of the values of its constituent factors, is the surplus of the expanded capital over the capital originally advanced. The means of production on the one hand, labour-power on the other, are merely the different modes of existence which the value of the original capital assumed when from being money it was transformed into the various factors of the labour-process. That part of capital then, which is represented by the means of production, by the raw material, auxiliary material and the instruments of labour, does not, in the process of production, undergo any quantitative alteration of value. I therefore call it the constant part of capital, or, more shortly, *constant capital*.

On the other hand, that part of capital, represented by labour-power, does, in the process of production, undergo an alteration of value. It both reproduces the equivalent of its own value, and also produces an excess, a surplus value, which may itself vary, may be more or less according to circumstances. This part of capital is continually being transformed from a constant into a variable magnitude. I therefore call it the variable part of capital, or, shortly, *variable capital*. The same elements of capital which, from the point of view of the labour-process, present themselves respectively as the objective and subjective factors, as means of production and labour-power, present themselves, from the point of view of the process of creating surplus value, as constant and variable capital.

The definition of constant capital given above by no means excludes the possibility of a change of value in its elements. Suppose the price of cotton to be one day sixpence a pound, and the next day, in consequence of a failure of the cotton crop, a shilling a pound. Each pound of the cotton bought at sixpence, and worked up after the rise in value, transfers to the product a value of one shilling ; and the cotton already spun before the rise, and perhaps circulating in the markets as yarn, likewise transfers to the product twice its original value. It is plain, however, that these changes of value are independent of the increment or surplus value added to the value of the cotton by the spinning itself. If the old cotton had never been spun, it could, after the rise, be resold at a shilling a pound instead of at sixpence. Further, the fewer the processes the cotton has gone through, the more certain is this result. We therefore find that speculators make it a rule when such sudden changes in value occur to speculate in that material on which the least possible quantity of labour has been spent : to speculate, therefore, in yarn rather than in cloth, in cotton itself, rather than in yarn. The change of value in the case we have been considering, originates, not in the process in which the cotton plays the part of a means of production, and in which it therefore functions as constant capital, but in the process in which the cotton itself is produced. The value of a commodity, it is true, is determined by the quantity of labour contained in it, but this quantity is itself limited by social conditions. If the time socially necessary for the production of any commodity alters—and a given weight of cotton represents, after a bad harvest, more labour than after a good one—all previously existing commodities of the same class are affected, because they are, as it were, only individuals of the species, and their value at any given time is measured by the labour socially necessary, i.e., by the labour necessary for their production under the then existing social conditions.

As the value of the raw material may change, so, too, may that of the instruments of labour, of the machinery, etc., employed in the process ; and consequently that portion of the value of the product transferred to it from them, may also change. If in consequence of a new invention, machinery of a particular kind can be produced by a diminished expenditure of labour, the old machinery becomes depreciated more or less and consequently transfers so much less value to the product. But here again, the change in value originates outside the process in which the machine is acting as a means of production. Once engaged in this process, the machine cannot transfer more value than it possesses apart from the process.

Just as a change in the value of the means of production, even after they have commenced to take a part in the labour process, does not alter their character as constant capital, so, too, a change in the proportion of constant to variable capital does not affect the respective functions of these two kinds of capital. The technical conditions of the labour-process may be revolutionised to such an extent that, where formerly ten men using ten implements of small value worked up a relatively small quantity of raw material, one man may now, with the aid of one expensive machine, work up one hundred times as much raw material. In the latter case we have an enormous increase in the constant capital, that is represented by the total value of the means of production used, and at the same time a great reduction in the variable capital, invested in labour-power. Such a revolution, however, alters only the quantitative relation between the constant and the variable capital, or the proportions in which the total capital is split up into its constant and variable constituents ; it has not in the least degree affected the essential difference between the two.

SIMPLE REPRODUCTION
(Vol. II, Ch. XX)
The Formulation of the Question

. . . So long as we looked upon the production of value and the value of products from the point of view of individual capital, it was immaterial for the analysis which was the natural form of the product in commodities, whether it was, for instance, that of a machine, of corn, or of looking-glasses. It was always but a matter of illustration, and any line of production could serve that purpose. What we had to consider was the immediate process of production itself, which presented itself at every point as the process of some individual capital. So far as reproduction was concerned, it was sufficient to assume that that portion of the product in commodities, which represented capital in the sphere of circulation, found an opportunity to reconvert itself into its elements of production and thus into its form of productive capital. It likewise sufficed to assume that both the labourer and the capitalist found in the market those commodities for which they spend their wages and surplus-value. This merely formal manner of presentation does not suffice in the study of the total social capital and of the value of its products. The reconversion of one portion of the value of the product into capital, the passing of another portion into the individual consumption of the capitalist and working classes, form a movement within the value of the product itself which is created by the total capital ; and this movement is not only a reproduction of value, but also of material, and is, therefore, as much conditioned on the relative proportions of the elements of value of the total social product as on its use-value, its material substance.

Simple reproduction on the same scale appears as an abstraction, inasmuch as the absence of all accumulation or reproduction on an enlarged scale is an irrelevant assumption in capitalist society, and, on the other hand, conditions of production do not remain exactly the same in different years (as was assumed). The assumption is that a social capital of a given magnitude produces the same quantity of value in commodities this year as last, and supplies the same quantity of wants, although the forms of the commodities may be changed in the process of reproduction. However, while accumulation does take place, simple reproduction is always a part of it and may, therefore, be studied in itself, being an actual factor in accumulation. . . .

The Two Departments of Social Production

The total product, and therefore the total production, of society, is divided into two great sections :

I. *Means of Production*, commodities having a form in which they must, or at least may, pass over into productive consumption.

II. *Means of Consumption*, commodities having a form in which they pass into the individual consumption of the capitalist and working classes.

In each of these two departments, all the various lines of production belonging to them form one single great line of production, the one that of the means of production, the other that of articles of consumption. The aggregate capital invested in each of these two departments of production constitutes a separate section of the entire social capital.

In each department, the capital consists of two parts :

(1) *Variable Capital*. This capital, so far as its value is concerned, is equal to the value of the social labour-power employed in this line of production, in other words equal to the sum of the wages paid for this labour-power. So far as its substance is concerned, it consists of the active labour-power itself, that is to say, of the living labour set in motion by this value of capital.

(2) *Constant Capital*. This is the value of all the means of production employed in this line. These, again, are divided into *fixed* capital, such as machines, instruments of labour, buildings, labouring animals, etc., and *circulating* capital, such as materials of production, raw and auxiliary materials, half-wrought articles, etc.

The value of the total annual product created with the capital of each of the two great departments of production consists of one portion representing the constant capital c consumed in the process of production and transferred to the product, and of another portion added by the entire labour of the year. This latter portion, again, consists of one part reproducing the advanced variable capital v, and of another representing an excess over the variable capital, the surplus-value s. And just as the value of every individual commodity, so that of the entire annual product of each department consists of c + v + s.

The portion c of the value, representing the constant capital *consumed* in production, is not identical with the value of the constant capital *invested* in production. It is true that the materials of production are entirely consumed and their values completely transferred to the product. But of the invested *fixed* capital, only a portion is consumed and its value transferred to the product. Another portion of the fixed capital, such as machines, buildings, etc., continues to exist and serve the same as before, merely depreciating to the extent of the annual wear and tear. This persistent portion of the fixed capital does not exist for us, when we consider the value of the product. It is a portion of the value of capital existing independently beside the new value in commodities produced by this capital. This was shown previously in the analysis of the value of the product of some individual capital (Volume I, Chapter VI). However, for the present we must leave aside the method of analysis employed there. We saw in the study of the value of the product of individual capital that the value withdrawn from the fixed capital by wear and tear was transferred to the product in commodities created during the time of wear, no matter whether any portion of this fixed capital is reproduced in its natural form out of the value thus transferred or not. At this point, however, in the study of the social product as a whole and of its value, we must for the present leave out of consideration that portion of value which is transferred from the fixed capital to the annual product by wear and tear, unless this fixed capital is reproduced *in natura* during the year. In one of the following sections of this chapter we shall return to this point.

We shall base our analysis of simple reproduction on the following diagram, in which c stands for constant capital, v for variable capital, and s for surplus value, the rate of surplus value between v and s being assumed at 100 per cent. The figures may indicate millions of francs, marks, pounds sterling, or dollars.

I. Production of Means of Production.

Capital...............4000 c + 1000 v=5000.

Product in Commodities..4000 c + 1000 v + 1000 s= 6000.

These exist in the form of means of production.

II. Production of Means of Consumption.

Capital................2000 c + 500 v=2500.

Product in Commodities..2000 c + 500 v + 500 s=3000.

These exist in articles of consumption.

Recapitulation : Total annual product in commodities :

I. 4000 c + 1000 v + 1000 s=6000 means of production.

II. 2000 c + 500 v + 500 s=3000 articles of consumption.

Total value 9000, exclusive of the fixed capital persisting in its natural form, according to our assumption.

Now, if we examine the transactions required on the basis of simple reproduction, where the entire surplus value is unproductively consumed, leaving aside for the present the mediation of the money circulation, we obtain at the outset three great points of vantage.

(1) The 500 v, representing wages of the labourers, and 500 s, representing surplus value of the capitalists, in department II, must be spent for articles of consumption. But their value exists in the articles of consumption to the amount of 1000, held by the capitalists of department II, which reproduce the 500 v and represent the 500 s. The wages and surplus value of department II, then, are exchanged within this department for products of this same department. By this means, a quantity of articles of consumption equal to 1000 (500 v + 500 s) disappear out of the total product of department II.

(2) The 1000 v and 1000 s of department I must likewise

be spent for articles of consumption, in other words, for some of the products of department II. Hence they must be exchanged for the remaining 2000 c of constant value, which is equal in amount to them. Department II receives in return an equal quantity of means of production, the product of I, in which the value of 1000 v and 1000 s of I is incorporated. By this means, 2000 c of II and (1000 v + 1000 s) of I disappear out of the calculation.

(3) Nothing remains now but 4000 c of I. These consist of means of production which can be used up only in department I. They serve for the reproduction of its consumed constant capital, and are disposed of by the mutual exchange between the individual capitalists of I, just as are the (500 v + 500 s) in II by an exchange between the capitalists and labourers, or between the individual capitalists, of II. . . .

ACCUMULATION AND REPRODUCTION ON AN ENLARGED SCALE
(Vol. II, Ch. XXI)

It has been shown in Volume I, how accumulation works in the case of the individual capitalist. By the conversion of the commodity-capital into money, the surplus-product, in which the surplus value is incorporated, is also monetised. The capitalist reconverts the surplus value thus monetised into additional natural elements of his productive capital. In the next cycle of production the increased capital furnishes an increased product. But what happens in the case of the individual capital, must also show in the annual reproduction of society as a whole, just as we have seen it done in the case of reproduction on a simple scale, where the successive precipitation of the depreciated elements of fixed capitals in the form of money, accumulated as a hoard, also makes itself felt in the annual reproduction of society.

If a certain individual capital amounts to 400 c + 100 v,

with an annual surplus value of 100 s, then the product in commodities amounts to 400 c + 100 v + 100 s. This amount of 600 is converted into money. Of this money, again, 400 c are converted into the natural form of constant capital, 100 v into labour power, and—provided that the entire surplus value is accumulated—100 s are converted into additional constant capital by their transformation into natural elements of productive capital. The following assumptions go with this case : (1) That this amount is sufficient under the given technical conditions either to expand the existing constant capital, or to establish a new industrial business. But it may also happen that surplus value must be converted into money and this money hoarded for a much longer time, before these steps may be taken, before actual accumulation, or expansion of production, can take place. (2) It is furthermore assumed that production on an enlarged scale has actually been in process previously. For in order that the money (the surplus value hoarded as money) may be converted into elements of productive capital, these elements must be available on the market as commodities. It makes no difference whether they are bought as finished products, or made to order. They are not paid for until they are finished, and at any rate, until actual reproduction on an enlarged scale, an expansion of hitherto normal production, has taken place so far as they are concerned. They had to be present potentially, that is to say, in their elements, for it required only an impulse in the form of an order, that is to say, a purchase preceding their actual existence and anticipating their sale, in order to stimulate their production. The money on one side in that case calls forth expanded reproduction on the other, because the possibility for it exists without the money. For money in itself is not an element of actual reproduction. . . .

A. Diagram of Simple Reproduction.

I. $4000 c + 1000 v + 1000 s = 6000$
II. $2000 c + 500 v + 500 s = 3000$ } Total, 9000.

B. Initial Diagram for Accumulation on an Expanded Scale.

I. 4000 c + 1000 v + 1000 s = 6000 ⎫
II. 1500 c + 750 v + 750 s = 3000 ⎬ Total, 9000.

Assuming that in diagram B one half of the surplus value of I, amounting to 500, is accumulated, we have first to accomplish the change of place between (1000 v + 500 s) I, or 1500 I (v + s), and 1500 II c. Department I then keeps 4000 c and 500 s, the last sum being accumulated. The exchange between (1000 v + 500 s) I and 1500 II c is a process of simple reproduction, which has been examined previously.

Let us now assume that 400 of the 500 I s are to be converted into constant capital, and 100 into variable capital. The transactions within the 400 s of I, which are to be capitalised, have already been discussed. They can be immediately annexed to I c, and in that case we get in department I

4400 c + 1000 v + 100 s (these last to be converted into 100 v).

Department II buys from I for the purpose of accumulation the 100 I s (existing in means of production), which thus become additional constant capital in department II, while the 100 in money, which this department pays for them, are converted into the money-form of the additional variable capital of I. We then have for I a capital of 4400 c + 1100 v (these last in money), a total of 5500.

Department II has now 1600 c for its constant capital. In order to be able to operate this, it must advance 50 v in money for the purchase of new labour power, so that its variable capital grows from 750 to 800. This expansion of the constant and variable capital of II by a total of 150 is supplied out of its surplus value. Hence only 600 of the 750 II s remain for the consumption of the capitalists of II, whose annual product is now distributed as follows :

II. 1600 c + 800 v + 600 s (fund for consumption), a total of 3000. The 150 s, produced in articles of consumption, which have been converted into (100 c + 50 v) II, pass entirely into the consumption of the labourers in this form, 100 being consumed by the labourers of I (100 I v), and 50 by the labourers of II (50 II v), as explained above. Department II, where the total product is prepared in a form suitable for accumulation, must indeed reproduce surplus value in the form of necessary articles of consumption exceeding the other portions by 100. If reproduction really starts on an expanded scale, then the 100 of variable money capital of I flow back to II through the hands of the labourers of I, while II transfers 100 s in commodities to I and at the same time 50 in commodities to its own labourers.

The change made in the arrangement for the purpose of accumulation now presents the following aspect :

I. 4400 c + 1100 v + 500 fund for consumption = 6000
II. 1600 c + 800 v + 600 fund for consumption = 3000

Total, as before, 9000

Of these amounts, the following are capital :

I. 4400 c + 1100 v (money) = 5500 ⎱ Total, 7900
II. 1600 c + 800 v (money) = 2400 ⎰

while production started out with

I. 4000 c + 1000 v = 5000 ⎱ Total, 7250
II. 1500 c + 750 v = 2250 ⎰

Now, if actual accumulation takes place on this basis, that is to say, if reproduction is actually undertaken with this increased capital, we obtained at the end of next year :

I. 4400 c + 1100 v + 1100 s = 6600 ⎱ Total, 9800.
II. 1600 c + 800 v + 800 s = 3200 ⎰

MARKET PRICES AND MARKET VALUES
(Vol. III, Ch. X)

. . . Whatever may be the way in which the prices of the various commodities are first fixed or mutually regulated, the law of value always dominates their movements. If the labour time required for the production of these commodities is reduced, prices fall ; if it is increased, prices rise, other circumstances remaining the same.

Aside from the fact that prices and their movements are dominated by the law of value, it is quite appropriate, under these circumstances, to regard the value of commodities not only theoretically, but also historically, as existing prior to the prices of production. This applies to conditions, in which the labourer owns his means of production, and this is the condition of the land-owning farmer and of the craftsman in the old world as well as the new. This agrees also with the view formerly expressed by me that the development of products into commodities arises through the exchange between different communes, not through that between the members of the same commune. It applies not only to this primitive condition, but also to subsequent conditions based on slavery or serfdom, and to the guild organisation of handicrafts, so long as the means of production installed in one line of production cannot be transferred to another line except under difficulties, so that the various lines of production maintain, to a certain degree, the same mutual relations as foreign countries or communistic groups.

In order that the prices at which commodities are exchanged with one another may correspond approximately to their values, no other conditions are required but the following : (1) The exchange of the various commodities must no longer be accidental or occasional ; (2) So far as the direct exchange of commodities is concerned, these commodities must be produced on both sides in sufficient quantities to meet mutual requirements, a thing easily learned by experience in trading, and therefore a natural outgrowth of continued trading ; (3) So far as selling is concerned, there must be no accidental or artificial monopoly which may enable either of the contracting sides to sell commodities above their value or compel others to sell below value. An accidental monopoly is one which a buyer or seller acquires by an accidental proportion of supply to demand.

The assumption that the commodities of the various spheres of production are sold at their value implies, of course, only that their value is the centre of gravity around which prices fluctuate, and around which their rise and fall tends to an equilibrium. We shall also have to note a *market value*, which must be distinguished from the individual value of the commodities produced by the various producers. Of this more anon. The individual value of some of these commodities will be below the market value, that is to say, they require less labour-time for their production than is expressed in the market value, while that of others will be above the market value. We shall have to regard the market-value on one side as the average value of the commodities produced in a certain sphere, and on the other side as the individual value of commodities produced under the average conditions of their respective sphere of production and constituting the bulk of the products of that sphere. It is only extraordinary combinations of circumstances under which commodities produced under the least or most favourable conditions regulate the market value, which forms the centre of fluctuation for the market prices, which are the same, however, for the same kind of commodities. If the ordinary demand is satisfied by the supply of commodities of average value, that is to say, of a value midway between the two extremes, then those commodities, whose individual value stands below the market value, realise an extra surplus-value, or surplus-profit, while those, whose individual value stands above the market value, cannot realise a portion of the surplus value contained in them. . . .

No matter what may be the way in which prices are regulated, the result always is the following :

(1) The law of value dominates the movements of prices, since a reduction or increase of the labour time required for production causes the prices of production to fall or to rise. It is in this sense that Ricardo (who doubtless realised that

his prices of production differed from the value of commodities) says that " the inquiry to which he wishes to draw the reader's attention relates to the effect of the variations in the relative value of commodities, and not in their absolute value."

(2) The average profit which determines the prices of production must always be approximately equal to that quantity of surplus value which falls to the share of a certain individual capital in its capacity as an aliquot part of the total social capital. Take it that the average rate of profit, and therefore the average profit, are expressed by an amount of money of a higher value than the money value of the actual average surplus value. So far as the capitalists are concerned in that case, it is immaterial whether they charge one another a profit of 10 or of 15 per cent. The one of these percentages does not cover any more actual commodity value than the other, since the overcharge in money is mutual. But so far as the labourer is concerned (the assumption being that he receives the normal wages, so that the raising of the average profit does not imply an actual deduction from his wages, in other words, does not express something entirely different from the normal surplus value of the capitalist), the rise in the price of commodities due to a raising of the average profit must be accompanied by a corresponding rise of the money expression for the variable capital. As a matter of fact, such a general nominal raising of the rate of profit and the average profit above the limit provided by the proportion of the actual surplus value to the total invested capital is not possible without carrying in its wake an increase of wages, and also an increase in the prices of the commodities which constitute the constant capital. The same is true of the opposite case, that of a reduction of the rate of profit in this way. Now, since the total value of the commodities regulates the total surplus value, and this the level of the average profit and the average rate of profit—always understanding this as a general law, as a principle regulating the fluctuations—it

follows that the law of value regulates the prices of production.

Competition first brings about, in a certain individual sphere, the establishment of an equal market value and market price by averaging the various individual values of the commodities. The competition of the capitals in the different spheres then results in the price of production which equalises the rates of profit between the different spheres. This last process requires a higher development of capitalist production than the previous process.

In order that commodities of the same sphere of production, the same kind, and approximately the same quality may be sold at their value, the following two requirements must be fulfilled :

(1) The different individual values must have been averaged into *one* social value, the above-named market value, and this implies a competition between the producers of the same kind of commodities, and also the existence of a common market, on which they offer their articles for sale. In order that the market price of identical commodities, which however are produced under different individual circumstances, may correspond to the market value, may not differ from it by exceeding it or falling below it, it is necessary that the different sellers should exert sufficient pressure upon one another to bring that quantity of commodities on the market which social requirements demand, in other words, that quantity of commodities whose market value society can pay. If the quantity of products exceeds this demand, then the commodities must be sold below their market value ; vice versa, if the quantity of products is not large enough to meet this demand, or, what amounts to the same, if the pressure of competition among the sellers is not strong enough to bring this quantity of products to market, then the commodities are sold above their market value. If the market value is changed, then there will also be a change in the conditions under which the total quantity of commodities can be sold. If the market value falls, then

the average social demand increases (always referring to the solvent demand) and can absorb a larger quantity of commodities within certain limits. If the market value rises, then the solvent social demand for commodities is reduced and smaller quantities of them are absorbed. Hence if supply and demand regulate the market price, or rather the deviations of market prices from market values, it is true, on the other hand, that the market value regulates the proportions of supply and demand, or the centre around which supply and demand cause the market prices to fluctuate.

If we look closer at the matter, we find that the conditions determining the value of some individual commodity become effective, in this instance, as conditions determining the value of the total quantities of a certain kind. For, generally speaking, capitalist production is from the outset a mass production. And even other, less developed, modes of production carry small quantities of products, the result of the work of many small producers, to market as co-operative products, at least in the main lines of production, concentrating and accumulating them for sale in the hands of relatively few merchants. Such commodities are regarded as co-operative products of an entire line of production, or of a greater or smaller part of this line.

We remark by the way that the " social demand," in other words, that which regulates the principle of demand, is essentially conditioned on the mutual relations of the different economic classes and their relative economic positions, that is to say, first, on the proportion of the total surplus value to the wages, and secondly, on the proportion of the various parts into which surplus value is divided (profit, interest, ground-rent, taxes, etc.). And this shows once more that absolutely nothing can be explained by the relation of supply and demand, unless the basis has first been ascertained, on which this relation rests. . . .

(2) To say that a commodity has a use-value is merely to say that it satisfies some social want. So long as we were dealing simply with individual commodities, we could

assume that the demand for any one commodity—its price implying its quantity—existed without inquiring into the extent to which this demand required satisfaction. But this question of the extent of a certain demand becomes essential, whenever the product of some entire line of production is placed on one side, and the social demand for it on the other. In that case it becomes necessary to consider the amount, the quantity, of this social demand.

In the foregoing statements referring to market value, the assumption was that the mass of the produced commodities remains the same given quantity, and that a change takes place only in the proportions of the elements constituting this mass and produced under different conditions, so that the market value of the same mass of commodities is differently regulated. Let us suppose that this mass is of a quantity equal to the ordinary supply, leaving aside the possibility that a portion of the produced commodities may be temporarily withdrawn from the market. Now, if the demand for this mass also remains the same, then this commodity will be sold at its market value ; no matter which one of the three aforementioned cases may regulate this market value. This mass of commodities does not only satisfy a demand, but satisfies it to its full social extent. On the other hand, if the quantity is smaller than the demand for it, then the market prices differ from the market values. And the first differentiation is that the market value is always regulated by the commodity produced under the least favourable circumstances, if the supply is too small, and by the commodity produced under the most favourable conditions, if the supply is too large. In other words, one of the extremes determines the market value, in spite of the fact that the proportion of the masses produced under different conditions ought to bring about a different result. If the difference between demand and supply of the product is very considerable, then the market price will likewise differ considerably from the market value in either direction. Now, the difference between the quantity of the produced commodities and the quantity of commodities which fixes their sale at their market value may be due to two reasons. Either the quantity itself varies, by decreasing or increasing, so that there would be a reproduction on a different scale than the one which regulated a certain market value. If so, then the supply changes while the demand remains unchanged, and we have a relative over-production or under-production. Or, the reproduction, and the supply, remain the same, while the demand is reduced or increased, which may take place for several reasons. If so, then the absolute magnitude of the supply is un-changed, while its relative magnitude, compared to the demand, has changed. The effect is the same as in the first case, only it acts in the opposite direction. Finally, if changes take place on both sides, either in opposite direc-tions, or, if in the same direction, not to the same extent, in other words, if changes take place on both sides which alter the former proportion between these sides, then the final result must always lead to one of the two above-mentioned cases.

The real difficulty in determining the meaning of the concepts supply and demand is that they seem to amount to a tautology. Consider first the supply, either the product on the market, or the product which can be supplied to the market. In order to avoid useless details, we shall consider only the mass annually reproduced in every given line of production and leave out of the question the varying faculty of some commodities to withdraw from the market and go into storage for consumption at a later time, for instance next year. This annual reproduction is expressed in a cer-tain quantity, in weight or numbers, according to whether this mass of commodities is measured continuously or discontinuously. They represent not only use-value satisfy-ing human wants, but these use-values are on the market in definite quantities. In the second place, this quantity of commodities has a definite market value, which may be expressed by a multiple of the market value of the individual commodity, or of the measure, which serve as units. There is, then, no necessary connection between the quantitative volume of the commodities on the market and their market value, since many commodities have, for instance, a high specific value, others a low specific value, so that a given sum of values may be represented by a very large quantity of some, and a very small quantity of other commodities. There is only this connection between the quantity of articles on the market and the market value of these articles : Given a certain basis for the productivity of labour in every particular sphere of production, the production of a certain quantity of articles requires a definite quantity of social labour time ; but this proportion differs in different spheres of production and stands in no internal relation to the usefulness of these articles or the particular nature of their use-values. Assuming all other circumstances to be equal, and a certain quantity a of some commodity to cost b labour time, a quantity na of the same commodity will cost nb labour time. Furthermore, if society wants to satisfy some demand and have articles produced for this purpose, it must pay for them. Since the production of commodities is accompanied by a division of labour, society buys these articles by devoting to their production a portion of its available labour time. Society buys them by spending a definite quantity of the labour time over which it disposes. That part of society, to which the division of labour assigns the task of employing its labour in the production of the desired article, must be given an equivalent for it by other social labour incorporated in articles which it wants. There is, however, no necessary, but only an accidental, connection between the volume of society's demand for a certain article and the volume represented by the production of this article in the total production, or the quantity of social labour spent on this article, the aliquot part of the total labour power spent by society in the production of this article. True, every individual article, or every definite quantity of any kind of commodities, contains,

perhaps, only the social labour required for its production,
and from this point of view the market value of this entire
mass of commodities of a certain kind represents only
necessary labour. Nevertheless, if this commodity has been
produced in excess of the temporary demand of society
for it, so much of the social labour has been wasted, and
in that case this mass of commodities represents a much
smaller quantity of labour on the market than is actually
incorporated in it. (Only when production will be under the
conscious and prearranged control of society, will society
establish a direct relation between the quantity of social
labour time employed in the production of definite articles
and the quantity of the demand of society for them.) The
commodities must then be sold below their market value,
and a portion of them may even become unsaleable. The
opposite takes place if the quantity of social labour employed in the production of a certain kind of commodities
is too small to meet the social demand for them. But if the
quantity of social labour spent in the production of a
certain article corresponds to the social demand for it, so
that the quantity produced is that which is the ordinary
on that scale of production and for that same demand, then
the article is sold at its market value. The exchange, or sale,
of commodities at their value is the rational way, the
natural law of their equilibrium. It must be the point of
departure for the explanation of deviations from it, not
vice versa the deviations the basis on which this law is
explained.

Now let us look at the other side, the demand.

Commodities are bought either as means of production or
means of subsistence, in order to be used for productive or
individual consumption. It does not alter matters that some
commodities may serve both ends. There is, then, a demand
for them on the part of the producers (who are capitalists in
this case, since we have assumed that the means of production have been transformed into capital) and on the part of
the consumers. It appears at first sight as though these

two sides ought to have a corresponding quantity of social demands offset by a corresponding quantity of social supplies in the various lines of production. If the cotton industry is to accomplish its annual reproduction on a given scale, it must produce the usual quantity of cotton and an additional quantity determined by the annual extension of reproduction through the necessities of accumulating capital, always assuming other circumstances to remain the same. This is also true of means of subsistence. The working class must find at least the same quantity of necessities on hand, if it is to continue living in the accustomed way, although these necessities may be of different kinds and differently distributed. And there must be an additional quantity to allow for the annual increase of population. This applies with more or less modification to the other classes.

It would seem, then, that there is on the side of demand a definite magnitude of social wants which require for their satisfaction a definite quantity of certain articles on the market. But the quantity demanded by these wants is very elastic and changing. Its fixedness is but apparent. If the means of subsistence were cheaper, or money wages higher, the labourers would buy more of them, and a greater " social demand " would be manifested for this kind of commodities, leaving aside the question of paupers, whose " demand " is even below the narrowest limits of their physical wants. On the other hand, if cotton were cheaper, the demand of the capitalists for it would increase, more additional capital would be thrown into the cotton industry, etc. It must never be forgotten that the demand for productive consumption is a demand of capitalists, under our assumption, and that its essential purpose is the production of surplus value, so that commodities are produced only to this end. Still this does not argue against the fact that the capitalist as a buyer, for instance of cotton, represents the demand for this cotton. Moreover it is immaterial to the seller of cotton, whether the buyer converts it into shirting or into guncotton, or whether he intends to make it into wads for his and the world's ears. But it *does* exert a considerable influence on the way in which the capitalist acts as a buyer. His demand for cotton is essentially modified by the fact that he disguises thereby his real demand, that of making profits. The limits within which the *need for commodities on the market*, the demand, differs quantitatively from the *actual social need*, varies naturally considerably for different commodities ; in other words, the difference between the demanded quantity of commodities and that quantity which would be demanded, if the money prices of the commodities, or other conditions concerning the money or living of the buyers, were different. . . .

THE LAW OF THE FALLING TENDENCY OF THE RATE OF PROFIT : THE THEORY OF THE LAW
(Vol. III, Ch. XIII)

With a given wage and working day, a certain variable capital, for instance of 100, represents a certain number of employed labourers. It is the index of this number. For instance, let 100 p.st. be the wages of 100 labourers for one week. If these labourers perform the same amount of necessary as of surplus labour, in other words, if they work daily as much time for themselves as they do for the capitalist, or, in still other words, if they require as much time for the reproduction of their wages as they do for the production of surplus value for the capitalist, then they would produce a total value of 200 p.st., and the surplus value would amount to 100 p.st. The rate of surplus value, $\frac{s}{v}$, would be 100 per cent. But we have seen that this rate of surplus value would express itself in considerably different rates of profit, according to the different volumes of constant capitals c and consequently of total capitals C. For the rate of profit is calculated by the formula $\frac{s}{C}$.

Take it that the rate of surplus value is 100 per cent. Now, if

c= 50, and v=100, then p$'=\frac{100}{150}$, or 66$\frac{2}{3}$%.
c=100, and v=100, then p$'=\frac{100}{200}$, or 50 %.
c=200, and v=100, then p$'=\frac{100}{300}$, or 33$\frac{1}{3}$%.
c=300, and v=100, then p$'=\frac{100}{400}$, or 25 %.
c=400, and v=100, then p$'=\frac{100}{500}$, or 20 %.

In this way, the same rate of surplus value, with the same degree of labour exploitation, would express itself in a falling rate of profit, because the material growth of the constant capital, and consequently of the total capital, implies their growth in value, although not in the same proportion.

If it is furthermore assumed that this gradual change in the composition of capital is not confined to some individual spheres of production, but occurs more or less in all, or at least in the most important ones, so that they imply changes in the organic average composition of the total capital of a certain society, then the gradual and relative growth of the constant over the variable capital must necessarily lead to *a gradual fall of the average rate of profit*, so long as the rate of surplus value, or the intensity of exploitation of labour by capital, remain the same. Now we have seen that it is one of the laws of capitalist production that its development carries with it a relative decrease of variable as compared with constant capital, and consequently as compared to the total capital, which it sets in motion. This is only another way of saying that the same number of labourers, the same quantity of labour power set in motion by a variable capital of a given value, consume in production an ever increasing quantity of means of production, such as machinery and all sorts of fixed capital, raw and auxiliary materials, and consequently a constant capital of ever increasing value and volume, during the same period of time, owing to the peculiar methods of production developing within the capitalist system. This progressive relative decrease of the variable capital as compared to the constant, and consequently to the total, capital is identical with the progressive higher organic composition of the average social capital. It is, in another way, but an expression of the progressive development of the productive powers of society, which is manifested by the fact that the same number of labourers, in the same time, convert an ever growing quantity of raw and auxiliary materials into products, thanks to the growing application of machinery and fixed capital in general, so that less labour is needed for the production of the same, or of more, commodities. This growing value and volume of constant capital corresponds to a progressive cheapening of products, although the increase in the value of the constant capital indicates but imperfectly the growth in the actual mass of use-values represented by the material of the constant capital. Every individual product, taken by itself, contains a smaller quantity of labour than the same product did on a lower scale of production, in which the capital invested in wages occupies a far greater space compared to the capital invested in means of production. The hypothetical series placed at the beginning of this chapter expresses, therefore, the actual tendency of capitalist production. This mode of production produces a progressive decrease of the variable capital as compared to the constant capital, and consequently a continuously rising organic composition of the total capital. The immediate result of this is that the rate of surplus value, at the same degree of labour exploitation, expresses itself in a continually falling average rate of profit. (We shall see later why this fall does not manifest itself in an absolute form, but rather as a tendency toward a progressive fall.) This progressive tendency of the average rate of profit to fall is, therefore, but a peculiar expression of capitalist production for the fact that the social productivity of labour is progressively increasing. This is not saying that the rate of profit may not fall temporarily for other reasons. But it demonstrates at least that it is the nature of the capitalist mode of production, and a logical necessity of its development, to give expression to the average rate of surplus value by a falling rate of average profit. Since the mass of the employed living labour is continually on the decline compared to the mass of materialised labour incorporated in productively consumed means of production, it follows that that portion of living labour, which is unpaid and represents surplus value, must also be continually on the decrease compared to the volume and value of the invested total capital. Seeing that the proportion of the mass of surplus value to the value of the invested total capital forms the rate of profit, this rate must fall continuously. . . .

The law of the falling tendency of the rate of profit, or of the relative decline of the appropriated surplus labour compared to the mass of materialised labour set in motion by living labour does not argue in any way against the fact that the absolute mass of the employed and exploited labour set in motion by the social capital, and consequently the absolute mass of the surplus labour appropriated by it, may grow. Nor does it argue against the fact that the capitals controlled by individual capitalists may dispose of a growing mass of labour and surplus labour, even though the number of the labourers employed by them may not grow.

Take for illustration's sake a certain population of working people, for instance, two millions. Assume, furthermore, that the length and intensity of the average working day, and the level of wages, and thereby the proportion between necessary and surplus labour, are given. In that case the aggregate labour of these two millions, and their surplus labour expressed in surplus value, represent always the same magnitude of values. But with the growth of the mass of the constant (fixed and circulating) capital, which this labour manipulates, the proportion of this produced quantity of values declines as compared to the value of this total capital. And the value of this capital grows with its mass, although not in the same proportion. This proportion, and consequently the rate of profit, falls in spite of the fact that the same mass of living labour is controlled as before, and the same amount of surplus labour absorbed by the capital. This proportion changes, not because the mass of living labour decreases, but because the mass of the materialised labour set in motion by living labour increases. It is a relative decrease, not an absolute one, and has really nothing to do with the absolute magnitude of the labour and surplus labour set in motion. The fall of the rate of profit is not due to an absolute, but only to a relative decrease of the variable part of the total capital, that is, its decrease as compared with, the constant part.

The same thing which applies to any given mass of labour and surplus labour, applies also to a growing number of labourers, and thus under the above assumptions, to any growing mass of the controlled labour in general and to its unpaid part, the surplus labour, in particular. If the labouring population increases from two million to three million, if, furthermore, the variable capital invested in wages also rises to three million from its former amount of two million, while the constant capital rises from four million to fifteen million, then the mass of surplus labour, and of surplus value, under the above assumption of a constant working day and a constant rate of surplus value, rises by 50 per cent, that is, from two million to three million. Nevertheless, in spite of this growth in the absolute mass of surplus labour and surplus value by 50 per cent, the proportion of the variable to the constant capital would fall from 2 : 4 to 3 : 15, and the proportion of the surplus value to the total capital, expressed in millions, would be

$$\text{I.} \quad 4\,c + 2\,v + 2\,s \,;\; C = 6,\; p' = 33\tfrac{1}{3}\%.$$
$$\text{II.} \quad 15\,c + 3\,v + 3\,s \,;\; C = 18,\; p' = 16\tfrac{2}{3}\%.$$

While the mass of surplus value has increased by one-half, the rate of profit has fallen by one-half. However, the profit is only the surplus value calculated on the total social capital, so that its absolute magnitude, socially considered, is the same as the absolute magnitude of the surplus value. In this case, the absolute magnitude of the profit would have grown by 50 per cent, in spite of its enormous relative decrease compared to the advanced total capital, or in spite of the enormous fall of the average rate of profit. We see, then, that in spite of the progressive fall of the rate of profit, there may be an absolute increase of the number of labourers employed by capital, an absolute increase of the labour set in motion by it, an absolute increase of the mass of surplus labour absorbed, a resulting absolute increase of the produced surplus value, and consequently an absolute increase in the mass of the produced profit. And this increase may be progressive. And it *may* not only be so. On the basis of capitalist production, it *must* be so, aside from temporary fluctuations. . . .

COUNTERACTING CAUSES
(Vol. III, Ch. XIV)

If we consider the enormous development of the productive powers of labour, even comparing but the last thirty years with all former periods ; if we consider in particular the enormous mass of fixed capital, aside from machinery in the strict meaning of the term, passing into the process of social production as a whole, then the difficulty, which has hitherto troubled the vulgar economists, namely that of finding an explanation for the falling rate of profit, gives way to its opposite, namely to the question : How is it that this fall is not greater and more rapid ? There must be some counteracting influences at work, which thwart and annul the effects of this general law, leaving to it merely the character of a tendency. For this reason we have referred to the fall of the average rate of profit as a tendency to fall.

The following are the general counterbalancing causes :

I. *Raising the Intensity of Exploitation*

The rate at which labour is exploited, the appropriation of surplus labour and surplus value, is raised by a prolongation of the working day and an intensification of labour.

These two points have been fully discussed in Volume I as
incidents to the production of absolute and relative surplus
value. There are many ways of intensifying labour, which
imply an increase of the constant capital as compared to the
variable, and consequently a fall in the rate of profit, for
instance setting a labourer to watch a larger number of
machines. In such cases—and in the majority of manipulations serving to produce relative surplus value—the same
causes, which bring about an increase in the rate of surplus
value, may also imply a fall in the mass of surplus value,
looking upon the matter from the point of view of the total
quantities of invested capital. But there are other means
of intensification, such as increasing the speed of machinery,
which, although consuming more raw material, and, so
far as the fixed capital is concerned, wearing out the
machinery so much faster, nevertheless do not affect the
relation of its value to the price of labour set in motion by
it. It is particularly the prolongation of the working day,
this invention of modern industry, which increases the mass
of appropriated surplus labour without essentially altering
the proportion of the employed labour power to the constant capital set in motion by it, and which tends to reduce
this capital relatively, if anything. For the rest, we have
already demonstrated—what constitutes the real secret of
the tendency of the rate of profit to fall—that the manipulations made for the purpose of producing relative surplus
value amount on the whole to this : That on one side as
much as possible of a certain quantity of labour is transformed into surplus value, and that on the other hand as
little labour as possible is employed in proportion to the
invested capital, so that the same causes, which permit the
raising of the intensity of exploitation, forbid the exploitation of the same quantity of labour by the same capital as
before. These are the warring tendencies, which, while
aiming at a raise in the rate of surplus value, have at the
same time a tendency to bring about a fall in the mass of
surplus value, and therefore of the rate of surplus value

produced by a certain capital. It is furthermore appropriate to mention at this point the extensive introduction of female and child labour, in so far as the whole family must produce a larger quantity of surplus value for a certain capital than before, even in case the total amount of their wages should increase, which is by no means general.

Whatever tends to promote the production of relative surplus value by mere improvements in methods, for instance in agriculture, without altering the magnitude of the invested capital, has the same effect. While the constant capital does not increase relatively to the variable in such cases, taking the variable capital as an index of the amount of labour power employed, the mass of the product *does* increase in proportion to the labour power employed. The same takes place, when the productive power of labour (whether its product passes into the consumption of the labourer or into the elements of constant capital) is freed from obstacles of circulation, of arbitrary or other restrictions which become obstacles in course of time, in short, of fetters of all kinds, without touching directly the proportion between the variable and the constant capital.

It might be asked, whether the causes checking the fall of the rate of profit, but always hastening it in the last analysis, include the temporary rise in surplus value above the average level, which recurs now in this, now in that line of production for the benefit of those individual capitalists, who make use of inventions, etc., before they are generally introduced. This question must be answered in the affirmative.

The mass of surplus value produced by a capital of a certain magnitude is the product of two factors, namely of the rate of surplus value multiplied by the number of labourers employed at this rate. Hence it depends on the number of labourers, when the rate of surplus value is given, and on the rate of surplus value, when the number of labourers is given. In short, it depends on the composite proportion of the absolute magnitudes of the variable

capital and the rate of surplus value. Now we have seen,
that on an average the same causes, which raise the rate of
relative surplus value, lower the mass of the employed
labour power. It is evident, however, that there will be a
more or less in this according to the definite proportion,
in which the opposite movements exert themselves, and
that the tendency to reduce the rate of profit will be particularly checked by a raise in the rate of absolute surplus
value due to a prolongation of the working day.

We saw in the case of the rate of profit, that a fall in the
rate was generally accompanied by an increase in the mass
of profit, on account of the increasing mass of the total
capital employed. From the point of view of the total
variable capital of society, the surplus value produced by it
is equal to the profit produced by it. Both the absolute
mass and the absolute rate of surplus value have thus increased. The one has increased, because the quantity of
labour power employed by society has grown, the other,
because the intensity of exploitation of this labour power
has increased. But in the case of a capital of a given magnitude, for instance 100, the rate of surplus value may increase, while the mass may decrease on an average ; for
the rate is determined by the proportion, in which the
variable capital produces value, while its mass is determined by the proportional part which the variable capital
constitutes in the total capital..

The rise in the rate of surplus value is a factor, which
determines also the mass of surplus value and thereby the
rate of profit, for it takes place especially under conditions,
in which, as we have seen, the constant capital is either not
increased at all relatively to the variable capital, or not
increased in proportion. This factor does not suspend the
general law. But it causes that law to become more of a
tendency, that is a law whose absolute enforcement is
checked, retarded, weakened, by counteracting influences.
Since the same causes, which raise the rate of surplus value
(even a prolongation of the working time is a result of large

scale industry), also tend to decrease the labour power employed by a certain capital, it follows that these same causes also tend to reduce the rate of profit and to check the speed of this fall. If one labourer is compelled to perform as much labour as would be rationally performed by two, and if this is done under circumstances, in which this one labourer can replace three, then this one will produce as much surplus labour as was formerly produced by two, and to that extent the rate of surplus value will have risen. But this one will not produce as much as formerly three, and to that extent the mass of surplus value will have decreased. But this reduction in mass will be compensated, or limited, by the rise in the rate of surplus value. If the entire population is employed at a higher rate of surplus value, the mass of surplus value will increase, although the population may remain the same. It will increase still more if the population increases at the same time. And although this goes hand in hand with a relative reduction of the number of labourers employed in proportion to the magnitude of the total capital, yet this reduction is checked or moderated by the rise in the rate of surplus value.

Before leaving this point, we wish to emphasise once more that, with a capital of a certain magnitude, the *rate* of surplus value may rise, while its *mass* is decreasing, and vice versa. The mass of surplus value is equal to the rate multiplied by the number of labourers ; however, this rate is never calculated on the total, but only on the variable capital, actually only for a day at a time. On the other hand, with a given magnitude of a certain capital, the *rate of profit* can never fall or rise, without a simultaneous fall or rise in the *mass of surplus value*.

II. *Depression of Wages Below their Value*

This is mentioned only empirically at this place, since it, like many other things, which might be enumerated here, has nothing to do with the general analysis of capital, but belongs in a presentation of competition, which is not given in this work. However, it is one of the most important causes checking the tendency of the rate of profit to fall.

III. *Cheapening of the Elements of Constant Capital*

Everything that has been said in the first part of this volume about the causes, which raise the rate of profit while the rate of surplus value remains the same, or independently of the rate of surplus value, belongs here. This applies particularly to the fact that, from the point of view of the total capital, the value of the constant capital does not increase in the same proportion as its material volume. For instance, the quantity of cotton, which a single European spinning operator works up in a modern factory, has grown in a colossal degree compared to the quantity formerly worked up by a European operator with a spinning wheel. But the value of the worked-up cotton has not grown in proportion to its mass. The same holds good of machinery and other fixed capital. In short, the same development, which increases the mass of the constant capital relatively over that of the variable, reduces the value of its elements as a result of the increased productivity of labour. In this way the value of the constant capital, although continually increasing, is prevented from increasing at the same rate as its material volume, that is, the material volume of the means of production set in motion by the same amount of labour power. In exceptional cases the mass of the elements of constant capital may even increase, while its value remains the same or even falls.

The foregoing bears upon the depreciation of existing capital (that is, of its material elements) which comes with the development of industry. This is another one of the causes which by their constant effects tend to check the fall of the rate of profit, although it may under certain circumstances reduce the mass of profit by reducing the mass of capital yielding a profit. This shows once more that the same causes, which bring about a tendency of the rate of profit to fall, also check the realisation of this tendency.

IV. *Relative Over-population*

The production of a relative surplus population is inseparable from the development of the productivity of labour expressed by a fall in the rate of profit, and the two go hand in hand. The relative over-population becomes so much more apparent in a certain country, the more the capitalist mode of production is developed in it. This, again, is on the one hand a reason, which explains why the imperfect subordination of labour to capital continues in many lines of production, and continues longer than seems at first glance compatible with the general stage of development. This is due to the cheapness and mass of the disposable or unemployed wage labourers, and to the greater resistance, which some lines of production, by their nature, oppose to a transformation of manufacture into machine production. On the other hand, new lines of production are opened up, especially for the production of luxuries, and these lines take for their basis this relative over-population set free in other lines of production by the increase of their constant capital. These new lines start out with living labour as their predominating element, and go by degrees through the same evolution as the other lines of production. In either case the variable capital constitutes a considerable proportion of the total capital and wages are below the average, so that both the rate and mass of surplus value are exceptionally high. Since the average rate of profit is formed by levelling the rates of profit in the individual lines of production, the same cause, which brings about a falling tendency of the rate of profit, once more produces a counterbalance to this tendency and paralyses its effects more or less.

V. *Foreign Trade*

To the extent that foreign trade cheapens partly the elements of constant capital, partly the necessities of life for which the variable capital is exchanged, it tends to raise the rate of profit by raising the rate of surplus value and lowering the value of the constant capital. It exerts itself generally in this direction by permitting an expansion of the scale of production. But by this means it hastens on one hand the process of accumulation, on the other the reduction of the variable as compared to the constant capital, and thus a fall in the rate of profit. In the same way the expansion of foreign trade, which is the basis of the capitalist mode of production in its stages of infancy, has become its own product in the further progress of capitalist development through its innate necessities, through its need of an ever expanding market. Here we see once more the dual nature of these effects. (Ricardo entirely overlooked this side of foreign trade.)

Another question, which by its special nature is really beyond the scope of our analysis, is the following : Is the average rate of profit raised by the higher rate of profit, which capital invested in foreign, and particularly in colonial, trade realises ?

Capitals invested in foreign trade are in a position to yield a higher rate of profit, because, in the first place, they come in competition with commodities produced in other countries with lesser facilities of production, so that an advanced country is enabled to sell its goods above their value even when it sells them cheaper than the competing countries. To the extent that the labour of the advanced countries is here exploited as a labour of a higher specific weight, the rate of profit rises, because labour which has not been paid as being of a higher quality is sold as such. The same condition may obtain in the relations with a certain country, into which commodities are exported and from which commodities are imported. This country may offer more

materialised labour in goods than it receives, and yet it
may receive in return commodities cheaper than it could
produce them. In the same way a manufacturer, who exploits a new invention before it has become general, under-
sells his competitors and yet sells his commodities above
their individual values, that is to say, he exploits the
specifically higher productive power of the labour employed by him as surplus value. By this means he secures
a surplus profit. On the other hand, capitals invested in
colonies, etc., may yield a higher rate of profit for the
simple reason that the rate of profit is higher there on
account of the backward development, and for the added
reason, that slaves, coolies, etc., permit a better exploitation
of labour. We see no reason, why these higher rates of
profit realised by capitals invested in certain lines and sent
home by them should not enter as elements into the average
rate of profit and tend to keep it up to that extent. We see
so much less reason for the contrary opinion, when it is
assumed that such favoured lines of investment are subject
to the laws of free competition. What Ricardo has in mind
as objections, is mainly this : With the higher prices realised
in foreign trade, commodities are bought abroad and sent
home. These commodities are sold on the home market,
and this can constitute at best but a temporary advantage
of the favoured spheres of production over others. This
aspect of the matter is changed, when we no longer look
upon it from the point of view of money. The favoured
country recovers more labour in exchange for less labour,
although this difference, this surplus, is pocketed by a certain class, as it is in any exchange between labour and
capital. So far as the rate of profit is higher, because it is
generally higher in the colonial country, it may go hand in
hand with a low level of prices, if the natural conditions are
favourable. It is true that a compensation takes place,
but it is not a compensation on the old level, as Ricardo
thinks.

However, this same foreign trade develops the capitalist

mode of production in the home country. And this implies
the relative decrease of the variable as compared to the
constant capital, while it produces, on the other hand, an
overproduction for the foreign market, so that it has once
more the opposite effect in its further course.

And so we have seen in a general way, that the same
causes, which produce a falling tendency in the rate of
profit, also call forth counter-effects, which check and partly
paralyse this fall. This law is not suspended, but its effect is
weakened. Otherwise it would not be the fall of the average
rate of profit, which would be unintelligible, but rather the
relative slowness of this fall. The law therefore shows itself
only as a tendency, whose effects become clearly marked
only under certain conditions and in the course of long
periods. . . .

UNRAVELLING THE INTERNAL CONTRADICTIONS OF THE LAW
(Vol. III, Ch. XV)

. . . A fall in the rate of profit and a hastening of accumulation are in so far only different expressions of the same process as both of them indicate the development of the
productive power. Accumulation in its turn hastens the fall
of the rate of profit, inasmuch as it implies the concentration of labour on a large scale and thereby a higher composition of capital. On the other hand, a fall in the rate of
profit hastens the concentration of capital and its centralisation through the expropriation of the smaller capitalists,
the expropriation of the last survivors of the direct producers who still have anything to give up. This accelerates
on one hand the accumulation, so far as mass is concerned,
although the rate of accumulation falls with the rate of
profit.

On the other hand, so far as the rate of self-expansion of
the total capital, the rate of profit, is the incentive of capitalist production (just as this self-expression of capital is its

only purpose), its fall checks the formation of new independent capitals and thus seems to threaten the development of the process of capitalist production. It promotes overproduction, speculation, crises, surplus capital, along with surplus population. Those economists who, like Ricardo, regard the capitalist mode of production as absolute, feel, nevertheless, that this mode of production creates its own limits, and therefore they attribute this limit, not to production, but to nature (in their theory of rent). But the main point in their horror over the falling rate of profit is the feeling, that capitalist production meets in the development of productive forces a barrier, which has nothing to do with the production of wealth as such ; and this peculiar barrier testifies to the finiteness and the historical, merely transitory character of capitalist production. It demonstrates that this is not an absolute mode for the production of wealth, but rather comes in conflict with the further development of wealth at a certain stage. . . .

The creation of surplus value, assuming the necessary means of production, or sufficient accumulation of capital, to be existing, finds no other limit but the labouring population, when the rate of surplus value, that is, the intensity of exploitation, is given ; and no other limit but the intensity of exploitation, when the labouring population is given. And the capitalist process of production consists essentially of the production of surplus value, materialised in the surplus product, which is that aliquot portion of the produced commodities, in which unpaid labour is materialised. It must never be forgotten, that the production of this surplus value—and the reconversion of a portion of it into capital, or accumulation, forms an indispensable part of this production of surplus value—is the immediate purpose and the compelling motive of capitalist production. It will not do to represent capitalist production as something which it is not, that is to say, as a production having for its immediate purpose the consumption of goods, or the production

of means of enjoyment for capitalists. This would be overlooking the specific character of capitalist production, which
reveals itself in its innermost essence.

The creation of this surplus value is the object of the
direct process of production, and this process has no other
limits but those mentioned above. As soon as the available
quantity of surplus value has been materialised in commodities, surplus value has been produced. But this production of surplus value is but the first act of the capitalist
process of production, it merely terminates the act of direct
production. Capital has absorbed so much unpaid labour.
With the development of the process, which expresses itself
through a falling tendency of the rate of profit, the mass of
surplus value thus produced is swelled to immense dimensions. Now comes the second act of the process. The entire
mass of commodities, the total product, which contains a
portion which is to reproduce the constant and variable
capital as well as a portion representing surplus value,
must be sold. If this is not done, or only partly accomplished,
or only at prices which are below the prices of production,
the labourer has been none the less exploited, but his
exploitation does not realise as much for the capitalist. It
may yield no surplus value at all for him, or only realise a
portion of the produced surplus value, or it may even mean
a partial or complete loss of his capital. The conditions of
direct exploitation and those of the realisation of surplus
value are not identical. They are separated logically as
well as by time and space. The first are only limited by the
productive power of society, the last by the proportional
relations of the various lines of production and by the
consuming power of society. This last-named power is not
determined either by the absolute productive power nor
by the absolute consuming power, but by the consuming
power based on antagonistic conditions of distribution,
which reduces the consumption of the great mass of the
population to a variable minimum within more or less
narrow limits. The consuming power is furthermore

restricted by the tendency to accumulate, the greed for an expansion of capital and a production of surplus value on an enlarged scale. This is a law of capitalist production imposed by incessant revolutions in the methods of production themselves, the resulting depreciation of existing capital, the general competitive struggle and the necessity of improving the product and expanding the scale of production, for the sake of self-preservation and on penalty of failure. The market must, therefore, be continually extended, so that its interrelations and the conditions regulating them assume more and more the form of a natural law independent of the producers and become ever more uncontrollable. This internal contradiction seeks to balance itself by an expansion of the outlying fields of production. But to the extent that the productive power develops, it finds itself at variance with the narrow basis on which the conditions of consumption rest. On this self-contradictory basis it is no contradiction at all that there should be an excess cf capital simultaneously with an excess of population. For while a combination of these two would indeed increase the mass of the produced surplus value, it would at the same time intensify the contradiction between the conditions under which this surplus value is produced and those under which it is realised. . . .

Conflict between the Expansion of Production and the Creation of Values

The development of the productive power of labour shows itself in two ways : First, in the magnitude of the already produced productive powers, in the volume of values and masses of requirements of production, under which new production is carried on, and in the absolute magnitude of the already accumulated productive capital ; secondly, in the relative smallness of the capital invested in wages as compared to the total capital, that is, in the relatively small quantity of living labour required for the reproduction and self-expansion of a given capital as compared to mass production. It is at the same time conditioned on the concentration of capital.

So far as the employed labour-power is concerned, the development of the productive powers shows itself once more in two ways : First, in the increase of surplus labour, that is, the reduction of the necessary labour time required for the reproduction of labour power ; secondly, in the decrease of the quantity of labour power (the number of labourers) employed in general for the purpose of setting in motion a given capital.

Both movements do not only go hand in hand, but are mutually conditioned on one another. They are different phenomena, through which the same law expresses itself. However, they affect the rate of profit in opposite ways. The total mass of profits is equal to the total mass of surplus values, the rate of profit $=\frac{s}{c}=\frac{\text{surplus value}}{\text{advanced total capital}}$. Now, surplus value, as a total, is determined first by its rate, secondly by the mass of labour simultaneously employed at this rate, or what amounts to the same, by the magnitude of the variable capital. One of these factors, the rate of surplus value, rises in one direction, the other factor, the number of labourers, falls in the opposite direction (relatively or absolutely). To the extent that the development of the productive power reduces the paid portion of the employed labour, it raises the surplus value by raising its rate ; but to the extent that it reduces the total mass of labour employed by a certain capital, it reduces the factor of numbers with which the rate of surplus value is multiplied in order to calculate its mass. Two labourers, each working 12 hours daily, cannot produce the same mass of surplus value as 24 labourers each working only 2 hours, even if they could live on air and did not have to work for themselves at all. In this respect, then, the compensation of the reduction in the number of labourers by means of an intensification of exploitation has certain impassable limits.

It may, for this reason, check the fall of the rate of profit, but cannot prevent it entirely.

With the development of the capitalist mode of production, the rate of profit therefore falls, while its mass increases with the growing mass of the employed capital. Given the rate, the absolute increase in the mass of capital depends on its existing magnitude. But on the other hand, if this magnitude is given, the proportion of its growth, the rate of its increment, depends on the rate of profit. The increase in the productive power (which, we repeat, always goes hand in hand with a depreciation of the productive capital) cannot directly increase the value of the existing capital, unless it increases, by raising the rate of profit, that portion of the value of the annual product which is reconverted into capital. So far as the productive power is concerned (since it has no direct bearing upon the *value* of the existing capital), it can accomplish this only by raising the relative surplus value, or reducing the value of the constant capital, so that those commodities which enter either into the reproduction of labour power or into the elements of constant capital are cheapened. Both of these things imply a depreciation of the existing capital, and both of them go hand in hand with a relative reduction of the variable as compared to the constant capital. Both things imply a fall in the rate of profit, and both of them check it. Furthermore, so far as an increased rate of profit causes a greater demand for labour, it tends to increase the working population and thus the material, whose exploitation gives to capital its real nature of capital.

Indirectly, however, the development of the productive power of labour contributes to the increase of the value of the existing capital, by increasing the mass and variety of use-values, in which the same exchange value presents itself and which form the material substance, the objective elements, of capital, the material objects of which the constant capital is directly composed and the variable capital at least indirectly. With the same capital and the same labour more things are produced, which may be converted into capital, aside from their exchange value. Things which may serve for the absorption of additional labour, and consequently of additional surplus labour, and which therefore may become additional capital. The amount of labour, which a certain capital may command, does not depend on its value, but on the mass of raw and auxiliary materials, of machinery and elements of fixed capital, of necessities of life, of which it is composed, whatever may be their value. As the mass of the employed labour, and thus of surplus labour, increases, so does the value of the reproduced capital and the surplus value newly added to it grow.

These two elements playing their rôle in the process of accumulation should not, however, be observed in their quiet existence side by side, as Ricardo does. They imply a contradiction, which expresses itself in antagonistic tendencies and phenomena. These antagonistic agencies cppose each other simultaneously.

Together with the incentives for an actual increase of the labouring population, which originates in the augmentation of that portion of the total social product which serves as capital, there are the effects of other agencies, which create merely a relative over-population.

Together with the fall of the rate of profit grows the mass of capitals, and hand in hand with it goes a depreciation of the existing capitals, which checks this fall and gives an accelerating push to the accumulation of capital values.

Together with the development of the productive power grows the higher composition of capital, the relative decrease of the variable as compared to the constant capital. These different influences make themselves felt, now more side by side in space, now more successively in time. Periodically the conflict of antagonistic agencies seeks vent in crises. The crises are always but momentary and forcible solutions of the existing contradictions, violent eruptions, which restore the disturbed equilibrium for a while.

The contradiction, generally speaking, consists in this that the capitalist mode of production has a tendency to develop the productive forces absolutely, regardless of value and of the surplus value contained in it and regardless of the social conditions under which capitalist production takes place ; while it has on the other hand for its aim the preservation of the value of the existing capital and its self-expansion to the highest limit (that is, an ever accelerated growth of this value). Its specific character is directed at the existing value of capital as a means of increasing this value to the utmost. The methods by which it aims to accomplish this comprise a fall of the rate of profit, a depreciation of the existing capital, and a development of the productive forces of labour at the expense of the already created productive forces.

The periodical depreciation of the existing capital, which is one of the immanent means of capitalist production by which the fall in the rate of profit is checked and the accumulation of capital value through the formation of new capital promoted, disturbs the existing conditions, within which the process of circulation and reproduction of capital takes place, and is therefore accompanied by sudden stagnations and crises in the process of production.

The relative decrease of variable capital as compared to the constant, which goes hand in hand with the development of the productive forces, gives an impulse to the growth of the labouring population, while it continually creates an artificial over-population. The accumulation of capital, so far as its value is concerned, is checked by the falling rate of profit, in order to hasten still more the accumulation of its use-value, and this, in its turn, adds new speed to the accumulation of its value.

Capitalist production is continually engaged in the attempt to overcome these immanent barriers, but it overcomes them only by means which again place the same barriers in its way in a more formidable size.

The real barrier of capitalist production is capital itself. It is the fact that capital and its self-expansion appear as the starting and closing point, as the motive and aim of production ; that production is merely production for *capital*, and not vice versa, the means of production mere means for an ever expanding system of the life process for the benefit of the *society* of producers. The barriers, within which the preservation and self-expansion of the value of capital resting on the expropriation and pauperisation of the great mass of producers can alone move, these barriers come continually in collision with the methods of production, which capital must employ for its purposes, and which steer straight toward an unrestricted extension of production, toward production for its own self, toward an unconditional development of the productive forces of society. The means, this unconditional development of the productive forces of society, comes continually into conflict with the limited end, the self-expansion of the existing capital. Thus, while the capitalist mode of production is one of the historical means by which the material forces of production are developed and the world-market required for them created, it is at the same time in continual conflict with this historical task and the conditions of social production corresponding to it.

Surplus of Capital and Surplus of Population

With the fall of the rate of profit grows the lowest limit of capital required in the hands of the individual capitalist for the productive employment of labour, required both for the exploitation of labour and for bringing the consumed labour time within the limits of the labour time necessary for the production of the commodities, the limits of the average social labour time required for the production of the commodities. Simultaneously with it grows the concentration, because there comes a certain limit where large capital with a small rate of profit accumulates faster than small capital with a large rate of profit. This increasing concentration in its turn brings about a new fall in the rate of profit at a certain climax. The mass of the small divided capitals is thereby pushed into adventurous channels, speculation, fraudulent credit, fraudulent stocks, crises. The so-called plethora of capital refers always essentially to a plethora of that class of capital which finds no compensation in its mass for the fall in the rate of profit—and this applies always to the newly formed sprouts of capital—or to a plethora of capitals incapable of self-dependent action and placed at the disposal of the managers of large lines of industry in the form of credit. This plethora of capital proceeds from the same causes which call forth a relative overpopulation. It is therefore a phenomenon supplementing this last one, although they are found at opposite poles, unemployed capital on the one hand, and unemployed labouring population on the other.

An over-production of capital, not of individual commodities, signifies therefore simply an over-accumulation of capital—although the over-production of capital always includes the over-production of commodities. In order to understand what this over-accumulation is (its detailed analysis follows later), it is but necessary to assume it to be absolute. When would an over-production of capital be absolute? When would it be an over-production which would not affect merely a few important lines of production, but which would be so absolute as to extend to every field of production?

There would be an absolute over-production of capital as soon as the additional capital for purposes of capitalist production would be equal to zero. The purpose of capitalist production is the self-expansion of capital, that is, the appropriation of surplus labour, the production of surplus value, of profit. As soon as capital would have grown to such a proportion compared with the labouring population, that neither the absolute labour time nor the relative surplus labour time could be extended any further (this last named extension would be out of the question even in the mere case that the demand for labour would be very strong, so that there would be a tendency for wages to rise) ; as soon as a point is reached where the increased capital produces no larger, or even smaller, quantities of surplus value than it did before its increase, there would be an absolute over-production of capital. That is to say, the increased capital C + $\triangle$ C would not produce any more profit, or even less profit, than capital C before its expansion by $\triangle$ C. In both cases there would be a strong and sudden fall in the average rate of profit, but it would be due to a change in the composition of capital which would not be caused by the development of the productive forces, but by a rise in the money-value of the variable capital (on account of the increased wages) and the corresponding reduction in the proportion of surplus labour to necessary labour.

In reality the matter would amount to this, that a portion of the capital would lie fallow completely or partially (be-cause it would first have to crowd some of the active capital out before it could take part in the process of self-expansion), while the active portion would produce values at a lower rate of profit, owing to the pressure of the unemployed or but partly employed capital. Matters would not be altered in this respect, if a part of the additional capital were to take the place of some old capital, crowding this into the position of additional capital. We should always have on one side the sum of old capitals, on the other that of the additional capitals. The fall in the rate of profit would then be accom-panied by an absolute decrease in the mass of profits, since under the conditions assumed by us the mass of the em-ployed labour power could not be increased and the rate of surplus value not raised, so that there could be no raising of the mass of surplus value. And the reduced mass of profits would have to be calculated on an increased total capital. But even assuming that the employed capital were to continue producing value at the old rate, the mass of profits, remaining the same, this mass would still be calculated on an increased total capital, and this would likewise imply a fall in the rate of profits. If a total capital of 1,000 yielded a profit of 100, and after its increase to 1,500 still yielded 100, then 1,000 in the second case would yield only $66\frac{2}{3}$. The self-expansion of the old capital would have been reduced absolutely. A capital of 1,000 would not yield any more under the new circumstances than formerly a capital of $666\frac{2}{3}$.

It is evident that this actual depreciation of the old capital could not take place without a struggle, that the additional capital $\triangle$ C could not assume the functions of capital without an effort. The rate of profit would not fall on account of competition due to the over-production of capital. The competitive struggle would rather begin, because the fall of the rate of profit and the over-production of capital are caused by the same conditions. The capitalists who are actively engaged with their old capitals would keep as much of the new additional capitals as would be in their hands in a fallow state, in order to prevent a depreciation of their original capital and a crowding of its space within the field of production. Or they would employ it for the purpose of loading, even at a momentary loss, the necessity of keeping additional capital fallow upon the shoulders of new intruders and other competitors in general.

That portion of $\triangle$ C which would be in new hands would seek to make room for itself at the expense of the old capital, and would accomplish this in part by forcing a portion of the old capital into a fallow state. The old capital would have to give up its place to the new and retire to the place of the completely or partially unemployed additional capital.

Under all circumstances, a portion of the old capital would be compelled to lie fallow, to give up its capacity of capital and stop acting and producing value as such. The competitive struggle would decide what part would have to go into this fallow state. So long as everything goes well, competition effects a practical brotherhood of the capitalist class, as we have seen in the case of the average rate of profit, so that each shares in the common loot in proportion to the magnitude of his share of investment. But as soon as it is no longer a question of sharing profits, but of sharing losses, everyone tries to reduce his own share to a minimum and load as much as possible upon the shoulders of some other competitor. However, the class must inevitably lose. How much the individual capitalist must bear of the loss, to what extent he must share in it at all, is decided by power and craftiness, and competition then transforms itself into a fight of hostile brothers. The antagonism of the interests of the individual capitalists and those of the capitalist class as a whole then makes itself felt just as previously the identity of these interests impressed itself practically on competition.

How would this conflict be settled and the " healthy " movement of capitalist production resumed under normal conditions ? The mode of settlement is already indicated by the mere statement of the conflict whose settlement is under discussion. It implies the necessity of making unproductive, or even partially destroying, some capital, amounting either to the complete value of the additional capital $\triangle$ C, or to a part of it. But a graphic presentation of this conflict shows that the loss is not equally distributed over all the individual capitals, but according to the fortunes of the competitive struggle, which assigns the loss in very different proportions and in various shapes by grace of previously captured advantages or positions, so that one capital is rendered unproductive, another destroyed, a third but relatively injured or but momentarily depreciated, etc.

But under all circumstances the equilibrium is restored by making more or less capital unproductive or destroying it. This would affect to some extent the material substance of capital, that is, a part of the means of production, fixed and circulating capital, would not perform any service as capital ; a portion of the running establishments would then close down. Of course, time would corrode and depreciate all means of production (except land)', but this particular stagnation would cause a far more serious destruction of means of production. However, the main effect in this case would be to suspend the functions of some means of production and prevent them for a shorter or longer time from serving as means of production.

The principal work of destruction would show its most dire effects in a slaughtering of the *values* of capitals. That portion of the value of capital which exists only in the form of claims on future shares of surplus value of profit, which consists in fact of creditor's notes on production in its various forms, would be immediately depreciated by the reduction of the receipts on which it is calculated. One portion of the gold and silver money is rendered unproductive, cannot serve as capital. One portion of the commodities on the market can complete its process of circulation and reproduction only by means of an immense contraction of its prices, which means a depreciation of the capital represented by it. In the same way the elements of fixed capital are more or less depreciated. Then there is the added complication that the process of reproduction is based on definite assumptions as to prices, so that a general fall in prices checks and disturbs the process of reproduction. This interference and stagnation paralyses the function of money as a medium of payment, which is conditioned on the development of capital and the resulting price relations. The chain of payments due at certain times is broken in a hundred places, and the disaster is intensified by the collapse of the credit system. Thus violent and acute crises are brought about, sudden and forcible depreciations, an actual stagnation and collapse of the process of reproduction, and finally a real falling off in reproduction.

At the same time still other agencies would have been at work. The stagnation of production would have laid off a part of the labouring class and thereby placed the employed part in a condition in which they would have to submit to a reduction of wages, even below the average. This operation has the same effect on capital as though the relative or absolute surplus value had been increased at average wages. The time of prosperity would have promoted marriages among the labourers and reduced the decimation of the offspring. These circumstances, while implying a real increase in population, do not signify an increase in the actual working population, but they nevertheless affect the relations of the labourers to capital in the same way as though the number of the actually working labourers had increased. On the other hand, the fall in prices and the competitive struggle would have given to every capitalist an impulse to raise the individual value of his total product above its average value by means of new machines, new and improved working methods, new combinations, which means, to increase the productive power of a certain quantity of labour, to lower the proportion of the variable to the constant capital, and thereby to release some labourers, in short, to create an artificial over-population. The depreciation of the elements of constant capital itself would be another factor tending to raise the rate of profit. The mass of the employed constant capital, compared to the variable, would have increased, but the value of this mass might have fallen. The present stagnation of production would have prepared an expansion of production later on, within capitalistic limits.

And in this way the cycle would be run once more. One portion of the capital which had been depreciated by the stagnation of its function would recover its old value. For the rest, the same vicious circle would be described once more under expanded conditions of production, in an expanded market, and with increased productive forces.

However, even under the extreme conditions assumed by us this absolute over-production of capital would not be an absolute over-production in the sense that it would be an absolute over-production of means of production. It would be an over-production of means of production *only to the extent that they serve as capital*, so that the increased value of its increased mass would also imply a utilisation for the production of more value.

Yet it would be an over-production, because capital would be unable to exploit labour to a degree required by

the " healthy, normal " development of the process of
capitalist production, a degree of exploitation which would
increase at least the mass of profit to the extent that the
mass of the employed capital would grow ; which would
therefore exclude any possibility of the rate of profit falling
to the same extent that capital grows, or of the rate of profits
falling even more rapidly than capital grows.

Over-production of capital never signifies anything else
but over-production of means of production—means of
production and necessities of life—which may serve as
capital, that is, serve for the exploitation of labour at a
given degree of exploitation ; for a fall in the intensity of
exploitation below a certain point calls forth disturbances
and stagnations in the process of capitalist production,
crises, destruction of capital. It is no contradiction that this
over-production of capital is accompanied by a more or less
considerable relative over-population. The same circumstances, which have increased the productive power of
labour, augmented the mass of produced commodities,
expanded the markets, accelerated the accumulation of
capital both as concerns its mass and its value, and lowered
the rate of profit, these same circumstances have also
created a relative over-population, and continue to create it
all the time, an over-population of labourers who are not
employed by the surplus capital on account of the low
degree of exploitation at which they might be employed,
or at least on account of the low rate of profit, which they
would yield with the given rate of exploitation.

If capital is sent to foreign countries, it is not done
because there is absolutely no employment to be had for it
at home. It is done, because it can be employed at a higher
rate of profit in a foreign country. But such capital is
absolute surplus capital for the employed labouring population and for the home country in general. It exists as such
together. with the relative over-population, and this is an
illustration of the way in which both of them exist side by
side and are conditioned on one another.

On the other hand, the fall in the rate of profit connected
with accumulation necessarily creates a competitive
struggle. The compensation of the fall in the rate of profit
by a rise in the mass of profit applies only to the total social
capital and to the great capitalists who are firmly installed.
The new additional capital, which enters upon its functions,
does not enjoy any such compensating conditions. It must
conquer them for itself, and so the fall in the rate of profit
calls forth the competitive struggle among capitalists, not
vice versa. This competitive struggle is indeed accompanied
by a transient rise in wages and a resulting further fall of
the rate of profit for a short time. The same thing is seen
in the over-production of commodities, the overstocking of
markets. Since the aim of capital is not to minister to certain
wants, but to produce profits, and since it accomplishes this
purpose by methods which adapt the mass of production
to the scale of production, not vice versa, conflict must
continually ensue between the limited conditions of consumption on a capitalist basis and a production which
for ever tends to exceed its immanent barriers. Moreover,
capital consists of commodities, and therefore the over-
production of capital implies an over-production of commodities. Hence we meet with the peculiar phenomenon
that the same economists, who deny the over-production of
commodities, admit that of capital. If it is said that there
is no general over-production, but that a disproportion
grows up between various lines of production, then this is
tantamount to saying that within capitalist production the
proportionality of the individual lines of production is
brought about through a continual process of dispropor-
tionality, that is, the interrelations of production as a whole
enforce themselves as a blind law upon the agents of production instead of having brought the productive process
under their common control as a law understood by
the social mind. It amounts furthermore to demanding
that countries, in which capitalist production is not yet
developed, should consume and produce at the same rate

as that adapted to countries with capitalist production. If it is said that over-production is only relative, then the statement is correct ; but the entire mode of production is only a relative one, whose barriers are not absolute, but have absoluteness only in so far as it is capitalistic. Otherwise, how could there be a lack of demand for the very commodities which the mass of the people want, and how would it be possible that this demand must be sought in foreign countries, in foreign markets, in order that the labourers at home might receive in payment the average amount of necessities of life ? This is possible only because in this specific capitalist inter-relation the surplus product assumes a form, in which its owner cannot offer it for consumption, unless it first reconverts itself into capital for him. Finally, if it is said that the capitalists would only have to exchange and consume those commodities among themselves, then the nature of the capitalist mode of production is forgotten, it is forgotten that the question is merely one of expanding the value of the capital, not of consuming it. In short, all these objections to the obvious phenomena of over-production (phenomena which do not pay any attention to these objections) amount to this, that the barriers of capitalist production are not absolute barriers of production itself and therefore no barriers of this specific, capitalistic, production. But the contradiction of this capitalist mode of production consists precisely in its tendency to an absolute development of productive forces, a development, which comes continually in conflict with the specific conditions of production in which capital moves and alone can move.

It is not a fact that too many necessities of life are produced in proportion to the existing population. The reverse is true. Not enough is produced to satisfy the wants of the great mass decently and humanely.

It is not a fact that too many means of production are produced to employ the able-bodied portion of the population. The reverse is the case. In the first place, too large a portion of the population is produced consisting of people who are really not capable of working, who are dependent through force of circumstances on the exploitation of the labour of others, or compelled to perform certain kinds of labour which can be dignified with this name only under a miserable mode of production. In the second place, not enough means of production are produced to permit the employment of the entire able-bodied population under the most productive conditions, so that their absolute labour time would be shortened by the mass and effectiveness of the constant capital employed during working hours.

On the other hand, there is periodically a production of too many means of production and necessities of life to permit of their serving as means for the exploitation of the labourers at a certain rate of profit. Too many commodities are produced to permit of a realisation of the value and surplus value contained in them under the conditions of distribution and consumption peculiar to capitalist production, that is, too many to permit of the continuation of this process without ever recurring explosions.

It is not a fact that too much wealth is produced. But it is true that there is periodical over-production of wealth in its capitalistic and self-contradictory form.

The barrier of the capitalist mode of production becomes apparent :

(1) In the fact that the development of the productive power of labour creates in the falling rate of profit a law which turns into an antagonism of this mode of production at a certain point and requires for its defeat periodical crises.

(2) In the fact that the expansion or contraction of production is determined by the appropriation of unpaid labour, and by the proportion of this unpaid labour to materialised labour in general, or, to speak the language of the capitalists, is determined by profit and by the proportion of this profit to the employed capital, by a definite rate of profit, instead of being determined by the relations of production to social wants, to the wants of socially developed

human beings. The capitalist mode of production, for this reason, meets with barriers at a certain scale of production which would be inadequate under different conditions. It comes to a standstill at a point determined by the production and realisation of profit, not by the satisfaction of social needs.

If the rate of profit falls, there follows on one hand an exertion of capital, in order that the capitalist may be enabled to depress the individual value of his commodities below the social average level and thereby realise an extra profit at the prevailing market prices. On the other hand, there follows swindle and a general promotion of swindle by frenzied attempts at new methods of production, new investments of capital, new adventures, for the sake of securing some shred of extra profit, which shall be independent of the general average and above it.

The rate of profit, that is, the relative increment of capital, is above all important for all new off-shoots of capital seeking an independent location. And as soon as the formation of capital were to fall into the hands of a few established great capitals, which are compensated by the mass of profits for the loss through a fall in the rate of profits, the vital fire of production would be extinguished. It would fall into a dormant state. The rate of profit is the compelling power of capitalist production, and only such things are produced as yield a profit. Hence the fright of the English economists over the decline of the rate of profit. That the bare possibility of such a thing should worry Ricardo, shows his profound understanding of the conditions of capitalist production. The reproach moved against him, that he has an eye only to the development of the productive forces regardless of " human beings," regardless of the sacrifices in human beings and capital *values* incurred, strikes precisely his strong point. The development of the productive forces of social labour is the historical task and privilege of capital. It is precisely in this way that it unconsciously creates the material requirements of a higher

424 MARX

mode of production. What worries Ricardo is the fact that
that rate of profit, the stimulating principle of capitalist
production, the fundamental premise and driving force of
accumulation, should be endangered by the development
of production itself. And the quantitative proportion means
everything here. There is indeed something deeper than
this hidden at this point, which he vaguely feels. It is here
demonstrated in a purely economic way, that is, from a
bourgeois point of view, within the confines of capitalist
understanding, from the standpoint of capitalist production
itself, that it has a barrier, that it is relative, that it is not
an absolute, but only a historical mode of production
corresponding to a definite and limited epoch in the
development of the material conditions of production. . . .

CONDITIONS OF DISTRIBUTION AND PRODUCTION
(Vol. III, Ch. LI)

The new value added by the annual new labour—and
thus also that portion of the annual product, in which this
value is represented and may be drawn out of the total fund
and separated from it—is divided into three parts, which
assume three different forms of revenue. These forms indicate that one portion of this value belongs, or goes to, the
owner of labour power, another portion to the owner of
capital, and a third portion to the owner of land. These,
then, are forms, or conditions, of distribution, for they express conditions, under which the newly produced total
value is distributed among the owners of the different
agencies of production.

To the ordinary mind these conditions of distribution
appear as natural conditions, as conditions arising from the
nature of all social production, from the laws of human production in general. While it cannot be denied that pre-
capitalist societies show other modes of distribution, yet
those modes are interpreted as undeveloped, imperfect,
disguised, differently coloured modes of these natural

conditions of distribution, which have not reached their purest expression and their highest form.

The only correct thing in this conception is this : Assuming some form of social production to exist (for instance, that of the primitive Indian communes, or that of the more artificially developed communism of the Peruvians), a distinction can always be made between that portion of labour, which supplies products directly for the individual consumption of the producers and their families—aside from the part which is productively consumed—and that portion of labour, which produces surplus products, which always serve for the satisfaction of social needs, no matter what may be the mode of distribution of this surplus product, and whoever may perform the function of a representative of these social needs. The identity of the various modes of distribution amounts merely to this, that they are identical, if we leave out of consideration their differences and specific forms and keep in mind only their common features as distinguished from their differences.

A more advanced, more critical mind, however, admits the historically developed character of the condition of distribution, but clings on the other hand so much more tenaciously to the unaltering character of the conditions of production arising from human nature and thus independent of all historical development.

On the other hand, the scientific analysis of the capitalist mode of production demonstrates that it is a peculiar mode of production, specifically defined by historical development ; that it, like any other definite mode of production, is conditioned upon a certain stage of social productivity and upon the historically developed form of the forces of production. This historical pre-requisite is itself the historical result and product of a preceding process, from which the new mode of production takes its departure as from its given foundation. The conditions of production corresponding to this specific, historically determined, mode of production have a specific, historical, passing character, and men enter

into them as into their process of social life, the process by
which they create their social life. The conditions of distribution are essentially identical with these conditions of
production, being their reverse side, so that both conditions
share the same historical and passing character.

In the study of conditions of distribution, the start is made
from the alleged fact, that the annual product is distributed
among wages, profit and rent. But if so expressed, it is a
misstatement. The product is assigned on one side to capital,
on the other to revenues. One of these revenues, wages,
never assumes the form of a revenue, a revenue of the
labourer, until it has first faced this labourer in the form of
capital. The meeting of the produced requirement of labour
and of the general products of labour as capital, in opposition to the direct producers, includes from the outset a
definite social character of the material requirements of
labour as compared to the labourers, and with it a definite
relation, into which they enter in production itself with the
owners of the means of production and among themselves.
The transformation of these means of production into
capital implies on their part the expropriation of the direct
producers from the soil, and thus a definite form of property
in land.

If one portion of the product were not transformed into
capital, the other would not assume the form of wages,
profit and rent.

On the other hand, just as the capitalist mode of production is conditioned upon this definite social form of the conditions of production, so it reproduces them continually. It
produces not merely the material products, but reproduces
continually the conditions of production, in which the
others are produced, and with them the corresponding
conditions of distribution.

It may indeed be said that capital (and the ownership of
land implied by it) is itself conditioned upon a certain mode
of distribution, namely the expropriation of the labourers
from the means of production, the concentration of these

means in the hands of a minority of individuals, the exclusive ownership of land by other individuals, in short
all those conditions, which have been described in the Part
dealing with Primitive Accumulation (Volume I, Chapter
XXVI). But this distribution differs considerably from the
meaning of "conditions of distribution," provided we invest
them with a historical character in opposition to conditions
of production. By the first kind of distribution is meant the
various titles to that portion of the product, which goes into
individual consumption. By conditions of distribution, on
the other hand, we mean the foundations of specific social
functions performed within the conditions of production
themselves by special agents in opposition to the direct
producers. They imbue the conditions of production themselves and their representatives with a specific social quality.
They determine the entire character and the entire movement of production.

Capitalist production is marked from the outset by two
peculiar traits.

(1) It produces its products as commodities. The fact
that it produces commodities does not distinguish it from
other modes of production. Its peculiar mark is that the
prevailing and determining character of its products is that
of being commodities. This implies, in the first place, that
the labourer himself acts in the rôle of a seller of commodities, as a free wage worker, so that wage labour is the
typical character of labour. In view of the foregoing
analyses it is not necessary to demonstrate again, that the
relation between wage labour and capital determines the
entire character of the mode of production. The principal
agents of this mode of production itself, the capitalist and
the wage worker, are to that extent merely personifications
of capital and wage labour. They are definite social characters, assigned to individuals by the process of social production. They are products of these definite social conditions
of production.

The character, first of the product as a commodity,

secondly of the commodity as a product of capital, implies all conditions of circulation, that is, a definite social process through which the products must pass and in which they assume definite social forms. It also implies definite relations of the agents in production, by which the formation of value in the product and its reconversion, either into means of subsistence or into means of production, is determined. But aside from this, the two above-named characters of the product as commodities, and of commodities as products of capital, dominate the entire determination of value and the regulation of the whole production by value. In this specific form of value, labour appears on the one hand only as social labour ; on the other hand, the distribution of this social labour and the mutual supplementing and circulation of matter in the products, the subordination under the social activity and the entrance into it, are left to the accidental and mutually nullifying initiative of the individual capitalists. Since these meet one another only as owners of commodities, and every one seeks to sell his commodity as dearly as possible (being apparently guided in the regulation of his production by his own arbitrary will), the internal law enforces itself merely by means of their competition, by their mutual pressure upon each other, by means of which the various deviations are balanced. Only as an internal law, and from the point of view of the individual agents as a blind law, does the law of value exert its influence here and maintain the social equilibrium of production in the turmoil of its accidental fluctuations.

Furthermore, the existence of commodities, and still more of commodities as products of capital, implies the externalisation of the conditions of social production and the personification of the material foundations of production, which characterise the entire capitalist mode of production.

(2) The other specific mark of the capitalist mode of production is the production of surplus value as the direct aim and determining incentive of production. Capital produces essentially capital, and does so only to the extent that it

produces surplus value. We have seen in our discussion of relative surplus value, and in the discussion of the transformation of surplus value into profit, that a mode of production peculiar to the capitalist period is founded upon this. This is a special form in the development of the productive powers of labour, in such a way that these powers appear as self-dependent powers of capital lording it over labour and standing in direct opposition to the labourer's own development. Production which has for its incentive value and surplus value implies, as we have shown in the course of our analyses, the perpetually effective tendency to reduce the labour necessary for the production of a commodity, in other words, to reduce its value, below the prevailing social average. The effort to reduce the cost price to its minimum becomes the strongest lever for the raising of the social productivity of labour, which, however, appears under these conditions as a continual increase of the productive power of capital.

The authority assumed by the capitalist by his personification of capital in the direct process of production, the social function performed by him in his capacity as a manager and ruler of production, is essentially different from the authority exercised upon the basis of production by means of slaves, serfs, etc.

Upon the basis of capitalist production, the social character of their production impresses itself upon the mass of direct producers as a strictly regulating authority and as a social mechanism of the labour process graduated into a complete hierarchy. This authority is vested in its bearers only as a personification of the requirements of labour standing above the labourer. It is not vested in them in their capacity as political or theoretical rulers, in the way that it used to be under former modes of production. Among the bearers of this authority, on the other hand, the capitalists themselves, complete anarchy reigns, since they face each other only as owners of commodities, while the social inter-relations of production manifest themselves to these capitalists only as an overwhelming natural law, which curbs their individual license.

It is only because labour is presumed as wage labour, and the means of production in the form of capital, only on account of this specific social form of these two essential agencies in production, that a part of the value (product) presents itself as surplus value and this surplus value as profit (rent), as a gain of the capitalists, as additional available wealth belonging to the capitalist. But only because they present themselves as his profit, do the additional means of production, which are intended for the expansion of reproduction, and which form a part of this profit, present themselves as new additional capital, and only for this reason does the expansion of the process of reproduction present itself as a process of capitalist accumulation.

Although the form of labour, as wage labour, determines the shape of the entire process and the specific mode of production itself, it is not wage labour which determines value. In the determination of value the question turns around social labour time in general, about that quantity of labour, which society in general has at its disposal, and the relative absorption of which by the various products determines, as it were, their respective social weights. The definite form, in which the social labour time enforces itself in the determination of the value of commodities, is indeed connected with the wage form of labour and with the corresponding form of the means of production as capital, inasmuch as the production of commodities becomes the general form of production only upon this basis.

Now let us consider the so-called conditions of distribution themselves. Wages are conditioned upon wage labour, profit upon capital. These definite forms of distribution have for their pre-requisites definite social characters on the part of the conditions of production, and definite social relations of the agents in production. The definite condition of distribution, therefore, is merely the expression of the historically determined condition of production.

And now let us take profit. This definite form of surplus value is a pre-requisite for the new creation of means of production by means of capitalist production. It is a relation which dominates reproduction, although it seems to the individual capitalist as though he could consume his entire profit as his revenue. But he meets barriers which hamper him even in the form of insurance and reserve funds, laws of competition, etc. These demonstrate to him by practice that profit is not a mere category in the distribution of the product for individual consumption. Furthermore, the entire process of capitalist production is regulated by the prices of products. But the regulating prices of production are in their turn regulated by the equalisation of the rate of profit and by the distribution of capital among the various social spheres of production in correspondence with this equalisation. Profit, then, appears here as the main factor, not of the distribution of products, but of their production itself, as a part in the distribution of capitals and of labour among the various spheres of production. The division of profit into profit of enterprise and interest appears as the distribution of the same revenue. But it arises primarily from the development of capital in its capacity as a self-expanding value, creating surplus value, it arises from this definite social form of the prevailing process of production. It develops credit and credit institutions out of itself, and with them the shape of production. In interest, etc., the alleged forms of distribution enter as determining elements of production into the price.

Ground-rent might seem to be a mere form of distribution, because private land as such does not perform any, or at least no normal, function in the process of production itself. But the fact that, first, rent is limited to the excess above the average profit, and, secondly, that the landlord is depressed by the ruler and manager of the process of production and of the entire social life's process to the position of a mere holder of land for rent, a usurer in land and collector of rent, is a specific historical result of the

capitalist mode of production. The fact that the earth
received the form of private property is a historical requirement for this mode of production. The fact that private
ownership of land assumes forms, which permit the capitalist
mode of production in agriculture, is a product of the
specific character of this mode of production. The income
of the landlord may be called rent, even under other forms
of society. But it differs essentially from the rent as it
appears under the capitalist mode of production.

The so-called conditions of distribution, then, correspond
to and arise from historically defined and specifically social
forms of the process of production and of conditions, into
which human beings enter in the process by which they
reproduce their lives. The historical character of these
conditions of distribution is the same as that of the conditions of production, one side of which they express. Capitalist distribution differs from those forms of distribution,
which arise from other modes of production, and every
mode of distribution disappears with the peculiar mode of
production, from which it arose and to which it belongs.

The conception which regards only the conditions of
distribution historically, but not the conditions of production, is, on the one hand, merely an idea begotten by the
incipient, but still handicapped, critique of bourgeois
economy. On the other hand it rests upon a misconception,
an identification of the process of social production with the
simple labour process, such as might be performed by any
abnormally situated human being without any social
assistance. To the extent that the labour process is a simple
process between man and nature, its simple elements remain
the same in all social forms of development. But every
definite historical form of this process develops more and
more its material foundations and social forms. Whenever
a certain maturity is reached, one definite social form is
discarded and displaced by a higher one. The time for the
coming of such a crisis is announced by the depth and
breadth of the contradictions and antagonisms, which

separate the conditions of distribution, and with them the definite historical form of the corresponding conditions of production, from the productive forces, the productivity, and development of their agencies. A conflict then arises between the material development of production and its social form.

V. I. Lenin

THE TEACHINGS OF KARL MARX

Published 1914, in the " Granat Russian Encyclopædia," in abbreviated form ; complete English edition, Martin Lawrence Ltd., 1931.

[This was an essay written for an encyclopædia. It is therefore extremely brief, but at the same time it is the most comprehensive summary of Marxism. Owing to the censorship, many vital passages were omitted when it was first published. The essay is in three parts ; the first deals with the life of Marx, and the third is a bibliography of Marxism. Only the second section, covering the whole range of Marx's theories, is reprinted here.]

THE TEACHINGS OF KARL MARX

Marxism is the system of the views and teachings of Marx. Marx was the genius who continued and completed the three chief ideological currents of the nineteenth century, represented respectively by the three most advanced countries of humanity : classical German philosophy, classical English political economy, and French

Socialism combined with French revolutionary doctrines. The remarkable consistency and unity of conception of Marx's views, acknowledged even by his opponents, which in their totality constitute modern materialism and modern scientific Socialism as the theory and programme of the labour movement in all the civilised countries of the world, make it necessary that we present a brief outline of his world conception in general before proceeding to the chief contents of Marxism, namely, the economic doctrine of Marx.

PHILOSOPHIC MATERIALISM

Beginning with the years 1844–1845, when his views were definitely formed, Marx was a materialist, and especially a follower of Feuerbach ; even in later times, he saw Feuerbach's weak side only in this, that his materialism was not sufficiently consistent and comprehensive. For Marx, Feuerbach's world-historic and " epoch-making " significance consisted in his having decisively broken away from the idealism of Hegel, and in his proclamation of materialism, which even in the eighteenth century, especially in France, had become " a struggle not only against the existing political institutions, and against . . . religion and theology, but also . . . against every form of metaphysics " (as " intoxicated speculation " in contradistinction to " sober philosophy "). [*Die Heilige Familie* in the *Literarischer Nachlass*.]

> For Hegel—wrote Marx, in the preface to the second edition of the first volume of *Capital*—the thought process (which he actually transforms into an independent subject, giving to it the name of " idea ") is the demiurge [creator] of the real. . . . In my view, on the other hand, the ideal is nothing other than the material when it has been transposed and translated inside the human head. [*Capital*, Vol. I.]

In full conformity with Marx's materialist philosophy, and expounding it, Engels wrote in *Anti-Dühring* (which Marx read in the manuscript) :

The unity of the world does not consist in its existence. . . .
The real unity of the world consists in its materiality, and this
is proved . . . by the long and laborious development of philosophy and natural science. . . . Motion is the form of existence
of matter. Never and nowhere has there been or can there be
matter without motion. . . . Matter without motion is just as
unthinkable as motion without matter. . . . If we enquire . . .
what thought and consciousness are, whence they come, we
find that they are products of the human brain, and that man
himself is a product of nature, developing in and along with
his environment. Obviously, therefore, the products of the
human brain, being in the last analysis likewise products of
nature, do not contradict the rest of nature, but correspond
to it.

Again : " Hegel was an idealist ; that is to say, for him
the thoughts in his head were not 'more or less abstract
reflections [in the original : *Abbilder*, images, copies ;
sometimes Engels speaks of " imprints "] of real things and
processes ; but, on the contrary, things and their evolution
were, for Hegel, only reflections in reality of the Idea that
existed somewhere even prior to the world."

In his *Ludwig Feuerbach*—in which Engels expounds his
own and Marx's views on Feuerbach's philosophy, and
which Engels sent to the press after re-reading an old manuscript, written by Marx and himself in 1844–1845, on Hegel,
Feuerbach, and the materialist conception of history—
Engels writes :

The great basic question of all, and especially of recen,
philosophy, is the question of the relationship between thought
and existence, between spirit and nature. . . . Which is prior
to the other : spirit or nature ? Philosophers are divided into
two great camps, according to the way in which they have
answered this question. Those who declare that spirit existed
before nature, and who, in the last analysis, therefore, assume
in one way or another that the world was created . . . have
formed the idealist camp. The others, who regard nature as
primary, belong to the various schools of materialism.

Any other use (in a philosophic sense) of the terms
idealism and materialism is only confusing. Marx decidedly

rejected not only idealism, always connected in one way
or another with religion, but also the views of Hume and
Kant, that are especially widespread in our day, as well
as agnosticism, criticism, positivism in various forms ; he
considered such philosophy as a " reactionary " concession
to idealism, at best as a " shamefaced manner of admitting
materialism through the back door while denying it before
the world." (On this question see, besides the above-mentioned works of Engels and Marx, a letter of Marx to
Engels, dated December 12, 1866, in which Marx, taking
cognisance of an utterance of the well-known naturalist,
T. Huxley, who " in a more materialistic spirit than he has
manifested in recent years " declared that " as long as we
actually observe and think, we cannot get away from
materialism," reproaches him for once more leaving a new
" back door " open to agnosticism and Humeism.) It is
especially important that we should note Marx's opinion
concerning the relation between freedom and necessity :
" Freedom is the recognition of necessity. Necessity is blind
only in so far as it is not understood " (Engels, *Anti-
Dühring*). This means acknowledgment of the objective
reign of law in nature and of the dialectical transformation
of necessity into freedom (at the same time, an acknowledgment of the transformation of the unknown but know-
able " thing-in-itself " into the " thing-for-us," of the
" essence of things " into " phenomena "). Marx and
Engels pointed out the following major shortcomings of
the " old " materialism, including Feuerbach's (and, *a
fortiori*, the " vulgar " materialism of Büchner, Vogt and
Moleschott) : (1) it was " predominantly mechanical," not
taking into account the latest developments of chemistry
and biology (in our day it would be necessary to add the
electric theory of matter) ; (2) it was non-historical, non-
dialectical (was metaphysical, in the sense of being anti-
dialectical), and did not apply the standpoint of evolution
consistently and all-sidedly ; (3) it regarded " human
nature " abstractly, and not as a " synthesis " of (definite,

concrete-historical) " social relationships "—and thus only " interpreted " the world, whereas it was a question of " changing " it, that is, it did not grasp the significance of " practical revolutionary activity."

DIALECTICS

Marx and Engels regarded Hegelian dialectics, the theory of evolution most comprehensive, rich in content and profound, as the greatest achievement of classical German philosophy. All other formulations of the principle of development, of evolution, they considered to be one-sided, poor in content, distorting and mutilating the actual course of development of nature and society (a course often consummated in leaps and bounds, catastrophes, revolutions).

Marx and I were almost the only persons who rescued conscious dialectics . . . [from the swamp of idealism, including Hegelianism] by transforming it into the materialist conception of nature. . . . Nature is the test of dialectics, and we must say that science has supplied a vast and daily increasing mass of material for this test, thereby proving that, in the last analysis, nature proceeds dialectically and not metaphysically [this was written before the discovery of radium, electrons, the transmutation of elements, etc.].

Again, Engels writes :

The great basic idea that the world is not to be viewed as a complex of fully fashioned objects, but as a complex of processes, in which apparently stable objects, no less than the images of them inside our heads (our concepts), are undergoing incessant changes, arising here and disappearing there, and which with all apparent accident and in spite of all momentary retrogression, ultimately constitutes a progressive development—this great basic idea has, particularly since the time of Hegel, so deeply penetrated the general consciousness that hardly any one will now venture to dispute it in its general form. But it is one thing to accept it in words, quite another thing to put it in practice on every occasion and in every field of investigation.

In the eyes of dialectic philosophy, nothing is established for all time, nothing is absolute or sacred. On everything and in everything it sees the stamp of inevitable decline ; nothing can resist it save the unceasing process of formation and destruction, the unending ascent from the lower to the higher—a process of which that philosophy itself is only a simple reflection within the thinking brain.

Thus dialectics, according to Marx, is " the science of the general laws of motion both of the external world and of human thinking."

This revolutionary side of Hegel's philosophy was adopted and developed by Marx. Dialectical materialism " does not need any philosophy towering above the other sciences." Of former philosophies there remain " the science of thinking and its laws—formal logic and dialectics." Dialectics, as the term is used by Marx in conformity with Hegel, includes what is now called the theory of cognition, or epistemology, or gnoseology, a science that must contemplate its subject matter in the same way—historically, studying and generalising the origin and development of cognition, the transition from *non*-consciousness to consciousness. In our times, the idea of development, of evolution, has almost fully penetrated social consciousness, but it has done so in other ways, not through Hegel's philosophy. Still, the same idea, as formulated by Marx and Engels on the basis of Hegel's philosophy, is much more comprehensive, much more abundant in content than the current theory of evolution. A development that repeats, as it were, the stages already passed, but repeats them in a different way, on a higher plane (" negation of negation ") ; a development, so to speak, in spirals, not in a straight line ; a development in leaps and bounds, catastrophes, revolutions ; " intervals of gradualness " ; transformation of quantity into quality ; inner impulses for development, imparted by the contradiction, the conflict of different forces and tendencies reacting on a given body or inside a given phenomenon or within a given society ; interdependence, and the closest, indissoluble connection between *all* sides of every phenomenon (history disclosing ever new sides), a connection that provides the one world-process of motion proceeding according to law— such are some of the features of dialectics as a doctrine of evolution more full of meaning than the current one. (See letter of Marx to Engels, dated January 8, 1868, in which he ridicules Stein's "wooden trichotomies," which it is absurd to confuse with materialist dialectics.)

MATERIALIST CONCEPTION OF HISTORY

Realising the inconsistency, the incompleteness, and the one-sidedness of the old materialism, Marx became convinced that it was necessary " to harmonise the science of society with the materialist basis, and to reconstruct it in accordance with this basis." If, speaking generally, material- ism explains consciousness as the outcome of existence, and not conversely, then, applied to the social life of man- kind, materialism must explain *social* consciousness as the outcome of *social* existence. " Technology," writes Marx in the first volume of *Capital*, " reveals man's dealings with nature, discloses the direct productive activities of his life, thus throwing light upon social relations and the resultant mental conceptions." In the preface to *A Contribution to the Critique of Political Economy*, Marx gives an integral formula- tion of the fundamental principles of materialism as applied to human society and its history, in the following words :

In the social production of the means of life, human beings enter into definite and necessary relations which are independent of their will—production relations which correspond to a definite stage of the development of their productive forces. The totality of these production relations constitutes the economic structure of society, the real basis upon which a legal and political super- structure arises and to which definite forms of social conscious- ness correspond. The mode of production of the material means of life, determines, in general, the social, political, and intellec- tual processes of life. It is not the consciousness of human beings that determines their existence, but, conversely, it is their social existence that determines their consciousness. At a certain

stage of their development, the material productive forces of
society come into conflict with the existing production relationships, or, what is but a legal expression for the same thing, with
the property relationships within which they have hitherto
moved. From forms of development of the productive forces,
these relationships turn into their fetters. A period of social
revolution then begins. With the change in the economic
foundation, the whole gigantic superstructure is more or less
rapidly transformed. In considering such transformations we
must always distinguish between the material changes in the
economic conditions of production, changes which can be
determined with the precision of natural science, and the legal,
political, religious, æsthetic, or philosophic, in short, ideological
forms, in which human beings become conscious of this conflict
and fight it out to an issue.

Just as little as we judge an individual by what he thinks of
himself, just so little can we appraise such a revolutionary
epoch in accordance with its own consciousness of itself. On
the contrary, we have to explain this consciousness as the outcome of the contradictions of material life, of the conflict
existing between social productive forces and production
relationships. . . . In broad outline we can designate the Asiatic,
the classical, the feudal, and the modern bourgeois forms of
production as progressive epochs in the economic formation of
society. [Compare Marx's brief formulation in a letter to Engels,
dated July 7, 1866 : " Our theory about the organisation of
labour being determined by the means of production."]

The discovery of the materialist conception of history, or,
more correctly, the consistent extension of materialism to
the domain of social phenomena, obviated the two chief
defects in earlier historical theories. For, in the first place,
those theories, at best, examined only the ideological motives
of the historical activity of human beings without investi-
gating the origin of these ideological motives, or grasping
the objective conformity to law in the development of the
system of social relationships, or discerning the roots of
these social relationships in the degree of development of
material production. In the second place, the earlier
historical theories ignored the activities of the *masses*,
whereas historical materialism first made it possible to
study with scientific accuracy the social conditions of the

life of the masses and the changes in these conditions. At best, pre-Marxist " sociology " and historiography gave an accumulation of raw facts collected at random, and a description of separate sides of the historic process. Examining the *totality* of all the opposing tendencies, reducing them to precisely definable conditions in the mode of life and the method of production of the various *classes* of society, discarding subjectivism and free will in the choice of various " leading " ideas or in their interpretation, showing how all the ideas and all the various tendencies, without exception, have their roots in the condition of the material forces of production, Marxism pointed the way to a comprehensive, an all-embracing study of the rise, development, and decay of socio-economic structures. People make their own history ; but what determines their motives, that is, the motives of people in the mass ; what gives rise to the clash of conflicting ideas and endeavours ; what is the sum total of all these clashes among the whole mass of human societies ; what are the objective conditions for the production of the material means of life that form the basis of all the historical activity of man ; what is the law of the development of these conditions?—to all these matters Marx directed attention, pointing out the way to a scientific study of history as a unified and true-to-law process despite its being extremely variegated and contradictory.

CLASS STRUGGLE

That in any given society the strivings of some of the members conflict with the strivings of others ; that social life is full of contradictions ; that history discloses to us a struggle among peoples and societies, and also within each nation and each society, manifesting in addition an alternation between periods of revolution and reaction, peace and war, stagnation and rapid progress or decline—these facts are generally known. Marxism provides a clue which enables us to discover the reign of law in this seeming

labyrinth and chaos : the theory of the class struggle.
Nothing but the study of the totality of the strivings of all
the members of a given society, or group of societies, can
lead to the scientific definition of the result of these strivings.
Now, the conflict of strivings arises from differences in the
situation and modes of life of the *classes* into which society is
divided.

> The history of all human society, past and present [wrote Marx
> in 1848, in *The Communist Manifesto* ; except the history of the
> primitive community, Engels added], has been the history of
> class struggles. Freeman and slave, patrician and plebeian,
> baron and serf, guild-burgess and journeyman—in a word,
> oppressor and oppressed—stood in sharp opposition each to the
> other. They carried on perpetual warfare, sometimes masked,
> sometimes open and acknowledged ; a warfare that invariably
> ended either in a revolutionary change in the whole structure
> of society or else in the common ruin of the contending classes.
> . . . Modern bourgeois society, rising out of the ruins of feudal
> society, did not make an end of class antagonisms. It merely
> set up new classes in place of the old ; new conditions of oppres-
> sion ; new embodiments of struggle. Our own age, the bourgeois
> age, is distinguished by this—that it has simplified class antagon-
> isms. More and more, society is splitting up into two great
> hostile camps, into two great and directly contraposed classes :
> bourgeoisie and proletariat.

Since the time of the great French Revolution, the class
struggle as the actual motive force of events has been most
clearly manifest in all European history. During the Restoration period in France, there were already a number of
historians (Thierry, Guizot, Mignet, Thiers) who, generalising events, could not but recognise in the class struggle
the key to the understanding of all the history of France.
In the modern age—the epoch of the complete victory of
the bourgeoisie, of representative institutions, of extended
(if not universal) suffrage, of cheap daily newspapers widely
circulated among the masses, etc., of powerful and ever-
expanding organisations of workers and employers, etc.—
the class struggle (though sometimes in a highly one-sided,
" peaceful," " constitutional " form), has shown itself still

more obviously to be the mainspring of events. The following passage from Marx's *Communist Manifesto* will show us what Marx demanded of social sciences as regards an objective analysis of the situation of every class in modern society as well as an analysis of the conditions of development of every class.

> Among all the classes that confront the bourgeoisie to-day, the proletariat alone is really revolutionary. Other classes decay and perish with the rise of large-scale industry, but the proletariat is the most characteristic product of that industry. The lower middle class—small manufacturers, small traders, handicraftsmen, peasant proprietors—one and all fight the bourgeoisie in the hope of safeguarding their existence as sections of the middle class. They are, therefore, not revolutionary, but conservative. Nay, more, they are reactionary, for they are trying to make the wheels of history turn backwards. If they ever become revolutionary, it is only because they are afraid of slipping down into the ranks of the proletariat ; they are not defending their present interests, but their future interests ; they are forsaking their own standpoint, in order to adopt that of the proletariat.

In a number of historical works Marx gave brilliant and profound examples of materialist historiography, an analysis of the position of *each* separate class, and sometimes of that of various groups or strata within a class, showing plainly why and how " every class struggle is a political struggle." The above quoted passage is an illustration of what a complex network of social relations and *transitional stages* between one class and another, between the past and the future, Marx analyses in order to arrive at the resultant of the whole historical development.

Marx's economic doctrine is the most profound, the most many-sided, and the most detailed confirmation and application of his teaching.

MARX'S ECONOMIC DOCTRINE

" It is the ultimate aim of this work to reveal the economic law of motion of modern society " (that is to say, capitalist, bourgeois society), writes Marx in the preface to the first volume of *Capital*. The study of the production relationships in a given, historically determinate society, in their genesis, their development, and their decay—such is the content of Marx's economic teaching. In capitalist society the dominant feature is the production of *commodities*, and Marx's analysis therefore begins with an analysis of commodity.

Value

A commodity is, firstly, something that satisfies a human need ; and, secondly, it is something that is exchanged for something else. The utility of a thing gives it *use-value*. Exchange-value (or simply, value) presents itself first of all as the proportion, the ratio, in which a certain number of use-values of one kind are exchanged for a certain number of use-values of another kind. Daily experience shows us that by millions upon millions of such exchanges, all and sundry use-values, in themselves very different and not comparable one with another, are equated to one another. Now, what is common in these various things which are constantly weighed one against another in a definite system of social relationships ? That which is common to them is that they are *products of labour*. In exchanging products, people equate to one another most diverse kinds of labour. The production of commodities is a system of social relationships in which different producers produce various products (the social division of labour), and in which all these products are equated to one another in exchange. Consequently, the element common to all commodities is not concrete labour in a definite branch of production, not labour of one particular kind, but *abstract* human labour— human labour in general. All the labour power of a given society, represented in the sum total of values of all commodities, is one and the same human labour power. Millions upon millions of acts of exchange prove this. Consequently, each particular commodity represents only a certain part of *socially necessary* labour time. The magnitude of the value is determined by the amount of socially necessary labour, or by the labour time that is socially requisite for the production of the given commodity, of the given use-value. ". . . Exchanging labour products of different kinds one for another, they equate the values of the exchanged products ; and in doing so they equate the different kinds of labour expended in production, treating them as homogeneous human labour. They do not know that they are doing this, but they do it." As one of the earlier economists said, value is a relationship between two persons, only he should have added that it is a relationship hidden beneath a material wrapping. We can only understand what value is when we consider it from the point of view of a system of social production relationships in one particular historical type of society ; and, moreover, of relationships which present themselves in a mass form, the phenomenon of exchange repeating itself millions upon millions of times. "As values, all commodities are only definite quantities of congealed labour time." Having made a detailed analysis of the twofold character of the labour incorporated in commodities, Marx goes on to analyse the *form of value and of money*. His main task, then, is to study the *origin* of the money form of value, to study the *historical process* of the development of exchange, beginning with isolated and casual acts of exchange (" simple, isolated, or casual value form," in which a given quantity of one commodity is exchanged for a given quantity of another), passing on to the universal form of value, in which a number of different commodities are exchanged for one and the same particular commodity, and ending with the money form of value, when gold becomes this particular commodity, the universal equivalent. Being the highest product of the development of exchange and of commodity production, money masks the social character of individual labour, and hides the social tie between the various producers who come together in the market. Marx analyses in great detail the various

functions of money ; and it is essential to note that here
(as generally in the opening chapters of *Capital*) what
appears to be an abstract and at times purely deductive
mode of exposition in reality reproduces a gigantic collection of facts concerning the history of the development of
exchange and commodity production.

> Money . . . presupposes a definite level of commodity ex-
> change. The various forms of money (simple commodity
> equivalent or means of circulation, or means of payment,
> treasure, or international money) indicate, according to the
> different extent to which this or that function is put into applica-
> tion, and according to the comparative predominance of one or
> other of them, very different grades of the social process of
> production. [*Capital*, Vol. I.]

Surplus Value

At a particular stage in the development of commodity
production, money becomes transformed into capital. The
formula of commodity circulation was C-M-C (commodity
—money—commodity) ; the sale of one commodity for
the purpose of buying another. But the general formula of
capital, on the contrary, is M-C-M (money—commodity—
money) ; purchase for the purpose of selling—at a profit.
The designation " surplus value " is given by Marx to the
increase over the original value of money that is put into
circulation. The fact of this " growth " of money in capitalist society is well known. Indeed, it is this " growth " which
transforms money into *capital*, as a special, historically
defined, social relationship of production. Surplus value
cannot arise out of the circulation of commodities, for this
represents nothing more than the exchange of equivalents ;
it cannot arise out of an advance in prices, for the mutual
losses and gains of buyers and sellers would equalise one
another ; and we are concerned here, not with what
happens to individuals, but with a mass or average or
social phenomenon. In order that he may be able to receive
surplus value, " Moneybags must . . . find in the market a
commodity whose use-value has the peculiar quality of

being a source of value "—a commodity, the actual process of whose use is at the same time the process of the creation of value. Such a commodity exists. It is human labour power. Its use is labour, and labour creates value. The owner of money buys labour power at its value, which is determined, like the value of every other commodity, by the socially necessary labour time requisite for its production (that is to say, the cost of maintaining the worker and his family). Having bought labour power, the owner of money is entitled to use it, that is, to set it to work for the whole day—twelve hours, let us suppose. Meanwhile, in the course of six hours (" necessary " labour time) the labourer produces sufficient to pay back the cost of his own maintenance, and in the course of the next six hours (" surplus " labour time), he produces a " surplus " product for which the capitalist does not pay him—surplus product or surplus value. In capital, therefore, from the viewpoint of the process of production, we have to distinguish between two parts : first, constant capital, expended for the means of production (machinery, tools, raw materials, etc.), the value of this being (all at once or part by part) transferred, unchanged, to the finished product ; and, secondly, variable capital, expended for labour power. The value of this latter capital is not constant, but grows in the labour process, creating surplus value. To express the degree of exploitation of labour power by capital, we must therefore compare the surplus value, not with the whole capital, but only with the variable capital. Thus, in the example just given, the rate of surplus value, as Marx calls this relationship, will be 6 : 6, i.e., 100 per cent.

There are two historical prerequisites to the genesis of capital : first, accumulation of a considerable sum of money in the hands of individuals living under conditions in which there is a comparatively high development of commodity production. Second, the existence of workers who are " free " in a double sense of the term : free from any constraint or restriction as regards the sale of their labour power ; free from any bondage to the soil or to the means of production in general—i.e., of propertyless workers, of " proletarians " who cannot maintain their existence except by the sale of their labour power.

There are two fundamental ways in which surplus value can be increased : by an increase in the working day (" absolute surplus value ") ; and by a reduction in the necessary working day (" relative surplus value "). Analysing the former method, Marx gives an impressive picture of the struggle of the working class for shorter hours and of governmental interference, first (from the fourteenth century to the seventeenth) in order to lengthen the working day, and subsequently (factory legislation of the nineteenth century) to shorten it. Since the appearance of *Capital*, the history of the working-class movement in all lands provides a wealth of new facts to amplify this picture.

Analysing the production of relative surplus value, Marx investigates the three fundamental historical stages of the process whereby capitalism has increased the productivity of labour ; (1) simple co-operation ; (2) division of labour, and manufacture ; (3) machinery and large-scale industry. How profoundly Marx has here revealed the basic and typical features of capitalist development is shown by the fact that investigations of the so-called " kustar " industry of Russia furnish abundant material for the illustration of the first two of these stages. The revolutionising effect of large-scale machine industry, described by Marx in 1867, has become evident in a number of " new " countries, such as Russia, Japan, etc., in the course of the last fifty years.

But to continue. Of extreme importance and originality is Marx's analysis of the *accumulation of capital*, that is to say, the transformation of a portion of surplus value into capital and the applying of this portion to additional production, instead of using it to supply the personal needs or to gratify the whims of the capitalist. Marx pointed out the mistake made by earlier classical political economy (from Adam Smith on), which assumed that all the surplus value which was transformed into capital became variable capital. In actual fact, it is divided into *means of production* plus variable capital. The more rapid growth of constant capital as compared with variable capital in the sum total of capital is of immense importance in the process of development of capitalism and in that of the transformation of capitalism into Socialism.

The accumulation of capital, accelerating the replacement of workers by machinery, creating wealth at the one pole and poverty at the other, gives birth to the so-called " reserve army of labour," to a "relative over-abundance" of workers or to " capitalist over-population." This assumes the most diversified forms, and gives capital the possibility of expanding production at an exceptionally rapid rate. This possibility, in conjunction with enhanced facilities for credit and with the accumulation of capital in the means of production, furnishes, among other things, the key to the understanding of the *crises* of over production that occur periodically in capitalist countries—first about every ten years, on an average, but subsequently in a more continuous form and with a less definite periodicity. From accumulation of capital upon a capitalist foundation we must distinguish the so-called " primitive accumulation " : the forcible severance of the worker from the means of production, the driving of the peasants off the land, the stealing of the communal lands, the system of colonies and national debts, of protective tariffs, and the like. " Primitive accumulation " creates, at one pole, the " free " proletarian : at the other, the owner of money, the capitalist.

The " *historical tendency of capitalist accumulation* " is described by Marx in the following well-known terms :

The expropriation of the immediate producers is effected with ruthless vandalism, and under the stimulus of the most infamous, the basest, the meanest, and the most odious of passions. Self-earned private property [of the peasant and the handicraftsman], the private property that may be looked upon as grounded on a coalescence of the isolated, individual, and independent worker with his working conditions, is supplemented by capitalist private property, which is maintained by the exploitation of others' labour, but of labour which in a formal sense is free. . . . What has now to be expropriated is no longer the labourer working on his own account, but the capitalist who exploits many labourers. This expropriation is brought about by the operation of the immanent laws of capitalist production, by the centralisation of capital. One capitalist lays a number of his fellow capitalists low. Hand in hand with this centralisation, concomitantly with the expropriation of many capitalists by a few, the co-operative form of the labour process develops to an ever-increasing degree ; therewith we find a growing tendency towards the purposive application of science to the improvement of technique ; the land is more methodically cultivated ; the instruments of labour tend to assume forms which are only utilisable by combined effort ; the means of production are economised through being turned to account only by joint, by social labour ; all the peoples of the world are enmeshed in the net of the world market, and therefore the capitalist régime tends more and more to assume an international character. While there is thus a progressive diminution in the number of the capitalist magnates (who usurp and monopolise all the advantages of this transformative process), there occurs a corresponding increase in the mass of poverty, oppression, enslavement, degeneration, and exploitation ; but at the same time there is a steady intensification of the wrath of the working class—a class which grows ever more numerous, and is disciplined, unified, and organised by the very mechanism of the capitalist method of production. Capitalist monopoly becomes a fetter upon the method of production which has flourished with it and under it. The centralisation of the means of production and the socialisation of labour reach a point where they prove incompatible with their capitalist husk. This bursts asunder. The knell of capitalist private property sounds. The expropriators are expropriated. [*Capital*, Vol. I.]

Of great importance and quite new is Marx's analysis, in the second volume of *Capital*, of the reproduction of social capital, taken as a whole. Here, too, Marx is dealing, not with an individual phenomenon, but with a mass phenomenon ; not with a fractional part of the economy of society, but with economy as a whole. Having corrected the above-mentioned mistake of the classical economists, Marx divides the whole of social production into two great sections : production of the means of production, and production of articles for consumption. Using figures for an example, he makes a detailed examination of the circulation of all social capital taken as a whole—both when it is reproduced in its previous proportions and when accumulation takes place. The third volume of *Capital* solves the problem of how the average rate of profit is formed on the basis of the law of value. An immense advance in economic science is this, that Marx conducts his analysis from the point of view of mass economic phenomena, of the aggregate of social economy, and not from the point of view of individual cases or upon the purely superficial aspects of competition —a limitation of view so often met with in vulgar political economy and in the contemporary " theory of marginal utility." First, Marx analyses the origin of surplus value, and then he goes on to consider its division into profit, interest, and ground-rent. Profit is the ratio between the surplus value and all the capital invested in an undertaking. Capital with a " high organic composition " (i.e., with a preponderance of constant capital over variable capital to an extent above the social average) yields a below-average rate of profit ; capital with a " low organic composition " yields an above-average rate of profit. Competition among the capitalists, who are free to transfer their capital from one branch of production to another, reduces the rate of profit in both cases to the average. The sum total of the values of all the commodities in a given society coincides with the sum total of the prices of all the commodities ; but in separate undertakings, and in separate branches of production, as a result of competition, commodities are sold, not in accordance with their values, but in accordance with the *prices of production*, which are equal to the expended capital plus the average profit.

In this way the well-known and indisputable fact of the divergence between prices and values and of the equalisation of profits is fully explained by Marx in conformity with

the law of value ; for the sum total of the values of all the
commodities coincides with the sum total of all the prices.
But the adjustment of value (a social matter) to price (an
individual matter) does not proceed by a simple and direct
way. It is an exceedingly complex affair. Naturally, therefore, in a society made up of separate producers of commodities, linked solely through the market, conformity to
law can only be an average, a general manifestation, a
mass phenomenon, with individual and mutually compensating deviations to one side and the other.

An increase in the productivity of labour means a more
rapid growth of constant capital as compared with variable
capital. Inasmuch as surplus value is a function of variable
capital alone, it is obvious that the rate of profit (the ratio
of surplus value to the whole capital, and not to its variable
part alone) has a tendency to fall. Marx makes a detailed
analysis of this tendency and of the circumstances that
incline to favour it or to counteract it. Without pausing
to give an account of the extraordinarily interesting parts of
the third volume of *Capital* that are devoted to the consideration of usurer's capital, commercial capital, and
money capital, I shall turn to the most important subject
of that volume, the theory of *ground-rent*. Due to the fact
that the land area is limited, and that in capitalist countries
it is all occupied by private owners, the production price
of agricultural products is determined by the cost of production, not on soil of average quality, but on the worst
soil, and by the cost of bringing goods to the market, not
under average conditions, but under the worst conditions.
The difference between this price and the price of production on better soil (or under better conditions) constitutes *differential* rent. Analysing this in detail, and showing
how it arises out of variations in the fertility of the individual
plots of land and in the extent to which capital is applied
to the land, Marx fully exposes (see also the *Theorien über den
Mehrwert* [*Theories of Surplus Value*], in which the criticism
of Rodbertus's theory deserves particular attention) the

error of Ricardo, who considered that differential rent is only obtained when there is a continual transition from better to worse lands. Advances in agricultural technique, the growth of towns, and so on, may, on the contrary, act inversely, may transfer land from one category into the other ; and the famous " law of diminishing returns," charging nature with the insufficiencies, limitations, and contradictions of capitalism, is a great mistake. Moreover, the equalisation of profit in all branches of industry and national economy in general, presupposes complete freedom of competition, the free mobility of capital from one branch to another. But the private ownership of land, creating monopoly, hinders this free mobility. Thanks to this monopoly, the products of agriculture, where a low organic composition of capital prevails, and, consequently, individually, a higher rate of profit can be secured, are not exposed to a perfectly free process of equalisation of the rate of profit. The landowner, being a monopolist, can keep the price of his produce above the average, and this monopoly price is the source of *absolute rent*. Differential rent cannot be done away with so long as capitalism exists ; but absolute rent *can* be abolished even under capitalism— for instance, by nationalisation of the land, by making all the land state property. Nationalisation of the land would put an end to the monopoly of private landowners, with the result that free competition would be more consistently and fully applied in the domain of agriculture. That is why, as Marx states, in the course of history the radical bourgeois have again and again come out with this progressive bourgeois demand of land nationalisation, which, however, frightens away the majority of the bourgeoisie, for it touches upon another monopoly that is highly important and " touchy " in our days—the monopoly of the means of production in general. (In a letter to Engels, dated August 2, 1862, Marx gives a remarkably popular, concise, and clear exposition of his theory of average rate of profit and of absolute ground-rent. See *Briefwechsel*, Vol. III, pp. 77–81 ;

also the letter of August 9, 1862, Vol. III, pp. 86–87). For the history of ground-rent it is also important to note Marx's analysis which shows how rent paid in labour service (when the peasant creates a surplus product by labouring on the lord's land) is transformed into rent paid in produce or rent in kind (the peasant creating a surplus product on his own land and handing this over to the lord of the soil under stress of " non-economic constraint ") ; then into monetary rent (which is the monetary equivalent of rent in kind, the *obrok* of old Russia, money having replaced produce thanks to the development of commodity production), and finally into capitalist rent, when the place of the peasant has been taken by the agricultural *entrepreneur* cultivating the soil with the help of wage labour. In connection with this analysis of the " genesis of capitalist ground-rent " must be noted Marx's profound ideas concerning the *evolution of capitalism in agriculture* (this is of especial importance in its bearing on backward countries, such as Russia).

The transformation of rent in kind into money rent is not only necessarily accompanied, but even anticipated by the formation of a class of propertyless day labourers, who hire themselves out for wages. During the period of their rise, when this new class appears but sporadically, the custom necessarily develops among the better situated tributary farmers of exploiting agricultural labourers for their own account, just as the wealthier serfs in feudal times used to employ serfs for their own benefit. In this way they gradually acquire the ability to accumulate a certain amount of wealth and to transform themselves even into future capitalists. The old self-employing possessors of the land thus gave rise among themselves to a nursery for capitalist tenants, whose development is conditioned upon the general development of capitalist production outside of the rural districts. [*Capital*, Vol. III.]

The expropriation of part of the country folk, and the hunting of them off the land, does not merely " set free " the workers for the uses of industrial capital, together with their means of subsistence and the materials of their labour ; in addition it creates the home market. [*Capital*, Vol. I.]

The impoverishment and the ruin of the agricultural population lead, in their turn, to the formation of a reserve army of labour for capital. In every capitalist country, " part of the rural population is continually on the move, in course of transference to join the urban proletariat, the manufacturing proletariat. . . . (In this connection, the term " manufacture " is used to include all non-agricultural industry.) This source of a relative surplus population is, therefore, continually flowing. . . . The agricultural labourer, therefore, has his wages kept down to the minimum, and always has one foot in the swamp of pauperism " (*Capital*, Vol. I). The peasant's private ownership of the land he tills constitutes the basis of small-scale production and causes the latter to flourish and attain its classical form. But such petty production is only compatible with a narrow and primitive type of production, with a narrow and primitive framework of society. Under capitalism, the exploitation of the peasants " differs from the exploitation of the industrial proletariat only in point of form. The exploiter is the same : capital. The individual capitalists exploit the individual peasants through mortgages and usury, and the capitalist class exploits the peasant class through state taxation ",(*Class Struggles in France*). " Peasant agriculture, the smallholding system, is merely an expedient whereby the capitalist is enabled to extract profit, interest, and rent from the land, while leaving the peasant proprietor to pay himself his own wages as best he may." As a rule, the peasant hands over to the capitalist society, i.e., to the capitalist class, part of the wages of his own labour, sinking " down to the level of the Irish tenant—all this on the pretext of being the owner of private property." Why is it that " the price of cereals is lower in countries with a predominance of small farmers than in countries with a capitalist method of production " ? (*Capital*, Vol. III.) The answer is that the peasant presents part of his surplus product as a free gift to society (i.e., to the capitalist class). " This lower price [of bread and other agricultural

products] is also a result of the poverty of the producers and
by no means of the productivity of their labour " (*Capital*,
Vol. III). Peasant proprietorship, the smallholding system,
which is the normal form of petty production, degenerates,
withers, perishes under capitalism.

Small peasants' property excludes by its very nature the
development of the social powers of production, of labour, the
social forms of labour, the social concentration of capital, cattle
raising on a large scale, and a progressive application of science.
Usury and a system of taxation must impoverish it everywhere.
The expenditure of capital in the price of the land withdraws
this capital from cultivation. An infinite dissipation of means of
production and an isolation of the producers themselves go
with it. [Co-operatives, i.e., associations of small peasants,
while playing an unusually progressive bourgeois rôle, only
weaken this tendency without eliminating it ; one must not
forget besides, that these co-operatives do much for the well-
to-do peasants and very little, almost nothing, for the mass of
the poor peasants, also that the associations themselves become
exploiters of wage labour.] Also an enormous waste of human
energy. A progressive deterioration of the conditions of production and a raising of the price of means of production is a
necessary law of small peasants' property. [*Capital*, Vol. III.]

In agriculture as in industry, capitalism improves the
production process only at the price of the " martyrdom of
the producers."

The dispersion of the rural workers over large areas breaks
down their powers of resistance at the very time when concentration is increasing the powers of the urban operatives in this
respect. In modern agriculture, as in urban industry, the increased productivity and the greater mobility of labour are
purchased at the cost of devastating labour power and making
it a prey to disease. Moreover, every advance in capitalist
agriculture is an advance in the art, not only of robbing the
worker, but also of robbing the soil. . . . Capitalist production,
therefore, is only able to develop the technique and the combination of the social process of production by simultaneously
undermining the foundations of all wealth—the land and the
workers. [*Capital*, Vol. I.]

SOCIALISM

From the foregoing it is manifest that Marx deduces the inevitability of the transformation of capitalist society into Socialist society wholly and exclusively from the economic law of the movement of contemporary society. The chief material foundation of the inevitability of the coming of Socialism is the socialisation of labour in its myriad forms, advancing ever more rapidly, and conspicuously so, throughout the half century that has elapsed since the death of Marx—being especially plain in the growth of large-scale production, of capitalist cartels, syndicates, and trusts ; but also in the gigantic increase in the dimensions and the power of finance capital. The intellectual and moral driving force of this transformation is the proletariat, the physical carrier trained by capitalism itself. The contest of the proletariat with the bourgeoisie, assuming various forms which grow continually richer in content, inevitably becomes a political struggle aiming at the conquest of political power by the proletariat (" the dictatorship of the proletariat "). The socialisation of production cannot fail to lead to the transfer of the means of production into the possession of society, to the " expropriation of the expropriators." An immense increase in the productivity of labour ; a reduction in working hours ; replacement of the remnants, the ruins of petty, primitive, individual production by collective and perfected labour—such will be the direct consequences of this transformation. Capitalism breaks all ties between agriculture and industry ; but at the same time, in the course of its highest development, it prepares new elements for the establishment of a connection between the two, uniting industry and agriculture upon the basis of the conscious use of science and the combination of collective labour, the redistribution of population (putting an end at one and the same time to rural seclusion and unsociability and savagery, and to the unnatural concentration of enormous masses of population in huge cities). A new kind of family life, changes in the position of women and in the upbringing of the younger generation, are being prepared by the highest forms of modern capitalism ; the labour of women and children, the break-up of the patriarchal family by capitalism, necessarily assume in contemporary society the most terrible, disastrous, and repulsive forms. Nevertheless,

> . . . large-scale industry, by assigning to women and to young persons and children of both sexes a decisive rôle in the socially organised process of production, and a rôle which has to be fulfilled outside the home, is building the new economic foundation for a higher form of the family and of the relations between the sexes. I need hardly say that it is just as stupid to regard the Christo-Teutonic form of the family as absolute, as it is to take the same view of the classical Roman form or of the classical Greek form, or of the Oriental form—which, by the by, constitute an historically interconnected developmental series. It is plain, moreover, that the composition of the combined labour personnel out of individuals of both sexes and various ages—although in its spontaneously developed and brutal capitalist form (wherein the worker exists for the process of production instead of the process of production existing for the worker) it is a pestilential source of corruption and slavery —under suitable conditions cannot fail to be transformed into a source of human progress. [*Capital*, Vol. I.]

In the factory system are to be found " the germs of the education of the future. . . . This will be an education which, in the case of every child over a certain age, will combine productive labour with instruction and physical culture, not only as a means for increasing social production, but as the only way of producing fully developed human beings " (*ibid.*, p. 522). Upon the same historical foundation, not with the sole idea of throwing light on the past, but with the idea of boldly foreseeing the future and boldly working to bring about its realisation, the Socialism of Marx propounds the problems of nationality and the State. The nation is a necessary product, an inevitable form, in the bourgeois epoch of social development. The working class cannot grow strong, cannot mature, cannot consolidate its forces, except by " establishing itself as the nation," except by being " national " (" though by no means in the bourgeois sense of the term "). But the development of capitalism tends more and more to break down the partitions that separate the nations one from another, does away with national isolation, substitutes class antagonisms for national antagonisms. In the more developed capitalist countries, therefore, it is perfectly true that " the workers have no fatherland," and that " united action " of the workers, in the civilised countries at least, " is one of the first conditions requisite for the emancipation of the workers " (*Communist Manifesto*). The State, which is organised oppression, came into being inevitably at a certain stage in the development of society, when this society had split into irreconcilable classes, and when it could not exist without an " authority " supposed to be standing above society and to some extent separated from it. Arising out of class contradictions, the State becomes

. . . the State of the most powerful economic class that by force of its economic supremacy becomes also the ruling political class, and thus acquires new means of subduing and exploiting the oppressed masses. The ancient State was therefore the State of the slave-owners for the purpose of holding the slaves in check. The feudal state was the organ of the nobility for the oppression of the serfs and dependent farmers. The modern representative State is the tool of the capitalist exploiters of wage labour. [Engels, *The Origin of the Family, Private Property, and the State*, a work in which the writer expounds his own views and Marx's.]

This condition of affairs persists even in the democratic republic, the freest and most progressive kind of bourgeois State ; there is merely a change of form (the government becoming linked up with the stock exchange, and the officialdom and the press being corrupted by direct or indirect means). Socialism, putting an end to classes, will thereby put an end to the State.

The first act, writes Engels in *Anti-Dühring*, whereby the State really becomes the representative of society as a whole, namely, the expropriation of the means of production for the benefit of society as a whole, will likewise be its last independent act as a State. The interference of the State authority in social relationships will become superfluous, and will be discontinued in one domain after another. The government over persons will be transformed into the administration of things and the management of the process of production. The State will not be " abolished " ; it will " die out."

The society that is to reorganise production on the basis of a free and equal association of the producers will transfer the machinery of State where it will then belong : into the museum of antiquities, by the side of the spinning-wheel and the bronze axe. [Engels, *The Origin of the Family, Private Property, and the State.*]

If, finally, we wish to understand the attitude of Marxian Socialism towards the small peasantry, which will continue to exist in the period of the expropriation of the expropriators, we must turn to a declaration by Engels expressing Marx's views. In an article on " The Peasant Problem in France and Germany," which appeared in the *Neue Zeit*, he says :

When we are in possession of the powers of the State, we shall not even dream of forcibly expropriating the poorer peasants, the smallholders (with or without compensation), as we shall have to do in relation to the large landowners. Our task as regards the smallholders will first of all consist in transforming their individual production and individual ownership into co-operative production and co-operative ownership, not forcibly, but by way of example, and by offering social aid for this purpose. We shall then have the means of showing the peasant all the advantages of this change—advantages which even now should be obvious to him.

TACTICS OF THE CLASS STRUGGLE OF THE PROLETARIAT

Having discovered as early as 1844–1845 that one of the chief defects of the earlier materialism was its failure to understand the conditions or recognise the importance of practical revolutionary activity, Marx, during all his life, alongside of theoretical work, gave unremitting attention to the tactical problems of the class struggle of the proletariat. An immense amount of material bearing upon this is contained in all the works of Marx and in the four volumes of his correspondence with Engels (*Briefwechsel*), published in 1913. This material is still far from having been collected, organised, studied, and elaborated. This is why we shall have to confine ourselves to the most general and brief remarks, emphasising the point that Marx justly considered materialism without *this* side to be incomplete, one-sided, and devoid of vitality. The fundamental task of proletarian tactics was defined by Marx in strict conformity with the general principles of his materialist-dialectical outlook. Nothing but an objective account of the sum total of all the mutual relationships of all the classes of a given society without exception, and consequently an account of the objective stage of development of this society as well as an account of the mutual relationship between it and other societies, can serve as the basis for the correct tactics of the class that forms the vanguard. All classes and all countries are at the same time looked upon not statically, but dynamically ; i.e., not as motionless, but as in motion (the laws of their motion being determined by the economic conditions of existence of each class). The motion, in its turn, is looked upon not only from the point of view of the past, but also from the point of view of the future ; and, moreover, not only in accordance with the vulgar conception of the " evolutionists," who see only slow changes—but dialectically : " In such great developments, twenty years are but as one day—and then may come days which are the concentrated essence of twenty years," wrote Marx to Engels (*Briefwechsel*, Vol. III, p. 127). At each stage of development, at each moment, proletarian tactics must take account of these objectively unavoidable dialectics of human history, utilising, on the one hand, the phases of political stagnation, when things are moving at a snail's pace along the road of the so-called "peaceful" development, to increase the class consciousness, strength, and fighting capacity of the most advanced class ; on the other hand, conducting this work in the direction of the "final aims" of the movement of this class, cultivating in it the faculty for the practical performance of great tasks in great days that are the "concentrated essence of twenty years." Two of Marx's arguments are of especial importance in this connection : one of these is in the *Poverty of Philosophy* and relates to the industrial struggle and to the industrial organisations of the proletariat ; the other is in *The Communist Manifesto*, and relates to the proletariat's political tasks. The former runs as follows :

> The great industry masses together in a single place a crowd of people unknown to each other. Competition divides their interests. But the maintenance of their wages, this common interest which they have against their employer, unites them in the same idea of resistance—combination. . . . The combinations, at first isolated, . . . [form into] groups, and, in face of constantly united capital, the maintenance of the association becomes more important and necessary for them than the maintenance of wages. . . . In this struggle—a veritable civil war—are united and developed all the elements necessary for a future battle. Once arrived at that point, association takes a political character.

Here we have the programme and the tactics of the economic struggle and the trade union movement for several decades to come, for the whole long period in which the workers are preparing for "a future battle." We must place side by side with this a number of Marx's references, in his correspondence with Engels, to the example of the British labour movement ; here Marx shows how, industry being in a flourishing condition, attempts are made "to buy the workers" (*Briefwechsel*, Vol. I, p. 136), to distract them from the struggle ; how, generally speaking, prolonged prosperity "demoralises the workers " (Vol. II, p. 218) ; how the British proletariat is becoming " bourgeoisified " ; how " the ultimate aim of this most bourgeois of all nations seems to be to establish a bourgeois aristocracy and a bourgeois proletariat side by side with the bourgeoisie " (Vol. II, p. 290) ; how the " revolutionary energy " of the British proletariat oozes away (Vol. III, p. 124) ; how it will be necessary to wait for a considerable time " before the British workers can rid themselves of seeming bourgeois contamination " (Vol. III, p. 127) ; how the British movement " lacks the mettle of the old Chartists " (1866 : Vol. III, p. 305) ; how the English workers are developing leaders of " a type that is half way between the radical bourgeoisie and the worker " (Vol. IV, p. 209, on Holyoake) ; how, due to British monopoly, and as long as that monopoly lasts, " the British worker will not budge " (Vol. IV, p. 433). The tactics of the economic struggle in connection with the general course (and *the outcome*) of the labour movement, are here considered from a remarkably broad many-sided, dialectical, and genuinely revolutionary outlook.

On the tactics of the political struggle, *The Communist Manifesto* advanced this fundamental Marxian thesis : " Communists fight on behalf of the immediate aims and interests of the working class,ᵉ but in their present movement they are also defending the future of that movement." That was why in 1848 Marx supported the Polish party of the " agrarian revolution "—" the party which initiated the Cracow insurrection in the year 1846." In Germany during 1848 and 1849 he supported the radical revolutionary democracy, nor subsequently did he retract what he had then said about tactics. He looked upon the German bourgeoisie as " inclined from the very beginning to betray the people " (only an alliance with the peasantry would have enabled the bourgeoisie completely to fulfil its tasks) " and to compromise with the crowned representatives of the old order of society." Here is Marx's summary account of the class position of the German bourgeoisie in the epoch of the bourgeois-democratic revolution—an analysis which, among other things, is an example of materialism, contemplating society in motion, and not looking only at that part of the motion which is directed *backwards*.

> Lacking faith in themselves, lacking faith in the people ; grumbling at those above, and trembling in face of those below . . . dreading a world-wide storm . . . nowhere with energy, everywhere with plagiarism . . .; without initiative . . .—a miserable old man, doomed to guide in his own senile interests the first youthful impulses of a young and vigorous people. . . . [*Neue Rheinische Zeitung*, 1848 ; see *Literarischer Nachlass*, Vol. III, p. 213.]

About twenty years afterwards, writing to Engels under the date of February 11, 1865 (*Briefwechsel*, Vol. III, p. 224), Marx said that the cause of the failure of the Revolution of 1848 was that the bourgeoisie had preferred peace with slavery to the mere prospect of having to fight for freedom. When the revolutionary epoch of 1848–9 was over, Marx was strongly opposed to any playing at Revolution (Schapper and Willich, and the contest with them), insisting on the need for knowing how to work under the new conditions, when new revolutions were in the making—quasi-" peacefully." The spirit in which Marx wanted the work to be carried on is plainly shown by his estimate of the situation in Germany during the period of blackest reaction. In 1856 he wrote (*Briefwechsel*, Vol. II, p. 108) : " The whole thing in Germany depends on whether it is possible to back the proletarian revolution by some second edition of the peasants' war." As long as the bourgeois-democratic revolution in Germany was in progress, Marx directed his whole attention, in the matter of tactics of the Socialist proletariat, to developing the democratic energy of the peasantry. He held that Lassalle's action was " objectively a betrayal of the whole working-class movement to the Prussians " (*Briefwechsel*, Vol. III, p. 210), among other things, because he " was

rendering assistance to the junkers and to Prussian national-
ism." On February 5, 1865, exchanging views with Marx
regarding a forthcoming joint declaration of theirs in the
press, Engels wrote (*Briefwechsel*, Vol. III, p. 217) : " In
a predominantly agricultural country it is base to confine
oneself to attacks on the bourgeoisie exclusively in the name
of the industrial proletariat, while forgetting to say even
a word about the patriarchal ' whipping rod exploitation '
of the rural proletariat by the big feudal nobility." During
the period from 1864 to 1870, in which the epoch of the
bourgeois-democratic revolution in Germany was being
completed, in which the exploiting classes of Prussia and
Austria were fighting for this or that method of completing
the revolution *from above*, Marx not only condemned
Lassalle for coquetting with Bismarck, but also corrected
Wilhelm Liebknecht who had lapsed into " Austrophilism "
and defended particularism. Marx insisted upon revolutionary tactics that would fight against both Bismarck
and " Austrophilism " with equal ruthlessness, tactics
which would not only suit the " conqueror," the Prussian
junker, but would forthwith renew the struggle with him
upon the very basis created by the Prussian military successes
(*Briefwechsel*, Vol. III, pp. 134, 136, 147, 179, 204, 210, 215,
418, 437, 440–1). In the famous address issued by the
International Workingmen's Association, dated September
9, 1870, Marx warned the French proletariat against an
untimely uprising ; but when, in 1871, the uprising actually
took place, Marx hailed the revolutionary initiative of the
masses with the utmost enthusiasm, saying that they were
" storming the heavens " (Letter of Marx to Kugelmann).
In this situation, as in so many others, the defeat of a
revolutionary onslaught was, from the Marxian standpoint
of dialectical materialism, from the point of view of the
general course and the *outcome* of the proletarian struggle,
a lesser evil than would have been a retreat from a position
hitherto occupied, a surrender without striking a blow,
as such a surrender would have demoralised the proletariat

and undermined its readiness for struggle. Fully recognising the importance of using legal means of struggle during periods of political stagnation, and when bourgeois legality prevails, Marx, in 1877 and 1878 when the Exception Law against the Socialists had been passed in Germany, strongly condemned the " revolutionary phrase-making " of Most ; but he attacked no less and perhaps even more sharply, the opportunism that, for a time, prevailed in the official Social-Democratic Party, which failed to manifest a spontaneous readiness to resist, to be firm, a revolutionary spirit, a readiness to resort to illegal struggle in reply to the Exception Law (*Briefwechsel*, Vol. IV, pp, 397, 404, 418, 422, and 424 ; also letters to Sorge).

V. I. Lenin

OUR PROGRAMME

Written 1899 ; first published 1925. English translation in " The Communist," July 1928.

[This article was written in 1899, for the third number of the *Rabochaia Gazeta*, which however never appeared, owing to police interference. The article is one of the earliest in which Lenin clearly stated the policy of an independent party with a clear revolutionary policy and free of opportunists. This was to be the continuous theme of his writings (in the journal *Iskra*, and in *What is to be Done ?*) during the following years, and was to lead to the splitting of the Russian Social Democratic Labour Party, at its Congress in London in 1903, into the " Bolshevik " (majority—following Lenin) and " Menshevik " (minority) sections.]

OUR PROGRAMME

INTERNATIONAL social democracy is at present going through a period of theoretical vacillations. Up to the present the doctrines of Marx and Engels were regarded as a firm foundation of revolutionary theory—nowadays voices are raised everywhere declaring these doctrines to be inadequate and antiquated. Anyone calling himself a social-democrat and having the intention to publish a social-democratic organ, must take up a definite attitude as regards this question, which by no means concerns German social-democrats alone.

We base our faith entirely on Marx's theory ; it was the first to transform socialism from a Utopia into a science, to give this science a firm foundation and to indicate the path which must be trodden in order further to develop` this science and to elaborate it in all its details. It discovered the nature of present-day capitalist economy and explained the way in which the employment of workers—the purchase of labour power—the enslavement of millions of those possessing no property by a handful of capitalists, by the owners of the land, the factories, the mines, etc., is concealed. It has shown how the whole development of modern capitalism is advancing towards the large producer ousting the small one, and is creating the prerequisites which make a socialist order of society possible and necessary. It has taught us to see, under the disguise of ossified habits, political intrigues, intricate laws, cunning theories, the class struggle, the struggle between, on the one hand, the various species of the possessing classes, and, on the other hand, the mass possessing no property, the proletariat, which leads all those who possess nothing. It has made clear what is the real task of a revolutionary socialist party—not to set up projects for the transformation of society, not to preach sermons to the capitalists and their admirers about improving the position of the workers, not the instigation of conspiracies, but the organisation of the class struggle of the proletariat and the carrying on of this struggle, the final aim of which is the seizure of political power by the proletariat and the organisation of a socialist society.

We now ask : What new elements have the touting " renovators " introduced into this theory, they who have attracted so much notice in our day and have grouped themselves round the German socialist Bernstein ? Nothing, nothing at all ; they have not advanced by a single step the science which Marx and Engels adjured us to develop ; they have not taught the proletariat any new methods of fighting ; they are only marching backwards in that they adopt the fragments of antiquated theories and are preaching to the proletariat not the theory of struggle but the theory of submissiveness—submissiveness to the bitterest enemies of the proletariat, to the governments and bourgeois parties who never tire of finding new methods of persecuting socialists. Plekhanov, one of the founders and leaders of Russian social-democracy, was perfectly right when he subjected to merciless criticism the latest " Criticism " of Bernstein, whose views have now been rejected even by the representatives of the German workers at the Party Congress in Hanover (October, 1899.—Ed.).

We know that on account of these words we shall be drenched with a flood of accusations ; they will cry out that we want to turn the Socialist Party into a holy order of the " orthodox," who persecute the " heretics " for their aberrations from the " true dogma," for any independent opinion, etc. We know all these nonsensical phrases which have become the fashion nowadays. Yet there is no shadow of truth in them, no iota of sense. There can be no strong socialist party without a revolutionary theory which unites all socialists, from which the socialists draw their whole conviction, which they apply in their methods of fighting and working. To defend a theory of this kind, of the truth of which one is completely convinced, against unfounded attacks and against attempts to debase it, does

not mean being an enemy of criticism in general. We by
no means regard the theory of Marx as perfect and inviol-
able ; on the contrary, we are convinced that this theory
has only laid the foundation stones of that science on which
the socialists must continue to build in every direction,
unless they wish to be left behind by life. We believe that it
is particularly necessary for Russian socialists to work out
the Marxist theory independently, for this theory only
gives general precepts, the details of which must be applied
in England otherwise than in France, in France otherwise
than in Germany, and in Germany otherwise than in
Russia. For this reason we will willingly devote space in
our paper to articles about theoretical questions, and we
call upon all comrades openly to discuss the matters in
dispute.

What are the main questions which arise in applying the
common programme of all social-democrats to Russia ?

We have already said that the essence of this programme
consists in the organisation of the class struggle of the
proletariat and in carrying on this struggle, the final aim
of which is the seizure of political power by the proletariat
and the construction of a socialist society. The class struggle
of the proletariat is divided into : The economic fight (the
fight against individual capitalists, or against the individual
groups of capitalists by the improvement of the position
of the workers) and the political fight (the fight against
the Government for the extension of the rights of the
people, i.e., for democracy, and for the expansion of the
political power of the proletariat). Some Russian social-
democrats (among them apparently those who conduct
the paper *Rabochaia Mysl*) regard the economic fight as
incomparably more important and almost go so far as to
postpone the political fight to a more or less distant future.
This standpoint is quite wrong. All social-democrats are
unanimous in believing that it is necessary to carry on an
agitation among the workers on this basis, i.e., to help the
workers in their daily fight against the employers, to direct

their attention to all kinds and all cases of chicanery, and in this way to make clear to them the necessity of unity. To forget the political for the economic fight would, however, mean a digression from the most important principle of international social-democracy ; it would mean forgetting what the whole history of the Labour movement has taught us. Fanatical adherents of the bourgeoisie and of the Government which serves it, have indeed repeatedly tried to organise purely economic unions of workers and thus to deflect them from the " politics " of socialism. It is quite possible that the Russian Government will also be clever enough to do something of the kind, as it has always endeavoured to throw some largesse or other sham presents to the people in order to prevent them becoming conscious that they are oppressed and are without rights.

No economic fight can give the workers a permanent improvement of their situation, it cannot, indeed, be carried on on a large scale unless the workers have the free right to call meetings, to join in unions, to have their own newspapers and to send their representatives to the National Assembly as do the workers in Germany and all European countries (with the exception of Turkey and Russia). In order, however, to obtain these rights, a political fight must be carried on. In Russia, not only the workers but all the citizens are deprived of political rights. Russia is an absolute monarchy. The Tsar alone promulgates laws, nominates officials and controls them. For this reason it seems as though in Russia the Tsar and the Tsarist Government were dependent on no class and cared for all equally. In reality, however, all the officials are chosen exclusively from the possessing class, and all are subject to the influence of the large capitalists who obtain whatever they want—the Ministers dance to the tune the large capitalists play. The Russian worker is bowed under a double yoke ; he is robbed and plundered by the capitalists and the landowners, and, lest he should fight against them, he is bound hand and foot by the police, his mouth is gagged and any attempt to

All who can nowhere find protection against the chicanery of
the officials and the police. (*Our Programme*)

defend the rights of the people is followed by persecution. Any strike against a capitalist results in the military and police being let loose on the workers. Every economic fight of necessity turns into a political fight, and social-democracy must indissolubly combine the economic with the political fight into a united class struggle of the proletariat.

The first and chief aim of such a fight must be the conquest of political rights, the conquest of political freedom. Since the workers of St. Petersburg alone have succeeded, in spite of the inadequate support given them by the socialists, in obtaining concessions from the Government within a short time—the passing of a law for shortening the hours of work—the whole working class, led by a united " Russian Social-Democratic Labour Party," will be able, through obstinate fighting, to obtain incomparably more important concessions.

The Russian working class will see its way to carrying on an economic and political fight alone, even if no other class comes to its help. The workers are not alone, however, in the political fight. The fact that the people is absolutely without rights and the unbridled arbitrary rule of the officials rouses the indignation of all who have any pretensions to honesty and education, who cannot reconcile themselves with the persecution of all free speech and all free thought ; it rouses the indignation of the persecuted Poles, Finns, Jews, Russian sects, it rouses the indignation of small traders, of the industrialists, the peasants, of all who can nowhere find protection against the chicanery of the officials and the police. All these groups of the population are incapable of carrying on an obstinate political fight alone ; if, however, the working class raises the banner of a fight of this kind it will be supported on all sides. Russian social-democracy will place itself at the head of all fights for the rights of the people, of all fights for democracy, and then it will be invincible.

These are our fundamental ideas which we shall develop systematically and from every point of view in our paper.

We are convinced that in this way we shall tread the
path which has been indicated by the " Russian Social-
Democratic Labour Party " in its " Manifesto."

V. I. Lenin

WHAT IS TO BE DONE ?

Published 1902. English edition, Martin Lawrence Ltd., 1931.

[This work, the sub-title of which is " Burning Questions
of Our Movement," was of great historical importance in
the development of the Russian Social Democratic Labour
Party. In his earlier articles and pamphlets, Lenin had
already sharply criticised the perversions of Marxist theory
which were at that time beginning to dominate the socialist
movement in Western Europe and were gathering influence in Russia. In *What is to be Done?* he showed the need
for a triple struggle—theoretical, political, economic—and
secondly, for a centralised revolutionary party to lead it.
The sections reprinted here cover the main theoretical issue
of the character and content of revolutionary agitation.]

WHAT IS TO BE DONE?

DOGMATISM AND "FREEDOM OF CRITICISM"

What is " Freedom of Criticism"?

"FREEDOM OF CRITICISM," this undoubtedly is the most
fashionable slogan at the present time, and the one most
frequently employed in the controversies between the
Socialists and democrats of all countries. At first sight,

nothing would appear to be more strange than the solemn
appeals by one of the parties to the dispute for freedom of
criticism. Can it be that some of the progressive parties
have raised their voices against the constitutional law of the
majority of European countries which guarantees freedom
to science and scientific investigation ? " Something must
be wrong here," an onlooker who has not yet fully appreciated the nature of the disagreements among the contro-
versialists will say when he hears this fashionable slogan
repeated at every cross-road. " Evidently this slogan is one
of the conventional phrases which, like a nickname, becomes
legitimatised by custom," he will conclude.

In fact, it is no secret that two separate tendencies have
been formed in international Social-Democracy.[1] The fight
between these tendencies now flares up in a bright flame,
and now dies down and smoulders under the ashes of imposing " resolutions for an armistice." What this " new "
tendency, which adopts a " critical " attitude towards
"obsolete doctrinaire" Marxism represents, has been *stated*
with sufficient precision by Bernstein, and *demonstrated* by
Millerand.

Social-Democracy must change from a party of the social
revolution into a democratic party of social reforms.
Bernstein has surrounded this political demand by a whole
battery of symmetrically arranged " new " arguments and

[1] This, perhaps, is the first occasion in the history of modern Socialism
that controversies between various tendencies within the Socialist movement have grown from national into international controversies; and
this is extremely encouraging. Formerly, the disputes between the
Lassalleans and the Eisenachers, between the Guesdists and the Possibilists, between the Fabians and the Social-Democrats, and between the
Narodniki and the Social-Democrats in Russia, remained purely
national disputes, reflected purely national features and proceeded, as
it were, on different planes. At the present time (this is quite evident
now) the English Fabians, the French Ministerialists, the German
Bernsteinists, and the Russian " Critics "—all belong to the same
family, all extol each other, learn from each other, and are rallying
their forces against " doctrinaire " Marxism. Perhaps, in this first real
battle with Socialist opportunism, international revolutionary Social-
Democracy will become sufficiently hardened to be able, at last, to put
an end to the political reaction, long reigning in Europe.

reasonings. The possibility of putting Socialism on a scientific basis and of proving that it is necessary and inevitable from the point of view of the materialist conception of history was denied ; the fact of increasing poverty, proletarianisation, the growing acuteness of capitalist contradictions, were also denied. The very conception of " *ultimate aim* " was declared to be unsound, and the idea of the dictatorship of the proletariat was absolutely rejected. It was denied that there is any difference in principle between liberalism and Socialism. *The theory of the class struggle* was rejected on the grounds that it could not be applied to strictly democratic society, governed according to the will of the majority, etc.

Thus, the demand for a decided change from revolutionary Social-Democracy to bourgeois reformism, was accompanied by a no less decided turn towards bourgeois criticism of all the fundamental ideas of Marxism. As this criticism of Marxism has been going on for a long time now, from the political platform, from university chairs, in numerous pamphlets, and in a number of scientific works, as the younger generation of the educational classes have been systematically trained for decades on this criticism, it is not surprising that the " new, critical " tendency in Social-Democracy should spring up, all complete, like Minerva from the head of Jupiter. This new tendency did not have to grow and develop, it was transferred bodily from bourgois literature to Socialist literature.

If Bernstein's theoretical criticism and political yearnings are still obscure to anyone, the trouble the French have taken to demonstrate the " new method " should remove all ambiguities. In this instance, also, France has justified its old reputation as the country in which " more than anywhere else the historical class struggles were always fought to a finish " [Engels, in his introduction to Marx's *Eighteenth Brumaire*]. The French Socialists have commenced, not to theorise, but to act. The more developed democratic political conditions in France have permitted them to put

Bernsteinism into practice immediately, with its inevitable consequences. Millerand has provided an excellent example of practical Bernsteinism. It is not surprising that he so zealously defends and praises Bernstein and Volmar ! Indeed, if Social-Democracy, in essentials, is merely a reformist party, and must be bold enough to admit this openly, then, not only has a Socialist the right to join a bourgeois cabinet, but he ought always to strive to obtain places in it. If democracy, in essence, means the abolition of class domination, then why should not a Socialist minister charm the whole bourgeois world by orations on class co-operation ? Why should he not remain in the cabinet even after the shooting down of workers by gendarmes has exposed, for the hundredth and thousandth time, the real nature of the democratic co-operation of classes ? Why should he not personally take part in welcoming the Tsar, for whom the French Socialists now have no other sobriquet than " Hero of the Gallows, Knout and Banishment " (*knouteur, pendeur et deportateur*) ? And the reward for this humiliation and self-degradation of Socialism in the face of the whole world, for the corruption of the Socialist consciousness of the working class—the only thing that can guarantee victory—the reward for this is, imposing *plans* for niggardly reforms, so niggardly in fact, that much more has been obtained even from bourgeois governments.

He who does not deliberately close his eyes cannot fail to see that the new " critical " tendency in Socialism is nothing more nor less than a new species of *opportunism*. And if we judge people not by the brilliant uniforms they deck themselves in, not by the imposing appellations they give themselves, but by their actions, and by what they actually advocate, it will be clear that " freedom of criticism " means freedom for an opportunistic tendency in Social-Democracy, the freedom to convert Social-Democracy into a democratic reformist party, the freedom to introduce bourgeois ideas and bourgeois elements into Socialism.

" Freedom " is a grand word, but under the banner of Free Trade the most predatory wars were conducted : under the banner of " free labour," the toilers were robbed. The term " freedom of criticism " contains the same inherent falsehood. Those who are really convinced that they have advanced science, would demand, not freedom for the new views to continue side by side with the old, but the substitution of the old views by the new views. The cry " Long live freedom of criticism," that is heard to-day, too strongly calls to mind the fable of the empty barrel.

We are marching in a compact group along a precipitous and difficult path, firmly holding each other by the hand. We are surrounded on all sides by enemies, and are under their almost constant fire. We have combined voluntarily, especially for the purpose of fighting the enemy and not to retreat into the adjacent marsh, the inhabitants of which, right from the very outset, have reproached us with having separated ourselves into an exclusive group, and with having chosen the path of struggle instead of the path of conciliation. And now several in our crowd begin to cry out : Let us go into this marsh ! And when we begin to shame them, they retort : How conservative you are ! Are you not ashamed to deny us the right to invite you to take a better road !

Oh yes, gentlemen ! You are free, not only to invite us, but to go yourselves wherever you will, even into the marsh. In fact, we think that the marsh is your proper place, and we are prepared to render *you* every assistance to get there. Only, let go of our hands, don't clutch at us, and don't besmirch the grand word " freedom " ; for we too are " free " to go where we please, free, not only to fight against the marsh, but also those who are turning towards the marsh. . . .

Criticism in Russia

The peculiar position of Russia in regard to the point we are examining is that *right from the very beginning* of the spontaneous labour movement on the one hand, and the change of progressive public opinion towards Marxism on the other, a combination was observed of obviously heterogeneous elements under a common flag for the purpose of fighting the common enemy (obsolete social and political views). We refer to the heyday of " legal Marxism." Speaking generally, this was an extremely curious phenomenon, that no one in the 'eighties, or the beginning of the 'nineties, would have believed possible. Suddenly, in a country ruled by an autocracy, in which the press is completely shackled, and in a period of intense political reaction in which even the tiniest outgrowth of political discontent and protest was suppressed, a *censored* literature springs up, advocating the theory of revolutionary Marxism, in a language extremely obscure, but understood by the " interest." The government had accustomed itself to regard only the theory of (revolutionary) Populism as dangerous without observing its internal evolution as is usually the case, and rejoicing at the criticism, levelled against it *no matter from what side it came.* Quite a considerable time elapsed (according to our Russian calculations) before the government realised what had happened and the unwieldly army of censors and gendarmes discovered the new enemy and flung itself upon him. Meanwhile, Marxian books were published one after another, Marxian journals and newspapers were published, nearly every one became a Marxist, Marxism was flattered, the Marxists were courted and the book publishers rejoiced at the extraordinary ready sale of Marxian literature. It is quite reasonable to suppose that among the Marxian novices who were carried away by this stream, there was more than one " author who got a swelled head. . . ."

We can now speak calmly of this period as of an event of the past. It is no secret that the brief appearance of Marxism on the surface of our literature was called forth by the alliance between people of extreme and of extremely moderate views. In point of fact, the latter were bourgeois

democrats ; and this was the conclusion (so strikingly confirmed by their subsequent " critical " development), that
intruded itself on the minds of certain persons even when
the " alliance " was still intact.

That being the case, does not the responsibility for the
subsequent "confusion" rest mainly upon the revolutionary Social-Democrats who entered into alliance with
these future " critics " ? This question, together with a
reply in the affirmative, is sometimes heard from people
with excessively rigid views. But these people are absolutely
wrong. Only those who have no reliance in themselves can
fear to enter into temporary alliances with unreliable
people. Besides, not a single political party could exist without entering into such alliances. The combination with the
legal Marxists was in its way the first really political alliance contracted by Russian Social-Democrats. Thanks to
this alliance an astonishingly rapid victory was obtained
over Populism, and Marxian ideas (even though in a vulgarised form) became very widespread. Moreover, the
alliance was not concluded altogether without " conditions." The proof: The burning by the censor, in 1895, of
the Marxian symposium, *Materials on the Problem of the
Economic Development of Russia.* If the literary agreement
with the legal Marxists can be compared with a political
alliance, then that book can be compared with a political
treaty.

The rupture, of course, did not occur because the
" allies " proved to be bourgeois democrats. On the contrary, the representatives of the latter tendency were the
natural and desirable allies of the Social-Democrats in so
far as their democratic tasks that were brought to the front
by the prevailing situation in Russia were concerned. But
an essential condition for such an alliance must be complete liberty for Socialists to reveal to the working class that
its interests are diametrically opposed to the interests of
the bourgeoisie. However, the Bernsteinist and " critical "
tendency to which the majority of the legal Marxists turned,

deprived the Socialists of this liberty and corrupted Socialist consciousness by vulgarising Marxism, by preaching the toning down of social antagonisms, by declaring the idea of the social revolution and the dictatorship of the proletariat to be absurd, by restricting the labour movement and the class struggle to narrow trade unionism and to a " practical " struggle for petty, gradual reforms. This was tantamount to the bourgeois democrat's denial of Socialism's right to independence, and, consequently, of its right to existence ; in practice it meant a striving to convert the nascent labour movement into a tail of the liberals.

Naturally, under such circumstances a rupture was necessary. But the " peculiar " feature of Russia manifested itself in that this rupture simply meant the closing to the Social-Democrats of access to the most popular and widespread " legal " literature. The " ex-Marxists " who took up the flag of " criticism," and who obtained almost a monopoly in the " sale " of Marxism, entrenched themselves in this literature. Catchwords like : " Against orthodoxy " and " Long live freedom of criticism " (now repeated by *Rabocheye Dyelo*) immediately became the fashion, and the fact that neither the censor nor the gendarmes could resist this fashion is apparent from the publication of *three* Russian editions of Bernstein's celebrated book (celebrated in the Herostratus sense) and from the fact that the books by Bernstein, Prokopovich and others were recommended by Zubatov [*Iskra*, No. 10]. And this tendency did not confine itself to the sphere of literature. The turn towards criticism was accompanied by the turn towards Economism that was taken by Social-Democratic practical workers.

The manner in which the contacts and mutual dependence between legal criticism and illegal Economism arose and grew is an interesting subject in itself, and may very well be treated in a special article. It is sufficient to note here that these contacts undoubtedly existed. The notoriety deservedly acquired by the *Credo* was due precisely to the frankness with which it formulated these contacts and laid down the fundamental political tendencies of Economism, viz. : Let the workers carry on the economic struggle (it would be more correct to say the trade union struggle, because the latter embraces also specifically labour politics), and let the Marxist intelligentsia merge with the liberals for the political " struggle." Thus, it turned out that trade union work " among the people " meant fulfilling the first part of this task, and legal criticism meant fulfilling the second part. . . .

The question now arises : Seeing what the peculiar features of Russian " criticism " and Russian Bernsteinism were, what should those who desired, in deeds and not merely in words, to oppose opportunism have done ? First of all, they should have made efforts to resume the theoretical work that was only just commenced in the period of legal Marxism, and that has now again fallen on the shoulders of the illegal workers. Unless such work is undertaken the successful growth of the movement is impossible. Secondly, they should have actively combated legal " criticism " that was corrupting people's minds. Thirdly, they should have actively counteracted the confusion and vacillation prevailing in practical work, and should have exposed and repudiated every conscious or unconscious attempt to degrade our programme and tactics. . . .

The Importance of the Theoretical Struggle

. . . The case of the Russian Social-Democrats strikingly illustrates the fact observed in the whole of Europe (and long ago observed in German Marxism) that the notorious freedom of criticism implies, not the substitution of one theory by another, but freedom from every complete and thought-out theory ; it implies eclecticism and absence of principle. Those who are in the least acquainted with the actual state of our movement cannot but see that the spread of Marxism was accompanied by a certain deterioration of theoretical standards. Quite a number of people, with very little, and even totally lacking in, theoretical training, joined the movement for the sake of its practical significance and its practical successes. We can judge, therefore, how tactless *Robocheye Dyelo* is when, with an air of invincibility, it quotes the statement of Marx that : " A single step of the real movement is worth a dozen programmes." To repeat these words in the epoch of theoretical chaos is sheer mockery. Moreover, these words of Marx are taken from his letter on the Gotha Programme, in which he *sharply condemns* eclecticism in the formulation of principles : " If you must combine," Marx wrote to the party leaders, " then enter into agreements to satisfy the practical aims of the movement, but do not haggle over principles, do not make ' concessions ' in theory." This was Marx's idea, and yet there are people among us who strive—in his name !— to belittle the significance of theory.

Without a revolutionary theory there can be no revolutionary movement. This cannot be insisted upon too strongly at a time when the fashionable preaching of opportunism is combined with absorption in the narrowest forms of practical activity. The importance of theory for Russian Social-Democrats is still greater for three reasons, which are often forgotten :

The first is that our party is only in the process of formation, its features are only just becoming outlined, and it has not yet completely settled its reckoning with other tendencies in revolutionary thought which threaten to divert the movement from the proper path. Indeed, in very recent times we have observed (as Axelrod long ago warned the Economists would happen) a revival of non-Social-Democratic revolutionary tendencies. Under such circumstances, what at first sight appears to be an " unimportant " mistake, may give rise to most deplorable consequences, and only the short-sighted would consider factional disputes and strict distinction of shades to be inopportune and superfluous. The fate of Russian Social-Democracy for many,

many years to come may be determined by the strengthening of one or the other " shade."

The second reason is that the Social-Democratic movement is essentially an international movement. This does
not mean merely that we must combat national chauvinism.
It means also that a movement that is starting in a young
country can be successful only on the condition that it
assimilates the experience of other countries. In order to
assimilate this experience, it is not sufficient merely to be
acquainted with it, or simply to transcribe the latest revolutions. A critical attitude is required towards this experience,
and ability to subject it to independent tests. Only those
who realise how much the modern labour movement has
grown in strength will understand what a reserve of theoretical forces and political (as well as revolutionary) experience is required to fulfil this task.

The third reason is that the national tasks of Russian
Social-Democracy are such as have never confronted any
other Socialist party in the world. Farther on we shall deal
with the political and organisational duties which the task
of emancipating the whole people from the yoke of autocracy imposes upon us. At the moment, we wish merely
to state that the *rôle of vanguard can be fulfilled only by a party
that is guided by an advanced theory.* . . .

TRADE UNION POLITICS AND SOCIAL DEMOCRATIC POLITICS

Political Agitation and its Restriction by the Economists

Everyone knows that the spread and consolidation of
the economic[1] struggle of the Russian workers proceeded

---

[1] In order to avoid misunderstanding we would state, that here, and
throughout this pamphlet, by economic struggle, we mean (in accordance with the meaning of the term as it has become accepted amongst
us) the " practical economic struggle " which Engels described as
" resistance to capitalism," and which in free countries is known as
the trade union struggle.

simultaneously with the creation of a " literature " exposing economic conditions, i.e., factory and industrial conditions. These "leaflets" were devoted mainly to the exposure of factory conditions, and very soon a passion for exposures was roused among the workers. As soon as the workers realised that the Social-Democratic circles desired to and could supply them with a new kind of leaflet that told the whole truth about their poverty-stricken lives, about their excessive toil and their lack of rights, correspondence began to pour in from the factories and workshops. This " exposure literature " created a sensation not only in the particular factory dealt with and the conditions of which were exposed in a given leaflet, but in all the factories to which news had spread about the facts exposed. And as the poverty and want among the workers in the various enterprises and in the various trades are pretty much the same, the " Truth about the life of the workers " roused the admiration *of all*. Even among the most backward workers, a veritable passion was roused to " go into print "—a noble passion to adopt this rudimentary form of war against the whole of the modern social system which is based upon robbery and oppression. And in the overwhelming majority of cases these " leaflets " were in truth a declaration of war, because the exposures had a terrifically rousing effect upon the workers ; it stimulated them to put forward demands for the removal of the most glaring evils, and roused in them a readiness to support these demands with strikes. Finally, the employers themselves were compelled to recognise the significance of these leaflets as a declaration of war, so much so that in a large number of cases they did not even wait for the outbreak of hostilities. As is always the case, the mere publication of these exposures made them effective, and they acquired the significance of a strong moral force. On more than one occasion the mere appearance of a leaflet proved sufficient to compel an employer to concede all or part of the demands put forward. In a word, economic (factory) exposures have been an important lever in the economic struggle and they will continue to be so as long as capitalism, which creates the need for the workers to defend themselves, exists. Even in the more progressive countries of Europe to-day, the exposure of the evils in some backward trade, or in some forgotten branch of domestic industry, serves as a starting point for the awakening of class-consciousness, for the beginning of a trade-union struggle, and for the spread of Socialism.

Recently, the overwhelming majority of Russian Social-Democrats were almost wholly engaged in this work of exposing factory conditions. It is sufficient to refer to the columns of *Rabochaya Mysl* to judge to what an extent they were engaged in it. So much so, indeed, that they lost sight of the fact that this, *taken by itself*, was not substantially Social-Democratic work, but merely trade-union work. As a matter of fact, these exposures merely dealt with the relations between the workers *in a given trade*, with their immediate employers, and all that it achieved was that the vendors of labour power learned to sell their " commodity " on better terms, and to fight the purchasers of labour power over a purely commercial deal. These exposures might have served (if properly utilised by revolutionaries) as a beginning and a constituent part of Social-Democratic activity, but they might also (and with subservience to spontaneity inevitably had to) have led to a "pure and simple " trade-union struggle and to a non-Social-Democratic labour movement. Social-Democrats lead the struggle of the working class not only for better terms for the sale of labour power, but also for the abolition of the social system which compels the propertyless class to sell itself to the rich. Social-Democracy represents the working class, not in its relation to a given group of employers, but in its relation to all classes in modern society, to the state as an organised political force. Hence, it not only follows that Social-Democrats must not confine themselves entirely to the economic struggle ; they must not even allow the organisation of economic exposures to become the predominant part of their activities. We must actively take up the political education of the working class, and the development of its political consciousness. *Now*, after *Zarya* and *Iskra* have made the first attack upon Economism " all are agreed " with this (although some agreed only nominally, as we shall soon prove).

The question now arises : What does political education mean ? Is it sufficient to confine oneself to the propaganda of working-class hostility to autocracy ? Of course not. It is not enough to *explain* to the workers that they are politically oppressed (any more than it was to *explain* to them that their interests were antagonistic to the interests of the employers). Advantage must be taken of every concrete example of this oppression for the purpose of agitation (in the same way as we began to use concrete examples of economic oppression for the purpose of agitation). And inasmuch as *political* oppression affects all sorts of classes in society, inasmuch as it manifests itself in various spheres of life and activity, in industrial life, civic life, in personal and family life, in religious life, scientific life, etc., etc., is it not evident that *we shall not be fulfilling our task* of developing the political consciousness of the workers if *we do not undertake* the organisation of the *political exposure of autocracy in all its aspects* ? In order to agitate over concrete examples of oppression, these examples must be exposed (in the same way as it was necessary to expose factory evils in order to carry on economic agitation).

One would think that this was clear enough. It turns out, however, that " all " are agreed that it is necessary to develop political consciousness *in all its aspects*, only in words. It turns out that *Rabocheye Dyelo*, for example, has not only failed to take up the task of organising (or to make a start in organising) in all-sided political exposure, but is even trying to *drag Iskra*, which has undertaken this task, *away from it*. Listen to this : " The political struggle of the working class is merely (it is precisely not " merely ") a more developed, a wider and more effective form of economic struggle." [Programme of *Rabocheye Dyelo* pubblished in No. 1, p. 3.] " The Social Democrats are now confronted with the task of, as far as possible, giving the economic struggle itself a political character." [Martynov, *Rabocheye Dyelo*, No. 10, p. 42.] " The economic struggle is the most widely applicable method of drawing the masses into active political struggle " (resolution passed by the congress of the League and "amendments" thereto). [*Two Congresses*, pp. 11 and 17.] As the reader will observe, all these postulates permeate *Rabocheye Dyelo*, from its very first number to the recently issued Instructions by the Editorial Committee, and all of them evidently express a single view regarding political agitation and the political struggle. Examine this view from the standpoint of the opinion prevailing among all Economists, that political agitation must *follow* economic agitation. Is it true that in general the economic struggle " is the most widely applicable method " of drawing the masses into the political struggle? It is absolutely untrue. All and sundry manifestations of police tyranny and autocratic outrage, in addition to the evils connected with the economic struggle, are equally " widely applicable " as a means of " drawing in " the masses. The tyranny of the Zemstvo chiefs, the flogging of the peasantry, the corruption of the officials, the conduct of the police towards the " common people " in the cities, the fight against the famine-stricken and the suppression of the popular striving towards enlightenment and knowledge, the extortion of taxes, the persecution of the religious sects, the severe discipline in the army, the militarist conduct towards the students and the liberal intelligentsia—all these and a thousand other similar manifestations of tyranny, though not directly connected with the " economic " struggle, do they, in general, represent a *less* " widely applicable " method and subject for political agitation and for drawing the masses into the political struggle ? The very opposite is the case. Of all the innumerable cases in which the workers suffer (either personally or those closely associated with them) from tyranny, violence, and lack of rights, undoubtedly only a relatively few represent cases of police tyranny in the economic struggle as such. Why then should we beforehand *restrict* the scope of political agitation by declaring *only one* of the methods to be " the most widely applicable," when Social-Democrats have other, generally speaking, not less " widely applicable " means ?

Long, long ago (a year ago ! . . .) *Rabocheye Dyelo* wrote :

> The masses begin to understand immediate political demands after one, or at all events, after several strikes ; immediately the government sets the police and gendarmerie against them [No. 7, p. 15, August 1900].

This opportunist theory of stages has now been rejected by the League, which makes a concession to us by declaring : " There is no need whatever to conduct political agitation right from the beginning, exclusively on an economic basis." [*Two Congresses*, p. 11.] This very repudiation of part of its former errors by the League will enable the future historian of Russian Social-Democracy to discern the depths to which our Economists have degraded Socialism better than any number of lengthy arguments ! But the League must be very naïve indeed to imagine that the abandonment of one form of restricting politics will induce us to agree to another form of restriction ! Would it not be more logical to say that the economic struggle should be conducted on the widest possible basis, that it should be utilised for political agitation, but that " there is no need whatever " to regard the economic struggle as the *most* widely applicable means of drawing the masses into active political struggle ? The League attaches significance to the fact that it substituted the phrase " most widely applicable method " by the phrase " a better method," contained in one of the resolutions of the Fouth Congress of the Jewish Labour League (Bund). We confess that we find it difficult

to say which of these resolutions is the better one. In our
opinion *both are bad*. Both the League and the Bund fall
into error (partly perhaps unconsciously, owing to the influence of tradition) concerning the economic, trade-unionist
interpretation of politics. The fact that this error is expressed
either by the word " better " or by the words " most widely
applicable " makes no material difference whatever. If the
League had said that " political agitation on an economic
basis " is the most widely applied (and not " applicable ")
method it would have been right in regard to a certain
period in the development of our Social-Democratic
movement. It would have been right in regard to the
Economists and to many (if not the majority) of the practical
Economists of 1898–1901 who have *applied* the method of
political agitation (to the extent that they applied it at all)
almost exclusively on an economic basis. Political agitation on
such lines was recognised, and as we have seen, even recommended by *Rabochaya Mysl*, and by the Self-Emancipation
group ! *Rabocheye Dyelo* should have *strongly condemned* the
fact that useful economic agitation was accompanied by the
harmful restriction of the political struggle, but, instead of
that, it declares the method most widely *applied* (*by the
Economists*) to be the most widely *applicable* ! It is not surprising, therefore, that when we describe these people as
Economists, they can do nothing else but pour abuse upon
us, and call us " mystifiers," " disrupters," " Papal
Nuncios," and " slanderers," go complaining to the world
that we have mortally offended them and declare almost
on oath that " not a single Social-Democratic organisation
is now tinged with Economism." Oh, these evil, slanderous
politicians ! They must have deliberately invented this
Economism, out of sheer hatred of mankind, in order
mortally to offend other people !

What do the words " to give the economic struggle itself
a political character," which Martynov uses in presenting
the tasks of Social-Democracy, mean concretely ? The
economic struggle is the collective struggle of the workers

against their employers for better terms *in the sale of their labour power*, for better conditions of life and labour. This struggle is necessarily a struggle according to trade, because conditions of labour differ very much in different trades, and, consequently, the fight to *improve* these conditions can only be conducted in respect of each trade (trade unions in the Western countries, temporary trade associations and leaflets in Russia, etc.). To give " the economic struggle itself a political character " means, therefore, to strive to secure satisfaction for these trade demands, the improvement of conditions of labour in each separate trade by means of "legislative and adminstrative measures" (as Martynov expresses it on the next page of his article, p. 43). This is exactly what the trade unions do and always have done. Read the works of the thoroughly scientific (and " thoroughly " opportunist) Mr. and Mrs. Webb and you will find that the British trade unions long ago recognised, and have long carried out the task of " giving the economic struggle itself a political character " ; they have long been fighting for the right to strike, for the removal of all juridical hindrances to the co-operative and trade-union movement, for laws protecting women and children, for the improvement of conditions of labour by means of sanitary and factory legislation, etc.

Thus, the pompous phrase : " To give the economic struggle *itself* a political character," which sounds so " terrifically " profound and revolutionary, serves as a screen to conceal what is in fact the traditional striving to *degrade* Social-Democratic politics to the level of trade-union politics ! On the pretext of rectifying *Iskra's* one-sidedness, which, it is alleged, places " the revolutionising of dogma higher than the revolutionising of life," we are presented with the *struggle for economic reform* as if it were something entirely new. As a matter of fact, the phrase " to give the economic struggle itself a political character " means nothing more than the struggle for economic reforms. And Martynov himself might have come to this simple conclusion had he only pondered over the significance of his own words. " Our party," he says, turning his heaviest guns against *Iskra*, " could and should have presented concrete demands to the government for legislative and administrative measures against economic exploitation, for the relief of unemployment, for the relief of the famine-stricken, etc." [*Rabocheye Dyelo*, No. 10, pp. 42, 43.] Concrete demands for measures—does not this mean demands for social reforms ? And again we ask the impartial reader, do we slander the *Rabocheye Dyeloists* (may I be forgiven for this clumsy expression !) when we declare them to be concealed Bernsteinists, for advancing their thesis about the necessity for fighting for economic reforms as a reason for their *disagreement* with *Iskra* ?

Revolutionary Social-Democracy always included, and now includes, the fight for reforms in its activities. But it utilises " economic " agitation for the purpose of presenting to the government, not only demands for all sorts of measures, but also (and primarily) the demand ·that it cease to be an autocratic government. Moreover, it considers it to be its duty to present this demand to the government, not on the basis of the economic struggle *alone*, but on the basis of all manifestations of public and political life. In a word, it subordinates the struggle for reforms to the revolutionary struggle for liberty and for Socialism, in the same way as the part is subordinate to the whole. Martynov, however, resuscitates the theory of stages in a new form, and strives to prescribe an exclusively economic, so to speak, path of development for the political struggle. By coming out at this moment, when the revolutionary movement is on the up-grade, with an alleged special " task " of fighting for reforms, he is dragging the party backwards, and is playing into the hands of both "economic " and liberal opportunism.

Shamefacedly hiding the struggle for reforms behind the pompous thesis " to give the economic struggle itself a political character," Martynov advanced, as if it were a special point, *exclusively economic* (in fact, exclusively factory) *reforms*. Why he did that, we do not know. Perhaps it was due to carelessness ? But if he indeed had only " factory " reforms in mind, then the whole of his thesis, which we have just quoted, loses all sense. Perhaps he did it because he thought it possible and probable that the government would agree to make " concessions " only in the economic sphere ? If that is what he thought, then it is a strange error. Concessions are also possible, and are made in the sphere of legislation concerning flogging, passports, land-compensation payments, religious sects, the censorship, etc., etc. " Economic " concessions (or pseudo-concessions) are, of course, the cheapest and most advantageous concessions) to make from the government's point of view, because by these means it hopes to win the confidence of the masses of the workers. Precisely for this very reason, Social-Democrats *must under no circumstances* create grounds for the belief (or the misunderstanding) that we attach greater value to economic reforms than to political reforms, or that we regard them as being particularly important, etc. . . .

Political Exposures and "Training in Revolutionary Activity"

In advancing against *Iskra* his " theory " of " raising the activity of the masses of the workers," Martynov, as a matter of fact, displayed a striving to *diminish* this activity, because he declared the very economic struggle before which all Economists grovel to be the preferable, the most important and " the most widely applicable means of rousing this activity, and the widest field for it." This error is such a characteristic one, precisely because it is not peculiar to Martynov alone. As a matter of fact, it is possible to "raise the activity of the masses of the workers" *only* provided this activity *is not restricted entirely* to " political agitation on an economic basis." And one of the fundamental conditions for the necessary expansion of political agitation is the organisation of *all-sided* political exposure. In *no other way* can the masses be trained in political consciousness and revolutionary activity except by means of such exposures. Hence, to conduct such activity is one of the most important functions of international Social-Democracy as a whole, for even in countries where political liberty exists, there is still a field for work of exposure, although in such countries the work is conducted in a different sphere. For example, the German party is strengthening its position and spreading its influence, thanks particularly to the untiring energy with which it is conducting a campaign of political exposure. Working-class consciousness cannot be genuinely political consciousness unless the workers are trained to respond to all cases of tyranny, oppression, violence and abuse, no matter *what class* is affected. Moreover, that response must be a Social-Democratic response, and not one from any other point of view. The consciousness of the masses of the workers cannot be genuine class consciousness, unless the workers learn to observe from concrete, and above all from topical, political facts and events, *every* other social class and *all* the manifestations of the intellectual, ethical and political life of these classes ; unless they learn to apply practically the materialist analysis and the materialist estimate of *all* aspects of the life and activity of *all* classes, strata and groups of the population. Those who concentrate the attention, observation and the consciousness of the working class exclusively, or even mainly, upon itself alone, are not Social-Democrats ; because, for its self-realisation the working class must not only have a theoretical . . . rather it would be more true to say : Not so much theoretical as a practical understanding acquired through experience of political life of the relationships between *all* classes of modern society. That is why the idea preached by our Economists, that the economic struggle is the most widely applicable means of drawing the masses into the political movement is so extremely harmful and extremely reactionary in practice. In order to become a Social-Democrat, a working man must have a clear picture in his mind of the economic nature and the social and political features of the landlord, of the priest, of the high state official and of the peasant, of the student and of the tramp ; he must know their strong and weak sides ; he must understand all the catchwords and sophisms by which each class and each stratum camouflages its egotistical strivings and its real " nature " ; he must understand what interests certain institutions and certain laws reflect and how they are reflected. The working man cannot obtain this " clear picture " from books. He can obtain it only from living examples and from exposures, following hot after their occurrence, of what goes on around us at a given moment, of what is being discussed, in whispers perhaps, by each one in his own way, of the meaning of such and such events, of such and such statistics, in such and such court sentences, etc., etc., etc. These universal political exposures are an essential and *fundamental* condition for training the masses in revolutionary activity.

Why is it that the Russian workers as yet display so little revolutionary activity in connection with the brutal way in which the police maltreat the people, in connection with the persecution of the religious sects, with the flogging of the peasantry, with the outrageous censorship, with the torture of soldiers, with the persecution of the most innocent cultural enterprises, etc. ? Is it because the " economic struggle " does not " stimulate " them to this, because such political activity does not " promise palpable results," because it produces little that is " positive " ? To advance this argument, we repeat, is merely to shift the blame to the shoulders of others, to blame the masses of the workers for our own philistinism (also. Bernsteinism). We must blame ourselves, our remoteness from the mass movement ; we must blame ourselves for being unable as yet to organise a sufficiently wide, striking and rapid exposure of these despicable outrages. When we do that (and we must and can do it), the most backward worker will understand, *or will feel*, that the students and religious sects, the muzhiks and the authors are being abused and outraged by the very same dark forces that are oppressing and crushing him at every step of his life, and, feeling that, he himself will be filled with an irresistible desire to respond to these things and then he will organise cat-calls against the censors one day, another day he will demonstrate outside the house of the provincial governor who has brutally suppressed peasant uprising, another day he will teach a lesson to the gendarmes in surplices who are doing the work of the Holy Inquisition, etc. As yet we have done very little, almost nothing, to *hurl* universal and fresh exposures among the masses of the workers. Many of us as yet do not appreciate the *bounden duty* that rests upon us, but spontaneously follow in the wake of the " drab every-day struggle," in the narrow confines of factory life. Under such circumstances to say that *Iskra* displays a tendency to belittle the significance of the forward march of the drab every-day struggle in comparison with the propaganda of brilliant and complete ideas [Martynov, p. 61]—means to drag the party backwards, to defend and glorify our unpreparedness and backwardness.

As for calling the masses to action, that will come of itself immediately that energetic political agitation, live and striking exposures are set going. To catch some criminal red-handed and immediately to brand him publicly will have far more effect than any number of "appeals to action" ; the effect very often will be such that it will be impossible to tell who exactly it was that " appealed " to the crowd, and who exactly suggested this or that plan of demonstration, etc. Calls for action, not in the general, but in the concrete, sense of the term, can be made only at the place of action ; only those who themselves go into action now can make appeals for action. And our business as Social-Democratic publicists is to deepen, expand and intensify political exposures and political agitation. A word in passing about " calls to action." *The only paper* that *prior to* the spring events, *called upon* the workers actively to intervene in a matter that certainly did *not promise* any *palpable results* for the workers, i.e., the drafting of the students into the army *was Iskra*. Immediately after the publication of the order of January 11 " Drafting the 183 Students into the Army," *Iskra* published an article about it (in its February issue, No. 2), and *before* any demonstration was started openly *called upon* " the workers to go to the aid of the students," called upon the " people " boldly to take up the government's open challenge. We ask : How is the remarkable fact to be explained that although he talks so much about " calling for action," and even suggests " calling for action " as a special form of activity, Martynov said not a word about *this* call ? After this, is not Martynov's allegation, that *Iskra* was *one-sided* because it did not sufficiently " call for " the struggle for demands " promising palpable results," sheer philistinism ?

Our Economists, including *Rabocheye Dyelo*, were successful because they disguised themselves as uneducated workers. But the working-class Social-Democrat, the working-class revolutionist (and their number is growing) will indignantly reject all this talk about fighting for demands " promising palpable results," etc., because he will understand that this is only a variation of the old song about adding a kopeck to the rouble. These working-class revolutionaries will say to their counsellors of the *Rabochaya Mysl* and *Rabocheye Dyelo* : You are wasting your time, gentlemen ; you are interfering with excessive zeal in a job that we can manage ourselves, and you are neglecting your own duties. It is silly of you to say that the Social-Democrats' task is to give the economic struggle itself a political character, for that is only the beginning, it is not the main task that Social-Democrats must fulfil. All over the world, including Russia, *the police themselves often give* the economic struggle a political character, and the workers are beginning to understand whom the government supports.[1]

The " economic struggle between the workers and the employers and the government," about which you make as much fuss as if you had made a new discovery, is being carried on in all parts of Russia, even the most remote, by the workers themselves who have heard about strikes, but who have heard almost nothing about Socialism. The " activity " you want to stimulate among us workers by advancing concrete demands promising palpable results, we are already displaying and in our every-day, petty trade-union work, we put forward concrete demands, very often without any assistance from the intellectuals whatever. But *such* activity is not enough for us ; we are not children to be fed on the sops of " economic " politics alone ; we want to know everything that everybody else knows, we want to learn the details of *all* aspects of political life and to take part *actively* in every political event. In order that we may do this, the intellectuals must talk to us less on what we already know, and tell us more about what we do not know and what we can never learn from our factory

[1] The demand " to give the economic struggle itself a political character " most strikingly expresses *subservience to spontaneity* in the sphere of political activity. Very often the economic struggle *spontaneously* assumed a political character, that is to say without the injection of the " revolutionary bacilli of the intelligentsia," without the intervention of the class-conscious Social-Democrats. For example, the economic struggle of the British workers assumed a political character without the intervention of the Socialists. The tasks of the Social-Democrats, however, are not exhausted by political agitation on the economic field; their task is to *convert* trade-union politics into the Social-Democratic political struggle, to *utilise* the flashes of political consciousness which gleam in the minds of the workers during their economic struggles for the purpose of *raising* them to the level of *Social-Democratic* political consciousness. The Martynovs, however, instead of raising and stimulating the spontaneously awakening political consciousness of the workers, *bow down before spontaneity* and repeat over and over again, until one is sick and tired of hearing it, that the economic struggle " stimulates " in the workers' minds thoughts about their own lack of political rights. It is unfortunate, gentlemen, that the spontaneously awakening trade-union political consciousness does not " *stimulate* " in your minds thoughts about your Social-Democratic tasks !

and " economic " experience, that is, you must give us
political knowledge. You intellectuals can acquire this
knowledge, and it is your *duty* to bring us that knowledge
in a hundred and a thousand times greater measure than
you have done up till now ; and you must bring us this
knowledge, not only in the form of arguments, pamphlets
and articles which sometimes—excuse my frankness !—
are very dull, but in the form of live *exposures* of what our
government and our governing classes are doing at this
very moment in all spheres of life. Fulfil this duty with
greater zeal, and *talk less about " increasing the activity of the
masses of the workers ! "* We are far more active than you
think, and we are quite able to support by open street
fighting demands that do not even promise any " palpable
results " whatever ! You cannot " increase " our activity,
because *you yourselves are not sufficiently active.* Be less subser-
vient to spontaneity, and think more about increasing *your
own* activity, gentlemen ! . . .

The Working Class as Champion of Democracy

We have seen that the organisation of wide political
agitation, and, consequently, of all-sided political exposures,
is an absolutely necessary *and paramount* task of activity,
that is, if that activity is to be truly Social-Democratic.
We arrived at this conclusion *solely* on the grounds of the
pressing needs of the working class for political knowledge
and political training. But this ground by itself is too
narrow for the presentation of the question, for it ignores
the general democratic tasks of Social-Democracy as a
whole, and of modern Russian Social-Democracy in particular. In order to explain the situation more concretely
we shall approach the subject from an aspect that is
" nearer " to the Economist, namely, from the practical
aspect. " Every one agrees " that it is necessary to develop
the political consciousness of the working class. But the
question arises, How is that to be done ? What must be

done to bring this about? The economic struggle merely brings the workers " up against " questions concerning the attitude of the government towards the working class. Consequently, *however much we may try* to " give to the economic struggle itself a political character " *we shall never be able* to develop the political consciousness of the workers (to the degree of Social-Democratic consciousness) by confining ourselves to the economic struggle, for *the limits of this task are too narrow.* The Martynov formula has some value for us, not because it illustrates Martynov's abilities to confuse things, but because it strikingly expresses the fundamental error that all the Economists commit, namely, their conviction that it is possible to develop the class political consciousness of the workers *from within*, that is to say, exclusively, or at least mainly, by means of the economic struggle. Such a view is radically wrong. Piqued by our opposition to them, the Economists refuse to ponder deeply over the origins of these disagreements, with the result that we absolutely fail to understand each other. It is as if we spoke in different tongues.

The workers can acquire class political consciousness *only from without*, that is, only outside of the economic struggle, outside of the sphere of relations between workers and employers. The sphere from which alone it is possible to obtain this knowledge is the sphere of relationships between *all* classes and the state and the government—the sphere of the inter-relations between *all* classes. For that reason, the reply to the question : What must be done in order that the workers may acquire political knowledge? cannot be merely the one which, in the majority of cases, the practical workers, especially those who are inclined towards Economism, usually content themselves with, i.e., " go among the workers." To bring political knowledge to the workers the Social-Democrats must *go among all classes of the population, must despatch units of their army in all directions.*

We deliberately select this awkward formula, we deliberately express ourselves in a simple, forcible way, not

because we desire to indulge in paradoxes, but in order to
" stimulate " the Economists to take up their tasks which
they unpardonably ignore, to ıake them understand the
difference between trade-union and Social-Democratic
politics, which they refuse to understand. Therefore, we
beg the reader not to get excited, but to hear us patiently
to the end.

Take the type of Social-Democratic circle that has been
most widespread during the past few years, and examine its
work. It has " contact with the workers," it issues leaflets
—in which abuses in the factories, the government's partiality towards the capitalists, and the tyranny of the police
are strongly condemned—and rests content with this. At
meetings of workers, there are either no discussions or
they do not extend beyond such subjects. Lectures and
discussions on the history of the revolutionary movement,
on questions of the home and foreign policy of our government, on questions of the economic evolution of Russia and
of Europe, and the position of the various classes in modern
society, etc., are extremely rare. Of systematically acquiring
and extending contact with other classes of society, no one
even dreams. The ideal leader, as the majority of the members of such circles picture him, is something more in the
nature of a trade-union secretary than a Socialist political
leader. Any trade-union secretary, an English one, for instance, helps the workers to conduct the economic struggle,
helps to expose factory abuses, explains the injustice of the
laws and of measures which hamper the freedom of strikes
and the freedom to picket, to warn all and sundry that a
strike is proceeding at a certain factory, explains the
partiality of arbitration courts which are in the hands of
the bourgeois classes, etc., etc. In a word, every trade-union
secretary conducts and helps to conduct " the economic
struggle against the employers and the government.". It
cannot be too strongly insisted that *this is not* enough to
constitute Social-Democracy. The Social-Democrat's ideal
should not be a trade-union secretary, but *a tribune of the*

people, able to react to every manifestation of tyranny and oppression, no matter where it takes place, no matter what stratum or class of the people it affects ; he must be able to group all these manifestations into a single picture of police violence and capitalist exploitation ; he must be able to take advantage of every petty event in order to explain his Socialistic convictions and his Social-Democratic demands *to all*, in order to explain to *all* and everyone the world historical significance of the struggle for the emancipation of the proletariat. . . .

We said that a Social-Democrat, if he really believes it is necessary to develop the political consciousness of the proletariat, must " go among all classes of the people." This gives rise to the questions : How is this to be done ? Have we enough forces to do this ? Is there a base for such work among all the other classes ? Will this not mean a retreat, or lead to a retreat from the class point of view ? We shall deal with these questions.

We must " go among all classes of the people " as theoreticians, as propagandists, as agitators, and as organisers. No one doubts that the theoretical work of Social-Democrats should be directed towards studying all the features of the social and political position of the various classes. But extremely little is done in this direction compared with the work that is done in studying the features of factory life. In the committees and circles, you will meet men who are immersed say in the study of some special branch of the metal industry, but you will hardly ever find members of organisations (obliged, as often happens, for some reason or other to give up practical work) especially engaged in the collection of material concerning some pressing question of social and political life which could serve as a means for conducting Social-Democratic work among other strata of the population. In speaking of the lack of training of the majority of present-day leaders of the labour movement, we cannot refrain from mentioning the point about training in this connection also, for it is also bound up with the " economic " conception of " close organic contact with the proletarian struggle." The principal thing, of course, is *propaganda and agitation* among all strata of the people. The Western-European Social-Democrats find their work in this field facilitated by the calling of public meetings, to which *all* are free to go, and by the parliament, in which they speak to the representatives of *all* classes. We have neither a parliament, nor the freedom to call meetings, nevertheless we are able to arrange meetings of workers who desire to listen to *a Social-Democrat.* We must also find ways and means of calling meetings of representatives of all and every other class of the population that desire to listen to a *Democrat* ; for he who forgets that " the Communists support every revolutionary movement," that we are obliged for that reason to emphasise *general democratic tasks before the whole people*, without for a moment concealing our Socialistic convictions, is not a Social-Democrat. He who forgets his obligation to *be in advance of everybody* in bringing up, sharpening and solving *every* general democratic question is not a Social-Democrat. . . .

To proceed. Have we sufficient forces to be able to direct our propaganda and agitation among *all* classes of the population ? Of course we have. Our Economists are frequently inclined to deny this. They lose sight of the gigantic progress our movement has made from (approximately) 1894 to 1901. Like real Khvostists, they frequently live in the distant past, in the period of the beginning of the movement. At that time, indeed, we had astonishingly few forces, and it was perfectly natural and legitimate then to resolve to go exclusively among the workers, and severely condemn any deviation from this. The whole task then was to consolidate our position in the working class. At the present time, however, gigantic forces have been attracted to the movement ; the best representatives of the young generation of the educated classes are coming over to us ; everywhere, and in all provinces, there are people who have taken part in the movement in the past, who desire to do so now, who are striving towards Social-Democracy, but who are obliged to sit idle because we cannot employ them (in 1894 you could count the Social-Democrats on your fingers). One of the principal political and organisational shortcomings of our movement is that we are *unable* to utilise all these forces, and give them appropriate work (we shall deal with this in detail in the next chapter). The overwhelming majority of these forces entirely lack the opportunity for " going to the workers," so there are no grounds for fearing that we shall deflect forces from our main cause. And in order to be able to provide the workers with real, universal, and live political knowledge, we must have " our own men," Social-Democrats, everywhere, among all social strata, and in all positions from which we can learn the inner springs of our state mechanism. Such men are required for propaganda and agitation, but in a still larger measure for organisation.

Is there scope for activity among all classes of the population ? Those who fail to see this also lag intellectually behind the spontaneous awakening of the masses. The labour movement has aroused and is continuing to arouse discontent in some, hopes for support for the opposition in others, and the consciousness of the intolerableness and inevitable downfall of autocracy in still others. We would be " politicians " and Social-Democrats only in name (as very often happens), if we failed to realise that our task is to utilise every manifestation of discontent, and to collect and utilise every grain of even rudimentary protest. This is quite apart from the fact that many millions of the peasantry, handicraftsmen, petty artisans, etc., always listen eagerly to the preachings of any Social-Democrat who is at all intelligent. Is there a single class of the population in which no individuals, groups or circles are to be found who are discontented with the state of tyranny, and therefore accessible to the propaganda of Social-Democrats as the spokesmen of the most pressing general democratic needs ? To those who desire to have a clear idea of what the

political agitation of a Social-Democrat *among all* classes
and strata of the population should be like, we would
point to *political exposures* in the broad sense of the word
as the principal (but of course not the sole) form of this
agitation.

> We must " arouse in every section of the population that is at
> all enlightened a passion for *political* exposure," I wrote in my
> article " Where to Begin " (*Iskra*, No. 4, May 1901), with which
> I shall deal in greater detail later.
> " We must not allow ourselves to be discouraged by the fact
> that the voice of political exposure is still feeble, rare and timid.
> This is not because of a general submission to political despot-
> ism, but because those who are able and ready to expose have
> no tribune from which to speak, because there is no audience
> to listen eagerly to and approve of what the orators say, and
> because the latter can nowhere perceive among the people
> forces to whom it would be worth while directing their com-
> plaint against the ' omnipotent' Russian government. . . .
> We are now in a position to set up a tribune for the national
> exposure of the tsarist government, and it is our duty to do so.
> That tribune must be a Social-Democratic paper. . . ."

The ideal audience for these political exposures is the
working class, which is first and foremost in need of universal and live political knowledge, which is most capable of
converting this knowledge into active struggle, even if it
did not promise " palpable results." The only platform from
which *public* exposures can be made is an All-Russian news-
paper. " Unless we have a political organ, a movement
deserving the name of political is inconceivable in modern
Europe." In this connection Russia must undoubtedly be
included in modern Europe. The press has long ago become
a power in our country, otherwise the government would
not spend tens of thousands of roubles to bribe it, and to
subsidise the Katkovs, and Meshcherskys. And it is no
novelty in autocratic Russia for the underground press to
break through the wall of censorship and *compel* the legal
and conservative press to speak openly of it. This was the
case in the 'seventies and even in the 'fifties. How much

broader and deeper are now the strata of the people willing
to read the illegal underground press, and to learn from
it " how to live and how to die," to use the expression of the
worker who sent a letter to *Iskra* [No. 7]. Political exposures
are as much a declaration of war against the *government* as
economic exposures are a declaration of war against the
employers. And the wider and more powerful this campaign of exposure will be, the more numerous and determined the social *class* which has *declared war in order to commence the war* will be, the greater will be the moral significance of this declaration of war. Hence, political exposures
in themselves serve as a powerful instrument for *disintegrating* the system we oppose, the means for diverting from
the enemy his casual or temporary allies, the means for
spreading enmity and distrust among those who preman-
ently share power with the autocracy.

Only a party that will *organise* real all-national exposures
can become the vanguard of the revolutionary forces in our
time. The word all-national has a very profound meaning.
The overwhelming majority of the non-working class ex-
posers (and in order to become the vanguard, we must
attract other classes) are sober politicians and cool business
men. They know perfectly well how dangerous it is to
" complain " even against a minor official, let alone
against the " omnipotent " Russian government. And they
will come *to us* with their complaints only when they see
that these complaints really have effect, and when they see
that we represent a *political* force. In order to become this
political force in the eyes of outsiders, much persistent and
stubborn work is required to *increase* our own consciousness,
initiative and energy. For this, it is not sufficient to stick
the label " vanguard " on " rearguard " theory and
practice.

But if we have to undertake the organisation of the
real all-national exposure of the government, then in what
way will the class character of our movement be expressed ?
—the over-zealous advocates of " close organic contact

with the proletarian struggle " will ask us. The reply is :
In that we *Social-Democrats* will *organise* these public exposures ; in that all the questions that are brought up by the
agitation will be explained in the spirit of Social-Democracy, without any deliberate or unconscious distortions of
Marxism ; in the fact that *the party* will carry on this universal political agitation, uniting into one inseparable whole
the pressure upon the government in the name of the whole
people, the revolutionary training of the proletariat—
while preserving its political independence—the guidance
of the economic struggle of the working class, the utilisation
of all its spontaneous conflicts with its exploiters, which
rouse and bring into our camp increasing numbers of the
proletariat ! . . .

V. I. Lenin

THE REVOLUTION OF 1905

*Articles published in Bolshevik journals during 1905 and 1906,
also a lecture delivered in Zurich in January 1917. English edition,
Martin Lawrence, Ltd., 1931.*

[During the Russian revolution of 1905 Lenin was in
Geneva, where he was editing the Bolshevik journals
Vperiod and later *Proletary*, the *Iskra* (which Lenin directed
from 1901–3) having come under Menshevik control since
1903. The first article, reprinted here, was written on Jan.
25, 1905, immediately after the massacre of the workers
in St. Petersburg on " Bloody Sunday," and was published
in *Vperiod*, Jan. 31, 1905. This was followed by other articles
on the various stages of the revolution. The lecture on the
1905 revolution delivered by Lenin in Zurich on January

22, 1917, covers the ground of these articles, and is therefore
the second document reprinted below. It is a complete
analysis of the 1905 revolution, which Lenin later described
as the " dress rehearsal " of the 1917 revolution.]

THE REVOLUTION OF 1905

THE BEGINNING OF THE REVOLUTION
IN RUSSIA

Geneva.
Wednesday, January 25.

Most important historic events are taking place in
Russia. The proletariat has risen against Tsarism. The
proletariat has been driven to the uprising by the Government. Now there is hardly room for doubt that the Government deliberately allowed the strike movement to develop
and a wide demonstration to be started in order to bring
matters to a head, and to have a pretext for calling out
the military forces. Its manœuvre was successful ! Thousands of killed and wounded—this is the toll of Bloody
Sunday, January 22, in Petersburg. The army vanquished
unarmed workers, women and children. The army overpowered the enemy by shooting prostrate workers. " We
have taught them a good lesson ! " cynically say the Tsar's
henchmen and their European flunkeys, the conservative
bourgeoisie.

Yes, it was a great lesson ! The Russian proletariat will
not forget this lesson. The most uneducated, the most
backward strata of the working class, who had naïvely
trusted the Tsar and had sincerely wished to put peacefully
before " the Tsar himself " the requests of a tormented
nation, were all taught a lesson by the military force led
by the Tsar and the Tsar's uncle, the Grand Duke Vladimir.

The working class had received a great lesson in civil

war ; the revolutionary education of the proletariat advanced in one day further than it could have advanced in months and years of drab, everyday, stupefied existence. The slogan of the heroic Petersburg proletariat, " liberty or death ! " rings like an echo throughout the whole of Russia. Events are developing with marvellous speed. The general strike in Petersburg is spreading. All industrial social and political life is paralysed. On Monday, January 23, the encounters between the workers and the military become more stubborn. Contrary to the false Government *communiqués*, blood is spilt in many parts of the capital. The Kolpino workers are rising. The proletariat is arming itself and the people. There are rumours that the workers have seized the Sestroretsk Arsenal. The workers are supplying themselves with revolvers, they are forging their tools into weapons, they are procuring bombs for a desperate fight for freedom. The general strike is spreading to the provinces. In Moscow 10,000 people have already ceased work. A general strike is to be called in Moscow to-morrow (Thursday, January 26). A revolt has broken out in Riga. The workers in Lodz are demonstrating, an uprising is being prepared in Warsaw, demonstrations of the proletariat are taking place in Helsingfors. In Baku, Odessa, Kiev, Kharkov, Kovno and Vilno, there is growing ferment among the workers and the strike is spreading. In Sebastopol the stores and arsenals of the navy department are ablaze, and the troops refuse to shoot on the rebellious sailors. There are strikes in Reval and in Saratov. In Radom, an armed encounter occurred between the workers and a detachment of reserves which had been called out.

The revolution is spreading. The government is already beginning to waver. From a policy of bloody repression it is trying to pass to economic concessions and to save itself by throwing a sop, by promising the nine-hour day. But the lesson of Bloody Sunday must not be forgotten. The demand of the rebellious Petersburg workers—the immediate convocation of a Constituent Assembly on the

basis of universal, direct, equal and secret suffrage—must
become the demand of all the striking workers. The
immediate overthrow of the Government—such was
the slogan raised in answer to the massacre of January
9, even by those Petersburg workers who believed in the
Tsar ; they raised this slogan through their leader, George
Gapon, who said after that bloody day : " We no longer
have a Tsar. A river of blood separates the Tsar from the
nation. Long live the fight for freedom ! "

Long live the revolutionary proletariat ! say we. The
general strike is rousing and mobilising larger and larger
masses of the working class and of the city poor. The arming
of the people is becoming one of the immediate problems
of the revolutionary moment.

Only an armed people can be a real stronghold of
national freedom. And the sooner the proletariat succeeds
in arming itself, and the longer it maintains its martial
position of striker and revolutionary, the sooner will
the army begin to waver, the soldiers will at last begin to
understand what they are doing, they will go over to the
side of the people against the monsters, against the tyrants,
against the murderers of defenceless workers and of their
wives and children. No matter what the outcome of the
present uprising in Petersburg will be, it will, in any case,
be the first step to a wider, more conscious, better prepared
uprising. The government may perhaps succeed in putting
off the day of reckoning, but the postponement will only
make the next step of the revolutionary attack more
powerful. Social-Democracy will take advantage of this
postponement in order to close the ranks of the organised
fighters, and to spread the news about the start made
by the Petersburg workers. The proletariat will join in
the fight, will desert mill and factory, and prepare arms
for itself. Into the midst of the city poor, to the millions
of peasants, the slogans of the struggle for freedom will
be carried more and more effectively. Revolutionary
committees will be formed in every factory, in every

section of the city, in every village. The people in revolt will overthrow all the government institutions of the Tsarist autocracy and proclaim the immediate convocation of the Constituent Assembly.

The immediate arming of the workers and of all citizens in general, the preparation and organisation of the revolutionary forces for annihilating the Government authorities and institutions—this is the practical basis on which all revolutionaries can and must unite, to strike a common blow. The proletariat must always go its independent way in close contact with the Social-Democrat party, always bearing in mind its great final goal, the goal of ridding mankind of all exploitation. But this independence of the Social-Democratic proletarian party will never cause us to forget the importance of a common revolutionary attack at the moment of actual revolution. We Social-Democrats can and must proceed independently of the revolutionaries of the bourgeois democracy, and guard the class independence of the proletariat. But we must go hand in hand with them in an uprising when direct blows are being struck at Tsarism, when resisting the troops, when attacking the Bastille of the accursed enemy of the entire Russian people.

The eyes of the proletariat of the whole world are anxiously turned towards the proletariat of all Russia. The overthrow of Tsarism in Russia, started so valiantly by our working class, will be the turning-point in the history of all countries, will make easier the task of the workers of all nations, in all states, in all parts of the globe. Therefore, let every Social-Democrat, let every class-conscious worker remember the great tasks of the all-national struggle that now rest on his shoulders. Let him not forget that he represents the needs and the interests of the entire peasantry too, of the entire mass of the toiling and exploited, of the entire people against the all-national enemy. The whole world is watching the example of the heroic proletarians of St. Petersburg.

Long live the Revolution !
Long live the proletariat in revolt !

LECTURE ON THE 1905 REVOLUTION

MY YOUNG FRIENDS AND COMRADES,

To-day is the twelfth anniversary of " Bloody Sunday,"
which is rightly regarded as the beginning of the Russian
Revolution.

Thousands of workers—not Social-Democrats, but
faithful, loyal people—led by the priest Gapon, stream
from all parts of the city to the centre of the capital, to
the square in front of the Winter Palace, in order to submit
a petition to the Tsar. The workers carry ikons, and their
leader, in a letter to the Tsar, has guaranteed his personal
safety and asked him to appear before the people.

Troops are called out. Uhlans and Cossacks hurl themselves against the crowd with drawn swords. They fire
on the unarmed workers, who on their bended knees
implore the Cossacks to let them go to the Tsar. On that
day, according to police reports, more than 1,000 were
killed and more than 2,000 were wounded. The indignation of the workers was indescribable.

Such is the bare outline of what took place on January
22, 1905, " Bloody Sunday."

In order that you may understand more clearly the
significance of this event, I will quote to you a few passages
from the workers' petition. The petition begins with the
following words :

> We workers, inhabitants of St. Petersburg, have come to
> Thee. We are unfortunate, reviled slaves. We are crushed by
> despotism and tyranny. At last, when our patience was ex-
> hausted, we ceased work and begged our masters to give us only
> that without which life is a torture. But this was refused. Every-
> thing seemed unlawful to the employers. We here, many thou-
> sands of us, like the whole of the Russian people, have no human
> rights whatever. Owing to the deeds of Thine officials we have
> become slaves.

The petition enumerates the following demands : amnesty, civic liberty, normal wages, the land to be gradually transferred to the people, convocation of a Constituent Assembly on the basis of universal and equal suffrage ; and it ends with the following words : " Sire, do not refuse aid to Thy people ! Throw down the wall that separates Thee from Thy people. Order and swear that our requests will be granted, and Thou wilt make Russia happy ; if not, we are ready to die on this very spot. We have only two roads : freedom and happiness, or the grave."

Reading it *now*, this petition of uneducated, illiterate workers, led by a patriarchal priest, creates a strange impression. Involuntarily one compares this naïve petition with the peaceful resolutions passed to-day by the social-pacifists, i.e., who claim to be Socialists, but who, in reality, are bourgeois phrase-mongers. The unenlightened workers of pre-revolutionary Russia did not know that the Tsar was the head of the *ruling class*, namely, the class of large landowners, who by a thousand ties, were already bound up with a big bourgeoisie who were ready to defend their monopoly, privileges and profits by every violent means. The social-pacifists of to-day, who—without jesting —pretend to be " highly educated " people, do not realise that it is just as foolish to expect a " democratic " peace from the bourgeois governments, which are waging an imperialist predatory war, as it was foolish to think that the bloody Tsar could be induced to grant reforms by peaceful petitions.

Nevertheless, the great difference between the two is that the present-day social-pacifists are to a large extent hypocrites, who, by mild suggestions, strive to divert the people from the revolutionary struggle, whereas the unenlightened workers in pre-revolutionary Russia proved by their deeds that they were straightforward people who, for the first time, had awakened to political consciousness.

It is this awakening of tremendous masses of the people to political consciousness and revolutionary struggle that marks the historic significance of January 22, 1905.

" There is not yet a revolutionary people in Russia," said Mr. Peter Struve, then leader of the Russian liberals and publisher abroad of an illegal, free organ—*two days before* " *Bloody Sunday*." To this " highly educated," supercilious and extremely stupid leader of the bourgeois reformists the idea that an illiterate peasant country could give birth to a revolutionary people seemed utterly absurd. The reformists of those days—like the reformists of to-day—were profoundly convinced that a real revolution was impossible !

Prior to January 22 (January 9, old style), 1905, the revolutionary party of Russia consisted of a small handful of people, and the reformists of those days (like the reformists of to-day) derisively called them a " sect." Several hundred revolutionary organisers, several thousand members of local organisations, half a dozen revolutionary papers appearing not more frequently than once a month, published mainly abroad, and smuggled into Russia under extraordinary difficulties and at the price of many sacrifices—such were the revolutionary parties in Russia, and revolutionary Social-Democracy in particular, prior to January 22, 1905. This circumstance gave the narrow-minded and overbearing reformists a formal justification for asserting that there was not yet a revolutionary people in Russia.

Within a few months, however, the picture completely changed. The hundreds of revolutionary Social-Democrats " suddenly " grew into thousands ; the thousands became leaders of between two and three millions of proletarians. The proletarian struggle gave rise to a strong ferment, often to revolutionary movements, among the peasant masses, fifty to a hundred million strong ; the peasant movement had its repercussion in the army and led to soldiers' uprisings, to armed clashes between one section of the army and another. In this manner, a colossal country, with a population of 130,000,000, entered into the revolution ; in this way slumbering Russia became transformed into a Russia of a revolutionary proletariat and a revolutionary people.

It is necessary to study this transformation to understand its possibilities, its ways and methods, so to speak.

The principal means by which this transformation was brought about was the mass strike. The peculiar feature of the Russian Revolution is that in its social content it was a *bourgeois-democratic* revolution, but in its methods of struggle it was a *proletarian* revolution. It was a bourgeois-democratic revolution, since the aim toward which it strove directly and which it could reach directly, with the aid of its own forces, was a democratic republic, an eight-hour day and the confiscation of the immense estates of the nobility—all measures achieved almost completely in the French bourgeois revolution in 1792 and 1793.

At the same time the Russian Revolution was also a proletarian revolution, not only in the sense that the proletariat was the leading force, the vanguard of the movement, but also in the sense that the specifically proletarian means of struggle—namely, the trike—was the principal instrument employed for rousing the masses and the most characteristic phenomenon in the wave-like rise of decisive events.

The Russian Revolution is the *first*, though certainly not the last, great revolution in history, in which the mass political strike played an extraordinarily great rôle. It can even be asserted that it is impossible to understand the events in the Russian Revolution and the changes that took place in its political forms, unless a study is made of the *statistics of strikes*, which alone provide the clue to these events and change in form.

I know perfectly well that statistics are very dry in a lecture and are calculated to drive an audience away.

Nevertheless, I cannot refrain from quoting a few figures, in order that you may be able to appreciate the objective foundation of the whole movement. The average number of persons involved in strikes in Russia during the last ten years preceding the revolution was 43,000 per annum. Consequently, the total number of persons involved in strikes during the whole decade preceding the revolution was 430,000. In January, 1905, which was the first month of the revolution, the number of persons involved in strikes was 440,000. There were more persons involved in strikes in one month than in the whole of the preceding decade !

In no capitalist country in the world—not even in advanced countries like England, the United States of America, or Germany, has such a tremendous strike movement been witnessed as that which occurred in Russia in 1905. The total number of persons involved in strikes rose to 2,800,000, twice the total number of factory workers in the country ! This, of course, does not prove that the urban factory workers of Russia were more educated, or stronger, or more adapted to the struggle than their brothers in Western Europe. The very opposite is true.

But it does prove how great the dormant energy of the proletariat can be. It shows that in a revolutionary epoch— I say this without exaggeration on the basis of the most accurate data of Russian history—the proletariat *can* develop fighting energy *a hundred times greater* than in normal, peaceful times. It shows that up to 1905, humanity did not yet know what a great, what a tremendous exertion of effort the proletariat is capable of in a fight for really great aims, and when it fights in a really revolutionary manner !

The history of the Russian Revolution shows that it is the vanguard, the chosen elements of the wage-workers who fought with the greatest tenacity and the greatest self-sacrifice. The larger the enterprises involved, the more stubborn the strikes were and the more often they repeated themselves during that year. The bigger the city the more significant was the rôle the proletariat played in the struggle. In the three large cities, St. Petersburg, Riga and Warsaw, where the workers were numerous and more class-conscious, the proportion of workers involved in strikes to the total number of workers was immeasurably larger than in other cities, and, of course, much larger than in the rural districts.

The metal workers in Russia—probably the same is true also in regard to the other capitalist countries—represent the vanguard of the proletariat. In this connection we note the following instructive fact : Taking all industries combined, the number of persons involved in strikes in 1905 was 160 per hundred workers employed, but in the *metal industry* the number was 320 per hundred ! It is calculated that in 1905 every Russian factory worker lost in wages in consequence of strikes, on the average ten roubles— approximately 26 francs at the pre-war rate of exchange— sacrificing this money, as it were, for the sake of the struggle. If we take the metal workers alone, we find that the loss in wages is *three times as great* ! The best elements of the working class marched in the forefront of the battle, leading after them the hesitating ones, rousing the dormant and encouraging the weak.

An outstanding feature was the manner in which economic strikes were interlaced with political strikes during the revolution.

It is quite evident that only when these two forms of strikes are closely linked up with each other can the movement acquire its greatest power. The broad masses of the exploited could not have been drawn into the revolutionary movement had they not seen examples of how the wage workers in the various branches of industry compelled the capitalists to improve their conditions. This struggle imbued the masses of the Russian people with a new spirit. Only then did the old serf-ridden, backward, patriarchal pious and obedient Russia cast off the old Adam ; only then did the Russian people obtain a really democratic and really revolutionary education.

When the bourgeois gentry and their uncritical chorus of satellites, the social-reformists, talk priggishly about the "education" of the masses, they usually mean something schoolmasterly, pedantic, something which demoralises the masses and imbues them with bourgeois prejudices.

The real education of the masses can never be separated from the independent, political, and particularly from the revolutionary struggle of the masses themselves. Only the struggle educates the exploited class. Only the struggle discloses to it the magnitude of its own power, widens its horizon, enhances its abilities, clarifies its mind, forges its will; and therefore, even reactionaries have to admit that the year 1905, the year of struggle, " the mad year," definitely buried patriarchal Russia.

We will examine more closely the relation between the metal workers and the textile workers in Russia during the strike struggle of 1905. The metal workers were the best paid, the most class-conscious and the best educated proletarians. The textile workers, who in 1905 were two and a half times more numerous than the metal workers, were the most backward and the worst-paid mass of workers in Russia, who in very many cases had not yet definitely severed their connections with their present kinsmen in the village. In this connection a very important fact comes to light.

The metal workers' strikes in 1905 show a preponderance of political over economic strikes, although at the beginning of the year this preponderance was not so great as it was toward the end of the year. On the other hand, among the textile workers were observed a great preponderance of economic strikes at the beginning of 1905, and only at the end of the year do we get a preponderance of political strikes. From this it follows quite obviously that the economic struggle, the struggle for immediate and direct improvement of conditions. is alone capable of rousing the backward strata of the exploited masses, gives them a real education and transforms them—during a revolutionary epoch—into an army of political fighters within the space of a few months.

Of course, for this to happen, the vanguard of the workers had to understand that the class struggle was not a struggle in the interests of a small upper stratum, as the reformists too often tried to persuade the workers to believe ; the proletariat had to come forward as the real vanguard of the majority of the exploited, drawing that majority into the struggle, as was the case in Russia in 1905 and as must certainly be the case in the coming proletarian revolution in Europe.

The beginning of 1905 brought with it the first great wave of strikes throughout the entire country. Already in the spring of that year we observe the awakening of the first big, not only economic, but also political *peasant movement* in Russia. The importance of this turning-point of history will be appreciated if it is borne in mind that it was only in 1861 that the peasantry in Russia was liberated from the severest bondage of serfdom, that the majority of the peasants are illiterate, that they live in indescribable poverty, oppressed by the landlords, deluded by the priests and isolated from each other by great distances and an almost complete absence of roads.

A revolutionary movement against Tsarism arose for the first time in Russia in 1825 and that revolution was represented almost entirely by noblemen. From that moment up to 1881, when Alexander the Second was assassinated by the terrorists, the movement was led by middle class intellectuals. They displayed the greatest spirit of self-sacrifice, and they aroused the astonishment of the whole world by their heroic, terroristic methods of struggle. Those sacrifices were certainly not made in vain. They certainly contributed—directly and indirectly— to the subsequent revolutionary education of the Russian people. But they did not and could not achieve their immediate aim—to call forth a popular revolution.

This was achieved only by the revolutionary struggle of the proletariat. Only the waves of mass strikes that swept over the whole country, coupled with the severe lessons of the imperialist Russo-Japanese war, roused the broad masses of peasants from their lethargic slumber. The word " striker " acquired an entirely new meaning among the peasants : it signified a rebel, a revolutionary, a term previously expressed by the word " student." As, however, the " student " belonged to the middle class, to the " learned," to the " gentry," he was alien to the people. On the other hand a " striker " was of the people ; he belonged to the exploited class ; when deported from St. Petersburg, he often returned to the village, where he told his fellow-villagers of the conflagration that had broken out in the cities that was to destroy the capitalists and nobility. A new type appeared in the Russian village—the class-conscious young peasant. He associated with " strikers," he read newspapers, he told the peasants about events in the cities, explained to his fellow villagers the meaning of political demands and called upon them to fight against the big landowners, the priests and the government officials.

The peasants would gather in groups to discuss their conditions and gradually they were drawn into the struggle. Gathering in large crowds they attacked the big landowners, set fire to their mansions and estates and looted their stores, seized grain and other foodstuffs, killed policemen and demanded that the huge estates belonging to the nobility be transferred to the people.

In the spring of 1905, the peasant movement was only in its inception ; it spread to only a minority of the counties, approximately one-seventh of the total were affected.

But the combination of the proletarian mass strikes in the cities with the peasant movement in the villages was sufficient to shake the " firmest " and last prop of Tsarism. I refer to the *Army.*

A series of *mutinies* in the navy and in the army broke out. Every fresh wave of strikes and of peasant movements during the revolution was accompanied by mutinies among the armed forces in all parts of Russia. The most well-known of these is the mutiny on the Black Sea cruiser, *Prince Potemkin*, which, after it was seized by the revolutionaries, took part in the revolution in Odessa. After the revolution was defeated, and the attempts to seize other ports (for instance, Feodosia in the Crimea) had failed, it surrendered to the Rumanian authorities in Constanza.

Permit me to relate to you in detail one little episode in the mutiny of the Black Sea Fleet, in order to give you a concrete picture of events at the apex of their development.

Gatherings of revolutionary workers and sailors were being organised more and more frequently. Since men in the armed forces were not permitted to attend workers' meetings, the workers began in masses to visit the military meetings. They gathered in thousands. The idea of joint action found a lively response. The most class-conscious companies elected deputies.

Then the military authorities decided to take action. The attempts of some of the officers to deliver " patriotic " speeches at the meetings had failed miserably : the seamen, who were accustomed to debating, put their officers to shameful flight. After these efforts had failed, it was decided to prohibit meetings altogether. In the morning of November 24, 1905, a company of soldiers, in full war kit, was posted at the gate of the naval barracks. Rear-Admiral Pisarevsky, in a loud voice, gave the order : " Permit no one to leave the barracks ! In case of disobedience, shoot ! " A sailor, named Petrov, stepped forth from the ranks of the company that received that order, loaded his rifle in everybody's view, and with one shot killed Lieutenant-Colonel Stein of the Brest-Litovsk Regiment, and with another wounded Rear-Admiral Pisarevsky. The command was given : " Arrest him ! " Nobody budged. Petrov threw his rifle to the ground and exclaimed : " Why don't you move ? Take me ! " He was arrested. The seamen, who rushed from every side, angrily demanded his release, and declared that they vouched for him. Excitement ran high.

" Petrov, the shot was an accident, wasn't it ? " asked one of the officers, trying to find a way out of the situation.

" What do you mean, an accident ? I stepped forward, loaded and took aim. Is that an accident ? "

" They demand your release. . . ."

And Petrov was released. The seamen, however, were not content with that ; all officers on duty were arrested, disarmed, and taken to company headquarters. . . . Seamen delegates, forty in number, conferred throughout the whole night. The decision was to release the officers, but never to permit them to enter the barracks again.

This little incident shows you clearly how events developed in the majority of the mutinies. The revolutionary ferment among the people could not but spread to the armed forces. It is characteristic that the leaders of the movement came from those elements in the navy and the army which had been recruited mainly from among the industrial workers and possessed most technical training, for instance, the sappers. The broad masses, however, were still too naïve, their mood was too passive, too good-natured, too Christian. They flared up very quickly ; any case of injustice, excessively harsh conduct on the part of the officers, bad food, etc., was enough to call forth revolt. But there was no persistence in their protest ; they lacked a clear perception of aim ; they lacked a clear understanding of the fact that only the most vigorous continuation of the armed struggle, only a victory over all the military and civil authorities, only the overthrow of the government and the seizure of power throughout the whole state could guarantee the success of the revolution.

The broad masses of the seamen and soldiers light-heartedly rose in revolt. But with equal light-heartedness they foolishly released the arrested officers. They allowed themselves to be pacified by promises and persuasion on the part of their officers ; in this way the officers gained precious time, obtained reinforcements, broke the power of the rebels, and then the most brutal suppression of the movement and the execution of the leaders followed.

It is instructive to compare the mutinies in Russia in 1905 with the mutinies of the Decembrists in 1825. At that time, the leaders of the political movement belonged almost exclusively to the officer class, particularly to the officers of the nobility ; they had become infected through contact with the democratic ideas of Europe during the Napoleonic Wars. The mass of the soldiers, who at that time were still serfs, remained passive.

The history of 1905 presents a totally different picture. The mood of the officers, with few exceptions, was either bourgeois-liberal reformist, or openly counter-revolutionary. The workers and peasants in military uniform were the soul of the mutinies ; the mutinies became a movement of the people. For the first time in the history of Russia the movement spread to the majority of the exploited. But on the one hand, the masses lacked persistence and determination, they were too much afflicted with the malady of trustfulness ; on the other hand, the movement lacked an organisation of revolutionary Social-Democratic workers in military uniform. The soldiers lacked the ability to take the leadership into their own hands, to place themselves at the head of the revolutionary army, and to assume the offensive against the government authorities.

These two shortcomings—we will say in passing—will slowly, perhaps, but surely, be removed, not only by the general development of capitalism, but also by the present war.

At all events, the history of the Russian Revolution, like the history of the Paris Commune of 1871, unfailingly teaches that militarism can never, under any circumstances, be vanquished and destroyed, except by a victorious struggle of one section of the national army against the other section. It is not sufficient simply to denounce, revile and to " repudiate " militarism, to criticise and to argue that it is harmful ; it is foolish peacefully to refuse to perform military service : the task is to keep the revolutionary consciousness of the proletariat in a state of high tension and to train its best elements, not only in a general way but concretely, so that when popular ferment reaches the higher pitch, they will put themselves at the head of the revolutionary army.

This lesson is taught us by daily experience in any capitalist state. Every " minor " crisis that such a state experiences shows us in miniature the elements and embryos of the battles which must inevitably take place on a large scale during a big crisis. What else, for instance, is a strike, if not a small crisis in capitalist society ? Was not the Prussian Minister for Internal Affairs, Herr von Puttkamer, right when he uttered his famous declaration : " Every strike discloses the hydra head of revolution " ? Does not the calling out of troops during strikes in all, even the most peaceful, the most " democratic "—save the mark—capitalist countries show *how* things will work in a *really great* crisis ?

But to return to the history of the Russian Revolution.

I have endeavoured to picture to you how the workers' strikes stirred the whole country and the broadest, most backward strata of the exploited, how the peasant movement began, and how it was accompanied by military uprisings.

In the autumn of 1905, the movement reached its zenith. On August 19 the Tsar issued a manifesto on the introduction of popular representation. The so-called Bulygin Duma was to be created on the basis of a suffrage embracing a remarkably small number of electors, and this peculiar " parliament " was supposed to have, not legislative, but only *advisory* powers !

The bourgeoisie, the liberals, the opportunists, were ready to embrace wholeheartedly this " grant " of a frightened Tsar. Like all reformists, our reformists of 1905 could not understand that historic situations arise when reforms and particularly mere promises of reforms pursue *only* one aim : to allay the unrest of the people, to force the revolutionary class to cease, or at least to slacken, its struggle.

Russian revolutionary Social-Democracy perfectly understood the true nature of the grant of an illusory constitution in August, 1905. This is why, without a moment's hesitation, it issued the slogans : " Down with the advisory Duma ! Boycott the Duma ! Down with the Tsarist government ! Continue the revolutionary struggle for the overthrow of this government ! Not the Tsar, but a provisional revolutionary government must convoke the first real popular representative assembly in Russia ! "

History proved that the revolutionary Social-Democrats were right by the fact that the Bulygin Duma was never convoked. It was swept away by the revolutionary storm before it assembled ; this storm forced the Tsar to promulgate a new electoral law, which provided for an increase in the number of electors, and to recognise the legislative character of the Duma.

In October and December, 1905, the rising tide of the Russian Revolution reached its highest level. The floodgates of the revolutionary power of the people opened wider than ever before. The number of persons involved in strikes—which in January, 1905, as I have already told you, was 440,000—reached over half a million in November, 1905 (in one single month, notice !). To this number, which applies *only* to factory workers, must be added several hundreds of thousands of railway workers, postal and telegraph employees, etc.

The Russian general railroad strike stopped railway traffic and most effectively paralysed the power of the government. The doors of the universities and lecture halls which in peace-time were used only to befuddle youthful heads with pedantic professorial wisdom and to turn them

into docile servants of the bourgeoisie and Tsarism, were
flung wide open and served as meeting-places for thousands
of workers, artisans and office workers, who openly and
freely discussed political questions.

Freedom of the press was won. The censorship was
simply ignored. No publisher dared send the copy to the
authorities, and the authorities did not dare take any
measures against this. For the first time in Russian history
revolutionary papers appeared freely in St. Petersburg
and other cities ; in St. Petersburg alone, three daily
Social-Democratic papers, with circulations ranging from
50,000 to 100,000, were published.

The proletariat marched at the head of the movement.
It set out to win the eight-hour day in a revolutionary
manner. The fighting slogan of the St. Petersburg proletariat was then : " *An eight-hour day and arms!* " It became
obvious to the growing mass of the workers that the fate
of the revolution could, and would, be decided only by
an armed struggle.

In the fire of battle a peculiar mass organisation was
formed, the famous *Soviets of Workers' Deputies*, meetings
of delegates from all factories. In several cities in Russia
these *Soviets of Workers' Deputies* began to play more and
more the rôle of a provisional revolutionary government,
the rôle of organs and leaders of rebellion. Attempts were
made to organise Soviets of Soldiers' and Sailors' Deputies,
and to combine them with the Soviets of Workers' Deputies.

For a period, several cities of Russia at that time represented something in the nature of small, local " republics," the state authorities were deposed, and the Soviet
of Workers' Deputies actually functioned as the new state
authority. Unfortunately, these periods were all too brief,
the " victories " were too weak, too isolated.

The peasant movement in the autumn of 1905 reached
still greater dimensions. *Over one-third* of the counties
throughout the country were affected by " peasant riots "
and real peasant uprisings. The peasants burned no less

than 2,000 estates and distributed among themselves
the provisions that the predatory nobility had robbed
from the people.

Unfortunately, this work was not done with sufficient
thoroughness : unfortunately, the peasants destroyed only
one-fifteenth of the total number of noblemen's estates,
only one-fifteenth part of what *they should have* destroyed,
in order to wipe from the face of the land of Russia the
shame of large feudal land ownership. Unfortunately,
the peasants were too scattered, too isolated from each
other in their actions ; they were too unorganised, not
aggressive enough, and therein lies one of the fundamental
reasons for the defeat of the revolution.

Among the oppressed peoples of Russia there flared up a
national movement for liberation. *Over one-half, almost three-
fifths (to be exact, 57 per cent.*) of the population of Russia
is subject to national oppression : they have not the right
to employ their native language, and are forcibly Russified.
For instance, the Mohammedans, who number tens of
millions among the population of Russia, with astonishing
rapidity, organised a Mohammedan League. Generally
speaking, all kinds of organisations sprang up and grew
at a colossal rate at that time.

To give the audience, particularly the youth, an example
of how at that time the national movement for liberation
rose in connection with the labour movement, I quote the
following case :

In December, 1905, the children in hundreds of Polish
schools burned all Russian books, pictures and portraits
of the Tsar, and attacked and drove out of the Russian
schools the Russian teachers and Russian schoolmasters,
shouting : " Get out of here ! Go back to Russia ! " The
Polish pupils in the secondary schools put forward the
following demands : (1) all secondary schools to be under
the control of a Soviet of Workers' Deputies ; (2) joint
pupils' and workers' meetings to be called within the school
buildings ; (3) the wearing of red blouses in the secondary

schools to be permitted as a token of membership in the
future proletarian republic ; etc.

The higher the tide of the movement rose, the more
vigorously and decisively did the reaction arm to fight
against the revolution. The Russian Revolution of 1905
confirmed the truth of what Karl Kautsky had written
in 1902 in his book *Social Revolution* (at that time he was
still a revolutionary Marxist and not a defender of social-
patriots and opportunists as at present). He wrote the
following :

> The coming revolution . . . will be less like a spontaneous
> uprising against the government and more like a protracted
> *civil war*.

This is exactly what happened ! This will, undoubtedly,
also happen in the coming European revolution !

The hatred of Tsarism was directed particularly against
the Jews. On the one hand, the Jews provided a particularly
high percentage (compared with the total of the Jewish
population) of leaders of the revolutionary movement.
In passing, it should be said to their merit that to-day
the Jews provide a relatively high percentage of representatives of internationalism compared with other nations.
On the other hand, Tsarism knew perfectly well how to
play up the most despicable prejudices of the most ignorant
strata of the population against the Jews, in order to
organise—if not to lead directly—pogroms, those atrocious
massacres of peaceful Jews, their wives and children,
which have roused such disgust throughout the whole
civilised world. Of course, I have in mind the disgust of
the truly democratic elements of the civilised world, and
those are *exclusively* the Socialist workers, the proletarians.

It is calculated that in 100 cities at that time 4,000 were
killed and 10,000 were mutilated. The bourgeoisie, even
in the freest republican countries of Western Europe,
know only too well how to combine their hypocritical
phrases about " Russian atrocities " with the most

shameless financial transactions, particularly with financial support of Tsarism and with imperialist exploitation of Russia through the export of capital, etc.

The climax of the Revolution of 1905 was reached in the December uprising in Moscow. A small handful of rebels, namely, of organised and armed workers—they numbered not more than *eight thousand*—for nine days resisted the Tsarist Government. The government dared not trust the Moscow garrison ; on the contrary, it had to keep it behind locked doors, and only on the arrival of the Semenovsky Regiment from St. Petersburg was it able to quell the rebellion.

The bourgeoisie are pleased to describe the Moscow uprising as something artificial and throw scorn upon it. In the German so-called " scientific " literature, for instance, Herr Professor Max Weber, in his great work on the political development of Russia, described the Moscow uprising as a " putsch." " The Lenin group," says this " highly learned " Herr Professor, " and a section of the Social-Revolutionaries had long prepared for this *senseless* uprising."

In order properly to appraise this professorial wisdom of the cowardly bourgeoisie, it is sufficient to recall the dry strike statistics. In January, 1905, there were only 13,000 persons involved in purely political strikes in Russia, whereas in October there were 330,000 and *in December the maximum was reached of 370,000 involved in purely political strikes*—in one month alone ! Let us recall the progress of the counter-revolution, the uprisings of the peasants and the soldiers, and we will soon come to the conclusion that the dictum of bourgeois science concerning the December uprising is not only absurd, but is a subterfuge on the part of the representatives of the cowardly bourgeoisie, which sees in the proletariat its most dangerous class enemy.

In reality, the whole development of the Russian Revolution inevitably led to an armed, decisive battle between the Tsarist Government and the vanguard of the class-conscious proletariat.

In my previous remarks I have already pointed out wherein lay the weakness of the Russian Revolution which led to its temporary defeat.

With the quelling of the December uprising the revolution began to subside. Even in this period, extremely interesting moments are to be observed ; suffice it to recall the twofold attempt of the most militant elements of the working class to stop the retreat of the revolution and to prepare for a new offensive.

But my time has nearly expired, and I do not want to abuse the patience of my audience. I think, however, that I have outlined the most important aspects of the revolution—its class character, its driving forces and its method of struggle—as fully as it is possible to deal with a large subject in a brief lecture.

A few brief remarks concerning the world significance of the Russian Revolution.

Geographically, economically, and historically, Russia belongs, not only to Europe, but also to Asia. This is why the Russian Revolution succeeded in finally rousing the biggest and the most backward country in Europe and in creating a revolutionary people led by a revolutionary proletariat. It achieved more than that.

The Russian Revolution gave rise to a movement throughout the whole of Asia. The revolutions in Turkey, Persia and China prove that the mighty uprising of 1905 left deep traces, and that its influence expressed in the forward movement of *hundreds and hundreds* of millions of people is ineradicable.

In an indirect way the Russian Revolution exercised influence also on the countries situated to the west. One must not forget that news of the Tsar's constitutional manifesto, reaching Vienna on October 30, 1905, played a decisive rôle in the final victory of universal suffrage in Austria.

A telegram bearing the news was delivered to the Congress of the Austrian Social-Democratic Party, which was then assembled, just as Comrade Ellenbogen—who at that time was not yet a social-patriot but a comrade— was making his report on the political strike. This telegram was placed before him on the table. The discussion was immediately stopped. Our place is in the streets !—this was the cry that resounded in the meeting hall of the delegates of Austrian Social-Democracy. The following days witnessed monster street demonstrations in Vienna and barricades in Prague. The victory of universal suffrage in Austria was decided.

Very often we meet Western Europeans who argue about the Russian Revolution as if events, relationships, and methods of struggle in that backward country have very little resemblance to Western European relationships and, therefore, can hardly have any practical significance.

There is nothing more erroneous than such an opinion.

No doubt the forms and occasions for the impending battles in the coming European revolution will, in many respects, differ from the forms of the Russian Revolution.

Nevertheless, the Russian Revolution—precisely because of its proletarian character in that particular sense to which I referred—was the *prologue* to the coming European revolution. Undoubtedly this coming revolution can only be a proletarian revolution in the profounder sense of the word : a proletarian Socialist revolution even in its content. This coming revolution will show to an even greater degree on the one hand, that only stern battles, only civil wars, can free humanity from the yoke of capital ; on the other hand, that only class-conscious proletarians can and will come forth in the rôle of leaders of the vast majority of the exploited.

The present grave-like stillness in Europe must not deceive us. Europe is charged with revolution. The monstrous horrors of the imperialist war, the suffering caused by the high cost of living, engender everywhere a revolutionary spirit ; and the ruling classes, the bourgeoisie with its servitors, the governments, are more and more moving into a blind alley from which they can never extricate themselves without tremendous upheavals.

Just as in 1905 a popular uprising against the Tsarist government commenced under the leadership of the proletariat with the aim of achieving a democratic republic, so the coming years, precisely because of this predatory war, will lead in Europe to popular uprisings under the leadership of the proletariat against the power of finance capital, against the big banks, against the capitalists ; and these upheavals cannot end otherwise than with the expropriation of the bourgeoisie, with the victory of Socialism.

We of the older generation may not live to see the decisive battles of this coming revolution. But I can certainly express the hope that the youth who are working so splendidly in the Socialist movement of Switzerland, and of the whole world, will be fortunate enough not only to fight, but also to win, in the coming proletarian revolution.

Opposite: Popular uprisings under the leadership of the proletariat. (*The Revolution of 1905*)

V. I. Lenin

IMPERIALISM : THE HIGHEST STAGE OF CAPITALISM

Published in Petrograd, 1917. English edition, Martin Lawrence Ltd., 1933.

[This was written by Lenin in 1916, in Zurich. Its immediate aim was to show that " the war of 1914–18 was on both sides imperialist " ; that imperialism is a " direct continuation of the fundamental properties of capitalism in general." The book traces the growth of trusts and monopolies in the chief capitalist countries, and shows how this development inevitably leads to war. It is also of great importance for its examination of the sources of opportunism in the international labour movement. Parts of the later chapters are given below ; in these conclusions are drawn and the theory of imperialism stated.]

IMPERIALISM: THE HIGHEST STAGE OF CAPITALISM

IMPERIALISM AS A SPECIAL STAGE OF CAPITALISM

(Ch. VII)

WE MUST now try to draw certain conclusions, to sum up what has been said about imperialism. Imperialism emerged as a development and direct continuation of the fundamental properties of capitalism in general. But capitalism became capitalist imperialism, only at a definite, very high stage of its development, when certain of its fundamental properties had begun to change into their opposites, when the features of a period of transition from capitalism to a higher socio-economic system had begun to take shape and reveal themselves all along the line. Economically fundamental in this process is the replacement of capitalist free competition by capitalist monopolies. Free competition is the fundamental property of capitalism and of commodity production generally. Monopoly is the direct opposite of free competition ; but we have seen the latter being transformed into monopoly before our very eyes, creating large-scale production and squeezing out small-scale production, replacing large-scale by larger-scale production, finally leading to such a concentration of production and capital that monopoly has been and is the result : cartels, syndicates and trusts, and, merging with them, the capital of a dozen or so banks manipulating thousands of millions. And at the same time the monopolies, which have sprung from free competition, do not eliminate it, but exist alongside of it and over it, thereby giving rise to a number of very acute and bitter antagonisms, points of friction, and conflicts. Monopoly is the transition from capitalism to a higher order.

If it were necessary to give the briefest possible definition of imperialism, we should have to say that imperialism is the monopoly stage of capitalism. Such a definition would include the essential point, for, on the one hand, finance capital is bank capital of the few biggest monopolist banks, merged with the capital of the monopolist combines of industrialists ; on the other hand, the division of the world is the transition from a colonial policy which has extended without hindrance to territories unoccupied by any capitalist power, to a colonial policy of monopolistic possession of the territories of the world, which has been completely divided up.

But too brief definitions, although convenient, since they sum up the main points, are nevertheless inadequate, because very fundamental features of the phenomenon to be defined must still be deduced. And so, without forgetting the conditional and relative value of all definitions, which can never include all the connections of a fully developed phenomenon, we must give a definition of imperialism that will include the following five essential features :

1. The concentration of production and capital, developed to such a high stage that it has created monopolies which play a decisive rôle in economic life.

2. The merging of bank capital with industrial capital and the creation, on the basis of this " finance capital," of a financial oligarchy.

3. The export of capital, as distinguished from the export of commodities, becomes of particularly great importance.

4. International monopoly combines of capitalists are formed which divide up the world.

5. The territorial division of the world by the greatest capitalist powers is completed.

Imperialism is capitalism in that stage of development in which the domination of monopolies and finance capital has taken shape ; in which the export of capital has acquired pronounced importance ; in which the division of the world by the international trusts has begun, and in which the partition of all the territory of the earth by the greatest capitalist countries has been completed.

We shall see later how imperialism may and must be defined differently when consideration is given not only to the fundamental, purely economic factors—to which the above definition is limited—but also to the historical place of this stage of capitalism in relation to capitalism in general, or to the relations between imperialism and the two basic tendencies in the labour movement. The point to be noted just now is that imperialism, as understood in this sense, undoubtedly represents a special stage in the development of capitalism. In order to enable the reader to obtain as well-grounded an impression of imperialism as possible we have expressly tried to quote as much as possible from *bourgeois* economists, who are obliged to admit the particularly indisputable and established facts regarding the newest capitalist economy. With the same object we have produced detailed statistics which reveal to what extent bank capital, etc., has grown, showing just how the transition from quantity to quality, from developed capitalism to imperialism, has expressed itself. Needless to say, all the boundaries in nature and in society are conditional and changing, and it would be absurd to dispute, for instance, over the year or decade in which imperialism became " definitely " established.

In defining imperialism, however, we have to enter into controversy, primarily, with Karl Kautsky, the principal Marxist theoretician of the epoch of the so-called Second International—that is, of the twenty-five years between 1889 and 1914.

Kautsky, in 1915 and even in November 1914, decisively attacked the fundamental ideas expressed in our definition of imperialism. He declared that imperialism must not be regarded as a " phase " or as an economic stage, but as a policy ; a definite policy " preferred " by finance capital ; that imperialism cannot be " identified " with " contemporary capitalism " ; that if by imperialism is meant " all the phenomena of contemporary capitalism "—cartels, protectionism, the rule of the financiers, and colonial policy— then the question whether imperialism is necessary to capitalism becomes reduced to the " rankest tautology," for in that case, imperialism is " naturally a vital necessity for capitalism," and so on. The most accurate way to present Kautsky's ideas is to quote his own definition of imperialism, which is directly opposed to the substance of the ideas which we set forth (for the objections of the German Marxists, who for many years have been propounding such ideas, have been known to Kautsky as the objections of a definite tendency in Marxism for a long time).

Kautsky's definition is as follows :

> Imperialism is a product of highly developed industrial capitalism. It consists in the striving of every industrial capitalist nation to bring under its control and to annex larger and larger *agrarian* [Kautsky's italics] regions, irrespective of what nations inhabit them.

This definition is utterly worthless because it is one-sided, i.e., it arbitrarily brings out the national question alone (admittedly, it is extremely important in itself as well as in its relation to imperialism) ; arbitrarily and *incorrectly* it connects this question *only* with the industrial capital in the countries which annex other nations ; in an equally arbitrary and incorrect manner it emphasises the annexation of agrarian regions.

Imperialism is a striving for annexations—this is what the *political* part of Kautsky's definition amounts to. It is correct, but very incomplete, for politically, imperialism is generally a striving towards violence and reaction. We are interested here, however, in the *economic* aspect of the question, which Kautsky *himself* introduced into *his own* definition. The errors in the definition of Kautsky are clearly evident. The characteristic feature of imperialism is *not* industrial capital, *but* finance capital. It is not an accident that in France, it was precisely the extraordinarily rapid development of *finance* capital and the weakening of industrial capital, that, from 1880 onwards, gave rise to a sharpening of annexationist (colonial) policy. The characteristic feature of imperialism is precisely the fact that it strives to annex *not only* agrarian but even the most industrialised regions (the German appetite for Belgium ; the French appetite for Lorraine), first, because the fact that the world is already partitioned makes it necessary, in the event of a *re-partition*, to stretch out one's hand to *any* kind of territory, and second, because an essential feature of imperialism is the rivalry between a number of great powers in striving for hegemony, i.e., for the seizure of territory, not so much for their own direct advantage as to weaken the adversary and undermine *his* hegemony (for Germany, Belgium is chiefly necessary as a base against England ; for England, Bagdad as a base against Germany, etc.).

Kautsky refers especially—and repeatedly—to the Englishmen who, he alleges, have established the purely political meaning of the word " imperialism " in his, Kautsky's, sense. We take up the work by the Englishman, Hobson, *Imperialism*, which appeared in 1902, and therein we read (p. 324) :

> The new imperialism differs from the older, first, in substituting for the ambition of a single growing empire the theory and the practice of competing empires, each motived by similar lusts of political aggrandisement and commercial gain ; secondly in the dominance of financial or investing over mercantile interests.

We see that Kautsky is absolutely wrong in factually referring to Englishmen in general (unless he meant the vulgar British imperialists, or the avowed apologists for imperialism). We see that Kautsky, while pretending that he is continuing to defend Marxism, is really taking a step backward in comparison with the *social-liberal* Hobson, who rightly takes account of two " historically concrete " (Kautsky virtually ridicules historical concreteness by his definition) features of modern imperialism : (1) the competition between *several* imperialisms and (2) the predominance of the financier over the merchant. Yet if it were chiefly a question of the annexation of an agrarian country by an industrial one, the rôle played by the merchant would be predominant.

But Kautsky's definition is not only wrong and un-Marxian. It serves as a basis for a whole system of views which all along the line run counter to Marxian theory and practice ; we shall refer to this again. The argument about words which Kautsky raises as to whether the newest stage of capitalism should be called imperialism or the stage of finance capital is really not serious. Call it what you will, it makes no difference. The important thing is that Kautsky detaches the policy of imperialism from its economics, speaks of annexations as being a policy " preferred " by finance capital, and opposes to it another bourgeois policy which he alleges to be possible on the same basis of finance capital. It would follow that monopolies in economics are compatible with methods which are neither monopolistic,

nor violent, nor annexationist, in politics. It would follow
that the territorial division of the world, which was completed precisely during the period of finance capital and
which represents the main feature of the present peculiar
forms of rivalry between the greatest capitalist states, is
compatible with a non-imperialist policy. The result is a
slurring-over and a blunting of the most profound contradictions of the newest stage of capitalism, instead of an
exposure of their depth. The result is bourgeois reformism
instead of Marxism.

Kautsky enters into controversy with the German apologist of imperialism and annexations, Cunow, who clumsily
and cynically argues that : imperialism is modern capitalism ; the development of capitalism is inevitable and progressive ; therefore imperialism is progressive ; therefore we
should bow down before imperialism and chant its praises.
This is something like the caricature of the Russian Marxists
which the Narodniks drew in 1894–1895. They used to
argue that if the Marxists considered capitalism inevitable
and progressive in Russia, they ought to open up a public-
house and start breeding capitalism ! Kautsky retorts to
Cunow : No, imperialism is not modern capitalism, but
only one of the forms of the policy of modern capitalism.
This policy we can and must fight ; we can and must fight
against imperialism, annexations, etc.

The retort sounds quite plausible. But in effect it is a
more subtle and disguised (and, therefore, more dangerous)
preaching of conciliation with imperialism, for unless the
" struggle " against the policy of the trusts and banks strikes
at the economic bases of the trusts and banks, it reduces
itself to bourgeois reformism and pacifism, to an innocent
and benevolent expression of pious hopes. Kautsky's theory,
which has nothing in common with Marxism, avoids mentioning existing conditions, and ignores the most important
of them instead of revealing them in their full depth.
Naturally, such a " theory " can only serve the purpose of
defending unity with the Cunows !

From a purely economic point of view, says Kautsky, it is not impossible that capitalism will pass through yet another new phase, that of the extension of the policy of the cartels to foreign policy, the phase of ultra-imperialism, i.e., of a super-imperialism, a union of world imperialisms and not struggles among them ; a phase when wars shall cease under capitalism, a phase of " the joint exploitation of the world by an internationally combined finance capital."

We shall have to deal with this " theory of ultra-imperialism " later to show in detail how decisively and utterly it departs from Marxism. Meanwhile, in keeping with the general plan of the present work, we must examine the exact economic data on this question. Is " ultra-imperialism " possible " from the purely economic point of view," or is this ultra-nonsense ?

If by the purely economic point of view is meant a " pure " abstraction, then all that can be said resolves itself into the following proposition : evolution is proceeding towards monopoly ; therefore the trend is towards a single world monopoly, single world trust. This is indisputable, but it is also as completely devoid of meaning as is the statement that " evolution is proceeding " towards the manufacture of foodstuffs in laboratories. In this sense the " theory " of ultra-imperialism is no less absurd than a " theory of ultra-agriculture " would be.

If, on the other hand, we are discussing the " purely economic " conditions of the epoch of finance capital as an historically concrete epoch of the beginning of the twentieth century, then the best reply to the lifeless abstractions of " ultra-imperialism " (which serve an exclusively reactionary aim : that of diverting attention from the depth of *existing* contradictions) is to contrast them with the concrete economic realities of present-day world economy. Kautsky's meaningless talk about ultra-imperialism encourages, amongst other things, the profoundly mistaken idea, which only brings grist to the mill of the apologists of imperialism, that the domination of finance capital *weakens* the unevenness and contradictions within world economy, whereas in reality it *strengthens* them.

Richard Cawler, in his little book, *An Introduction to World Economy*, attempted to compile the chief, purely economic data necessary to understand, in a concrete way, the inter-relations within world economy at the turn of the nineteenth century. He divides the world into five " main economic regions " : (1) Central Europe (the whole of Europe with the exception of Russia and Great Britain) ; (2) Great Britain ; (3) Russia ; (4) Eastern Asia ; (5) America. He includes the colonies in the " regions " of the states to which they belong and " puts aside " a few countries not distributed according to regions, such as Persia, Afghanistan and Arabia in Asia, Morocco and Abyssinia in Africa, etc.

We observe three regions with highly developed capitalism (with a high development of means of communication, trade and industry) : the Central European, the British, and the American. Among them are three states which dominate the world : Germany, Britain, the United States. Imperialist rivalry and the struggle between these countries have become very keen because Germany has only an insignificant area and few colonies ; the creation of " Central Europe " is still a matter for the future, and it is being born in the midst of desperate struggles. For the moment the distinctive feature of all Europe is political disintegration. In the British and American regions, on the contrary, political concentration is very highly developed, but there is a tremendous disparity between the immense colonies of the former and the insignificant colonies of the latter. In the colonies, capitalism is only beginning to develop. The struggle for South America becomes more and more bitter.

Here is a summary of the economic data he gives on these regions :

Principal Econ. Regions of the World	Area (in mill. sq. km.)	Pop. (in mills.)	Transport		Trade Imp. and Exp. (in bill. Mks.)	Industry		
			Rlwys. (in thous. km.)	Merch. fleet (in mill. tons)		Yearly Output of Coal (in mill. tons)	Output of Pig Iron (in mill. tons)	No. of Cotton Spindles (in mills.)
1. Cent. European . .	27·6 (23·6)[1]	388 (146)	204	8	41	251	15	26
2. British .	28·9 (28·6)	398 (355)	140	11	25	249	9	51
3. Russian .	22·	131	63	1	3	16	3	7
4. East. Asian .	12·	389	8	1	2	8	0·02	2
5. American .	30·	148	379	6	14	245	14	19

There are two regions where capitalism is poorly developed : Russia and Eastern Asia. In the former the density of population is low, in the latter it is very high ; in the former, political concentration is high, in the latter it does not exist. The partition of China has only just begun, and the struggle for it between Japan, the U.S.A., etc., is continually gaining in intensity.

Compare this reality, the vast diversity of economic and political conditions, the extreme disparity in the rate of growth of the various countries, the frenzied struggles among the imperialist states, with Kautsky's stupid little fable about " peaceful " ultra-imperialism. Is this not the reactionary attempt of a frightened petty-bourgeois to hide from stern reality ? Do not the international cartels, which seem to Kautsky to be the embryos of " ultra-imperialism " (as the manufacture of tablets in a laboratory " might " seem to be ultra-agriculture in embryo) present an example of the division and the *re-division* of the world, the transition from peaceful division to non-peaceful and vice versa ? Is not American and other finance capital, which peacefully divided up the whole world, with Germany's participation (for instance in the international rail syndicate, or in the international mercantile shipping trust) now *re-dividing* the world on the basis of a new alignment of forces

[1] The figures in parentheses show the area and population of the colonies.

which are being changed by methods altogether *non-peaceful* ?

Finance capital and the trusts are aggravating instead of diminishing the differences between the rates of development of the various parts of world economy. When the alignment of forces is changed, how else, *under capitalism*, can a solution of the contradictions be found, except through *force* ?

Railway statistics provide remarkably exact data on the different rates of growth of capitalism and finance capital in world economy. In the last decades of imperialist development, the total length of railways has changed as follows :

RAILROADS
(in thousands of kilometres)

	1890	1913	Increase
Europe . . .	224	346	122
United States . .	268	411	143
Colonies (total) . .	82 }	210 }	128 }
Independent or semi-dependent states of Asia	} 125	} 347	} 222
and America . .	43 }	137 }	94 }
Total . .	617	1,104	487

The development of railways has been most rapid in the colonies and in the independent (and semi-independent) states of Asia and America. It is known that here the finance capital of the four or five biggest capitalist states reigns fully. Two hundred thousand kilometres of new railway lines in the colonies and in the other countries of Asia and America represent more than 40 billion marks in capital, newly invested on particularly advantageous terms, with special guarantees of a good return, with profitable orders for steel mills, etc., etc.

Capitalism is growing most rapidly in the colonies and in trans-oceanic countries. Amongst the latter *new* imperialist powers are emerging (Japan). The struggle of world imperialisms is becoming acute. The tribute levied by

finance capital on the most profitable colonial and trans-
oceanic enterprises is increasing. In dividing up this
" booty," an exceptionally large share goes to countries
which, as far as rate of development of productive forces
is concerned, do not always stand at the top of the list. In
the case of the greatest powers, considered with their
colonies, the total length of railways (in thousands of kilometres) was as follows :

	1890	1913	Increase
United States . .	268	413	145
British Empire . .	107	208	101
Russia . . .	32	78	46
Germany . . .	43	68	25
France . . .	41	63	22
Total . .	491	830	339

Thus, about eighty per cent of the total railways are concentrated in the hands of the five greatest powers. But the
concentration of the *ownership* of these railways, the concentration of finance capital, is immeasurably more important ;
French and English millionaires, for example, own an
enormous amount of stocks and bonds in American,
Russian and other railways.

Thanks to its colonies, Great Britain has increased " its "
network of railways by 100,000 kilometres, four times as
much as Germany. At the same time, it is known that the
development of productive forces in Germany during this
period, and especially the development of the coal and iron
industries, has been incomparably more rapid than in
England—not to mention France or Russia. In 1892,
Germany produced 4·9 million tons of pig iron, and Great
Britain 6·8 million tons ; but in 1912, Germany produced
17·6 million tons against Great Britain's 9 million, an overwhelming superiority over England ! The question arises,
is there, *under capitalism*, any means of eliminating the disparity between the development of productive forces and

the accumulation of capital on the one side, and the partition of colonies and " spheres of influence " by finance capital on the other side—other than war ?

PARASITISM AND THE DECAY OF CAPITALISM

(Ch. VIII)

We have now to examine another very important aspect of imperialism, to which, usually, too little attention is paid in the majority of discussions on this subject. One of the shortcomings of the Marxist, Hilferding, is that he took a step backward in comparison with the non-Marxist, Hobson. We refer to parasitism, inherent in imperialism.

As we have seen, the most deep-rooted economic foundation of imperialism is monopoly. This is capitalist monopoly, i.e., monopoly which has grown out of capitalism, and exists in the general capitalist environment of commodity production and competition, in permanent and insoluble contradiction to this general environment. Nevertheless, like any monopoly, it inevitably gives rise to a tendency towards stagnation and decay. In proportion as monopoly prices become fixed, even temporarily, so the stimulus to technical, and consequently to all other progress, to advance, tends to disappear ; and to that extent also the *economic* possibility arises of artificially retarding technical progress. For instance, in America a certain Owens invented a machine which revolutionised the manufacture of bottles. The German bottle-manufacturing cartel purchased Owens's patents, but pigeon-holed them and held up their practical application. Certainly, monopoly under capitalism can never completely, and for any length of time, eliminate competition on the world market (and this is one of the reasons why the theory of ultra-imperialism is absurd). Of course, the possibility of reducing cost of production and increasing profits by introducing technical improvements is an influence in the direction of change.

Nevertheless, the *tendency* towards stagnation and decay, inherent in monopoly, continues in turn to operate in individual branches of industry ; in individual countries, for certain periods of time, it gains the upper hand.

The monopoly of ownership of very extensive, rich or well-situated colonies, works in the same direction.

Moreover, imperialism is an immense accumulation of money capital in a few countries, which, as we have seen, amounts to 100 or 150 billion francs in securities. Hence the extraordinary growth of a class, or rather of a stratum, of *rentiers*, i.e., persons who live by "clipping coupons," who take absolutely no part in any enterprise, and whose profession is idleness. The exportation of capital, one of the most essential economic bases of imperialism, still further isolates this rentier stratum from production and sets the seal of parasitism on the whole country living on the exploitation of the labour of several overseas countries and colonies.

> In 1893—writes Hobson—the British capital invested abroad represented about 15 per cent of the total wealth of the United Kingdom.

Let us remember that by 1915 this capital had increased about two and a half times.

> Aggressive imperialism—says Hobson further on—which costs the tax-payer so dear, which is of so little value to the manufacturer and trader . . . is a source of great gain to the investor. . . . The annual income Great Britain derives from commissions on her whole foreign and colonial trade, import and export, is estimated by Sir R. Giffen [the statistician] at £18,000,000 for 1899, taken at 2½ per cent, upon a turnover of £800,000,000.

Considerable as this sum is, it cannot entirely explain the aggressive imperialism of Great Britain. This is explained by the 90 to 100 million pounds revenue from " invested " capital, the income of the rentier class.

The income of the rentiers is *five times* as great as the revenue obtained from the foreign trade of the greatest

" trading " country in the world ! This is the essence of imperialism and imperialist parasitism.

For this reason the term " rentier state " (*Rentnerstaat*) or usurer state is coming into general use in the economic literature on imperialism. The world has become divided into a handful of usurer states and a vast majority of debtor states.

> The premier place among foreign investments—says Schulze-Gaevernitz—is taken by those invested in politically dependent, or closely allied countries. England makes loans to Egypt, Japan, China, South America. Her war fleet plays the part of sheriff in case of necessity. England's political power protects her from the anger of her debtors. . . .

Sartorius von Waltershausen in his work, *The National Economic System of Foreign Capital Investments*, cites Holland as the model rentier state, and points out that England and France are now becoming such. Schilder believes that five industrial nations are " definitely avowed creditor nations " : England, France, Germany, Belgium and Switzerland. Holland does not appear on this list simply because it is " less industrialised." The United States is the creditor only of other American countries.

> England—writes Schulze-Gaevernitz—is gradually being transformed from an industrial state into a creditor state. Notwithstanding the absolute increase in industrial production and exports, the relative importance of revenue from interest and dividends, profits from issues, commissions and speculation is on the increase, when the whole national economy is taken into account. In my opinion it is this fact which is at the economic base of imperialist expansion. The creditor is more firmly tied to the debtor than the seller is to the buyer.

In regard to Germany, A. Lansburgh, the editor of *Die Bank*, in 1911, in an article entitled, " Germany As A Rentier State," wrote the following :

> People in Germany like to sneer at the inclination observed in France for people to become rentiers. But they forget meanwhile

that, as far as the middle class is concerned, the situation in Germany is becoming more and more like that in France.

The rentier state is a state of parasitic decaying capitalism, and this circumstance cannot fail to be reflected in all the social-political conditions of the affected countries in general, and particularly in the two fundamental tendencies in the working-class movement. To demonstrate this as clearly as possible, we shall let Hobson speak—a most " reliable " witness, since he cannot be suspected of partiality for " orthodox Marxism " ; moreover, he is an Englishman who is very well acquainted with the situation in the country which is richest in colonies, in finance capital, and in imperialist experience.

With the Boer War fresh in his mind, Hobson describes the connection between imperialism and the interests of the financiers, their growing profits from armaments, supplies, etc., and writes as follows :

> While the directors of this definitely parasitic policy are capitalists, the same motives appeal to special classes of the workers. In many towns most important trades are dependent upon government employment or contracts ; the imperialism of the metal and shipbuilding centres is attributable in no small degree to this fact.

In this writer's opinion there are two circumstances which weakened the power of the ancient empires : (1) " economic parasitism " and (2) the formation of armies composed of subject peoples.

> There is first the habit of economic parasitism, by which the ruling state has used its provinces, colonies, and dependencies in order to enrich its ruling class and to bribe its lower classes into acquiescence.

And we would add that the economic possibility of such corruption, whatever its form may be, requires monopolistically high profits.

As for the second circumstance, Hobson writes :

One of the strangest symptoms of the blindness of imperialism is the reckless indifference with which Great Britain, France and other imperial nations are embarking on this perilous dependence. Great Britain has gone farthest. Most of the fighting by which we have won our Indian Empire has been done by natives ; in India, as more recently in Egypt, great standing armies are placed under British commanders ; almost all the fighting associated with our African dominions, except in the southern part, has been done for us by natives.

The prospect of a dismemberment of China evokes the following economic evaluation by Hobson :

The greater part of Western Europe might then assume the appearance and character already exhibited by tracts of country in the south of England, in the Riviera, and in the tourist-ridden or residential parts of Italy and Switzerland, little clusters of wealthy aristocrats drawing dividends and pensions from the Far East, with a somewhat larger group of professional retainers and tradesmen and a large body of personal servants and workers in the transport trade and in the final stages of production of the more perishable goods : all the main arterial industries would have disappeared, the staple foods and manufactures flowing in as tribute from Asia and Africa. . . .

We have foreshadowed the possibility of even a larger alliance of Western states, a European federation of great powers which, so far from forwarding the cause of world-civilisation, might introduce the gigantic peril of a Western parasitism, a group of advanced industrial nations, whose upper classes drew vast tribute from Asia and Africa, with which they support great tame masses of retainers, no longer engaged in the staple industries of agriculture and manufacture, but kept in the performance of personal or minor industrial services under the control of a new financial aristocracy. Let those who would scout such a theory as undeserving of consideration examine the economic and social condition of districts in Southern England to-day which are already reduced to this condition, and reflect upon the vast extension of such a system which might be rendered feasible by the subjection of China to the economic control of similar groups of financiers, investors, and political and business officials, draining the greatest potential reservoir of profit the world has ever known, in order to consume it in Europe. The situation is far too complex, the play of world-forces far too incalculable, to render this or any other single interpretation of the future very probable ; but the influences which govern the imperialism of Western Europe to-day are moving in this direction, and, unless counteracted or diverted, make towards some such consummation.

Hobson is quite right. If the forces of imperialism were not counteracted they would lead to just that. He correctly appraises the significance of a " United States of Europe," in the present, imperialist stage. But it must be added that *even within* the labour movement, the opportunists, who for the moment have been victorious in most countries, are " working " systematically and undeviatingly in this very direction. Imperialism, which means the partition of the world and the exploitation not of China alone ; which means monopolistically high profits for a handful of very rich countries, creates the economic possibility of corrupting the upper strata of the proletariat, and thereby fosters, gives form to and strengthens opportunism. However, we must not lose sight of the forces which counteract imperialism generally and opportunism in particular, which, naturally, the social-liberal Hobson does not see.

The German opportunist, Gerhard Hilderbrand, who at one time was expelled from the party for defending imperialism, but would to-day make a good leader of the so-called " Social-Democratic " Party of Germany, serves as a good supplement to Hobson by his advocacy of a " United States of Western Europe " (without Russia) for the purpose of " joint " action against . . . the African Negroes, the " great Islamic movement " ; for the " maintenance of a powerful army and navy " against a " Sino-Japanese coalition," etc.

The description of " British imperialism " in Schulze-Gaevernitz's book reveals the same parasitical traits. The national income of Great Britain approximately doubled between 1865 and 1898, while the income " from abroad " increased *ninefold* in the same period. While the " merit " of imperialism is that it " trains the Negro to work " (not without coercion, of course . . .), the "danger" of imperialism is that Europe will shift the burden of physical toil—first agricultural and mining, then heavy industrial labour—on to the coloured peoples, and itself be content with the rôle of rentier, and in this way, perhaps, pave the way for the economic and, later, the political emancipation of the coloured races.

An increasing proportion of land in Great Britain is being taken out of cultivation and used for sport, for the diversion of the rich. It is said of Scotland—the most aristocratic place for hunting and other sport—that it " lives on its past and Mr. Carnegie " (an American billionaire). Britain annually spends £14,000,000 on horse-racing and fox-hunting alone. The number of rentiers in Great Britain is about a million. The percentage of producers among the population is becoming smaller.

Year	Population of England and Wales (in millions)	No. of workers employed in basic industries (in millions)	Per cent of the population
1851 . .	17·9	4·1	23
1901 . .	32·5	5·0	15

And, in speaking of the British working class, the bourgeois student of " British imperialism at the beginning of the twentieth century " is obliged to distinguish systematically between the " *upper stratum* " and the " *lower proletarian stratum proper.*" The upper stratum furnishes the main body of co-operators, of trade unionists, of members of sporting clubs and of numerous religious sects. The right to vote, which in Great Britain is still " *sufficiently restricted to exclude the lower proletarian stratum proper,*" is adapted to their level ! In order to present the condition of the British working class in the best light, only this upper stratum—which constitutes only a *minority* of the proletarian—is generally spoken of. For instance : " The problem of unemployment is mainly a London problem and that of the lower proletarian stratum, *with whom politicians are little concerned.* . . ." It would be better to say : with whom the bourgeois politicians and the " Socialist " opportunists are little concerned.

Another one of the peculiarities of imperialism connected with the facts that we are describing, is the decline in emigration from imperialist countries, and the increase in immigration (influx of workers and transmigration) to these countries from the more backward countries, where wages are lower. As Hobson observes, emigration from Great Britain has been declining since 1884. In that year the number of emigrants was 242,000, while in 1900 the number was 169,000. German emigration reached its highest point in the decade 1881–1890 with a total of 1,453,000 emigrants. In the following two decades it fell to 554,000 and 341,000. On the other hand there was an increase in the number of workers entering Germany, from Austria, Italy, Russia and other countries. According to the 1907 census, there were 1,342,294 foreigners in Germany, of whom 440,800 were industrial workers and 257,329 were agricultural workers. In France, the workers employed in the mining industry are " in great part " foreigners : Polish, Italian and Spanish. In the United States, immigrants from Eastern and Southern Europe are engaged in the most poorly paid occupations, while American workers provide the highest percentage of foremen and of the better-paid workers. Imperialism has the tendency to create privileged sections even among the workers, and to separate them from the main proletarian masses.

It must be observed that in Great Britain the tendency of imperialism to split the workers, to strengthen opportunism among them, and cause temporary decay in the working-class movement, revealed itself much earlier than the end of the nineteenth and beginning of the twentieth centuries ; for two important distinguishing features of imperialism were observed in Great Britain in the middle of the nineteenth century, viz., vast colonial possessions and a monopolist position in world markets. For several decades Marx and Engels systematically traced this connection between opportunism in the labour movement and the imperialist features of British capitalism. For example, on October 7, 1858, Engels wrote to Marx :

> . . . the British working class is actually becoming more and more bourgeois, and it seems that this most bourgeois of all nations wants to bring matters to such a pass as to have a bourgeois aristocracy and a bourgeois proletariat *side by side* with the bourgeoisie. Of course this is to some extent justifiable for a nation which is exploiting the whole world.

Almost a quarter of a century later, in a letter dated August 11, 1881, Engels speaks of the " very worst English . . . [trade unions.—*Ed.*] which allow themselves to be led by men sold to, or at least paid by the middle class." In a letter to Kautsky, dated September 12, 1882, Engels wrote :

> You ask me what the English workers think of the colonial policy ? The same as they think about politics in general. There is no labour party here, there are only conservatives and liberal radicals, and the workers enjoy with them the fruits of the British world market and colonial monopoly. [Engels sets forth the same ideas in his preface to the second edition of *The Condition of the Working Class in England*, published in 1892.]

Here causes and effects are clearly shown. Causes : (1) exploitation of the whole world by this country ; (2) its monopolistic position in the world market ; (3) its colonial monopoly. Effects : (1) bourgeoisification of a part of the British proletariat ; (2) a part of the proletariat permits itself to be led by people who are bought by the bourgeoisie, or who at least are paid by it. The imperialism of the beginning of the twentieth century completed the partition of the world by a very few states, each of which to-day exploits (in the sense of drawing super-profits from) a part of the world only a little smaller than that which England exploited in 1858. Each of them, by means of trusts, cartels, finance capital, and the relations between debtor and creditor, occupies a monopoly position on the world market.

Each of them enjoys to some degree a colonial monopoly. (We have seen that out of 75 million square kilometres of *total* colonial area in the world, 65 million, or 86 per cent, is concentrated in the hands of six powers ; 61 million, or 81 per cent, belongs to three powers.)

The distinctive feature of the present situation is the prevalence of economic and political conditions which could not but intensify the irreconcilability between opportunism and the general and basic interests of the labour movement. Imperialism has grown from an embryo into a dominant system ; capitalist monopolies occupy first place in national economics and politics ; the partition of the world has been completed. On the other hand, instead of an undivided monopoly by Britain, we see a few imperialist powers fighting among themselves for the right to share in this monopoly, and this struggle is characteristic of the whole period of the beginning of the twentieth century.

Opportunism cannot now triumph completely in the labour movement of any country for many decades as it did in England in the second half of the nineteenth century, but in several countries it has finally grown ripe, over-ripe and rotten, and has become completely merged with bourgeois policy as " social-chauvinism."

CRITIQUE OF IMPERIALISM

(Ch. IX)

By the critique of imperialism, in the broad sense of the term, we mean the attitude of the different classes of society towards imperialist policy in connection with their general ideology.

The enormous dimensions of finance capital concentrated in a few hands and creating an extremely extensive and close network of ties and relationships, which subordinates to itself not only the bulk of the medium and small, but even very smallest capitalists and petty owners, on the one hand,

and an intense struggle waged against other national-state groups of financiers for the partition of the world and domination over other countries, on the other hand—cause the possessing classes to go over as one to the side of imperialism. The signs of the times are a " general " enthusiasm regarding its prospects, a passionate defence of imperialism, and every possible camouflage of its real nature. The imperialist ideology is also permeating the working class. There is no Chinese Wall between it and the other classes. The leaders of the present so-called " Social-Democratic " Party of Germany are justly called social-imperialists ; that is, Socialists in words and imperialists in deeds ; and as early as 1902, Hobson noted the existence of " Fabian imperialists " in England who belonged to the opportunist " Fabian Society."

The bourgeois scholars and publicists usually present their defence of imperialism in a somewhat veiled form, obscure the fact that it is in complete domination, and conceal its deep roots ; they strive to concentrate attention on special aspects and characteristics of secondary importance, and do their utmost to distract attention from the main issue by advancing absolutely ridiculous schemes for " reform," such as police supervision of the trusts or banks, etc. Less frequently, cynical and frank imperialists speak out and are bold enough to admit the absurdity of the idea of " reforming " the fundamental features of imperialism.

We will give an example. The German imperialists attempt, in the *Archives of World Economy*, to trace the movements for national emancipation in the colonies, particularly, of course, in colonies other than German. They note the ferment and protest movements in India ; the movement in Natal (South Africa), in the Dutch East Indies, etc. One of them, commenting on an English report of the speeches delivered at a conference of subject peoples and races, held on June 28–30, 1910, consisting of representatives of various peoples under foreign domination in Africa, Asia and Europe, writes as follows :

We are told that we must fight against imperialism ; that the dominant states must recognise the right of subjugated peoples to self-government ; that an international tribunal should supervise the fulfilment of treaties concluded between the great powers and the weaker peoples. Beyond the expression of these pious hopes the conference does not go. We see no trace of a realisation of the fact that imperialism is indissolubly bound up with capitalism in its present form and that therefore (! !) it is hopeless to fight directly against imperialism, except perhaps if the fight is confined to protests against certain of its most hateful excesses.

Since reforming the bases of imperialism is an illusion, a " pious hope," since the bourgeois representatives of oppressed nations do not go " further," the bourgeois representatives of the oppressing nations do go " further," but backward, to servility to imperialism, concealed by a pretence to " science." " Logic," indeed !

The question as to whether it is possible to change the bases of imperialism by reforms, whether to go forward to a further aggravation and accentuation of the contradictions it engenders, or backwards towards allaying them, is a fundamental question in the critique of imperialism. The fact that the political characteristics of imperialism are reaction all along the line and increased national oppression, in connection with oppression by the financial oligarchy and the elimination of free competition, has given rise to a petty-bourgeois-democratic opposition to imperialism in almost all imperialist countries since the beginning of the twentieth century. And the break with Marxism made by Kautsky and the broad international Kautskyist tendency consists in the very fact that Kautsky not only did not trouble to, and did not know how to, take a stand against this petty-bourgeois reformist opposition, which is reactionary in its economic basis, but, on the contrary, in practice became identified with it.

In the United States, the imperialist war waged against Spain in 1898 gave rise to an " anti-imperialist " opposition by the last of the Mohicans of bourgeois democracy. They

declared this war " criminal " ; they denounced the
annexation of foreign territories as a violation of the Constitution, and decried the " jingo treachery " by means
of which Aguinaldo, leader of the native Filipinos, was
deceived (he was promised liberty for his country, but later
American troops were landed there and the Philippines
were annexed). They quoted the words of Lincoln :

> When the white man governs himself, that is self-government ;
> but when he governs himself and also governs another man,
> that is more than self-government—that is despotism.

But as long as all this criticism shrank from recognising
the indissoluble bond between imperialism and the trusts,
and, therefore, between imperialism and the foundations
of capitalism ; as long as it shrank from aligning itself with
the forces being engendered by large-scale capitalism and
its development, it remained a " pious hope."

This also, in the main, is the position of Hobson in his
criticism of imperialism. Hobson anticipated Kautsky in
protesting against the " inevitability of imperialism," and
in making an appeal showing the need to " raise the consuming capacity " of the people (under capitalism !). The
petty-bourgeois point of view in the critique of imperialism,
the omnipotence of the banks, the financial oligarchy, etc.,
is that adopted by authors whom we have repeatedly
quoted, such as Agahd, Lansburgh, L. Eschwege, and,
among French writers, Victor Bérard, author of a superficial book entitled *England and Imperialism*, which appeared
in 1900. All of these, who make no claim whatever to being
Marxists, contrast imperialism with free competition and
democracy ; they condemn the Bagdad railway adventure
as leading to disputes and war, utter " pious hopes " for
peace, etc., including the compiler of international stock
issue statistics, A. Neymarck, who, after calculating the
hundreds of billions of francs of " international " securities,
exclaimed in 1912 :

> Is it possible to believe that peace can be disturbed ? . . . that, in the face of these enormous figures . . . any one would risk starting a war ?

Such simplicity of mind on the part of bourgeois economists is not surprising. Besides, *it is in their interest* to pretend to be so naïve and to talk " seriously " about peace under imperialism. But what remains of Kautsky's Marxism when, in 1914-1915-1916, he takes the same bourgeois-reformist point of view and affirms that " we are all agreed " (imperialists, pseudo-Socialists, and social-pacifists) with regard to peace ? Instead of an analysis of imperialism and an exposure of the depths of its contradictions, we have nothing but a reformist " pious hope " of side-stepping and evading them.

Here is an example of Kautsky's economic critique of imperialism. He takes the statistics of British export and import trade with Egypt for 1872 and 1912. These statistics show that this import and export trade has grown more slowly than British exports and imports as a whole. From this, Kautsky concludes :

> We have no reason to suppose that British trade with Egypt would have developed less, as a result of the operation of economic factors alone, without the military occupation of Egypt. . . . The efforts of present-day states to expand can best be satisfied not by the violent methods of imperialism, but by peaceful democracy.

This argument of Kautsky's which is repeated in every key by his Russian armour-bearer (and Russian sponsor of social-chauvinists) Mr. Spectator, constitutes the basis of Kautsky's critique of imperialism, and that is why we must deal with it in greater detail. We shall begin with a quotation from Hilferding, whose conclusions Kautsky, on many occasions, including April 1915, declared, " have been unanimously accepted by all Socialist theoreticians."

... It is not the business of the proletariat—wrote Hilferding—to contrast the more progressive capitalist policy with the policy, now overcome, of the era of free trade and of hostility towards the state. The reply of the proletariat to the economic policy of finance capital, to imperialism, cannot be free trade, but Socialism alone. The aim of proletarian policy cannot now be the idea of restoring free competition—now become a reactionary ideal—but only the complete abolition of competition by the abolition of capitalism.

Kautsky broke with Marxism by advocating what is, in the period of finance capital, a " reactionary ideal," " peaceful democracy," " the simple weight of economic factors " ; for, *objectively*, this ideal drags us back from monopoly to non-monopoly capitalism, and is a reformist swindle.

Trade with Egypt (or with any other colony or semi-colony) " would have developed better " *without* military occupation, without imperialism, without finance capital. What does this mean ? That capitalism would develop more rapidly if free competition were not restricted by monopolies in general, nor by the " ties " nor the yoke (i.e., again the monopoly), of finance capital, nor by the monopolist possession of colonies by individual countries ?

Kautsky's arguments can have no other sense ; and *this* " sense " is nonsense. But suppose that it is so, that free competition, without any sort of monopoly, *would* develop capitalism and trade more rapidly, is it not a fact that the more rapidly capitalism and trade develop, the greater is the concentration of production and capital which *gives rise* to monopoly ? And monopolies have *already* come into being—precisely *out of* free competition ! Even if monopolies have now begun to retard progress, this is not an argument in favour of free competition, which became impossible after it gave birth to monopolies.

However one may twist Kautsky's argument, there is nothing in it but reaction and bourgeois reformism. Even if we correct this argument and say, as Spectator says, that

the trade of the British colonies with Britain is now developing more slowly than their trade with other countries, that
likewise does not save Kautsky ; for Britain *also* is being
beaten by monopoly, by imperialism, only by that of other
countries (America, Germany). It is well known that the
cartels have given rise to a new and original form of protective tariffs—goods suitable for export are protected
(Engels noted this in Volume III of *Capital*). It is well
known, too, that the cartels and finance capital have a
system peculiar to themselves of exporting goods at "dumping prices," or " dumping," as the English call it : within
the country the cartel sells its products at a monopolistically
high price ; abroad it disposes of them at a fraction of this
price to undermine a competitor, to increase its own production to the maximum, etc. If German trade with the
British colonies is developing more rapidly than that of
Britain, it only proves that German imperialism is younger,
stronger, better organised, and more highly developed than
the British, but this by no means proves the " superiority "
of free trade, for it is not free trade fighting against protection and colonial dependence, but one imperialism fighting
another, one monopoly against another, one finance capital
against another. The superiority of German imperialism
over British imperialism is stronger than the wall of colonial
frontiers or of protective tariffs. To derive from this any
" argument " *in favour* of free trade and " peaceful democracy " is insipidity, it is to vulgarise the essential features
and qualities of imperialism, to substitute petty-bourgeois
reformism for Marxism. . . .

Kautsky's theoretical critique of imperialism has therefore nothing in common with Marxism and serves no purpose other than as a preamble to propaganda for peace and
unity with the opportunists and the social-chauvinists, for
the very reason that this critique evades and obscures
precisely the most profound and basic contradictions of
imperialism : the contradictions of monopolies existing side
by side with free competition ; the contradictions between

the immense " operations " (and immense profits) of finance capital and " fair " trade on the open market ; between combines and trusts on the one hand and non-trustified industry on the other, etc.

The notorious theory of " ultra-imperialism," invented by Kautsky, is equally reactionary. Compare his arguments on this subject in 1915 with Hobson's arguments of 1902. Kautsky writes :

. . . whether it is possible that the present imperialist policy might be supplanted by a new ultra-imperialist policy, which would introduce the joint exploitation of the world by an internationally combined finance capital in place of the mutual rivalries of national finance capitals ? Such a new phase of capitalism is at any rate conceivable. Is it realisable ? Sufficient evidence is not yet available to enable us to answer this question.

Hobson writes :

Christendom thus laid out in a few great federal empires, each with a retinue of uncivilised dependencies, seems to many the most legitimate development of present tendencies, and one which would offer the best hope of permanent peace on an assured basis of inter-imperialism.

Kautsky called ultra-imperialism or super-imperialism what Hobson thirteen years before had called inter-imperialism. Except for coining a new and clever word by replacing one Latin prefix by another, Kautsky's progress in " scientific " thought consists only in his temerity at labelling as Marxism what Hobson in effect described as the cant of English parsons. After the Boer War it was quite natural that this most worthy caste should exert its main effort to *console* the British petty-bourgeoisie and the workers, who had lost many of their relatives on the battle-fields of South Africa and who were paying higher taxes in order to guarantee still higher profits for the British financiers. And what better consolation could there be than the theory that imperialism is not so bad, that it stands close to inter- (or ultra-) imperialism, which can assure permanent peace ? No matter what the good intentions of the British clergy or of the sugary Kautsky may have been, the objective, that is, the real social significance of his " theory," is this and this alone : a most reactionary consolation of the masses by holding out hopes for a possible permanent peace under capitalism, by distracting their attention from the sharp antagonisms and acute problems of the present and directing their attention to illusory perspectives of some sort of new " ultra-imperialism " of the future. Other than delusion of the masses, there is nothing in Kautsky's " Marxian " theory.

Indeed, it is enough to keep clearly in mind well-known and indisputable facts to become convinced of the complete falsity of the perspectives which Kautsky is trying to hold out to the German workers (and the workers of all countries). Let us take India, Indo-China and China. It is well known that these three colonial and semi-colonial countries, inhabited by six or seven hundred million human beings, are subjected to the exploitation of the finance capital of several imperialist powers : Great Britain, France, Japan, the United States, etc. Let us assume that these imperialist countries form alliances against one another in order to protect and extend their possessions, interests, and " spheres of influence " in these Asiatic states ; these will be " inter-imperialist," or " ultra-imperialist " alliances. Let us assume that *all* the imperialist powers conclude an alliance for the " peaceful " partition of these Asiatic countries ; this alliance would be " internationally united finance capital." Actual examples of such an alliance may be seen in the history of the twentieth century, for instance, in the relations of the powers with China. We ask, is it " conceivable," assuming that the capitalist system remains intact (and this is precisely the assumption that Kautsky does make), that such alliances would not be short-lived, that they would preclude friction, conflicts and struggles in any and every possible form ?

It suffices to state this question clearly to make any other reply than a negative one impossible ; for there can be *no other* conceivable basis, under capitalism, for partition of spheres of influence, of interests, of colonies, etc., than a calculation of the *strength* of the participants, their general economic, financial, military and other strength. Now, the relative strength of these participants is not changing uniformly, for under capitalism there cannot be an *equal* development of different undertakings, trusts, branches of industry or countries. Half a century ago, Germany was a pitiable nonentity as compared with Britain so far as capitalist strength was concerned. The same with Japan as compared with Russia. Is it " conceivable " that in ten or twenty years' time the relative strength of the imperialist powers will have remained *un*changed ? Absolutely inconceivable.

Therefore, " inter-imperialist " or " ultra-imperialist " alliances, in the realities of capitalism and not in the petty-bourgeois phantasies of English clergymen or the German " Marxist " Kautsky, no matter in what form these alliances be concluded, whether of one imperialist coalition against another or of a general alliance of *all* the imperialist powers, *inevitably* can be only " breathing spells " between wars. Peaceful alliances prepare the ground for wars and in their turn grow out of wars. One is the condition of the other, giving rise to alternating forms of peaceful and non-peaceful struggle *on one and the same* basis, that of imperialist connections and inter-relations of world economics and world politics. But the sage Kautsky, in order to pacify the workers and to reconcile them with the social-chauvinists who have deserted to the side of the bourgeoisie, *breaks* one link of a whole chain from the others, separates to-day's peaceful (and ultra-imperialist, nay ultra-ultra-imperialist) alliance of *all* the powers for the " pacification " of China (remember the suppression of the Boxer Rebellion) from the non-peaceful conflict of to-morrow, which will prepare the ground for another " peaceful " general alliance for the partition, say, of Turkey, on the day after to-morrow, etc.,

etc. Instead of showing the vital connection between periods of imperialist peace and periods of imperialist wars, Kautsky puts before the workers a lifeless abstraction solely in order to reconcile them to their lifeless leaders.

An American writer, Hill, in his *History of Diplomacy in the International Development of Europe,* points out in his preface the following periods of modern diplomatic history : (1) the revolutionary period ; (2) the constitutional movement ; (3) the present period of " commercial imperialism."

Another writer divides the history of Great Britain's " foreign policy " since 1870 into four periods : (1) the Asiatic period : struggle against Russia's advance in Central Asia towards India ; (2) the African period (approximately 1885–1902) : struggles against France over the partition of Africa (the Fashoda affair, 1898, a hair's-breadth from a war with France) ; (3) the second Asiatic period (treaty with Japan against Russia) ; and (4) the " European " period, chiefly directed against Germany.

" The political skirmishes of outposts are fought on the financial field," wrote Riesser, the banker, in 1905, showing how French finance capital operating in Italy was preparing the way for a political alliance between the two countries, how a struggle was developing between Germany and Britain over Persia, a struggle among all the European capitalists over Chinese loans, etc. Behold, the living reality of peaceful " ultra-imperialist " alliances in their indissoluble connection with ordinary imperialist conflicts !

The glossing over of the deepest contradictions of imperialism by Kautsky, which inevitably becomes a decking-out of imperialism, leaves its traces also in this writer's critique of the political features of imperialism. Imperialism is the epoch of finance capital and of monopolies which introduce everywhere the striving for domination, not for freedom. The result of these tendencies is reaction all along the line, whatever the political system, and extreme intensification of antagonisms in this domain also. Particularly acute also becomes national oppression and the striving

for annexation, i.e., the violation of national independence
(for annexation is nothing else than a violation of the right
of nations to self-determination). Hilferding justly draws
attention to the relation between imperialism and the
intensification of national oppression.

> But in the newly opened-up countries—he writes—the im-
> ported capital intensifies antagonisms and excites the constantly
> growing resistance of the people, who are awakened to national
> consciousness against the intruders. This resistance can easily
> become transformed into dangerous measures directed against
> foreign capital. Former social relations become completely
> revolutionised. The agrarian fetters that for a thousand years
> have bound the " nations beyond the pale of history " are
> broken, and they themselves are drawn into the capitalist
> whirlpool. Capitalism itself gradually provides the vanquished
> with the ways and means for their emancipation. And they set
> out to achieve that goal which once was the highest for the
> European nations : the construction of a national united state
> as a means to economic and cultural freedom. This movement
> for independence threatens European capital precisely in its
> most valuable and most promising fields of exploitation, and
> European capital can maintain its denomination only by con-
> stantly increasing its military forces.

To this must be added that it is not only in newly
opened-up countries, but also in the old ones, that imperialism is leading to annexation, to increased national
oppression, and, consequently, also to more stubborn resistance. While objecting to the growth of political reaction
caused by imperialism, Kautsky leaves in the dark a question which has become very urgent, that of the impossibility of unity with the opportunists in the epoch of imperialism. While objecting to annexations, he presents his
objections in such a form as will be most acceptable and
least offensive to the opportunists. He addresses himself
directly to a German audience, yet he obscures the most
timely and important points, for instance, that Alsace-
Lorraine is an annexation by Germany. In order to appraise
this " mental aberration " of Kautsky's, we shall take the

following example. Let us suppose that a Japanese is condemning the annexation of the Philippine Islands by the Americans. Are there many who will believe that he is protesting because he abhors annexations in general, and not because he himself has a desire to annex the Philippines ? And shall we not be constrained to admit that the " fight " the Japanese is waging against annexations can be regarded as sincere and politically honest only if he fights against the annexation of Korea by Japan, and demands for Korea freedom of separation from Japan ?

Kautsky's theoretical analysis of imperialism and his economic and political critique of imperialism are permeated *through and through* with a spirit absolutely irreconcilable with Marxism, a spirit that obscures and glosses over the most basic contradictions of imperialism, and strives to preserve at all costs the crumbling unity with opportunism in the European labour movement.

V. I. Lenin

THE STATE AND REVOLUTION

First published early 1918. English edition, Martin Lawrence Ltd., 1934.

[In the preface which he wrote in August 1917, Lenin observed that " the question of the State is acquiring at present a particular importance, both as theory, and from the point of view of practical politics." This was when Lenin was in Finland, after the July rising in Petrograd, and less than three months before the November revolution. *The State and Revolution* is the most comprehensive study of revolutionary theory in relation to the State, both capitalist and proletarian. It is one of the most essential works of Marxism ; it explains the whole development of the revolution in Russia, the dictatorship of the proletariat, the building up of the productive forces and the stages towards classless society—all in advance of events, on the basis of the analysis made by Marx and Engels of the theory of the State and the experience of previous revolutions. It has only been possible to reprint chapters I and V. The titles of the other chapters are : II. The Experiences of 1848–51 ; III. Experience of the Paris Commune of 1871 ; IV. Supplementary Explanations by Engels ; and VI. Vulgarisation of Marx by the Opportunists. Lenin originally intended to write a seventh chapter : Experience of the Russian Revolutions of 1905 and 1917 (i.e., March 1917). But, as he says in a postscript, dated December 13, 1917, to the first edition : " Outside of the title, I did not succeed in writing a single line of the chapter ; what ' interfered ' was the political crisis—the eve of the October revolution of 1917. . . . It is more pleasant and useful to go through the ' experience of the revolution ' than to write about it." This final chapter was never written.]

THE STATE AND REVOLUTION

CLASS SOCIETY AND THE STATE
(Ch. I)

1. The State as the Product of the Irreconcilability of Class Antagonisms

WHAT IS NOW HAPPENING to Marx's doctrine has, in the course of history, often happened to the doctrines of other revolutionary thinkers and leaders of oppressed classes struggling for emancipation. During the lifetime of great revolutionaries, the oppressing classes have visited

relentless persecution on them and received their teaching
with the most savage hostility, the most furious hatred, the
most ruthless campaign of lies and slanders. After their
death, attempts are made to turn them into harmless icons,
canonise them, and surround their *names* with a certain halo
for the " consolation " of the oppressed classes and with
the object of duping them, while at the same time emascu-
lating and vulgarising the *real essence* of their revolutionary
theories and blunting their revolutionary edge. At the
present time, the bourgeoisie and the opportunists within
the labour movement are co-operating in this work of
adulterating Marxism. They omit, obliterate, and distort
the revolutionary side of its teaching, its revolutionary
soul. They push to the foreground and extol what is, or
seems, acceptable to the bourgeoisie. All the social-
chauvinists are now " Marxists "—joking aside ! And more
and more do German bourgeois professors, erstwhile
specialists in the demolition of Marx, speak now of the
" national-German " Marx, who, they aver, has educated
the labour unions which are so splendidly organised for
conducting the present predatory war !

In such circumstances, the distortion of Marxism being
so widespread, it is our first task to *resuscitate* the real
teachings of Marx on the State. For this purpose it will be
necessary to quote at length from the works of Marx and
Engels themselves. Of course, long quotations will make
the text cumbersome and in no way help to make it popular
reading, but we cannot possibly avoid them. All, or at any
rate, all the most essential passages in the works of Marx
and Engels on the subject of the State must necessarily
be given as fully as possible, in order that the reader may
form an independent opinion of all the views of the founders
of scientific Socialism and of the development of those views
and in order that their distortions by the present predominant " Kautskyism " may be proved in black and
white and rendered plain to all.

Let us begin with the most popular of Engels' works,

Der Ursprung der Familie, des Privateigentums und des Staats,
the sixth edition of which was published in Stuttgart as
far back as 1894. We must translate the quotations from
the German originals, as the Russian translations, although
very numerous, are for the most part either incomplete
or very unsatisfactory.

Summarising his historical analysis Engels says :

> The State is therefore by no means a power imposed on
> society from the outside ; just as little is it " the reality of the
> moral idea," " the image and reality of reason," as Hegel
> asserted. Rather, it is a product of society at a certain stage
> of development ; it is the admission that this society has become
> entangled in an insoluble contradiction with itself, that it is
> cleft into irreconcilable antagonisms which it is powerless to
> dispel. But in order that these antagonisms, classes with con-
> flicting economic interests, may not consume themselves and
> society in sterile struggle, a power apparently standing above
> society becomes necessary, whose purpose is to moderate the
> conflict and keep it within the bounds of " order " ; and this
> power arising out of society, but placing itself above it, and
> increasingly separating itself from it, is the State.

Here we have, expressed in all its clearness, the basic
idea of Marxism on the question of the historical rôle and
meaning of the State. The State is the product and the
manifestation of the *irreconcilability* of class antagonisms.
The State arises when, where, and to the extent that the
class antagonisms *cannot* be objectively reconciled. And,
conversely, the existence of the State proves that the class
antagonisms *are* irreconcilable.

It is precisely on this most important and fundamental
point that distortions of Marxisms arise along two main
lines.

On the one hand, the bourgeois, and particularly the
petty-bourgeois, idealogists, compelled under the pressure
of indisputable historical facts to admit that the State only
exists where there are class antagonisms and the class
struggle, " correct " Marx in such a way as to make it
appear that the State is an organ for *reconciling* the classes.

According to Marx, the State could neither arise nor maintain itself if a reconciliation of classes were possible. But with the petty-bourgeois and philistine professors and publicists, the State—and this frequently on the strength of benevolent references to Marx !—becomes a conciliator of the classes. According to Marx, the State is an organ of class *domination*, an organ of *oppression* of one class by another ; its aim is the creation of " order " which legalises and perpetuates this oppression by moderating the collisions between the classes. But in the opinion of the petty-bourgeois politicians, order means reconciliation of the classes, and not oppression of one class by another ; to moderate collisions does not mean, they say, to deprive the oppressed classes of certain definite means and methods of struggle for overthrowing the oppressors, but to practise reconciliation.

For instance, when, in the Revolution of 1917, the question of the real meaning and rôle of the State arose in all its vastness as a practical question demanding immediate action on a wide mass scale, all the Socialist-Revolutionaries and Mensheviks suddenly and completely sank to the petty-bourgeois theory of " reconciliation " of the classes by the " State." Innumerable resolutions and articles by politicians of both these parties are saturated through and through with this purely petty-bourgeois and philistine theory of " reconciliation." That the State is an organ of domination of a definite class which *cannot* be reconciled with its antipode (the class opposed to it)—this petty-bourgois democracy is never able to understand. Its attitude towards the State is one of the most telling proofs that our Socialist-Revolutionaries and Mensheviks are not Socialists at all (which we Bolsheviks have always maintained), but petty-bourgeois democrats with a near-Socialist phraseology.

On the other hand, the " Kautskyist " distortion of Marx is far more subtle. " Theoretically," there is no denying that the State is the organ of class domination, or that class antagonisms are irreconcilable. But what is forgotten or glossed over is this : if the State is the product of the irreconcilable character of class antagonisms, if it is a force standing *above* society and " increasingly separating itself from it," then it is clear that the liberation of the oppressed class is impossible not only without a violent revolution, *but also without the destruction* of the apparatus of State power, which was created by the ruling class and in which this " separation " is embodied. As we shall see later Marx drew his theoretically self-evident conclusion from a concrete historical analysis of the problems of revolution. And it is exactly this conclusion which Kautsky —as we shall show fully in our subsequent remarks—has " forgotten " and distorted.

2. Special Bodies of Armed Men, Prisons, Etc.

Engels continues :

> In contrast with the ancient organisation of the *gens*, the first distinguishing characteristic of the State is the grouping of the subjects of the State *on a territorial basis*. . . .

Such a grouping seems " natural " to us, but it came after a prolonged and costly struggle against the old form of tribal or gentilic society.

> . . . The second is the establishment of a *public force*, which is no longer absolutely identical with the population organising itself as an armed power. This special public force is necessary, because a self-acting armed organisation of the population has become impossible since the cleavage of society into classes. . . . This public force exists in every State ; it consists not merely of armed men, but of material appendages, prisons and repressive institutions of all kinds, of which gentilic society knew nothing. . . .

Engels develops the conception of that "power" which is termed the State—a power arising from society, but placing itself above it and becoming more and more separated from it. What does this power mainly consist of? It consists of special bodies of armed men who have at their disposal prisons, etc.

We are justified in speaking of special bodies of armed men, because the public power peculiar to every State is not " absolutely identical " with the armed population, with its " self-acting armed organisation."

Like all the great revolutionary thinkers, Engels tries to draw the attention of the class-conscious workers to that very fact which to prevailing philistinism appears least of all worthy of attention, most common and sanctified by solid, indeed, one might say, petrified prejudices. A standing army and police are the chief instruments of State power. But can this be otherwise?

From the point of view of the vast majority of Europeans at the end of the nineteenth century whom Engels was addressing, and who had neither lived through nor closely observed a single great revolution, this cannot be otherwise. They cannot understand at all what this " self-acting armed organisation of the population " means. To the question, whence arose the need for special bodies of armed men, standing above society and becoming separated from it (police and standing army), the Western European and Russian philistines are inclined to answer with a few phrases borrowed from Spencer or Mikhailovsky, by reference to the complexity of social life, the differentiation of functions, and so forth.

Such a reference seems " scientific " and effectively dulls the senses of the average man, obscuring the most important and basic fact, namely, the break-up of society into irreconcilably antagonistic classes.

Without such a break-up, the " self-acting armed organisation of the population " might have differed from the primitive organisation of a herd of monkeys grasping sticks, or of primitive men, or men united in a tribal form of society, by its complexity, its high technique, and so forth, but would still have been possible.

It is impossible now, because society, in the period of civilisation, is broken up into antagonistic, and, indeed, irreconcilably antagonistic classes, which, if armed in a " self-acting " manner, would come into armed struggle with each other. A State is formed, a special power is created in the form of special bodies of armed men, and every revolution, by shattering the State apparatus, demonstrates to us how the ruling class aims at the restoration of the special bodies of armed men at *its* service, and how the oppressed class tries to create a new organisation of this kind, capable of serving not the exploiters, but the exploited.

In the above observation, Engels raises theoretically the very same question which every great revolution raises practically, palpably, and on a mass scale of action, namely, the question of the relation between special bodies of armed men and the " self-acting armed organisation of the population." We shall see how this is concretely illustrated by the experience of the European and Russian revolutions.

But let us return to Engels' discourse.

He points out that sometimes, for instance, here and there in North America, this public power is weak (he has in mind an exception that is rare in capitalist society, and he speaks about parts of North America in its pre-imperialist days, where the free colonist predominated), but that in general it tends to become stronger :

> It [the public power] grows stronger, however, in proportion as the class antagonisms within the State grow sharper, and with the growth in size and population of the adjacent States. We have only to look at our present-day Europe, where class struggle and rivalry in conquest have screwed up the public power to such a pitch that it threatens to devour the whole of society and even the State itself.

This was written as early as the beginning of the 'nineties of last century, Engels' last preface being dated June 16, 1891. The turn towards imperialism, understood to mean complete domination of the trusts, full sway of the large banks, and a colonial policy on a grand scale, and so forth, was only just beginning in France, and was even weaker in North America and in Germany. Since then the " rivalry in conquest " has made gigantic progress—especially as, by the beginning of the second decade of the twentieth century, the whole world had been finally divided up between these " rivals in conquest," i.e., between the great predatory powers. Military and naval armaments since then have grown to monstrous proportions, and the predatory war of 1914–1917 for the domination of the world by England or Germany, for the division of the spoils, has brought the " swallowing up " of all the forces of society by the rapacious State power nearer to a complete catastrophe.

As early as 1891 Engels was able to point to " rivalry in conquest " as one of the most important features of the foreign policy of the great powers, but in 1914–1917, when this rivalry, many times intensified, has given birth to an imperialist war, the rascally social-chauvinists cover up their defence of the predatory policy of " their " capitalist classes by phrases about the " defence of the fatherland," or the " defence of the republic and the revolution," etc. !

3. The State as an Instrument for the Exploitation of the Oppressed Class

For the maintenance of a special public force standing above society, taxes and State loans are needed.

> Having at their disposal the public force and the right to exact taxes, the officials now stand as organs of society *above* society. The free, voluntary respect which was accorded to the organs of the gentilic form of government does not satisfy them, even if they could have it. . . .

Special laws are enacted regarding the sanctity and the inviolability of the officials. " The shabbiest police servant . . . has more authority " than the representative of the clan, but even the head of the military power of a civilised State " may well envy the least among the chiefs of the clan the unconstrained and uncontested respect which is paid to him."

Here the question regarding the privileged position of the officials as organs of State power is clearly stated. The main point is indicated as follows : what is it that places them *above* society ? We shall see how this theoretical problem was solved in practice by the Paris Commune in 1871 and how it was slurred over in a reactionary manner by Kautsky in 1912 :

> As the State arose out of the need to hold class antagonisms in check, but as it, at the same time, arose in the midst of the conflict of these classes, it is, as a rule, the State of the most powerful, economically dominant class, which by virtue thereof becomes also the dominant class politically, and thus acquires new means of holding down and exploiting the oppressed class. . . .

Not only the ancient and feudal States were organs of exploitation of the slaves and serfs, but

> the modern representative State is the instrument of the exploitation of wage-labour by capital. By way of exception, however, there are periods when the warring classes so nearly attain equilibrium that the State power, ostensibly appearing as a mediator, assumes for the moment a certain independence in relation to both. . . .

Such were, for instance, the absolute monarchies of the seventeenth and eighteenth centuries, the Bonapartism of the First and Second Empires in France, and the Bismarck régime in Germany.

Such, we may add, is now the Kerensky government in republican Russia after its shift to persecuting the revolutionary proletariat, at a moment when the Soviets, thanks to the leadership of the petty-bourgeois democrats, have *already* become impotent, while the bourgeoisie is *not yet* strong enough to disperse them outright.

In a democratic republic, Engels continues, "wealth wields its power indirectly, but all the more effectively," first, by means of "direct corruption of the officials" (America); second, by means of "the alliance of the government with the stock exchange" (France and America).

At the present time, imperialism and the domination of the banks have "developed" to an unusually fine art both these methods of defending and asserting the omnipotence of wealth in democratic republics of all descriptions. If, for instance, in the very first months of the Russian democratic republic, one might say during the honeymoon of the union of the "Socialists"—Socialist-Revolutionaries and Mensheviks—with the bourgeoisie, Mr. Palchinsky obstructed every measure in the coalition cabinet, restraining the capitalists and their war profiteering, their plundering of the public treasury by means of army contracts; and if, after his resignation, Mr. Palchinsky (replaced, of course, by an exactly similar Palchinsky) was "rewarded" by the capitalists with a "soft" job carrying a salary of 120,000 roubles per annum, what was this? Direct or indirect bribery? A league of the government with the capitalist syndicates, or "only" friendly relations? What is the rôle played by the Chernovs, Tseretelis, Avksentyevs and Skobelevs? Are they the "direct" or only the indirect allies of the millionaire treasury looters?

The omnipotence of "wealth" is thus more *secure* in a democratic republic, since it does not depend on the poor political shell of capitalism. A democratic republic is the best possible political shell for capitalism, and therefore, once capital has gained control (through the Palchinskys, Chernovs, Tseretelis and Co.) of this very best shell, it establishes its power so securely, so firmly, that *no* change, either of persons, or institutions, or parties in the bourgeois republic can shake it.

We must also note that Engels quite definitely regards universal suffrage as a means of bourgeois domination.

Universal suffrage, he says, obviously summing up the long experience of German Social-Democracy, is " an index of the maturity of the working class ; it cannot, and never will, be anything else but that in the modern State."

The petty-bourgeois democrats, such as our Socialist-Revolutionaries and Mensheviks, and also their twin brothers, the social-chauvinists and opportunists of Western Europe, all expect " more " from universal suffrage. They themselves share, and instil into the minds of the people, the wrong idea that universal suffrage " in the *modern* State " is really capable of expressing the will of the majority of the toilers and of assuring its realisation.

We can here only note this wrong idea, only point out that this perfectly clear, exact and concrete statement by Engels is distorted at every step in the propaganda and agitation of the " official " (i.e., opportunist) Socialist parties. A detailed analysis of all the falseness of this idea, which Engels brushes aside, is given in our further account of the views of Marx and Engels on the " modern " State.

A general summary of his views is given by Engels in the most popular of his works in the following words :

> The State, therefore, has not existed from all eternity. There have been societies which managed without it, which had no conception of the State and State power. At a certain stage of economic development, which was necessarily bound up with the cleavage of society into classes, the State became a necessity owing to this cleavage. We are now rapidly approaching a stage in the development of production at which the existence of these classes has not only ceased to be a necessity, but is becoming a positive hindrance to production. They will disappear as inevitably as they arose at an earlier stage. Along with them the State will inevitably disappear. The society that organises production anew on the basis of a free and equal association of the producers will put the whole State machine where it will then belong : in the museum of antiquities, side by side with the spinning-wheel and the bronze axe.

It is not often that we find this passage quoted in the propaganda and agitation literature of contemporary Social-Democracy. But even when we do come across it, it is generally quoted in the same manner as one bows before an icon, i.e., it is done merely to show official respect for Engels, without any attempt to gauge the breadth and depth of revolutionary action presupposed by this relegating of " the whole State machine . . . to the museum of antiquities." In most cases we do not even find an understanding of what Engels calls the State machine.

4. The " Withering Away " of the State and Violent Revolution

Engels' words regarding the " withering away " of the State enjoy such popularity, they are so often quoted, and they show so clearly the essence of the usual adulteration by means of which Marxism is made to look like opportunism, that we must dwell on them in detail. Let us quote the whole passage from which they are taken :

The proletariat seizes State power, and then transforms the means of production into State property. But in doing this, it puts an end to itself as the proletariat, it puts an end to all class differences and class antagonisms, it puts an end also to the State as the State. Former society, moving in class antagonisms, had need of the State, that is, an organisation of the exploiting class at each period for the maintenance of its external conditions of production ; therefore, in particular, for the forcible holding down of the exploited class in the conditions of oppression (slavery, bondage or serfdom, wage-labour) determined by the existing mode of production. The State was the official representative of society as a whole, its embodiment in a visible corporate body ; but it was this only in so far as it was the State of that class which itself, in its epoch, represented society as a whole : in ancient times, the State of the slave-owning citizens ; in the Middle Ages, of the feudal nobility ; in our epoch, of the bourgeoisie. When ultimately it becomes really representative of society as a whole, it makes itself superfluous. As soon as there is no longer any class of society to be held in subjection ; as soon as, along with class domination and the struggle for individual existence based on the former anarchy of production, the collisions and excesses arising from these have also been abolished, there is nothing more to be repressed, and a special repressive force, a State, is no longer necessary. The first act in which the State really comes forward as the representative of society as a whole —the seizure of the means of production in the name of society —is at the same time its last independent act as a State. The interference of a State power in social relations becomes superfluous in one sphere after another, and then becomes dormant of itself. Government over persons is replaced by the administration of things and the direction of the processes of production. The State is not " abolished," *it withers away.* It is from this standpoint that we must appraise the phrase " people's free State "—both its justification at times for agitational purposes, and its ultimate scientific inadequacy—and also the demand of the so-called Anarchists that the State should be abolished overnight.

Without fear of committing an error, it may be said that of this argument by Engels so singularly rich in ideas, only one point has become an integral part of Socialist thought among modern Socialist parties, namely, that, unlike the Anarchist doctrine of the " abolition " of the State, according to Marx the State " withers away." To emasculate Marxism in such a manner is to reduce it to opportunism, for such an " interpretation " only leaves the hazy conception of a slow, even, gradual change, free from leaps and storms, free from revolution. The current popular conception, if one may say so, of the " withering away " of the State undoubtedly means a slurring over, if not a negation, of revolution.

Yet, such an " interpretation " is the crudest distortion of Marxism, which is advantageous only to the bourgeoisie ; in point of theory, it is based on a disregard for the most important circumstances and considerations pointed out in the very passage summarising Engels' idea, which we have just quoted in full.

In the first place, Engels at the very outset of his argument says that, in assuming State power, the proletariat by that very act " puts an end to the State as the State." One is " not accustomed " to reflect on what this really means. Generally, it is either ignored altogether, or it is considered as a piece of " Hegelian weakness " on Engels' part. As a matter of fact, however, these words express succinctly the experience of one of the greatest proletarian revolutions—the Paris Commune of 1871, of which we shall speak in greater detail in its proper place. As a matter of fact, Engels speaks here of the destruction of the bourgeois State by the proletarian revolution, while the words about its withering away refer to the remains of *proletarian* statehood *after* the Socialist revolution. The bourgeois State does not " wither away," according to Engels, but is " put an end to " by the proletariat in the course of the revolution. What withers away after the revolution is the proletarian State or semi-state.

Secondly, the State is a " special repressive force." This splendid and extremely profound definition of Engels' is given by him here with complete lucidity. It follows from this that the " special repressive force " of the bourgeoisie for the suppression of the proletariat, of the millions of workers by a handful of the rich, must be replaced by a " special repressive force " of the proletariat for the suppression of the bourgeoisie (the dictatorship of the proletariat). It is just this that constitutes the destruction of " the State as the State." It is just this that constitutes the " act " of " the seizure of the means of production in the name of society." And it is obvious that such a substitution of one (proletarian) " special repressive force " for another (bourgeois) " special repressive force " can in no way take place in the form of a " withering away."

Thirdly, as to the " withering away " or, more expressively and colourfully, as to the State " becoming dormant," Engels refers quite clearly and definitely to the period *after* " the seizure of the means of production (by the State) in the name of society," that is, *after* the Socialist revolution. We all know that the political form of the "State" at that time is complete democracy. But it never enters the head of any of the opportunists who shamelessly distort Marx that when Engels speaks here of the State " withering away," or " becoming dormant," he speaks of *democracy*.

At first sight this seems very strange. But it is " unintelligible " only to one who has not reflected on the fact that democracy is *also* a State and that, consequently, democracy will *also* disappear when the State disappears. The bourgeois State can only be " put an end to " by a revolution. The State in general, i.e., most complete democracy, can only " wither away."

Fourthly, having formulated his famous proposition that " the State withers away," Engels at once explains concretely that this proposition is directed equally against the opportunists and the Anarchists. In doing this, however, Engels puts in the first place that conclusion from his proposition about the " withering away " of the State which is directed against the opportunists.

One can wager that out of every 10,000 persons who have read or heard about the " withering away " of the State, 9,990 do not know at all, or do not remember, that Engels did not direct his conclusions from this proposition against the Anarchists *alone*. And out of the remaining ten, probably nine do not know the meaning of a " people's free State " nor the reason why an attack on this watchword contains an attack on the opportunists. This is how history is written ! This is how a great revolutionary doctrine is imperceptibly adulterated and adapted to current philistinism ! The conclusion drawn against the Anarchists has been repeated thousands of times, vulgarised, harangued about in the crudest fashion possible until it has acquired the strength of a prejudice, whereas the conclusion drawn against the opportunists has been hushed up and " forgotten " !

The " people's free State " was a demand in the programme of the German Social-Democrats and their current slogan in the 'seventies. There is no political substance in this slogan other than a pompous middle-class circumlocution of the idea of democracy. In so far as it referred in a lawful manner to a democratic republic, Engels was prepared to " justify " its use " at times " from a propaganda

point of view. But this slogan was opportunist, for it not
only expressed an exaggerated view of the attractiveness
of bourgeois democracy, but also a lack of understanding
of the Socialist criticism of every State in general. We are
in favour of a democratic republic as the best form of the
State for the proletariat under capitalism, but we have no
right to forget that wage slavery is the lot of the people
even in the most democratic bourgeois republic. Furthermore, every State is a " special repressive force " for the
suppression of the oppressed class. Consequently, *no* State
is either " free " or " people's State." Marx and Engels
explained this repeatedly to their party comrades in the
'seventies.

Fifthly, in the same work of Engels, from which every
one remembers his argument on the " withering away " of
the State, there is also a disquisition on the significance of
a violent revolution. The historical analysis of its rôle
becomes, with Engels, a veritable panegyric on violent
revolution. This, of course, " no one remembers " ; to talk
or even to think of the importance of this idea is not considered good form by contemporary Socialist parties, and
in the daily propaganda and agitation among the masses
it plays no part whatever. Yet it is indissolubly bound up
with the " withering away " of the State in one harmonious
whole.

Here is Engels' argument :

   . . . That force, however, plays another rôle (other than
that of a diabolical power) in history, a revolutionary rôle ;
that, in the words of Marx, it is the midwife of every old society
which is pregnant with the new ; that it is the instrument with
whose aid social movement forces its way through and shatters
the dead, fossilised political forms—of this there is not a word
in Herr Dühring. It is only with sighs and groans that he
admits the possibility that force will perhaps be necessary for
the overthrow of the economic system of exploitation—unfortunately ! because all use of force, forsooth, demoralises the
person who uses it. And this in spite of the immense moral
and spiritual impetus which has resulted from every victorious

revolution ! And this in Germany, where a violent collision—
which indeed may be forced on the people—would at least
have the advantage of wiping out the servility which has
permeated the national consciousness as a result of the humiliation of the Thirty Years' War. And this parson's mode of
thought—lifeless, insipid and impotent—claims to impose
itself on the most revolutionary Party which history has known ?

How can this panegyric on violent revolution, which
Engels insistently brought to the attention of the German
Social-Democrats between 1878 and 1894, i.e., right to
the time of his death, be combined with the theory
of the " withering away " of the State to form one
doctrine ?

Usually the two views are combined by means of eclecticism, by an unprincipled, sophistic, arbitrary selection (to
oblige the powers that be) of either one or the other argument, and in ninety-nine cases out of a hundred (if not more
often), it is the idea of the " withering away " that is
specially emphasised. Eclecticism is substituted for dialectics—this is the most usual, the most widespread phenomenon to be met with in the official Social-Democratic
literature of our day in relation to Marxism. Such a substitution is, of course, nothing new ; it may be observed
even in the history of classic Greek philosophy. When
Marxism is adulterated to become opportunism, the substitution of eclecticism for dialectics is the best method of
deceiving the masses ; it gives an illusory satisfaction ; it
seems to take into account all sides of the process, all the
tendencies of development, all the contradictory factors
and so forth, whereas in reality it offers no consistent and
revolutionary view of the process of social development at
all.

We have already said above, and shall show more fully
later, that the teaching of Marx and Engels regarding the
inevitability of a violent revolution refers to the bourgeois
State. It *cannot* be replaced by the proletarian State (the
dictatorship of the proletariat) through " withering away,"

but, as a general rule, only through a violent revolution. The panegyric sung in its honour by Engels and fully corresponding to the repeated declarations of Marx (remember the concluding passages of the *Poverty of Philosophy* and *The Communist Manifesto*, with its proud and open declaration of the inevitability of a violent revolution ; remember Marx's *Critique of the Gotha Programme* of 1875 in which, almost thirty years later, he mercilessly castigates the opportunist character of that programme)—this praise is by no means a mere " impulse," a mere declamation, or a polemical sally. The necessity of systematically fostering among the masses *this* and just this point of view about violent revolution lies at the root of the *whole* of Marx's and Engels' teaching. The neglect of such propaganda and agitation by both the present predominant social-chauvinist and the Kautskyist currents brings their betrayal of Marx's and Engels' teaching into prominent relief.

The replacement of the bourgeois by the proletarian State is impossible without a violent revolution. The abolition of the proletarian State, i.e., of all States, is only possible through " withering away."

Marx and Engels gave a full and concrete exposition of these views in studying each revolutionary situation separately, in analysing the lessons of the experience of each individual revolution.

THE ECONOMIC BASE OF THE WITHERING AWAY OF THE STATE

(Ch. V)

A most detailed elucidation of this question is given by Marx in his *Critique of the Gotha Programme* (letter to Bracke, May 15, 1875, printed only in 1891 in the *Neue Zeit*, IX-1, and in a special Russian edition). The polemical part of this remarkable work, consisting of a criticism of Lassalleanism, has, so to speak, over-shadowed its positive part, namely, the analysis of the connection between the development of Communism and the withering away of the State.

1. Formulation of the Question by Marx

From a superficial comparison of the letter of Marx to Bracke (May 15, 1875) with Engels' letter to Bebel (March 28, 1875), analysed above, it might appear that Marx was much more " pro-state " than Engels, and that the difference of opinion between the two writers on the question of the State is very considerable.

Engels suggests to Bebel that all the chatter about the State should be thrown overboard ; that the word " State " should be eliminated from the programme and replaced by " community " ; Engels even declares that the Commune was really no longer a State in the proper sense of the word. And Marx even speaks of the " future State in Communist society," i.e., he is apparently recognising the necessity of a State even under Communism.

But such a view would be fundamentally incorrect. A closer examination shows that Marx's and Engels' views on the State and its withering away were completely identical, and that Marx's expression quoted above refers merely to this withering away of the State.

It is clear that there can be no question of defining the exact moment of the *future* withering away—the more so as it must obviously be a rather lengthy process. The apparent difference between Marx and Engels is due to the different subjects they dealt with, the different aims they were pursuing. Engels set out to show to Bebel, in a plain, bold and broad outline, all the absurdity of the current superstitions concerning the State, shared to no small degree by Lassalle himself. Marx, on the other hand, only touches upon *this* question in passing, being interested mainly in another subject—the *evolution* of Communist society.

The whole theory of Marx is an application of the theory of development—in its most consistent, complete, well considered and fruitful form—to modern capitalism. It was natural for Marx to raise the question of applying this theory both of the *coming* collapse of capitalism and to the *future* development of *future* Communism.

On the basis of what *data* can the future development of future Communism be considered?

On the basis of the fact that *it has its origin* in capitalism, that it develops historically from capitalism, that it is the result of the action of a social force to which capitalism *has given birth*. There is no shadow of an attempt on Marx's part to conjure up a Utopia, to make idle guesses about that which cannot be known. Marx treats the question of Communism in the same way as a naturalist would treat the question of the development of, say, a new biological species, if he knew that such and such was its origin, and such and such the direction in which it changed.

Marx, first of all, brushes aside the confusion the Gotha Programme brings into the question of the interrelation between State and society.

" Contemporary society " is the capitalist society—he writes —which exists in all civilised countries, more or less free of mediæval admixture, more or less modified by each country's particular historical development, more or less developed. In contrast with this, the " contemporary State " varies with every State boundary. It is different in the Prusso-German Empire from what it is in Switzerland, and different in England from what it is in the United States. The " contemporary State " is therefore a fiction.

Nevertheless, in spite of the motley variety of their forms, the different States of the various civilised countries all have this in common : they are all based on modern bourgeois society, only a little more or less capitalistically developed. Consequently, they also have certain essential characteristics in common. In this sense, it is possible to speak of the " contemporary State " in contrast to the future, when its present root, bourgeois society, will have perished.

Then the question arises : what transformation will the State undergo in a Communist society ? In other words, what social functions analogous to the present functions of the State will then still survive ? This question can only be answered scientifically, and however many thousand times the word people is combined with the word State, we get not a flea-jump closer to the problem. . . .

Having thus ridiculed all talk about a " people's State," Marx formulates the question and warns us, as it were, that to arrive at a scientific answer one must rely only on firmly established scientific data.

The first fact that has been established with complete exactness by the whole theory of development, by science as a whole—a fact which the Utopians forgot, and which is forgotten by the present-day opportunists who are afraid of the Socialist revolution—is that, historically, there must undoubtedly be a special stage or epoch of *transition* from capitalism to Communism.

2. Transition from Capitalism to Communism

Between capitalist and Communist society—Marx continues —lies the period of the revolutionary transformation of the former into the latter. To this also corresponds a political transition period, in which the State can be no other than *the revolutionary dictatorship of the proletariat.*

This conclusion Marx bases on an analysis of the rôle played by the proletariat in modern capitalist society, on the data concerning the development of this society, and on the irreconcilability of the opposing interests of the proletariat and the bourgeoisie.

Earlier the question was put thus : to attain its emancipation, the proletariat must overthrow the bourgeoisie, conquer political power and establish its own revolutionary dictatorship.

Now the question is put somewhat differently : the transition from capitalist society, developing towards Communism, towards a Communist society, is impossible without a " political transition period," and the State in this period can only be the revolutionary dictatorship of the proletariat.

What, then, is the relation of this dictatorship to democracy ?

We have seen that *The Communist Manifesto* simply places side by side the two ideas : the " transformation of the proletariat into the ruling class " and the " establishment of democracy." On the basis of all that has been said above, one can define more exactly how democracy changes in the transition from capitalism to Communism.

In capitalist society, under the conditions most favourable to its development, we have more or less complete democracy in the democratic republic. But this democracy is always bound by the narrow framework of capitalist exploitation, and consequently, always remains, in reality, a democracy for the minority, only for the possessing classes, only for the rich. Freedom in capitalist society always remains just about the same as it was in the ancient Greek republics : freedom for the slave-owners. The modern wage-slaves, owing to the conditions of capitalist exploitation, are so much crushed by want and poverty that " democracy is nothing to them," " politics is nothing to them " ; that, in the ordinary peaceful course of events, the majority of the population is debarred from participating in social and political life.

The correctness of this statement is perhaps most clearly proved by Germany, just because in this State constitutional legality lasted and remained stable for a remarkably long time—for nearly half a century (1871–1914)—and because Social-Democracy in Germany during that time was able to achieve far more than in other countries in " utilising legality," and was able to organise into a political party a larger proportion of the working class than anywhere else in the world.

What, then, is this largest proportion of politically conscious and active wage-slaves that has so far been observed in capitalist society ? One million members of the Social-Democratic Party—out of fifteen million wage-workers ! Three million organised in trade unions—out of fifteen million !

Democracy for an insignificant minority, democracy for the rich—that is the democracy of capitalist society. If we look more closely into the mechanism of capitalist democracy, everywhere, both in the " petty "—so-called petty—details of the suffrage (residential qualification, exclusion of women, etc.), and in the technique of the representative institutions, in the actual obstacles to the right of assembly (public buildings are not for " beggars " !), in the purely capitalist organisation of the daily Press, etc., etc.—on all sides we see restriction after restriction upon democracy. These restrictions, exceptions, exclusions, obstacles for the poor, seem slight, especially in the eyes of one who has himself never known want and has never been in close contact with the oppressed classes in their mass life (and nine-tenths, if not ninety-nine hundredths, of the bourgeois publicists and politicans are of this class), but in their sum total these restrictions exclude and squeeze out the poor from politics and from an active share in democracy.

Marx splendidly grasped this *essence* of capitalist democracy, when, in analysing the experience of the Commune, he said that the oppressed were allowed, once every few years, to decide which particular representatives of the oppressing class should be in parliament to represent and repress them !

But from this capitalist democracy—inevitably narrow, subtly rejecting the poor, and therefore hypocritical and false to the core—progress does not march onward, simply smoothly, and directly, to " greater and greater democracy," as the liberal professors and petty-bourgeois opportunists would have us believe. No, progress marches onward, i.e., toward Communism, through the dictatorship of the proletariat ; it cannot do otherwise, for there is no one else and no other way to *break the resistance* of the capitalist exploiters.

But the dictatorship of the proletariat—i.e., the organisation of the vanguard of the oppressed as the ruling class for the purpose of crushing the oppressors—cannot produce merely an expansion of democracy. *Together* with an immense expansion of democracy which *for the first time* becomes democracy for the poor, democracy for the people, and not democracy for the rich folk, the dictatorship o the proletariat produces a series of restrictions of liberty in the case of the oppressors, the exploiters, the capitalists. We must crush them in order to free humanity from wage-slavery ; their resistance must be broken by force ; it is clear that where there is suppression there is also violence, there is no liberty, no democracy.

Engels expressed this splendidly in his letter to Bebel when he said, as the reader will remember, that " as long as the proletariat still *needs* the State, it needs it not in the interests of freedom, but for the purpose of crushing its antagonists ; and as soon as it becomes possible to speak of freedom, then the State, as such, ceases to exist."

Democracy for the vast majority of the people, and suppression by force, i.e., exclusion from democracy, of the exploiters and oppressors of the people—this is the modification of democracy during the *transition* from capitalism to Communism.

Only in Communist society, when the resistance of the capitalists has been completely broken, when the capitalists have disappeared, when there are no classes (i.e., there is no difference between the members of society in their relation to the social means of production), *only then* " the State ceases to exist," and " *it becomes possible to speak of freedom.*" Only then a really full democracy, a democracy without any exceptions, will be possible and will be realised. And only then will democracy itself begin to *wither away* due to the simple fact that, freed from capitalist slavery, from the untold horrors, savagery, absurdities and infamies of capitalist exploitation, people will gradually *become accustomed* to the observation of the elementary rules of social life that have been known for centuries and repeated for thousands of years in all school books ; they will become accustomed to observing them without force, without compulsion, without subordination, without the *special apparatus* for compulsion which is called the State.

The expression " the State *withers away*," is very well chosen, for it indicates both the gradual and the elemental nature of the process. Only habit can, and undoubtedly will, have such an effect ; for we see around us millions of times how readily people get accustomed to observe the necessary rules of life in common, if there is no exploitation, if there is nothing that causes indignation, that calls forth protest and revolt and has to be *suppressed*.

Thus, in capitalist society, we have a democracy that is curtailed, poor, false ; a democracy only for the rich, for the minority. The dictatorship of the proletariat, the period of transition to Communism, will, for the first time, produce democracy for the people, for the majority, side by side with the necessary suppression of the minority—the exploiters. Communism alone is capable of giving a really complete democracy, and the more complete it is the more quickly will it become unnecessary and wither away of itself.

In other words : under capitalism we have a State in the proper sense of the word, that is, special machinery for the suppression of one class by another, and of the majority by the minority at that. Naturally, for the successful discharge of such a task as the systematic suppression by the exploiting minority of the exploited majority, the greatest ferocity and savagery of suppression are required, seas of blood are required, through which mankind is marching in slavery, serfdom, and wage-labour.

Again, during the *transition* from capitalism to Communism, suppression is *still* necessary ; but it is the suppression of the minority of exploiters by the majority of exploited. A special apparatus, special machinery for suppression, the " State," is *still* necessary, but this is now a transitional State, no longer a State in the usual sense, for the suppression of the minority of exploiters, by the majority of the wage slaves of *yesterday*, is a matter comparatively so easy, simple and natural that it will cost far less bloodshed than the suppression of the risings of slaves, serfs or wage labourers, and will cost mankind far less. This is compatible with the diffusion of democracy among such an overwhelming majority of the population, that the need for *special machinery* of suppression will begin to disappear. The exploiters are, naturally, unable to suppress the people without a most complex machinery for performing this task ; but *the people* can suppress the exploiters even with very simple " machinery," almost without any " machinery," without any special apparatus, by the simple *organisation of the armed masses* (such as the Soviets of Workers' and Soldiers' Deputies, we may remark, anticipating a little).

Finally, only Communism renders the State absolutely unnecessary, for there is *no one* to be suppressed—" no one " in the sense of a *class*, in the sense of a systematic struggle with a definite section of the population. We are not Utopians, and we do not in the least deny the possibility and inevitability of excesses on the part of *individual persons*, nor the need to suppress *such* excesses. But, in the first place, no special machinery, no special apparatus of repression is needed for this ; this will be done by the armed people itself, as simply and as readily as any crowd of civilised people, even in modern society, parts a pair of combatants or does not allow a woman to be outraged. And, secondly, we know that the fundamental social cause of excesses which consists in violating the rules of social life is the exploitation of the masses, their want and their poverty. With the removal of this chief cause, excesses will inevitably begin to " *wither away*." We do not know how quickly and in what succession, but we know that they will wither away. With their withering away, the State will also *wither away*.

Without going into Utopias, Marx defined more fully what can *now* be defined regarding this future, namely, the difference between the lower and higher phases (degrees, stages) of Communist society.

3. First Phase of Communist Society

In the *Critique of the Gotha Programme*, Marx goes into some detail to disprove the Lassallean idea of the workers' receiving under Socialism the " undiminished " or " full product of their labour." Marx shows that out of the whole of the social labour of society, it is necessary to deduct a reserve fund, a fund for the expansion of production, for the replacement of worn-out machinery and so on ; then also, out of the means of consumption must be deducted a fund for the expenses of management, for schools, hospitals, homes for the aged, and so on.

Instead of the hazy, obscure, general phrase of Lassalle's —" the full product of his labour for the worker "—Marx gives a sober estimate of exactly how a Socialist society will have to manage its affairs, Marx undertakes a *concrete* analysis of the conditions of life of a society in which there is no capitalism, and says :

> What we are dealing with here [analysing the programme of the party] is not a Communist society which has *developed* on its own foundations, but, on the contrary, one which is just *emerging* from capitalist society, and which therefore in all respects—economic, moral and intellectual—still bears the birthmarks of the old society from whose womb it sprung.

And it is this Communist society—a society which has just come into the world out of the womb of capitalism, and which, in all respects, bears the stamp of the old society— that Marx terms the " first," or lower, phase of Communist society.

The means of production are no longer the private property of individuals. The means of production belong to the whole of society. Every member of society, performing a certain part of socially-necessary work, receives a certificate from society to the effect that he has done such and such a quantity of work. According to this certificate, he receives from the public warehouses, where articles of consumption are stored, a corresponding quantity of products. Deducting that proportion of labour which goes to the public fund, every worker, therefore, receives from society as much as he has given it.

" Equality " seems to reign supreme.

But when Lassalle, having in view such a social order (generally called Socialism, but termed by Marx the first phase of Communism), speaks of this as " just distribution " and says that this is " the equal right of each to an equal product of labour," Lassalle is mistaken, and Marx exposes his error.

" Equal right," says Marx, " we indeed have here " ; but it is *still* a " bourgeois right," which, like every right, *presupposes inequality*. Every right is an application of the *same* measure to *different* people who, in fact, are not the same and are not equal to one another ; this is why " equal right " is really a violation of equality, and an injustice. In effect, every man having done as much social labour as every other, receives an equal share of the social products (with the above-mentioned deductions).

But different people are not alike : one is strong, another is weak ; one is married, the other is not ; one has more children, another has less, and so on.

> . . . With equal labour—Marx concludes—and therefore an equal share in the social consumption fund, one man in fact receives more than the other, one is richer than the other, and so forth. In order to avoid all these defects, rights, instead of being equal, must be unequal.

The first phase of Communism, therefore, still cannot produce justice and equality ; differences, and unjust differences, in wealth will still exist, but the *exploitation* of man by man will have become impossible, because it will be impossible to seize as private property the *means of production*, the factories, machines, land, and so on. In tearing down Lassalle's petty-bourgeois, confused phrase about " equality " and " justice " *in general*, Marx shows the *course of development* of Communist society, which is forced at first to destroy *only* the " injustice " that consists in the means of production having been seized by private individuals, and which *is not capable* of destroying at once the further injustice consisting in the distribution of the articles of consumption " according to work performed " (and not according to need).

The vulgar economists, including the bourgeois professors and also " our " Tugan-Baranovsky, constantly reproach the Socialists with forgetting the inequality of people and with " dreaming " of destroying this inequality. Such a reproach, as we see, only proves the extreme ignorance of the gentlemen propounding bourgeois ideology.

Marx not only takes into account with the greatest accuracy the inevitable inequality of men ; he also takes into account the fact that the mere conversion of the means of production into the common property of the whole of society (" Socialism " in the generally accepted sense of the word) *does not remove* the defects of distribution and the inequality of " bourgeois right " which *continue to rule* as long as the products are divided " according to work performed."

> But these defects—Marx continues—are unavoidable in the first phase of Communist society, when, after long travail, it first emerges from capitalist society. Justice can never rise superior to the economic conditions of society and the cultural development conditioned by them.

And so, in the first phase of Communist society (generally called Socialism) " bourgeois right " is *not* abolished in its entirety, but only in part, only in proportion to the economic transformation so far attained, i.e., only in respect of the means of production. " Bourgeois right " recognises them as the private property of separate individuals. Socialism converts them into common property. *To that extent*, and to that extent alone, does " bourgeois rights " disappear.

However, it continues to exist as far as its other part is concerned ; it remains in the capacity of regulator (determining factor) distributing the products and allotting labour among the members of society. " He who does not work, shall not eat "—this Socialist principle is *already* realised ; " for an equal quantity of labour, an equal quantity of products "—this Socialist principle is also *already* realised. However, this is not yet Communism, and this does not abolish " bourgeois right," which gives to unequal individuals, in return for an equal (in reality unequal) amount of work, an equal quantity of products.

This is a " defect," says Marx, but it is unavoidable during the first phase of Communism ; for, if we are not to fall into Utopianism, we cannot imagine that, having overthrown capitalism, people will at once learn to work for society *without any standards of right* ; indeed, the abolition of capitalism *does not immediately lay* the economic foundations for *such* a change.

And there is no other standard yet than that of " bourgeois right." To this extent, therefore, a form of State is still necessary, which, while maintaining public ownership of the means of production, would preserve the equality of labour and equality in the distribution of products.

The State is withering away in so far as there are no longer any capitalists, any classes, and, consequently, no *class* can be suppressed.

But the State has not yet altogether withered away, since there still remains the protection of " bourgeois right " which sanctifies actual inequality. For the complete extinction of the State, complete Communism is necessary.

4. Higher Phase of Communist Society

Marx continues :

In a higher phase of Communist society, when the enslaving subordination of individuals in · the division of labour has disappeared, and with it also the antagonism, between mental and physical labour ; when labour has become not only a means of living, but itself the first necessity of life ; when, along with the all-round development of individuals, the productive forces too have grown, and all the springs of social wealth are flowing more freely—it is only at that stage that it will be possible to pass completely beyond the narrow horizon of bourgeois rights, and for society to inscribe on its banners : from each according to his ability : to each according to his needs !

Only now can we appreciate the full correctness of Engels' remarks in which he mercilessly ridiculed all the absurdity of combining the words " freedom " and " state." While the State exists there is no freedom. When there is freedom, there will be no State.

The economic basis for the complete withering away of the State is that high stage of development of Communism when the antagonism between mental and physical labour disappears, that is to say, when one of the principal sources of modern *social* inequality disappears—a source, moreover, which it is impossible to remove immediately by the mere conversion of the means of production into public property, by the mere expropriation of the capitalists.

This expropriation will make a gigantic development of the productive forces *possible*. And seeing how incredibly, even now, capitalism *retards* this development, how much progress could be made even on the basis of modern technique at the level it has reached, we have a right to say, with the fullest confidence, that the expropriation of the capitalists will inevitably result in a gigantic development of the productive forces of human society. But how rapidly this development will go forward, how soon it will reach the point of breaking away from the division of labour, of removing the antagonism between mental and physical labour, of transforming work into the " first necessity of life "—this we do not and *cannot* know.

Consequently, we have a right to speak solely of the inevitable withering away of the State, emphasising the protracted nature of this process and its dependence upon the rapidity of development of the *higher phase* of Communism ;

leaving quite open the question of lengths of time, or the concrete forms of withering away, since material for the solution of such questions is *not available*.

The State will be able to wither away completely when society has realised the rule : " From each according to his ability ; to each according to his needs," i.e., when people have become accustomed to observe the fundamental rules of social life, and their labour is so productive, that they voluntarily work *according to their ability*. " The narrow horizon of bourgeois rights," which compels one to calculate, with the hard-heartedness of a Shylock, whether he has not worked half an hour more than another, whether he is not getting less pay than another—this narrow horizon will then be left behind. There will then be no need for any exact calculation by society of the quantity of products to be distributed to each of its members ; each will take freely " according to his needs."

From the bourgeois point of view, it is easy to declare such a social order " a pure Utopia," and to sneer at the Socialists for promising each the right to receive from society, without any control of the labour of the individual citizen, any quantity of truffles, automobiles, pianos, etc. Even now, most bourgeois " savants " deliver themselves of such sneers, thereby displaying at once their ignorance and their self-seeking defence of capitalism.

Ignorance—for it has never entered the head of any Socialist to " promise " that the highest phase of Communism will arrive ; while the great Socialists, in *foreseeing* its arrival, presupposed both a productivity of labour unlike the present and a person not like the present man in the street, capable of spoiling, without reflection, like the seminary students in Pomyalovsky's book, the stores of social wealth, and of demanding the impossible.

Until the " higher " phase of Communism arrives, the Socialists demand the *strictest* control, *by society and by the State*, of the quantity of labour and the quantity of consumption ; only this control must *start* with the expropriation of the capitalists, with the control of the workers over the capitalists, and must be carried out, not by a State of bureaucrats, but by a State of *armed workers*.

Self-seeking defence of capitalism by the bourgeois ideologists (and their hangers-on like Tsereteli, Chernov and Co.) consists in that they *substitute* disputes and discussions about the distant future for the essential imperative questions of present-day policy : the expropriation of the capitalists, the conversion of *all* citizens into workers and employees of *one* huge " syndicate "—the whole State —and the complete subordination of the whole of the work of this syndicate to the really democratic State of the *Soviets of Workers' and Soldiers' Deputies*.

In reality, when a learned professor, and following him some philistine, and following the latter Messrs. Tsereteli and Chernov, talk of the unreasonable Utopias, of the demagogic promises of the Bolsheviks, of the impossibility of " introducing " Socialism, it is the higher stage or phase of Communism which they have in mind, and which no one has ever promised, or even thought of " introducing," for the reason that, generally speaking, it cannot be " introduced."

And here we come to that question of the scientific difference between Socialism and Communism, upon which Engels touched in his above-quoted discussion on the incorrectness of the name " Social-Democrat." The political difference between the first, or lower, and the higher phase of Communism will in time, no doubt, be tremendous ; but it would be ridiculous to emphasise it now, under capitalism, and only, perhaps, some isolated Anarchist could invest it with primary importance (if there are still some people among the Anarchists who have learned nothing from the Plekhanov-like conversion of the Kropotkins, the Graveses, the Cornelissens, and other " leading lights " of Anarchism to social-chauvinism or Anarcho-*Jusquaubout*-ism, as Gé, one of the few Anarchists still preserving honour and conscience, has expressed it).

But the scientific difference between Socialism and Communism is clear. What is generally called Socialism was termed by Marx the " first " or lower phase of Communist society. In so far as the means of production become *public* property, the word " Communism " is also applicable here, providing we do not forget that it is *not* full Communism. The great significance of Marx's elucidations consists in this : that here, too, he consistently applies materialist dialectics, the doctrine of development, looking upon Communism as something which evolves *out of* capitalism. Instead of artificial, " elaborate " scholastic definitions and profitless disquisitions on the meaning of words (what Socialism is, what Communism is), Marx gives an analysis of what may be called stages in the economic ripeness of Communism.

In its first phase or first stage Communism *cannot* as yet be economically ripe and entirely free of all tradition and of all taint of capitalism. Hence the interesting phenomenon of Communism retaining, in its first phase, " the narrow horizon of bourgeois rights." Bourgeois rights, with respect to distribution of articles of *consumption*, inevitably presupposes, of course, the existence of the *bourgeois State*, for rights are nothing without an apparatus capable of *enforcing* the observance of the rights.

Consequently, for a certain time not only bourgeois rights, but even the bourgeois State remains under Communism, without the bourgeoisie !

This may look like a paradox, or simply a dialectical puzzle for which Marxism is often blamed by people who would not make the least effort to study its extraordinarily profound content.

But, as a matter of fact, the old surviving in the new confronts us in life at every step, in nature as well as in society. Marx did not smuggle a scrap of " bourgeois " rights into Communism of his own accord ; he indicated what is economically and politically inevitable in a society issuing *from the womb* of capitalism.

Democracy is of great importance for the working class
in its struggle for freedom against the capitalists. But democracy is by no means a limit one may not overstep ; it is
only one of the stages in the course of development from
feudalism to capitalism, and from capitalism to Communism.

Democracy means equality. The great significance of the
struggle of the proletariat for equality, and the significance
of equality as a slogan, are apparent, if we correctly interpret it as meaning the abolition of *classes*. But democracy
means only *formal* equality. Immediately after the attainment of equality for all members of society *in respect of* the
ownership of the means of production, that is, of equality
of labour and equality of wages, there will inevitably arise
before humanity the question of going further from formal
equality to real equality, i.e., to realising the rule, " From
each according to his ability ; to each according to his
needs." By what stages, by means of what practical
measures humanity will proceed to this higher aim—this
we do not and cannot know. But it is important to realise
how infinitely mendacious is the usual bourgeois presentation of Socialism as something lifeless, petrified, fixed once
for all, whereas in reality, it is *only* with Socialism that there
will commence a rapid, genuine, real mass advance, in
which first the *majority* and then the whole of the population
will take part—an advance in all domains of social and
individual life.

Democracy is a form of the State—one of its varieties.
Consequently, like every State, it consists in organised,
systematic application of force against human beings. This
on the one hand. On the other hand, however, it signifies
the formal recognition of the equality of all citizens, the
equal right of all to determine the structure and administration of the State. This, in turn, is connected with the
fact that, at a certain stage in the development of democracy, it first rallies the proletariat as a revolutionary class
against capitalism, and gives it an opportunity to crush,

to smash to bits, to wipe off the face of the earth the bourgeois State machinery—even its republican variety : the
standing army, the police, and bureaucracy ; then it substitutes for all this a *more* democratic, but still a State
machinery in the shape of armed masses of workers, which
becomes transformed into universal participation of the
people in the militia.

Here " quantity turns into quality " : *such* a degree of
democracy is bound up with the abandonment of the
framework of bourgeois society, and the beginning of its
Socialist reconstruction. If *everyone* really takes part in the
administration of the State, capitalism cannot retain its
hold. In its turn, capitalism, as it develops, itself creates
pre-requisites for " everyone " *to be able* really to take part
in the administration of the State. Among such pre-requisites
are universal literacy, already realised in most of the advanced capitalist countries, then the " training and dis-
ciplining " of millions of workers by the huge, complex,
and socialised apparatus of the post office, the railways, the
big factories, large-scale commerce, banking, etc., etc.

With such *economic* pre-requisites it is perfectly possible,
immediately, within twenty-four hours after the overthrow
of the capitalists and bureaucrats, to replace them, in the
control of production and distribution, in the business of
control of labour and products, by the armed workers, by
the whole people in arms. (The question of control and
accounting must not be confused with the question of the
scientifically educated staffs of engineers, agronomists and
so on. These gentlemen work to-day, obeying the capitalists ; they will work even better to-morrow, obeying the
armed workers.)

Accounting and control—these are the *chief* things necessary for the organising and correct functioning of the *first
phase of* Communist society. *All* citizens are here transformed
into hired employees of the State, which is made up of the
armed workers. *All* citizens become employees and workers
of *one* national State " syndicate." All that is required is

that they should work equally, should regularly do their share of work, and should receive equal pay. The accounting and control necessary for this have been *simplified* by capitalism to the utmost, till they have become the extraordinarily simple operations of watching, recording and issuing receipts, within the reach of anybody who can read and write and knows the first four rules of arithmetic.

When the *majority* of the people begin everywhere to keep such accounts and maintain such control over the capitalists (now converted into employees) and over the intellectual gentry, who still retain capitalist habits, this control will really become universal, general, national ; and there will be no way of getting away from it, there will be " nowhere to go."

The whole of society will have become one office and one factory, with equal work and equal pay.

But this " factory " discipline, which the proletariat will extend to the whole of society after the defeat of the capitalists and the overthrow of the exploiters, is by no means our ideal, or our final aim. It is but a *foothold* necessary for the radical cleansing of society of all the hideousness and foulness of capitalist exploitation, *in order to advance further*.

From the moment when all members of society, or even only the overwhelming majority, have learned how to govern the State *themselves*, have taken this business into their own hands, have " established " control over the insignificant minority of capitalists, over the gentry with capitalist leanings, and the workers thoroughly demoralised by capitalism—from this moment the need for any government begins to disappear. The more complete the democracy, the nearer the moment when it begins to be unnecessary. The more democratic the " State " consisting of armed workers, which is " no longer a State in the proper sense of the word," the more rapidly does *every* State begin to wither away.

For when *all* have learned to manage, and independently

are actually managing by themselves social production, keeping accounts, controlling the idlers, the gentlefolk, the swindlers and similar " guardians of capitalist traditions," then the escape from this national accounting and control will inevitably become so increasingly difficult, such a rare exception, and will probably be accompanied by such swift and severe punishment (for the armed workers are men of practical life, not sentimental intellectuals, and they will scarcely allow anyone to trifle with them), that very soon the *necessity* of observing the simple, fundamental rules of every-day social life in common will have become a *habit*.

The door will then be wide open for the transition from the first phase of Communist society to its higher phase, and along with it to the complete withering away of the State.

Opposite: The situation was ripe for revolution. (*On the Eve of October*)

V. I. Lenin

ON THE EVE OF OCTOBER

*Articles and letters written in the weeks preceding November 7,
1917 ; some only published after the Revolution. English edition,
Martin Lawrence Ltd., 1932.*

[First from Finland, and then after his return to Petrograd, Lenin urged on the Central Committee of the Bolsheviks that the situation was ripe for revolution—" armed
uprising is inevitable and has fully matured." The Central
Committee hesitated, and even after a majority decision
in favour of an uprising, the two dissentients, Kamenev
and Zinoviev, published a declaration against it. The letters
printed below show Lenin's application of the Marxist
theory of revolution, and his insistence on action at " the
crucial point of the maturing revolution."]

ON THE EVE OF OCTOBER

MARXISM AND UPRISING

AMONG the most vicious and perhaps most widespread
distortions of Marxism practised by the prevailing " Socialist " parties, is to be found the opportunist lie which says
that preparations for an uprising, and generally the treatment of an uprising as an art, is " Blanquism."

Bernstein, the leader of opportunism, long since gained sad notoriety by accusing Marxism of Blanquism ; and our present opportunists, by shouting about Blanquism, in reality do not in any way improve or " enrich " the meagre " ideas " of Bernstein.

To accuse Marxists of Blanquism for treating uprising as an art ! Can there be a more flagrant distortion of the truth, when there is not a single Marxist who denies that it was Marx who expressed himself in the most definite, precise and categorical manner on this score ; that it was Marx who called uprising nothing but an *art*, who said that uprising must be treated as an art, that one must *gain* the first success and then proceed from success to success without stopping the *offensive* against the enemy and making use of his confusion, etc., etc.

To be successful, the uprising must be based not on a conspiracy, not on a party, but on the advanced class. This is the first point. The uprising must be based on the revolutionary upsurge of the people. This is the second point. The uprising must be based on the *crucial point* in the history of the maturing revolution, when the activity of the vanguard of the people is at its height, when the *vacillations* in the ranks of the enemies, and *in the ranks of the weak, half-hearted, undecided friends of the revolution are at their highest point*. This is the third point. It is in pointing out these three conditions as the way of approaching the question of an uprising, that Marxism differs from Blanquism.

But once these conditions exist, then to refuse to treat the uprising *as an art* means to betray Marxism and the revolution.

To show why this very moment must be recognised as the one when it is obligatory for the party to recognise the uprising as placed on the order of the day by the course of objective events, and to treat uprising as an art—to show this, it will perhaps be best to use the method of comparison and to draw a parallel between July 16–17 and the September days.

On July 16–17 it was possible, without trespassing against the truth, to put the question thus : it would have been more proper to take power, since our enemies would anyway accuse us of revolt and treat us as rebels. This, however, did not warrant a decision to take power at that time, because there were still lacking the objective conditions for a victorious uprising.

1. We did not yet have behind us the class that is the vanguard of the revolution. We did not yet have a majority among the workers and soldiers of the capitals. Now we have a majority in both Soviets. It was created *only* by the history of July and August, by the experience of ruthless punishment meted out to the Bolsheviks, and by the experience of the Kornilov affair.

2. At that time there was no general revolutionary upsurge of the people. Now there is, after the Kornilov affair. This is proven by the situation in the provinces and by the seizure of power by the Soviets in many localities.

3. At that time there were no *vacillations* on a serious, general, political scale among our enemies and among the undecided petty bourgeoisie. Now the vacillations are enormous ; our main enemy, the imperialism of the Allies and of the world (for the " Allies " are at the head of world imperialism), has begun to vacillate between war to a victory and a separate peace against Russia. Our petty-bourgeois democrats, having obviously lost their majority among the people, have begun to vacillate enormously, rejecting a bloc, i.e. a coalition with the Cadets.

4. This is why an uprising on July 16–17 would have been an error : we would not have retained power either physically or politically. Not physically, in spite of the fact that at certain moments Petrograd was in our hands, because our workers and soldiers would not have *fought and died* at that time for the sake of holding Petrograd ; at that time people had not yet become so " brutalised " ; there was not in existence such a burning hatred both towards the Kerenskys and towards the Tseretelis and·Chernovs ; and

our own people were not yet hardened by the experience of the Bolsheviks being persecuted, while the Socialist-Revolutionaries and Mensheviks took part in the persecuting.

We could not have retained power July 16–17 politically, for, *before the Kornilov affair*, the army and the provinces could and would have marched against Petrograd.

Now the picture is entirely different.

We have back of us the majority of a *class* that is the vanguard of the revolution, the vanguard of the people, and is capable of drawing the masses along.

We have back of us a *majority* of the people, for Chernov's resignation, far from being the only sign, is only the most striking, the most outstanding sign showing that the peasantry *will not receive land* from a bloc with the S.-R.'s, or from the S.-R.'s themselves. And in this lies the essence of the popular character of the revolution.

We are in the advantageous position of a party which knows its road perfectly well, while *imperialism as a whole*, as well as the entire bloc of the Mensheviks and the S.-R.'s, is vacillating in an extraordinary manner.

Victory is assured to us, for the people are now very close to desperation, and we are showing the whole people a sure way out, having demonstrated to the whole people the significance of our leadership during the " Kornilov days," and then having *offered* the bloc politicians a compromise which they *rejected* at a time when their vacillations continued uninterruptedly.

It would be a very great error to think that our compromise offer has *not yet* been rejected, that the " *Democratic Conference* " *still* may accept it. The compromise was offered from *party to parties*. It could not have been offered otherwise. The *parties* have rejected it. The Democratic Conference is nothing but a *conference*. One must not forget one thing, namely, that this conference does not represent the *majority* of the revolutionary people, the poorest and most embittered peasantry. One must not forget the self-evident truth that this conference represents a *minority of the people*.

It would be a very great error, a very great parliamentary idiocy on our part, if we were to treat the Democratic Conference as a parliament, for even *if* it were to proclaim itself a parliament, the sovereign parliament of the revolution, it would not be able to *decide* anything. The decision lies *outside* of it, in the workers' sections of Petrograd and Moscow.

We have before us all the objective prerequisites for a successful uprising. We have the advantages of a situation where *only* our victory in an uprising will put an end to the most painful thing on earth, the vacillations that have sickened the people ; a situation where *only our* victory in an uprising will *put an end* to the game of a separate peace against the revolution by openly offering a more complete, more just, more immediate peace *in favour of* the revolution.

Only our party, having won a victory in an uprising, *can* save Petrograd, for if our offer of peace is rejected, and we obtain not even a truce, then *we* shall become " defensists," then we shall place ourselves *at the head of the war parties*, we shall be the most " warring " party, and we shall carry on a war in a truly revolutionary manner. We shall take away from the capitalists all the bread and all the shoes. We shall leave them crumbs. We shall dress them in bast shoes. We shall send all the bread and all the shoes to the front.

And then we shall save Petrograd.

The resources, both material and spiritual, of a truly revolutionary war are still immense in Russia ; there are ninety-nine chances in a hundred that the Germans will at least grant us a truce. And to secure a truce at present means to conquer the *whole world*.

Having recognised the absolute necessity of an uprising of the workers of Petrograd and Moscow for the sake of saving the revolution and of saving Russia from being " separately " divided among the imperialists of both coalitions, we must first adapt our political tactics at the conference to the conditions of the maturing uprising ; secondly, we must prove that we accept, and not only in words, the idea of Marx about the necessity of treating uprising as an art.

At the conference, we must immediately consolidate the Bolshevik fraction without worrying about numbers, without being afraid of leaving the vacillators in the camp of the vacillating : they are more useful *there* to the cause of revolution than in the camp of the resolute and courageous fighters.

We must compose a brief declaration in the name of the Bolsheviks in which we sharply emphasise the irrelevance of long speeches, the irrelevance of " speeches " generally, the necessity of quick action to save the revolution, the absolute necessity of breaking completely with the bourgeoisie, of completely ousting the whole present government, of completely severing relations with the Anglo-French imperialists who are preparing a " separate " partition of Russia, the necessity of all power immediately passing into the hands of *revolutionary democracy headed by the revolutionary proletariat.*

Our declaration must be the briefest and sharpest formulation of this conclusion ; it must connect up with the points in the programme of peace to the people, land to the peasants, confiscation of scandalous profits, and a halt to the scandalous damage to production done by the capitalists.

The briefer, the sharper the declaration, the better. Only two more important points must be clearly indicated in it, namely, that the people are tired of vacillations, that they are tortured by the lack of decisiveness on the part of the S.-R.'s and Mensheviks ; and that we are definitely severing relations with these *parties* because they have betrayed the revolution.

The other point. In offering an immediate peace without annexations, in breaking at once with the Allied imperialists and with all imperialists, we obtain either an immediate truce or a going over of the entire revolutionary proletariat to the side of defence, and a truly just, truly revolutionary war will then be waged by revolutionary democracy under the leadership of the proletariat.

Having made this declaration, having appealed for *decisions* and not talk ; for *actions*, not writing resolutions, we must *push* our whole fraction *into the factories and barracks* : its place is there ; the pulse of life is there ; the source of saving the revolution is there ; the moving force of the Democratic Conference is there.

In heated, impassioned speeches we must make our programme clear and we must put the question this way : either the conference accepts it *fully*, or an uprising follows. There is no middle course. Delay is impossible. The revolution is perishing.

Having put the question this way, having concentrated our entire fraction in the factories and barracks, *we shall correctly estimate the best moment to begin the uprising.*

And in order to treat uprising in a Marxist way, i.e. as an art, we must at the same time, without losing a single moment, organise the staff of the insurrectionary detachments ; designate the forces ; move the loyal regiments to the most important points ; surround the Alexander theatre; occupy Peter and Paul Fortress ; arrest the general staff and the government ; move against the military cadets, the Wild Division, etc., such detachments as will die rather than allow the enemy to move to the centre of the city ; we must mobilise the armed workers, call them to a last desperate battle, occupy at once the telegraph and telephone stations, place *our* staff of the uprising at the central telephone station, connect it by wire with all the factories, the regiments, the points of armed fighting, etc.

Of course, this is all by way of an example, to *illustrate* the idea that at the present moment it is impossible to remain loyal to the revolution *without treating uprising as an art.*

Written September 26–27, 1917.

THE CRISIS HAS MATURED

. . . What, then, is to be done ? We must *aussprechen, was ist*, " say what is," admit the truth, that in our Central

Committee and at the top of our party there is a tendency in favour of *awaiting* the Congress of Soviets, *against* the immediate seizure of power, *against* an immediate uprising. We must *overcome* this tendency or opinion.

Otherwise the Bolsheviks would *cover themselves with shame for ever* ; they would be *reduced to nothing* as a party.

For to miss such a moment and to " await " the Congress of Soviets is either *absolute idiocy* or *complete betrayal*.

It is a complete betrayal of the German workers. Indeed, we must not wait for the *beginning* of their revolution ! ! When it begins, even the Liberdans will be in favour of " supporting " it. But it *cannot* begin as long as Kerensky, Kishkin and Co. are in power.

It is a complete betrayal of the peasantry. To have the Soviets of *both capitals* and to allow the uprising of the peasants to be suppressed means *to lose, and justly so,* all the confidence of the peasant ; it means to become in the eyes of the peasants equal to the Liberdans and other scoundrels.

To " await " the Congress of Soviets is absolute idiocy, for this means losing *weeks*, whereas weeks and even days now decide *everything*. It means timidly to *refuse* the seizure of power, for on November 14–15 it will be impossible (both politically and technically, since the Cossacks will be mobilised for the day of the foolishly " appointed "[1] uprising).

To " await " the Congress of Soviets is idiocy, for the Congress *will give nothing, it can give nothing* !

The " moral " importance ? Strange indeed ! The " importance " of resolutions and negotiations with the Liberdans when we know that the Soviets are *in favour* of the peasants and that the peasant uprising *is being suppressed* ! ! Thus, we will reduce the *Soviets* to the rôle of miserable chatterers. First vanquish Kerensky, then call the Congress.

The victory of the uprising is now *secure* for the Bolsheviks:

[1] To "call" the Congress of Soviets for November 2, in order to decide upon the seizure of power—is there any difference between this and a foolishly " appointed " uprising? Now we can seize power, whereas November 2–11 you will not be allowed to seize it.

(1) we can[1] (if we do not " await " the Soviet Congress) launch a *sudden* attack from three points, from Petrograd, from Moscow, from the Baltic fleet; (2) we have slogans whose support is guaranteed: down with the government that suppresses the uprising of the peasants against the landowners ! (3) we have a majority *in the country*; (4) complete disorganisation of the Mensheviks and S.-R.'s; (5) we are technically in a position to seize power in Moscow (which might even be the one to start, so as to deal the enemy a surprise blow); (6) we have *thousands* of armed workers and soldiers in Petrograd who can seize *at once* the Winter Palace, the General Staff Building, the telephone exchange and all the largest printing establishments. They will not be able to drive us out from there, whereas there will be such propaganda *in the army* that it will be *impossible* to fight against this government of peace, of land for the peasants, etc.

If we were to attack at once, suddenly, from three points, in Petrograd, Moscow, and the Baltic fleet, there are ninety-nine out of a hundred chances that we would gain a victory with fewer victims than on July 16–18, because *the troops will not advance* against the government of peace. Even if Kerensky has *already* " loyal " cavalry, etc., in Petrograd, when we attack from two sides and when the army is in sympathy *with us*, Kerensky will be compelled to *surrender*. If, with chances like the present, we do not seize power, then all talk of Soviet rule becomes a *lie*.

To refrain from seizing power at present, to " wait," to " chatter " in the Central Committee, to confine ourselves to " fighting for the organ " (of the Soviet), to " fighting for the Congress," means to *ruin the revolution*.

Seeing that the Central Committee has left *even without an answer* my writings insisting on such a policy since the beginning of the Democratic Conference, that the Central Organ *is deleting* from my articles references to such

---

[1] What has the party done by way of *studying* the location of the troops, etc. ? What has it done for the carrying out of the uprising as " an art " ? Only talk in the Central Committee, etc. ! !

glaring errors of the Bolsheviks as the shameful decision to participate in the pre-parliament, as giving seats to the Mensheviks in the Presidium of the Soviets, etc., etc.—seeing all that, I am compelled to recognise here a " gentle " hint as to the unwillingness of the Central Committee even to consider this question, a gentle hint at gagging me and at suggesting that I retire.

I am compelled to *tender my resignation from the Central Committee*, which I hereby do, leaving myself the freedom of propaganda *in the lower ranks* of the party and at the Party Congress.

For it is my deepest conviction that if we " await " the Congress of Soviets and let the present moment pass, we *ruin* the revolution.

Written October 12, 1917.

P.S. A whole series of facts has proven that even the Cossack troops will not move against the government of peace ! And how many are they ? Where are they ? And will not the entire army delegate units in *our favour* ?

LETTER TO THE MEMBERS OF THE CENTRAL COMMITTEE

COMRADES !

I am writing these lines on the evening of the 6th. The situation is extremely critical. It is as clear as can be that delaying the uprising now really means death.

With all my power I wish to persuade the comrades that now everything hangs on a hair, that on the order of the day are questions that are not solved by conferences, by congresses (even by Congresses of Soviets), but only by the people, by the masses, by the struggle of armed masses.

The bourgeois onslaught of the Kornilovists, the removal of Verkhovsky show that we must not wait. We must at any price, this evening, to-night, arrest the Ministers, having disarmed (defeated if they offer resistance) the military cadets, etc.

We must not wait ! We may lose everything !

The immediate gain from the seizure of power at present is : defence of *the people* (not the congress, but the people, in the first place, the army and the peasants) against the Kornilovist government which has driven out Verkhovsky and has hatched a second Kornilov plot.

Who should seize power ?

At present this is not important. Let the Military Revolutionary Committee seize it, or " some other institution " which declares that it will relinquish the power only to the real representatives of the interests of the people, the interests of the Army (immediate offer of peace), the interests of the peasants (take the land immediately, abolish private property), the interests of the hungry.

It is necessary that all the boroughs, all regiments, all forces should be mobilised and should immediately send delegations to the Military Revolutionary Committee, to the Central Committee of the Bolsheviks, insistently demanding that under no circumstances is power to be left in the hands of Kerensky and Co. until the 7th, by no means !—but that the matter must absolutely be decided this evening or to-night.

History will not forgive delay by revolutionists who could be victorious to-day (and will surely be victorious to-day), while they risk losing much to-morrow, they risk losing all.

If we seize power to-day, we seize it not against the Soviets but for them.

Seizure of power is the point of the uprising ; its political task will be clarified after the seizure.

It would be a disaster or formalism to wait for the uncertain voting of November 7. The people have a right and a duty to decide such questions not by voting but by force ; the people have a right and duty in critical moments of a revolution to give directions to their representatives, even their best representatives, and not to wait for them.

This has been proven by the history of all revolutions, and the crime of revolutionists would be limitless if they let go the proper moment, knowing that upon them depends the *saving of the revolution*, the offer of peace, the saving of Petrograd, the saving from starvation, the transfer of the land to the peasants.

The government is tottering. We must *deal it the death blow* at any cost.

To delay action is the same as death.

Written November 6, 1917.

J. Stalin

THE OCTOBER REVOLUTION

Articles and speeches on the Soviet Revolution, published in various Soviet journals between 1918 and 1927. English edition, Martin Lawrence Ltd., 1934.

[Two of these articles are reprinted below. The first, on the National Question, was published in *Pravda*, November 6 and 19, 1918. It shows the Marxist attitude to the national question—this " is only part of the general question of the transformation of the existing order of society " ; and that the Russian Revolution has changed the content of the national question " into a general question of liberating the oppressed nations, colonies and semi-colonies from imperialism." The second article, on the " middle strata," brings out the importance to the revolution of its " reserves," possible allies—in Russia, chiefly the peasantry. This was published in *Pravda*, Nov. 7, 1923.]

THE OCTOBER REVOLUTION

THE OCTOBER REVOLUTION AND THE NATIONAL QUESTION

THE NATIONAL QUESTION is not something that is self-sufficient, fixed once for all time. Being only part of the general question of the transformation of the existing order of society, the national question is wholly determined by the conditions of the social environment, the character of the government of the country and, generally, by the whole course of social development. This is particularly noticeable during revolutionary epochs, when the national question and the national movement rapidly change their content in full view of everyone, according to the course and outcome of the revolution.

I. *The February Revolution and the National Question*

In the epoch of the bourgeois revolution in Russia (dating from February 1917) the national movement in the borderlands bore the character of a bourgeois emancipatory movement. The nationalities of Russia, for ages oppressed and exploited by the " old régime," now for the first time felt that they possessed strength and hurled themselves into the combat with their oppressors. " Liquidate national oppression " was the slogan of the movement. The borderlands of Russia were instantly covered with " all-national " institutions. The movement was headed by the national bourgeois-democratic intelligentsia: " National Councils " in Latvia, in the Esthonian region, in Lithuania, Georgia, Armenia, Azerbaijan, in the cities of the Caucasus, in Kirghizstan and the Middle Volga region ; the " Rada " in the Ukraine and in White Russia ; " Sfatul Tarei " in Bessarabia ; " Kurultai " in the Crimea and in Bashkiria ; the " Autonomous Government " in Turkestan—such were the " all-national " institutions around which the national bourgeoisie was gathering strength. The question at issue was emancipation from tsarism as the " basic cause " of national oppression, and the formation of national bourgeois States. The right of nations to self-determination was interpreted to mean the right of the national bourgeoisie in the borderlands to take power into its own hands and make use of the February Revolution for the purpose of forming its " own " national state. The above-mentioned bourgeois institutions did not contemplate and could not contemplate developing the revolution further. At the same time it was overlooked that naked, barefaced, imperialism was coming to take the place of tsarism, and that this imperialism was a stronger and more dangerous enemy of nationalities, was the basis of a new national oppression.

The abolition of tsarism and the coming into power of the bourgeoisie did not, however, lead to the abolition of national oppression. The old, coarse form of national oppression gave way to a new, refined, yet more dangerous, form of oppression. The government of Lvov-Miliukov-Kerensky not only did not break with the policy of national oppression but organised a new campaign against Finland (dispersion of the Sejm in the summer of 1917) and the Ukraine (destruction of the cultural institutions of the Ukraine). More than that. This government, imperialist by nature, called on the population to continue the war in order to subjugate new lands, new colonies and nationalities. It was impelled to take this course not only by its intrinsic imperialist character but also by the existence of the old imperialist States in Western Europe which were irresistibly endeavouring to subjugate new lands and nationalities and threatened to constrict its sphere of influence. A struggle by the imperialist States to subjugate the small nationalities as a condition of the existence of these States was the picture revealed in the course of the imperialist war. The annihilation of tsarism and the appearance on the scene of the Miliukov-Kerensky government wrought virtually no improvement in this ungainly picture. Naturally, in so far as the " all-national " institutions in the borderlands displayed a tendency towards political independence, they encountered the irresistible opposition of the imperialist government of Russia. However, in so far as they consolidated the power of the national bourgeoisie and remained deaf to the vital interests of " their own "

workers and peasants, they evoked grumbling and discontent among the latter. The so-called " national regiments " only poured oil on the flames ; they were powerless
as against the danger from above, and merely intensified
and aggravated the danger from below. The " all-national "
institutions were left without defence against the blows
dealt from without as well as against an explosion within.
The budding bourgeois national States began to fade before
blossom-time.

Thus the old bourgeois-democratic interpretation of the
principle of self-determination became a fiction and lost its
revolutionary meaning. In such conditions there could
clearly be no question of the abolition of national oppression and of the independence of small and national States.
It was becoming obvious that the liberation of the toiling
masses of the oppressed nationalities and the abolition of
national oppression were inconceivable without a break
with imperialism, without overthrowing " one's own "
national bourgeoisie and without the seizure of power by
the toiling masses themselves.

This became especially apparent after the October
Revolution.

II. *The October Revolution and the National Question*

The February Revolution concealed in its bosom irreconcilable inner contradictions. The revolution was accomplished through the efforts of workers and peasants
(soldiers), whereas, as a result of the revolution, power
passed, not to the workers and peasants, but to the bourgeoisie. By making the revolution the workers and peasants
wanted to put an end to the war, wanted to secure peace,
whereas the bourgeoisie, which assumed power, strove to
use the revolutionary ardour of the masses to continue the
war, was against peace. The economic ruin of the country
and the food crisis demanded the expropriation of capital
and of the industrial enterprises for the benefit of the

workers, the confiscation of the landlord estates for the benefit of the peasants, whereas the bourgeois Miliukov-Kerensky government was standing guard over the interests of the landlords and capitalists, resolutely protecting the latter against attack by workers or peasants. That was a bourgeois revolution, effected at the hands of the workers and peasants for the benefit of " their own " exploiters.

Meanwhile the country continued to groan under the burden of the imperialist war, of economic disintegration and of the collapse of the food supply. The front was falling to pieces and was fast melting away. Factories and mills were stopping work. Famine was on the increase in the country. The February Revolution with its inner contradictions proved obviously inadequate to " save the country." The Miliukov-Kerensky government proved obviously incapable of solving the basic problems of the revolution.

A new, *socialist* revolution was necessary to lead the country out of the impasse of imperialist war and economic ruin.

This revolution came about as a result of the October insurrection.

By overthrowing the power of the landlords and the bourgeoisie and placing a government of the workers and peasants in its stead, the October Revolution at one blow solved the contradictions of the February Revolution. The abolition of landlord-kulak omnipotence and the transfer of the use of the land to the toiling masses of the villages ; the expropriation of the factories and mills, and their transfer to the management of the workers ; the break with imperialism and the termination of the predatory war ; the publication of the secret treaties and the exposure of the policy of foreign territorial annexations ; finally the proclamation of self-determination for the toiling masses of the oppressed nations and the recognition of the independence of Finland constitute the principal measures carried into effect by the Soviet government in the course of the revolution.

This was a truly *socialist* revolution.

The revolution which started at the centre could not be long confined to the narrow territory of the central area. After being victorious at the centre, it was absolutely bound to spread to the border regions. And, indeed, the revolutionary wave, from the very first days of the revolution, spread from the North throughout the whole of Russia, engulfing one borderland after another. However, here it struck a rampart in the form of the " national councils " and regional " governments " (Don, Kuban, Siberia) which had been formed prior to October. The fact of the matter was that these " national governments " would not hear of a socialist revolution. Bourgeois by nature, they had no intention whatever of destroying the old bourgeois world ; on the contrary, they considered it their duty to exert all their energy to preserve and consolidate it. Imperialist in essence, they had not the slightest intention of breaking with imperialism ; on the contrary, they were never averse to capturing and subjugating bits and morsels of " foreign " nationalities, whenever an opportunity to do so presented itself. No wonder then that these " national governments " in the borderlands declared war on the socialist government at the centre. Once they had declared war, they naturally became hotbeds of reaction, to which everything counter-revolutionary in Russia gravitated. It is no secret to anyone that all the counter-revolutionaries cast out of Russia rushed to these hotbeds, and that there, around these hotbeds, they formed white guard " national " regiments.

However, in addition to " national " governments, the borderlands also have national workers and peasants. Even before the October Revolution they were organised in their own revolutionary Soviets of Deputies, after the model of the Soviet of Deputies obtaining in the central parts of Russia, and never severed their connections with their brothers in the North. They, too, strove for victory over the bourgeoisie ; they, too, fought for the triumph of socialism. No wonder the conflict between them and

" their own " national governments increased from day to day. The October Revolution only consolidated the alliance between the workers and peasants of the borderlands and the workers and peasants of Russia, inspiring them with faith in the triumph of socialism. And the war of the " national governments " against the Soviet government brought their conflict with these " governments " to a complete break with them, brought them to open rebellion against them.

Thus was formed the socialist alliance between the workers and peasants of all Russia against the counter-revolutionary alliance of the national-bourgeois " governments " of Russia's borderlands.

Some people depict the struggle of the borderland " governments " as a struggle for national liberation and against the " soulless centralism " of the Soviet government. This, however, is wrong. No government in the world ever granted such extensive decentralisation, no government in the world ever afforded its peoples such plenary national freedom as does the Soviet government of Russia. The struggle of the borderland " governments " was and remains a struggle of the bourgeois counter-revolution against socialism. The national flag is tacked on to the cause only to deceive the masses, only as a popular flag which conveniently covers up the counter-revolutionary designs of the national bourgeoisie.

However, the struggle of the " national " and regional " governments " proved to be an unequal, struggle. Attacked from two quarters—from without by the Soviet government, and from within by " their own " workers and peasants—the " national governments " had to retreat after the very first battles. The uprising of the Finnish workers and agricultural labourers and the flight of the bourgeois " Senate " ; the uprising of the Ukrainian workers and peasants and the flight of the bourgeois " Rada " ; the uprising of the workers and peasants in the Don region, in Kuban in Siberia and the downfall of

Kaledin, of Kornilov and of the Siberian " government " ; the uprising of the poor of Turkestan and the flight of the " autonomous government " ; the agrarian revolution in the Caucasus and the utter helplessness of the " national councils " of Georgia, Armenia and Azerbaijan—these are facts of common knowledge demonstrating the complete isolation of the borderland " governments " from " their own " masses. Having been completely defeated, the " national governments " were " forced " to appeal to the imperialists of Western Europe, to the age-long oppressors and exploiters of the small nations of the whole world, for aid against " their own " workers and peasants.

Such was the beginning of the period of foreign intervention in, and occupation of, the borderlands—a period revealing once more the counter-revolutionary nature of the " national " and regional " governments."

Only now has it become obvious to all that the national bourgeoisie is striving not for the liberation of " its own people " from national oppression but for the liberty of wringing profits from it, for the liberty of preserving its own privileges and capital.

Only now has it become obvious that the liberation of the oppressed nationalities is inconceivable without breaking with imperialism, without overthrowing the bourgeoisie of the oppressed nations, without power passing into the hands of the toiling masses of those nationalities.

Thus the old bourgeois conception of the principle of self-determination with the slogan " All Power to the National Bourgeoisie " was exposed and rejected by the very course of the revolution. The socialist conception of self-determination with the slogan " All Power to the Toiling Masses of the Oppressed Nations " obtained full recognition and opportunity of application.

Thus the October Revolution, after putting an end to the old bourgeois emancipatory national movement, inaugurated the era of a new socialist movement of the workers and peasants of the oppressed nations, directed against all—which signifies also national—oppression, against the rule of the bourgeoisie, whether " its own " or foreign, against imperialism in general.

III. The International Importance of the October Revolution

After being victorious in the central part of Russia and taking possession of a number of borderlands, the October Revolution could not stop short at the territorial boundaries of Russia. In the atmosphere of imperialist world war and general discontent among the lower classes, it could not but spread to the neighbouring countries. The break with imperialism and the liberation of Russia from the pre-datory war, the publication of the secret treaties and the solemn abrogation of the policy of seizing foreign soil, the proclamation of national freedom and the recognition of the independence of Finland, the declaration of Russia as a " Federation of Soviet National Republics " and the militant battle-cry of a resolute struggle against im-perialism broadcast all over the world by the Soviet govern-ment in millions of pamphlets, newspapers and leaflets in the mother tongues of the peoples of the East and West—all this could not fail to have its effect on the enslaved East and the bleeding West.

And, in truth, the October Revolution is the first revolu-tion in the history of the world that has broken the sleep of centuries of the toiling masses of the oppressed nations of the East and drawn them into the struggle against world imperialism. The formation of workers' and peasants' soviets in Persia, China and India, modelled after the soviets in Russia, is sufficiently convincing proof of this.

The October Revolution is the first revolution in the world that provided the workers and peasants of the West with a living and salutary example and urged them on to the path of real liberation from the yoke of war and

imperialism. The uprising of the workers and soldiers in
Austria-Hungary and Germany, the formation of Soviets
of Workers' and Soldiers' Deputies, the revolutionary
struggle of the nations of Austria-Hungary against national
oppression are quite eloquent proofs of this.

That the struggle in the East and even in the West has
not yet succeeded in shedding the bourgeois-nationalist
features is not at all the point at issue—the point is that the
struggle against imperialism *has begun*, that it goes on and
is inevitably bound to reach its logical termination.

Foreign intervention and the policy of occupation pur-
sued by the " foreign " imperialists only intensify the revolutionary crisis, drawing new nations into the struggle and
extending the area of revolutionary clashes with imperialism.

Thus the October Revolution, by establishing ties between the nations of the backward East and the advanced
West, draws them together into the joint camp of the
struggle against imperialism.

The national question thus grows from the partial
question of struggling against national oppression to the
general question of liberating the nations, colonies and
semi-colonies from imperialism.

The mortal sin of the Second International and its
leader Kautsky consists incidentally in this : that they
were always deviating towards a bourgeois conception of
national self-determination, that they did not understand
the revolutionary meaning of the latter, that they did not
know how, or did not want, to put the national question on
the revolutionary basis of an open struggle against imperialism, that they did not know how, or did not want, to
link the national question to the question of liberating the
colonies.

The thick-headedness of the Austrian Social-Democrats of
the type of Bauer and Renner consists indeed in that they
failed to understand the indissoluble bond between the
national question and the question of power, and tried to

separate the national question from politics and confine it within the scope of cultural and educational questions, oblivious of the existence of such " trifles " as imperialism and the colonies enslaved by it.

It is said that the principles of self-determination and of the " defence of the fatherland " have been abrogated by the very course of events in the conditions of an ascendant socialist revolution. In fact it is not self-determination and the " defence of the fatherland " that have been abrogated, but their bourgeois interpretation. It is sufficient to cast a glance at the occupied regions, languishing under the yoke of imperialism and yearning for liberation ; sufficient to cast a glance at Russia conducting a revolutionary war for the defence of the socialist fatherland against the pirates of imperialism ; sufficient to ponder the events that are now transpiring in Austria-Hungary ; sufficient to glance at the enslaved colonies and semi-colonies, that have already organised soviets in their respective countries (India, Persia, China)—one need but cast a glance at all this to realise the full revolutionary significance of the principle of self-determination in its socialist interpretation.

Indeed the great international importance of the October Revolution consists mainly in that this revolution :

(1) has widened the scope of the national question, transforming it from a partial question of struggling against national oppression into a general question of liberating the oppressed nations, colonies and semi-colonies from imperialism ;

(2) has ushered in vast opportunities and disclosed the actual means for this liberation, thus considerably facilitating the task of the oppressed nations of the West and East to accomplish their liberation and drawing them into the common channel of a victorious struggle against imperialism ;

(3) has thereby erected a bridge between the socialist West and the enslaved East, by setting up a new front of revolutions extending from the proletarians of the West on

through the Russian Revolution to the oppressed nations of the East *against* world imperialism.

This, in effect, explains the indescribable enthusiasm now displayed by the toiling and exploited masses of the East and West with regard to the Russian proletariat.

This largely explains the brutal fury with which the imperialist robbers of the whole world have hurled themselves against Soviet Russia.

THE OCTOBER REVOLUTION AND THE QUESTION OF THE MIDDLE STRATA

The question of the middle strata undoubtedly presents one of the fundamental questions of the workers' revolution. The middle strata are the peasantry and the petty labouring populace of the cities. In this category must also be classified the oppressed nationalities, which consist nine-tenths of middle strata. As you see, these are precisely the strata which, by their economic position, are situated between the proletariat and the capitalist class. The relative importance of these strata is determined by two circumstances : in the first place, these strata represent the majority, or, at any rate, a considerable minority of the population of the existing States ; second, they represent the important reserves from among which the capitalist class recruits its army against the proletariat. The proletariat cannot maintain power without the sympathy and support of the middle strata, primarily of the peasantry, especially in a country like our union of republics. The proletariat cannot even seriously think of seizing power unless these strata have at least been neutralised, unless these strata have already had time to divorce themselves from the capitalist class, if they still constitute, in their mass, an army of the capitalists. Hence the struggle for the middle strata, the struggle for the peasantry, which passes like a coloured thread through the whole fabric of our revolution, from 1905 to 1917, a struggle which is far from over and which will go on in the future as well.

The Revolution of 1848 in France suffered defeat because, among other things, it failed to evoke sympathetic response among the French peasants. The Paris Commune fell because, among other things, it encountered the opposition of the middle strata, especially of the peasantry. The same must be said of the Russian Revolution of 1905. Some of the vulgar Marxists, with Kautsky at their head, basing themselves on the experience of the European revolutions, arrived at the conclusion that the middle strata, especially of the peasantry, were well-nigh born enemies of the workers' revolution, and that it was necessary on that account to steer towards a more lengthy period of development, as a result of which the proletariat would become the majority of the nation whereby the actual conditions prerequisite to a victory of the workers' revolution would be created. On the basis of this conclusion, these vulgar Marxists warned the proletariat against a " premature " revolution. On the basis of this conclusion, they, for " considerations of principle," placed these middle strata at the complete disposal of the capitalists. On the basis of this conclusion, they prophesied to us the doom of the Russian October Revolution, referring to the fact that the proletariat constituted a minority in Russia, that Russia was a peasant country and that on that account a victorious workers' revolution was impossible in Russia.

It is characteristic that Marx himself evaluated the middle strata, especially the peasantry, quite differently. Whereas the vulgar Marxists, after giving up the peasantry and placing it at the complete disposal of capital, vociferously swaggered about their " unswerving adherence to principles "—Marx, most consistent of all Marxists in questions of principle, insistently advised the party of the Communists not to lose sight of the peasantry, to win it over to the side of the proletariat and to make sure of its support in the coming proletarian revolution. It is well known that in the 'fifties, after the defeat of the February Revolution in France and in Germany, Marx wrote to Engels, and through him to the Communist Party of Germany, as follows :

> The whole thing in Germany will depend on the possibility to back the proletarian revolution by some second edition of the Peasant War.

This was written about the Germany of the 'fifties, a peasant country, in which the proletariat formed an insignificant minority, in which the proletariat was less organised than in the Russia of 1917, and in which the peasantry, owing to its position, was less disposed to support a proletarian revolution than was the case in the Russia of 1917.

The October Revolution undoubtedly presented the happy combination of a " peasant war " and a " proletarian revolution " of which Marx wrote, all the chatterboxes and their " principles " notwithstanding. The October Revolution proved that such a combination is both possible and feasible. The October Revolution proved that the proletariat can seize power and maintain it, provided it is able to wrest the middle strata, especially the peasantry, from the capitalist classes, provided it knows how to transform these strata from reserves of capitalism into reserves of the proletariat.

In brief : the October Revolution was the first of all the revolutions of the world to advance to the forefront the question of the middle strata, primarily the peasantry, and to settle it victoriously, all the " theories " and lamentations of the heroes of the Second International notwithstanding.

This constitutes the first service of the October Revolution, if one may speak altogether of services in this case.

However, matters did not rest there. The October Revolution went further, trying to rally the oppressed

nationalities round the proletariat. It was stated above
that these nationalities consist nine-tenths of peasants
and the petty labouring populace of the cities. However,
this does not fully characterise the concept " oppressed
nationality." The oppressed nationalities are usually
oppressed not only as peasantry and the labouring populace of the cities but also as nationalities, i.e. as workers
of a definite statehood, language, culture, manner of life,
customs and habits. The double weight of oppression
cannot but revolutionise the toiling masses of the oppressed
nationalities, cannot but urge them on to the struggle
against the principal force of oppression—to the struggle
against capital. This circumstance served as the base on
which the proletariat succeeded in realising the combination of a " proletarian revolution " and not only a " peasant
war " but also a " national war." All this could not fail to
extend the field of action of the proletarian revolution far
beyond the confines of Russia, could not fail to jeopardise
the most deep-seated reserves of capitalism. If the struggle
for the middle strata of a given dominating nationality
means the struggle for the immediate reserves of capitalism,
the struggle for the liberation of the oppressed nationalities
could not but be transformed into a struggle for the conquest of the separate, most deep-seated reserves of capitalism, into a struggle for the liberation of the colonial and
partly disfranchised nations from the yoke of capitalism.
This latter struggle is not over by far—besides, it has not
yet had time to yield even the first decisive successes.
However, this struggle for the deep-seated reserves owes
its commencement to the October Revolution, and it will
undoubtedly develop step by step, commensurate with the
development of imperialism, commensurate with the
increase in power of our union of republics, commensurate
with the development of the proletarian revolution in the
West.

In brief : the October Revolution has actually initiated
the struggle of the proletariat for the deep-seated reserves

of capitalism from among the masses of the people in the oppressed and partly disfranchised countries ; it was the first to raise the standard of struggle for winning these reserves—this constitutes its second service.

Winning the peasantry proceeded in our country under the banner of socialism. The peasantry, which had received land at the hands of the proletariat, which had defeated the landlords with the aid of the proletariat, and which had risen to power under the leadership of the proletariat, could not but feel, could not but understand that the process of its liberation proceeded, and would proceed in the future, under the banner of the proletariat, under its Red Banner. This circumstance could not fail to transform the banner of socialism, which was formerly a bogey to the peasantry, into a standard attracting its attention and facilitating its liberation from wretchedness, destitution and oppression. The same must be said with even more emphasis in regard to the oppressed nationalities. The call to struggle for the liberation of the nationalities, a call reenforced by facts such as the liberation of Finland, the evacuation of troops from Persia and China, the formation of the Union of Republics, open moral support to the peoples of Turkey, China, Hindustan, Egypt—this call was first sounded by the people who were the victors in the October Revolution. The fact that Russia, which formerly served as the symbol of oppression in the eyes of the oppressed nationalities, has now, after it has become socialist, been transformed into a symbol of liberation, cannot be described as a mere chance. Nor is it accidental that the name of Comrade Lenin, the leader of the October Revolution, is now the most cherished name of the downtrodden, browbeaten peasants and revolutionary intelligentsia of the colonial and semi-enfranchised countries. If formerly Christianity was considered an anchor of salvation among the oppressed and downtrodden slaves of the vast Roman Empire, now things are heading towards a point where socialism can serve (and is already beginning to serve !) as a banner of liberation for the many millions in the vast colonial States of imperialism. It is hardly susceptible of doubt that this circumstance considerably facilitated the struggle to combat the prejudices against socialism and opened the road to the ideas of socialism in the most remote corners of the oppressed countries. If formerly it was difficult for a socialist to show himself with open visor among the non-proletarian middle strata of the oppressed or oppressing countries, to-day he can openly propagate the idea of socialism among these strata and expect to be listened to and perhaps even followed, for he possesses so cogent an argument as the October Revolution. This is also a result of the October Revolution.

In brief : the October Revolution cleared the path to the ideas of socialism for the middle non-proletarian peasant strata of all nationalities and tribes ; it popularised the banner of socialism among them—which constitutes the third service of the October Revolution.

Opposite: The Executive Committee of the Communist International. Joseph Stalin appears in the middle.

J. Stalin

FOUNDATIONS OF LENINISM

A lecture delivered in April 1924 ; published in a collection of Stalin's works, 1926. English edition, " Leninism," Allen & Unwin, Ltd., 1928. Another translation was published by the Co-operative Publishing Society of Foreign Workers in the U.S.S.R., 1935 ; the section given below is from this edition.

[This was a lecture delivered by Stalin at Sverdlov University, in April, 1924. In the introduction, Stalin defines Leninism as " the Marxism of the epoch of imperialism and of the proletarian revolution." The lecture covers the Historical Roots of Leninism ; Method ; Theory ; the Dictatorship of the Proletariat ; the Peasant Problem ; the National Question ; Strategy and Tactics ; the Party, and Style in the Work. It is the most important study of Leninism that exists, bringing out the development of Marxism made by Lenin " in a period of fully developed imperialism ; in a period when the proletarian revolution was already under way . . ." The section reprinted below, on The Party, shows the development of the revolutionary party of the proletariat under Lenin's guidance, and the part played by the Party both before and after the revolution.]

FOUNDATIONS OF LENINISM

THE PARTY

In the pre-revolutionary period, in the period of more or less peaceful development, when the parties of the Second International were the predominant force in the labour movement and parliamentary forms of struggle were regarded as the principal forms, the Party neither had nor could have that great and decisive importance which it acquired afterwards in the midst of open revolutionary battles. In defending the Second International against the attacks that were made upon it, Kautsky says that the parties of the Second International are instruments of peace and not of war, that for that very reason they were powerless to take any far-reaching steps during the war, during the period of revolutionary action by the proletariat. That is absolutely true. But what does it prove? It proves that the parties of the Second International are not suitable for the revolutionary struggle of the proletariat, that they are not militant parties of the proletariat leading the workers to power, but an election apparatus suitable for parliamentary elections and parliamentary struggle. This, properly speaking, explains why, in the days when the opportunists of the Second International were dominant, it was not the Party but the parliamentary fraction that was the fundamental political organisation of the proletariat. It is well known that the Party at that time was really an appendage or an auxiliary of the parliamentary fraction. It is superfluous to add that under such circumstances and with such a Party at its head, it was utterly impossible to prepare the proletariat for revolution.

With the dawn of the new period, however, matters

changed radically. The new period is a period of open collisions between the classes, a period of revolutionary action by the proletariat, a period of proletarian revolution ; it is the period of the immediate mustering of forces for the overthrow of imperialism, for the seizure of power by the proletariat. This period confronts the proletariat with new tasks of reorganising all Party work on new, revolutionary lines ; of educating the workers in the spirit of the revolutionary struggle for power ; of preparing and moving up the reserves ; of establishing an alliance with the proletarians of neighbouring countries ; of establishing durable contact with the liberation movement in the colonies and dependent countries, etc., etc. To imagine that these new tasks can be fulfilled by the old Social-Democratic parties, brought up as they were in the peaceful atmosphere of parliamentarism, can lead only to hopeless despair and to inevitable defeat. To have such tasks to shoulder under the leadership of the old parties is tantamount to being left completely disarmed. It goes without saying that the proletariat could not accept such a position.

Hence the necessity for a new party, a militant party, a revolutionary party, bold enough to lead the proletarians to the struggle for power, with sufficient experience to be able to orientate itself in the complicated problems that arise in a revolutionary situation, and sufficiently flexible to steer clear of any submerged rocks on the way to its goal.

Without such a party it is futile to think of overthrowing imperialism and achieving the dictatorship of the proletariat.

This new party is the party of Leninism.

What are the special features of this new party ?

(1) *The Party as the Vanguard of the Working Class*

The Party must first of all constitute the *vanguard* of the working class. The Party must absorb all the best elements of the working class, their experience, their revolutionary spirit and their unbounded devotion to the cause of the proletariat. But in order that it may really be the vanguard, the Party must be armed with a revolutionary theory, with a knowledge of the laws of the movement, with a knowledge of the laws of revolution. Without this it will be impotent to guide the struggle of the proletariat and to lead the proletariat. The Party cannot be a real Party if it limits itself to registering what the masses of the working class think or experience, if it drags along at the tail of the spontaneous movement, if it does not know how to overcome the inertness and the political indifference of the spontaneous movement, or if it cannot rise above the transient interests of the proletariat, if it cannot raise the masses to the level of the class interests of the proletariat. The Party must take its stand at the head of the working class, it must see ahead of the working class, lead the proletariat and not trail behind the spontaneous movement. The parties of the Second International which preach " tailism " are the exponents of bourgeois politics which condemn the proletariat to being a tool in the hands of the bourgeoisie. Only a party which adopts the point of view of the vanguard of the proletariat, which is capable of raising the masses to the level of the class interests of the proletariat, is capable of diverting the working class from the path of craft unionism and converting it into an independent political force. The Party is the political leader of the working class.

I have spoken above of the difficulties encountered in the struggle of the working class, of the complicated nature of this struggle, of strategy and tactics, of reserves and manœuvring operations, of attack and defence. These conditions are no less complicated, perhaps more so, than war operations. Who can understand these conditions, who can give correct guidance to the vast masses of the proletariat? Every army at war must have an experienced General Staff if it is to avoid certain defeat. All the more reason therefore why the proletariat must have such a

General Staff if it is to prevent itself from being routed by its mortal enemies. But where is this General Staff? Only the revolutionary party of the proletariat can serve as this General Staff. A working class without a revolutionary party is like an army without a General Staff. The Party is the Military Staff of the proletariat.

But the Party cannot be merely a *vanguard*. It must at the same time be a unit of the *class*, be part of that class, intimately bound to it with every fibre of its being. The distinction between the vanguard and the main body of the working class, between Party members and non-Party workers, will continue as long as classes exist, as long as the proletariat continues replenishing its ranks with newcomers from other classes, as long as the working class as a whole lacks the opportunity of raising itself to the level of the vanguard. But the Party would cease to be a party if this distinction were widened into a rupture : if it were to isolate itself and break away from the non-Party masses. The Party cannot lead the class if it is not connected with the non-Party masses, if there is no close union between the Party and the non-Party masses, if these masses do not accept its leadership, if the Party does not enjoy moral and political authority among the masses. Recently, two hundred thousand new workers joined our Party. The remarkable thing about this is that these workers did not *come* into the Party, but were rather *sent* there by the mass of other non-Party workers who took an active part in the acceptance of the new members and without whose approval no new member was accepted. This fact proves that the broad masses of non-Party workers regard our Party as *their* Party, as a Party near *and dear* to them, in the expansion and consolidation of which they are vitally interested and to whose leadership they willingly entrust their destinies. It goes without saying that without these intangible moral ties connecting the Party with the non-Party masses, the Party could never become the decisive force of its class. The Party is an inseparable part of the working class.

We are the party of a class—says Lenin—and therefore *almost the entire class* (and in times of war, during the period of civil war, the entire class) must act under the leadership of our Party, must link itself up with our Party as closely as possible. But we would be guilty of Manilovism and "khvostism" if we believed that at any time under capitalism nearly the whole class, or the whole class, would be able to rise to the level of the class consciousness and degree of activity of its vanguard, of its socialist party. No sensible Socialist has ever yet doubted that under capitalism even the trade union organisations (which are more primitive and more accesible to the intelligence of the undeveloped strata) are unable to embrace nearly the whole, or the whole, working class. To forget the distinction between the vanguard and the whole of the masses gravitating towards it, to forget the constant duty of the vanguard to *raise* these increasingly widening strata to this advanced level, only means deceiving oneself, shutting one's eyes to the immensity of our tasks and narrowing them. (*Collected Works*, Russian edition, Vol. VI, pp. 205–206.)

(2) *The Party as the Organised Detachment of the Working Class*

The Party is not only the *vanguard* of the working class. If it desires really to lead the struggle of the class it must at the same time be the *organised* detachment of its class. Under the capitalist system the Party's tasks are huge and varied. The Party must lead the struggle of the proletariat under the exceptionally difficult circumstances of inner as well as outer development ; it must lead the proletariat in its attack when the situation calls for an attack, it must withdraw the proletariat from the blows of a powerful opponent when the situation calls for retreat ; it must imbue the millions of unorganised non-Party workers with the spirit of discipline and system in fighting, with the spirit of organisation and perseverance. But the Party can acquit itself of these tasks only if it itself is the embodiment of discipline and organisation, if it itself is the *organised* detachment of the proletariat. Unless these conditions are fulfilled it is idle to talk about the Party really leading the vast masses of the proletariat. The Party is the organised detachment of the working class.

The conception of the Party as an organised whole has become firmly fixed in Lenin's well-known formulation of the first point of our Party rules in which the Party is regarded as the *sum total* of the organisations and the Party member as a member of one of the organisations of the Party. The Mensheviks, who had objected to this formulation as early as 1903, proposed to substitute for it a " system " of self-enrolment in the Party, a " system " of conferring the " title " Party member upon every "professor" and " high school student," upon every " sympathiser " and " striker " who gave support to the Party in one way or another, but who did not belong and had no inclination to belong to any one of the Party organisations. We need not stop to prove that had this odd " system " become firmly entrenched in our Party it would have been inundated with professors and students, it would have degenerated into a widely diffused, amorphous, disorganised " body " lost in a sea of " sympathisers," that would have obliterated the line of demarcation between the Party and the class and would have frustrated the aim of the Party to raise the unorganised masses to the level of the vanguard. It goes without saying that under such an opportunist " system " our Party would not have been able to accomplish its mission as the organising nucleus of the working class during the course of our revolution.

> From Martov's point of view—says Lenin—the boundary line of the Party remains absolutely unfixed inasmuch as " every striker could declare himself a member of the Party." What advantage is there in this diffuseness? Spreading wide a "title." The harmfulness of it lies in that it introduces the *disruptive* idea of identifying the class with the Party. (*Collected Works*, Russian edition, Vol. VI, p. 211.)

But the Party is not merely the *sum total* of Party organisations. The Party at the same time represents a single system of these organisations, their formal unification into a single whole, possessing higher and lower organs of leadership, with submission of the minority to the majority, where decisions on questions of practice are obligatory upon all members of the Party. Unless these conditions are fulfilled the Party is unable to form a single organised whole capable of exercising systematic and organised leadership of the struggle of the working class.

> *Formerly*—says Lenin—our Party was not a formally organised whole, but only the sum total of separate groups. Therefore, no other relations except that of ideological influence were possible between these groups. *Now*, we have become an organised Party, and this implies the creation of a power, the conversion of the authority of ideas into the authority of power, the subordination of the lower Party bodies to the higher Party bodies. (*Ibid.*, p. 291.)

The principle of the minority submitting to the majority, the principle of leading Party work from a centre, has been a subject of repeated attacks by wavering elements who accuse us of " bureaucracy," " formalism," etc. It hardly needs to be proved that systematic work of the Party, as one whole, and the leadership of the struggle of the working class would have been impossible without the enforcement of these principles. On the organisational question, Leninism stands for the strict enforcement of these principles. Lenin terms the fight against these principles " Russian nihilism " and " gentleman's anarchism " which deserve only to be ridiculed and thrown aside.

This is what Lenin has to say about these wavering elements in his book entitled *One Step Forward, Two Steps Backward* :

> The Russian nihilist is especially addicted to this gentleman's anarchism. To him the Party organisation appears to be a monstrous " factory," the subordination of the part to the whole and the submission of the minority to the majority appears to him to be " serfdom " . . . the division of labour under the

leadership of a centre evokes tragi-comical lamentations about people being reduced to mere " cogs and screws " . . . the bare mention of the Party rules on organisation calls forth a contemptuous grimace and some disdainful . . . remark to the effect that we could get along without rules. . . . It seems clear, however, that these outcries against the alleged bureaucracy are an attempt to conceal the dissatisfaction with the personnel of these centres, a fig leaf. . . . " You are a bureaucrat because you were appointed by the Congress without my consent and against my wishes : you are a formalist because you seek support in the formal decisions of the Congress and not in my approval : you act in a crudely mechanical way, because your authority is the ' mechanical ' majority of the Party Congress and you do not consult my desire to be co-opted ; you are an autocrat because you do not want to deliver power into the hands of the old gang."[1] (*Collected Works*, Russian edition, Vol. VI, pp. 310 and 287.)

(3) *The Party as the Highest Form of Class Organisation of the Proletariat*

The Party is the organised detachment of the working class. But the Party is not the only organisation of the working class. The proletariat has in addition a great number of other organisations which are indispensable in its correct struggle against the capitalist system—trade unions, co-operative societies, factory and shop organisations, parliamentary fractions, non-Party women's associations, the press, cultural and educational organisations, youth leagues, military revolutionary organisations (in times of direct revolutionary action), soviets of deputies as the State form of organisation (where the proletariat is in power), etc. Most of these organisations are non-Party and only a certain part of these adhere directly to the Party, or represent its offshoots. All these organisations, under certain conditions, are absolutely necessary for the working class, as without them it is impossible to consolidate the

[1] The " old gang " here referred to is that of Axelrod, Martov, Potresov and others who would not submit to the decisions of the Second Congress and who accused Lenin of being a " bureaucrat."—J. S.

class position of the proletariat in the diversified spheres of struggle, and without them it is impossible to steel the proletariat as the force whose mission it is to replace the bourgeois order by the socialist order. But how can unity of leadership become a reality in the face of such a multiplicity of organisations ? What guarantee is there that this multiplicity of organisations will not lead to discord in leadership ? It might be argued that each of these organisations carries on its work in its own field in which it specialises and cannot, therefore, interfere with the others. That, of course, is true. But it is likewise true that the activities of all these organisations ought to be directed into a single channel, as they serve *one* class, the class of the proletariat. The question then arises : who is to determine the line, the general direction along which the work of all these organisations is to be conducted ? Where is that central organisation which is not only able, having the necessary experience, to work out such a general line, but also capable, because of its authority, of prevailing upon all these organisations to carry out this line, in order to attain unity of direction and preclude the possibility of working at cross purposes ?

This organisation is the party of the proletariat.

The Party possesses all the necessary qualifications for this purpose because, in the first place, it is the common meeting ground of the best elements in the working class that have direct connections with the non-Party organisations of the proletariat and very frequently lead them ; because, secondly, the Party, as the meeting ground of the best members of the working class, is the best school for training leaders of the working class, capable of directing every form of organisation of their class ; because, thirdly, the Party, as the best school for training leaders of the working class, is, by reason of its experience and authority, the only organisation capable of centralising the leadership of the struggle of the proletariat and in this way of transforming each and every non-Party organisation of the working class into an auxiliary body, a transmission belt linking it with the class. The Party is the highest form of class organisation of the proletariat.

This does not mean, of course, that non-Party organisations like trade unions, co-operative societies, etc., must be formally subordinated to Party leadership. It means simply that the members of the Party who belong to these organisations and doubtless exercise influence in them should do all they can to persuade these non-Party organisations to draw nearer to the Party of the proletariat in their work and voluntarily accept its political guidance.

That is why Lenin says that " the Party is the *highest* form of class association of proletarians " whose political leadership ought to extend to every other form of organisation of the proletariat. (" *Left-Wing* " *Communism, etc.,* Chap. VI.)

That is why the opportunist theory of the " independence " and " neutrality " of the non-Party organisations, which theory is the progenitor of *independent* parliamentarians and publicists who are *isolated* from the Party, and of *narrow-minded* trade unionists and co-operative society officials who have become petty bourgeois, is wholly incompatible with the theory and practice of Leninism.

(4) *The Party as the Weapon of the Dictatorship of the Proletariat*

The Party is the highest form of organisation of the proletariat. The Party is the fundamental leading element within the class of the proletariat and within the organisations of that class. But it does not follow by any means that the Party can be regarded as an end in itself, as a self-sufficing force. The Party is not only the highest form of class association of the proletarians ; it is at the same time a *weapon* in the hands of the proletariat *for* the achievement of the dictatorship where that has not yet been achieved ; *for* the consolidation and extension of the dictatorship where it has already been achieved. The Party would not rank so high in importance and it could not overshadow all other forms of organisation of the proletariat if the latter were not face to face with the question of power, if the conditions of imperialism, the inevitability of wars and the presence of a crisis did not demand the concentration of all the forces of the proletariat on one point and the gathering together of all the threads of the revolutionary movement in one spot, to overthrow the bourgeoisie and to establish the dictatorship of the proletariat. The proletariat needs the Party first of all as its General Staff, which it must have for the successful seizure of power. Needless to say, the Russian proletariat could never have established its revolutionary dictatorship without a Party capable of rallying around itself the mass organisations of the proletariat and of centralising the leadership of the entire movement during the progress of the struggle.

But the proletariat needs the Party not only to achieve the dictatorship, it needs it still more to maintain, consolidate and extend its dictatorship in order to attain complete victory for socialism.

> Certainly almost everyone now realises—says Lenin—that the Bolsheviks could not have maintained themselves in power for two and a half years, and not even for two and a half months, without the strictest discipline, the truly iron discipline, in our Party, and without the fullest and unreserved support rendered it by the whole mass of the working class, that is, by all those belonging to this class who think, who are honest, self-sacrificing, influential, and capable of leading and attracting the backward masses. (" Left-Wing " Communism, etc., Chap. II.)

Now what is meant by " maintaining " and " extending " the dictatorship? It means imbuing these millions of proletarians with the spirit of discipline and organisation : it means creating among the proletarian masses a bulwark against the corrosive influences of petty-bourgeois spontaneity and petty-bourgeois habits ; it means that the organising work of the proletarians in re-educating and remoulding the petty-bourgeois strata must be reinforced ; it means that assistance must be given to the masses of the proletarians in educating themselves so that they may become a force capable of abolishing classes and of preparing the ground for the organisation of socialist production. But it is impossible to accomplish all this without a Party, which is strong by reason of its cohesion and discipline.

> The dictatorship of the proletariat—says Lenin—is a persistent struggle—sanguinary and bloodless, violent and peaceful, military and economic, educational and administrative—against the forces and traditions of the old society. The force of habit of millions and of tens of millions is a terrible force. Without an iron party steeled in the struggle, without a party enjoying the confidence of all that is honest in the given class, without a party capable of keeping track of and influencing the mood of the masses, it is impossible to conduct such a struggle successfully. (" *Left-Wing* " *Communism, etc.*, Chap. V.)

The proletariat needs the Party *for* the purpose of achieving and maintaining the dictatorship. The Party is the instrument of the dictatorship of the proletariat.

From this it follows that when classes disappear and the dictatorship of the proletariat dies out, the Party will also die out.

(5) *The Party as the Expression of Unity of Will, Which is Incompatible With the Existence of Factions*

The achievement and maintenance of the dictatorship of the proletariat are impossible without a party strong in its cohesion and iron discipline. But iron discipline in the Party is impossible without unity of will and without absolute and complete unity of action on the part of all members of the Party. This does not mean, of course, that the possibility of a conflict of opinion within the Party is thus excluded. On the contrary, iron discipline does not preclude but presupposes criticism and conflicts of opinion within the Party. Least of all does it mean that this discipline must be " blind " discipline. On the contrary, iron discipline does not preclude but presupposes conscious and voluntary submission, for only conscious discipline can be truly iron discipline. But after a discussion has been closed, after criticism has run its course and a decision has been made, unity of will and unity of action of all Party members become indispensable conditions without which Party unity and iron discipline in the Party are inconceivable.

> In the present epoch of intensified civil war—says Lenin—the Communist Party can discharge its duty only if it is organised with the highest degree of centralisation; ruled by iron discipline bordering on military discipline, and if its Party centre proves to be a potent authoritative body invested with broad powers and enjoying the general confidence of the Party members. (*Conditions of Affiliation to the Communist International.*)

This is the position in regard to discipline in the Party in the period of struggle preceding the establishment of the dictatorship.

The same thing applies, but to a greater degree, to discipline in the Party after the establishment of the dictatorship.

In this connection, Lenin said :

> Whoever in the least weakens the iron discipline of the party of the proletariat (especially during its dictatorship) actually aids the bourgeoisie against the proletariat. (" *Left-Wing* " *Communism, etc.*, Chap. V.)

It follows that the existence of factions is incompatible with Party unity and with its iron discipline. It need hardly be emphasised that the existence of factions leads to the creation of a number of centres, and the existence of a number of centres connotes the absence of a common centre in the Party, a breach in the unity of will, the weakening and disintegration of discipline, the weakening and disintegration of the dictatorship. It is true that the parties of the Second International, which are fighting against the dictatorship of the proletariat and have no desire to lead the proletariat to power, can permit themselves the luxury of such liberalism as freedom for factions, for they have no need whatever of iron discipline. But the parties of the

Communist International, which organise their activities on the basis of the task of achieving and strengthening the dictatorship of the proletariat, cannot afford to be "liberal" or to permit the formation of factions. The Party is synonymous with unity of will, which leaves no room for any factionalism or division of authority in the Party.

Hence Lenin's warning on the "danger of factionalism from the point of view of Party unity and of the realisation of unity of will in the vanguard of the proletariat as the primary prerequisite for the success of the dictatorship of the proletariat," which is embodied in a special resolution of the Tenth Congress of our Party, *On Party Unity*.

Hence Lenin's demand for the "complete extermination of all factionalism" and the "immediate dissolution of all groups, without exception, that had been formed on the basis of this or that platform" on pain of "unconditional and immediate expulsion from the Party." (*Cf.* the resolution, *On Party Unity*.)

(6) *The Party Is Strengthened by Purging Itself of Opportunist Elements*

The opportunist elements in the Party are the source of Party factionalism. The proletariat is not an isolated class. A steady stream of peasants, small tradesmen and intellectuals, who have become proletarianised by the development of capitalism, flows into the ranks of the proletariat. At the same time the upper strata of the proletariat—principally the trade union leaders and labour members of parliament—who have been fed by the bourgeoisie out of the super-profits extracted from the colonies, are undergoing a process of decay.

This stratum of the labour aristocracy or of workers who have become bourgeois—says Lenin—who have become quite petty-bourgeois in their mode of life, in their earnings, and in their outlook, serve as the principal bulwark of the Second International, and, in our days, the principal *social* (not military) *support of the bourgeoisie.* They are the real *agents of the bourgeoisie in the labour movement*, the labour lieutenants of the capitalist class, channels of reformism and chauvinism. (*Imperialism*, Preface to the French and German editions.)

All these petty-bourgeois groups somehow or other penetrate into the Party into which they introduce an element of hesitancy and opportunism, of disintegration and lack of self-confidence. Factionalism and splits, disorganisation and the undermining of the Party from within are principally due to them. Fighting imperialism with such " allies " in one's rear is as bad as being caught between two fires, coming both from the front and rear. Therefore, no quarter should be given in fighting such elements, and their relentless expulsion from the Party is a condition precedent for the successful struggle against imperialism.

The theory of " overcoming " opportunist elements by ideological struggle within the Party ; the theory of " living down " these elements within the confines of a single Party are rotten and dangerous theories that threaten to reduce the Party to paralysis and chronic infirmity, that threaten to abandon the Party to opportunism, that threaten to leave the proletariat without a revolutionary party, that threaten to deprive the proletariat of its main weapon in the fight against imperialism. Our Party could not have come out on to the high road, it could not have seized power and organised the dictatorship of the proletariat, it could not have emerged victorious from the civil war, if it had had within its ranks people like Martov and Dan, Potresov and Axelrod. Our Party succeeded in creating true unity and greater cohesion in its ranks than ever before, mainly because it undertook in time to purge itself of opportunist pollution and expelled the liquidators and Mensheviks from its ranks. The proletarian parties develop and become strong by purging themselves of opportunists and reformists, social-imperialists and social-chauvinists, social-patriots and social-pacifists. The Party becomes strong by ridding itself of opportunist elements.

With reformists and Mensheviks in our ranks—says Lenin—
we cannot be victorious in the proletarian revolution *nor can* we
defend it against attack. This is clearly so in principle. It is
strikingly confirmed by the experiences of Russia and Hungary.
. . . Russia found itself in a tight corner *many* a time, when the
Soviet régime would certainly have been overthrown had the
Mensheviks, reformists or petty-bourgeois democrats remained
within our Party. . . . It is generally admitted that in Italy
events are heading towards decisive battles of the proletariat
with the bourgeoisie for the capture of State power. At such a
time not only does the removal of the Mensheviks, reformists
and Turatists from the Party become absolutely necessary, but
it may even prove useful to remove certain excellent Communists who might and who do waver in the direction of desiring
to maintain " unity " with the reformists—to remove these
from all responsible positions. . . . On the eve of the revolution
and in the midst of the desperate struggle for victory, the
slightest hesitancy within the Party is apt to *ruin* everything,
to disrupt the revolution and to snatch the power out of the
hands of the proletariat, since that power is as yet insecure and
the attacks upon it are still too violent. The retirement of wavering leaders at such a time does not weaken but strengthens the
Party, the labour movement and the revolution. (*Collected
Works*, Russian edition, Vol. XXV, pp. 462–4.)

Note: The following glossaries were prepared at the time of the original publication of *The Handbook of Marxism*. The reader will therefore note the absence of any dates subsequent to 1935.

GLOSSARY OF NAMES

Aristotle (384–322 B.C.). Celebrated Greek philosopher, called by Marx " the Hegel of the ancient world."

Axelrod, P. B. (1850–1928). Russian Menshevik leader after the Social Democratic Labour Party split in 1903.

Babeuf, F. N. (1760–97). A radical republican (Jacobin) in the great French Revolution, guillotined for plotting for a Communist state.

Bakunin, M. A. (1814–76). Famous Russian revolutionary and leader of the Anarchist wing of the First International.

Bauer, Bruno (1809–82). " Young Hegelian " philosopher.

Bauer, Otto (1882–   ). Leader of Austrian Social Democracy, and prominent theoretician of the Second International.

Bebel, Auguste (1840–1913). One of the founders of the German Social Democratic Party. Leader of the Second International before the war.

Berkeley, G. (1684–1753). Famous idealist philosopher.

Bernstein, Eduard (1850–   ). Prominent German Social Democrat, member of the Reichstag, leader of the Second International.

Bismarck, Otto von (1815–98). Chancellor of the German Empire. Author of the *Anti-Socialist Laws*.

Blanc, Louis. French Utopian Socialist and historian, who entered the French Provisional Government in 1848 as a " workers' representative."

Blanqui, A. (1805–81). French revolutionary Socialist who advocated " putchist " tactics as a substitute for mass action.

Bonaparte, Louis (1808–73). Nephew of Napoleon I. He was elected French President in 1848, and proclaimed himself Emperor in 1851 by *coup d'état*. Overthrown in 1870, after defeat in Franco-Prussian war.

Buchanan, G. W. (1854–1924). British Ambassador to Russia, 1910–18.

Büchner, L. (1824–99). German doctor, materialist writer.

Caussidière (1808–61). French revolutionary.

Chernov, Victor (1876–   ). Leader of the Russian Socialist Revolutionary Party. Opponent of the Bolsheviks.

Chkheidze, N. S. (1864–1926). Menshevik leader from the Caucasus.

Dan, F. J. (1871–   ). Menshevik leader.

Danton, G. (1759–94). A Jacobin leader in the great French Revolution.

Darwin, Charles (1809–1882). English naturalist, famous for his development of the theory of Evolution.

David, E. (1863–   ). German Social Democrat opportunist.

Denikin. Tsarist general ; in 1918–19 commanded the counter-revolutionary forces in South Russia.

Descartes (1596–1650). French philosopher, whose work contains elements of both materialism and idealism.

Desmoulins, Camille (1760–94). A Jacobin leader in the great French Revolution.

Diderot (1713–84). French materialist philosopher.

Dietzgen, Joseph (1828–88). German socialist and self-educated philosopher. A tanner by trade.

Favre, Jules. French Foreign Minister, in the Thiers Government, February 1871.

Feuerbach, Ludwig (1804–72). " Young Hegelian " philosopher who turned to materialism, influencing Marx and Engels.

Fichte, J. G. (1762–1814). German idealist philosopher.

Fourier C. (1772–1837). French Utopian Socialist.

Gapon, G. (died 1906). A priest who organised the mass demonstration on " Bloody Sunday " which precipitated the 1905 Revolution.

Goethe, W. (1749–1832). German classical writer.

Golay, Paul. French Socialist. During the war edited a socialist paper in Lausanne.

Gompers, S. (1850–1924). Reactionary president of the American Federation of Labour.

Gorter, H. (1864–1927). Dutch left-wing Socialist, later Communist.

Guchkov, A. I. (1862–   ). Rich Moscow capitalist. Minister of War in the First Provisional Government, 1917.

Guizot (1787–1874). French Conservative. Representative of the Finance aristocracy.

Habakkuk. Hebrew prophet.

Haeckel, Ernst (1834–1919). German biologist.

Hegel, G. W. F. (1770–1831). German philosopher who developed the dialectical theory as an idealist.

Hilferding, Rudolph (1877–   ). Leading theoretician of German Social-Democracy. Attempted to reconcile Marxism with opportunism.

Hobbes, T. (1588–1697). English materialist philosopher.

Hobson, J. A. (1858–   ). English economist.

Höglund, Z. (1884–   ). Leader of Swedish Left Socialist Party before the war. For a short time Communist.

Holyoake, G. J. (1817–1906). English co-operator.

Hume, David (1711–76). English " sceptical " philosopher.

Huxley, T. H. (1825–95). English biologist, " Agnostic " philosopher.

Jouhaux, L. (1876–   ). Secretary of the French General Confederation of Labour and leader of the Amsterdam (trade union) International.

Kant, Emmanuel (1724–1804). Classical German philosopher.

Kautsky, Karl (1854–   ). Former leading Marxist theoretician, sank into Opportunism during the Great War, and opposed the Bolshevik Revolution.

Kerensky, A. F. (1881–   ). Socialist-Revolutionary, Premier in the Provisional Government that was overthrown by the Bolshevik Revolution.

Kornilov, L. G. (1876–1918). Tsarist General. Marched on Petrograd in September 1917, in an unsuccessful attempt to set up a military dictatorship.

Kropotkin, P. A. (1842–1921). Founder of Anarcho-Communism.

Lamarck, J. (1744–1829). French naturalist.

Lamartine, A. (1790–1869). French poet.

Laplace, P. (1749–1827). French astronomer and mathematician.

Lassalle, Ferdinand (1825–64). One of the outstanding leaders of the early German labour movement. Orator, publicist ; non-Marxist.

Ledru-Rollin, A. (1807–74). Bourgeois Republican leader.

Legien, K. (1861–1920). German reformist Trade Union leader.

Liebknecht, Karl (1871–1919). Left German Social-Democrat ; militant Internationalist and opponent of the Imperialist War ; murdered by German officers.

Liebknecht, Wilhelm (1826–1900). One of the founders of German Social-Democracy. Father of Karl Liebknecht.

Lincoln, Abraham (1809–65). United States President and leader of the Capitalist North in the Civil War.

Linnaeus, C. (1741–83). Swedish naturalist.

Locke, J. (1632–1704). English materialist philosopher.

Lunacharsky, A. V. (1875–1934). Bolshevik. People's Commissar for Education after the Boshevik Revolution.

Lvov, Prince (1861–1925). Large landowner and member of the Provisional Government, 1917.

Macaire. Type of swindler from French play.
Mach, Ernst. German eclectic philosopher who vacillated between idealism and materialism.
Maine, H. S. (1822–88). English jurist and historian.
Malpighi, M. (1628–94). Italian anatomist.
Martov, L. (1873–1923). Leader of the Mensheviks at the Russian Social Democratic Labour Party split in 1903.
Martynov, A. S. (1865–1934). Theorist of " Economism," later Menshevik. Became a Bolshevik after the Bolshevik Revolution.
Metternich (1773–1859). Chancellor of the Austrian empire, and leader of the European reaction.
Mignet, F. (1796–1884). French historian.
Miliukov, P. (1859–　　). Leader of Constitutional Democratic Party (" Cadets ") and of Russian Liberalism. Bitter opponent of the Soviet Government.
Millerand, A. (1859–　　). French politician. First Socialist to join a bourgeois cabinet (1899–1902). Later expelled from the Socialist Party.
Moleschott (1822–93). Dutch naturalist with materialist views.
Moll, Joseph. German watchmaker, member of the Communist League. In London associated with Chartist movement. Fell in the German revolutionary struggles of 1849.
Montesquieu, C. (1689–1755). French historian.

Newton, Isaac (1642–1727). Mathematician, astronomer, physicist. Famous for his work on Gravitation.
Noske. German Social-Democrat who suppressed the revolutionary risings of the German workers after the war.

Ostwald. German chemist, writer on philosophical questions.
Owen, Robert (1771–1858). English Utopian Socialist. Pioneer of the Co-operative Movement.

Philippe, Louis (1773–1850). Duke of Orleans. Became " King of the French " as a result of July 1830 revolution. Deposed by February 1848 revolution.
Plekhanov, George (1856–1918). Founder of Russian Marxism. Supported Lenin in his controversies with the idealists, but became a social-patriot during the war, and opposed the Bolshevik revolution.

Potresov, A. N. (1869–   ). Old Russian Social-Democrat. Leader of extreme right wing of the Mensheviks. Social-patriot during the war.

Proudhon, P. J. (1809–65). Petty-bourgeois Utopian Socialist.

Rakovsky, C. (1873–   ). Rumanian Socialist, then Communist and Soviet official ; later in Trotskyist opposition.

Rasputin, Gregory (1872–1916). Siberian priest who attained great influence at the Russian Court.

Renan, E. (1823–92). French historian.

Renner, Karl (1871–   ). Leading theorist of Opportunism in the Austrian Social-Democratic Party.

Ricardo, David (1772–1823). English banker and economist.

Robespierre, Maximilien (1758–1794). French Jacobin ; leader in the Great French Revolution.

Rodbertus-Jagetzow (1805–75). A rich Prussian landowner, theorist of " Prussian Junker " socialism.

Roland-Holst, Henrietta (1869–   ). Dutch writer and Marxist.

Romanov. Family name of the Russian Tsar Nicholas II.

Rousseau, J. J. (1712–78). French writer, author of the *Social Contract* ; expressed bourgeois revolt against the rule of the feudal aristocracy.

Royer-Collard, P. (1763–1845). French Liberal.

Saint-Just, A. L. (1767–94). Jacobin. Outstanding figure in the French revolution.

Saint-Simon (1760–1825). French Utopian Socialist.

Say, Jean Baptiste (1767–1832). Leading French economist, and apologist of free-trade capitalism.

Scheidemann, P. (1865–   ). Right Wing German Social-Democrat. Together with Noske he organised the crushing of the Spartacist rising in 1919.

Sismondi (1773–1842). French historian and economist.

Skobelev, M. I. (1885–   ), Menshevik, member of the Fourth Duma.

Smith, Adam (1723–90). Classical English economist.

Stirner, Max (1808–56). Associated with " Young Hegelians."

Strauss, D. F. (1800–74). German " Young Hegelian " philosopher.

Struve, Peter (1870–   ). Russian economist. Originally opportunist Social-Democrat, later Liberal.

Sun-Yat-Sen. Leader of Chinese bourgeois revolution. Founded Kuomintang Party in 1912. In control of Canton from 1916 until his death in 1925.

Thiers, A. (1797–1877). Leader of government that suppressed the Paris Commune in 1871.

Thierry, A. (1795–1856). French historian.

Trochu, L. J. (1815–96). Military Governor of Paris, after September 4, 1870, President of the " Government of National Defence."

Trotsky, L. (1879–   ). Leading Russian Social-Democrat, who vacillated between the Bolsheviks and Mensheviks after the Party split in 1903, being continually in opposition to Lenin. He joined the Bolshevik Party just before the Bolshevik Revolution and filled leading posts during the Civil War. Later he became a leader of anti-party fractional struggles and was expelled from the Party. From 1928 carried on active campaign from various countries against the Soviet Union, and in the Moscow trials of 1936 and 1937 was stated by certain of the accused to be the organiser from abroad of groups of terrorists and wreckers inside the Soviet Union, in conjunction with Nazi agents.

Tseretelli, I. G. (1882–   ). Menshevik. Became a Minister of the First Coalition Government in May 1917.

Turati, F. (1857–   ). Leader of right wing in Italian Socialist Party.

Turgenev, I. S. (1818–83). Famous Russian novelist.

Vogt, Karl (1817–98). German naturalist, vulgar materialist and petty-bourgeois democrat.

Vollner, G. von (1850–1922). German Social-Democrat and outstanding defender of Imperialism.

Zubatov (1864–1917). Head of the Tsarist Secret Police in Moscow.

GLOSSARY OF UNFAMILIAR TERMS

Anti-Socialist Laws (Germany). Introduced by Bismarck in 1878 to suppress the Social-Democratic organisation. The organisation, however, developed, and when elections were held after the repeal of these laws in 1890, the Social Democratic Party secured 1½ million votes.

Artel. A group of workers or peasants engaged in co-operative production.

Black Hundreds. The most reactionary landlord group in Russia under the Tsars.

Boxer Rebellion. Chinese national revolt against foreign oppression (1900).

Bund. The Jewish Labour League in Poland and Russia, established in 1897.

Cadets. Constitutional-Democratic Party in Russia.

Decembriseur. Member of " Society of December 10th," described by Marx in his *Eighteenth Brumaire.*

Duma. Russian " parliament " granted by Tsar after 1905 revolution.

Gotha Programme. Programme adopted by the German Social-Democratic Party on the occasion of its formation by the amalgamation of the two previously existing workers' parties (1875).

Guildmaster. A full member of a craft guild.

Holy Alliance. Alliance of counter-revolutionary monarchies of Russia, Austria and Prussia. Founded in 1815.

Jacobins. Radical Republicans, the most radical party representing the petty-bourgeoisie in the French Revolution, 1789.

Junkers. Large landowners of Prussia.

Kienthal (Switzerland). The second international conference of Socialist groups opposing the war was held there in 1916.

Kulak. Rich peasant, also village usurer and exploiter.

Kustar industry. Small-scale home industry, mainly handicraft.

Legitimists. Supporters of the older or " legitimate " branch of the Bourbon Royal family of France, who represented particularly the landlords.

Liquidators. Reformist Socialist—Mensheviks—who proposed the liquidation of the underground party organisation and instead favoured only legal activities.

Lumpenproletariat. Literally " Ragged proletariat," but applied to good-for-nothing, declassed workers.

Muzhik, mujik. Russian peasant.

Narodniks. A Russian petty-bourgeois revolutionary group.

Octobrists. A Russian (constitutional) political party formed in 1905, when the Tsar promised a Duma.

Orleanists. Supporters of the junior branch of the Bourbons (descendants of Louis Philippe). The Party of the merchants, bankers and landlords.

Phalanstères. Socialist colonies planned by Charles Fourier.

Prætorian. In ancient Rome, the personal bodyguard of a general or emperor.

Sachsenwald. The extensive estate presented to the German Chancellor Bismarck.

Spartacus League. The anti-war organisation of Karl Liebknecht during the war. (He signed his illegal leaflets " Spartacus"—Spartacus was the leader of a slave revolt in ancient Rome.)

Tuileries. Traditional residence of the French Kings.

Vedas. Hindu Sacred Books.

White Guards. The general term used by the Bolsheviks (the " Reds ") to describe the counter-revolutionary forces (the " Whites ") after November 1917.

Zemstvo. Elected provincial representative assembly in Russia. The zemstvos were used by the Liberal bourgeoisie for agitation against the autocracy.

Zimmerwald (Switzerland). The first international conference of Socialist groups opposing the war was held there in 1915.